P9-CDU-987

INDUSTRIAL RELATIONS RESEARCH ASSOCIATION SERIES

Research Frontiers in Industrial Relations and Human Resources

EDITED BY

David Lewin

Olivia S. Mitchell

Peter D. Sherer

Preparation of this volume was supported in part by the provision of editorial and copyediting services to the IRRA by the UCLA Institute of Industrial Relations, David Lewin, Director.

First edition

Library of Congress Catalog Card Number: 50-13564

ISBN 0-913447-53-6

INDUSTRIAL RELATIONS RESEARCH ASSOCIATION SERIES
- Proceedings of the Annual Meeting (Summer publication)
- Proceedings of the Spring Meeting (Fall publication)
- Annual Research Volume
- Membership Directory (every fourth year)

IRRA Newsletter (published quarterly)

Inquiries and other communications regarding membership, meetings, publications, and general affairs of the Association, copyright requests, as well as notice of address changes should be addressed to the IRRA national office.

INDUSTRIAL RELATIONS RESEARCH ASSOCIATION
7226 Social Science Building, University of Wisconsin, 1180 Observatory Drive, Madison, WI 53706 U.S.A. Telephone 608/262-2762

CONTENTS

III. Labor Markets

IV. Industrial Relations and Human Resource Regulation

PREFACE

The production of a volume such as this one would not have been possible without the major contributions of many individuals. This includes the twenty-three authors and coauthors of papers contained in the volume who, for the most part, cooperated willingly and promptly with the many demands made upon them by the editors. It says something important about the commitment of industrial relations/human resource scholars that only one of the papers originally planned to be included in the 1992 IRRA research volume was not delivered by its author. To the contributors to this volume we express our appreciation and gratitude, and we encourage others in our field to do the same.

Acknowledgement should also be given to members of the Editorial Committee of the IRRA, who encouraged us to pursue this volume, and in particular to the Editor-in-Chief of the Association, Professor John F. Burton, Jr. Professor Burton and his colleagues on the Editorial Committee made sure that we toed the line in terms of meeting Association deadlines and related requirements for publication of this volume.

In October, 1991, a pre-publication conference on this volume was held at the University of Pennsylvania's Wharton School. That conference served as a refereeing step for papers presented in this volume. Professor Peter Cappelli of the Wharton School was instrumental to the planning and coordination of that conference, and we acknowledge his efforts in this regard along with the contributions of the thirty or so scholars who participated in the conference.

Finally, we acknowledge and express our gratitude to Kay Hutchison, IRRA National Office Administrator, Jane Wildhorn, Director of Publications for the UCLA Institute of Industrial Relations, and Maryann McGuire and Betsy Ryan, staff members of the UCLA Institute of Industrial Relations. Their administrative, editorial, and copyediting skills are outstanding and contributed in a major way to the completion of this volume.

DAVID LEWIN
OLIVIA S. MITCHELL
PETER D. SHERER

CHAPTER 1

Introduction and Overview

DAVID LEWIN
UCLA

OLIVIA S. MITCHELL
Cornell University

PETER D. SHERER
University of Pennsylvania

About every decade or so, the annual research volume of the Industrial Relations Research Association (IRRA) is devoted to an assessment of research in major topic areas within the field. Typically, these volumes have provided lengthy comprehensive research summaries in a few topic areas (see, for example, Chamberlain, et al. 1958; Ginsburg, et al. 1970; Aaron, et al. 1971; Kochan, et al. 1982).

For the 1992 annual research volume, which assesses scholarly work done in the 1980s, the editors have taken a somewhat different approach, in part because research summaries of specialty areas within industrial relations (IR) have been published with increased frequency in recent years (see, for example, Freeman 1986; Stagner 1981; Stieber, et al. 1981), and also because new IR topics have drawn scholarly attention (see, for example, Mitchell and Zaidi 1990; Katz 1991). This last point is perhaps implied by the title of the present volume, which for the first time (in the IRRA Series) includes the phrase "human resources" (HR).

In addition to the editors' introductory chapter, the 1992 IRRA research volume contains 16 chapters subsumed under four major topic headings: (1) unions, collective bargaining, and dispute resolution; (2) human resource management; (3) labor market research; and (4) the regulation of IR-HR. Of particular note, the author(s) of each chapter has been asked to provide (a) a selective summary of recent research in his/her topic area, (b) some new evidence about the topic, and (c) an agenda for future research on the topic. It is our hope that this collection of research agendas, and the editors' attempt to integrate them in this opening chapter, will be of special value to a new generation of IR-HR scholars, who will help to shape the field during the 1990s and beyond the year 2000. In the pages to follow, we review and comment on some of the key ideas, empirical findings, and research agendas offered by authors of papers in the 1992 IRRA research volume.

Unions, Bargaining, and Dispute Resolution

In few areas of industrial relations have recent changes been as notable or dramatic as in the area of unions and collective bargaining. As is well known, union density declined in most developed nations of the world (save especially Canada) during the 1980s (Chaison and Rose 1991). In the U.S., private sector union membership fell from 20.1 to 12.4 percent of the work force between 1980 and 1989 (and to 12.1 percent by 1991). Further, collective bargaining during the 1980s was often characterized by such terms as "concession bargaining," "givebacks," "two-tier pay plans," "lump-sum payments," "the death of pattern bargaining," and the like.

Despite these developments, or perhaps in part because of them, the 1980s witnessed a plethora of research on the economic outcomes of unions and collective bargaining. Such research has a longstanding tradition in industrial relations, with the bulk of it taking the form of union wage impact studies using a neoclassical economic framework of analysis (Rees 1977). In the 1970s, union wage impact research advanced markedly through the use of individual (as distinct from firm and industry) level data sets, and through the development and application of more complex measurement models, including simultaneous equation models. During the 1980s, researchers' attention turned toward the measurement of union impacts on the economic performance of firms. This work is also grounded in neoclassical theory, but it goes considerably further than wage impact research in explaining the economic consequences of unionism and bargaining. In brief, empirical studies conducted during the 1980s yielded evidence of significant negative effects of unions on firm profitability, capital investment, research and development expenditures, and market value (Clark 1984; Voos and Michel 1986; Becker and Olson 1987; Hirsch 1992). Firms with double-breasted (union and nonunion operations) typically reduced their investments in unionized operations and increased their investments in nonunion operations during the 1980s (Verma 1985; Kochan, Katz, and McKersie 1986). Additionally, some of this research used event analysis to show that the announcements of strikes by unionized firms were significantly associated with declines in the stock prices of struck firms (Becker and Olson 1986; Abowd 1989). Similarly, announcements of union representation elections in nonunion firms were significantly associated with declines in the stock prices of these firms (Becker and Olson 1987). Taken as a whole, this work helps to account for the significant decline in U.S. private sector unionism during the 1980s.

Somewhat offsetting this research and its attendant conclusions about unionism and collective bargaining is the well-known work of Freeman and Medoff (1984), which uses exit-voice theory (developed by Hirschman 1970) to explain how and why unionized and nonunionized firms can coexist in the same industry. In brief, according to Freeman and Medoff, unionism lowers workers' quit rates and raises workers' job tenure (experience), thereby giving employers incentives to invest in worker training (human capital), with consequent increases in productivity that are roughly offset by bargained increases in labor costs (pay and benefits). This work has been vigorously critiqued for its conceptual and empirical limitations (Reder 1985; Addison 1985), and for failing adequately to address the concept of loyalty that forms part of the conceptual framework (developed by Hirschman 1970) in which the work is ostensibly grounded (Boroff and Lewin 1991; Lewin 1990). In any case, the collective voice "face" of unionism, as developed by Freeman and Medoff, squares far less closely with the decline of U.S. unionism and the export of U.S. jobs during the 1980s than does the so-called monopoly "face" of unionism.

As the 1980s drew to a close, researchers increasingly turned their attention toward international/comparative studies of the economic outcomes of unionism and other institutional forms of worker participation in the enterprise. Some of this research uses the aforementioned exit-voice framework of analysis (Blanchflower and Freeman 1992), and much of it focuses on the economic consequences of works councils and codetermination in Western

European nations (Lewin and Mitchell 1992). For the most part, these economic consequences are reported to be neutral to modestly negative (Bain 1992). However, to date this international/ comparative research has dealt hardly at all with changes in work rules and practices under unionism, works councils, or codetermination—that is, with industrial relations outcomes as distinct from economic outcomes.

Collective Bargaining and Industrial Relations Outcomes

On the U.S. scene, the decline of unionism and the rise of concession bargaining (and all that this term implies) during the 1980s are often claimed to have produced major changes in work rules and work practices in unionized workplaces. Yet as Harry Katz and Jeffrey Keefe point out, such rules and practices have long been diverse. This is particularly true in the U.S. (on which Katz and Keefe focus), given its (continuing) traditions of decentralized bargaining, the workplace focus of bargaining, and the importance of local unions.

But is there more or less diversity in work rules and practices in unionized U.S. workplaces today than previously? Katz and Keefe provide answers to this question by systematically examining collective bargaining contract provisions that prevailed in 1975 and 1989 in the U.S. They find that, during this period, the incidence and scope of grievance procedures remained relatively stable, the incidence of union-management cooperation committees rose substantially, and the incidence of quality of working life (QWL) initiatives rose slightly. However, they also find significant increases in the incidence of lump-sum and two-tier pay provisions, and significant strengthening of both managements' rights clauses and seniority provisions between 1975 and 1989. The authors contend that these developments are better explained by a "transformation" model than by yo-yo, rigidification, maturity, and business cycles models of workplace industrial relations.

Katz and Keefe turn next to the question of how work rules and work practices in unionized settings affect industrial relations outcomes. Prior to the 1980s, they point out, answers to this question came largely in the form of case studies, with their attendant limitations on generalizability. The 1980s witnessed the emergence of quantitative studies of work rules and practices, which were intended to develop more "scientific" answers to this question. This objective has perhaps been most notably achieved by research on workplace grievance activity, which finds that grievance rates are significantly negatively associated with labor productivity and product quality, and significantly positively associated with unit production costs. Researchers have been less successful, according to Katz and Keefe, in measuring the effects of work restructuring, team forms of work organization, and other recent employee involvement/participation initiatives on industrial relations outcomes. This conclusion needs to be qualified because it rests in part on the contradictory findings that emanate from relevant studies. However, the conclusion also rests in part on the fact that researchers have gained access to relatively few organizations and workplaces for the purposes of quantitatively studying the effects of new work rules and work practices on industrial relations outcomes.

Katz and Keefe also briefly address the effects of workplace industrial relations practices on the economic (as distinct from the industrial relations) performance of firms. Here their contribution is mainly theoretical, as they offer a conceptual framework which specifies that work rules and practices may affect firms' economic outcomes directly as well as indirectly through their effects on industrial relations outcomes. Empirically, according to these authors, there is little evidence of the effects of workplace industrial relations practices, especially new practices, on firms' economic performance—a conclusion which may apply to international/comparative research as well as to U.S.-focused research.

In sum and following Katz and Keefe, researchers would do well to devote greater effort to measuring the effects of new work rules and practices on industrial relations outcomes and firms' economic outcomes. In addition, as the authors point out, there is a paucity of research on (unionized and nonunion) workers' perceptions of and attitudes towards recent changes in work rules and work practices. Popular literature presupposes that such changes spur workers to work harder and/or smarter, but evidence on this score is scant indeed. Thus, Katz and Keefe's proposal that more systematic attention be paid to workers' responses to changes in workplace industrial relations seems particularly well-founded.

Strike Models and Outcomes

Paralleling the decline of unionism in the U.S. during the 1980s, and not unrelated to it, was the precipitous decline in strike activity.

Also as with unionism, however, there was a resurgence during the 1980s of research on strikes. Bruce Kaufman reviews and assesses this research, which ranges across a wide variety of disciplines and fields, and he offers readers a good news-bad news story.

The good news, says Kaufman, comes in the form of theoretical contributions to the study of strikes provided by scholars from several disciplines. In particular, these include joint cost, symmetric information, and information uncertainty models developed by economists, expectancy-value theory and cognitive script models developed by psychologists, resource mobilization theory developed by organizational studies specialists, and political event models developed by political scientists. Kaufman's review and assessment of this disparate theoretical work on strikes is comprehensive and approaches the status of a meta-analysis.

Additional good news comes in the form of empirical studies of strikes, with the most notable feature being the use of comprehensive micro-level data at the level of the bargaining unit and firm. These data enabled researchers to match individual strike outcomes, including the absence or presence of a strike, with various firm, union, and industry-specific characteristics that were previously unexamined. A related advantage of this work, notes Kaufman, is that it permits the matching of strikes with the expiration of individual bargaining agreements, thereby controlling for variation in the opportunity to strike. In particular, this empirical research examined the impact of strikes on inflation and COLA clauses, state bargaining laws and alternative methods of dispute resolution, the availability and generosity of AFDC and UI payments to strikers, economic conditions in the firm's product and labor market, the relationship between cyclical fluctuations in strike frequency and duration, and the impact of strikes on industry-level output and prices.

The bad news about the 1980s research on strikes, says Kaufman, takes the forms of disciplinary parochialism, remoteness from real world events, and the perhaps surprising absence of studies of the decline in strike activity and the growth of replacement workers for strikers. Proceeding from this assessment, Kaufman calls for more multidisciplinary research on strikes to enhance and integrate our understanding of this social phenomenon, enhanced use of the "go and see" case approach to the study of strikes, and a refocusing on the real world issues of strike declines and replacement workers. Pointedly and in line with Mitchell's agenda for future research on fringe benefits and social insurance presented later in this volume, Kaufman doubts that current academic reward systems will support the type of research on strikes which he advocates for the 1990s.

Grievance Procedures in the Union and Nonunion Sectors

As suggested by Katz and Keefe, the grievance procedure is the centerpiece of collective bargaining agreements in the U.S. Almost all industrial union contracts and a majority of craft union contracts contain such a procedure. What appeared to be new in the 1980s was the growth of formal grievance (or grievance-like) procedures in nonunion firms. Some researchers conclude that such procedures are adopted by nonunion firms largely to forestall unionization, but other researchers dispute this conclusion (Feuille and Delaney 1992).

The paper by Richard Peterson assesses recent grievance procedure research along several dimensions, in particular, the determinants, personal outcomes, and organizational outcomes of grievance filing. Prior to the 1980s, most grievance procedure research dealt with the characteristics of grievance filers and the dynamics of grievance settlement. That research featured a plethora of case studies and a large literature on grievance arbitration.

The focus of grievance procedure research shifted during the 1980s to emphasize more conceptual and systematic empirical approaches to this form of workplace conflict resolution. These included applications of exit-voice theory to unionized grievance procedures, applications of procedural justice and distributive justice concepts to unionized and nonunion grievance procedures, applications of contingency theory to the grievance-arbitration process, modeling of the grievance procedure within a compensating wage differentials framework, and the modeling and measurement of grievance procedure effectiveness.

The systems approach to grievance procedure research utilized by Lewin and Peterson (1988) led to the identification of certain determinants of grievance filing, settlement, and post-grievance settlement outcomes. Further, many of the recent studies reviewed by Peterson seem to support this systems approach. For example, certain personal, technological, organizational, and labor-management characteristics have been shown to be systematically related to grievance filing, the speed of grievance settlement, the level of grievance settlement, and decisions in favor of the employee-grievant (or employer).

But perhaps most telling about grievance procedure research conducted during the 1980s are the results of studies which focused on the outcomes of grievance filing and settlement for grievance filers, both in unionized and nonunion settings. This work employed quasi-experimental research designs to match within-organization samples of grievance filers and nonfilers prior to, during, and following periods of grievance filing. Filers and nonfilers were compared in terms of measured performance ratings, promotion rates, and work attendance, none of which differed significantly during the pre-grievance filing period or during the grievance filing and settlement period. However, in the post-grievance settlement period (typically one to two years), the job performance, promotion rate, and work attendance of grievance filers declined significantly relative to comparable measures for nonfilers. Further, both voluntary and involuntary turnover among grievance filers in the post-grievance settlement period were significantly higher than among nonfilers. Moreover, and of special importance, similar findings resulted from comparisons of supervisors of grievance filers with supervisors of nonfilers along the aforementioned dimensions before, during, and after grievance filing and settlement.

One interpretation of these findings is that employees who file grievances and the supervisors of those employees suffer reprisals for being involved in grievance activity (Lewin 1990). Such reprisals conflict with the notion that grievance procedures provide a form of industrial democracy in the workplace, and also do not square with the idea that voice exercised through grievance filing is negatively associated with employee exit from the firm. Moreover, if grievance filers do not suffer reprisals relative to nonfilers but, instead, are systematically poorer performers than nonfilers (or, in other words, a "true performance" interpretation of the data reviewed by Peterson), then the findings from exit-voice-based studies of grievance procedures are further called into question.

Peterson concludes his chapter by calling for longitudinal research using larger samples of firms and workers to assess the generalizability of these important findings. This is an especially formidable challenge in nonunion settings, given that nonunion firms jealously guard their internal dispute resolution data and that quasi-public records of workplace dispute settlement, such as those created via arbitration awards, are far less common in nonunion than in unionized firms. Consistent with Katz and Keefe's recommendations about future research on changes in work rules and practices, Peterson also proposes that researchers pay more attention to unionized and nonunion workers' perceptions of workplace dispute settlement processes and outcomes. For this purpose, says Peterson, concepts of procedural and distributive justice should prove to be especially useful.

Human Resource Management

Human Resource Strategy and Choice

The idea that human resource decisions of firms can be subjected to strategic choices seemed to have come of age in the 1980s. Prior to that time, research and practice focused on components of the "personnel management" process—selection, rewards, appraisal, discipline—and was characterized by a short-term, reductionist, and often nonempirical orientation. Further and through the 1970s, industrial relations and personnel management stood apart from each other as separate fields, and scholarly interchange and crossover were rare. But as Peter Cappelli and Harbir Singh point out, a view of industrial relations as a "closed" field—closed to the behavioral sciences—emerged in some quarters during the 1970s, whereas personnel management appeared increasingly open to models, concepts, and analytical frameworks applied by scholars from several social science disciplines.

In addition, the 1980s featured a plethora of popular writings which claimed that human resources could be used—managed—to achieve competitive advantage for the firm. While these writings may be discounted for their lack of scientific underpinnings, they nevertheless reflected the influence of new competitive forces, stemming largely from international sources and deregulation, on personnel management generally and on the utilization, assessment, and motivation of employees in particular. Hence, during the 1980s, the short-term, quick-fix orientation to personnel management practice appeared increasingly to give way to longer-term, strategically driven human resource management policies and practices.

But just how strong is the link between human resource management and business strategy, either in research or practice? Cappelli and Singh conclude that the human resource (or human resource/industrial relations) strategy literature has been largely divorced from the mainstream business strategy literature, though occasional points of convergence and even a few direct linkages between the two sets of literature can be found. Despite this assessment, Cappelli and Singh envision a coming marriage between business strategy and human resource strategy based on mutual recognition of the competitive advantage that human resources potentially create for the firm—or, in other words, a "human resource-based view of strategy."

Cappelli and Singh begin their paper by tracing the evolution of strategy as a concept. Early on, Schelling's (1963) game theory perspective viewed strategy as the influence exerted by one party (firm) on another party's (opponent's or firm's) behavior. Chandler's (1962) historical perspective viewed strategy as the firm's goals together with its attendant policies and action plans, and the firm's structure was said to follow from its strategy. Ansoff (1965), Andrews (1971), and others subsequently broadened the concept of strategy to include many more actions on the part of firms than were identified by Schelling and Chandler. Later, Caves and Porter (1978) and Porter (1980) further expanded and refined notions of competitive strategy, drawing on earlier work by Bain (1956). In these authors' view, firms restricted competition and enhanced their profits by correctly analyzing and using key forces associated with the market structure of their respective industries, such as entry barriers and the bargaining power of suppliers.

Cappelli and Singh then identify the historical points of convergence between business strategy and human resources/industrial relations strategy. Just as firms use market position to gain "excess" profits, Commons (1919) and others (for example, Hendricks 1975) showed how unions strategically gained superior wages and greater job security for workers by "taking wages out of competition," thereby creating entry barriers. Cappelli and Singh observe, however, that the most direct linkage to the business strategy literature was the pre-1980s personnel management literature on manpower planning. More recently, Walker (1980) and others advocated the notion of strategic human resource management in which all major human resource activities in a firm are related to the firm's business strategy. This approach led to several studies which attempted to assess the "fit" of human resource strategy with business strategy as well as the consequences associated with such fit. Nevertheless, say Cappelli and Singh, this notion of fit has proven to be elusive because there are very few conceptual and empirically verified propositions about the behaviors and attitudes required by the business strategy and produced by the human resource strategy of a firm.

With the publication of works by Kochan, McKersie, and Cappelli (1984) and Kochan, Katz, and McKersie (1986), human resources/industrial relations moved further into the strategy arena. A strategic view of industrial relations was proposed by these authors to explain the movement away from the post-World War II union model. For these researchers, the impetus toward change came from management and its strategic decisions about human resources, only some of which occurred through traditional collective bargaining. Subsequent industrial relations strategy research focused on management actions in the areas of union avoidance and collective bargaining.

Cappelli and Singh then suggest that human resources/industrial relations and business strategy have common ground to jointly develop a resource-based view of strategy. While much of the early work on strategy assumed that the internal capital assets of a firm could be used against competitors, as needed, Cappelli and Singh document the growing interest in a resource-based approach to strategy in which internal human assets (resources) provide competitive advantage to the firm in the form of enhanced profits and restrictions on competition (Rumelt 1979). From this perspective, internal human assets are potentially distinctive, even unique, and may be difficult for competitors to imitate. The authors undergird this view by identifying and discussing differences in the ways that firms select, replace, compensate, develop, assess, and use teamwork in managing human resources. A firm's particular set (or bundle) of human resource policies and practices will generally be difficult for competitors to imitate, say Cappelli and Singh, because scarce specialized skills and capabilities are required to do so.

Cappelli and Singh propose a research agenda which differs from prior work on human resource strategy. Specifically, they propose that research attention should initially be focused on firms with employment systems that create human resources and competencies which produce competitive advantage. Then, contend Cappelli and Singh, researchers should examine how such firms adapt their business strategies to fit the human assets and resources created by their employment systems. Whether or not such a "best practice" or "benchmarking" research approach can produce valid generalizations about human resource strategy and competitive advantage is open to question, however, because it appears to exclude firms with certain types of employment systems and firms which have not achieved competitive advantage—a restriction of range problem perhaps comparable to that associated with single firm case studies.

Pay, Participation, and Performance

Barry Gerhart, George Milkovich, and Brian Murray review and assess the vast literature on compensation that was produced during the 1980s. While they note the resurgence of interest by economists and sociologists in compensation, these authors identify a distinct human resource approach to compensation. Its key features are the organization as the sampling unit and a focus on the strategic choices of the firm; a multidimensional perspective on pay that focuses on its level, mix, structure, and process; recognition that pay needs to be considered in its interaction with other attributes of the employment relationship, particularly such process elements as employee participation in decision making and employee empowerment; and empirical validation of theoretical propositions.

As Gerhart, Milkovich, and Murray observe, prior to the 1980s the vast majority of human resource research on compensation was at the individual level of analysis and was concerned with the motivational or psychological bases and effects of pay. During the 1980s, there was a decided push toward organizational level analyses which took a strategic-contingency approach to compensation. Firms were seen as having a compensation scheme or bundles of pay policies and practices that fit their business strategies at various stages of their respective product life cycles. Thus, from this perspective, firms were seen as having discretion, to greater or lesser degrees, over the various attributes of pay.

As these authors also indicate, a great deal of work has been done on firms' strategic choices of pay level. The particular focus has been to explain why some firms pay more than others—what economists refer to as "efficiency wages." Economic explanations of these wage levels rest on the notion that the firm selects a wage in excess of the market-clearing or "going" rate in order to achieve higher employee job performance. For example, Akerloff (1984) contends that firms give employees "high" wages in order to make them feel obligated to the firm and thereby increase their levels of effort at work. Yet Gerhart, Milkovich, and Murray note that there have been few tests of this and related economic explanations of firm decisions regarding pay levels. Moreover, these authors differentiate the human resource approach from the economic approach to pay by suggesting that the efficiency-inducing consequences of particular pay levels is an empirical matter and should not be accepted, *a priori*.

Gerhart, Milkovich, and Murray argue further, however, that a strategic view of compensation will not yield its highest payoffs from studying pay levels. Although firms appear to have considerable discretion in setting pay levels, they face considerable product and labor market constraints on pay decisions. Hence, the authors contend that the "real action" in the sense of where a strategic perspective on compensation may be more fruitful is in studying the mix of pay across organizations. Decisions about pay mix are not so clearly constrained by market forces and cost structures, and pay mix involves many decisions that can differentiate firms. Indeed, firms differ in their use of merit pay versus merit bonuses, profit sharing, stock ownership, wage and salary versus benefits, flexible benefits, and more. The authors also suggest that an understanding of firms' strategic decisions on pay mix can best be obtained through competing tests of economic and organizational-based theories, for example, transactions cost, agency, and institutional theories.

Finally, Gerhart, Milkovich, and Murray discuss the increasing interrelationship of pay and participation in research and practice. Their literature review suggests that "pay is not the whole story," and that there are numerous process considerations in improving organizational effectiveness. Indeed, the authors argue that compensation innovations, especially those that involve more contingent compensation or financial empowerment, have worked best when joined with nonfinancial participation, information sharing, team building, integration, employee rights, and other initiatives which can be referred to as psychological empowerment. Thus, a matching or contingency perspective is claimed here, too; financial empowerment has to fit with psychological empowerment. However, as the authors observe, many compensation innovations, particularly those that make pay more variable, may not empower employees so much as they put them at risk. And, it is not clear that organizations are fully succeeding at empowering their employees through participation, teams, and other "innovative" practices.

The human resource approach to compensation offered by Gerhart, Milkovich, and Murray yields a broad research agenda. It implies that there will be competing explanations of firm-level compensation decisions, that firms make numerous compensation decisions, and that various other human resource decisions and practices are linked to compensation decisions and practices. Sorting out explanations of these many and varied compensation decisions should attract the interest of researchers from a wide range of disciplines and fields during the 1990s.

HR Practices and Productive Labor-Management Relations

As noted by Gerhart, Milkovich, and Murray, much of the evidence about the effects of employee participation in decision making on human resource management and organizational outcomes has been derived from narrow outcome measures, cross-sectional studies, and occasional longitudinal studies. These limitations are largely overcome by Casey Ichniowski, whose paper begins with a detailed account of a labor relations transformation in a U.S. paper mill between 1976 and 1990.

For the first six years of the period, the paper mill's grievance rates and strike frequency were among the highest in the industry, and its productivity and return on capital stock were among the lowest in the industry. Between 1975 and 1980, manning levels in this mill rose by about 27 percent, and between 1975 and 1982 the mill had seven different general managers. By 1983, there were only one or two workers per each of the mill's 94 job classifications.

In light of these results, management sought sweeping changes in the mill's human resource practices in the 1983 contract negotiations with its two United Paperworkers International Union (UPIU) locals. Following a two and one-half month strike, the parties signed a collective bargaining agreement which featured a new "team concept" to include broad, flexible jobs with but four instead of 94 classifications; compensation increases in an era of freezes and cuts elsewhere; training programs to develop the worker multiskilling necessary for broadly defined job clusters; attitude surveys and manager "listening" sessions with workers to replace certain past practices regarding communication and dispute resolution (but not the grievance procedure); and guaranteed job and wage security (no employee was to lose his job or have his wage rate cut as a result of the agreement). Ichniowski documents the dramatic business performance and human resource management performance changes brought about by implementation of the team concept in the paper mill that he studied. These included major increases in productivity (tons of paper produced per day) and operating profitability, and major reductions in grievance rates, accident rates, and strike activity (no strikes took place between 1983 and 1990). Labor relations in this mill changed from highly adversarial to highly cooperative, and the change endured over a seven-year period.

In the remainder of his paper, Ichniowski places this case experience in larger perspective and provides a detailed analysis of why the well-known agency (or shirking, free riding, contracting) problem did not seem to materialize in this mill. He concludes in part that the combination of multiskilling and employment security motivated employees to believe that the results of their new efforts would redound to them rather than being withheld from them or distributed only to others (such as shareholders). But Ichniowski also concludes in part that psychological and sociological forces operated in this mill in such a way as to penalize workers who did not offer new ideas or otherwise participate actively in the team concept. In other words, workers who may have been inclined not to make the new effort required by the team concept had costs imposed on them by other workers in this mill, which reduced (if it did not eliminate) the free rider phenomenon.

In offering this interpretation of the paper mill experience he describes and in attempting to generalize from it, Ichniowski in a sense is revivifying the concept of group norms, which has long held a prominent place in the industrial relations literature (at least since the Hawthorne experiments). Moreover, in his proposed research agenda, Ichniowski calls for ethnographic studies of workplace norms and culture based on extensive contact with workers as perhaps the best way of more fully developing constructs of multiskilling, employment security, and performance-based compensation, and of gaining a better understanding of the interplay between human resource practices and economic performance of the firm. In other words, Ichniowski calls for a return to the "long-standing interdisciplinary, hands-on, field research tradition of industrial relations"—a position not often associated with newer industrial relations scholars, but one that squares closely with the position outlined earlier by Kaufman with respect to future research on strikes.

Internal Labor Markets

The types of industrial relations and human resource management changes in the paper mill described by Ichniowski are in a sense treated more generally by Paul Osterman in his paper on internal labor markets. Osterman reviews research and changes in internal labor markets during the last decade, and offers an agenda for future research. He begins by discussing advances in research on internal labor markets since the classic works of Kerr (1954), Dunlop (1957), and Doeringer and Piore (1971). According to Osterman, there is now greater understanding of variation in internal labor markets beyond those associated with blue-collar unionized settings; well-structured explanations of the rise of internal labor markets have been offered by economists and sociologists; and research methodologies used to study internal labor markets have broadened to include representative samples, archival data, and advanced statistical analysis.

Osterman then broaches the question, "What has happened to internal labor markets in recent years and what explains changes in their character?" He first considers the claim that internal labor markets have been dismantled by comparing 1979 and 1988 Current Population Survey data on length of employee job tenure. He concludes that these data do not support the claim of an aggregate movement away from long-term employment relationships in the U.S., which Osterman takes as a proxy for internal labor markets. To the contrary, Osterman notes, job tenure for women increased during the 1980s, and only middle-aged men experienced a lowering of their average job tenure during this period. Still, as Osterman observes, these data do not tell the whole story. Work arrangements that have secondary labor market characteristics, such as temporary or contingent jobs, increased markedly during the 1980s, and women are disproportionately represented in such arrangements.

Osterman then considers the contrasting claim that internal labor markets in the U.S. have evolved to an even more developed (or internalized) stage. Here Osterman is referring to high or mutual commitment-type internal labor markets traditionally associated with firms such as IBM and Digital Equipment Corporation. This type of internal labor market is characterized by employment security in exchange for flexible deployment, contingent compensation, team structures, and direct communications with employees. Yet, as Osterman further notes, the high-commitment-type internal labor market seems presently to be in turmoil, and some of the very firms most associated with using and promoting it are now transforming and, in some cases, even disbanding it.

Osterman poses three questions about the state of internal labor markets which can serve as a guide for future research: why have some firms stayed with the blue-collar union model of internal labor markets, why have some firms moved to a high-commitment model of internal labor markets, and why do some firms that have historically followed a high-commitment model of internal labor markets seem to be moving away from it? Osterman considers three major sets of factors bearing upon these questions: (1) performance; (2) customs, norms and politics; and (3) the broader external environment.

Overall, Osterman judges performance considerations to provide the best answer to the aforementioned questions, but he is cognizant of important divisions in thought about how internal labor markets operate and about the relation of internal labor markets to performance. Osterman observes that economists typically view internal labor markets as control mechanisms which provide greater accountability than less structured arrangements and which, in turn, lead to better organizational performance. Thus, the dominant economics perspective on internal labor markets emphasizes monitoring, incentives, and other mechanisms for reducing agency costs as ways to improve performance. In contrast, sociological and organizational behavior approaches to internal labor markets generally emphasize the role of employee commitment and citizenship in organizational performance.

The next set of factors discussed by Osterman includes customs, norms and politics. While custom has long been known to play a role in internal labor markets (Dunlop 1957), Osterman expands this category of factors to include the emulation or mimicry models of organizational institutionalists and the politics and power models of organizational behavior specialists. Interestingly, Osterman observes, intraorganizational power may be as much an explanation of why some internal labor markets have not changed as of why some other internal labor markets have changed.

The last set of factors taken up by Osterman has to do with the broader external environment, particularly the role of national culture and the educational system in explaining the state of internal labor markets. In this regard, Osterman emphasizes the value of international comparisons and differences in sorting out competing explanations of the state of contemporary internal labor markets.

Osterman's work offers a rich and important agenda for research on internal labor markets. For starters, we still do not have a full understanding of the character of internal labor markets. While there is much speculation in this regard, there is little in the way of statistical research that details the character of new and evolving forms of internal labor markets. There is also a pressing need to sort out empirically which theories and sets of explanations best provide an understanding of why firms have the internal labor markets they do and why and how these change. Such sorting out, notes Osterman, will also be important in examining the role of internal labor markets in the competitive strategy of the firm.

International Human Resource Studies

Thomas Kochan, Lee Dyer, and Rosemary Batt propose a framework and an agenda for research on international human resources. According to these authors, a framework and an agenda are needed because the extant literature on international human resources lacks theoretical depth and is too applied and focused on the particular concerns of multinational corporations.

The authors begin by identifying a series of "starting point" questions: Under what conditions do human resources serve as a source of competitive advantage to firms and national economies? What actions do firms and countries take to gain competitive advantage from human resources? How do strategic actions affect stakeholders in the firm? Within a country, how much diffusion is there of human resource practices that have competitive advantage? Are human resource practices that perform well in one country transferable to another country? All of these questions require us to have a more fundamental and deeper understanding of what explains competitive advantage to a firm and a nation.

Kochan, Dyer, and Batt turn first to classical and neoclassical economics for an understanding of what explains competitive advantage. The authors view these theories as providing parsimonious but insufficient explanations of how human resources serve as a source of competitive advantage. They contend that economic explanations focus almost entirely on how the firm minimizes labor costs in order to compete on product price. Yet, there is growing awareness that firms compete on more than just price; firms compete, *inter alia*, on quality, the capacity to innovate, and speed to market. Given that firms have these (and other) multiple objectives, a view of the firm which focuses only on labor cost minimization as a driver of price competition will not suffice.

Kochan, Dyer, and Batt then consider how competitive advantage is created through human resources. Turning to human capital theory, the authors contend that while it provides general awareness that a firm and a country need to have a well-educated and trained labor force, the theory is not helpful in showing the linkages between investments in human capital and skill, productivity, and wages. There is increasing recognition that firms are turning more to interdependent bundles or packages of training, compensation, employment staffing and security, work organization, trust and employee relations rather than to a menu of isolated and independently made human resource choices. Kochan, Dyer, and Batt also point out that research is increasingly making it clear that firms that enjoy competitive advantage fit human resources to the nature of technology or production. Further, the authors consider the role of financial markets, corporate governance structures, and government policies to promote competitive advantage through human resources.

According to Kochan, Dyer, and Batt, the field of international human resources must move from a sole interest in employers to an accompanying consideration of the effects of human resource policies on employee interests and welfare. They argue that economic arguments to the effect that social welfare and equity will be optimized when individuals are paid the value of their marginal products does not allow us adequately to address how a firm and a country can distribute wealth. Firms, unions, the state, and other organizations typically have different, often conflicting, views about the ways in which national wealth should be distributed. The authors then consider the diffusion of human resources and suggest that economic and other explanations that focus almost entirely on a firm's capacity to diffuse innovations do not suffice. Typically in organizations as well as societies, there are systemic social and political barriers to and facilitators of the diffusion of human resource innovations.

Kochan, Dyer, and Batt next address the matter of the transferability of human resource practices across nations. As the authors observe, this issue has been part of the long-standing debate, initiated by Kerr, Dunlop, Harbison, and Myers (1964), on whether or not countries around the world are converging toward a single model of human resources (or industrial relations) because of the technological imperatives of industrialization. While convergence theory has fallen out of favor, contemporary debates have focused on the transferability of human resource practices from one country (usually Japan) to another (usually the U.S.). Kochan, Dyer, and Batt hypothesize that human resource practices must be conceived of as interdependent bundles or packages if they are to have similar effects across countries.

The research agenda forwarded by Kochan, Dyer, and Batt contains a stimulating set of questions which will hopefully serve to mobilize scholars in human resources, industrial relations, political economy, sociology, business strategy and other fields to advance the theoretical and empirical study of international human resources.

Labor Market Research

Compensation, Productivity, and the New Economics of Personnel

Much labor market research of the 1970s explored the determinants of average wage and employment patterns, with a special focus on econometric problems arising in the process of measuring and estimating these models. While pay and employment continued to be the subject of labor market research in the 1980s, a new theme pervaded the analysis. Instead of focusing on wage outcomes, researchers studied how particular pay and employment contracts are structured and their incentive effects on worker and firm behavior.

Edward Lazear's paper on compensation, productivity, and the new economics of personnel offers a summary and synthesis of this rich new body of labor market research. The central contribution of this literature, according to Lazear, is that certain real-world phenomena have been recognized and incorporated in labor market models for the first time, in particular, the difficulty of monitoring employee output. Because employers often cannot observe employee productivity with great precision, they find it profitable to devise compensation schemes that motivate workers to put forth effort even when monitoring costs make it difficult to tell in the short run whether or not the work is getting done. Such pay schemes include piecework arrangements, upward-sloping pay profiles, tournament or relative performance systems in which only a few can reach the top, and profit-sharing plans. Also, according to Lazear, efficient compensation systems should encourage a worker whose productivity is below target to leave the firm in order to ensure continued firm profitability. This conceptual framework is offered to explain the existence of pensions, severance pay, and private disability schemes which induce exit by those who can no longer perform effectively on the job.

This theoretical research on new and complex pay systems enriches our understanding of the many different ways in which pay is delivered to workers, and also offers provocative explanations of why pay profiles differ so much between firms and across occupations. Unfortunately, distinguishing empirically between these hypotheses has been difficult, sometimes because of theoretical considerations. Thus, for instance, upward sloping wage profiles may be compatible with effort inducement, but also can be rationalized by the existence of on-the-job training and perhaps employees' desire to insure against low productivity in old age. Also, if workers are not risk-neutral (and which one of us is?), many theoretical predictions are also muddied. One of the research tasks awaiting labor market analysts of the 1990s is to nest these different models linking pay to productivity so that clear refutable hypotheses may be derived and tested.

Another issue confronting analysts of compensation schemes is that frequently the real world is too complex to support tidy tests of one theory versus another. For instance, as Lazear points out, the existence of monitoring costs makes it unlikely that workers on piece rate will receive 100 percent commission independent of quality controls. The role of luck is also critical in determining which pay pattern will prevail, as is the ability of workers to collude or harm their co-workers and their feelings about pay equity. In general, it is fair to say that existing empirical research has not yet firmly established the relative contribution of one or another explanation of specific compensation systems observed in the real world. It is interesting that Lazear believes that the best evidence available on some of the theories comes from chicken breeders and professional golfers! Better data on productivity and compensation is a necessary prerequisite for pushing empirical testing further in this field.

While a great deal remains to be done in explaining links between pay and productivity, this literature offers much to intrigue researchers. The work has relevance for a wide range of topics, including what formerly were called dual labor market structures and have been reborn as efficiency wage models, turnover and promotion rules, academic tenure, and, perhaps most of all, the meaning of a job. What is certainly clear, as Lazear points out, is that jobs cannot be defined independently of the effort expended and compensation anticipated by workers. The new economics of personnel thus appears to offer a conceptual framework which is redefining older economic notions of work and pay.

Race and Gender Pay Differentials

The decade of the 1970s featured a plethora of theoretical and empirical research on pay differentials by race and sex. During the 1980s, somewhat less attention was devoted to these subgroups of the work force as researchers conducted in-depth studies of wage structures and the increasing pay gaps between low- and high-wage workers. Nevertheless, the motivation for studying race/sex pay differentials remains strong, since puzzling and contradictory developments marked pay patterns during the 1980s. Thus, black workers' earnings relative to whites' fell over the last decade while, in contrast, women's pay rates relative to men's rose steadily over the last ten years.

In attempting to explain these trends, Francine Blau and Lawrence Kahn show that returns to education and skill increased over the decade of the 1980s. This was primarily due to a decline in the demand for low-skilled workers and a reduction in unionization. This shift apparently reduced many minorities' wages because educational quality was low; even more disturbing, there is some evidence that the relative quality of schooling may have deteriorated for blacks entering the job market during the 1980s as compared to whites. Another factor that may explain falling relative wages for blacks is the suggestion in the literature reviewed by Blau and Kahn that an increased supply of college-educated blacks drove down their relative pay. In contrast, relative pay for women rose over the decade because they were employed in industries which grew relatively faster and because they developed more on-the-job experience.

To further evaluate these findings, the authors present new estimates of log wage equations for different race/sex groups using Current Population Survey data from 1972, 1982, and 1989. Their results confirm the aforementioned finding that changes in industry mix had positive effects on women's relative pay. However, these industry mix findings do not explain why relative pay for black men deteriorated during the 1980s. This is puzzling in light of other scholars' conclusions, and is a finding which remains to be explored in future research.

In addition to the industry mix explanation, there is also evidence that labor force composition changes explain some of the relative pay trends during the 1980s. Employment rates varied across population subgroups and over time, meaning that comparisons of pay should recognize and correct for possible systematic sample selectivity. Blau and Kahn suggest that the white work force became "more selective" over the 1980s, particularly for younger people, so some and perhaps most of the deterioration in black/white pay rates over time would have been eliminated if this were taken into account. For women, on the other hand, labor force participation rates continued to increase over the 1980s, implying that selectivity probably worked in the other direction: that is, the female/male pay ratio would probably have improved even more dramatically had it not been for women's increased labor market attachment.

The 1970s generated much research on government antidiscrimination policy, but research output on this topic withered during the 1980s, corresponding with decreased federal government enforcement efforts. Antidiscrimination efforts at the state government level included the enactment of comparable worth policies, which many researchers concluded serve to equalize female/male pay while lowering employment in affected occupations. As Blau and Kahn point out, these studies "remind us that such policies also impose costs."

One of the strengths of this chapter is the frequent reference to international findings regarding pay differentials by sex and ethnic groups. Such international comparisons are critical in arriving at a better understanding of how the U.S. labor market operates. For example, we learn that the U.S. wage distribution penalizes those with below-average skills more harshly than is the case in other industrialized countries. Such insights are central if we are to evaluate the long-term consequences of increasing internationalization of the labor market. Blau and Kahn also recommend that future research on pay differentials be more carefully integrated with recent developments, described in an earlier chapter by Lazear, in labor market theory and the new economics of personnel.

Immigration

What are the economic costs and benefits from immigration to the United States? George Borjas succinctly addresses this question and summarizes reasons why economists' view of immigration changed so dramatically during the 1980s. While not everyone will agree with Borjas's economics, and some may disagree with his stress on economic factors to the exclusion of social and demographic factors, the chapter is a clear and well-argued statement of what has been learned, and what remains to be learned, in immigration economics.

One explanation of the controversy surrounding immigration research is the fact that at the end of the 1970s, most saw immigration through rose-colored glasses. At that time, notes Borjas, it was generally agreed that immigrants lacked skills on arrival to the U.S., but assimilated quickly and contributed positively to national well-being. Their children did even better, the story went, overtaking their parents and many other groups as well. The facts appear to have changed by the end of the 1980s, however, mostly for the worse. Borjas reports that skills of recent immigrants fell sharply as compared to previous cohorts of immigrants, and their labor market performance was much worse. Not only did more recent immigrants fail to catch up with native-born Americans, their children are also doing worse. Borjas rounds out this disturbing new view of immigration by showing that immigrants depend on welfare programs far more than in the past, and that recent immigration may have widened pay differentials between skilled and unskilled workers.

Borjas offers several explanations for the turnabout in immigration evidence. A useful contribution of his work is to clarify the importance of identification assumptions in empirical earnings models of immigrants and native-born workers. Past researchers used a single cross-section survey of many cohorts of immigrants, concluding that people who had been in the U.S. longer were well assimilated since their pay levels exceeded those of recent migrants. In contrast, Borjas arrives at a very different answer by carefully distinguishing cohort and assimilation effects, exploiting repeated cross-section and panel data sets. Thus recent cohorts are seen as earning less because they are inherently less skilled, rather than merely recent entrants. He links this conclusion to an assessment of immigrants' countries of origin, and ties the decline in immigrants' skills to the fact that recent immigrants are Latin American and Asian, rather than European. This last conclusion is buttressed by an economic migration model in which Borjas posits that immigrants of the 1980s were those with the least to gain in their home countries; hence recent immigrants are seen to be "negatively selected," in contrast to those who came before and were "positively selected."

One of the most valuable elements of this paper is Borjas's organizing framework. He poses three central questions that he believes future immigration research should address more thoroughly: (1) How do immigrants do in the U.S. economy? (2) What is the impact of immigration on native workers' opportunities? and (3) Does the U.S. benefit from immigration? This format is exactly what is needed to clarify what has been done right in the past (and what has not), and also clearly points to what remains to be done. For example, more needs to be understood regarding women workers' role in migration, and the importance of the underground economy in which many illegal aliens are found. To date there has been too little linkage of the immigration literature with studies of international trade, a subject requiring more future attention. Nevertheless, Borjas's findings on the causes and consequences of immigration will certainly command center stage in the continuing policy debate on this key national issue.

Work Force Preparedness

Much has been said about worker quality in the industrial relations literature of the past decade, and this is the subject of John Bishop's research on work force preparedness. Two questions are central to his chapter: (1) Does schooling and academic achievement increase productivity? and (2) Are returns to schooling improving over time? Bishop answers both questions affirmatively, drawing from an impressive and diverse body of literature spanning psychology, education, economics, and human resources.

Focusing initially on the academic-productivity relationship, Bishop points out that other researchers have found it difficult to tie these together, especially when workers' productivity is represented by their earnings. Indeed, he finds no link between pay and demonstrated competence in math, science, or language arts, at least for young men, and offers two explanations of this finding. One emphasizes employers' inability to detect academic competence and tie it to performance on the job, while the other relies on the sort of long-term contracts, described by Lazear, in which wage earnings at any given period do not necessarily reflect that period's productivity. Nonetheless, Bishop contends that academic achievement does enhance worker productivity based on the analysis of several data sets which measure such productivity in unusually fine detail. The contribution of this section of his chapter, then, is to draw our attention to the need for further human capital investment irrespective of its measured impact on wage earnings.

Turning to trends in returns to schooling over time and lacking direct productivity data, Bishop relies on earnings data and concludes, as do others in this volume, that there is a widening pay gap between more and less well-educated U.S. workers. Of particular note are high rates of pay among those with technical training, including scientists and engineers, computer programmers, and others employed in these fields. Based on this finding, plus the finding that the supply of college graduates is dwindling, Bishop concludes that the payoff to higher education is not likely to decline in the near future.

The research agenda which flows from Bishop's work is a rich and varied one. He recommends more work to devise improved educational tests, more analysis of how employers use "objective" data in setting their recruiting, hiring, training, and turnover targets, and better linkage of schooling achievements to workplace productivity. Readers will also be likely to think of related questions of their own; Why, for instance, do young women's wages appear to reward schooling achievement, while young men's do not? Is it likely that educational testing of the sort that Bishop recommends will be tolerated in an educational system which has been moving away from, instead of toward, standardized tests over the last decade? Clearly, researchers from diverse fields will have to cooperate on multidisciplinary research during the next decade in order to answer these questions. Without such cooperation, further progress on work force preparedness may falter, even though it is perhaps the most important issue facing the labor market of the future.

Industrial Relations and Human Resource Regulation

The Role of the State in Industrial Relations

The initial paper in this section deals not with a particular topic or subject of regulation but instead with the role of the state. Roy Adams examines this role, using a variety of historical and contemporary evidence from several developed countries. He points out that during much of the 19th century, the role of the state (central government) in advanced economies was largely to outlaw restraints of trade so as to spur private market activity. Between the late 19th and the mid-20th centuries, most central governments undertook measures to support private-sector unionism and collective bargaining, but often with limitations on strike activity.

Following World War II, the role of central governments in developed nations expanded considerably with most of them undertaking new policy measures to spur economic growth, regulate the labor market, and enhance industrial democracy, including (in Western Europe) works councils and codetermination. At roughly the same time, notes Adams, most developed nations (except the U.S.) adopted policies of neocorporatism or tripartism to formulate and implement incomes policies and, more broadly, to define the terms of the social contract.

By the 1980s, much of this had changed and deregulation proceeded apace in developed countries with consequent implications for industrial relations. According to Adams, deregulation initiatives in the United States and Britain during the 1980s substantially undermined unions and collective bargaining to the point where their future viability is called into question. While some readers may disagree with this interpretation, they are more likely to concur with Adams' proposition that government should properly be viewed as making strategic choices with respect to industrial relations.

Indeed, Adams proceeds from this proposition to distinguish two distinct perspectives on the role of government as an actor in the industrial relations system (Dunlop 1958). One perspective is *normative*, which views the proper role of the state in economic affairs as looking after the public interest—the state is the agent of the public. The other perspective is *positive*, which appears to mean that there is no "proper" role for the state. Instead, the "positive analyst" asks why the state does what it does—in the present case, why it does what it does with respect to industrial relations.

Adams clearly favors the positive approach to research on government regulation of industrial relations, and the remainder of his paper is largely a call for a new conceptualization of the role of the state which invokes this positive tradition and which relies on the tools of political science. But rather than concluding on this note, Adams goes on to identify and describe some leading frameworks and theories used by political scientists and public policy analysts to conceptualize the role of the state—frameworks which he believes are of particular relevance to industrial relations.

One of these is pluralism which calls attention to the multiple institutions that often represent the state and to the notion that the state is not a neutral actor but, instead, has interests of its own. Adams suggests that Australian research employing regulatory life cycle theory and U.S. research on strategic choice theory in industrial relations fit well within this pluralism framework, though Adams vigorously criticizes the latter for its alleged failure adequately to conceptualize the role of the state.

Another political science-based framework for analyzing the role of the state reviewed by Adams is that of Marxist and quasi-Marxist thought, which is typically posed as an alternative to pluralism. A version of this school of thought is reflected in the critical legal studies (CRITS) literature, which came to prominence in the U.S. during the 1980s and which is more fully analyzed by Finkin later in this volume. In brief, CRITS advocates claim that the "state" has undermined U.S. unions and retarded labor's potential for developing a radical agenda by "wrongfully" substituting an individualistic for a collective employment relationship. A less extreme conceptualization of the role of the state, according to Adams, is offered by French regulation theory which invokes the concept of "regimes of accumulation" to analyze the fit of a society's industrial relations and business systems to its economic and regulatory systems. Using this concept as a point of departure, Adams suggests that the dominant challenge to national governments in the 1990s will be to develop public policies which support the type of high-commitment work and employment systems that "appear to accord with the new realities of international economic competition." As the authors of several other papers in this volume point out, however, high-commitment work and employment systems do not necessarily fit every nation, industry, firm, work group, or individual employee.

The last political science-based theory reviewed by Adams is statist theory, which seeks to explain why government policy is often contradictory and thus apparently poses a threat to itself. The leading example of such contradiction is said to have been the British government's simultaneous support of and opposition to shopfloor bargaining during the 1970s and 1980s. Adams' review of this experience leads him to conclude that, during periods of stability the state seeks to maintain public order and thus support its articulated policies—in this case, opposing shopfloor bargaining. During turbulent times however, the state seeks accommodations with various interest groups, which in the British case resulted in agreements with labor unions that ostensibly supported shopfloor bargaining.

While hardly fully embracing any of the political science-based theories of the role of the state that he reviews, Adams commends them to the attention of scholars interested in explaining why the state "does what it does" with respect to the regulation of industrial relations. More generally, Adams recommends that industrial relations scholars develop a better understanding of the role of government as an actor—a positive actor—in the industrial relations system. To this end, scholars could well begin with the question, "Why does industrial relations/human resource regulation come into being?"

The Regulation of Labor-Management Relations

There is little doubt that, during the past decade or so, the focus of U.S. regulation in the area of labor-management relations shifted away from union-management relations and toward employee-employer relations. Such issues as wrongful termination, employee drug testing, employee AIDS testing, employee polygraph testing, and access to personnel file information, among others, have drawn increased attention from U.S. courts and state legislatures, if not the federal Congress. In fact, the decade of the 1980s was also notable for the shift from the federal government to state governments as the locus of most major actions insofar as the regulation of the employment relationship in the U.S. is concerned.

Matthew Finkin not only documents both of these shifts, he shows how they were paralleled by developments in labor law scholarship during the 1980s. Whereas in the 1960s labor law scholarship focused on collective bargaining, the "issue" of union power, and the appropriateness of the Taft-Hartley Act as a national labor policy, by the 1980s labor law scholarship had become far more specialized to focus on such issues as wrongful termination and particular categories of employment discrimination—as examples, age, sex, race, and handicapped status. In the area of union-management relations, Finkin points out that recent regulatory developments and recent labor law research have focused on the issue of substitutes for unionism and unionized employees in the form of, on the one hand, employer-initiated employee involvement/participation plans and, on the other hand, replacements for striking workers.

But Finkin's paper does far more than this. He analyzes such recently emergent areas of labor law scholarship as nontraditional legal writing (including in the area of law and economics), critical legal studies (CRITS), feminism, critical race theory, and "storytelling" (by which is meant the interpretation of law through the narration of personal experience). Finkin's main conclusion about these developments is that they run a substantial risk of being judged as non-scholarship, that is, of advocating personal political and intellectual preferences without an adequate basis in law. Worse still, says Finkin, the bulk of recent labor law scholarship may be "out of touch with real workplace legal problems." Readers can judge the validity of this conclusion for themselves, but it is a major contribution of Finkin's chapter to show how larger social, economic, and political factors substantially influenced both the regulation of U.S. labor-management relations and labor law scholarship during the 1980s.

Finkin's paper was the subject of discussion comments by Clyde W. Summers at a conference on the 1992 IRRA research volume held at the University of Pennsylvania's Wharton School in October 1991 (that conference served as a refereeing step for the papers in the volume). Professor Summers observed that the literature in the areas of CRITS and law and economics, which otherwise differ markedly, take on the quality of fundamentalism and ignore other values. In the case of CRITS, strong emphasis is placed on the alleged incoherence of traditional industrial pluralism in U.S. labor law and on judicial interpretations of the law which serve to manipulate employee discontent and undermine labor's radical potential. In the case of law and economics, the dominant emphasis is on the uses of labor law (and the law more broadly) to support market efficiency, thereby limiting the law's role in individual and collective employment relationships. Both Finkin and Summers are troubled by the single-mindedness of these respective schools of labor law scholarship, and by both schools' tendency to offer philosophically-based broad generalizations as scholarship.

Proceeding from Finkin's paper, Summers proposed that future labor law scholarship be concerned with codifying employee representation rights in the absence of unionism, determining appropriate uniform law in the area of employment-at-will, more fully defining the right of privacy in the employment relationship, and formulating procedures to enforce new statutory employment rights (also see Summers 1991). Interestingly, this research agenda could be reformulated to focus on the policies and procedures through which the law, together with market forces, can (or should) provide individual and collective voice to employees in the employment relationship. Neither Finkin nor Summers pay much attention to the large literature on employee voice that developed during the 1980s (Lewin and Mitchell 1992)—which supports, though not quite in the way he intended, Finkin's observation about the increasing compartmentalization of labor law scholarship.

Again proceeding from Finkin's paper, Summers and John F. Burton, Jr., Chair of the IRRA Editorial Committee and also a Wharton conference participant, emphasized the role of law students in determining legal scholarship. This is because law students manage and edit law reviews, and are usually the authors of (unsigned) notes, articles, and book reviews that appear in law journals. These facts came as a surprise to other (non-legally trained) participants in the Wharton conference, as they no doubt will to many readers of this volume. Scholars from disciplines and fields other than law might care to speculate about how scholarship in their respective areas of specialization might differ from what it is at present (or what it will be in future) if graduate students were "in charge" of major journals.

OSHA and Workers' Compensation

Despite twenty years of federal regulation, the U.S. workplace appears at least as dangerous as it ever was. Industry-specific injury rates throughout the 1980s were in many cases higher than in all previous years, and the annual number of workdays lost rose by almost one-third since the mid-1970s. Why has the record been so dismal in making jobs safer? According to Robert Smith, recent research offers some answers to this question, though there does not yet appear to be a simple or single explanation readily amenable to policy change.

A central problem plaguing research on workplace safety is the lack of good data. Statistics do not exist by which to compare work injuries prior to and following the 1970 Occupational Safety and Health Act (OSHA). In addition, the U.S. Department of Labor risk data are quite imperfect, capturing fewer than one-third of the trauma-induced work-related deaths reported by other government agencies. Finally, the Occupational Safety and Health Administration twice implemented policy changes in the 1980s which altered firms' tendencies to report injuries. Most important among these changes was the use of employer injury logs to target the firms that would receive in-depth inspections in 1981 (which appears to have induced underreporting), and the imposition of new penalties for underreporting injuries in 1986 (which seems to have decreased underreporting).

Numerous empirical studies in the last decade have examined how OSHA and workers' compensation programs affect risk levels in the workplace. Smith reviews the best of the recent studies linking workplace injury rates and the probability of OSHA inspection and concludes that there is no evidence for a powerful "threat" or deterrent OSHA effect prior to an inspection. He also finds little evidence of the occurrence of an inspection on subsequent years' injury patterns. A large part of the explanation for this null finding is that OSHA fines remain quite low, averaging less than $300, and most firms have a small chance of being inspected.

If low OSHA fines cannot increase workplace safety, then it might be thought that the workers' compensation program would do better. This is because firms with higher injury rates are generally required to pay more under the workers' compensation program, thereby presumably forcing companies with dangerous jobs to do more to make the jobs safer. However, the program is far from perfectly experience rated, with changes in risk sometimes taking four years to be reflected in premiums.

Smith also notes that the workers' compensation statistics should be viewed with caution. This is because there is some evidence that employers underreport serious injuries, while workers overreport injuries and remain home longer when benefit levels are more generous. About the only solid evidence of the workers' compensation program's effects on "real" safety levels is that higher benefit levels are associated with lower medical cost reimbursements.

In describing what remains to be done in this area, Smith calls for better firm-level work injury data, more precisely measured workers' compensation premium rates, and firm-specific OSHA inspection probabilities. He recommends that researchers seek to disentangle true program effects from "reporting" effects in order to determine what might improve workplace safety. Finally, Smith cautions that many work injuries can be attributed to worker carelessness or transient conditions, and suggests that regulatory standards can be expected to reduce work injuries by at most 25 percent even in the best of situations. Of particular interest here would be studies that examine the effects of new work rules and procedures (of the type described earlier in this volume by Katz and Keefe) on workplace injuries. In any case, making the workplace safer seemingly will require a combination of old and new policies designed to affect outcomes directly as well as through changes in working conditions.

Social Insurance and Benefits

Daniel Mitchell reviews developments in the literature on social insurance and employee benefits over the last ten years. Because this field is so broad, he sensibly limits most of his discussion to the two major components of the benefits/social insurance package, namely, retirement income and health care insurance. Mitchell begins with an overview of the stylized facts about and history of employer-provided benefits and social insurance. He then goes on to critique what has been learned about the causes of health care cost inflation and developments in the pension arena.

One valuable contribution of this paper is its portfolio approach to employer-provided benefits and social insurance. Too often researchers investigate pensions alone or Social Security payments as a freestanding subject, or focus on the rising costs of health care, without paying enough attention to the mix of private versus social benefits and the costs and trade-offs among elements of the benefits package. Mitchell's historical perspective is quite instructive, tracing the spurts and starts of employer initiatives against the backdrop of federal programs in related areas. His international perspective is also informative, emphasizing that the U.S. split between public and private provision is by no means the only way to structure benefits, nor is it necessarily the most sensible.

Readers of this chapter may particularly enjoy but also challenge Mitchell's interpretation of past research, which is both dubious and damning. He condemns much previous research as useless because of the tendency to develop untestable complex economic models and for the pursuit of what he regards as dead-end questions, such as the effects of Social Security on savings rates and the effects of unemployment insurance on the duration of unemployment. Another of Mitchell's concerns is that researchers have not communicated their findings to policymakers and practitioners in the last decade. He also suggests that researchers in the 1980s were either not interested in issues of fairness and equity or were "uncomfortable" in talking about these matters with policymakers.

While some may join with him in lamenting the disappearance of what he calls old-style institutionalists, Mitchell's harsh assessment of past research is perhaps unduly negative. In each benefit area, there have been numerous studies of not only the efficiency but also the equity ramifications of changing benefits policy. Thus, in the health area, for example, a great deal was learned from creative efforts by RAND Corporation studies during the 1980s of health insurance experiments, and much thought went into evaluating alternative health care systems. Mitchell also downplays studies exploring the welfare economics of various tax and benefits policies along with labor supply. Further, it can be argued that Mitchell overlooks some of the "new institutionalism"-type research on efficiency wages, pensions, long-term contracting in the labor market, and the like—issues which are addressed by Lazear elsewhere in this volume.

Nevertheless, Mitchell offers some thought-provoking prescriptions for what benefits researchers should examine in the years ahead. For example, he forecasts that the future of job-linked benefits is grim in light of increased employee mobility, corporate restructuring, and deregulated competition. Surely this view merits increased research attention, particularly in light of the internationalization of the labor market. In keeping with the traditions of the IRRA, Mitchell also calls for more discussion among policymakers, academic researchers, and practitioners insofar as social insurance and benefits are concerned. While few academics would disagree with this view, it should be recognized that researchers frequently find that their real world counterparts will not always be willing to sit across a table to discuss research questions with them. This is occasionally due to a communications gap, as some academics have trouble using language accessible to the lay public. But it may be that a more important obstacle to such discussions is that academics and others are not interested in the same questions; even when they are, they tend to have very different standards for data collection and statistical testing. Nonetheless, better research on employee benefits and social insurance must be contingent on improved access to firm-side data, and improvements along these lines would surely be welcome.

Concluding Thoughts

In its scope of coverage, presentation of new evidence, and delineation of future agendas, this volume may well stand apart from others published by the IRRA which have reviewed prior decades' worth of research—though final judgments in this regard are better left to readers than to the editors. Nevertheless, and recognizing that this is the last "research review" volume to be published by the IRRA in the 20th century, we end this introductory chapter with a few concluding observations.

First, the decline of unionism in the U.S. and in most industrialized nations during the late 20th century should cause industrial relations/human resource (IR/HR) scholars to reconsider their "focal" interests. Whereas from the immediate post-World War II period to about the late 1960s union-management relations provided a core research focus for IR/HR scholars, developments since then strongly suggest that the employment relationship is and should be at the core of IR/HR researchers' focal interests irrespective of the extent or type of unionism that may characterize a nation, an industry, a firm, or a group of workers. In this regard, the behavior and perceptions of workers in response to changes in work rules and practices (of the type analyzed by Katz and Keefe), the dynamics and consequences of newer type workplace dispute resolution procedures (such as those analyzed by Peterson), and macro- and micro-level determinants of strikes (of the type analyzed by Kaufman) clearly merit the close attention of IR/HR scholars.

Second, the proposition (forwarded by Cappelli and Singh) that the strategic management of human resources can provide a competitive advantage to the firm offers a broad-ranging research agenda for IR/HR scholars. To illustrate, various initiatives in compensation and reward systems (of the type described by Gerhart, Milkovich, and Murray), team-based work arrangements (of the type described by Ichniowski), and internal labor market practices (of the type described by Osterman) have been undertaken in the belief that they enhance the performance of the firm. Whether they in fact do so, and whether the firm's choice of particular human resource practices or packages is systematically contingent on the fit of such practices/packages to the firm's business strategy, structural characteristics or other variables, are empirical questions which IR/HR scholars appear to be well equipped to address. Kochan, Dyer, and Batt forcefully advocate that IR/HR scholars address these and related issues in international/comparative settings—in part so as to avoid conclusions and generalizations based largely on American exceptionalism.

Third, the functioning of labor markets remains an essential theoretical and empirical area of inquiry irrespective of the degree of unionization in a particular economy or labor market. Whether or not certain compensation initiatives, such as the payment of efficiency wages (of the type analyzed by Lazear), actually improve the functioning of labor markets and/or the performance of the firm is an undeniably important research question. But so too are questions regarding the role of wages, new compensation initiatives, and non-money rewards in moderating race and sex discrimination (as analyzed by Blau and Kahn), inducing or retarding immigration (as analyzed by Borjas), and overcoming weaknesses (especially in the U.S.) in work force preparedness (as analyzed by Bishop).

Fourth, government regulation of IR/HR and the labor market appears to continue apace despite an overall trend toward industry and "problem" deregulation in developed and developing nations. The fundamental question in this regard (raised by Adams) is "Why and for what purposes does the (nation) state regulate IR/HR?" A related question is "Why are particular dimensions of IR/HR—for example, labor-management relations (as analyzed by Finkin), occupational safety (as analyzed by Smith), and pension/health benefits (as analyzed by Mitchell)—treated separately by political bodies rather than as components of larger portfolios within which potentially cost-efficient and socially equitable trade-offs might be made?" IR/HR scholars would do well to turn their attention to these admittedly large scale, big picture research questions so that they can help advance national discussion and debate about the issues which underlie these questions.

In conclusion, the employment relationship remains at the heart of IR/HR studies even as the incidence of unionism and collective bargaining continue to decline. The challenge to researchers in this field is to show that they have something important to contribute to the development of new theory and research methodology, to national IR/HR policy making, and to the determination of firm-level IR/HR policy and practice. We believe that the ideas, empirical findings, and research agendas offered by the authors of papers in this volume constitute important contributions in these respects.

References

Aaron, Benjamin. 1992. "Employee Voice: A Legal Perspective," *California Management Review* 34 (Spring): 124-138.

Aaron, Benjamin, Paul S. Meyer, John Crispo, Garth L. Mangum, and James L. Stern. 1971. *A Review of Industrial Relations Research in the 1970s: Volume II*. Madison, WI: Industrial Relations Research Association.

Abowd, John M. 1989. "The Effect of Wage Bargains on the Stock Market Value of Firms," *American Economic Review* 79 (September): 678-690.

Addison, John T. 1985. "What Do Unions Really Do? A Review Article," *Journal of Labor Research* 6 (Spring): 127-146.

Akerloff, George. 1984. "Gift-Exchange and Efficiency Wage Theory: Four Views," *American Economic Review* 77 (May): 79-83.

Andrews, Kenneth R. 1971. *The Concept of Corporate Strategy*. Homewood, IL: Irwin.

Ansoff, Igor. 1965. *Corporate Strategy*. New York: McGraw Hill.

Bain, Joe S. 1956. *Barriers to New Competition*. Cambridge, MA: Harvard University Press.

Bain, Trevor. 1992. "Employee Voice: A Comparative International Perspective," paper presented to the Forty-Fourth Annual Meeting of the Industrial Relations Research Association, New Orleans, LA.

Becker, Brian E., and Craig A. Olson. 1987. "Labor Relations and Firm Performance," in Morris M. Kleiner, Richard N. Block, Myron Roomkin, and Sidney W. Salsburg, eds., *Human Resources and the Performance of the Firm*. Madison, WI: Industrial Relations Research Association: 43-85.

Becker, Brian E., and Craig A. Olson. 1986. "The Impact of Strikes on Shareholder Equity," *Industrial and Labor Relations Review* 39 (April): 425-438.

Blanchflower, David G., and Richard B. Freeman. 1992. "Unionism in the United States and Other Advanced OECD Countries," *Industrial Relations* 31 (Winter): 56-79.

Boroff, Karen, and David Lewin. 1991. "Loyalty, Voice, and Intent to Exit a Nonunion Firm: A Conceptual and Empirical Analysis." Los Angeles: UCLA Institute of Industrial Relations Working Paper #211.

Caves, Richard E., and Michael E. Porter. 1978. "Market Structure, Oligopoly, and Stability of Market Shares," *Journal of Industrial Economics* 26 (Spring): 289-313.

Chaison, Gary N., and Joseph B. Rose. 1991. "The Macrodeterminants of Union Growth and Decline," in George Strauss, Daniel G. Gallagher, and Jack Fiorito, eds., *The State of the Unions*. Madison, WI: Industrial Relations Research Association: 3-45.

Chandler, Alfred D. 1962. *Strategy and Structure: Chapters in the History of American Industrial Enterprise*. Cambridge, MA: M.I.T. Press.

Clark, Kim B. 1984. "Unionization and Firm Performance: The Impact on Profits, Growth, and Productivity," *American Economic Review* 74 (December): 893-919.

Commons, John R. 1919. *Industrial Goodwill*. New York: McGraw-Hill.

Doeringer, Peter B., and Michael J. Piore. 1971. *Internal Labor Markets and Manpower Analysis*. Lexington, MA: Heath.

Dunlop, John T. 1958. *Industrial Relations Systems*. New York: Henry Holt.

Dunlop, John T. 1957. *The Theory of Wage Determination*. London: MacMillan.

Feuille, Peter, and John Thomas Delaney. 1992. "The Individual Pursuit of Organizational Justice: Grievance Procedures in Nonunion Workplaces," in Gerald G. Ferris and Kenneth M. Rowland, eds., *Research in Personnel and Human Resource Management, vol. 10*. Greenwich, CT: JAI Press, forthcoming.

Freeman, Richard B. 1986. "Unionism Comes to the Public Sector," *Journal of Economic Literature* 24 (March): 41-86.

Freeman, Richard B., and James L. Medoff. 1986. *What Do Unions Do?* New York: Basic Books.

Ginsburg, Woodrow L., E. Robert Livernash, Herbert S. Parnes, and George Strauss. 1970. *A Review of Industrial Relations Research in the 1970s: Volume I*. Madison, WI: Industrial Relations Research Association.

Hendricks, Wallace. 1975. "Labor Market Structure and Union Wage Levels," *Economic Inquiry* 13 (September): 401-416.

Hirsch, Barry T. 1992. "Firm Investment Behavior and Collective Bargaining Strategy," *Industrial Relations* 31 (Winter): 95-121.

Hirschman, Albert O. 1970. *Exit, Voice, and Loyalty*. Cambridge, MA: Harvard University Press.

Katz, Harry C., ed. 1991. *The Future of Industrial Relations*. Ithaca, NY: New York State School of Industrial and Labor Relations, Cornell University.

Kerr, Clark. 1954. "The Balkanization of Labor Markets," in E. Wight Bakke, ed., *Labor Mobility and Economic Opportunity*. Cambridge, MA: MIT Press: 92-110.

Kerr, Clark, John T. Dunlop, Frederick Harbison, and Charles A. Myers. 1964. *Industrialism and Industrial Man*, 2nd ed. New York: Oxford University Press.

Kochan, Thomas A., Harry C. Katz, and Robert B. McKersie. 1986. *The Transformation of American Industrial Relations*. New York: Basic Books.

Kochan, Thomas A., Robert B. McKersie, and Peter Cappelli. 1984. "Strategic Choice and Industrial Relations Theory," *Industrial Relations* 23 (Winter): 16-39.

Lewin, David. 1992. "Conflict Resolution and Management in Contemporary Work Organizations: Theoretical Perspectives and Empirical Evidence," in Samuel B. Bacharach, Ronald L. Seeber, and David J. Walsh, eds., *Research in the Sociology of Organizations, Vol. 12*. Greenwich, CT: JAI Press, forthcoming.

Lewin, David. 1990. "Grievance Procedures in Nonunion Workplaces: An Empirical Analysis of Usage, Dynamics, and Outcomes," *Chicago-Kent Law Review* 66 (3): 823-844.

Lewin, David, and Daniel J.B. Mitchell. 1992. "Systems of Employee Voice: Theoretical and Empirical Perspectives," *California Management Review* 34 (Spring): 95-111.

Lewin, David, and Richard B. Peterson. 1988. *The Modern Grievance Procedure in the United States*. Westport, CT: Greenwood Press.

Mitchell, Daniel J.B., and Mahmood Zaidi. 1990. "A Symposium: The Economics of Human Resource Management," *Industrial Relations* 29 (Spring): 155-163.

Porter, Michael E. 1980. *Competitive Strategy: Techniques for Analyzing Industries and Competitors*. New York: Free Press.

Reder, Melvin W. 1985. "Comment on *What Do Unions Do?*," by Richard B. Freeman and James L. Medoff, *Industrial and Labor Relations Review* 38 (January): 256-258.

Rees, Albert. 1977. *The Economics of Trade Unions*, rev. ed. Chicago, IL: University of Chicago Press.

Rumelt, Richard P. 1979. "Evolution of Strategy: Theory and Models," in Dan E. Schendel and Charles W. Hofer, eds., *Strategy Management: A New View of Business Policy and Planning*. Boston, MA: Little Brown, 196-215.

Schelling, Thomas C. 1963. *The Strategy of Conflict*. Cambridge, MA: Harvard University Press.

Stagner, Ross, ed. 1981. "Special Issue: Psychologists and Unions," *International Review of Applied Psychology* 30 (April), entire issue.

Steiber, Jack, Robert B. McKersie, and D. Quinn Mills. 1981. *U.S. Industrial Relations 1950-80: A Critical Assessment*. Madison, WI: Industrial Relations Research Association.

Summers, Clyde W. 1991. "Unions Without Majorities: The Potentials of the NLRA," *Proceedings of the Forty-Third Annual Meeting*, Industrial Relations Research Association. Madison, WI: Industrial Relations Research Association: 154-162.

Verma, Anil. 1985. "Relative Flow of Capital to Union and Nonunion Plants Within a Firm," *Industrial Relations* 24 (Fall): 395-405.

Voos, Paula B., and Lawrence R. Mishel. 1986. "The Union Impact on Profits: Evidence from Industry Price-Cost Margin Data," *Journal of Labor Economics* 4 (January): 105-133.

Walker, James A. 1980. *Human Resource Planning*. New York: McGraw-Hill.

Part I

Unions, Bargaining, and Dispute Resolution

CHAPTER 2

Collective Bargaining and Industrial Relations Outcomes: The Causes and Consequences of Diversity

HARRY C. KATZ
Cornell University

JEFFREY H. KEEFE
Rutgers University

> "No matter what standards of comparison are used, there is great diversity in the character and results of collective bargaining. There are many differences in the economic and technological environment. Managements differ in attitudes and policies, and so do unions. . . . Generalizations that unions actually or always have this or that particular effect are highly hazardous" (Slichter, Healy, and Livernash 1960).

The 1980s witnessed the elaboration of a new research literature assessing the effects of work rules and work practices on industrial relations and economic outcomes. This research was spurred by efforts to understand how unionized settings were reorganizing to confront growing domestic nonunion and foreign competition. For example, researchers studying unionized work sites that implemented employee involvement programs, team systems, or reduced job classifications discovered a sizeable diversity in work rules and work practices across the union sector. They were thereby led to examine the sources of industrial relations diversity as well as its consequences.

This chapter reviews this burgeoning literature. First, it examines the evidence for the diversity we have mentioned. Specifically, it considers two kinds of diversity that have been found in collective bargaining practice: cross-sectional variation, where collective bargaining practices vary across plants, firms, and industries at a given point in time; and longitudinal variation, where they vary significantly over time.

Next, it focuses on how work rules and work practices evolved after 1975 in the union sector in the United States, and reviews a number of the many hypotheses offered in recent research to explain the sources of the wide cross-sectional and longitudinal variation revealed in our data. Then it assesses the abundant recent research evaluating the effects on economic performance of the variation in collective bargaining practices and, in particular, of recent modifications in rules and practice.

Much of the new research reviewed here focuses on the connections between collective bargaining practices and firm performance. The chapter ends by identifying both gaps in the research concerning how collective bargaining has affected workers' interests and measurement and conceptual weaknesses in the new line of research.

Defining Terms and the Causal Map

Terms

The research in this domain focuses on three categories of variables: work rules and practices, industrial relations outcomes, and economic outcomes. There are many potential variables and measures within each of the three categories. Table 1 focuses on the variables that have been measured in the recent literature, and for clarification purposes lists some of the examples that have been used to measure components of work organization, dispute resolution, and pay procedures, such as the number of job classifications or the use of team systems.

In some of the new literature, industrial relations outcomes are considered measures of industrial relations performance, just as economic outcomes are considered measures of economic performance. As we discuss later, however, many of the industrial relations outcomes and work rules and practices might also be considered economic outcomes. Nevertheless, how these variables are labeled is less important than the causal map that is used to test hypotheses or interpret data.

Causal Map

The standard causal map relates work rules and practices, industrial relations outcomes, and economic outcomes. The notion is that

TABLE 1
Variables Measured in Recent Literature

Key Categories	Measured Variables	Examples
Work rules and practices	Dispute resolution procedures Pay procedures Work organization	Role of seniority in overtime allocation Number of job classifications Use of pay-for-knowledge Team systems
Industrial relations "performance" outcomes	Absentee rates Grievance rates Worker attitudes Management attitudes Union role Strike frequency	
Economic "performance" outcomes	Productivity Product quality Production flexibility	

work rules and practices exert both direct effects and indirect effects (through industrial relations outcomes) on economic performance. For instance, the use of team systems may directly lead to higher productivity in a plant by reducing scrap or lowering staffing and also lead to lower grievance rates, which might indirectly increase productivity.

It might also be the case that factors other than work rules or practices lead to better industrial relations outcomes in a plant (or firm) and that these improvements produce improvements in economic performance. For example, fear that the plant may soon close or the arrival of a new plant manager might improve relations between management and the union, thus reducing grievance or absentee rates which, in turn, could lead to better productivity or product quality.

Researchers want to know whether work rules and practices and industrial relations outcomes exert statistically significant effects on economic performance. Most importantly, researchers would like to know the economic magnitude of these effects (i.e., the size of the coefficients in regressions explaining economic performance). For example, in addition to learning whether the lowering of grievance rates or the introduction of work teams improves productivity, researchers want to know the magnitude of change.

The Diversity in Industrial Relations Practices and Outcomes Across Unionized Settings in the United States

The Source of Local Variation

An earlier institutional literature discussed the variation in collective bargaining practices and the tenor of labor-management relations (often alleged to be the source of the variation in practice) across unionized firms. See, for example, Harbison and Dubin (1947), Golden and Parker (1949), and Harbison and Coleman (1951). During the 1960s and 1970s, however, the mission of industrial relations research changed from explaining diversity to testing general propositions; an example of this new trend was the immense number of union wage-effect studies made possible by newly collected data and computerized statistical programs.

In practice, over the 1960s and early 1970s, collective bargaining of economic issues was often centralized (or at least in many cases was becoming relatively more centralized over this period). This centralization gave further impetus to researchers' focus on general economic outcomes.

At the local level, however, collective bargaining remained centered on work rules, grievances, supervision, and the informal systems of shop floor control. The local union strategy for shopfloor representation during this period is best characterized as job control unionism. Under this system unions and management negotiated highly formalized local contracts and a quasi-judicial grievance procedure to adjudicate disputes during the term of those contracts. Workers' earnings were determined by the wages attached to their job classifications. Lifetime income, access to better working conditions, employment security during periods of slack work, and protection from arbitrary treatment flowed from this system of highly delineated job classifications and seniority rules regulating the process of vacancy allocations and training opportunities. Management, through local contractual language and agreements, sought to preserve its right to manage and to restrict the unions influence only to mandatory issues of bargaining. Work rule concessions at the shop floor level, however, were often traded by labor relations managers eager to prevent work stoppages.

New Quantitative Evidence of Diversity

In contrast to earlier research, a novel aspect of the new literature is that it quantitatively documents a wide diversity in the work rules and work practices and industrial relations outcomes across unionized plants and firms—even across work groups and work areas within the same unionized plant. Not only does this new literature provide quantitative evidence of this variation, it uses this data to assess the effects exerted by work rules and work practices (and industrial relations outcomes) on economic performance. An example of this literature is research examining the diversity in grievance activity.

Diversity in Grievance Activity

Data show wide variation in grievance filing within the same industry and even within the same firm. For example, data from General Motors plants covered by the same national labor agreement and operating with similar technologies reveal wide variation in grievance rates. Katz, Kochan, and Gobeille (1983) find that in the same year, grievances per 100 workers varied from a low of 24 in one plant to a high of 450 in another. Ichniowski (1986) finds wide variation in grievance rates across paper mills.

Where consistent measures are available across unionized companies, similar extensive variation is reported. There also is evidence of wide variation of grievance activity across industries as reported by Lewin and Peterson (1988, p. 87). In reviewing the grievance literature Gordon and Miller (1984, p. 122) report highly diverse grievance rates, but caution that there is no uniform, valid, or reliable standard for measuring or classifying grievances.

A qualitative literature also identifies substantial variation in the administration of the grievance procedure (see Kuhn 1961). Grievances are often used to influence collective bargaining agendas and outcomes as grievance rates significantly increase just prior to negotiations (Lewin and Peterson 1988, p. 193). Disputes over contract interpretation can properly be conceptualized as part of the continuous collective bargaining process.

Fractional shop floor bargaining utilizes the grievance procedure as one element in the ongoing contest between work groups and supervisors, often with an end result of day-to-day accommodations. Fractional bargaining has been shown to be widespread and enduring (Kuhn 1961; Lewin and Peterson 1988, p. 193). In fact, one of the purposes of recent employee participation programs is to normalize and open up the process of fractional bargaining.

Correlations across Industrial Relations Measures and Components

The new data reveal substantial intercorrelation across various measures and components of industrial relations practice and performance. For example, Katz, Kochan, and Gobeille (1983) and Katz, Kochan, and Weber (1985) report correlations among plant-level industrial relations outcomes that are large and statistically significant. These correlations lend support to the notion that various components of shop floor industrial relations reinforce one another. The correlations suggest the spillover of behavior, attitudes, or conflict on the shop floor.

Union vs. Nonunion Practices

Even in the face of the wide diversity revealed within unionized plants, the new data also show that there are strong and consistent commonalities in union practice. In particular, the research shows that union practices differ markedly from work rules and practices in nonunion firms and plants (Verma 1983; Arthur 1990; Eaton and Voos 1991).

It is interesting to note that much less research has surfaced to date that documents quantitatively or qualitatively the extent of diversity that exists in the work rules and practices of nonunion plants and firms. The absence of the sort of formal documentation of work practices that derives from the presence of a collective bargaining agreement in the union sector may be a partial explanation for this. It also may be harder to measure some aspects of nonunion practices given that grievance rates and formal contractual work rules do not exist. We also sense that nonunion firms have been less willing to grant researchers access to their work sites.

Trends in Work Rules and Work Practices

The literature just reviewed primarily focuses on the variation in collective bargaining practices across plants at a given point in time. Collective bargaining practices and contractual language also appear to vary substantially over time (longitudinal variation). The next section analyzes how collective bargaining changed in the United States after 1975. It relies heavily on descriptive data accumulated in surveys of major collective bargaining agreements conducted by the Bureau of National Affairs (BNA). This review of recent trends also refers to other research examining these trends.

This section frequently refers to data from BNA's *Basic Patterns of Union Contracts* (1975; 1989). The BNA samples 400 labor contracts primarily drawn from manufacturing. The section will discuss recent trends in collective bargaining practices and contractual language concerning: grievance administration; union-management cooperation and employee participation; management and union rights; work force adjustment and seniority; and wage rules and work schedules. These issues have long been central trends in American collective bargaining; however, they have occurred within the broader context of declining private-sector unionism and collective bargaining. During the last decade, the decline of private-sector unionism accelerated, with union density falling from 24 percent to 12 percent, while the actual number of union members declined for the first time since the New Deal.

Grievance Administration

The BNA data reported in Table 2 reveal that grievance and arbitration procedures remain a central part of a substantial share of

TABLE 2

Grievance Procedures and Disciplinary Standards

Collectively Bargained Work Rule Provisions	1975	1989	Percentage Change
Discipline & Discharge			
Just cause provision	79%	86%	*9%
Specific grounds	66	75	*14
Notice to union for discharge	43	54	*26
Notice to union for discipline	29	50	*72
Grievances & Arbitration			
Grievance procedure	98	99	1
Number of steps in grievance procedure — 1	6	7	17
Number of steps in grievance procedure — 2	18	21	17
Number of steps in grievance procedure — 3	48	48	0
Number of steps in grievance procedure — 4	25	21	−16
Number of steps in grievance procedure — 5	3	3	0
Conciliation and mediation prior to arbitration	5	4	−20
Expedited arbitration	74	72	−3
Pay for union representatives for grievance time	49	55	*12
Job security provision for union reps	44	36	*−18
Restrictions on arbitrators	80	82	3
Restrictions on scope of arbitration	65	95	*46
Arbitration expense shared equally	81	82	1

*Significant difference $p < .01$.

collective bargaining agreements. Furthermore, the BNA data show that the parties did not radically modify grievance procedures in recent years. Lewin and Peterson (1988, p. 209), in their thorough examination of the grievance procedure and its usage, also find little evidence that employers or unions wish to abandon or substantially modify existing grievance and disciplinary procedures.

Nevertheless, the BNA data show that there were some changes made in grievance and arbitration procedures. In the area of employee discipline and discharge, for example, the parties have continued to codify the arbitral standard of just cause for discipline (note the 9 percent rise in the frequency of just cause provisions). Management also continues to expand its use of the contract to provide general notice for specific rule infractions (see the 14 percent rise in the use of specific grounds provisions). Unions more frequently have negotiated notification requirements for employee discipline and discharge which, if handled properly by the union, can add a level of protection to both parties from duty of fair representation suits.

Lewin and Peterson (1988) report positive outcomes from expedited grievance procedures, which speed up grievance settlement, heighten perceptions of the importance of grievance issues, and raise the sense of equity of grievance settlements. Almost three-fourths of collective bargaining agreements provide for expedited grievance procedure, yet, as revealed in the data in Table 2, there is no indication that they became more widespread from 1975 to 1989. Furthermore, although there has been a renewed interest in grievance mediation in recent years, the BNA data show no major movement toward its adoption.

Union-Management Cooperation and Employee Participation

There is extensive recent industrial relations research examining new labor-management efforts to expand cooperation and participation. This literature includes several literature reviews (Cooke 1990; Levine and Tyson 1990; Eaton and Voos 1991). Rather than duplicate these reviews, we identify some trends revealed in the research and suggest several areas where future research needs to focus. Before we get started, however, we need to clarify some terms.

By union-management cooperation, we mean a set of institutional processes and procedures established to improve relations and solve problems outside, but alongside, the traditional collective bargaining relationship. We use the term employee participation to cover programs that involve hourly employees in discussions about improving the work environment and group performance under such names as quality of work life (QWL), employee involvement, and quality circles. The forum for this type of participation is often regular weekly or biweekly meetings that usually take place on company time and at company expense, but do not necessarily entail any fundamental work reorganization. Consequently, these programs are often referred to as off-line participation.

In contrast, team systems involve work reorganizations, often including job classification reductions, job rotation, job enlargement, and reductions in direct supervision. Teams emphasize group participation in problem solving and group responsibility in accomplishing work tasks and achieving organizational goals.

The BNA data reported in Table 3 indicate dramatic growth in the frequency of pledges of cooperation (from 14 percent of contracts in 1975 to 53 percent in 1989). The growth in joint committees on special problems or mutual interests is less spectacular. The BNA data also indicate that only 6 percent of the sampled collective bargaining agreements in 1989 formally provide for quality of work life programs, yet this represents an upward trend from none in 1975 to 2 percent in 1983 and 4 percent in 1986. QWL and other employee participation programs represent a relatively new innovation in industrial relations as very few QWL programs existed in either the union or nonunion sector prior to the late 1970s, and most have been implemented since 1980 (Eaton and Voos 1991).

While there has been much descriptive research on the new participation programs, a number of key issues need further clarification. Research needs include measuring the dimensions of participation. How do employees participate? Do joint committees make decisions that are implemented? What are the problems that the committees address? What is the appropriate unit of analysis: work group, department, establishment, or company? How are committees selected? Do the committees have mandates or constituents? How does employee participation influence the tenor of labor-management relations? The discrepancy between the prevalence of pledges and committee provisions as revealed in Table 3 raises some interesting issues worthy of exploration.

TABLE 3

Management Rights, Labor-Management Cooperation, and Participation

Collectively Bargained Work Rule Provisions	1975	1989	Percentage Change
Union-Management Cooperation			
Pledge of cooperation	14%	53%	*279%
Joint committees on specific problems	8	15	*88
Joint committees on mutual interests	3	8	*167
Quality of work life program	0	6	*
Management Rights Clauses			
Direct work force	74	76	3
Manage business	74	72	−3
Control production	34	37	9
Frame company rules	27	37	*37
Determine employees' duties	11	27	*145
Close or relocate plant	22	16	*−27
Change technology	19	14	*−26
Restrictions on Management Rights			
General	36	53	*47
Subcontracting	40	54	*35
Supervisory performance of work	57	56	−2
Technological changes	19	27	*42
Plant shutdown or relocation	17	25	*47
Union Rights & Restrictions Clauses			
Access by union representatives	58	55	−5
Bulletin board rights	68	69	1
Access to information	58	61	5
No union activity on company time	25	23	−8
No solicitation of membership on company time	15	16	7
No dues collection on company time	9	9	0

*Significant difference $p < .01$.

Industrial relations research needs to address under what conditions cooperative pledges are negotiated and, in particular, whether pledges are tradeoffs for union concessions. Furthermore, the functioning of joint labor-management committees should be more thoroughly investigated, as should the way joint union-management processes influence intraorganizational bargaining and strategic alignments within union and management organizations. We also need to examine whether and how these union-management efforts at cooperation spill over to the bargaining relationship or shop floor work organization.

Eaton and Voos (1991) compare the nature and extent of workplace innovations in union and nonunion companies. They find that nonunion companies make greater use of profit sharing, but union companies are more likely to use team systems and employee participation programs. They conclude that the union sector leads the nonunion sector with regard to workplace innovations that are more likely to improve the economic performance of work organizations. The research literature on workplace innovations and economic performance, however, has too few studies and too many weaknesses to reach definite conclusions. One source of variation in these studies is the measure of output. Cooke (1990) reports that studies that employ independent measures of output usually find no significant performance effect from workplace innovations, while those studies that rely on managerial appraisals of performance often find a positive performance result.

Management Rights

At the same time that cooperative commitments have grown, the BNA data also indicate that management has contractually reinforced its rights to frame company rules and to determine employee duties. For example, note in Table 3 the substantial increase in management rights clauses concerning control of production, framing of company rules, and the determination of employee duties. Management rights clauses concerning termination of employee duties, for example, appeared in 11 percent of contracts in 1975 and 27 percent of contracts in 1989. The frequency of union rights clauses, as revealed in Table 3, did not change substantially from 1975 to 1989. The strengthening of management's right to manage at the same time the parties are pledging greater cooperation raises some intriguing questions for investigation.

The acceleration of worker displacement during the 1980s increased union concern over management rights issues involving subcontracting, technological change, and facility relocation and shutdown. Adding further impetus to collective bargaining over these issues were several court and NLRB decisions that restricted the scope of the 8(a)(5) duty to bargain obligation.[1] It would be interesting to know if any of the new contract clauses restricting management rights to subcontract, to introduce new technology, to relocate, or to shut down were an outgrowth of these legal decisions.

On the other hand, these contract clauses may have simply incorporated language reflecting the employer's obligation to supply advance notice required by the federal WARN Act (Worker Adjustment and Retraining Notification Act of 1988) or the state-level predecessors of WARN. Industrial relations research needs to improve our understanding about how changes in the legal environment influence union-management relations on this and other topics.

Issues such as subcontracting and technological change have also been the focus of some union-management cooperation committees, which have yielded mixed and diverse outcomes. Controversies over subcontracting and outsourcing, for example, have produced several notable successes for joint union-management committees. One of the earliest cases was GM's Packard Electric Division (Kochan, Katz, and McKersie 1986). Cutcher-Gershenfeld (1991) reports on a similar process implemented between Xerox and ACTWU.

In contrast to joint efforts concerning subcontracting, technology committees generally have not produced significant outcomes. For example, the joint union-management technology committees negotiated between CWA and the former Bell System companies barely got started prior to AT&T divestiture in 1984, and since then these committees have not functioned. Thomas (1991) reports on the technology committees negotiated between Boeing and the IAM, which have produced few modifications in technology implementation.

The aggregated BNA data, unfortunately, are unable to tell us whether language granting management clearer rights to manage certain issues helps spur cooperation on other matters or whether strengthening management rights provisions represents an alternative to union-management cooperation.

Work Force Adjustment and Seniority

Beginning in 1979, major structural changes in the U.S. economy combined with a deep recession to cause dramatic and permanent employment declines in a number of basic industries. In response to these massive dislocations, a number of collective bargaining agreements adopted worker adjustment programs modeled on the Armour Automation Fund. For example, the UAW-Ford and the UAW-GM 1982 contracts contained pilot adjustment programs to aid workers displaced by a plant shutdown; these programs were later given permanent status, and are now funded by company contributions. These and other adjustment programs are described in Doeringer et al. (1991).

The BNA data reported in Table 4 show a small increase in the frequency of income maintenance provisions (from 48 percent of

TABLE 4

Work Force Adjustment and Seniority Provisions

Collectively Bargained Work Rule Provisions	1975	1989	Percentage Change
Income Maintenance			
Income maintenance provisions	48%	52%	8%
Work or pay guarantees	6	13	*117
Severance pay	37	40	8
SUB	17	14	−18
Seniority			
Probationary periods	71	83	*17
Senority lists required	60	70	*17
Vacancies must be posted	52	64	*23
Seniority in Promotions			
Applied in some degree	69	74	*7
Sole factor	4	5	25
Determining factor	34	43	*26
Secondary factor	25	25	0
Equal with other factors	4	1	*−75
Seniority in Transfers			
Applied in some degree	48	59	*23
Sole factor	5	8	*60
Determining factor	26	36	*38
Secondary factor	14	14	0
Equal with other factors	2	1	−50
Layoff and Rehire Procedures			
Seniority applied in layoffs	85	87	2
Exceptions to seniority allowed in layoffs	46	47	2
Advance notice of layoff required	44	49	*11
Recall specified	75	81	*8
Bumping permitted	53	59	*11
Worksharing provided	20	18	−10
Seniority in Layoffs			
Applied in some degree	85	87	2
Sole factor	42	46	10
Determining factor	30	28	−7
Secondary factor	11	12	9

*Significant difference $p < .01$.

contracts in 1975 to 52 percent in 1989). Work or pay guarantees, much talked about topics, increased in frequency from 6 percent to 13 percent of contracts from 1975 to 1989.

Central to any discussion of work force adjustment is the principle of seniority allocation, particularly during an era of increasingly scarce union-sector job opportunities. The BNA data, reported in Table 4, indicate that seniority rules regulating transfers and promotions were strengthened from 1975 to 1989. For example, provisions stipulating that among the pool of qualified employees seniority will be the determining factor for promotions and transfers increased from 34 percent of contracts in 1975 to 43 percent in 1989.

Seniority also continued as a dominant criterion in the allocation of layoffs. In 1989, 89 percent of collective bargaining agreements applied seniority in layoffs. During this period unions also gained more widely provisions requiring advance notice of layoffs, specifying recall procedures, and permitting bumping of less senior workers. Meanwhile, from 1975 to 1989, management more frequently secured probationary periods for new employees (from 71 percent of contracts in 1975 to 83 percent in 1989). Unions, on the other hand, gained more frequent posting of seniority lists (from 60 percent of contracts in 1975 to 70 percent in 1989) and posting of job vacancies (from 52 percent in 1975 to 64 percent in 1989). Note that although Foulkes (1980) found that seniority often governed many staffing decisions in large nonunion companies, seniority has been shown to be more important in both layoffs and promotions under collective bargaining (Olson and Berger 1983; Abraham and Medoff 1984, 1985; Abraham and Farber 1988).

Wage Rules and Work Schedules

Central features of the New Deal collective bargaining system were the Annual Improvement Factor (AIF) and the Cost of Living Adjustment (COLA) clauses first negotiated between GM and the UAW in 1948. Since 1982, however, in the contracts covering the Big Three auto companies and the United Auto Workers, a regular AIF has been abandoned. In these contracts the 3 percent AIF deferred annual wage increase was replaced by lump sum bonuses and profit sharing. Furthermore, in the auto and many other contracts in the 1980s, the COLA was deferred and the base year was modified (Katz 1985, p. 56). The BNA data reported in Table 5 indicate a

TABLE 5

Wage Rules and Work Schedules

Collectively Bargained Work Rule Provisions	1975	1989	Percentage Change
Wage Administration & Wage Rule			
Deferred increase	88%	77%	*−13%
Cost of living	36	26	*−28
Lump sums	0	22	*
Wage reopening	8	9	13
Two-tier	0	28	*
Wage progression	43	44	2
Reporting pay	71	78	*10
Call back, call-in	62	67	*8
Temporary transfer	52	64	*23
Wage incentive	35	33	−6
Job classifications change procedures	51	58	*14
Shift differential	82	85	4
Hazard duty	7	13	*86
Travel expenses	21	31	*48
Work clothes	19	33	*74
Tools	10	25	*150
Paid Holidays & Vacations			
8 days or less holidays	29	18	*−38
9, 10, or 11 days holidays	61	51	*−16
12 or more days holidays	10	32	*220
3 weeks vacation	85	89	*5
4 weeks vacation	76	85	*12
5 weeks vacation	42	61	*45
6 weeks vacation	10	21	*110
Work Schedules			
Work schedule provisions	97	96	−1
Daily schedule specified	82	85	4
Weekly schedule specified	64	61	−5
Monday thru Friday schedule specified	48	39	*−19
Daily overtime provisions	95	94	−1
Weekly overtime provisions	66	69	5
Sixth day overtime provisions	17	22	29
Seventh day overtime provisions	18	26	*44
Saturday overtime provisions	52	51	−2
Sunday overtime provisions	68	65	−4
Layoffs to avoid weekly overtime prohibited	24	24	0
Pyramiding of overtime prohibited	64	66	3
Advance notice required	23	26	13
Distribution of overtime provisions	58	63	*9
Lunch time specified	42	61	*45
Paid lunch	6	24	*300
Lunch less than one-half hour	4	7	*75
Half hour lunch	27	34	*26
Hour lunch	11	12	9
Rest periods	29	44	*52
Clean-up time	14	21	*50
Average Workrule Change ($p < .05$)	1609	1625	*12

*Significant difference $p > .01$.

sizeable movement away from deferred wage increases and COLA toward lump sums and two-tier pay systems during the last 15 years. Note, for example, that the use of lump sums rises from zero to 22 percent of the contracts over the period. Erickson (1992) analyzes the use of lump sums in aerospace contracts. Recent data, however, shows a decline in the use of (non-merging) two-tier wage systems from 1985 to 1990 (Bureau of National Affairs 1991).

Collectively bargained wage incentives have not declined over the last 15 years, and the use of wage incentives has become more strongly linked with unionism during this period (Keefe 1991c, 1991d). Nonunion firms, on the other hand, are more likely to adopt profit sharing and merit pay as their preferred contingent pay mechanisms. The systematically lower hourly wages paid under merit plans, which serve as a substitute for more costly incentive and standard rate methods of pay, make them particularly attractive systems of compensation in the nonunion sector. With the growth of the nonunion sector, it is interesting to note that pay secrecy has been reintroduced for hourly workers. As the union sector loses its leading influence in wage setting, there are indications that nonunion employers are also shifting away from using industry standards for wage setting and returning to traditional community wage setting methods.

Although there have been well publicized union concessions on paid time off, most notably, the surrendering of nine paid personal holidays by the UAW in the 1982 auto negotiations, these events apparently mask a general trend in collective bargaining agreements toward more paid time off. Note that the data in Table 5 reveal that paid holidays and vacation time significantly increased during the 15-year period. Table 5 also shows that management has not made major alterations in scheduling procedures, particularly the payment of overtime wages. Rather, the procedures for allocating overtime are increasingly spelled out in the collective bargaining agreement. The frequency of contractual clauses providing paid lunch periods, rest periods, and clean-up time also has increased.

In the early 1980s, after several years of concession bargaining, some business journals suggested that collective bargaining contracts were becoming less formal and went on to predict that we would witness a return to the one-page collective bargaining agreement. The BNA data, however, do not support the notion that collective bargaining contracts have become less formal as the contracts in 1989 contain more specific language than the 1975 contracts. For the issues included in our tables, the unweighted prevalence of each contract provision rose from 1975 to 1989, and the increase is statistically significant at the 5 percent level.

In the various topic areas in the BNA data there are some changes made from 1975 to 1989 that favor management, and others that appear to favor unions. What explains the nature of these changes in contract clauses? In particular, why did management gain on some issues while unions gained on others?

It is, of course, possible that this variability results from the aggregate nature of the data. More microanalysis may be needed to clearly identify bargaining power shifts or tradeoffs under way over this period. Alternatively, the variability in advantage may be explained by the fact that in many unionized industries both employers and unions have lost bargaining power. As unionized employers face increased domestic and foreign competition, they have lost control over product markets that they once dominated, which allowed for mark-up pricing. Now they must confront greater uncertainty, instability, and declining market shares. At the same time, unions have steadily lost their ability to take wages out of competition and are now forced to compete in labor markets dominated by nonunion labor. Particularly in such a period of change one might expect erratic and varying bargaining outcomes as the parties experiment with new methods to reverse their mutual decline. One could also adopt a systems transformation argument (discussed more fully later in this chapter) and argue that it is not surprising that some recent changes favor management while others favor unions if system switches are under way. In a switch to a new system of industrial relations one would expect tradeoffs in bargaining that yield gains to both sides. Or the BNA data may be measuring an average of transformed and untransformed collective bargaining relationships. Again, more microcomparisons would be needed to explain outcomes. Clearly, these issues should be the subject for further research.

What Explains the Diversity that Exists in Work Rules and Practices Across Union Plants and Firms?

The data discussed in the preceding two sections of the chapter reveal wide variation across plants and across time in collective bargaining outcomes. There has been extensive research analyzing the causes of the diversity in industrial relations practices and outcomes. This is not just an intellectual curiosity. Given the competitive challenges confronting the union sector, industrial relations professionals are eager for advice regarding how they could shift industrial relations practices in directions that yield positive returns to workers and firms.

Business Cycle

The business cycle has been shown to strongly affect the incidence of strikes, wages, and other industrial relations and labor market outcomes. Cyclical movement of strike frequency, for example, has been found across time and countries (Hibbs 1976; Kaufman 1982). In the new research, cyclical movements are apparent in a variety of industrial relations outcome measures. For example, Katz (1985, see especially Figure 5.1) finds sizeable cyclical movement in the grievance and absentee rates in General Motors plants in the 1970s. Cappelli and Chauvin (1991) also find cyclical movements in auto grievance rates.

The reasons why grievance and absentee rates (and other industrial relations outcomes) move with the economy are not readily apparent, and the new research does not shed much new light on this question. It might be that as the economy expands and bargaining leverage shifts to the work force and unions (as a result of lower unemployment rates and the higher cost of work stoppages to management), the work force takes advantage of its bargaining leverage by more readily challenging managerial authority, which could spur a rise in grievance or absentee rates.

The Tenor of Labor-Management Relations

Another explanation for variation in industrial relations outcomes across union settings is that industrial relations performance is shaped by how well labor and management get along at a particular site. In this account, it is the overall tenor of labor-management relations that critically shapes outcomes. One version of this explanation was offered by Walton and McKersie (1965, p. 189), who claimed that the tenor of labor-management relations varies across a continuum, with "conflict" relations at one extreme and "collusion" relations at the other. Harbison and Coleman (1951) earlier categorized collective bargaining relationships into the following three types: armed truce, working harmony, and union-management cooperation.

On the contemporary scene, the most common range in the tenor of relations is between adversarial (conflict) and cooperative relationships. An adversarial relationship is said to involve high grievance and absentee rates, rigid application of rules, conflict attitudes, and in other ways high levels of conflict. There are three major explanations in the research literature of the causes of variation in the tenor of labor-management relations.

The maturation thesis. In the 1940s and 1950s, a number of institutionalists argued that relations between unions and management in the United States were proceeding through a transition from conflict relations to a more "mature" collective bargaining relationship (Ross 1948). The claim was that although American management had initially fiercely opposed unionization, management had come to accept unions and had learned the helpful role that unions could play. In particular, management had allegedly learned that unions (and perhaps most importantly, the effective operation of the grievance procedure) could bring stability to shop floor labor-management relations, and that unionization was consistent with reasonably high economic performance.

One could generalize this maturation account and argue that in other countries, the tenor of labor-management relations also is likely to be conflictual during and shortly after unionization. Yet over time an accommodation generally emerges between the two sides, bringing growing cooperation and stabilization.

There are a number of problems with this maturation hypothesis, not the least of which is the difficulty in explaining the extreme hostility management exhibited towards unions in the United States during the 1980s (and in earlier periods). Furthermore, the maturation view, with its sanguine prediction regarding union effects on economic performance, has great difficulty explaining the substantial competitive problems American unionized sites confronted from both nonunion and international competition from the mid-1970s on.

The rigidification thesis. A more pessimistic account of union effects argues that over time the tenor of labor-management relations tends to worsen and rigidify. The claim here is that as union work rules and practices accumulate, they become inflexible and increasingly constraining in the face of changes in the economic environment.

Evidence in support of an age-rigidification effect on work practices comes from Verma (1983, p. 129), who shows that the old plants of one company have more rigid and formal work rules and practices than the company's newer plants. Note that Verma's data include nonunion plants, and that these plants also exhibit age effects. There are, for instance, more job classifications and wage grades in the old nonunion plants than the new nonunion plants. Thus, it may be more appropriate (and fairer to unions) to speak of an age effect on industrial relations outcomes across union and nonunion plants rather than a union-sector rigidification effect.

Alternatively, the age effect may simply be capturing the previous dominance and later erosion of Tayloristic management principles favoring highly delineated job classifications and extensive monitoring of worker performance. In other words, rules did not accumulate; rather, older plants were born as more rule-bound institutions.

A yo-yo model. The above accounts yield nearly opposite predictions regarding the course of the tenor of labor-management relations over time at a given site. Yet both claim there is a consistent trend in the tenor of labor-management relations. A sharply contrasting view is espoused by those arguing that labor-management relations often shift between cooperation and conflict. Hammer and Stern (1986) describe such a "yo-yo" path in their account of employee involvement and labor representation on the board of directors of Rath Meatpacking. One can generalize their account and claim that many unionized settings experience periodic ups and downs in the tenor of the labor-management relationship. Such a yo-yo model is consistent with wide variation in industrial relations outcomes and strong correlations across components of industrial relations outcomes at a given point in time at a site; thus, it is consistent with the data discussed earlier finding diversity and strong correlations across industrial relations outcomes.

Transformation Argument

A yo-yo model is extremely pessimistic regarding the possibility of reshaping labor-management relations. More importantly, it has a hard time explaining why the extent of diversity in industrial relations outcomes widened in the 1980s. Some researchers have a contrasting view of an evolutionary course within labor-management relations—one that has a particular historical dynamic and not the dynamic found in either the rigidification or maturation views.

The transformation proponents claim that the 1980s marked a special period when the union sector was struggling to reshape practices so as to respond to environmental pressures. Kochan, Katz, and McKersie (1986) describe a shift away from traditional "New Deal" industrial relations to a new industrial relations system that puts greater emphasis on strategic and workplace issues and processes. Some of the key industrial relations practices in the new system are more contingent pay, team systems of work organization, worker employment security and career development, and worker and union participation in business and strategic decisions.[2]

Similar comparisons of new and traditional work practices are found in Heckscher (1988) and Zuboff (1988). In the transformation account, the diversity that became apparent in the new micro data is explained in part by variation in the extent to which plants have transformed to the new system.

Not only does the transformation argument have a particular evolutionary account of American industrial relations, but it emphasizes a "systems" account of industrial relations practices and change. The transformation proponents emphasize that new practices fit together and reinforce one another as a system. For example, a systems view is presented in Katz's (1985) claim that recent changes in auto labor relations are distinguished by the extent to which they go beyond previous "amendments" to the old auto industrial relations system. The transformationists are thereby led into a discussion of "patterns" of industrial relations, and in this way their arguments are similar to others who utilize patterns to explain union and non-union practices.

Patterns of Industrial Relations

One can put the transformationists' argument into historical and cross-sectional context by analyzing union and nonunion work practices in terms of patterns (or systems). Edwards (1979), for example, traces the historical evolution of American work organization and managerial practice and describes a number of key industrial relations system types. In analyzing British industrial relations, Fox (1974) identifies five patterns of union practice. Use of patterns to explain contemporary U.S. practice includes Osterman (1988),

Strauss (1990), and Sherer (1992). Cutcher-Gershenfeld (1991) distinguishes between traditional, transitional, and transformational labor relations patterns across work groups within one facility. Katz and Kochan (1992) compare the new participatory (i.e., transformed) union pattern to other union and nonunion patterns of industrial relations. Although the number and specific content of the industrial relations patterns described by these authors are not identical, there are many similarities in these accounts, such as their emphasis on the strategic uncertainty and structural instability in the current industrial relations environment (Streeck 1987).

Links Between Business and Industrial Relations Strategy

Another explanation for diversity in industrial relations derives from the links between business and industrial relations strategy. The claim is that particular business strategies are associated with particular industrial relations strategies either because business strategies cause industrial relations choices, or because industrial relations practices constrain business choices, or a combination of these interactions. For example, Cappelli (1985) argues that airline company product strategies (market segments) led to divergent industrial relations concessions in the 1980s. Arthur (1992) claims that the market strategies of steel minimills correlate with the industrial relations patterns in those mills. Similarly, Kochan, Katz, and McKersie (1986) differentiate between a high-wage/high-quality strategy and a low-wage/low-cost strategy.

Much more research needs to be focused on clarifying and testing these alleged links between business and industrial relations strategies. Among other things, research should examine more closely the source of any connection between business and industrial relations strategies. What is the path and method of causation in any linkage? Furthermore, is it truly accurate to speak in terms of actual strategies or are organizational actions more appropriately described through ad hoc accounts? For further discussion of the weaknesses in the strategic linkage literature, see Lewin (1987a).

Effects of Industrial Relations on Economic Outcomes

Industrial Relations Matters

Perhaps the most important contribution of the new literature is its assessment of the effects exerted by work rules and practices and other industrial relations variables on economic performance. The research employs the standard causal path to make this evaluation. These empirical studies use both cross-sectional and longitudinal data to control for the effects of other determinants of economic outcomes such as plant size or the business cycle and isolate the independent contribution of industrial relations.

This research is extremely important to practitioners and policymakers in light of the changes under way in American industrial relations practice. Even doubters of the transformation argument would agree that it is extremely valuable to know whether, and the extent to which, new industrial relations practices are significantly altering economic performance. In the past there were many case-study or descriptive assessments of these industrial relations changes. A classic illustration is Guest (1979).

The weakness of the earlier qualitative or case accounts lies in their inability to control for the effects of other events on economic performance. Without controlling for the effects of other independent variables it is impossible to assess the independent contribution of the industrial relations changes. This problem is particularly troubling given the likelihood that many other things are changing along with work practices and other industrial relations variables. In fact, it could even be argued that plants (or work groups) where industrial relations are changing are most likely sites experiencing extensive other changes.

The new literature also benefits from the fact that it relies on quantitative data to assess the effects of industrial relations variables. Typically, these quantitative data come from sources independent from the actors involved in the industrial relations events and thus are a great improvement from the assessments provided in qualitative studies. Given the large stakes for the participants in making (and defending) industrial relations change, there is likely to be substantial bias in the qualitative data typically relied on in case studies and descriptive accounts.[3]

The new research shows that industrial relations do affect economic performance and that the effects are economically and statistically significant. Some of this literature analyzes the consequences of lower grievance rates. For example, Katz, Kochan, and Gobeille (1983) and Katz, Kochan, and Weber (1985) find that high levels of grievance activity adversely influence product quality and plant productivity at General Motors. Cutcher-Gershenfeld (1991) finds evidence that variation in grievance activity across work groups in a facility affects economic performance. Norsworthy and Zabala (1985) find that higher grievance activity is associated with lower total factor productivity and higher unit costs in the automobile industry. After controlling for various other factors that affect productivity in a sample of paper mills, Ichniowski (1986) finds that productivity at the plants having the average number of grievances was 1.2 percent lower than the productivity at plants with no grievances.

Grievance systems may influence employer costs by reducing hiring and training costs. Freeman and Medoff (1984) claim that grievance procedure coverage reduces quits and increases job tenure. Yet the precise mechanism whereby grievance activity influences economic performance has not been fully explained.

Worker attitudes and work rules also appear to exert sizeable effects on economic performance. Norsworthy and Zabala (1985) estimate that a 10 percent annual improvement in worker attitudes and behavior would have translated into a 3 to 5 percent reduction in the annual unit costs of production between 1959 and 1976 in U.S. manufacturing industries. Katz, Kochan, and Keefe (1987) find that General Motors plants with work rules that give management more discretion and increase work pace have lower labor costs.

An interesting recent extension of the research discussed in this section is provided in Arthur's (1990, 1992) hypothesis that economic performance is affected both by the fit between the components of an industrial relations system and the fit between a firm's business and industrial relations strategies. Arthur finds evidence from steel minimills that both types of fit matter.

Economic Payouts to Work Restructuring and Increased Worker and Union Involvement

Labor and management have extensively restructured work at a number of companies and launched participatory processes in the hopes that these changes will yield sizeable economic payouts and improve the competitiveness of union plants. The new literature suggests that industrial relations changes have not always worked as the participants hoped and the payouts to such changes may have been modest in some sites. For instance, Katz, Kochan, and Keefe (1987) find that plants that used work teams at General Motors had lower productivity (note that their data stop in 1986). Keefe and Katz (1990) report that management efforts to reduce job classifications for assembly line workers did not have positive effects on either productivity or product quality. Katz, Kochan, and Gobeille (1983), with earlier data, find limited returns from the quality of working life programs in General Motors plants. Many of these programs appear to plateau about 18 months after implementation, with many disappearing within several years.

Yet the evidence on the effects of teams and job classification consolidation is not clear-cut. Cutcher-Gershenfeld (1991) finds evidence that work organization and employee participation, particularly as expressed through differences in industrial relations patterns, exert substantial effects on economic performance. Eaton and Voos (1991) report that several studies find a significant productivity advantage from team systems in manufacturing. The new research suggests that at some companies, increases in worker involvement and work restructuring have led to substantial (and statistically significant) improvements in economic performance. Katz, Kochan, and Keefe (1987) find that greater worker and union participation in the process of introducing technology was associated with increased productivity and improved product quality at GM.[4] There also is evidence that management evaluations of the benefits from worker participation are more favorable than independently measured outcomes (Voos 1987; Cooke 1990).

Furthermore, team work organizations have operated productively in the construction and utility industries for many decades. These work groups, however, are never called teams. Examining the functioning of these work organizations and making comparisons with newly formed in-plant teams may yield useful insights.

Among the ranks of labor and management, team systems of work organization have been highly controversial. In the auto industry, they serve as a major focal point of opposition by the New Directions caucus in the UAW. Some observers (Parker and Slaughter 1988; Fucini 1990) claim that teams have negative outcomes for workers. For example, Parker and Slaughter argue that teams foster "management by stress" as team members confront peer pressure or fears of job loss. Clearly, evaluation of team systems from the workers' viewpoint as well as in terms of economic performance is a critical subject for further research.

International Data and Issues

A major source of the pressure for change in U.S. industrial relations is international competition. Fittingly, there is a sizeable literature that qualitatively compares industrial relations practices across countries, much of it concluding that there are marked differences across countries (Dore 1973; Streeck 1984; Turner 1992). The observation of persistent differences in shop floor industrial relations practice across countries is contrary to earlier predictions of convergence in industrial relations practices made by Kerr, Dunlop, Harbison, and Myers (1960) and others.

Much of the comparative industrial relations research literature in recent years extols the virtues of the German or Japanese industrial relations systems, which are said to yield superior economic performance. Yet this conclusion is nearly always based on indirect evidence such as the relatively successful performance of German or Japanese firms or economies, case studies, or industry comparisons. There is very little quantitative cross-national data comparing industrial relations outcomes and the effects of industrial relations on economic performance. An exception is the research of MacDuffie and Krafcik (1992) analyzing productivity in automobile assembly plants in a number of countries.

There also is some qualitative evidence that work rules and practices have begun to converge across industrialized countries. In many countries unionized settings are witnessing the expansion of team systems, more contingent compensation, participation processes, and the replacement of formal bargaining with informal communication between workers and managers (Windolf 1989). Analyzing the extent and persistence of this convergence is one of the key issues for future comparative industrial relations research.

Impact of Industrial Relations Practices and Changes on Workers

What are the effects of work practices and recent changes in these practices on workers? A partial answer comes from the extensive research assessing the effects of unions on compensation (reviewed in this volume by Lazear).

Evidence in the New Literature

The new literature analyzed here does include some assessment of how practices affect workers. For instance, as mentioned earlier, the new research examines variations in absentee and grievance rates and the factors that influence this variation. The new literature also includes some information regarding work pace and job conditions (Keefe 1991a). The data in Katz, Kochan, and Keefe (1987), for example, include measures of the degree of managerial discretion, employee involvement in decisions, and work pace.

Studies of new technology also include some data on workers' views of work practices and conditions. Milkman and Pullman (1991) and Keefe, Eaton, Milkman, and Pullman (1991), for instance, include survey responses of hourly auto workers regarding how new technology and plant modernization influence auto worker alienation.

The Paucity of Data on Workers' Perceptions

Overall, however, the new literature includes relatively little data on work conditions as reported by workers. It would be very valuable to hear workers' views concerning the work rules and practices that make up the raw data for the new literature. In particular, worker views may help answer one of the central debates surrounding work restructuring: the extent to which participatory processes or work restructuring requires workers to work harder or smarter.

Critics of new team systems, participation programs, or Japanese production methods claim that these practices essentially entail a speed-up in the pace of work (Parker and Slaughter 1988). Objective measures of work pace (which are largely missing in the new literature) would help answer this question. Furthermore, it would be extremely helpful to know what workers think. Extending the new literature to include worker views is a central task for future research.

Effects of Work Practices on Unions and their Role in New Work Systems

The new literature does include research evaluating how work practices affect unions. In particular, there is growing research evaluating the influence of teams, participation processes, and other new practices on unions (Eaton, Gordon, and Keefe 1992). Kochan, Katz, and Mower (1984), for instance, analyze workers' and union officers' assessments of the consequences of participation programs for local unions. Walton, Cutcher-Gershenfeld, and McKersie (forthcoming) examine the evolving role of shop committeemen and other union officers in locations where labor-management relations have become more integrative and informal. Kochan,

Katz, and McKersie (1986) claim that at some firms the union has become more involved in strategic issues and has thereby altered its function.

Future Research Directions

Explaining Diversity in the Union Sector

The literature in this domain is growing, yet a number of critical gaps remain. Perhaps the greatest shortfall in the new literature is its inability to account for the wide diversity within the union sector in industrial relations practices and effects. The research has gone far toward showing the existence of diversity, but has not explained well the source of that diversity.

Union-Nonunion Differences

Further research also needs to examine the nature and consequences of union-nonunion work rule and work practice differences. Research journals in the field continue to be inundated with union-nonunion wage studies, but contain few comparisons of work rules and practices across the sectors (Lewin 1987b). The lack of research may be due to difficulties in gaining access and collecting data from the nonunion sector. Researchers will have to work harder at gaining access and might benefit by working more closely with colleagues from the field of human resource management who may already have such access.

The Effects on Economic Outcomes

The new literature has made some progress toward understanding how work rules and practices influence economic performance. Yet much more needs to be done on this issue in light of the extensive changes under way in American practices and the critical policy relevance of the research evaluation. Industrial relations professionals now engaged in these work rule changes need the assistance of researchers to understand which changes are likely to succeed.

One of the factors impeding the value of researchers' advice to practitioners on this issue is the weak quantitative measures of worker participation processes and work restructuring. Yet, without such measures it is impossible to derive reliable estimates of the effects of ongoing changes at the workplace. Again, researchers will have to work harder at refining their measures and taking advantage of research opportunities. The continuation and elaboration of participation and work restructuring at so many union workplaces at least provides the opportunity for more research.

In particular, it would be informative if researchers would extend their quantitative analysis of economic impacts across national borders. This could facilitate more reliable assessment of the economic consequences of differences in industrial relations practice. Again, the policy relevance of this question suggests that a high priority should be attached to this line of research. Comparative data analysis also could help answer the old, yet still critical, question regarding the extent to which there is convergence in industrial relations practice across countries.

Modeling Difficulties

If they turn to these questions, researchers should bear in mind the problems that plague statistical analysis of work rules and practices, work restructuring, and participation processes. As mentioned earlier, it is extremely difficult to measure many of the relevant variables.

Furthermore, there are difficult "selection" and "identification" statistical problems associated with assessing the economic impacts of work rules and practices. For example, it is not obvious whether worker participation causes economic performance or vice versa. Enhanced worker participation in decisions may lead to improved productivity. Yet it is also possible that management and labor will turn to worker participation and expand it more extensively in plants that initially have poor productivity. Thus, to statistically identify the independent effects of worker participation across a sample of plants the researcher might estimate a two-stage regression model in which one equation includes worker participation as an independent variable explaining economic performance while another equation uses independent variables to explain worker participation. The problem is that it is extremely difficult to come up with a simple equation to explain the diffusion of worker participation, let alone measure many of the relevant explanatory variables.

It may also be the case that use of regressions to assess the impact of work rules and practices or participation processes on economic outcomes is a fundamentally flawed methodology. Linear regression may be inappropriate if work rules and practices come in packages and do not, in fact, vary marginally across plants or firms. This is the very claim made by those who view industrial relations in terms of systems or patterns (see the earlier discussion for references to this literature). If industrial relations patterns dominate, then researchers need to test the consequences of moving from one pattern (or system) to another rather than test the effects of marginal changes in one component of an industrial relations pattern (such as the number of grievances or the number of job classifications). This does not mean that statistical analysis cannot be used to assess the influence of industrial relations on economic outcomes. Rather, researchers may need to use statistical techniques other than traditional regression analysis.

The policy importance of the research should not induce researchers to overstate the conclusiveness of their findings, given these measurement and statistical problems. Nevertheless, even with all the difficulties associated with research in this domain, there is much to be done. The questions are important, the extent of change under way in current practice is large, and the stakes are high. As a result, research in this area should, and most likely will, grow.

Endnotes

[1] In 1981, the Supreme Court's decision in *First National Maintenance* held that an employer's decision to close a portion of its operations is not a mandatory subject of bargaining. In 1984, the NLRB in *Otis Elevator II* held that an employer that transfers work from one plant to another has no statutory duty to bargain with the union about the decision itself, unless that decision rests solely on an attempt to reduce labor costs, or that a specific contract clause requires bargaining.

[2] The comparable traditional work rules and practices include wage formulas, numerous job classifications, highly cyclical seniority-based layoffs, and arms-length relations between labor and management.

[3] This not intended to convey that there is little to be learned from the case study approach. Yet case studies may be particularly weak at identifying the effects of industrial relations change on economic performance.

[4] With regard to the latter finding, keep in mind that, as noted earlier, unions in general have had little influence on the diffusion of new technology (Keefe 1991b) and have passively accepted most technological change (Slichter, Healy, and Livernash 1960).

References

Abraham, Katharine, and Henry Farber. "Returns to Seniority in Union and Non-union Jobs: A New Look at the Evidence." *Industrial and Labor Relations Review* 42, 1 (1988), pp. 3-17.

Abraham, Katharine, and James Medoff. "Length of Service and Layoffs in Union and Non-union Work Groups." *Industrial and Labor Relations Review* 38, 1 (1984), 87-97.

———. "Length of Service and Promotions in Union and Non-union Work Groups." *Industrial and Labor Relations Review* 38, 3 (1985), pp. 408-20.

Arthur, Jeffrey B. "Industrial Relations and Business Strategies in American Steel Minimills." Unpublished Ph.D. dissertation, Ithaca, NY: Cornell University, 1990.

———. "Link Between Business Strategy and Industrial Relations Systems in American Steel Minimills." *Industrial and Labor Relations Review* 45 (April 1992), pp. 488-506.

Bureau of National Affairs. *Basic Patterns of Union Contracts*, 8th ed.; 12th ed. Washington, D.C.: BNA, 1975; 1989.

———. *Employer Bargaining Objectives 1991.* Washington, D.C.: BNA, 1990.

Cappelli, Peter. "Competitive Pressures and Labor Relations in the Airline Industry." *Industrial Relations* 24 (Fall 1985), pp. 316-38.

Capelli, Peter, and Keith Chauvin. "A Test of an Efficiency Model of Grievance Activity." *Industrial and Labor Relations Review* 45 (October 1991), pp. 3-14.

Cooke, William N. *Labor-Management Cooperation: New Partnerships or Going In Circles?* Kalamazoo, MI: W.E. Upjohn Institute for Employment Research, 1990.

Cutcher-Gershenfeld, Joel. "The Impact on Economic Performance of a Transformation in Workplace Relations." *Industrial and Labor Relations Review* 44 (January 1991), pp. 241-260.

Doeringer, Peter, Kathleen Christensen, Patricia Flynn, Douglas Hall, Harry Katz, Jeffrey Keefe, Christopher Ruhm, Andrew Sum, and Michael Useem. *Turbulence in the American Workplace.* New York: Oxford University Press, 1991.

Dore, Ronald. *British Factory-Japanese Factory.* Berkeley: University of California Press, 1973.

Eaton, Adrienne E., Michael E. Gordon, and Jeffrey H. Keefe. "The Impact of Quality of Work Life Programs and Grievance System Effectiveness on Union Commitment." *Industrial and Labor Relations Review* 45 (April 1992), pp. 591-604.

Eaton, Adrienne E., and Paula Voos. "Unions and Contemporary Innovations in Work Organization, Compensation, and Employee Participation." In *Unions and Competitiveness*, ed. Paula Voos and Lawrence Mishel, New York: M.E. Sharpe, 1991, pp. 173-216.

Edwards, Richard C. *Contested Terrain.* New York: Basic Books, 1979.

Erickson, Christopher L. "Wage Rule Formation in the Aerospace Industry." *Industrial and Labor Relations Review* 45 (April 1992), pp. 507-22.

Foulkes, F. E. *Personnel Policies in Large Non-union Companies.* Englewood Cliffs, NJ: Prentice-Hall, 1980.

Fox, Alan. *Beyond Contract: Work, Power and Trust Relations.* London: Faber and Faber, 1974.

Freeman, Richard B., and James L. Medoff. *What Do Unions Do?* New York: Basic Books, 1984.

Fucini, Joseph J., and Suzy Fucini. *Working for the Japanese.* New York: Free Press, 1990.

Golden, Clinton S., and Virginia D. Parker. *Causes of Industrial Peace.* New York: Harper, 1949.

Gordon, Michael, and Sandra Miller. "Grievances: A Review of the Research and Practice." *Personnel Psychology* 37, 2 (1984), pp. 117-46.

Guest, Robert H. "Quality of Work Life—Learning from Tarrytown." *Harvard Business Review* 57 (August 1979), pp. 276-87.

Hammer, Tove, and Robert N. Stern. "A Yo-Yo Model of Cooperation: Union Participation in Management at the Rath Packing Company." *Industrial and Labor Relations Review* 39 (April 1986), pp. 337-49.

Harbison, Frederick H., and James S. Coleman. *Goals and Strategy in Collective Bargaining.* New York: Harper, 1951.

Harbison, Frederick H., and Robert Dubin. *Patterns of Union-Management Relations.* Chicago: Science Research Associates, 1947.

Heckscher, Charles. *The New Unionism: Employee Involvement in the Changing Corporation*. New York: Basic Books, 1988.

Hibbs, Douglas A., Jr. "Industrial Conflict in Advanced Industrial Societies." *American Political Science Review* 70 (December 1976), 1033-58.

Ichniowski, Casey. "The Effects of Grievance Activity on Productivity." *Industrial and Labor Relations Review* 40 (October 1986), pp. 75-89.

Katz, Harry C. *Shifting Gears: Changing Labor Relations in the U.S. Automobile Industry*. Cambridge, MA: MIT Press, 1985.

Katz, Harry C., and Thomas A. Kochan. *An Introduction to Collective Bargaining and Industrial Relations*. New York: McGraw-Hill, 1992.

Katz, Harry C., Thomas A. Kochan, and Kenneth R. Gobeille. "Industrial Relations Performance, Economic Performance, and QWL Programs: An Interplant Analysis." *Industrial and Labor Relations Review* 37, 1 (1983), pp. 3-17.

Katz, Harry C., Thomas A. Kochan, and Mark Weber. "Assessing the Effects of Industrial Relations and Quality of Working Life Efforts on Organizational Effectiveness." *Academy of Management Journal* 28 (September 1985), pp. 509-27.

Katz, Harry C., Thomas A. Kochan, and Jeffrey H. Keefe. "Industrial Relations Performance and Productivity in the U.S. Automobile Industry." *Brookings Papers on Economic Activity* 3 (1987), pp. 685-715.

Kaufman, Bruce E. "The Determinants of Strikes in the United States, 1900-1977." *Industrial and Labor Relations Review* 35 (July 1982), pp. 474-90.

Keefe, Jeffrey H. "Numerically Controlled Machine Tools and Worker Skills." *Industrial and Labor Relations Review* 44 (April 1991a), pp. 503-19.

________. "Do Unions Influence Technological Diffusion?" *Industrial and Labor Relations Review* 44 (January 1991b), pp. 261-74.

________. "Do Unions Hinder Technological Change?" In *Unions and Competitiveness*, ed. Paula Voos and Lawrence Mishel, New York: M.E. Sharpe, 1991c.

________. "Why Are Wage Incentives Obsolete?" Working paper, Institute of Management and Labor Relations, Rutgers University, September 1991d.

Keefe, Jeffrey H., and Harry C. Katz. "Job Classifications and Plant Performance." *Industrial Relations* 29 (Winter 1990), pp. 111-18.

Keefe, Jeffrey, Adrienne Eaton, Ruth Milkman, and Cydney Pullman. "Auto Workers and Alienation: The Effects of Technological Change." Working paper, Institute of Management and Labor Relations, Rutgers University, April 1991.

Kerr, Clark, John T. Dunlop, Frederick Harbison, and Charles A. Myers. *Industrialism and Industrial Man*. New York: Oxford University Press, 1960.

Kochan, Thomas A., Harry C. Katz, and Nancy R. Mower. *Worker Participation and American Unions: Threat or Opportunity?* Kalamazoo, MI: W.E. Upjohn Institute for Employment Research, 1984.

Kochan, Thomas A., Harry C. Katz, and Robert B. McKersie. *The Transformation of American Industrial Relations*. New York: Basic Books, 1986.

Kuhn, James W. *Bargaining in Grievance Settlement*. New York: Columbia University Press, 1961.

Levine, David I., and Laura D'Andrea Tyson. "Participation, Productivity, and the Firm's Environment." In *Paying for Productivity: A Look at the Evidence*, ed. Alan S. Blinder, Washington, D.C.: Brookings Institution, 1990, pp. 183-243.

Lewin, David. "Industrial Relations as a Strategic Variable." In *Human Resources and the Performance of the Firm*, ed. Morris M. Kleiner et al., Madison, WI: Industrial Relations Research Association, 1987a, pp. 1-41.

________. "Dispute Resolution in the Non-union Firm: A Theoretical and Empirical Analysis." *Journal of Conflict Resolution* 213, 3 (1987b), pp. 465-502.

Lewin, David, and Richard Peterson. *The Modern Grievance Procedure in the United States*. New York: Quorum Books, 1988.

MacDuffie, John Paul, and John F. Krafcik. "Flexible Production Systems and Manufacturing Performance." In *Transforming Organizations*, eds. Thomas A. Kochan and Michael Useem, New York: Oxford University Press, 1992, pp. 209-25.

Milkman, Ruth, and Cydney Pullman. "Technological Change in an Auto Assembly Plant." *Work and Occupations* 18 (May 1991), pp. 123-47.

Nosworthy, J.R., and Craig A. Zabala. "Work Attitudes, Worker Behavior, and Productivity in the U.S. Automobile Industry, 1959-1976." *Industrial and Labor Relations Review* 38 (July 1985), pp. 544-57.

Olson, Craig, and Chris Berger. "The Relationship Between Seniority, Ability, and the Promotion of Union and Non-union Workers." In *Advances in Industrial Relations*, eds. D.B. Lipsky and J.M. Douglas, Greenwich, CT: JAI Press, 1983, pp. 91-129.

Osterman, Paul. *Employment Futures*. New York: Oxford University Press, 1988.

Parker, Mike, and Jane Slaughter. *Choosing Sides: Unions and the Team Concept*. Boston: South End Press, 1988.

Ross, Arthur. *Trade Union Wage Policy*. Berkeley and Los Angeles: University of California Press, 1948.

Sherer, Peter. "Beyond the Employment Relationship: The Diversity in Labor Relationships and Labor Forms." Unpublished paper, Wharton School, University of Pennsylvania, 1992.

Slichter, Sumner H., James J. Healy, and E. Robert Livernash. *The Impact of Collective Bargaining on Management*. Washington, D.C.: Brookings Institution, 1960.

Strauss, George. "Towards the Study of Human Resource Policy." In *Reflections on the Transformation of Industrial Relations*, eds. James Chelius and James Dworkin. Metuchen, NJ: IMLR Press, Rutgers University, 1990, pp. 73-95.

Streeck, Wolfgang. *Industrial Relations in West Germany: A Case Study of the Car Industry*. New York: St. Martin's Press, 1984.

________. "The Uncertainties of Management in the Management of Uncertainty: Employers, Labor Relations and Industrial Adjustment in the 1980s." *Work, Employment & Society* 1, 3 (1987), pp. 281-308.

Thomas, Robert. "Technological Choice and Union-Management Cooperation." *Industrial Relations* 30, 2 (1991), pp. 167-92.

Turner, Lowell. *Democracy at Work*. Ithaca, NY: Cornell University Press, 1992.

Verma, Anil. "Union and Non-union Industrial Relations at the Plant Level." Unpublished Ph.D. dissertation, MIT, Cambridge, MA, 1983.

Voos, Paula V. "Managerial Perceptions of the Economic Impact of Labor Relations Programs." *Industrial and Labor Relations Review* 40 (January 1987), pp. 195-208.

Walton, Richard E., and Robert B. McKersie. *A Behavioral Theory of Labor Negotiations*. New York: McGraw-Hill, 1965.

Walton, Richard E., Joel Cutcher-Gershenfeld, and Robert B. McKersie. *Negotiating the Social Contract: A Theory of Negotiated Change in Labor-Management Relations*, forthcoming.

Windolf, Paul. "Productivity Coalitions and the Future of Corporatism." *Industrial Relations* 28 (Winter 1989), pp. 1-20.

Zuboff, Shoshana. *In the Age of the Smart Machine*. New York: Basic Books, 1988.

CHAPTER 3

Research on Strike Models and Outcomes in the 1980s: Accomplishments and Shortcomings

BRUCE E. KAUFMAN
Georgia State University

One of the boom areas of industrial relations research in the 1980s was the subject of strikes. Even as the number of strikes in the United States fell to the lowest level in the post-World War II period, the volume of articles and books published on the subject was double that of the previous decade. Equally remarkable was the broad multidisciplinary nature of strike research, for while economists authored the majority of studies, IR scholars from disciplines such as sociology, psychology, management, and law also made significant contributions.

In this chapter I survey the academic research literature on strikes, with emphasis on the period from 1980 to date.[1] Some consideration of earlier work is necessary, however, for the sake of continuity and perspective. Three broad topical areas are examined: theoretical studies that seek to identify the root cause of strikes or the factors that determine the timing, size, and duration of strikes; empirical studies that attempt to explain the time-series or cross-section variation of strike activity; and empirical studies that assess the impact of strikes on such things as inflation, industrial production, and employee psychological health. For each area I summarize the major studies published and their principal contributions and conclusions. The chapter ends with a summary of what I consider to be the major insights gained from this body of research, its major shortcomings, and suggested directions for future research.

Significant Strike Developments in the 1980s

Before plunging into the research literature it is useful to review major strike trends and events of the 1980s. In this regard, three aspects of the strike record of the 1980s are worth noting.

The first is the time-series variation in strike activity. Figure 1 shows the annual number of major work stoppages (1,000 workers or more) in the United States each year from 1950 through 1990.[2] The white bars represent periods of recession. The most obvious feature of Figure 1 is the dramatic fall-off in strike activity that occurred in the 1980s. During the ten-year period 1971-1980, an annual average of 269 major work stoppages took place involving 1.3 million workers, while from 1981 to 1990 only 68 major strikes occurred per year, on average, involving 475 thousand workers—levels of conflict roughly one-fourth of those experienced in the previous decade. To some extent the decline in strike activity reflects the concomitant decline in union membership (from 22 million in 1980 to 16 million in 1990), but clearly other factors were

FIGURE 1
Pattern of Strike Activity in the United States, 1950-1990

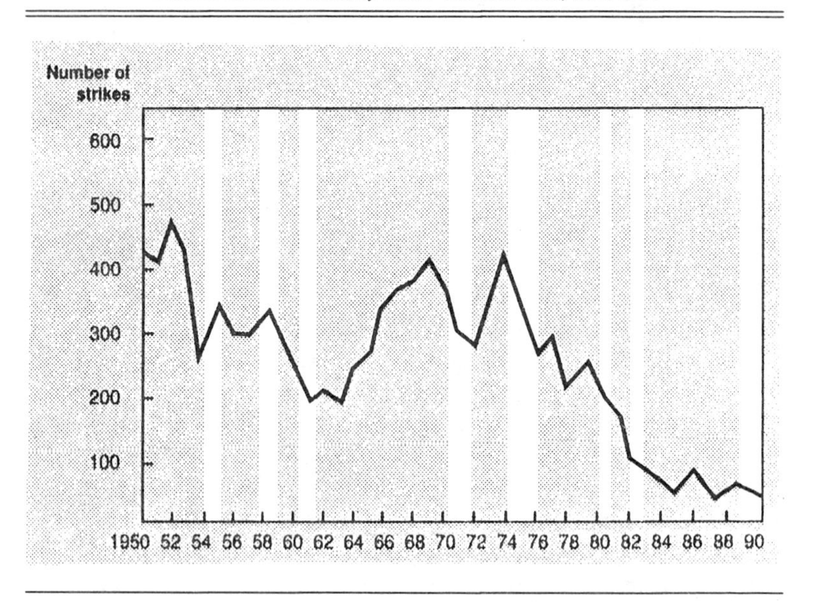

Source: Bureau of Labor Statistics, *Monthly Labor Review* (various issues).

also at work. It should be noted that this situation contrasts markedly with that in Canada where strike activity fluctuated around a stable trend over the decade and union membership grew from 3.4 to 4.0 million.

Figure 1 also illustrates a second noteworthy aspect of the strike record of the 1980s—namely, the lack of correspondence between the level of strike activity and the business cycle. The data in Figure 1 reveal a fairly close correlation between peaks and troughs in the business cycle and strike cycle for years prior to 1980. Indeed, if there is one fact about strikes that has been researched and documented more thoroughly than any other, it is that the volume of strike activity tends to increase in years of prosperity and decline in years of recession. Given this finding, the 1980s stand out as a clear exception, for after 1982 the economy experienced an eight-year business cycle expansion, while the number of strikes declined by one-half. The only precedent for this pattern is the 1920s, when strikes (and union membership) also declined precipitously during a period of sustained economic growth.

The third feature of the strike record of the 1980s is the cross-section distribution of strikes by industry. Several previous studies have demonstrated that strike activity tends to be concentrated among relatively few industries (Ross 1961; Kaufman 1983). This was certainly true in the 1980s as well. Ranked by total workers involved between 1982 and 1990, the five centers of conflict were (in order of importance): communications, government, transportation equipment, transportation, and construction. Together these industries accounted for 63 percent of workers involved in major strikes.

To introduce a theme that I return to later, it is necessary to get behind the numbers to develop a true appreciation for the causes and dynamics of strikes. Toward that end, I examined all the citations on strikes in the United States in the annual index of the *Wall Street Journal* for the years 1981-1990 and compiled a list of the most frequently mentioned disputes. Among the leaders were: the air traffic controllers' strike (PATCO-FAA); the copper strike at Phelps-Dodge; the meatpacking strike at Hormel; the baseball strikes in 1981, 1985, and 1990; the strikes at Continental and Eastern Airlines; the two strikes at Greyhound Bus Lines in 1983 and 1990; a series of strikes involving television and motion picture writers and actors; the strikes at AT&T and selected Bell companies; the strike at USX (the longest steel strike in the post-war period); and the bitter strike between Pittston Coal Co. and the United Mine Workers union.

A reading of the press accounts of these strikes reveals several important themes or events that are at least in part unique to the 1980s. Certainly the most important was the widespread use of striker replacements, a tactic that allowed many companies to defeat the strike or bust the union. A second characteristic endemic to many of the major strikes of the 1980s was the issue of "give-backs," where the give-backs took the form of wage concessions, copayments for health insurance, relaxed work rules, and greater flexibility on subcontracting of work. A third event that featured prominently in a number of strikes was the disrupting influence that industry deregulation had on established bargaining relationships and bargaining structures. Finally, a number of these strikes degenerated into long and bitter tests of strength, marred by considerable violence and ill will between the parties. The Hormel, Phelps-Dodge, Eastern, and Pittston strikes were of this genre, a type of industrial conflict not seen on a large scale since the New Deal years.

Strike Models

In this section I present an overview of the major theories and models that have been advanced to account for the occurrence of strikes. Although the literature is diverse and contains significant overlap across studies, from a conceptual point of view it is possible to distinguish four broad categories of strike theories: economic, behavioral, organizational, and political.

Economic

Most of the work on formal models of strikes has been done by economists. Economic strike models are generally distinguished by several features, including: the model is an application of bargaining theory; the bargaining is over the division of the economic rent (surplus) generated by the firm; the organizational security of the union is accepted as a "given"; the bargainers are imbued with a high degree of rationality; and the decision to strike is treated as an exercise in cost-benefit analysis. Given these common features, there nevertheless appeared in the literature of the 1980s five distinct types of economic strike models, each of which focused on a different aspect of the causation of strikes. Each of these models is summarized below. Before proceeding, however, it is necessary to briefly discuss two early (pre-World War II) explanations for strikes—explanations that have heavily influenced modern thinking on this subject.

The first explanation for strikes comes from the work of John Hicks (1932). Hicks portrayed his theory of strikes in a well-known diagram. The major feature of the diagram is the downward sloping resistance curve for the union and an upward sloping concession curve for the firm. The two intersect at a wage of *W* after a strike of *S* days. Two aspects of this outcome deserve brief comment. First, the model does not claim that a strike of *S* days will actually occur. The reason is that the settlement point *W,S* is an inefficient (or non-Pareto optimal) bargaining outcome—both sides would be better-off if they agreed to *W* and skipped the costs of the strike altogether.[3] Thus, according to Hicks, the challenge facing the union negotiator is to accurately assess the location and shape of the employer's concession curve, while the challenge facing the firm's negotiator is to do the same with respect to the union's resistance curve. If they accurately estimate each other's bargaining strengths and weaknesses, both sides will realize the wage *W* is the best that can be gained in the negotiations and will agree to that wage without a strike.

We now come to two questions that have preoccupied economists to the present day. The first is why strikes occur. Hicks gave three reasons. The most important is that they originate from a faulty assessment by one or both sides of the benefits and costs of a strike (i.e., the position and shape of the resistance and concession curves), implying strikes are in essence a bargaining mistake.[4] Another reason cited by Hicks is that the strike weapon must occasionally be used to impress upon the employer the union's resolve and the credibility of its bargaining power, while a third is the existence of a divergence of estimates between the union leadership and the rank and file over the size of the wage increase that can be realistically gained from the employer.

The second question is why strikes fluctuate with changes in variables exogenous to the union and firm, such as the inflation rate, unemployment rate, or availability of welfare payments for strikers. Hicks gave no answer to this question, and one is not immediately obvious. The reason is that a change in an exogenous variable, such as the unemployment rate, alters the benefits and costs of a strike for both sides, shifts the concession and resistance curves, and thereby alters the wage/strike-length intersection point. The net effect, however, should be a change in the negotiated wage, not a change in the probability of a strike (since both parties can presumably estimate the new W and agree to it without having to suffer a strike). The challenge, then, is to explain why miscalculations in bargaining are correlated with changes in these exogenous variables, an endeavor that has received much research effort in recent years.

While Hicks's theory has come to dominate economic theorizing on strikes in recent years, in the pre-World War II period an alternative explanation for strikes developed by institutionally oriented labor economists was more frequently cited in the literature. This perspective looks at strikes, not as a miscalculation, but as a deliberately timed exercise of bargaining power on the part of workers. This view is exemplified by the discussion of strikes in Adams and Sumner's (1905) labor problems text. They note that workers use the strike as a weapon to induce employers to improve labor conditions in prosperous times and stave off reductions in labor conditions in bad times. As to why strikes occur, Adams and Sumner argue that it is employees who generally initiate a strike and, thus, attention must be focused on their motives. In this regard they distinguish two different situations. One is during recessions and depressions when strikes are, in their words (p. 183), "a resentful rebellion against conditions regarded as too grievous to be longer endured." The second case is in times of prosperity when the strike "becomes a business proposition, a deliberate demand formulated when the time is ripe."

Through the mid-1960s the bargaining power perspective dominated economic thinking on the subject of strikes. It was used in an influential article by Rees (1952), for example, to address the second question posed above—why strikes fluctuate with changes in exogenous variables such as the business cycle. Rees argued that unions are most likely to strike when their bargaining power is greatest, giving them the best chance to win the strike on favorable terms. Thus, during recessions unions are in a weak bargaining position and strike only in unavoidable situations, while the reduction of unemployment that accompanies an economic expansion increases the bargaining power and willingness of unions to strike, causing them to aggressively press for both rectification of past grievances and new, more liberal contract terms.

Critics have argued that Rees's explanation for the cyclical behavior of strikes is wanting because, even though the union has more bargaining power at the cycle peak, the two sides should still be able to determine the intersection of their resistance and concession curves, agree to the resulting wage rate, and avoid a costly strike. From this perspective, the bargaining power argument is a dead end unless one can show why variations in bargaining power lead to systematic miscalculations on the part of unions and employers. Economists have generally concluded that this task is unproductive and have forsaken bargaining power theories in favor of other, more Hicksian-oriented approaches. (For an exception, see Card and Olson 1992.) These alternative models are what I now consider.

Imperfect information model. The first class of economic models, and the one that is closest to Hicks's in spirit and construction, is the "imperfect information" model. This model assumes that both the union and firm have imperfect information about current and future economic conditions and, thus, that strikes occur due to a miscalculation of the benefits and costs of a strike. The major challenge confronting this model is to explain, then, why the probability of a miscalculation varies systematically over time or across industries. Two recent studies along this line are Mauro (1982) and Kaufman (1981).

Mauro argues that miscalculations arise in bargaining because the union and firm give different weights to specific economic variables in the estimation of the resistance and concession curves. The firm, he argues, may know the entire universe of economic variables that influence its concession curve and the resistance curve of the union, but in estimating these curves it tends to give a large weight to variables that are important to it (e.g., producer prices) and tends to exclude or underemphasize variables important to the union's position (e.g., unemployment). Assuming the union makes the same type of estimation error, it is then inevitable that strikes or "mistakes" sometimes occur in collective bargaining. This perspective also explains why strike rates systematically vary over the business cycle. For example, Mauro's regression results show that a lower rate of unemployment is associated with a greater frequency of strikes. As discussed above, a strict interpretation of Hicks's model makes this result hard to explain. However, if the firm underestimates the extent to which the decline in unemployment bolsters the union's bargaining power and negotiating demands, it will miscalculate the true position and shape of the union's resistance curve, offer too little in the way of concessions, and thus increase the probability that a strike will occur.

A second example of a strike model that relies on divergent estimates of benefits and costs is provided by Kaufman (1981). Kaufman posits that strikes vary over time in a cyclical manner around a steady state or "natural" rate of strike activity. (The size of the natural rate reflects structural factors, such as the size of union membership, the structure of bargaining, the legal framework, etc.) If both the union and firm correctly forecast the rate of inflation over the 30- to 40-month duration of most collective bargaining contracts, each will adjust its wage demand/offer accordingly, leaving the benefits and costs of striking in real terms unchanged. In fact, however, unions are generally unable to fully anticipate movements in the inflation rate, leading them to demand too small a wage increase in the early part of the expansion phase of the business cycle (since they underestimate the coming rise in prices) and too large a wage increase at the end of the expansion phase (since they forecast continued high inflation, even though actual inflation begins to decline). The result is to first cause a narrowing of the distance separating the real wage demands of the two sides and, later, an enlargement of this distance, leading to a corresponding cycle in strikes. In particular, this model predicts that the peak of the strike cycle should occur shortly after the peak of the business cycle as firms experience a softening of sales, leading them to toughen their bargaining position, while the wage demands of unions continue to escalate, both to make up for the loss of real wages over the last contract and to keep up with expected high inflation over the next contract.

It is evident that both models provide an explanation for why strikes vary with economic conditions. Neither is problem-free, however. Mauro, for example, posits that the negotiators place different weights on economic variables in the concession and resistance curves, but offers no explanation for why this occurs. Kaufman's results critically depend on the inability of unions to accurately forecast inflation over the duration of collective bargaining contracts, an assumption that proponents of rational expectations in macroeconomics may quarrel with. It also provides no explanation for the oft-found relationship between the unemployment rate and inflation rate.

Information uncertainty model. A second model of strikes is the "information uncertainty" model. Major work on this line of thinking includes Siebert and Addison (1981), Cousineau and Lacroix (1986), and Gramm, Hendricks, and Kahn (1988). These authors view strikes as the result of miscalculations in bargaining, as in the imperfect information models, but differ as to the source of the miscalculation. The imperfect information models assume that the strike arises from the fact that the estimated values of the variables used to estimate the resistance and concession curves by the bargainers are biased from their mean values. The information uncertainty model, on the other hand, assumes that both bargainers know the mean values of the relevant variables and instead focus on two other features of the bargainers' information set: the amount of information that needs to be processed and the degree of uncertainty (the size of the variance) associated with the variables.

Siebert and Addison develop this line of thinking in what they call an "accident" model of strikes. They argue that strikes are much like road accidents. No individual auto accident is predictable *ex ante*, they claim, but certain conditions (e.g., rainy weather, higher speed limits) that make driving either more difficult or reduce the margin for error have a definite and predictable relationship to the frequency of accidents in the aggregate. They make the same type of argument with respect to the frequency of strikes. For example, any environmental change (e.g., a new workplace safety law, a new economic threat to the firm or union) that increases the number of issues on the bargaining table is likely to increase the frequency of strikes by adding to the complexity of the negotiations and reducing the amount of negotiating time available to any one issue. A second such factor is sudden and/or large changes in one or more aspects of the external environment, such as the rate of unemployment or inflation, for these introduce greater uncertainty into each side's benefit-cost calculations and thus increase the chances of a miscalculation and strike.

The information uncertainty model has several strengths. These include a certain amount of innate plausibility, an applicability to both time-series and cross-section variation in strike rates, and a significant amount of support from empirical studies. The major drawback of the model is its limited relevance to strikes other than those over economic issues during a contract renegotiation (e.g., renegotiation strikes over work rules or wildcat strikes over safety).

Asymmetric information model. A third type of strike model focuses on asymmetries in the information available to the bargaining part. The first published paper of this genre was Hayes (1984), which was then extended by Tracy (1986), Hart (1989), Card (1990), Booth and Cressy (1990), and others.[5] According to this theory, strikes are not a mistake due to divergent estimates of benefits and costs but, rather, a screening device used by unions to sort out firms based on their level of profitability. The rationale is the following. Some firms have high profits while others have low profits, but all have an incentive to tell the union they are in the latter group in order to gain a less expensive labor contract. The union's challenge is to identify the high-profit firms so that it can extract higher wages from them. How this is done, it is argued, is to confront all firms with a choice: pay a high wage and avoid a strike or pay a lower wage but suffer a strike of some specified length (i.e., to present firms with a downward-sloping concession schedule). If this wage/strike trade-off is properly constructed, it can be shown that the high-profit firms have an incentive to reveal their true profit position and pay the higher wage (because the forgone profits of a strike outweigh the higher wage costs), while the low-profit firm has no choice but to take a strike if it is to convince the union that it is a low-profit firm. Strikes, therefore, are not a bargaining mistake but an efficient way for unions (at least *ex ante*) to distinguish between more and less profitable firms.

According to Tracy (1987) and Abowd and Tracy (1989), the information asymmetry model leads to three major hypotheses: variables that increase the expected size of firm profits should decrease strike activity; variables that lead to a greater degree of uncertainty about future profits should increase strike activity; and variables that improve the alternative labor market opportunities of union members should also increase strikes. Abowd and Tracy use these hypotheses to argue, for example, that strike rates in an industry should be higher, *ceteris paribus*, the greater is the industry concentration ratio and the proportion of the industry work force unionized, in the former case because firms earn higher profits and in the latter because union workers have (allegedly) greater alternative labor market opportunities. A fourth hypothesis of the model, as noted by Kennan and Wilson (1988) and McConnell (1989), is that the size of the wage settlement should be inversely related to strike duration.

Of the economic strike models reviewed here, the asymmetric information model has been the one that has received the most attention in the last half of the 1980s. A number of economists (e.g., Kennan 1986; Tracy 1987) have also voiced the opinion that it holds the greatest promise for future theoretical work on strikes. My own assessment is significantly less enthusiastic (also see Fernandez and Glazer 1991). No evidence has been presented that strikes actually perform a screening function nor that the uncertainty of unions regarding firms' profitability is sufficiently large to generate a significant number of strikes. It is also likely that *both* the union and firm possess private information, but incorporating this in the model seriously compromises its predictive ability.

Union political model. The fourth class of economic strike model is what I refer to as the "union political" model. It was originally developed by Ashenfelter and Johnson (1969), with some subsequent elaboration by Farber (1978). The Ashenfelter-Johnson (A-J) model, while a product of the late 1960s, proved to be one of the most frequently cited theoretical works in the strike literature of the 1980s and was often used to guide or motivate empirical studies of strikes.

Ashenfelter and Johnson claim that a more fruitful approach to the study of strikes requires recognition that there are not two but three parties involved in labor-management negotiations: the management, the union leadership, and the union rank and file.[6] Based on this insight, which they attribute to Ross's (1948) work on trade union wage policy, A-J develop a formal bargaining model. They assume the goal of the firm is to maximize the present value of profits, the goal of the union leadership is to win reelection to office, and the goal of the rank and file is to win "more" at the bargaining table. A-J argue that the two parties that actually do the bargaining, the management of the firm and the union leadership, generally have realistic expectations of the benefits and costs of a strike and can generally reach a peaceful settlement. The problem, however, is that the union leadership must represent the wage aspirations of the rank and file in the negotiations, for if they do not they risk being defeated for office in the next union election.[7]

A-J do not state explicitly how the rank and file form their wage expectations, but posit that they are often more extreme than those of the leadership and decline over time as a function of strike duration. Hence, rather than risk electoral defeat, the union leadership will demand a relatively higher wage in negotiations than they realistically think the union can win without a strike. The firm, in turn, will find it more profitable to take a strike than agree to this inflated set of demands. As the strike progresses, however, the wage demands of the rank and file gradually fall and at some point the firm finds it profitable to end the strike and agree on the union's terms. In effect, then, the strike serves to equilibrate the wage expectations of the rank and file with what the firm is willing to pay.

The root cause of strikes, according to this model, is unrealistically high wage expectations on the part of the union rank and file. With regard to the occurrence of strikes, the model predicts that a strike will take place whenever the minimum wage demand that the union is willing to settle for at the strike deadline exceeds the maximum wage the firm is willing to pay. Finally, the occurrence of strikes will fluctuate over the business cycle and across firms and industries to the extent that one or more variables cause a systematic variation in the rank and file's minimally acceptable nonstrike wage increase or in their rate of concession during a strike.

Despite the popularity of the A-J model, it suffers from a number of conceptual problems (see Shalev 1980; Siebert, Addison, and Bertrand 1985). First, it is able to derive a determinate solution only by making the bargaining process one-sided (the union makes offers which the firm decides to accept or reject). The process by which the union forms its wage demands is also *ad hoc*. Finally, although the model ostensibly incorporates the political nature of union wage policy into the bargaining process, it is done in a way that yields no substantively interesting insights about the cause of strikes (because the union leadership always follows the wage preferences of the rank and file).

Given the popularity of the A-J model with strike researchers, and the serious conceptual defects with it, it is surprising that few studies have attempted to extend or refine the model. The major exception is a study by Swint and Nelson (1980). They take the basic A-J framework but then introduce utility functions for the management and union bargainers. The net effect is to open up the possibility that the management and union leaders may pursue a wage policy that promotes their self-interests over the interests of the people they represent (the stockholders and union rank and file). Among other results, Swint and Nelson claim to show that union members may actually gain higher (not lower) wages by striking.

Joint cost model. The fifth type of economic strike model found in the literature of the 1980s is known as the "joint cost" model. It was independently developed in concurrent articles by Kennan (1980) and Neumann and Reder (1980).

The idea behind the joint cost models is straightforward; i.e., the greater the joint costs of a strike, the greater the motivation of the union and firm to compromise their demands in order to avoid an expensive "mistake." The most elaborated rationale for this proposition is provided by Reder and Neumann (1980). They argue that the union and firm become involved in a long-term bargaining relationship. Since strikes impose costs on both sides, the bargainers have an incentive to develop "protocols" (i.e., rules and conventions) that resolve disputes over unforeseen contingencies. Since the development and operationalization of these protocols (e.g., a COLA clause, binding arbitration of grievances) is itself a costly activity, it generally will not pay a firm and union to cover all strike-threatening situations. Thus, firms and unions will divide resources and resolve disputes through two means, strikes and nonstrike protocols, where the proportion of each that is used depends on their relative cost. When strike costs are high, the union and firm will thus avoid using this method of dispute resolution and find some less costly alternative, leading to low observed strike rates (such as in the steel industry with the adoption of the Experimental Negotiating Agreement).

The major conceptual shortcoming of the joint cost model is that it considers only the costs of a strike to the two sides and not the benefits. Clearly, however, the decision to strike involves a comparison of both and to omit the benefit side of the calculation risks serious error in empirical work. As shall be argued later, issues of principle and organizational survival often give particular saliency to certain bargaining outcomes that are mutually opposed from the perspective of the union and firm), making a strike nearly inevitable and quite lengthy, even in the face of massive financial losses to both sides. On an empirical level, the joint cost model also seems to be of limited relevance to time-series studies of strikes. The greater frequency of strikes during a business cycle peak, for example, must necessarily imply a diminution of the joint costs facing the union and firm from a strike. While it is plausible that strike costs to workers are reduced in good times (e.g., due to the greater availability of alternative jobs, less fear of replacement by nonstrikers), it is also plausible that the costs to firms are greater (e.g., forgone sales will be greater and inventory stocks will be lower). The net effect is that the theory is not able to unambiguously explain the behavior of strikes over the business cycle.

Behavioral

The second class of strike models is behavioral. Behavioral models have several common features, including: considerable attention given to the influence of psychological processes and structures on the goals and behaviors of the bargainers and to the dynamics of the negotiation process; a focus on not only the distributive nature of bargaining (e.g., bargaining over a sum of money), but also on what Walton and McKersie (1965) call "attitudinal structuring" (defining the nature of the relationship between the union and firm) and "intraorganizational bargaining" (resolving disputes among factions within the union and company organization); and a significant concern with the role that psychological and social considerations play in facilitating or impeding collective action by workers and in determining the ability of both the firm and union to mobilize their members to initiate and sustain strike action.

As with the economic models, a significant body of behaviorally oriented work on strikes appeared in the years prior to 1980 and must be considered in a discussion of more recent research on the subject. There is a key difference between the two literatures, however. While in the 1980s the work on strikes by economists expanded greatly, similar work by behaviorally oriented researchers on the subject of strikes noticeably diminished. What appears to have happened is that the amount of behavioral research on the subjects of negotiation and conflict mushroomed but the type of negotiation and conflict examined shifted from a labor-management context (collective bargaining and strikes) to an intraorganizational context (superior-subordinate or worker-worker negotiation and conflict). It is not coincidental that this shift in research orientation occurred at the same time that behavioral researchers largely forsook the field of industrial relations for the newly emergent field of organizational behavior.

Before examining the 1980s behavioral research on strikes, a brief review of antecedent work is necessary. The two most significant works are by Stagner and Rosen (1965) and Walton and McKersie (1965).

Stagner and Rosen's work on strikes is the most explicitly psychological. They identify three psychological concepts key to understanding the occurrence of strikes: perception, motivation, and frustration. Perception is important because people act on the basis of the set of information available to them and how this information is interpreted. The important point for understanding the genesis of strikes, Stagner and Rosen claim, is that workers and managers perceive a given set of facts quite differently: to workers a demand for a wage concession is interpreted as an attempt by the company to make more money at their expense, while to the managers a wage cut is necessary to remain competitive. Motivation is important because each person in his/her role as a worker or manager acts out of a desire to satisfy various needs; for workers it is needs such as a higher income, a safer place to work, freedom from oppressive supervision; for managers it is greater profits, preserving freedom of decision making, and so on. Finally, frustration enters the equation because when people's efforts to satisfy their needs are blocked they react with frustration. Frustration, in turn, often leads to aggressive behavior as people attempt to remove the obstacle. Strikes thus originate out of an aggressive impulse generated by misperceptions and frustrations. Strikes are more likely to occur, in turn, when economic, social, or organizational conditions create or amplify misperceptions, lead to blocked and/or conflicting needs, and facilitate the expression of resultant frustration through collective action.

The title of Walton and McKersie's book, *A Behavioral Theory of Labor Negotiations* (1965), clearly stakes out the study's behavioral orientation, an approach they justify as follows:

> We conceive of labor negotiations as an example of social negotiations. . . . We chose the term 'social negotiations' because we wish to stress attitudinal and organizational aspects of this process . . . not treated in many theories of bargaining or games (p. 3).

More so than Stagner, however, they attempt to incorporate and analyze the impact of attitudinal and organizational factors in a formal model of the bargaining process. They follow Hicks and the economists in their analysis of distributive bargaining (the only type to be discussed in detail here) by arguing that both the union and management negotiators decide whether to strike or settle based on a comparison of the benefits and costs of a strike, but they then introduce the behavioral dimension by framing the calculation of benefits and costs in terms of subjective expected utility (SEU) theory. Accordingly, perception enters the model through each party's estimation of the utility gains and costs from different wage demands, estimates that each party attempts to alter to their advantage through a range of bargaining tactics, such as bluffing, threats, and commitment. Similarly, motivation enters their model by influencing the utility values attached to particular outcomes. Winning a wage increase at least as large as that won by workers at a competing firm may take on a very large utility value for the union negotiator, thus "motivating" him/her to pursue this demand aggressively; whereas a wage increase above this amount will quickly decline in utility value and its motivational pull. Walton and McKersie (p. 56) conclude that strikes occur "because the negotiators are not clear about the intentions of the other side," a point of view similar to Hicks's. The difference is that they develop in much more detail why each side may be unclear about the other's intentions, and how the dynamics of the bargaining process lead to this confusion.

We now come to consideration of the behavioral strike theory literature of the 1980s. As indicated earlier, this literature is relatively sparse. Several works, nonetheless, have made contributions in this area.

One is a paper by Kelly and Nicholson (1980). After a review of four conceptual approaches to explaining strikes (what they identify as environmental, institutional, sociological, and psychological theories), Kelly and Nicholson develop a model that endeavors to integrate all the important variables and causal relationships contained in these four theories. They argue that such a model must begin with a consideration of the social-psychological context of strikes (thus giving it a heavy behavioral orientation). They label this context the "industrial relations climate," which is itself composed of four factors: frames of reference, intergroup perceptions, perceptions of climate and conflict, and economic conditions. Out of these factors emerges a "trigger" that readies individual workers for collective action, but whether such action occurs is made a function of what Kelly and Nicholson identify as "structural facilitators and inhibitors" (e.g., community attitudes towards strikes, social cleavages among the workers). The second major component of their model pertains to the "strike process," which involves three groups of subprocesses: interparty bargaining, intraparty bargaining, and strike maintenance (e.g., the ability to maintain worker solidarity, keep out strikebreakers, etc.). The third conceptual component of their model relates to "strike outcomes," which they classify as substantive, procedural, and climate.

The second study of interest is Waddington's (1986) case study of a strike at the Ansells Brewery Co. The purpose of the study is to understand why the workers decided to strike, particularly when the parent company announced beforehand that the brewery would be closed in the event of a walkout (a threat subsequently made good). Waddington argues that in hindsight it is clear that the workers miscalculated management's resolve, a conclusion consistent with Hicks's position. The interesting part of the paper is that Waddington then goes on to provide a social-psychological explanation for why they made this miscalculation. He argues that workers are faced with a complex decision made in an environment of great uncertainty and conflicting claims. To resolve this cognitive complexity, people search for a way to order all the information they receive and establish logical cause-effect relationships. They do this by adopting a "cognitive script" (a mental model that abscribes motives to actors, saliency to certain facts or events, and probabilities to future actions and outcomes), where a particular script is chosen based on past experience, the influence of significant social others, and its perceived congruency with reality.

In the case of the brewery strike, the workers' cognitive script was heavily influenced by the low trust relationship between management and the union and the perception that the company's threat to close the plant was a bluff (since the company had threatened to do so before but had backed down). The end result was that workers ignored or downgraded management's warnings about the need to stem losses and boost productivity and interpreted the threat to close the plant as tactical opportunism. In retrospect it was clear that management's position had fundamentally changed due to heightened competition in its product market, but workers failed to perceive and act upon this knowledge because it was fundamentally at odds with their view of the world. Thus, a decision to strike that seemed rational *ex ante* proved foolhardy *ex post*.

A third study with a significant behavioral component is Hoyt Wheeler's book *Industrial Conflict: An Integrative Theory* (1985). The behavioral orientation of Wheeler's theory is indicated in the introduction when he states: "We have had available from economic theory sound and well-tested notions relating to the calculative side of human behavior. What has been lacking has been theory of comparable quality dealing with aspects of human nature that have nothing to do with cost-benefit calculations" (p. 3). As Wheeler conceptualizes it, strikes are an act of aggression on the part of a group of employees against the employer. His model is divided into two parts. The first part focuses on the individual employee and attempts to explain the factors that cause an employee to be predisposed to pursue aggressive action; the second focuses on the group level and attempts to explain the conditions that facilitate a coming together of individual employees for the purpose of collective action (a strike) against the company.

With respect to the first part of the model, the propensity of the individual employee to pursue aggressive action is tied to four conceptual "pillars" of behavior: the first is that human beings have innate predispositions and instincts; the second is that one of these predispositions is to pursue material and social dominance at work; the third holds that a gap between an employee's expectations and achievement as to material and social dominance is highly likely to ready him/her for aggressive action; and the fourth is that there exist three separate paths—frustration-aggression, threat, and rational-calculation—that lead from a predisposition to pursue aggressive action to actual readiness for aggression. Regarding these three paths, frustration-aggression is held to be the most common precipitator of strikes. In this scenario, if the employee is prevented from achieving his/her material and social needs, a feeling of frustration develops which is focused upon the employer. A strike, then, relieves this frustration in two ways: it gains greater material and social resources for the employee, thus reducing the expectations-achievement gap; and, second, it provides a cathartic release of emotions (e.g., resentment, hate, a desire to punish) associated with a state of frustration, thus helping to restore the individual to a psychological equilibrium.

As noted above, the second part of Wheeler's model pertains to the conditions necessary to translate individual readiness for aggressive behavior to collective action. This aspect of the model, it will be seen, relates directly to the concerns of the organizational models to be discussed shortly. The essential point is that no matter how dissatisfied or frustrated employees may be, a strike will not occur unless they are willing and able to act as a group and collectively walk off the job. Wheeler identifies three conditions that facilitate occurrence of collective action: first, the greater is the proportion of the employees who feel aggrieved; second, the fewer are the inhibitions to collective action; and third, the greater are the psychological and social bonds among the employees. (Also see Batstone, Boraston, and Frenkel 1978.)

In the last chapter of the book, Wheeler attempts to use his integrative theory to explain several of the regularities commonly found in empirical strike studies. He argues, for example, that the positive association between inflation-induced declines in real wages and strike activity reflects the emergence of a larger expectations-achievement gap. He claims his theory also rationalizes the negative relationship between the unemployment rate and strike activity on the grounds that higher unemployment reduces employee expectations and temporarily inhibits the expression of frustrated/aggressive behavior (i.e., aggressiveness remains latent during recessions but becomes manifest when economic conditions favor strike action). Finally, Wheeler's theory explains cross-industry strike rates on the basis of factors that facilitate collective action, create expectation-achievement gaps, or encourage feelings of frustration/aggression on the part of employees.

A fourth body of strike theory that has a significant behavioral component pertains to the determinants of strike "militancy" (see Schutt 1982; Martin 1986; and Ng 1991). Militancy is defined to mean a favorable attitude toward striking. Martin, for example, posits a social background category that relates attitudes toward strike action to a worker's age, race, sex, and other such sociodemographic variables; an economic category that ties militancy to the economic rewards (or lack thereof) from work; a political category that relates militancy to community and public support for strike action; and a "militancy" category that incorporates the effect of underlying individual attitudes and values toward strikes. The argument of these studies is that it is possible to identify causal links between specific variables (e.g., employee gender/age, community attitudes) and strike militancy. One complication noted by the authors, however, is that *ex ante* surveys of strike intentions (such as in Schutt's and Martin's studies) may not translate into strike action. Nor is it clear that attitudes are independent variables, for they may reflect instrumental considerations of benefits and costs.[8]

A final study to mention is Kaufman's (1981) application of Cross's (1969) bargaining model to the subject of strikes. Cross develops reaction functions for two bargainers who are negotiating over a sum of money. (Cross does not specifically consider the subject of strikes.) The reaction functions form a set of differential equations which can be solved to yield both the terms of the settlement and the length of the negotiations. The behavioral aspect of the model enters in two ways: first, because it is assumed both parties maximize subjective expected utility, thus providing an avenue for bargaining tactics such as bluffing, threats, and commitment to affect the bargaining outcome; and second because it is assumed that neither party knows the shape of the other's concession schedule, causing the bargaining to take place in an environment of "bounded rationality." Since each bargainer will most likely estimate the opponent's rate of concession with error, the model assumes that in each session of bargaining the two negotiators modify their demands as a proportion of the difference between what the opponent was expected to offer and the actual offer. Given that both sides are likely to start out the bargaining with demands higher than either realistically expects to win (due to bluffing and the knowledge of experienced negotiators that it is easier to lower a demand than raise it once a concession has been made), the negotiations take the form of an incremental, step-by-step convergence toward a settlement point as each party seeks to concede no more than is absolutely necessary.

The implications of this model for strikes are several. One is that the negotiation process must perforce be an incremental process of convergence, for any attempt by one party to move directly to the predicted point of settlement will only cause the other to raise its demand further. Given this insight, a second implication is that a strike is more likely when the period of bargaining is shorter; the initial demands of the two sides are wider; the expected rates of concession by both sides are more divergent; and the joint costs of a strike are smaller.[9] Finally, the model suggests that strike rates should decline over successive bargaining rounds for a given union/company pair as each becomes more familiar with the tactics and concession behavior of the other (also see Schnell and Gramm 1987; Montgomery and Benedict 1989).

Organizational

The third class of strike theories is organizational. The common denominator of these theories is the focus on strikes as a form of collective action and the role that workplace organization and various structural factors of a social, economic, and political nature play in facilitating and shaping such action. As might be expected, organizational theories of strikes have primarily been the domain of sociologists, although social psychologists and institutional labor economists have also made significant contributions in this area. The starting place for organizational theories of strikes is the observation that they represent a form of group behavior and, as such, require that people act in a concerted manner in pursuit of a common goal. This line of thought naturally leads to a consideration of the factors that motivate and facilitate group action and the role of formal organizations such as trade unions in this process. We briefly consider these two aspects in that order.

The factors that determine the conditions under which individuals will coalesce into a group and initiate some type of collective action have been a focus of investigation for many years. Research of the 1940s and 1950s identified a number of such factors. A basic precondition for group action, for example, was held to be the existence of a community of interests among the workers, for only if they shared a common sense of grievance, frustration, or aspiration would they be motivated to strike en masse. The development of this community of interests was, in turn, more likely in certain situations than others. In one of the most influential early "sociological" studies of strikes, for example, Kerr and Siegel (1954) argued that collective action is more likely in industries (e.g., coal mining, logging, longshoring) where workers form a relatively homogeneous group in terms of work skills, social backgrounds, and demographic characteristics, and where they live in communities largely isolated from the broader society. In another study, Moore (1954) argued that strike rates differ across occupations because the innate characteristics of some types of jobs (unpleasant or unsafe working conditions in steel or auto manufacture) lead to a greater sense of dissatisfaction or alienation among employees. A third facilitating factor identified by Taft (1954) was ideology, most particularly the degree to which the workers and their leaders subscribe to a conservative "business union" philosophy or a more radical socialist/communist philosophy. Finally, a fourth factor identified by Whyte (1951) was cross-sectional variation among firms and industries in personnel or "human relations" practices, the idea being that abusive or exploitive management practices help to create the necessary community of interests for strike action.

Research on organizational/sociological determinants of strikes largely faded from the literature in the 1960s and early 1970s. Since then, however, a modest revival has occurred. The more recent literature is distinguished from the earlier by a shift away from a preoccupation with the structural antecedents of strikes and toward a greater concern with identifying the necessary and sufficient conditions required for collective action, be it war, revolution, or striking (Tilly and Haimson 1989). A particular catalyst for this shift in emphasis was Olsen's (1965) book *The Logic of Collective Action.* Olsen argued that collective activities such as a strike contain a free rider problem in that people, acting to maximize their individual utility, desire to share in the benefits won from a strike but do not want to share in the costs of conducting the strike. Olsen's conclusion, then, was that effective collective action requires elimination of the free rider problem, such as through compulsion (e.g., union shop agreements) or "selective incentives" to individuals in the form of social sanctions and pressures to join in the strike. The success of the latter option, he claimed, declined with group size, implying that large work groups should have less success in mounting a strike than smaller sized groups.

Several strands of literature have emerged in recent years that attempt to provide an alternative explanation for collective action, generally by modifying or rejecting outright Olsen's economic model of individual self-interested rationality (see Oliver and Marwell 1988). For example, the most popular alternative theory of collective action to appear in the 1970s and 1980s is resource mobilization theory (Jenkins 1983; McCarthy and Zald 1987). This theory holds that the impetus for a collective form of action such as a strike is the desire on the part of a group of individuals to end exploitation or injustice. This motivation remains latent, however, until social, political, or economic conditions change in such a way that resources become available for the subordinate group to successfully challenge the hegemony of the dominant group. An example is the strike wave that followed the election of the pro-labor Roosevelt administration and the pickup in the economy after 1933 (see Cohen 1990; Goldfield 1991); another (but in the reverse direction) is the sharp decline in strikes in the 1980s that followed the Reagan administration's hard line on the air traffic controllers' strike (Northrup 1984), the antilabor rulings of the NLRB, and the large-scale job losses in heavily unionized industries.

Resource mobilization theory by itself does not, however, explain away the free rider problem nor the finding of most empirical studies that the propensity to strike is a positive function of the size of the bargaining unit. Several authors, therefore, have attempted to develop models of individual behavior that are consistent with both resource mobilization theory and the findings of empirical research. One effort in this direction is by Klanderman (1984, 1986). He uses expectancy-value theory to explain individual predisposition to engage in collective action (an approach that introduces a distinct behavioral element to the theory). The basic idea is that people are more likely to strike when the goals of the strike have a high valence (utility) to them and when they believe their participation will significantly improve the chances of success. Resource mobilization thus can be separated into two parts: "consensus mobilization" in which the strike leaders attempt to heighten individual estimates of the legitimacy of the strike and the gains to be derived from it (e.g., by documenting adverse pay or working conditions, whipping up anti-employer sentiments) and "action mobilization" in which the strike leaders endeavor to make the perceived social and financial gains to the individual from participation (and costs from nonparticipation) as high as possible (e.g., through appeals to worker solidarity, threats of social ostracism, or job demotion).

As noted in the introduction to this section, a second aspect of organizational theories of strikes centers on the impact of union organization on the frequency, size, and duration of work stoppages. Early work in this area was Shorter and Tilly's (1974) book on strikes in France, followed by two articles by David Snyder (1975, 1977). Snyder's work, in turn, precipitated a number of additional contributions, including Edwards (1981), Cronin (1978), Kaufman (1982), Skeels (1982), Franzosi (1989), and Cohn and Eaton (1989).

Snyder claims that strike frequency and size are causally related in a positive direction to the size of union membership, in large part because formal organization facilitates the mobilization of resources for collective action. He further claimed that when unions and collective bargaining are "noninstitutionalized," such as in pre-World War II America, or in France or Italy until recent years, that changing economic conditions have relatively little impact on strikes while fluctuations in union strength and density are the dominant influence (along with political factors, for reasons discussed in the next section).

Later writers dispute several aspects of Snyder's organizational theory. For example, Kaufman (1982), Skeels (1982), and Cohn and Eaton (1989) argue that in a noninstitutionalized system it often takes a strike to force the employer to recognize the union, implying that the causation often runs from strikes to union membership. Likewise, they maintain that union membership may have a negative impact on strike frequency in several ways not recognized by Snyder. A justification for the Wagner Act, for example, was that its encouragement of unionization would reduce recognition strikes, often the source of the bloodiest and most violent labor disputes. Formal union organization may also reduce strikes to the extent that it prevents spontaneous wildcat strikes by disaffected elements of the rank and file. A third reason is that the strike frequency associated with a given level of union membership is likely to decrease over time as the unions become bureaucratized, the bargaining relationship between the two parties becomes institutionalized, and union leaders lose their missionary zeal.[10] Finally, they agree with Snyder that fluctuations in union membership have a larger role in explaining strike patterns in a noninstitutionalized system (since union security is more problematic), but argue that a major unresolved issue is whether these fluctuations in union membership are themselves reflective of underlying changes in economic and political variables (or "resources"), suggesting that changes in union membership in the short run may better be thought of as an intervening variable rather than a truly independent variable.

The final point to be made about organizational theories of strikes is that they bear a close intellectual kinship to the bargaining power model originally developed by institutionally oriented economists. In particular, both bargaining power and resource mobilization theories focus on the strike as a form of collective action; the dependence of strikes on the extent and cohesiveness or worker organization (which is itself a function of economic, political, and social resources); the asymmetry between management and unions in the initiation of strike action; and the important role of psychological factors (e.g., discontent, inequity, frustration) as a nonrational (or noninstrumental) trigger of strikes. Thus, while Hicksian-based economic models focus on factors that cause miscalculations in bargaining between an established union and firm, the bargaining power/organizational models focus on those factors that facilitate or inhibit the formation of workers' organizations and the power resources available to them.

The two approaches lead, in turn, to fundamentally different predictions about the relationship of strikes to the business cycle. The Hicksian-based models, for example, tie the occurrence of strikes to the amount of *change* in business conditions, for it is the relative variation in unemployment or prices that influences the probability of a miscalculation in bargaining. A clear implication, then, is that a fall in the unemployment rate should lead to an initial rise in strike activity (because it precipitates more miscalculations), but that in the long run the level of strike activity should be independent of the *level* of the unemployment rate (i.e., the same number of miscalculations should occur at a steady state unemployment rate of 3 percent or 10 percent). The bargaining power/organizational models, however, predict that strike activity is a positive function of the power resources of unions and, thus, the level of strike activity will be *permanently* higher for any given steady state rate of unemployment (or other economic variable).

Political

The fourth class of strike theories is political. These theories focus on either the impact of political events on the decision to strike or the use of the strike by workers to win demands through the political process. As suggested below, there is a significant overlap between the political and organizational theories, given that political events have a major impact on workers' ability to mobilize for collective action. For the purpose of this review, the literature on political theories may be divided into four groups.

The first group focuses on the interrelationship between strikes, the integration of the working class in the national polity, and the political party in power of the national government. Two early studies first deserve mention. One is by Ross and Hartmann (1960). They argue that workers and their unions have two alternative methods to achieve their demands: through collective bargaining with the employer or political action with the government. They conclude from a historical analysis of strike trends in over a dozen countries that worker access to political power (say through a labor party in control of the national government) is a major deterrent to strike action since unions can achieve their demands with greater effectiveness and loss cost through the legislative process.

The second study is Shorter and Tilly's (1974) historical analysis of strikes in France and other industrialized countries. They argue that the characteristics of strikes and their causes are fundamentally affected by whether strikes are used as a weapon against employers in an economic contest of strength, such as in the United States, or as a political influence tool meant to persuade or pressure elected officials, as in France. In the former case strikes tend to be long, drawn-out affairs that are called by the union when economic conditions give workers the best tactical advantage, while in the latter case strikes take the form of a short protest timed to have the greatest impact on elected officials.[11]

In recent years these conjectures have been examined in several empirical studies, but only a modest amount of conceptual work has appeared along these lines. One exception is a study by David Snyder (1977) which, in turn, precipitated several other articles during the 1980s. Based on Shorter and Tilly's work, Snyder argued that the American working class had not achieved entry into the polity prior to World War II and, hence, strikes had a political objective and fluctuated with the political climate. After World War II, however, labor did gain effective political representation and strikes thus lost their political overtones and fluctuated mainly in tune with economic conditions. Edwards (1981), Kaufman (1982),

Skeels (1982), and several other writers challenged this thesis on two counts. First, they argue a lack of historical evidence exists to support the contention that pre-World War II strikes in America had (with a few exceptions) political objectives and, second, they claim that if labor achieved polity entrance after the war, then one could logically argue that strikes should still fluctuate with the political climate as unions use the political process when Democrats control the legislative and/or executive branches (the Ross and Hartmann argument).

A second study of relevance is by Korpi and Shalev (1980). They argue that earlier political strike theories (e.g., Ross and Hartmann 1960; Hibbs 1976) need to be modified in several respects. They agree that if unions gain effective representation in the political process they will transfer their collective demands from the industrial to the political arena, thus reducing the level of strike activity. The key indicator of such representation, however, is not the presence of a labor-oriented political party, but the extent of resource redistribution from capital to labor that the party in power undertakes. They also argue that economic variables (e.g., the unemployment rate, rate of inflation) are not independent determinants of strikes since a pro-labor government will adopt economic policies that favor lower unemployment and higher inflation.

The second strand of literature on political theories of strikes focuses on the strike as an outcome of a political contest between management and workers over control of the labor process. Representative of this body of work are Edwards and Scullion (1982), Lichtenstein (1985), Edwards (1986), and Wallace (1989). Generally written from a sociological/Marxist perspective, these authors see strikes less as an outcome of formal bargaining than a day-to-day political struggle between workers and managers on the shopfloor to define and defend their respective levels of power and authority and the terms of the wage/effort bargain. Strikes, in this view, are inherent to the system of capitalist production; they can be reduced through joint labor-management collaboration but never eliminated entirely.

The third strand of political theorizing on strikes centers on the internal political process in unions. This subject is explored in early work by Fisher and McConnell (1954) and Ross and Hartmann (1960). Both studies contend that the incidence of strikes is positively related to the amount of political competition and fractiousness in unions, the reason being that union leaders are driven to greater militancy in both bargaining and shopfloor relations with management when they perceive a threat to their survival in office. The most oft-cited study that appeals to the internal union political process as a source of strikes is by Ashenfelter and Johnson (1969) although, as indicated earlier, their theory on this matter is largely empty of substantive content. Another pre-1980s study of note is Roomkin (1976) which found that strike frequency is higher the more decentralized is the political structure of the union. Studies published in the 1980s that address the union political dimension are sparse. Case studies of the air traffic controllers' strike (Northrup 1984) and Hormel strike (Hage and Klauda 1989) both illustrate the pivotal role played by the union leadership in determining whether a strike occurs. Several studies also suggest how a strike can be used by union leaders to further their personal agendas and/or the goals of the union as an organization. Stagner and Elfal (1982) and Mellor (1990), for example, find evidence that a strike increases commitment to the union and political support for the leadership, while Golden (1990) argues that union leaders sometimes call strikes to protect the organizational security of the union even if doing so risks a "heroic defeat." While these studies are suggestive, the interplay between the goals of the union as an organization, the personal goals of the leadership, and the goals of the membership in the decision to strike remains vastly underexplored.

The fourth type of political theory pertains to the impact on strike activity of government legislation. One channel of influence between legislation and strikes is suggested by resource mobilization theory—legislation that either adds to or subtracts from the resources available to workers to mount effective collective action. Passage of laws in many states in the 1960s and 1970s permitting collective bargaining among public employees is a prime example of such a link (Olson 1988); proposed legislation to ban striker replacements is another (Gramm 1992). A second channel of influence that legislation has on strikes is to the extent it restricts the range of issues that can be bargained over or the amount that the union is permitted to win in bargaining. An example of the former is Executive Order 10988 which approved collective bargaining in the federal sector but prohibited bargaining over wages; an example of the latter is wage-price controls. The short-run effect of both actions is presumably to reduce strike activity by reducing either the issues in dispute or the size of the area of disagreement. Finally, legislation also affects strike activity to the extent it limits the ability of unions to call a strike or mandates that alternative forms of dispute resolution, such as binding arbitration, be used to resolve bargaining impasses. An example of the former is the Railway Labor Act; an example of the latter is public-sector bargaining laws of many states. An issue of particular interest during the 1980s in this regard was the extent to which legislated prohibitions on union recognition and/or the right to strike in the public sector result in a reduction in the incidence of strikes (Ichniowski 1982, 1988; Olson 1986; Partridge 1988).

Empirical Research

In this section I provide a brief overview of the empirical research on strikes, again with emphasis on the literature that appeared in the 1980s. The discussion of empirical research is divided into four subsections: methodological considerations, time-series studies, cross-sectional studies, and "other" studies.

Methodological Considerations

It is useful to begin with a consideration of methodological issues (also see Stern 1978). First a word about quantitative techniques and data.

Twenty-five years ago, strike studies tested hypotheses largely through a descriptive analysis of annual strike statistics obtained from government reports. Since then the quantitative study of strikes has undergone a veritable revolution. The first innovation was the use of ordinary least squares (OLS) multiple regression to analyze quarterly data on aggregate strike activity (Ashenfelter and Johnson 1969). By the end of the 1970s a second innovation appeared which was the replacement of aggregate, economy-wide strike data with national data disaggregated to the level of major issue and industry (Shalev 1980; Kaufman 1981). Data on contract expirations were also introduced at this time, permitting the researcher to conceptually divide strike movements into two parts: the part due to a change in the "opportunity to strike" (in the number of potential strike situations) and that due to a change in the "propensity to strike" (the probability of conflict in a given bargaining situation). The third innovation was the development of micro-level strike data in which the level of observation was the bargaining unit (Farber 1978; Mauro 1982; Swidinsky and Vanderkamp 1982). The permitted analysis of strike outcomes at the individual company level and a matching-up of the occurrence of a strike with the relevant contract expiration, as well as the introduction on the right-hand side of the regression equation of a host of independent variables of a company-specific nature. The development of micro-level data also led to the replacement of OLS with logit and probit regression techniques. Finally, hazard functions were also popularized in the mid-1980s for analysis of strike duration (Kennan 1985).

A second methodological issue concerns the measurement of the dependent variable in empirical studies. Strikes have three dimensions: frequency, size, and duration. Most empirical studies analyze these measures separately, and many only consider one of the dimensions and neglect the others. Several studies published in the 1980s suggest, however, that researchers need to be more attentive to this issue. Dilts (1986), for example, compared various "flow" measures of strikes with various "stock" measures and found a low correlation between the two groups. Korpi and Shalev (1980) and Walsh (1983) also showed that the various dimensions of strikes vary significantly across countries, implying that a cross-national comparison of only one or two dimensions may be quite misleading. A third consideration pertains to disaggregation of the strike measure by size, major issue, and contract issue. Kaufman (1981) and Flaherty (1983) showed, for example, that renegotiation strikes over economic issues are significantly more sensitive to economic variables than are those that occur during the term of an agreement over noneconomic issues (e.g., safety or grievances). Skeels, McGrath, and Arshanapalli (1988) also showed that the impact of variables such as the unemployment rate and rate of change of real wages on strike activity systematically differs by size of strike, an important result given the decision of the U.S. government in 1981 to collect data only on strikes of 1,000+ workers. (But see Garen and Krislov 1988 for conflicting evidence.) Finally, strikes exhibit several distinct temporal patterns, each of which is likely to have a different behavioral explanation. Examples include a seasonal variation, a year-to-year variation, a fluctuation over the business cycle, episodic "waves" (Cronin 1978; Kaufman 1982), long-run "Kondratieff cycles" (Screpanti 1987), and a secular time trend.

A final methodological issue to touch on concerns various measurement problems affecting the independent variables. Comparison of results across studies remains problematic given the penchant of researchers to use different sets of independent variables. The specification of independent variables also frequently differs, such as with the specification of the real wage change variable (e.g., polynomial distributed lag, annual percentage change, percentage change over the length of the contract). A third problem concerns the construct validity of the independent variables (see Wheeler 1984; Gallagher and Gramm 1991). Leigh (1983), for example, uses the industry injury rate as a proxy for workers' degree of risk preference, while Kaufman (1982) and Skeels (1982) use dummy variables to capture the impact of employers' welfare capitalism practices on strike activity. While perhaps no alternative is available to these constructs, the link between the conceptual variable and the actual measure may be quite weak and subject to bias.

Time-Series Studies

Empirical research on the time-series behavior of strike activity dates back more than 80 years (Cross 1980). The 1980s saw a major expansion in this line of research. The general aim of these studies is to account for the cyclical and secular pattern in strike activity, such as exhibited in Figure 1. Given the voluminous and diverse nature of this literature, the best I can do is offer a brief overview of the most salient findings. This discussion focuses first on research regarding strike frequency and size, followed by a discussion of research on the determinants of strike duration.

One fact emerges indisputably from empirical strike studies—that at least in the United States and Canada the frequency and size of strikes is related to the economic environment. For these two countries the most important economic variables are the unemployment rate and the past rate of change of real wages. Nearly all studies find that strikes decrease during periods of higher than average unemployment (other things equal), while they increase during periods of less than average growth in real wages, such as during a period of unanticipated inflation. (See Shalev 1980; Kaufman 1981; Gunderson, Kervin, and Reid 1986; Vroman 1989. An exception is Gramm 1986.) Importantly, this result seems to hold true for both the pre-World War II period, when bargaining arrangements were relatively uninstitutionalized, and in the post-war period, when union-management relations had developed a high degree of formalization (Kaufman 1982; Skeels 1982). It must be noted, however, that these relationships are weaker at the industry level (Kaufman 1983) and for strikes over noneconomic issues (Kaufman 1981; Byrne and King 1986; Naples 1987) and during the term of an existing contract (Flaherty 1983). More disconcerting, the impact of these economic variables on strikes also appears to differ considerably across countries (Paldham and Pederson 1982; Beggs and Chipman 1987), although problems related to data comparability and historical/institutional idiosyncrasies preclude a definitive conclusion as of yet (see Korpi and Shalev 1980; Shalev 1983; Walsh 1983).

In no particular order, other findings include:[12]

- Increased volatility in product and labor market variables (e.g., capacity utilization, producer prices, inflation expectations) are associated with increased strike activity.
- The presence of an escalator (COLA) clause in a union contract reduces the impact of inflation in causing strikes, although bargaining over the initial adoption of a COLA clause is associated with a greater probability of a strike.
- Strikes fluctuate with changes in union membership, but whether the changes in union membership have an independent impact on strikes' net of economic and political variables is unclear.
- The amount of strike activity is directly related to the number of contract expirations.
- In North America there is little evidence that changes in the political party in power have any discernable impact on strike activity. Changes in the balance of bargaining power or disruptions to bargaining relationships caused by political events have a clear impact on strikes, however.
- Some studies find negative state dependence in strikes (i.e., the probability of a strike occurring in a contract negotiation is lower if a strike occurred in the previous round of negotiations), while others find positive state dependence (at least for short-to-medium duration strikes).
- Strikes have a distinct seasonal variation, with the most strike-prone months being in the summer (net of the volume of contract expirations).

- Several studies have found that a deterioration in relative wages (e.g., the wage of workers in one industry relative to the national average) has a positive impact on strikes.
- Strikes are less likely, other things equal, when product market conditions facing the firm are robust but labor market conditions facing the workers are poor (implying both sides face large costs of striking).
- Neither the level nor change in profits has a consistent relationship to strikes.

After languishing for many years, research on the time-series behavior of strike duration experienced a modest boom in the 1980s. Kennan (1985) examined major (1,000+ workers) contract renegotiation strikes over wages in the U.S. manufacturing sector for the 1968-76 period. He found that the probability of settlement for a strike in progress declined until the ninetieth day of duration, after which it began to increase. A similar analysis by Harrison and Stewart (1989) using Canadian data found that the settlement rate declined throughout. The two studies found identical results, however, regarding the cyclical behavior of strike duration. In particular, both studies found that while strike frequency is procyclical, strike duration is counter-cyclical (i.e., during recessions there are fewer but longer lasting strikes). The generalizability of this result has been recently called into doubt by McConnell (1990), however, who found no cyclical pattern in duration for a large sample of U.S. strikes. Finally, several recent studies have analyzed the relationship between strike duration and the terms of the settlement. McConnell (1989) found that the wage settlement declines with duration (consistent with the predictions of the asymmetric information model), while Card (1990) found that the wage settlement increased with duration until a strike length of 99 days or more was reached, after which the wage settlement declined. A study by Lacroix (1986), on the other hand, found that a strike had no net impact on the negotiated wage.

Cross-section Studies

A second major thrust of empirical research has been to identify the determinants of cross-sectional variation in strike activity, such as across industries, states (provinces), or unions. The most popular approach is to estimate a pooled time-series, cross-section regression equation, where the dependent variable is a measure of strike activity for *i* firms or industries over *j* years, and the independent variables measure different organizational characteristics of the union and firm (or industry), demographic characteristics of the work force, conditions in the firm's particular product and labor market, national economic conditions, and so on (on this subject see Owusu-Gyapong 1986). A second, less frequently used approach is to focus on a particular industry (e.g., state government) or occupation (e.g., teachers) and estimate a cross-sectional regression equation with observations drawn from various states or administrative units (such as school districts).

Empirical research done in the 1980s of a cross-sectional nature is smaller in volume than the time-series literature. It is also less satisfactory in three respects. One is that no overarching conceptual framework exists to guide the organization and specification of cross-sectional research; second, that the theoretical link between many of the individual independent variables (e.g., industry sales concentration) and the occurrence of strikes is relatively weak; and, third, that cross-study comparisons are hampered by the plethora of different variables, equation specifications, and data samples.

Despite these limitations, a number of conclusions can be gleaned from this literature. Among the principal findings are the following:[13]

- Strikes are more likely to occur the longer the duration of the preceding contract.
- The fewer the issues being negotiated (such as in a contract reopener over wages), the lower is the probability of a strike.
- Negotiations that serve as a pattern setter for other firm/union pairs have a higher probability of a strike.
- Larger bargaining units are more likely to have a strike.
- A larger variance in the firm's financial performance is associated with a larger strike propensity.
- More highly unionized industries have more strike activity.
- Firms/industries that employ a larger proportion of women are less strike prone.

- Firms/industries with greater risk of injury or fatality are more strike prone.
- Firms/industries that pay a higher wage rate relative to other firms/industries have a lower probability of a strike.
- Considerable variation exists across two- and three-digit SIC industries in the propensity to strike, holding all other measurable variables constant.
- Firms that can inventory or stockpile goods are more likely to have a strike.

Less agreement exists with respect to other variables. Some variables (e.g., industry concentration, worker education, inventory/sales ratio) are included in a number of studies, but the signs and statistical significance of the estimated coefficients vary considerably. In other cases, the relevant variables (e.g., bargaining structure, number of competing unions in an industry, proportion of white-collar workers) have been included in sufficiently few studies that it is impossible to draw a reliable conclusion.

Of the various theoretical perspectives reviewed in this paper, one that gains a considerable amount of support from cross-sectional studies is the joint cost model. Hutchens, Lipsky, and Stern (1990), for example, use the joint cost theory to predict the impact of transfer payments on interstate strike activity. They document that striker eligibility for unemployment insurance and welfare benefits varies considerably across the 50 states and argue that the states with the most liberal rules should have the greatest number of strikes, other things equal. They rationalize this on the basis that greater transfer payments significantly reduce the strike costs to workers and only incrementally boost the costs to employers (through higher UI or federal and state taxes), implying that total strike costs, and thus the incentive to settle, are reduced. They test this hypothesis with a pooled time-series regression model estimated with state data for the years 1960-74. They find, consistent with the theory, that greater UI eligibility is associated with higher strike rates. A second example is a study by Olson (1984). He finds that strike rates among public school teachers in Pennsylvania are higher in those districts where school days lost due to strikes are rescheduled. He argues that this supports the joint cost theory, since rescheduling lost school days means the teachers and school board suffer a smaller reduction in, respectively, pay and state aid (which is allotted to school districts based on school days taught). (Also see Maki 1986.)

Other Empirical Studies

A large number of empirical studies on strikes, or the conclusions therefrom, are not easily fit into the time-series/cross-section discussion above. Due to space constraints I will mention the most important of these but forgo all but the briefest of remarks as to their purpose and principal conclusions.

Studies by Gramm (1987), Card (1988), and McConnell (1990) provide estimates of the "propensity to strike" (strikes as a percent of contract expirations). McConnell's data are apparently the most complete. She found a strike rate of 13.8 percent across 29 industries for the period 1970-1981. By comparison, Kaufman (1977) calculated a strike propensity for the manufacturing sector for the earlier 1954-1975 period of 16.5 percent. Apparently the propensity to strike dropped significantly in the 1980s. Based on unpublished strike data, I calculate for the years 1987-1989 a strike propensity in manufacturing of roughly 8 percent.[14]

A number of studies examined the impact on strikes of various pieces of legislation or legal restrictions on the right to strike (Zimmer and Jacobs 1981; Peterson 1981; Ichniowski 1982; Northrup 1984; Tomkiewicz and Brenner 1985; Olson 1986; Gunderson, Kervin, and Reid 1988; Olson 1988; Ichniowski 1988; Gunderson and Melino 1990). Most of this literature pertained to public-sector strikes. Several conclusions emerge: that compulsory interest arbitration significantly reduces strike activity; that a statutory denial of the right to strike (or to bargain collectively) is frequently ineffective in preventing strikes; and the incidence of illegal strikes is negatively related to the size of penalties and the probability of enforcement.

Two laboratory studies of interest to strike researchers are Farber and Brazerman (1989) and Sopher (1990). Farber and Brazerman conclude that neither divergent expectations nor asymmetric information are quantitatively important contributors to strikes, but that the incremental nature of the concession process is. Sopher finds that strikes occur even when the bargainers have complete information concerning the benefits and costs of disagreement, a finding that also casts doubt on the importance of asymmetric or divergent information. He tentatively attributes the occurrence of strikes in his experiment to the desire of the bargainers to establish a reputation for "toughness" and the time it takes to learn an opponent's "type."

Other diverse studies are the following. Horn, McGuire, and Tomkiewicz (1982) and Chermash (1982) conclude that strikes are more likely in collective bargaining situations characterized by a lack of communication and collaboration between management and union officials. Hodson, Ziegler, and Bump (1983) and Gramm and Schnell (1991) examine the factors that determine workers' willingness to cross a picket line. Ng and Maki (1988) find that strikes in Canada are less likely when the union involved is American-based, but whether the company is American or Canadian makes no difference. Rose (1991) finds strikes are less effective in conglomerate firms. Perone (1984) uses an input-output table to develop a measure of union bargaining "leverage" in strike situations. Rubin (1988) finds that strikes reduce income inequality among wage earners. Delaney (1983) finds that a dispute resolved by arbitration or striking results in the same increase in teachers' salaries. Ondrich and Schnell (1992) find that the greater the number of unresolved issues, the smaller the conditional settlement probability of a strike. Gersuny (1981) examines the role of work hazards as a cause of strikes; Jones (1986) examines the role of the news media in the outcome of strikes; Gennard (1981) analyzes the impact on household income and saving of strikes; and Grant and Wallace (1991) examine the determinants of violence in labor disputes. Finally, several book-length case studies of strikes were published, including Friedman and Meredeen (1980); Wilsher, Macintyre, and Jones (1985); Hage and Klauda (1989); and Marmo (1990).

The Impact of Strikes

The third component of the strike literature I examine is the empirical literature on the impact of strikes on workers, consumers, individual firms, and industries. Much of this literature is concerned with the economic impact of strikes, although some studies have also examined various social/psychological effects.

The fundamental purpose of the strike is to serve as a method of dispute resolution in collective bargaining. In this role the strike has always been regarded with pronounced ambivalency. On one hand, the strike has been strongly defended as a basic democratic right of labor and the best means by which companies and unions can resolve their differences without the intervention of a third party, such as government. On the other hand, strikes impose economic and social costs on the participants to the strike and on neutral third parties—costs which arouse opposition to the use of the strike and a continued search for alternative methods of dispute resolution. It is particularly the third party costs of strikes that have been of concern to policymakers, as witnessed by the national emergency dispute provisions of the Taft-Hartley Act and the plethora of federal and state laws that restrict or ban altogether the right to strike among public-sector employees.

The costs of strikes, both to the participants and third parties (e.g., consumers, nonstruck firms, the economy), have been a subject of academic research since the early 1950s. The 1980s saw a minor boomlet in this area, with several theoretical studies of strike effectiveness (Carter, Hueth, Mamer, and Schmitz 1987; Fuess 1990) and a number of impressive empirical studies of strike impact.

The conclusions of the early literature referenced above were that strikes frequently impose significant financial costs on the workers and firm directly involved in the dispute, but only negligible costs in most cases on the public at large. The research of the 1980s has reaffirmed this conclusion and, if anything, shown that the third party cost of strikes has declined over time.[15] Several studies, for example, examined the impact of strikes on the share price of individual firms and found a significant negative impact (see Neumann 1980; Greer, Martinez, and Reusser 1980; Becker and Olson 1986; Davidson, Worrell, and Garrison 1988; and DeFusco and Fuess 1991). Representative of these studies is the finding of Becker and Olson that the occurrence of a strike of average duration involving 1,000 or more workers during the 1962-1982 period lowered the company's stock price 4.1 percent, or $72 to $87 million (1980) dollars. DeFusco and Fuess examined the share price of both struck and nonstruck carriers in the industry. They found that struck carriers suffered a 2.3 percent decrease in share price, while nonstruck carriers experienced an increase. The latter finding reflects the windfall gain in customers and profits experienced by the competitors of the struck carrier.

Although individual firms may be adversely affected by a strike, the evidence indicates that the adverse impact on industry output and prices is transitory in length and modest to negligible in size for all but a handful of strikes (for exceptions, see Maki 1983; Northrup 1984). Neumann and Reder (1984), for example, examined the impact of strikes on output in 63 three-digit SIC industries over the 1955-1977 period. They found that the occurrence of strikes had no statistically significant impact on output in 43 industries and a statistically negative, but very small, impact in 19 industries. Two other studies of interest are Gunderson and Melino (1987) and Paarsch (1990). Gunderson and Melino examined the impact of strikes on output and prices in the North American auto industry, while Paarsch examined the same variables in the British Columbia lumber industry. These studies found some tendency for production to increase prior to a large strike, reflecting the decision of both consumers and producers to build up inventories of the good in anticipation of a work stoppage (also see Ackerman 1979). If the strike shuts down a significant portion of industry capacity, these studies find that industry output falls and the price of the good rises, but only modestly and until the work stoppage ends. For small size strikes, no output effect at the industry level is apparent. Once a large strike ends, industry output increases and the price falls as producers temporarily increase production above the normal level to make up for the backlog of demand and depleted inventory levels.

A small literature has also developed on the impact of strikes on the level and growth of productivity (and the reciprocal effect of productivity growth on the occurrence of strikes). Flaherty (1987), for example, argues that strikes may be associated with lower productivity growth for a direct and indirect reason—direct to the extent that strikes disrupt production, and indirect to the extent they signal dissatisfaction or unrest on the shopfloor (possibly due to management's attempt to improve work efficiency). He finds a negative relationship between strike rates and productivity growth, although the relationship is not able to explain much of the post-1973 decline in U.S. productivity growth (also see Naples 1981; Kendrick 1982). McHugh (1991) finds that strikes have a larger negative impact on the productivity of supplier industries than on the struck industry itself, while Knight (1989) finds (using British data) that strikes may have a positive impact on productivity to the extent they vent repressed grievances or call attention to poor management practices.

In ending this section it is useful to mention a number of other empirical studies that examine some noneconomic effects of strikes. MacBride, Lancee, and Freeman (1981), Stoner and Arora (1987), and Smith (1989) examine the impact of a strike on the psychological well-being of the workers involved in the dispute. Their findings indicate that strikes can be extremely stressful events, with the level of stress a positive function of the duration of the strike and a negative function of family and community support. Other studies, such as Pfuhl (1983), Norman and Malla (1984), and Vispo and Shore (1985), examine the effect of a strike on customers or clients of the struck organization. Pfuhl finds a lack of evidence, for example, that crime rates increase during police strikes. Finally, Gilson, Spencer, and Granville (1989) examine the impact of a strike on local community attitudes toward the strikers and unions.

Evaluation and Suggestions for Future Research

Having reviewed the strike literature of the 1980s, it is time to close with a brief assessment of its strengths and weaknesses and several suggestions for the direction of future research.

My evaluation of strike research contains both good news and bad news for the field of industrial relations and academic research. First the good news. As noted in the beginning of this chapter, the 1980s witnessed a resurgence of interest in the subject of strikes. Since few subjects are nearer and dearer to the field of industrial relations than strikes, one has to regard this as a positive development. I am also impressed with the breadth and depth of theoretical and empirical research during the 1980s on the subject of strikes.

In terms of theory, economists were the most prolific contributors to strike research and in a number of cases made substantive additions. The 1980s saw, for example, the development of three new strike models (joint cost, asymmetric information, information uncertainty) and a significant formalization of a fourth (imperfect information). Relatively little progress, however, was made in extending a fifth economic model—the union political model. Although these models suffer from a narrow conceptualization of collective bargaining and strikes, they nevertheless have succeeded in pinpointing several root causes of strikes and have offered a rich array of hypotheses for empirical testing.

Progress was also made in the behavioral, organizational, and political areas. The most impressive study was Wheeler's behavioral/organizational model of strikes. Although Wheeler's model lacked the mathematical formalization found in economic models, he nevertheless succeeded in integrating a number of diverse theories and perspectives into a highly plausible explanation of strikes, and one that yields testable hypotheses. A second important contribution was by social psychologists, such as Klanderman's application of expectancy-value theory to strikes and Waddington's notion of cognitive scripts. Both approaches are promising, I think, because they help explain the apparent pecuniary irrationality of many strikes. A third area of progress, and one largely due to the work of sociologists, was the increased attention given to the economic versus political orientation of strikes and the impact that different institutional arrangements have on the volume and shape of strike activity across nations and time.

Some impressive progress was also made on the empirical front. Most notable was the appearance of numerous studies using comprehensive micro-level data on strikes at the level of the bargaining unit or firm. These data sets advanced the empirical analysis of strikes by permitting researchers to match up individual strike outcomes (strike or no-strike) with a host of firm-, union-, and industry-specific characteristics that had heretofore been unexploited. A second advantage of firm-level data is that it also matches up the occurrence of strikes with the expiration of individual contracts, thus controlling for variations in the opportunity to strike.

Other advances in empirical research that deserve mention are the following. One is the disaggregation of strikes by industry, major issue, and contract status. It was shown conclusively in the 1980s that the behavioral determinants of strikes differ significantly by type of strike. Except possibly for the case of long-run historical studies or cross-country comparisons, aggregate strike data is now outmoded as a subject of empirical analysis. A second advance concerns the greater theoretical grounding of empirical studies. Prior to the 1980s, a number of empirical strike studies had a disturbing atheoretical, "curve-fitting" flavor. My impression is that over the last decade scholars have taken much greater pains to rigorously deduce hypotheses from some type of theoretical base and to then test these hypotheses with a more carefully specified empirical model. Finally, I think the empirical literature of the 1980s produced some results that represented true additions to knowledge. Examples include the impact on strikes of inflation and

COLA clauses, state bargaining laws and alternative methods of dispute resolution, the availability and generosity of AFDC and UI payments to strikers, economic conditions in the firm's product and labor market, the inverse relationship between cyclical fluctuations in strike frequency and duration, and the impact of strikes on industry-level output and prices.

Now for the bad news. Strike research, like much of academic research in general, suffers from a number of shortcomings. First is a disciplinary parochialism. Economists seem to studiously ignore the work of sociologists and social psychologists, while the latter two often caricature or misrepresent the work of economists. I recognize that the production of knowledge, like the production of other goods, benefits from a division of labor, but I think a good case can be made that the degree of disciplinary specialization has been carried to excess. Economists, for example, need to give greater attention to the forces inhibiting or facilitating collective action and the psychological saliency imparted to certain bargaining outcomes by considerations of principle and justice, while sociologists and psychologists would do well to accept that at least a portion of the decision to strike is made on the basis of instrumental calculations of benefits and costs, as presumed in economic models.

A second shortcoming of the strike literature is its academic insularity and corresponding remoteness from the events, institutions, and practices of the real world of labor-management relations. With the exception of several case studies, I found no indication in all of the strike literature of the 1980s that the author's theoretical or empirical work was in any way informed by personal observation or participation in a strike, interviews with company or union officials, case studies or strikes, or descriptions of strikes contained in the popular press. Again, I recognize that a person can make a significant contribution to science without having actually experienced the event he/she is writing about. It also seems apparent, however, that much of the strike literature is sadly divorced from reality because the researcher has not the slightest experience or practical familiarity with the subject. Academic researchers, for example, develop highly complex theoretical models of questionable relevance (e.g., the asymmetric information model), largely because they are motivated by the desire to extend theory for its own sake rather than to solve or explain a real world event or practice. Empirical studies are likewise distinguished by their concentration on academic issues of research methodology and statistical techniques, in the process reducing the explanation of strikes to an arcane exercise in data analysis.

A third criticism of the strike literature of the 1980s is that it omits consideration of a number of the most important or controversial developments of the decade, such as listed in the beginning section in this chapter. For example, it was noted that the level of strike activity in the 1980s plummeted to the lowest level of the post-World War II period and, furthermore, remained at this level even as the economic environment changed in ways that historically has led to increased strike rates (lower unemployment, higher inflation). To the best of my knowledge, however, no academic study has been published that either examines or attempts to explain this anomaly. A second example concerns the issue of striker replacement. A highly charged issue of the 1980s was the use of striker replacements by companies, a practice featured in many of the strikes listed at the beginning of this chapter. Recently proposed legislation has been introduced in Congress to ban this practice (Gramm 1992). Again, this subject is almost entirely missing from the industrial relations literature (but see papers by Gramm 1990; LeRoy 1991). Finally, a third example concerns the strategic use of the strike by companies to oust their unions, another feature of many of the strikes listed earlier. Although this practice obviously has important implications for bargaining models and public policy, academic research has so far ignored it. In part this lacuna reflects the inevitable lag between events and published research, but it also reflects in equal part the narrow, out-of-touch state of academic research.

Contrary to Wheeler's (1984) recent critique of strike research (macro-level studies in particular), I continue to believe that the academic research of the 1980s has made a significant contribution to the advancement of knowledge on this subject—advancements such as those outlined above. I am sympathetic to the basic thrust of Wheeler's complaint, however, and agree that much more could be learned about strikes than has been to date. His proposed solution for the reinvigoration of strike research is to turn away from macro-level strike studies and focus on strikes at the micro-level. I personally do not feel that gets to the heart of the problem. The heart of the problem, I believe, is that the criteria for promotion and tenure, the financial reward system, and the culture in academe all encourage a sterile scholasticism that places more value on theoretical and statistical sophistication than relevance and applicability to real world events. Thus, whether the analysis and data are macro- or micro-level makes little difference to the style and orientation of the product that is produced—it still will give primary emphasis to "science building" and will make only a modest contribution to "problem solving."

What strike research most desperately needs is a marriage of the case study "go and see" approach of the early institutionalists with the deductive/econometric approach of modern day scholars. Will academic researchers leave the ivory tower to acquaint themselves with the real world complexity and dynamics of strikes through case study research? I personally doubt it. Rather, I believe that most scholars (particularly younger ones writing a dissertation or facing the tenure decision) will realize that the payoff to this research strategy is low and will instead pursue the path of disciplinary specialization and technical sophistication.

The implication for industrial relations as a field is thus a decidedly mixed one. That a growing number of scholars are interested in strikes and other forms of collective action is surely a positive sign. Counterbalanced on the other side, however, is the disciplinary parochialism of much of this research and its lack of relevance to pragmatic issues of practice and policy. Strike research thus epitomizes both the promise and failure of industrial relations as a field of study.

Endnotes

[1] The strike literature of the 1970s is reviewed in Feuille and Wheeler (1981). More recent cross-disciplinary reviews include Wheeler (1985), Gallagher and Gramm (1991), and Goddard (1992). A review of the economic strike literature is provided in Hirsch and Addison (1986), Kennan (1986), and Kennan and Wilson (1990).

[2] Due to budget cutbacks, the Bureau of Labor Statistics (BLS) in 1981 stopped collecting data on strikes of all sizes and restricted its attention to only major (1,000+) work stoppages. Published summaries of strikes disaggregated by industry, major issue, and other such characteristics were also discontinued. The industry data cited later in this section are from unpublished tables provided by BLS.

[3] One side may still emerge from a strike as a net monetary gainer. Evidence on this matter is sparse, but three studies (Eaton 1972; Gennard 1982; Card and Olson 1992) find that a strike (particularly a short one) is often a good investment for workers, while Carter et al. (1987) find that a strike may also lead to increased profit (by causing a large increase in the product price).

[4] Numerous writers (e.g., Ashenfelter and Johnson 1969; McConnell 1990) suggest that strikes occur in the Hicks model because of irrationality. A careful reading of Hicks suggests, however, that the cause is an incorrect decision due to imperfect information—a fundamentally different factor. Thus, a union and firm may decide to strike based on faulty estimates of the benefits and costs, a decision that *ex post* may appear misguided but one that is still based on self-interested, maximizing behavior.

[5] The asymmetric information model is one of a number of game theoretic "strategic" bargaining models recently developed by economists. See Kennan and Wilson (1989, 1990).

[6] It has become near universal in the strike literature to attribute to A-J the insight that strikes may occur due to a divergence of estimates between the union leadership and rank and file (e.g., Gartner 1985), when in fact Hicks explicitly noted this point twice in his chapter on industrial disputes.

[7] Although A-J assume the union leadership's wage demands are more moderate than the rank and file's, evidence suggests the reverse is often the case. For example, the national emergency dispute provisions of the Taft-Hartley Act require a vote of the membership on the company's last contract offer before a strike may commence after the expiration of the 80-day cooling-off period, a stipulation that presumably reflects the belief that union leaders are more militant than the rank and file. Likewise, in the 1989 UPS/Teamsters negotiations, the union leadership recommended rejection of the proposed contract but the membership voted to accept it. Finally, Gunderson, Kervin, and Reid (1986) find strikes are lower when a mandatory strike vote by the union membership is required.

[8] A distinction made in the union joining literature (e.g., Shore and Newton 1992) is between "instrumental" and "committed" behavior, a distinction that has not been applied to the decision to strike but which seems quite relevant. Instrumental behavior originates from short-run, self-interested motives that are based on a calculative weighing of benefits and costs, while committed behavior originates from deeper-felt, relatively fixed values, principles, and ideologies. Economic models generally presume behavior is instrumental, while behaviorally oriented models provide a greater role for committed behavior, such as that motivated by feelings of militancy.

[9] Kennan (1986, p. 1100) dismisses the meaningfulness of these predictions because they are based on an "irrational model" (i.e., it is irrational for each side to consistently demand more than they expect the other side to concede). While Kennan has a legitimate point, his objection also illustrates the narrow conception of human behavior used by economists and their willingness to label as "irrational" what may well have a sound social-psychological basis. Evidence in support of the Cross model is provided in Farber and Bazerman's (1989) study. They cite two explanations for the failure of the bargainers to reach a voluntary settlement: a reluctance to concede where the optimal offers for the arbitrator are far apart in fear that concessions could come back to haunt them, and cognitive limitations that prevent each bargainer from accurately interpreting the opponent's behavior.

[10] With regard to the effect of trade unions on strikes, Adams and Sumner (1905) observe: "The trade union makes for the regulation, not the suppression of strikes; for their encouragement in season, for their discouragement out of season; but on the whole its influence is conservative . . . as our trade unions get stronger and older, it is very probable that the strike will be even more vigorously restricted, because it is the new and poorly organized unions which foment strikes" (pp. 182-83). Also see Lester 1958.

[11] Brett and Goldberg (1979) show that wildcat strikes in the coal mining industry had something of the same motivation, although in this case the strikes were intended to pressure top management of the companies to intervene in the settlement of mine-level grievances.

[12] These conclusions are synthesized from the following studies: Shalev (1980); Mitchell (1981); Edwards (1981); Kaufman (1981); Swidinsky and Vanderkamp (1982); Mauro (1982); Skeels (1982); Kaufman (1982); Moore and Pearce (1982); Hendricks and Kahn (1985); Gunderson, Kervin, and Reid (1986); Cousineau and Lacroix (1986); Gramm (1986); Tracy (1986, 1987); Schnell and Gramm (1987); Gramm, Hendricks, and Kahn (1988); McConnell (1989, 1990); Card (1990); and Skeels and McGrath (1991).

[13] These conclusions are synthesized from the following studies: Reder and Neumann (1980); Swidinsky and Vanderkamp (1982); Leigh (1983, 1984); Kaufman (1983); Gunderson, Kervin, and Reid (1986); Tracy (1987); Card (1988); Abowd and Tracy (1989); McConnell (1990).

[14] Calculated by dividing workers involved in major strikes in manufacturing for 1987-1989 by the number of workers covered under new major contract settlements for the same period (as given in *Current Wage Developments*). This figure probably overstates the true propensity to strike since some strikes in the numerator occurred during the term of an existing contract.

[15] One indication is the decline of national emergency strikes (Rehmus 1990). None occurred in the 1980s.

References

Abowd, John M., and Joseph S. Tracy. "Market Structure, Strike Activity, and Union Wage Settlements." *Industrial Relations* 28, 2 (1989), pp. 227-50.

Ackerman, John A. "The Impact of the Coal Strike of 1977-78." *Industrial and Labor Relations Review* 32, 2 (1979), pp. 175-88.

Adams, Thomas S., and Helen L. Sumner. *Labor Problems*. New York: MacMillan, 1905.

Ashenfelter, Orley, and George E. Johnson. "Bargaining Theory, Trade Unions, and Industrial Strike Activity." *American Economic Review* 59, 1 (1969), pp. 35-49.

Batstone, Eric, Ian Boraston, and Stephen Frenkel. *The Social Organization of Strikes*. Oxford: Basil Blackwell, 1978.

Becker, Brian E., and Craig A. Olson. "The Impact of Strikes on Shareholder Equity." *Industrial and Labor Relations Review* 39, 3 (1986), pp. 425-38.

Beggs, John J., and Bruce J. Chipman. "Australian Strike Activity in an International Context." *Journal of Industrial Relations* 29, 2 (1987), pp. 137-50.

Booth, Alison, and Robert Cressy. "Strikers with Asymmetric Information: Theory and Evidence." *Oxford Bulletin of Economics and Statistics* 52 (August 1990), pp. 269-92.

Brett, Jeane, and Stephen B. Goldberg. "Wildcat Strikes in Bituminous Coal Mining." *Industrial and Labor Relations Review* 32, 4 (1979), pp. 465-83.

Byrne, Dennis M., and Randall H. King. "Wildcat Strikes in U.S. Manufacturing 1960-1977." *Journal of Labor Research* 7 (Fall 1986), pp. 387-402.

Card, David. "Longitudinal Analysis of Strike Activity." *Journal of Labor Economics* 6, 2 (1988), pp. 147-76.

________. "Strikes and Wages: A Test of an Asymmetric Information Model." *Quarterly Journal of Economics* 105 (August 1990), pp. 625-59.

Card, David, and Craig Olson. "Bargaining Power, Strike Durations, and Wage Outcomes: An Analysis of Strikes in the 1880s." Working Paper No. 294. Princeton: Industrial Relations Section, Princeton University, 1992.

Carter, Colin, Darrell Hueth, John Mamer, and Andrew Schmitz. "Agricultural Labor Strikes and 1987 Farmer's Income." *Economic Inquiry* 25 (1987), pp. 121-33.

Chermesh, Ran. "Strike Proneness and Characteristics of Industrial Relations Systems at the Organization Level: A Discriminant Analysis." *Journal of Management Studies* 19, 4 (1982), pp. 413-35.

Cohen, Isaac. "Political Climate and Two Airline Strikes: Century Air in 1932 and Continental Airlines in 1983-1985." *Industrial and Labor Relations Review* 43, 2 (1990), pp. 308-23.

Cohn, Samuel, and Adrienne Eaton. "Historical Limits on Neoclassical Strike Theories: Evidence from 1989 French Coal Mining, 1890-1935." *Industrial and Labor Relations Review* 42, 4 (1989), pp. 649-62.
Cronin, James. "Theories of Strikes: Why Can't They Explain the British Experience?" *Journal of Social History* 12, 2 (1978), pp. 194-220.
Cross, Ira B. "Strike Statistics." *Journal of the American Statistical Association* 11, 82 (1908), pp. 168-94.
Cross, John. *The Economics of Bargaining*. New York: Basic Books, 1969.
Cousineau, Jean Michel, and Robert Lacroix. "Imperfect Information and Strikes: An Analysis of Canadian Experience, 1967-1982." *Industrial and Labor Relations Review* 39, 3 (1983), pp. 377-87.
Davidson, Wallace N. III, Dan L. Worell, and Sharon H. Garrison. "Effect of Strike Activity on Firm Value." *Academy of Management Journal* 31, 2 (1988), pp. 387-94.
Delaney, John T. "Strikes, Arbitration, and Teacher Salaries: A Behavioral Analysis." *Industrial and Labor Relations Review* 36, 3 (1983), 431-46.
DeFusco, Richard A., and Scott M. Fuess, Jr. "The Effects of Airline Strikes on Struck and Nonstruck Carriers. *Industrial and Labor Relations Review* 44, 2 (1991), pp. 324-33.
Dilts, David. "Strike Activity in the United States: An Analysis of Stocks and Flows." *Journal of Labor Research* 7, 2 (1986), pp. 187-200.
Eaton, B. Curtis. "The Worker and the Profitability of the Strike." *Industrial and Labor Relations Review* 26, 1 (1972), pp. 670-79.
Edwards, P.K. *Strikes in the United States, 1881-1974*. New York: St. Martin's Press, 1981.
________. *Conflict at Work: A Materialist Analysis of Workplace Relations*. Oxford: Basil Blackwell, 1986.
Edwards, P.K., and Hugh Scullion. *The Social Organization of Industrial Conflict*. Oxford: Basil Blackwell, 1982.
Farber, Henry. "Bargaining Theory, Wage Outcomes, and the Occurrence of Strikes: An Econometric Analysis." *American Economic Review* 68, 3 (1978), pp. 262-71.
Farber, Henry, and Max H. Bazerman. "Divergent Expectations as a Cause of Disagreement in Bargaining: Evidence from a Comparison of Arbitration Schemes." *Quarterly Journal of Economics* 104 (February 1989), pp. 99-120.
Fernandez, Raquel, and Jacob Glazer. "Striking for a Bargain Between Two Completely Informed Agents." *American Economic Review* 81, 1 (1991), pp. 240-52.
Feuille, Peter, and Hoyt N. Wheeler. "Will the Real Industrial Conflict Please Stand Up?" In *U.S. Industrial Relations 1950-1980: A Critical Assessment,* ed. Jack Stieber, Robert McKersie, and D. Quinn Mills. Madison: Industrial Relations Research Association 1981.
Fisher, Lloyd, and Grant McConnell. "Internal Conflict and Labor-union Solidarity." In *Industrial Conflict*, eds. Arthur Kornhauser, Robert Dubin, and Arthur Ross. New York: McGraw-Hill, 1954.
Flaherty, Sean. "Contract Status and the Economic Determinants of Strike Activity." *Industrial Relations* 22, 1 (1983), pp. 20-33.
________. "Strike Activity, Worker Militancy, and Productivity Change in Manufacturing." *Industrial and Labor Relations Review* 40, 4 (1987), pp. 585-600.
Franzosi, Roberto. "One Hundred Years of Strike Statistics: Methodological and Theoretical Issues in Quantitative Strike Research." *Industrial and Labor Relations Review* 42, 3 (1989), pp. 348-62.
Friedman, Henry, and Sander Meredeen. *The Dynamics of Industrial Conflict*. London: Croom-Helm, 1980.
Fuess, Scott M., Jr. "Strike Strategies and the Minimum Effective Union." *Journal of Labor Research* 11, 1 (1990), pp. 59-72.
Gallagher, Daniel, and Cynthia Gramm. "Integrating Behavioral and Economic Perspectives of Strike Activity: Promise or Illusion?" Unpublished paper. Harrisonburg: James Madison University, 1991.

Gartner, Manfred. "Strikes and the Real Wage Employment Nexus: A Hicksian Analysis of Industrial Disputes and Pay." *Journal of Labor Research* 6, 3 (1985), pp. 323-36.

Garren, John, and Joseph Krislov. "An Examination of the New American Strike Statistics in Analysing Aggregate Strike Incidence." *British Journal of Industrial Relations* 26, 1 (1988), pp. 75-84.

Gennard, John. "The Effect of Strike Activity on Households." *British Journal of Industrial Relations* 19, 3 (1981), pp. 327-44.

________. "The Financial Costs and Returns of Strikes." *British Journal of Industrial Relations* 20, 2 (1982), pp. 247-56.

Gersuny, Carl. *Work Hazards and Industrial Conflict*. Hanover: University Press of New England, 1981.

Gilson, C.H.J., I.S. Spencer, and S. Granville. "The Impact of a Strike on the Attitudes and Behavior of a Rural Community." *Relations Industrielles* 44, 4 (1989), pp. 785-803.

Goddard, John. "Strikes as Collective Voice: Towards an Integrative Theory of Strike Activity." *Proceedings*, Industrial Relations Research Association. Madison: IRRA, forthcoming 1992.

Golden, Miriam A. *A Rational Choice Analysis of Union Militancy with Applicaton to the Cases of British Coal and Fiat*. Ithaca: Western Societies Program Occasional Paper No. 26, Center for International Studies, Cornell University, 1990.

Goldfield, Michael. "The Economy, Strikes, Union Growth, and Public Policy During the 1930s." *Proceedings*, Annual Spring Meeting, Industrial Relations Research Association. Madison, WI: IRRA, forthcoming.

Gramm, Cynthia L. "The Determinants of Strike Incidence and Severity: A Micro Level Study." *Industrial and Labor Relations Review* 39, 3 (1986), pp. 361-76.

________. "New Measures of the Propensity to Strike During Contract Negotiations, 1971-1980." *Industrial and Labor Relations Review* 40, 3 (1987), pp. 406-17.

________. "Employers' Decisions to Operate During Strikes: Consequences and Policy Implications." Unpublished paper. Huntsville: University of Alabama at Huntsville, 1990.

________. "Labor's Legislative Initiatives to Restrict Permanently Replacing Strikers." Paper presented at the 1992 Meetings of the Industrial Relations Research Association. New Orleans, 1992.

Gramm, Cynthia, Wallace Hendricks, and Lawrence Kahn. "Inflation Uncertainty and Strikes." *Industrial Relations* 27, 1 (1988), pp. 114-29.

Gramm, Cynthia, and John F. Schnell. "Difficult Choices: Crossing the Picket Line During the 1987 National Football League Strike." Unpublished paper, 1991.

Grant, Don S., and Michael Wallace. "Why Do Strikes Turn Violent?" *American Journal of Sociology* 96, 5 (1991), pp. 1117-50.

Greer, Charles R., Stanley A. Martine, and Ted A. Reusser. "The Effect of Strikes on Shareholder Returns." *Journal of Labor Research* 1, 2 (1980), pp. 217-30.

Gunderson, Morley, and Angelo Melino. "Estimating Strike Effects in a General Model of Prices and Quantities." *Journal of Labor Economics* 5, 1 (1987), pp. 1-19.

________. "The Effects of Public Policy on Strike Duration." *Journal of Labor Economics* 8, 3 (1990), 295-316.

Gunderson, Morley, John Kervin, and Frank Reid. "Logit Estimates of Strike Incidence from Canadian Contract Data." *Journal of Labor Economics* 4, 2 (1986), pp. 257-76.

Hage, Dave, and Paul Klauda. *No Retreat, No Surrender: Labor's War at Hormel*. New York: William Morrow, 1989.

Harrison, Alan, and Mark Stewart. "Cyclical Fluctuations in Strike Durations." *American Economic Review* 79, 4 (1989), pp. 827-41.

Hart, Oliver, "Bargaining and Strikes." *Quarterly Journal of Economics* 104 (February 1989), pp. 25-43.

Hayes, Beth. "Unions and Strikes with Asymmetric Information." *Journal of Labor Economics* 2, 1 (1984), pp. 57-83.

Hendricks, Wallace, and Lawrence M. Kahn. *Wage Indexation in the United States: Cola or Uncola?* Cambridge: Ballinger, 1985.
Hibbs, Douglas A. "Industrial Conflict in Advanced Industrial Societies." *The American Political Science Review* 70, 4 (1976), pp. 1033-58.
Hicks, John R. *The Theory of Wages*. London: MacMillan, 1932.
Hirsch, Barry T., and John T. Addison. *The Economic Analysis of Unions: New Approaches and Evidence*. Boston: Allen and Unwin, 1986.
Hodson, Randy, Deborah Ziegler, and Barbara Bump. "Who Crosses the Picket Line? An Analysis of the CWA Strike of 1983." *Labor Studies Journal* (Fall 1987), pp. 19-37.
Horn, Robert N., William J. McGuire, and Joseph Tomkiewicz. "Work Stoppages by Teachers: An Empirical Analysis." *Journal of Labor Research* 3, 4 (1982), pp. 487-96.
Hutchens, Robert, David Lipsky, and Robert Stern. *Strikers and Subsidies: The Influence of Government Transfer Programs on Strike Activity*. Kalamazoo: W.E. Upjohn Institute, 1990.
Ichniowski, Casey. "Arbitration and Police Bargaining: Prescriptions for the Blue Flu." *Industrial Relations* 21, 2 (1982), pp. 149-66.
________. "Police Recognition Strikes: Illegal and Ill Fated." *Journal of Labor Research* 9, 2 (1988), pp. 183-97.
Jenkins, J. Craig. "Resource Mobilization Theory and the Study of Social Movements." *Annual Review of Sociology* 9 (1983), pp. 527-53.
Jones, Nicholas. *Strikes and the Media*. New York: Basil Blackwell, 1986.
Kaufman, Bruce E. 'The Propensity to Strike in American Manufacturing." In *Proceedings*, Thirtieth Annual Winter Meeting, Industrial Relations Research Association. Madison, WI: IRRA, 1977.
________. "Bargaining Theory, Inflation, and Cyclical Strike Activity in Manufacturing." *Industrial and Labor Relations Review* 34, 3 (1981), pp. 333-55.
________. "The Determinants of Strikes in the United States, 1900-1977." *Industrial and Labor Relations Review* 35, 4 (1982), pp. 473-90.
________. "The Determinants of Strikes Over Time and Across Industries." *Journal of Labor Research* 4, 2 (1983), pp. 159-76.
________. "Interindustry Trends in Strike Activity." *Industrial Relations* 22, 1 (1983), pp. 45-57.
Kelly, John E., and Nigel Nicholson. "The Causation of Strikes: A Review of Theoretical Approaches and the Potential Contribution of Social Psychology." *Human Relations* 33, 12 (1990), pp. 853-83.
Kendrick, John W. *Interindustry Differences in Productivity Growth*. Washington: American Enterprise Institute, 1982.
Kennan, John. "Pareto Optimality and the Economics of Strike Duration." *Journal of Labor Research* 1, 1 (1980), pp. 77-94.
________. "The Duration of Contract Strikes in U.S. Manufacturing." *Journal of Econometrics* 28 (1985), pp. 5-28.
________. "The Economics of Strikes." In *Handbook of Labor Economics*, Vol. 2, eds. Orley Ashenfelter and Richard Layard. New York: Elsevier Science Publishers, 1986.
Kennan, John, and Robert Wilson. "Strategic Bargaining Models and Interpretation of Strike Data." *Journal of Applied Econometrics* 4 (Supplement, 1989), pp. S87-S130.
________. "Can Strategic Bargaining Models Explain Collective Bargaining Data?" *American Economic Review* 80, 2 (1990), pp. 405-09.
Kerr, Clark, and Abraham Siegel. "The Interindustry Propensity to Strike—An International Comparison." In *Industrial Conflict*, eds. Arthur Kornhauser, Robert Dubin, and Arthur Ross. New York: McGraw-Hill, 1954.
Klanderman, P.G. "Mobilization and Participation in Trade Union Action: An Expectancy-Value Approach." *Journal of Occupational Psychology* 57 (1984), pp. 107-20.
________. "Psychology and Trade Union Participation: Joining, Acting, Quitting." *Journal of Occupational Psychology* 59 (1986), pp. 89-204.

Knight, K. G. "Labour Productivity and Strike Activity in British Manufacturing Industries: Some Quantitative Evidence." *British Journal of Industrial Relations* 27 (November 1989), pp. 365-74.
Korpi, Walter, and Michael Shalev. "Strikes, Power, and Politics in the Western Nations, 1900-76." In *Political Power and Social Theory*. Vol. 1. New York: JAI Press, 1980.
Lacroix, Robert. "A Microeconomic Analysis of the Effect of Strikes on Wages." *Relations Industrielles* 41, 1 (1986), p. 111-26.
Leigh, J. Paul. "Risk Preference and the Interindustry Propensity to Strike." *Industrial and Labor Relations Review* 36, 2 (1983), pp. 271-85.
________. "A Bargaining Model and Empirical Analysis of Strike Activity Across Industries." *Journal of Labor Research* 5, 2 (1984), pp. 127-38.
LeRoy, Michael. "Strike Crossovers and Striker Replacements: An Empirical Test of the NLRB's No Presumption Policy." *Arizona Law Review* 33 (1991), pp. 1-45.
Lester, Richard. *As Unions Mature*. Princeton: Princeton University Press, 1958.
Lichtenstein, Nelson. "UAW Bargaining Strategy and Shop Floor Conflict: 1946-1970." *Industrial Relations* 24, 3 (1985), pp. 360-81.
MacBride, Arlene, William Lancee, and Stanley Freeman. "The Psychological Impact of a Labour Dispute." *Journal of Occupational Psychology* 54 (1985), pp. 125-33.
Maki, Dennis R. "A Note on the Output Effects of Canadian Postal Strikes." *Canadian Journal of Economics* 16 (February 1983), pp. 149-54.
________. "The Effect of the Cost of Strikes on the Volume of Strike Activity." *Industrial and Labor Relations Review* 39, 4 (1986), pp. 552-63.
Marmo, Michael. *More Profile than Courage: The New York City Transit Strike of 1966*. Albany: State University of New York Press, 1990.
Martin, James E. "Predictors of Individual Propensity to Strike." *Industrial and Labor Relations Review* 39, 2 (1986), pp. 214-27.
Mauro, Martin J. "Strikes as a Result of Imperfect Information." *Industrial and Labor Relations Review* 35, 4 (1982), pp. 522-38.
McCarthy, John D., and Mayer N. Zald. "Resource Mobilization and Social Movements: A Partial Theory." In *Social Movements in an Organizational Society*, eds. John D. McCarthy and Martin N. Zald. New Brunswick, NJ: Transaction Books, 1987.
McConnell, Sheena. "Strikes, Wages, and Private Information." *American Economic Review* 79, 4 (1989), pp. 801-15.
________. "Cyclical Fluctuations in Strike Activity." *Industrial and Labor Relations Review* 44, 1 (1990), p. 130-43.
McHugh, Richard. "Productivity Effects of Struck and Nonstruck Industries." *Industrial and Labor Relations Review* 44, 4 (1991), pp. 722-32.
Mellor, Steven. "The Relationship Between Membership Decline and Union Commitment: A Field Study of Local Unions in Crisis." *Journal of Applied Psychology* 75, 1 (1990), pp. 258-67.
Mitchell, Daniel J. B. "A Note on Strike Propensities and Wage Developments." *Industrial Relations* 20, 1 (1981), pp. 123-27.
Montgomery, Edward, and Mary Ellen Benedict. "The Impact of Bargainer Experience on Teacher Strikes." *Industrial and Labor Relations Review* 42, 3 (1989), pp. 380-92.
Moore, Wilbert E. "Occupational Structure and Industrial Conflict." In *Industrial Conflict*, eds. Arthur Kornhauser, Robert Dubin, and Arthur Ross. New York: McGraw-Hill, 1954.
Moore, William J., and Douglas K. Pearce. "A Comparative Analysis of Strike Models During Periods of Rapid Inflation: 1967-1977." Journal of Labor Research 3, 1 (1982), pp. 39-53.
Naples, Michele I. "Industrial Conflict and Its Implications for Productivity Growth." *American Economic Review* 72 (May 1981), pp. 36-41.
________. "An Analysis of Defensive Strikes." *Industrial Relations* 26, 1 (1987), pp. 96-105.

Naylor, Robin. "Strikes, Free Riders, and Social Custom." *Quarterly Journal of Economics* 104 (November 1989), pp. 771-85.

Neuman, George R. "The Predictability of Strikes: Evidence from the Stock Market." *Industrial and Labor Relations Review* 33, 4 (1980), pp. 525-35.

Neumann, George R., and Melvin Reder. "Output and Strike Activity in U.S. Manufacturing: How Large are the Losses?" *Industrial and Labor Relations Review* 37, 2 (1984), pp. 197-211.

Ng, Ignace. "Predictors of Strike Voting Behavior." *Journal of Labor Research* 12, 2 (1991), pp. 123-34.

Ng, Ignace, and Dennis Maki. "Strike Activity of U.S. Institutions in Canada." *British Journal of Industrial Relations* 26, 1 (1988), pp. 63-73.

Norman, Ross, and Ashok Malla. "The Effect of a Mental Health Strike on General Hospital Psychiatric Services." *Psychological Medicine* 14, 4 (1984), pp. 913-24.

Northrup, Herbert. "The Rise and Demise of PATCO." *Industrial and Labor Relations Review* 37, 2 (1984), pp. 167-84.

Owusu-Gyapong, Anthony. "Alternative Estimating Techniques for Panel Data on Strike Activity." *Review of Economics and Statistics* 68, 3 (1986), pp. 526-31.

Olson, Craig. "The Role of Rescheduled School Days in Teacher Strikes." *Industrial and Labor Relations Review* 37, 4 (1984), pp. 515-28.

________. "Strikes, Strike Penalties, and Arbitration in Six States." *Industrial and Labor Relations Review* 39, 4 (1986), pp. 539-51.

________. "Dispute Resolution in the Public Sector." In *Public Sector Bargaining*, 2nd ed., eds. Benjamin Aaron et al. Washington: Bureau of National Affairs, 1988.

Oliver, Pamela, and Gerald Marwell. "The Paradox of Group Size in Collective Action: A Theory of the Critical Mass II." *American Sociological Review* 53, 1 (1988), pp. 1-8.

Ondrich, Jan, and John F. Schnell. "Strike Duration and the Degree of Disagreement." *Industrial Relations*, forthcoming 1992.

Paarsch, Harry J. "Work Stoppages and the Theory of the Offset Factor: Evidence from the British Columbian Lumber Industry." *Journal of Labor Economics* 8, 3 (1990), pp. 387-418.

Paldam, Martin, and Peder J. Pedersen. "The Macroeconomic Strike Model: A Study of Seventeen Countries, 1948-1975." *Industrial and Labor Relations Review* 35, 4 (1982), pp. 504-21.

Partridge, Dane M. "A Reexamination of the Effectiveness of No-Strike Laws for Public School Teachers." *Journal of Collective Negotiations in the Public Sector* 17, 4 (1988), pp. 257-66.

Perone, Luca. "Positional Power, Strikes, and Wages." *American Sociological Review* 43, 3 (1984), pp. 412-26.

Peterson, Andrew A. "Deterring Strikes by Public Employees: New York's Two for One Salary Penalty and the 1979 Prison Guard Strike." *Industrial and Labor Relations Review* 34, 4 (1981), pp. 545-62.

Pfuhl, Edwin N. "Police Strikes and Conventional Crime: A Look at the Data." *Criminology* 21, 4 (1983), pp. 489-503.

Reder, Melvin W., and George R. Neumann. "Conflict and Contract: The Case of Strikes." *Journal of Political Economy* 88 (October 1980), pp. 867-86.

Rees, Albert. "Industrial Conflict and Business Fluctuations." *Journal of Political Economy* 60, 5 (1952), pp. 371-82.

Rehmus, Charles M. "Emergency Strikes Revisited." *Industrial and Labor Relations Review* 43, 2 (1990), pp. 175-90.

Roomkin, Myron. "Union Structure, Internal Control, and Strike Activity." *Industrial and Labor Relations Review* 29, 2 (1976), pp. 198-217.

Rose, David C. "Are Strikes Less Effective in Conglomerate Firms?" *Industrial and Labor Relations Review* 45, 1 (1991), pp. 131-44.

Ross, Arthur M. *Trade Union Wage Policy*. Berkeley: University of California Press, 1948.

________. "The Prospects for Industrial Conflict." *Industrial Relations* 1 (October 1961), pp. 241-51.

Ross, Arthur M., and Paul T. Hartman. *Changing Patterns of Industrial Conflict.* New York: John Wiley and Sons, 1960.
Rubin, Beth. "Inequality in the Working Class: The Unanticipated Consequences of Union Organization and Strikes." *Industrial and Labor Relations Review* 4, 4 (1988), pp. 533-66.
Schnell, John F., and Cynthia Gramm. "Learning by Striking: Estimates of the Teetotaler Effect." *Journal of Labor Economics* 5, 2 (1987), pp. 221-41.
Schutt, Russell K. "Models of Militancy: Support for Strikes and Work Actions Among Public Employees." *Industrial and Labor Relations Review* 35, 3 (1982), pp. 406-22.
Screpanti, Ernesto. "Long Cycles in Strike Activity: An Empirical Investigation." *British Journal of Industrial Relations* 25, 1 (1987), pp. 99-124.
Shalev, Michael. "Trade Unionism and Economic Analysis: The Case of Industrial Conflict." *Journal of Labor Research* 1, 1 (1980), pp. 133-74.
________. Strikes and the Crisis: Industrial Conflict and Unemployment in the Western Nations." *Economic and Industrial Democracy* 4 (1983), pp. 417-60.
Shore, Lynn, and Lucy Newton. "A Model of Union Membership: Instrumentality, Commitment, and Opposition." *Academy of Management Review* 17, 2 (1992), pp. 275-98.
Shorter, Edward, and Charles Tilly. *Strikes in France, 1830-1968.* New York: Cambridge University Press, 1974.
Siebert, W. Stanley, and John T. Addison. "Are Strikes Accidental?" *Economic Journal* 91 (June 1981), pp. 389-404.
Siebert, W. Stanley, John T. Addison, and Philip Bertrand. "The Union Political Model: A New Twist." *Southern Economic Journal* 51 (July 1985), pp. 23-33.
Skeels, Jack. "The Economic and Organizational Basis of Early United States Strikes." *Industrial and Labor Relations Review* 35, 4 (1982), pp. 491-503.
Skeels, Jack, and Paul McGrath. "A Test of Uncertainty, Expectations, and Error Response in Two Strike Models." *Journal of Labor Research* 12, 3 (1991), pp. 205-22.
Skeels, Jack, Paul McGrath, and Ganagadha Arshanapalli. "The Importance of Strike Size in Strike Research." *Industrial and Labor Relations Review* 41, 4 (1988), pp. 582-91.
Smith, Leigh M. "Is it Fitting? Comments on the LISREL Analysis by Stoner and Arora of Variables Affecting the Psychosocial Health of Strikers." *Journal of Occupational Psychology* 62 (1989), pp. 257-62.
Snyder, David. "Instrumental Setting and Industrial Conflict: Comparative Analyses of France, Italy, and the United States." *American Sociological Review* 40, 3 (1975), pp. 259-78.
________. "Early North American Strikes: A Reinterpretation." *Industrial and Labor Relations Review* 30, 3 (1977), pp. 325-41.
Sopher, Barry. "Bargaining and the Joint Cost Theory of Strikes: An Experimental Study." *Journal of Labor Economics* 8, 1, pt. 1 (1990), pp. 48-74.
Stagner, Ross, and Hjalmar Rosen. *The Psychology of Union-Management Relations.* Belmont: Wadsworth, 1965.
Stagner, Ross, and Boaz Elfal. "Internal Union Dynamics During a Strike: A Quasi-Experimental Study." *Journal of Applied Psychology* 67, 1 (1982), pp. 37-44.
Stern, Robert N. "Methodological Issues in Quantitative Strike Analysis." *Industrial Relations* 17, 1 (1978), pp. 32-42.
Stoner, Charles R., and Raj Arora. "An Investigation of the Relationship Between Selected Variables and the Psychological Health of Strike Participants." *Journal of Occupational Psychology* 60 (1987), pp. 61-71.
Swidinsky, Robert, and John Vanderkamp. "A Microeconometric Analysis of Strike Activity in Canada." *Journal of Labor Research* 3, 4 (1982), pp. 455-72.
Swint, Michael J., and William B. Nelson. "Self-Motivated Bargaining and Rational Strikes: A Multiparty Model and Its Implications for Industrial Strike Activity." *Southern Economic Journal* 47, 2 (1980), pp. 317-31.
Taft, Philip. "Ideologies and Industrial Conflict." In *Industrial Conflict*, eds. Arthur Kornhauser, Robert Dubin, and Arthur Ross. New York: McGraw-Hill, 1954, pp. 257-65.

Tilly, Charles, and Leopold Haimson. *Strikes, Wars, and Revolutions in an International Perspective*. New York: Cambridge University Press, 1989.

Tomkiewicz, Joseph, and O.C. Brenner. "Why Don't Teachers Strike?" *Journal of Collective Negotiations in the Public Sector* 14, 2 (1985), pp. 183-90.

Tracy, Joseph S. "An Investigation into the Determinants of U.S. Strike Activity." *American Economic Review* 76, 3 (1986), pp. 423-36.

________. "An Empirical Test of an Asymmetric Information Model of Strikes." *Journal of Labor Economics* 5, 2 (1987), pp. 149-73.

Vispo, Raul, and Denise Shore. "Strike and Stress in a Maximum Security Hospital." *Psychiatric Quarterly* 57, 2 (1985), pp. 111-20.

Vroman, Susan B. "A Longitudinal Analysis of Strike Activity in U.S. Manufacturing: 1957-1984." *American Economic Review* 79, 4 (1989), pp. 816-26.

Waddington, David. "The Ansells Brewery Dispute: A Social-Cognitive Approach to the Study of Strikes." *Journal of Occupational Psychology* 59 (September 1986), pp. 231-46.

Wallace, Michael. "Aggressive Economism, Defensive Control: Contours of American Militancy, 1947-81." *Economic and Industrial Democracy* 10 (1989), pp. 7-34.

Walsh, Kenneth. *Strikes in Europe and the United States: Measurement and Incidence*. New York: St. Martin's, 1983.

Walton, Richard E., and Robert B. McKersie. *A Behavioral Theory of Labor Negotiations*. New York: McGraw-Hill, 1965.

Wheeler, Hoyt N. "Comment: Determinants of Strikes." *Industrial and Labor Relations Review* 37, 2 (1984), pp. 263-69.

________. *Industrial Conflict: An Integrative Theory*. Columbia: University of South Carolina Press, 1985.

Wilsher, Peter, Donald Macintyre, and Michael Jones. *Strike: Thatcher, Scargill, and the Miners*. London: Andre Deutsch, 1985.

Zimmer, Lynn, and James B. Jacobs. "Challenging the Taylor Law: Prison Guards on Strike." *Industrial and Labor Relations Review* 34, 4 (1981), pp. 531-44.

CHAPTER 4

The Union and Nonunion Grievance System

RICHARD B. PETERSON
University of Washington

Union Grievance Research

Background

What is meant by the term "grievance?" In the work situation, a grievance is any employee or managerial complaint about the employment relationship. A grievance recognized by management may be raised directly by the employee with his or her immediate supervisor, higher management, the personnel department, an ombudsman, or a civil service commission or panel. The common charge is that the employer action is in violation of the organization's policies and procedures, civil rules, personnel ordinances, or applicable state or federal law. In a union setting, it is alleged that the employer has violated one or more provisions of the collective bargaining agreement between the union and management.

Lewin and Peterson (1988) identified 22 empirical studies on the union grievance process that were published in North America between the end of World War II and 1979. Only a few of the studies offered conceptual models of the grievance procedure (Peach and Livernash 1974; Thomson and Murray 1976). Most studies did not generate testable hypotheses as part of their research design. As for developing a theory in the field, Thomson's 1974 observation that "so far no theory of the grievance process has evolved" still held in 1979. What contributions did researchers in the 1980s provide toward our understanding of the grievance process, as well as the association between the grievance process and such variables as grievance filing rates, propensity to file, personal outcomes for the grievant, and organizational outcomes?

Several computer searches were done covering the literature on the union grievance procedure, grievance mediation, and the non-union grievance process published between 1980 and 1989. We narrowed the list to those studies that were either conceptual or reported results of empirical research in these three topic areas. Thus, we will not comment on the descriptive literature that spells out the functions and operations of these three grievance processes.

We shall not include those studies of the grievance process published since 1989 in order to allow their inclusion in a review of the 1990s' research on the grievance system in the workplace. However, there have been some six or seven such studies published between 1990 and early 1992. This review chapter also will not include work by Greenberg and his associates in the field of psychology using laboratory simulations of due process systems or the legal literature on procedural and substantive due process. While important in their own right, they are tangential to our study of the work setting grievance process.

Review and Critique of Union Grievance Process Literature

Three reviews and critiques of the union grievance system research were published during the 1980s. Peterson and Lewin (1982) reviewed the literature from 1948 to 1981. They categorized the empirical research into the following categories: demographic differences between grievants and nongrievants, effects of management and union leadership patterns on grievance incidence, organizational characteristics and grievance activity, personality traits and grievance procedure, and comparison and contrast of grievance activity within and between sectors and industries. The authors proposed a research agenda that would include: (1) identification of a conceptual framework and set of hypotheses, (2) measurement of grievance procedure effectiveness, and (3) provision of longitudinal analyses within and across bargaining relationships.

Lewin and Peterson (1988, Chapter 2) reviewed and assessed the state of research through 1987 on the union grievance procedure that updated their earlier (1982) article. They drew the following conclusions from their review and assessment. First, the volume of research on grievance procedures was relatively small, but there was a resurgence of interest in the topic in the preceding decade. Second, the trend over the postwar years was to use more than one dependent variable, compared to the early years. Third, the research was shifting from studying demographic characteristics of grievants toward grievance procedure dynamics and outcomes. Finally, more recent research used larger grievant and employer samples, as compared to the case study and single plant sites of earlier years.

However, as of 1988, no theory of the grievance procedure had emerged. Moreover, the field lacked any systematic model that had been tested across a number of studies that would allow generalization. For a detailed summary of the union grievance studies published from the late 1940s through 1987, see Table 2.1 (pp. 49-58) in Lewin and Peterson (1988).

Gordon and Miller (1984) wrote an excellent critique of the empirical research on the union grievance process from a psychometric perspective. The authors identified the following problem areas with that research: not using common formulas for measuring grievance rate; no common standards for what constitutes excessive, average, and scant grievance activity; no common method of classifying grievances across studies; failure of researchers to recognize the complexity of actors affecting grievance settlement; questionable reliability of grievance data over time; problems of internal and external validity; lack of common standards for identifying environmental variables; and the lack of theory in the field. These reviews and critiques were helpful in encouraging better quality research as the years progressed during the 1980s.

Model Presentation and/or Testing

As previously mentioned, the vast majority of early postwar studies in this field did not provide any conceptual model to guide the research or identify testable hypotheses. Grievance research in the 1980s moved ahead in addressing these criticisms of the earlier studies. Klass (1989b) presented an integrative framework or model for examining both the determinants of grievance filing and the impact of the grievance system on employee behavior. Figure 1 identifies the variables in his model.

Klass identifies 17 different variables relating to both determinants of grievance activity and the grievance system's impact on employee behavior. The variables begin with workplace characteristics and employee characteristics on the left side of his integrative

FIGURE 1

Determinants of Grievance Activity and the Grievance System's Impact on Employer Behavior: An Integrative Perspective

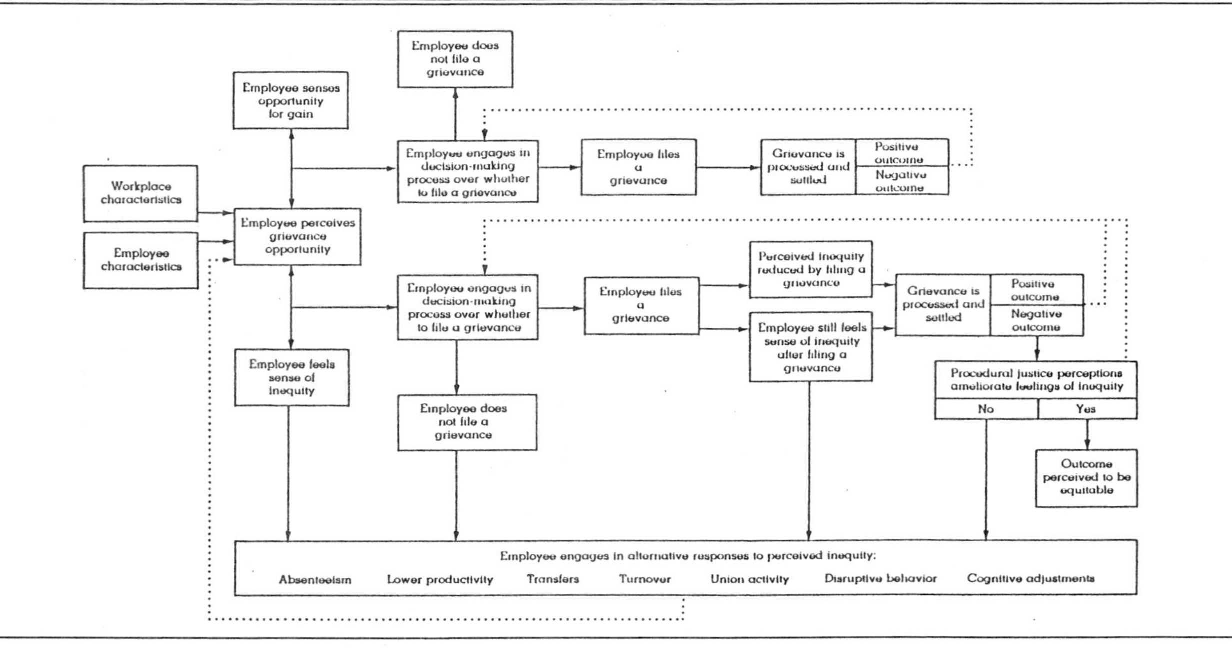

Source: Klass (1989b, p. 449).

model to both procedural and substantive outcomes on the right side. He did not test the framework, but offered seven propositions as a way of encouraging other researchers to test the model.

Peterson and Lewin (1982) and Lewin (1981) have provided the most comprehensive models of the grievance process to date. Their Partial Model of the Grievance Procedure identified seven variables that would help to explain the characteristics of the grievance procedure. The authors then developed a Systems Model of the Grievance Procedure (see Figure 2) that was tested in their large scale study of the grievance procedure in four sectors/industries in the United States (Lewin and Peterson 1988). Their Systems Model of the Grievance Procedure includes seven input variables (external, management, union and employee characteristics, management and union grievance policies, and characteristics of the labor-management relationship), two transformational variables (grievance procedure characteristics and grievance resolution), and one output measure (post-grievance resolution behavior). Each variable is measured by use of two or more subvariables. The focus of their model is on how effectively the grievance process is functioning, not whether or not the grievant wins or loses his or her case.

Four other studies (Allen and Keaveny 1985; Knight 1985; Labig and Helburn 1986; Meyer and Cooke 1988) presented and tested more limited models of the union grievance system than the models discussed earlier. More will be said about these studies when we discuss the empirical research on the union grievance procedure in the following sections of this chapter.

Grievance Rates and Propensity to File

It would be helpful if our review of the empirical studies of the union grievance procedure could be categorized by research method or by the dependent variables used in the various studies. This is not possible, given the large number of variables used and the heavy focus on surveys and analysis of grievance and personnel records. Thus, the next four sections of this review provide the best categorization of this diffuse body of empirical studies of the union grievance system published in the 1980s. The studies summarized here include both U.S. and Canadian research sites.

Seven studies were published during the 1980s that focused on either factors relating to the grievance rate or propensity of the

FIGURE 2

A Systems Model of the Grievance Procedure

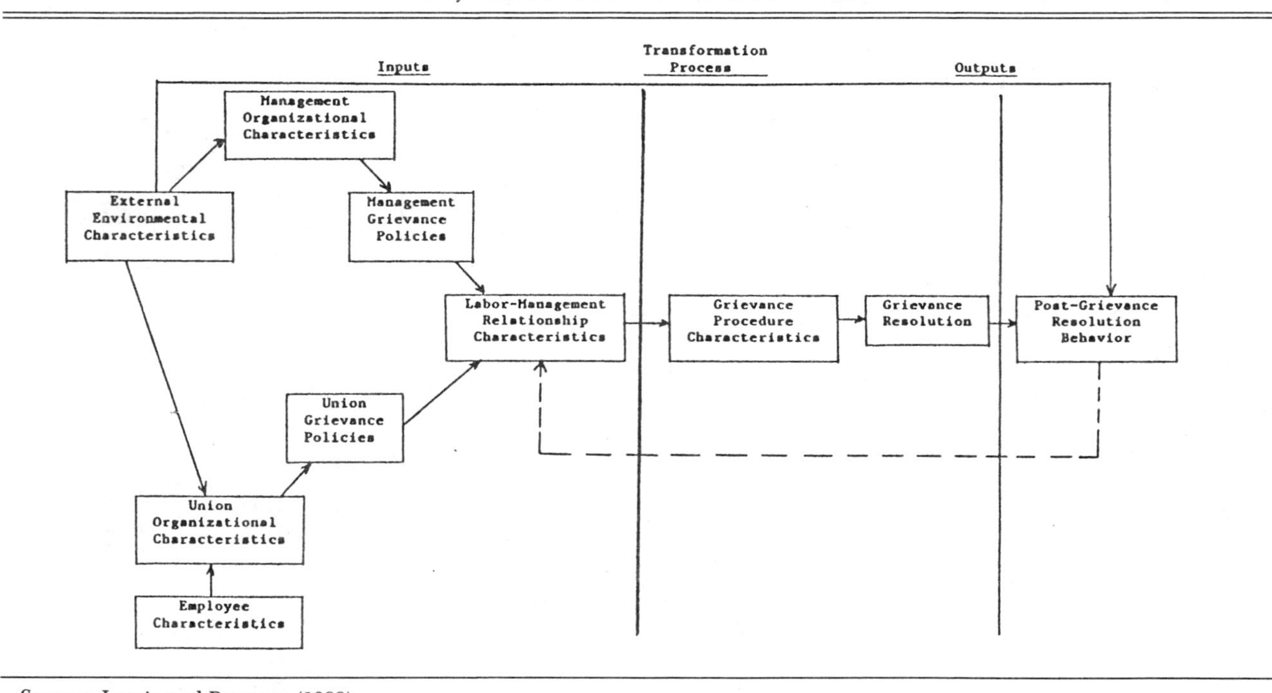

Source: Lewin and Peterson (1988).

employee to file a grievance. It should be noted that a number of early postwar studies had used the grievance rate as a key dependent variable. Unfortunately, the results of the earlier studies had been inconclusive in terms of demographic or organizational factors that related significantly to grievance rate (Labig and Helburn 1986). Labig and Helburn tested a model of policy influences on grievance rates based on data collected from 120 union and management officials using interviews with matched pairs of officials. They found only partial support for their model. The following variables were significantly related to the grievance rate: union encouragement of grievances, the existence of performance and disciplinary standards, management's attitudes toward union leaders, union rivalry, management maintaining initial grievance position, and management willingness to consult with union leaders.

Gandz and Whitehead (1982) tested the hypothesis that there will be higher grievance incidence under conflict, as opposed to cooperative labor-management relationships, at the bargaining group level using survey data from industrial relations officials and line managers and supervisors in 118 Canadian bargaining units. Most parts of their hypothesis were supported by the results of the four-year study.

Knight (1985) used systems analysis to help explain differences in the grievance rate between two synthetic fiber plants in the Southeast United States owned by the same firm. He used interviews, direct observation, and analysis of grievance records. The major finding was that a grievance was four times more likely to end in arbitration in the high grievance rate plant.

Nelson and Reiman (1983), in their study of grievance rates in a large auto components manufacturing plant, found support for earlier work by Sayles (1958) that the type of technology was strongly related to grievance rates. Grievance rates were significantly higher in batch technology operations than for the other two (single unit and mass assembly) technologies. When work technology was held constant, work group size was negatively related to grievance rate.

Muchinsky and Maassarani (1980), following up on the important study by Peach and Livernash (1974) in the steel industry, tested their data in the public sector. Like Peach and Livernash, they found that work environment variables impacted the level of grievances. It also appeared that the length of the bargaining relationship was important in explaining grievance rates.

The study by Allen and Keaveny (1985) used filing a grievance as the dependent variable when using data from the 1977 Quality of Employment Survey. Their independent measures included individual attitudes, employer and union characteristics, job dissatisfaction level, perceived instrumentality in filing a grievance, and some demographic factors. The researchers found age was the only demographic factor significantly related to grievance filing. Grievants also were less satisfied with their job than non-grievants. The grievants were also likely to be more active in the union, but less satisfied with it than the non-grievants.

A very interesting study was done by Gordon and Bowlby (1989) using a series of vignettes with union members and nonmembers in a large southern utility company. Two hypotheses were used in the separate tests of reactance and attribution theories. Both studies found that intent to pursue a grievance was significantly related to the threat inherent in management actions and the extent to which dispositional attributions appear to be valid explanations for such actions.

It is difficult to offer any overarching conclusions from the review of these studies other than to say that the focus on demographic and attitudinal characteristics of grievants has not proved to be very fruitful. Equally so, the use of grievance rates as the dependent variable hides other important factors that need to be considered.

Personal Outcomes of Grieving

Surprisingly, few of the earlier studies of the grievance process had looked at what happened to employees who had used the grievance process in terms of personal outcomes. Researchers during the 1980s gave much more attention to this topic. Some of the research focused on whether the grievant won or lost the case, while another stream of studies looked at subsequent outcomes that might be explained, at least in part, by the employee having used the grievance procedure.

There are eight studies that best fit under this category. Dalton and Todor (1981) studied the grievance procedure in a large West Coast plant. They found that 52 percent, 30.9 percent, and 17.1 percent of the grievances in the plant were settled at the first, second, and third steps of the grievance procedure. The most common issues included suspensions, seniority, transfer, and a miscellaneous category. Nothing was mentioned about the number of grievances won, lost, or ending in a compromise.

Studies testing the effect of gender on grievance administration outcomes (particularly addressing the arbitration process) were published in the 1980s (e.g., Bemmel's work). Dalton and Todor (1985) used two samples of grievances from a western public utility and a large western labor union to test two hypotheses relating to gender. The hypotheses assumed that favorable outcomes of a grievance for an employee would vary according to the gender of (1) the grievant, and (2) the adjudication dyad. They found no support for Hypothesis 1 that there would be systematic differences in workplace justice outcomes based on the grievant's gender. There was support for Hypothesis 2; namely, that grievants drawn from the union grievance files were significantly more likely to win than their counterparts at the public utility company. However, there were striking similarities between the two sample populations in the pattern of outcomes by dyad.

Another study by Gordon and Bowlby (1988) is discussed here, even though it covers issues beyond the personal outcome of the grievance. The researchers used questionnaires for samples of members belonging to seven different local unions in the public and private sectors. The three dependent variables included the person's view of the grievance system's ability to provide distributive justice, procedural justice, as well as the union member's overall assessment of their grievance system. Gordon and Bowlby found that the level of grievance settlement was not significantly associated with union members' and officials' attitudes toward the effectiveness of the grievance system. Grievances concerning discharge and work assignments improved member-union relations, while grievances over staffing issues had no impact. Finally, the grievant winning or partially winning the grievance was positively associated with all three dependent measures.

Meyer and Cooke (1988) tested six hypotheses related to management, workers, and unions on the dependent variable of grievance resolution. The level of clarity of the grievance was used as a moderating variable. They analyzed formal grievance records donated by Ford-UAW Local 400 to the Walter P. Reuther Memorial Library covering the years 1949-1959. Their empirical results provided modest support for their theoretical model: they found that clarity of rights and facts played an important limiting role in the resolution of grievances, but that even in cases of high clarity, political and economic factors can influence the resolution. The results supported more specific hypotheses about the impact of economic considerations, workplace characteristics, and union political factors.

What other factors might affect the grievance resolution? Ng and Dastmalchian (1989) carried out a study of 1,160 grievances resolved short of arbitration in one Canadian federal department. Their sample was drawn from grievances at 15 work sites over a two-year period. Their analysis showed that: grievances were most likely to be granted by management at the lower, rather than higher, steps of the grievance procedure; higher paid employees were more likely than lower paid employees to have their grievances at least partially granted; and grievance outcomes varied by issue. Grievants were more successful if the issue dealt with working conditions. On the other hand, grievances regarding job assignments led to less favorable outcomes for the grievant.

Another helpful study by Klass (1989a) was based on all grievances in the personnel files of a public sector organization in the United States for the years 1979-1985. Klass used four independent variables (past performance, tenure, discussion record, and grievance filed) and three control variables (number of grievances denied previously, grievance type, and grievance source). The dependent measure compared those grievances resulting in an employee win or partial win vs. management denying the grievance.

Klass found no evidence that previous work history affected the grievance outcome at the first step of the procedure, but that at the second and third steps those grievants with better work performance and longer tenure had more favorable outcomes. It was not clear to Klass that work history should have been a factor in grievance resolution in many of the cases.

Klass and De Nisi (1989) studied the linkage between grievance filing and subsequent performance appraisal ratings in one public sector organization over a seven-year period using panel data techniques. They tested four hypotheses. They broke down the grievances into two groups: grievances against organizational policy and grievances against supervisors. The researchers assumed that grievances against supervisors, as opposed to organizational policy, would adversely affect the grievant's subsequent performance ratings from that supervisor. They found that PA ratings of employees who filed grievances against their supervisors received significantly lower ratings after filing the grievance. The subsequent rating was even lower in cases where the employee won the grievance. Finally, there was no significant effect on the performance rating if the grievance was against organizational policy or if a different supervisor than the one grieved against completed the subsequent performance appraisal.

Lewin and Peterson (1987; 1988), in a grant funded by the National Science Foundation, studied personal outcomes of grieving by using samples of grievants and non-grievants from four organizations. Each organization was drawn from one of the four industries/sectors included in the larger study. The four industries/sectors included the steel industry (blue collar), retail department stores (white collar), public school teachers (government), and nurses in non-profit hospitals. Data was collected over a three-year period (year before grievance filed, year of grievance filing, and year after grievance filing). The personal outcomes included job performance ratings, promotion rates, attendance, and turnover. Interestingly, the grievants had better records than the non-grievant samples the year before filing. However, by the year after filing the grievance, the grievants had significantly lower performance ratings, promotion rates, poorer work attendance, and higher turnover than the non-grievants. The negative effects were even more noticeable for employees who pursued their grievances to higher steps of the procedure and those who won their grievances.

The negative effects even applied to the immediate supervisors of the grievant group when compared to those supervisors/managers who were not direct parties to grievance activity in the four organizations. If these findings can be generalized, it raises important questions about the negative aftereffects for grievants and their supervisors alike. Are the costs of grieving, even in a union context, too great to ensure the operation of a workplace justice system? Some of the studies reported in this section raise important questions that need to be addressed by future researchers. These questions will be discussed in our conclusions.

The Grievance Process and Organizational Outcomes

A real contribution of some of the 1980s' research in this field was the focus on organizational impacts associated with grievance activity. Does the grievance process have organizational (employer) costs and benefits too? If so, what are they? Four studies were uncovered that fall within this domain. Katz, Kochan, and Gobeille (1983) performed a study that analyzed the relationship among plant-level measures of industrial relations performance, economic performance, and quality of working life programs at 18 General Motors plants over a ten-year period. We will only comment on that part of the study dealing with grievance activity. The researchers found that the grievance rate was intercorrelated significantly and positively with the number of discipline cases, absenteeism, number of contract demands, and negotiation time. There was a negative relationship between grievance rate and cooperative work climate. Furthermore, the grievance rate was negatively related to both measures of product quality and direct labor efficiency. Finally, they found fewer grievances reported in the five best rated QWL plants than the five lowest rated QWL plants.

Katz, Kochan, and Weber (1985) provided an extension of their earlier study using seven additional GM plants, but limiting the analysis to the 1978-1980 period. They found that the grievance rates correlated positively and significantly with absentee and disciplinary action rates, while there was a negative association with salaried employees' attitudes, participation in the suggestion program, and QWL program involvement. Once again, grievance activity was negatively related to the two measures of plant economic performance.

A third study by Norsworthy and Zabala (1985) linked grievance rates with several measures of firm production performance using data from the U.S. automobile industry for the 1959-1976 period as part of their larger tests of two models of the production process. Their analysis showed that higher grievance rates were associated with lower productivity of production workers, lower total factor productivity, and higher unit costs of production.

The final study by Ichniowski (1986) tested the relationship between grievance rates and company productivity in nine union paper plants as well as a nonunion plant owned by the same company. Monthly performance results showed that the more grievances filed in a mill, the lower the mill's productivity. Moreover, the nonunion mill had significantly lower productivity than the union mills. There seems to be a consensus across these studies that high grievance rates are costly to the company. However, a high grievance rate may be only symptomatic of broader problems that exist in the labor-management relationship or in the firm itself.

Ichniowski and Lewin (1987) provide an excellent summation of that part of the grievance research literature published between 1960 and 1986 that links with firm performance.

What can we say about the importance of these studies? The most useful conclusion is that heavy grievance activity is associated with a number of unfavorable outcomes for management including poor labor productivity, poor firm performance, absenteeism, and so forth. Heavy grievance activity also seems to be symptomatic of troubled employee and union-management relations.

Miscellaneous Studies

There were a number of studies published during the 1980s that don't fit clearly under the earlier headings. Briggs (1982) was interested in identifying steps that unions and management could take to improve the grievance process. He sent questionnaires to matched pairs of union and municipal-sector management officials involved in grievance administration in the State of California. His conclusions were: both management and unions could do more in training supervisors and stewards in the grievance procedure, shop stewards could take more advantage of their authority to resolve grievances at the first and second steps of the procedure, and management could give first-level supervisors more authority to resolve grievances at the lower steps.

Dalton and Todor's (1982) study involved examining the relationship between the grievance behaviors of union stewards and the stewards' company commitment, union commitment, and overall satisfaction using data from the same western public utility mentioned earlier. They found that company commitment and overall satisfaction were negatively related to number of grievances filed, frequency of steward encouraging employee to file grievance even when the employee had shown no inclination to do so, and frequency of cases where the steward files grievance over objections of employees. Union commitment was negatively related to the frequency of steward consulting with the grievant's supervisor where the case was resolved before filing. Finally, they found that the steward's commitments to the union and company were unrelated.

Clark (1989) looked at perceptions of the grievance procedure, along with other independent measures, and its link with the quality of the union-management relationship using a sample of the membership of the National Association of Letter Carriers. Clark found that favorable perceptions of the effectiveness of the grievance procedure were significantly and positively associated with perceived quality of the union-management relationship.

Knight (1986, 1987) carried out two different studies on the grievance process. The first one focused on the role of feedback in the grievance process using questionnaires and interviews from eight workplace level case studies in four industries. He found that grievance feedback is one of the factors that contributes to grievance resolution. A second finding was that although previous grievance settlements and arbitration decisions were commonly referred to during grievance negotiations, the use and impact of feedback varied significantly between union and management.

Knight's second study looked at the issue of the duty of fair representation in conjunction with the grievance process. The questionnaire was sent to officials in nine industrial unions in the province of British Columbia. He found that employees were increasingly threatening to file fair representation complaints during the three-year period prior to the study, and that explicit threats to file such claims were most likely to be made at the final grievance step. Knight concluded that fair representation complaints were: (1) reflective of political factionalism within the union, and (2) a measure of economic decisions adversely affecting individuals, but (3) not a sign of inadequate union representation.

Moore (1981) used grievance records filed between 1977 and 1979 with the Environment Component of the Public Service Alliance of Canada. He identified six possible grievance outcomes for the employee. He broke up the 228 grievances into those that could be adjudicated vs. those that could not be adjudicated under the Public Service Staff Relations Act. Moore concluded that justice was more likely to be denied where there were restrictions on the types of grievances eligible for adjudication.

Sulzner (1980) was interested in determining what impact, if any, the negotiated grievance procedure might have on U.S. federal personnel policy and practice. He found that nearly two-thirds of the interviewees thought that the grievance procedure had an impact on those personnel policies and practices. However, the interview findings were inconsistent with published surveys of federal labor-management relations. Sulzner concluded that the trend in future years might show greater impact as the parties gain experience in working under the negotiated grievance system.

Fryxell and Gordon (1989) used their existing data to examine the extent to which workplace justice and job satisfaction predicted satisfaction by union members with their union and employer. Workplace justice was defined in terms of procedural and distributive justice afforded by their organization's grievance system, and a new variable regarding beliefs about a moral order in the workplace. Nine hypotheses were tested. Fryxell and Gordon found that greater levels of procedural and distributive justice afforded by their grievance system were predictors of satisfaction with their union. Belief in a moral order at the workplace was shown to be the strongest predictor of employee satisfaction with management.

The last two studies reported here focus on the effectiveness of the grievance procedure. Hayford and Pegnetter (1980) compared the language of the union grievance procedure in 17 contracts in four states with that of the civil service appeal system for state employees in the same states. The authors concluded that the union grievance procedure was the better of the two systems. The union procedure allowed a broader scope of issues to be adjudicated. Other benefits included greater assurance of competent employee representation, mutual selection of adjudicator, employee perceptions of the neutrality of the adjudication, and enhanced finality of the adjudication.

The last study, by Lewin and Peterson (1988), was the most thorough treatment of the union grievance procedure published during the 1980s. We have already commented on their Systematic Model of the Grievance Process and summarized that part of their study focused on personal outcomes for grievants. They studied the grievance process in the four industries/sectors already noted. They used surveys, interviews, and archival records. Unlike many earlier studies, Lewin and Peterson used multi-measures of grievance procedure effectiveness, including some that had never been used before such as perceived importance of issues and perceived equity of grievance settlement.

The conceptual model, presented earlier, was tested both within and across industry/sector. There was considerable support for the Systems Model of the Grievance Process based on correlational and regression analysis. The strongest support for the full model of grievance procedure effectiveness was found in nonprofit hospitals and steel. Variance explained in grievance procedure effectiveness ranged from 30 to 60 percent for the regression analysis. This study showed that the concept of grievance procedure effectiveness can be operationalized and measured. *The Modern Grievance Procedure in the United States* (1988) provides the full detail of their study.

Having commented on the vast majority of union grievance studies published in the 1980s in the United States and Canada, what broad conclusions can we draw? First, there was a noticeable drop in the number of studies that were interested in identifying demographic and organizational variables that differentiated grievants from non-grievants. When compared to earlier years, this is understandable: there were very few variables identified across studies, and there was little systematic use of the same set variables across studies.

Second, a number of the recent studies took the grievance process out of the black box or closed system to relate the process to personal outcomes for the grievant (e.g., Klass and De Nisi 1989; Lewin and Peterson 1988) or organizational outcomes (e.g., Ichniowski 1986; Katz, Kochan, and Gobeille 1983). Such studies, one would hope, would encourage union and management officials to focus greater attention on how to make the union grievance system work better than it has to date. It has been discouraging to find out from interviewing both union and employer officials responsible for administering grievances that few of them use their grievance data to solve, much less identify, problems in the grievance relationship or the labor-management relationship.

One of the most discouraging findings is that, if the findings are generalizable, the employee who grieves takes risks in filing, and particularly in winning, grievances—even if a union is present. Thus, the employee may gain consideration, and even win his or her case, but is not necessarily immune to subsequent negative treatment by the employer.

Third, it became more common for the researchers to use conceptual models as a base for testing their data. This meant that *a priori* statement of testable hypotheses became more prevalent during the 1980s. Thus it became easier to draw conclusions based on results over several studies.

Fourth, some of the recent union grievance research (e.g., Clark 1989; Fryxell and Gordon 1989) focused on the views of union members and nonmembers rather than limiting the perspective to that of union and management officials only. Gordon and his colleagues, in particular, placed the grievance procedure within the broader scope of workplace justice by asking employees how satisfied they were with the state of procedural justice and distributive justice, and their overall view of the grievance procedure operation in their organization.

Fifth, the trend has been in the direction of using more than one method of collecting data for any given study. Admittedly, some of the 1980s studies relied principally on questionnaire data, but there were other studies that used combinations of survey feedback, interviews, company and union grievance records, personnel file data, and economic performance indicators. Researchers are strongly encouraged to use either the Klass or the Lewin and Peterson models as a base for their own research on the union grievance procedure. Only in so doing will it be possible to make broad generalizations from the variety of empirical studies that will be done in the coming years.

Sixth, the issue of grievance procedure effectiveness was given more attention than previously. Much more research needs to be done on grievance procedure rate as the dependent measure. Lewin and Peterson's (1988) work goes the furthest by identifying six measures of effectiveness, including grievance rate, step level of settlement, speed of settlement, arbitration rate, importance of issue, and equity of settlement. Their research goes beyond these measures by incorporating subsequent treatment of the grievant regarding performance rating, promotion rate, attendance, and voluntary and involuntary turnover data. It is increasingly clear that such judgments need to be made using multiple measures of effectiveness and allowing more parties to take part in the assessments.

Seventh, while we have not commented on issues concerning statistical rigor in this review, the union grievance research in the 1980s, on the whole, employed more sophisticated statistical tests in analyzing the survey data than was true earlier. Some of the studies used a variety of statistical tests including factor analysis, multiple regression, and logit analysis. It is possible that earlier research used inappropriate statistics (e.g., using parametric tests where nonparametric statistics were appropriate). While the use of multiple tests doesn't eliminate such problems, the use of regressions allows us to explain what variance in the dependent measure is accounted for by the independent variables used in the particular study. Many of the significant correlations reported in previous studies accounted for very little explanation. When a study finds that three to six independent variables explain 40 to 60 percent of the variance in a dependent variable like grievance procedure effectiveness, we can really make some linkages of association. This is particularly so if there is a minimal problem of covariation.

Eighth, several studies tested the findings from earlier research in this field (e.g., Muchinsky and Maassarani 1980; Nelson and Reiman 1983) related to Sayles' (1958) study of technological effects and Peach and Livernash's (1974) work identifying the importance of workplace variables in explaining level of grievance activity. Such research should be encouraged.

Finally, some of the studies focused on the relationship between the operation of the grievance procedure and the state of labor-management relations (e.g., Gandz and Whitehead 1982; Ng and Dastmalchian 1989). This association is particularly important, as it may prod union and management to view the grievance administration record as a key indicator of the health of the union-management relationship. Such research findings give both parties evidence that their own behaviors may be more costly to their own side than they previously thought. All in all, over 30 union grievance research studies published in the 1980s were found through the computer search. This is a considerable increase over the output of the entire period of 1945-1979.

Grievance Mediation

We now turn our attention to the topic of grievance mediation and the research that was done on the topic during the 1980s. Gregory and Rooney define grievance mediation as "any effort on the part of a neutral person to assist two parties in reaching agreement on a grievance that is moving toward or is actually at impasse. The role of the neutral person, who is usually a state or federal mediator, is one of assistance and persuasion. He attempts to resolve the impasse through encouraging the parties to resolve the grievance voluntarily" (1980, p. 503).

Whereas mediation or med-arb had been used for some years as means of gaining resolution to grievance disputes short of arbitration, an innovation emerged in the late 1970s. Mediation became formally recognized as a distinct step in the grievance procedure handled by someone other than the person who will serve as the arbitrator if the grievance cannot be settled by the parties at the mediation step. Stephen Goldberg and his associates are most commonly identified with this model of grievance mediation. Their initial work began in the U.S. coal industry in the late 1970s in response to major problems in workplace relations in that industry.

We found only five empirical studies in this area. None of the studies is really based on a model of variables that would be associated with the effectiveness of grievance mediation, though Brett and Goldberg (1983) go further than the other researchers in this area. Gregory and Rooney (1980) studied the broader use of mediation in the grievance process. They initially did an informal poll of mediators in the state of Michigan. The poll showed that the state mediators reported success in resolving 83 percent of private-sector grievance cases and 84 percent of public-sector cases through grievance mediation. They then analyzed 60 completed grievance mediation cases handled by the Detroit Office of the Michigan Employment Relations Commission in 1979. Gregory and Rooney reported that 58.3 percent of the grievances were settled by mediation. Only 16.6 percent of the sampled cases eventually required arbitration.

Bowers, Seeber, and Stallworth (1982) canvassed samples of state and federal mediators to identify those factors that were related to successful grievance mediation. The respondents found the following factors helpful to grievance mediation success: low case loads, support by peers and supervisors in their agency for engaging in grievance mediation, dissatisfaction of the parties with grievance arbitration, clarity in defining the issue, restricting the mediator's authority to the specified issue(s), the mediator supplying written recommendations only at the request of the parties, and using joint sessions with the parties to clear grievance settlement recommendations.

The most thorough study was done by Brett and Goldberg (1983) based on experiments with grievance mediation over two separate six-month periods in four union districts in the states of

Virginia, Kentucky, Indiana, and Illinois. The results strongly supported grievance mediation as an alternative to arbitration. The researchers found that 89 percent of the cases referred to mediation were resolved short of arbitration, cases resolved through mediation took considerably less time to complete, the average cost of the third party's fees and expenses was only $295 vs. $1,034 for arbitrating non-discharge cases in the districts at that time, and surveys showed that union and employer officials using both processes favored grievance mediation over grievance arbitration. For further detail, the reader is encouraged to read the full article, as well as three other articles that were published on the subject in 1982 and 1983 by Goldberg and his colleagues.

Ury, Brett, and Goldberg (1988) updated their work on grievance mediation in their book, *Getting Disputes Resolved*. They reported that from November 1980 through June 1988, 827 coal industry grievances were mediated (only 20 percent went to arbitration). Other results were: the average cost per grievance mediation had dropped below 20 percent of that of arbitration ($330 vs. $1,692 per case), and the average time lapse from request for mediation to final resolution was only 24 days.

They also reported results for the use of grievance mediation in a variety of industries outside the coal industry including manufacturing, telecommunication, urban mass transit, retail sales, petroleum refining, electric power, local government, and public education. Between May 1983 and June 1988 there were 276 grievances that were appealed to arbitration. Approximately 81 percent of those cases were resolved short of arbitration (through mediation or dropping of the case by one party). The average cost of mediation ($435 per case) was approximately 30 percent of that of arbitration. Finally, the time lapse for mediation resolution was only 10 percent of that of grievance arbitration.

Silberman (1989) described two pilot projects on grievance mediation between Thrifty Corporation and Local 770 of the United Food and Commercial Workers Union and between Southwestern Bell Telephone Company and Local 6 of the Communication Workers of America, but offered no rigorous analysis of either program.

What can we conclude from these studies of grievance mediation? The major conclusion is that research so far shows that grievance mediation has real benefits as a dispute resolution technique. The use of mediation as a step prior to arbitration has advantages over going to arbitration in terms of lower cost, shorter time lapse, and satisfaction of union and management officials who have used both processes. Further research in this area is constrained by two factors. First, Ury, Brett, and Goldberg (1988) report that only approximately four percent of collective bargaining agreements in the late 1980s included grievance mediation language. Second, it is common that not all grievance issues are eligible for coverage by grievance mediation. Often the labor market parties do not use the grievance mediation option in cases dealing with discharge or management rights, for instance. It is hoped that the use of grievance mediation can be enlarged in the coming years in terms of both number of parties involved and types of issues that can be addressed. This would open up more research opportunities for evaluating the process and a broader data set on which to base our generalizations.

The one area where research on grievance mediation is more equivocal concerns the reactions of the grievants to the process. The grievants in Brett and Goldberg (1983) expressed a broader range of reaction than did either the union or management officials. Some grievants may prefer a straight win, and find that compromises growing out of mediation are less satisfying to them.

Nonunion Grievance Procedure

If we were reviewing the research literature on the grievance process for the postwar decades through the 1970s, it is doubtful that we would even include any discussion of the nonunion grievance procedure. However, this is no longer true. A number of American companies during the late 1970s instituted formal nonunion grievance systems, often as part of their new human resource management strategy (see Kochan, Katz, and McKersie 1986). These new grievance processes were, on the whole, more formal and encompassing than earlier processes like open door policies and appeal to levels above the employee's own supervisor. Berenbeim's (1980) Conference Board Survey reported on the presence of nonunion grievance systems among the 652 firms responding to his survey. Approximately 50 percent of the companies surveyed at that time had instituted a formal grievance procedure for their nonunion staff. Most of the programs were found to have been instituted quite recently.

Readers who want a thorough review and critique of the literature on the nonunion grievance process in the United States might read Peterson and Lewin's 1990 article. Three books were also published during the 1980s on the subject (Ewing 1989; McCabe 1988; Westin 1988). The thrust of the books is to categorize and describe the various nonunion grievance processes in selected American companies. Ewing, for example, evaluates the individual programs based on a set of standards that he spells out in Chapter 3 of his book.

McCabe (1988) does an excellent review of the post-World War II literature regarding grievance and appeal systems, drawing from a broad reading in the field. Our review of the research literature, however, will draw primarily from the five empirical studies during the 1980s included in Peterson and Lewin's 1990 article "The Non-Union Grievance Procedure: A Viable System of Due Process?"

Berenbeim (1980) asked for company experiences with their nonunion grievance procedures as part of his comprehensive survey. He reported that the number of grievances filed ranged from one-tenth of one percent to as high as 43 percent of employees. Second, the overwhelming number of responding firms reported that less than five percent of their employees had used the complaint procedure during the preceding year. Finally, Berenbeim found that production and clerical staff were the most frequent grievers.

A study by Drost and O'Brien (1983) queried production employees of a mid-Atlantic firm about their reactions to a roundtable committee grievance process including both employee and managerial representatives. The assessment of the 87 respondents was generally unfavorable. A majority of the employees were unfamiliar with the structure and function of the roundtable. More than half of the respondents felt that management would "hold it against" employees who grieved. Finally, many of the respondents believed that management's response to the grievance was neither timely nor addressed to the real problem.

Coombe (1984) studied three peer review grievance systems at General Electric, Control Data, and the Adolph Coors Company. The General Electric program was implemented at their Columbia, Maryland plant. The process is limited to grievances based on interpretation and application of existing company policies and procedures. Management was pleased by the work of the peer review panels in handling the first 20 grievances under the new system. The responsible management official also believed that the employees were enthusiastic about the peer review process.

The second study focused on the more extensive program at Control Data Corporation. The early experience with the CDC Peer Review Program showed that 50 cases were tendered for consideration by the peer panels, but only six of the cases went to the peer panel because the other cases were resolved through mediation.

Coombe described and evaluated the peer review program at the Coors Brewing Company. He found that in 89 complaints handled in 1982, 68 percent of the decisions favored management, approximately 17 percent modified or reduced the discipline, and approximately 23 percent overturned the management decision.

McCollum and Norris (1984) studied nonunion grievance systems in a large number of Southern manufacturing companies in the states of Alabama and Georgia. Their data is based on interviews and survey responses from 49 private-sector firms. They found that 1.3 grievances per 100 employees were resolved at the terminal step of the various grievance and complaint procedures. McCollum and Norris tested four hypotheses relating to company size, recency of grievance machinery, part of a parent firm vs. independent operation, and percent of grievances resolved by top management in the process and the extent of grievance machinery. The only significant regression support was for a positive link between company size and extent of grievance machinery (determined by the researchers' scoring system).

Lewin (1987) presented and tested a model of the nonunion grievance procedure in several organizations. His findings were, in general, similar to those found in the Lewin and Peterson (1988) study of the union grievance procedure.

The final study by Lo Bosco (1985) reported the results of a survey sent out to one hundred human resource managers by *Personnel* magazine. Sixty-two percent of the respondents' companies had formal nonunion grievance procedures. Five of the firms provided binding arbitration by a third-party neutral as the terminal step. Almost one-half of responding companies stated that all grievances would be considered under their grievance system. Four out of five respondents were favorable in assessing the effectiveness of their grievance procedure.

Making any definitive conclusions about the effectiveness of the nonunion procedure, based on this research, is premature. Only one of the five studies used *a priori* hypothesis testing. The researchers, in most cases, relied on data from management representatives who, one might expect, would have a favorable assessment of the process that they designed or administered. Most of the studies did not use rigorous research designs, but relied on survey and interview data that was not likely to offer deep insights into the functioning or success of the nonunion grievance process. One should not be surprised by these comments, given that such grievance processes are relatively new and early research in a field rarely offers the most penetrating research insights.

Directions for Future Research

What directions might be taken by industrial relations researchers in the future? A number of suggestions could be made about future research on the union grievance procedure, grievance mediation, and the nonunion grievance procedure. It might be best to treat each of the three topics separately, because they are at different stages of research development at the present time. However, the reader will note that a suggestion made in regard to one of the topics may have applicability to one or both of the other two topic areas.

As a person with education and previous work experience in industrial relations, my bias is towards improving the functioning of workplace governance systems. Thus policy and practice should be given at least equal weight with academic research goals in terms of the type of research desired on grievance processes. This does not rule out the possibility of rigorous research designs existing along with the addressing of important questions to improve workplace governance, but at times it may be necessary to compromise somewhat on research design in order to address the significant policy and practice issues. So what suggestions can be made?

Union Grievance Procedure

We begin with the union grievance procedure. The quality and quantity of published research in this area is already ahead of that in the other two. Earlier work by Sayles (1958), Kuhn (1961), Peach and Livernash (1974), Thompson and Murray (1976), and Slichter, Healy, and Livernash (1988) has laid important foundations for research. One can fully expect that future research might build on the best of the most recent research studies as well. One suggestion is to use model building as a base for any studies in this field. If most of the research in this field had been based on one or several models of the grievance process, we could have drawn some clear conclusions across studies, while dropping a number of variables that have not proved useful. In particular, the models of Klass (1989a; 1989b) and Lewin and Peterson (1988) are useful starting points for using more systematic ways of identifying variables and relationships between them. Such models are stepping stones to the development of a theory of the grievance process.

Another suggestion is that future research aimed at assessing the effectiveness of the union grievance procedure be multidimensional in nature. Ideally, studies should use multiple research methods (e.g., surveys, interviews, grievance and personnel records) from a greater variety of sources (union officials, management representatives, employees, and grievants themselves) than were used previously. We cannot necessarily assume that if union and management officials are satisfied with the process, the same holds for bargaining group employees or grievants themselves. No one study so far has captured all of the key parties.

Peterson and Lewin (1982) called for more longitudinal studies of the union grievance procedure in their IRRA paper. Their 1988 study, like some of the other research reviewed earlier, used a three-year period. Future research might go even further in identifying the environmental and internal forces over the period studied that may have influenced the operation of the union grievance process in the firm(s) studied. The grievance process fits into a broad framework of workplace relations at a given point of time in the history of a given society. We know that labor arbitration was used much less in the 1980s than in previous years. It would be naive to generalize that its declining use was due to unions and employers improving their relationship or better human resource management in the nonunion sector. The major restructuring in manufacturing, the considerable loss of union membership since 1979, a major recession in the early 1980s, globalization and international competition, and "hard-ball" tactics by some American employers during the past 12 years provide most of the reasons for the decline.

Furthermore, a study that stops when the grievance is resolved or dropped fails to capture the possible costs to the employee who files a grievance. If human relations deteriorates between the grievant and his or her supervisor afterwards, or management uses retribution, important facets of due process are lost. It would seem that altogether too many of the early postwar studies of the grievance process focused only on short-term results for the grievant, or considered only the interest of the union and/or employer.

What about the area of comparative cross-national research on the union grievance procedure? American researchers who have looked at the grievance process have rarely ventured outside the United States for their sample populations. And yet most advanced industrial countries use some form or other for processing grievances—many of them without as heavy a recourse as the United States' highly formal and legalistic mechanisms where win-lose is given greater credence and emphasis. What can we learn from the experience with grievance administration of other countries? The authors of the chapters in this volume were asked to address this subject in our reviews. We reviewed the table of contents of the *British Journal of Industrial Relations* and the *Journal of Industrial Relations* (Australia) for the period 1980-1989, but since few articles were published on union and nonunion grievance procedures during this period, we did not devote a separate section to non-North American applications.

We encourage more research focusing on Western Europe, Japan, and other parts of the world. Labor lawyers have published a number of books, monographs, and articles describing the grievance resolution processes found in these countries. Arbitration, as the final step in the grievance procedure, is less common outside of North America. Labor courts are used as the terminal step in a number of countries (e.g., Scandinavia and France). In many countries, the collective bargaining agreement does not spell out the rights and responsibilities of the union and management to the degree we find in the United States and Canada. The "law of the shop" in some countries allows for less documentation on lower steps of the grievance procedure. Little is known about the grievance process in Japan because of the seeming reticence of the parties to use a formal procedure that is viewed as litigious.

Comparative grievance research, therefore, would offer a fruitful direction for intercountry research collaboration. How do different systems compare in terms of cost, elapsed time, resolution, and satisfaction of parties and the grievant with the procedural and distributive elements of the union grievance procedures?

Finally, we suggest that future researchers be encouraged to do more testing of the grievance procedure in the public and professional sectors. The vast majority of the work to date has been based on the private sector experience. Furthermore, even in the private sector, we need to determine whether production and clerical staff differ in their assessment of the union grievance process.

Grievance Mediation

We have very little to say about needs to address in future research on grievance mediation. The research results are very consistent so far; namely, that the use of ad hoc grievance mediation as a separate grievance step prior to arbitration has notable benefits over grievance arbitration in terms of costs, time lapse, and party satisfaction with the process. We should encourage further research outside of the organizations covered by Goldberg and his associates. Their research is an excellent model for others to follow. Longitudinal analysis of this type could also assess whether initial favorable reaction by the parties of grievance mediation holds over time. The limiting factor so far is that the parties, in most cases, do not allow all grievance issues to use the grievance mediation process. Many contracts spell out those issues that are included (or excluded). Is there real justification for doing so? We don't know yet. Perhaps future studies can provide answers to such questions.

Nonunion Grievance Process

What about directions for future research in the nonunion grievance procedure? It is in this area that future research might be of most value to policymakers and practitioners, not to discount the concern of academics interested in workplace governance systems. Can nonunion grievance and appeal systems meet the procedural and distributive standards of justice expected of union grievance procedure? Research to answer this question is lacking so far.

Peterson and Lewin (1990) offer some hypotheses that should be tested in the field for answering the question raised here. So far there is very little known about how well such systems work in organizations, though one might expect that mixed composition peer committees and procedures providing binding arbitration by a neutral-third party would provide greater procedural and distributive justice than informal appeals to higher management or "open door" systems. One of the potential flaws in most nonunion grievance procedures is that while grievances must be based on alleged violations of the language or interpretation of company policies and procedures, employees are seldom a party to determining those policies and procedures. Moreover, these policies and procedures are rarely as encompassing as the language in most labor contracts because employers generally prefer to exercise wide managerial discretion in dealing with their employee staff.

We encourage researchers in this area to look at the best of the research covering the union grievance procedure as a base for collecting survey, interview, and grievance data in nonunion firms operating under a variety of grievance procedure models. Optimally, companies will be willing to allow researchers access to their organizations. It is especially important that researchers gain insights and answers from the nonunion staff and grievants themselves. Early research ventures with companies suggest that at least some of the firms are willing to participate as long as anonymity and confidentiality are respected by the researchers. Some of the models of the union grievance process can be adapted as a base for hypothesis testing. Other researchers might do experimental studies to create the necessary laboratory conditions to test key variables covering the grievance process.

Current developments in the workplace raise major questions concerning issue of "voice" in America in the coming years. Some management spokespeople write and talk about "employee empowerment" in the 1990s giving the employees more voice in the job than was true in the 1980s in many firms and industries. The assumption is that the post-baby-boomer work force would involve many employers and jobs chasing fewer job candidates. It may happen later in this decade, but as of early 1992 the reality is far different. National unemployment is over seven percent. Major company restructuring continues to result in more layoffs and voluntary and not so voluntary retirements. Employees, managers, and even executives, even when still employed, fear that they will be hit next.

Employees who fear loss of their jobs are, with relatively few exceptions, unlikely to call attention to themselves by grieving alleged violations of the collective bargaining agreement or company policies and procedures. Thus, a good case can be built that even when the employee has a nonunion or union grievance procedure available, he or she is reluctant to use it. With only 16 percent of the labor force covered by union membership, and civil service rules covering perhaps another 10 to 15 percent, most American employees and managers have only a limited voice in the workplace today.

The proliferation of nonunion grievance procedures in recent years may offer a counterbalance, but there is so little research to date on these programs that we can offer very little in the way of definitive judgments. Discussions so far suggest that many employers have used such nonunion grievance mechanisms as a way of discouraging union organization while still allowing wide management discretion in dealing with employees. Even if the firm has good intentions, employee use of such procedures is much less frequent than in the unionized sector because of shortcomings in the process (fear of retribution, limit of issues that can be grieved, lack of free access to legal and procedural expertise, and absence of finality by neutral arbitrator). Managers, with few exceptions, are not even covered by the nonunion grievance process. Thus, employees in general have less voice in their job than they did prior to 1980.

This leads us to the major question: can the vast majority of employers really offer a viable grievance procedure that meets or exceeds the basic features of procedure and substantive due process? Future research needs to compare the union and nonunion appeal processes to answer whether one or both is meeting commonly accepted standards developed by Epstein and others. If, in particular, the nonunion grievance system is failing to do so, national policy should change to provide basic elements of due process in the private and public workplace. Comparative studies of the nonunion and union systems would provide the data necessary to determine whether we need new labor policy in this area.

There is a full kettle of research that needs to be tended on all facets of the grievance process in the workplace. We hope that the person reviewing this research area for the 1990s will be able to answer a number of the questions raised here.

References

Allen, Robert E., and Timothy J. Keaveny. "Factors Differentiating Grievants and Non-grievants." *Human Relations* 38 (June 1985), pp. 519-34.

Aram, John D., and Paul F. Salipante, Jr. "An Evaluation of Organizational Due Process in the Resolution of Employee/Employer Conflict." *Academy of Management Review* 6 (April 1981), pp. 197-204.

Berenbeim, Ronald. *Non-Union Complaint Systems: A Corporate Appraisal.* Report No. 770. New York: The Conference Board, 1980.

Bowers, Mollie H., Ronald L. Seeber, and Lamont E. Stallworth. "Grievance Mediation: A Route to Resolution for the Cost-Conscious 1980s." *Labor Law Journal* 33 (August 1982), pp. 459-66.

Brett, Jeanne M., and Stephen B. Goldberg. "Grievance Mediation in the Coal Industry." *Industrial and Labor Relations Review* 37 (October 1983), pp. 49-69.

Briggs, Steven. "The Steward, the Supervisor, and the Grievance Process." In *Proceedings of the Thirty-Fourth Annual Meeting, Industrial Relations Research Association.* Madison, WI: IRRA, 1982, pp. 313-19.

Clark, Paul F. "Determinants of the Quality of Union-Management Relations: An Exploratory Study of Union Member Perceptions." *Journal of Collective Negotiations in the Public Sector* 18, no. 2 (1989), pp. 103-16.

Coombe, John D. "Peer Review: The Emerging Successful Application." *Employee Relations Law Journal* 9 (Spring 1984), pp. 659-71.

Dalton, Dan R., and William D. Todor. "Win, Lose, Draw: The Grievance Process in Practice." *Personnel Administrator* 26 (May-June 1981), pp. 25-9.

________. "Antecedents of Grievance Filing Behavior: Attitude/Behavioral Consistency and the Union Steward." *Academy of Management Journal* 25 (March 1982), pp. 158-69.

________. "Composition of Dyads as a Factor in the Outcome of Workplace Justice: Two Field Assessments." *Academy of Management Journal* 28 (September 1985), pp. 704-12.

Drost, Donald A., and Fabius P.O. O'Brien. "Are There Grievances Against Your Non-Union Grievance Procedure?" *Personnel Administrator* (January 1983), pp. 36-40, 42.

Ewing, David W. *Justice on the Job; Resolving Grievances in the Non-Union Workplace.* Boston, MA: Harvard Business School Press, 1989.

Fryxell, Gerald E., and Michael E. Gordon. "Workplace Justice and Job Satisfaction as Predictors of Satisfaction." *Academy of Management Journal* 32 (December 1989), pp. 851-66.

Gandz, Jeffrey, and J. David Whitehead. "The Relationship Between Industrial Relations Climate and Grievance Initiation and Resolution." *Proceedings of the Thirty-Fourth Annual Meeting, Industrial Relations Research Association.* Madison, WI: IRRA, 1982, pp. 320-28.

Gordon, Michael E., and Roger L. Bowlby. "Propositions about Grievance Settlements: Finally, Consultation with Grievants." *Personnel Psychology* 41 (Spring 1988), pp. 107-23.

________. "Reactions and Intentionality Attributions as Determinants of the Intent to File a Grievance." *Personnel Psychology* 42 (Summer 1989), pp. 309-29.

Gordon, Michael E., and Sandra J. Miller. "Grievances: A Review of Research and Practice." *Personnel Psychology* 37 (Spring 1984), pp. 117-46.

Gregory, Gordon A., and Robert E. Rooney, Jr. "Grievance Mediation: A Trend in the Cost-Conscious Eighties." *Labor Law Journal* 31 (August 1980), pp. 502-08.

Hayford, Stephen L., and Richard Pegnetter. "Grievance Adjudication for Public Employees." *Arbitration Journal* 35 (September 1980), pp. 22-9.

Ichniowski, Casey. "The Effects of Grievance Activity on Productivity." *Industrial and Labor Relations Review* 40 (October 1986), pp. 75-89.

Ichniowski, Casey, and David Lewin. "Grievance Procedures and Firm Performance." In *Human Resources and the Performance of the Firm*, ed. Morris Kleiner et al. IRRA Research Series. Madison, WI: IRRA, 1987, pp. 159-94.

Katz, Harry C., Thomas A. Kochan, and Kenneth R. Gobeille. "Industrial Relations Performance, Economic Performance, and QWL Programs: An Interplant Analysis." *Industrial and Labor Relations Review* 37 (October 1983), pp. 3-17.

Katz, Harry C., Thomas A. Kochan, and Mark Weber. "Assessing the Effects of Industrial Relations Systems and Efforts to Improve the Quality of Working Life on Organizational Effectiveness." *Academy of Management Journal* 28 (September 1985), pp. 509-26.

Klass, Brian S. "Managerial Decision-Making About Employee Grievances: The Impact of the Grievant's Work History." *Personnel Psychology* 42 (Spring 1989a), pp. 53-68.

________. "Determinants of Grievance Activity and the Grievance System's Impact on Employer Behavior: An Integrative Perspective." *Academy of Management Review* 14 (July 1989b), pp. 445-58.

Klass, Brian S., and Angelo DeNisi. "Managerial Reactions to Employee Dissent: The Impact of Grievance Activity on Performance Ratings." *Academy of Management Journal* 32 (December 1989), pp. 705-17.

Knight, Thomas R. "Toward A Contingency Theory of the Grievance-Arbitration System." In *Advances in Industrial and Labor Relations*, vol. 2, ed. David B. Lipsky, Greenwich, CT: JAI Press, 1985, pp. 269-318.

________. "Feedback and Grievance Resolution." *Industrial and Labor Relations Review* 39 (July 1986), pp. 585-98.

________. "The Role of the Duty of Fair Representation in Union Grievance Decisions." *Relations Industrielles* 42 (Autumn 1987), pp. 716-33.

Kochan, Thomas, Harry Katz, and Robert B. McKersie. *The Transformation of American Industrial Relations*. New York: Basic Books, 1986.

Kuhn, James W. *Bargaining in Grievance Settlement: The Power of Industrial Work Groups*. New York: Columbia University Press, 1961.

Labig, Chalmer E., and I. B. Helburn. "Union and Management Policy Influence on Grievance Initiation." *Journal of Labor Research* 7 (Summer 1986), pp. 269-84.

Lewin, David. "Theoretical Perspectives on the Modern Grievance Procedure." Paper presented at the Conference on New Approaches to Labor Unions, Virginia Polytechnic and State University, Blacksburg, VA, October 1981.

________. "Dispute Resolution in the Non-Union Firm: A Theoretical and Empirical Analysis." *Journal of Conflict Resolution* 31 (September 1987), pp. 465-502.

Lewin, David, and Richard B. Peterson. "Behavioral Outcomes of Grievance Activity." Working paper, Columbia University Graduate School of Business, September 1987.

________. *The Modern Grievance Procedure in the United States*. Westport, CT: Quorum Books, 1988.

Lo Bosco, Maryellen. "Consensus on . . .Non-Union Grievance Procedures." *Personnel* 62 (January 1985), pp. 61-5.

McCabe, Douglas. *Corporate Non-Union Complaint Procedures and Systems: A Strategic Human Resources Management Analysis*. New York: Praeger, 1988.

McCollum, James K., and Dwight Norris. "Non-Union Grievance Machinery in Southern Industry." *Personnel Administrator* 29 (November 1984), pp. 106-14, 131.

Meyer, David, and William Cooke. "Economic and Political Factors in Formal Grievance Resolution." *Industrial Relations* 27 (Fall 1988), pp. 318-35.

Moore, William R. "Justice and the Grievance Procedure in the Federal Public Service." *Relations Industrielles* 36 (October 1981), pp. 848-62.

Muchinsky, Paul M., and Mounawar A. Maassarani. "Work Environment Effects on Public Sector Grievances." *Personnel Psychology* 33 (Summer 1980), pp. 403-14.

Nelson, Nels, and Bernard Reiman. "Work Environment and Grievance Rates in a Manufacturing Plant." *Journal of Management* 9 (Fall/Winter 1983), pp. 145-58.

Ng, Ignace, and Ali Dastmalchian. "Determinants of Grievance Outcomes: A Case Study." *Industrial and Labor Relations Review* 42 (April 1989), pp. 393-403.

Norsworthy, J. R., and Craig A. Zabala. "Worker Attitudes, Worker Behavior, and Productivity in the U.S. Automobile Industry, 1959-1976." *Industrial and Labor Relations Review* 38 (July 1985), pp. 544-57.

Peach, David A., and E. Robert Livernash. *Grievance Initiation and Resolution: A Study in Basic Steel*. Boston: Graduate School of Business Administration, Harvard University, 1974.

Peterson, Richard B., and David Lewin. "The Non-Union Grievance Procedure: A Viable System of Due Process?" *Employee Responsibilities and Rights Journal* 3 (March 1990), pp. 1-18.

———. "A Model for Research and Analysis of the Grievance Process." *Proceedings of the Thirty-Fourth Annual Meeting, Industrial Relations Research Association*. Madison, WI: IRRA, 1982, pp. 303-12.

Sayles, Leonard. *Behavior of Industrial Work Groups*. New York: John Wiley, 1958.

Silberman, Allan D. "Breaking the Mold of Grievance Resolution: A Pilot Program in Mediation." *The Arbitration Journal* 44 (December 1989), pp. 40-5.

Slichter, Sumner, James Healy, and E. Robert Livernash. *The Impact of Collective Bargaining on Management*. Washington, D.C.: Bureau of National Affairs, 1988.

Sulzner, George T. "The Impact of Grievance and Arbitration Processes on Federal Personnel Policies and Practices: The View from Twenty Bargaining Units." *Journal of Collective Negotiations in the Public Sector* 9, no. 2 (1980), pp. 143-56.

Thomson, Andrew W.J. *The Grievance Procedure in the Private Sector*. Ithaca, NY: New York State School of Labor and Industrial Relations, Cornell University, 1974.

Thomson, Andrew W.J., and Victor F. Murray. *Grievance Procedures*. Westmead, England: Saxon House, 1976.

Ury, William, Jeanne M. Brett, and Stephen B. Goldberg. *Getting Disputes Resolved*. San Francisco: Jossey-Bass, 1988.

Westin, Alvin. *Resolving Employment Disputes Without Litigation*. Washington, D.C.: Bureau of National Affairs, 1988.

Part II

Human Resource Management

CHAPTER 5

Integrating Strategic Human Resources and Strategic Management

PETER CAPPELLI AND HARBIR SINGH
University of Pennsylvania

The recent interest in thinking about human resources in a strategic context parallels and has been driven in part by the development of business strategy/strategic management. While the fields of strategic management and human resources have largely ignored each other, they appear to have followed similar paths. Both fields, however, now seem to be converging on a common set of questions with the exciting possibility of contributing to each other's development. The emerging effort in strategic management to identify the sources of competitive advantage within the firm and in human resources to determine the consequences of employment practices point toward an integrated approach where business strategy may be explained in part by employee management issues.

Strategy as a Concept

The word strategy derives from the Greek word "strategos," which referred to the role of the general leading the army. The concept of strategy was first used to describe Philip and Alexander's defeat of the Greeks in Macedonia. Historical accounts of the defeat indicated that Philip and Alexander were successful due to their superior strategy—deceptive maneuvers and a surprise attack—despite a great mismatch in resources (Quinn 1978). Strategy as a concept played a significant part in military history and also in areas such as international diplomacy and negotiation. Contemporary academic discussions of strategy may begin with Schelling's (1960) notion of strategy as the effort to influence the behavior of those with which one is in conflict. And the field of strategic management has its origins in the work of Chandler (1962), whose historical study of U.S. organizations first identified corporate strategies associated with product markets as the guiding principle for changes in organizational structure. Chandler defined strategy as the statement of the firm's goals and its policies and plans for achieving those goals.[1]

Ansoff (1965) later defined corporate strategy as the firm's mission, its concept of business, and the scope of product markets in which the firm participates. These considerations provided a guiding principle for the firm to select the markets in which it will participate. Both Chandler and Ansoff saw strategy as being concerned with the relationship of the firm to its competitors and markets. Andrews (1971) extended the notion of strategy to a wider set of issues and practices, describing it as "the pattern of decisions in a company that determines and reveals its objectives, purposes, or goals, produces principal policies and plans for achieving these goals, and defines the range of business the company should pursue, the kind of economic and human organization it is or intends to be, and the nature of the economic and noneconomic contribution it intends to make to its shareholders, employees, customers and communities." This rather long sentence reveals the multiple considerations incorporated into early strategy research. It also helps to explain some of the apparent confusion in understanding the notion of strategy in employee relations (see later), where it is sometimes used to describe product market decisions, sometimes policies toward unions, and at other times general decision processes.

Perhaps the area of strategic management research that has the highest profile is "competitive strategy" at the business unit level. Here the goal is to position the firm with respect to its competitors in order to defend against market pressures. This work began with Bain's (1959) empirical observation that profit rates varied considerably across industries and were related to industry structure. Prior to Bain, economists theorized that only by establishing a monopoly position could a firm generate above normal returns. Bain suggested that barriers to easy entry would allow incumbent firms to set higher prices and therefore generate superior profits. His analysis focuses on the conditions under which entry barriers exist.

Caves and Porter (1977) and Porter (1980) extended Bain's work to show how firms derive superior profits from characteristics associated with the market structure of their industry. They suggest that firms that erect barriers around their industry (i.e., a "strategic group" of competitors who follow the same strategy in an industry) can defend against market forces, price above competitive levels, and bank above normal profits. In perhaps the best known of these studies, Porter (1980) describes five forces that impact the business unit's competitive strategy: entry, threat of substitution, bargaining power of buyers, bargaining power of suppliers, and rivalry among current competitors. Firms that correctly analyze their position in relationship to these five forces and use them to erect or maintain mobility barriers will restrict competition and gain superior profits.

The clearest links between the ideas in competitive strategy and employment issues have been in labor relations, especially collective bargaining, with efforts to explain the level of settlements across industries. Research on bargaining structure in industrial relations predates the industry structure research and makes similar arguments, albeit from the point of view of the union rather than the firm (e.g., Commons 1919): unions create above market wages by organizing all competitors in the same product market, imposing a monopoly wage, and effectively creating a barrier to low-cost entry in that market. The other relationship between competitive strategy and collective bargaining is with studies of collective bargaining outcomes. An employer's ability to pay has been a long-standing factor in explaining the variance across bargaining settlements, and industry structure has often been used to explain profitability/ability to pay and, in turn, variance in wage settlements (Hendricks 1975; Abowd and Tracy 1989).

But the most explicit link between competitive strategy research in strategic management and employment research has been on the personnel side. In outward looking approaches to strategic management such as competitive strategy research, human resources are viewed as complementary assets: a firm first chooses its competitive strategy based on market conditions and then assembles the assets to accomplish the strategy, such as human resources, which are fit to its strategy. As noted later, virtually all of the strategic research in personnel takes a contingency approach of fitting human resources to business strategy.

Strategy in Personnel

The roots of the strategic literature in personnel are quite clearly in manpower planning. In its simplest form, manpower planning looked at one aspect of personnel—staffing—and worked to align it with the demands of the organization as outlined in business plans. As Craft (1980) points out, the process rarely worked as expected and often failed to deliver even on its simplest demands. The overly mechanical aspects of this matching process and the fact that it was typically based on extrapolations from previous experience helped to divorce it from the more important and powerful levels of business decision making where basic business directions, including competitive strategy, were charted.

The beginnings of a "strategic" literature in this area were efforts to expand the range of the planning exercise to help address issues beyond simply meeting required levels of staffing. Walker (1980) extended the agenda for manpower planning by focusing it on specific business problems, such as a need for more technical expertise in an organization, and on how planning (specifically in the area of selection) could help address that problem. Schuler and Walker (1990) argue that the main difference between strategic human resources and traditional planning is that the former is focused on the short term while the latter takes a long-term approach. And because business problems tend to have a short-run orientation, strategic human resources can be part of solving business problems—the business strategy process—while planning cannot. What makes human resources strategic in the personnel framework, then, is the fact that it is working to serve a business strategy designed to solve specific business problems. The decision process itself does not involve strategy.[2]

Once solving specific business problems becomes part of the goal, then reaching the "right" plan for human resources becomes more problematic than in traditional planning models. Because business problems are often idiosyncratic and typically represent some change from previous practices, the appropriate plan for human resources is no longer straightforward. And because human resources is seen as serving business strategy, the key issue that has dominated virtually all subsequent research in human resource planning/strategic human resources is identifying the right "fit" between human resource practices and the strategic business goal of the organization. The concept of fit between strategy and practice differentiates strategic human resources from the vast array of "best practice" research in human resources; the latter argues that there exists a set of best practices that are beneficial largely independent of the situation, while the former stresses the match between circumstances and practices as the key factor in success.[3]

The strategic management literature had argued earlier that the issue of fit—between business strategy and organizational structure—was a crucial factor determining organizational performance (see Chandler 1960; Lorsch and Allen 1973; Galbraith and Nathanson 1978 for an early review). The basic notion was that the effects of organizational structure in terms of control should reinforce the basic goals of the organization. Nathanson and Cassano (1982) and Hambrick (1983), for example, found that performance was based on the fit between strategy and the nature of diversification. Galbraith and Nathanson (1978) include performance measures and other factors related to human resources as part of a model of the fit with business strategy. From that point, it was a relatively short step to complete frameworks for thinking about the relationship between human resources and business strategy. Tichy, Fombrun, and Devanna (1982) provide one of the earliest of the strategic human resource frameworks. Their basic approach of identifying a taxonomy of business strategies and the human resource practices that reinforce those strategies has been followed by the majority of researchers in this area (see Smith 1982; Dyer 1984; Burack 1985 for examples).[4]

The dominant research question in this area basically asks whether fit matters, and here there are two related hypotheses. The first asks whether human resource practices are in fact related to business strategy. Most of this research has been done within the field of strategic management, not human resources, and is a byproduct of more general arguments about links to strategy (e.g., Gupta and Govindarajan 1984; Kerr 1985). Schuler and Jackson (1989) present one of the first exceptions to the many case study tests of human resource fit in presenting survey data showing a relationship between human resource practices and broad business strategies. Kobrin (1992) also uses survey data to examine the fit between human resources and the extent of globalization in business strategy among multinational firms. MacDuffie (1992) finds a relationship between the systems of work organization and production strategies where the latter is king.

The second and more difficult empirical question raised by the issue of fit is whether organizations with a better fit between human resource practices and business strategy have better performance.

Smith and Ferris (1988) find that firms where HR is more integrated into the process of strategy formation have higher levels of performance, and Ferris et al. (1990) find that construction firms with higher levels of strategic planning have higher performance. The assumption here is that by doing strategic planning and integrating HR, firms are more likely to get it right and make HR consistent with business strategy. But an alternative hypothesis might be that firms that are doing better have the resources to plan for the future. MacDuffie and Kochan (1991) represents the best attempt to address this issue. They find a strong relationship between the fit of human resource systems and manufacturing systems in the auto industry; production is highest only where there is high investment in employee training *and* a "lean" production system that can make use of such training.[5]

The Concept of Fit

The notion of fit is a deceptively simple idea. Some of its complexities have been examined explicitly in organizational research, especially with regard to contingency theories (see Tosi and Slocum 1984; Van de Ven and Drazin 1985), but fit is an even more complicated matter in human resources strategy because the arguments combine hypotheses from two different fields.

The underpinnings of the concept of fit come from coherence theories of truth that argue that the truth of any statement depends on its relationship to a prior system of statements (see Hempel 1935 for a discussion). Perhaps the most common contemporary examples of this view are formal models of behavior in fields like economics where the truth of an hypothesis is seen as depending on whether it coheres or conforms to a series of propositions that are typically specified in the form of a system of equations.[6]

Consider, for example, the most typical "tests" of human resource strategy that argue that different business goals or corporate strategies should be associated with a unique set of human resource practices. Such hypotheses are based on the following unspoken assertions:

(I) A particular business strategy demands a unique set of responses from employees (behaviors and attitudes) in order to succeed.

(II) A particular set of human resource policies produces a unique set of responses from employees.

Any argument about fit is really an hypothesis about the relationship between propositions I and II. And that hypothesis cannot be true unless both propositions are also true. For example, an hypothesis suggesting that firms pursuing a low-price market niche are more likely to be antiunion assumes the proposition that low-price strategies need to be reinforced by low labor costs *and* that anitiunion policies are associated with lower labor costs. If either proposition is false, then the results cannot be interpreted.

This description of the propositions within an hypothesis of fit suggests the main difficulty facing attempts to do research on strategy and human resources: we do not have a well-developed and empirically verified body of propositions associated with categories I and II. Until we can know more about what business strategies demand of human resources and what responses are associated with given human resource practices, it may be difficult to find relationships between them. Among the first recommendations for future research, therefore, should be to develop research on these background propositions.

The other unarticulated component of arguments about fit is an underlying or "background" theory of firms that creates the need for fit. In most instances, that unstated theory is based on a view of competitive markets. The assumption is that a lack of fit is associated with inefficiencies, competitive markets will drive firms with less effective practices out of business, and business strategies that are not reinforced by appropriate human resource practices will be less effective. All that survives to be observed, therefore, will be firms with good fit. This may in some cases be a reasonable assumption, but it is important to bear in mind that obviously it does not hold in certain industries or markets (e.g., public utilities, regulated industries) and that its importance in any situation is an empirical matter. As Johnson, Sambharya, and Bobko (1989) found, for example, there was no real fit between competitive strategy and wages in airlines under regulation presumably because there was no market pressure to drive out inefficient firms with bad fits. That pressure was there after regulation ended and markets became competitive, however, and so was a relationship between competitive strategy and wages.

Another problem is that tests of fit between human resources and competitive strategy may not be robust to the specifications of strategy; the various taxonomies of business strategy may classify the same firms differently because they focus on unique aspects of business plans or positions. It is possible, therefore, to find links between HR practices and one business strategy framework and not with another. Taxonomies of strategy that have been developed for strategic management and applied to human resources do not necessarily identify the factors with the greatest impact on employment matters, an issue to be explored later. Bamberger, Bacharach, and Dyer (1989), for example, find that the existing strategy frameworks do not predict HR practices well because they ignore important contingencies (e.g., stage of a firm's development and whether it is high tech) that can be shown to influence human resource practices.[7]

Strategy and Labor Relations

There are many important ways in which industrial relations (IR) research differs from traditional personnel research. For the purpose of this chapter, perhaps the most important is that employment outcomes in a unionized setting cannot be conceptualized as being dictated entirely by management. For unionized firms, the process of fitting human resource policies and practices to business strategies is only the beginning of the problem. Where outcomes are the result of bilateral, competitive bargaining, the process of achieving those outcomes takes on characteristics very similar to the competitive strategy decisions associated earlier with management product market decisions.

Although the recent development of strategic research in industrial relations began independently from other disciplines, several of the themes in IR research have contemporary precedents in other fields. Perhaps the first of these are the arguments associated with political economy that attached greater importance to management as an actor in employment relations. Marglin (1976) argued, for example, that management had an interest in control as well as in lowering costs. And management made fundamental business decisions—including choices of technology—to affect the organization of work and reduce the control that workers could exert.

A second stream of research in labor history took a more empirical path and emphasized the variance in management practices across employers, especially during the New Deal period of rapid union growth. The most important of these is Harris's

(1982) account, which indicates that big business in the United States reacted to unions in quite disparate ways ranging from acceptance to uncompromising hostility. As scholars like Nelson (1989) note, these early choices not only shaped labor relations in the 1930s but continue to shape it today.

IR researchers in Britain developed their own arguments about strategy and labor relations that also focused on the role of management. The concern there was very similar to that of U.S. labor historians: that management was an important and neglected player in labor relations whose choices in relations with unions ultimately had long-run implications for labor relations (see Gospel and Littler 1982; Purcell 1983; Purcell and Sisson 1983 for examples). The focus of this research was to see the relationship between management's labor relations decisions and labor relations outcomes. At least some of the move toward studying management in the U.K. was also the result of broader political issues, specifically, a conservative attack in the House of Lords against the government-funded Industrial Relations Center at the University of Warwick objecting to its emphasis on studies of trade union problems.

The other important precedent to U.S. strategic research in industrial relations were studies of union organizing campaigns and the relationship between management tactics and election outcomes. A series of studies showed definitively that management unfair labor practices influenced election outcomes (e.g., Dickens 1983), that management's use of consultants (a proxy for aggressive tactics) also shaped election outcomes (e.g., Lawler 1984), and that management's bargaining tactics—or lack of bargaining—determined whether election victories ever led to union contracts (e.g., Cooke 1985).

This line of research helped focus attention on management as a research topic. And the linking theme in all of these union organizing studies was that management *decisions* were under study, not technology, structures, or characteristics of the environment associated with systems theory (Dunlop 1957). The other important aspect of research on these management decisions is that the decisions were quite clearly choices made from sets of feasible outcomes. It is difficult to argue, for example, that management *had no choice* but to break the law through unfair labor practices. Even where management believed that unfair labor practices were the only way to prevent a union victory and that a union victory would lead to bankruptcy, for example, few business leaders would argue that market pressures necessarily take precedence over the law.

Kochan, McKersie, and Cappelli (1984) marks for many the beginning of a strategic perspective on industrial relations research. It began with an empirical problem: the extent of change in U.S. industrial relations and the variance in practices could not be explained by the prevailing paradigm that focused on conditions in the environment outside union and management relations. The decline in union organizing success, for example, could not be understood without examining the management practices just described in addition to the changes in the economy and society. The paper argued that the actors in industrial relations—unions, management, and the government—in many cases had some discretion in their decisions and that these discretionary decisions could be thought of as strategic choices.

It is useful to think of strategic choices in the context of competitive strategy, and of unions and management as competitors. Following Schelling (1960), these strategic choices are decisions designed to gain an advantage in the relationship with the party with which one is in conflict. After noting that there could be three distinct levels of decision making in a given relationship, Kochan, McKersie, and Cappelli (1984) then identify some of the basic management strategic choices that could affect the relationship with unions, and argue for their impact on IR outcomes. The paper's main empirical example illustrates how business strategy choices at the corporate level drove collective bargaining outcomes in the tire industry. Kochan, Katz, and McKersie (1986) extend this framework to explain most of the major changes in U.S. labor relations in the past decade or so.

The main contribution of this analysis might be the identification of new mechanisms through which management could change specific union-management relationships. The empirical benefit of this approach is in helping explain the variance in outcomes across relationships. To understand average changes in a population of relationships, such as changes in U.S. labor relations as a whole, it is still necessary to examine developments common to that population—in the environment. As Lewin (1987) notes, for example, the decline in union membership in the United States should ultimately be traced back to common environmental issues such as changes in public opinion and management values, even though those developments are being played out at the labor relations level through changes in management strategy.

The strategic research since Kochan, McKersie, and Cappelli (1984) has generally been empirical investigations of management choices (Stratton and Reshef 1990 are an exception, looking at unions). This research can be divided into two sets. The first set examines the relationship between management strategic choices in labor relations and labor relations outcomes—the "middle tier" of the Kochan, McKersie, and Cappelli (1984) framework. This research is closest to competitive strategy in its approach. A good deal of this research focuses on union organizing; Lawler and West (1985) find, for example, that union victories are fewer where management takes an aggressive stance in organizing campaigns, as do Cappelli and Chalykoff (1986). Verma (1985) shows how the shift of investment and capital from union to nonunion plants within the same firm substantially reduced unionization in that firm. Fiorito, Lowman, and Nelson (1987) find that management choices about human resource policies also reduce union organizing success, substituting in some ways for unions.

Related studies examined the relationship between management labor relations choices and collective bargaining outcomes. Kawla (1987) finds a relationship between corporate business decisions and settlements in steel. Cappelli and Chalykoff (1986) find lower settlements at firms that report a strategy of union avoidance. Cooke and Meyer (1990) make one of the more interesting extensions of this line of research by asking about the factors that determine management labor relations strategies.

The second set of strategic studies has focused on the relationship between management's corporate-level business decisions, or competitive strategy, and labor relations outcomes. Cappelli (1985a) examines the business strategies of airlines after deregulation and finds a relationship with management's collective bargaining demands and, in turn, with collective bargaining outcomes. Because the introduction of product market competition meant that all airlines had to develop a strategy for addressing competition, documenting changes in strategy and assessing the effects associated with these new strategies was easier to do. Johnson, Sambharya, and Bobko (1989) find a statistical relationship between airline business strategy (using the Miles and Snow [1978] typology of business strategies) and airline wages that is independent of economic factors such as ability to pay. Nay (1991), on the other hand, fails to find a relationship between business strategy and wages in airlines after controlling for carrier circumstances. One difficulty with Nay's test is that the strategic choice arguments stated that strategy affects a carrier's ability to pay (financial performance), which in turn affects bargaining outcomes, so it is not surprising to find no links between strategy and outcomes when controlling for a carrier's ability to pay.

Kochan, McKersie, and Chalykoff (1986) find that firm-level business strategies affect union election outcomes, and Cappelli and McKersie (1987) find that business strategies can affect the rate of work rule change at the "work place" level of the three-tier framework. Whitaker (1986) looks at how plant location decisions changed labor relations in a U.K. firm; Cappelli (1985b) shows how the choice of dealing with new technology (closing outmoded union plants and opening new nonunion plants v. retooling the union plants) drove collective bargaining outcomes in the tire industry. Sorge and Streeck (1988) find a relationship between Porter's (1980) taxonomy of business strategies and approaches to the employment issues associated with technological change. And Arthur (1992) represents an interesting bridge between the industrial relations and human resources literature in that he finds relationships between business strategies and systems of employment practices, only one part of which is labor relations.

The research on corporate business strategy and labor relations outcomes is typically distinct from the strategic HR literature in that the business strategies in the former are often chosen at least in part because of the consequences for labor relations; in HR research, the business strategies may be constrained by HR issues but rarely seem designed to influence them.

One point that has been missing throughout the research on collective bargaining is the specification of the mechanisms through which strategic choices affect outcomes: How do management decisions translate into collectively bargained outcomes? In the personnel research, the mechanism is straightforward; management dictates the outcome, and if the relationship is not clear, it is because management did not make it so.[8] In the union setting, management decisions affect the environment for collective bargaining and, indirectly, settlement outcomes. The derived demand for labor is the most basic mechanism through which this transmission occurs. For example, a management's decision to close a plant or to reinvest/divest from a plant, contingent on a negotiated settlement level in the future, confronts labor unions with a change in the demand for labor. For those who see settlements as represented by the intersection of derived demand and union preference functions, management's strategic choice changes the derived demand function and leads to a different intersection point and settlement outcome.

Lewin (1987) finds problems with the notion of strategy in industrial relations—presumably with the research on strategy and human resources as well—in part because of an idiosyncratic definition of what constitutes strategy. Lewin asserts that strategies are decisions that are not based on a reaction to the environment external to the organization.[9] It is difficult to imagine any nonexistential decision that could qualify as being strictly independent of the external environment. The entire field of strategic management, which, as Porter (1980, p. 3) notes, centers on "relating a company to its environment," fails to meet this test. Given that unions are part of an organization's environment, virtually all management labor relations decisions would be defined out of the strategy set. With this definition as a straw man, it is not surprising that Lewin finds no existing IR research qualifying as strategic.[10]

Although unstated, what Lewin appears to want as a test of "strategy" are examples of management IR decisions that cannot be interpreted as consistent with economic rationality; "researchers must be able to show how the concept of strategic choice differs from the economist's concept of choice" (Lewin 1987, p. 36). But the economist's notion that actors weigh costs and benefits and make choices to maximize utility is perfectly consistent with strategy research. Strategy merely considers the different processes for maximizing utility demanded by situations where the behavior of others both affects one's own outcomes and can be influenced by one's actions. Economists who study oligopolies, management strategy, and related situations have made it clear for generations that there are no conflicts between such studies and economic rationality (e.g., game theory where utility maximization remains the goal).

Where the distinction between strategy and more routine economic decisions would be relevant is in situations where business decisions are made without any intention of influencing labor relations that nevertheless have an effect on labor relations.

Holding aside the empirical question of whether such decisions ever occur, would they count as strategic or not? They would appear to fit under the strategic heading in personnel/human resources where the criterion is whether the business decisions themselves are strategic. They would not appear to fit the heading as used in IR where the criterion is more procedural—the intent of influencing union behavior.

The Future: A Resource-Based View of Strategy

Recently, research in management strategy has developed in a direction that may offer an important role for human resources. The empirical problem is again to explain why certain firms are able to earn above normal profits: what accounts for their competitive advantage? These resource-based arguments look within the firm itself (as opposed to the firm's position in relation to competitors) to suggest that firms have resources or capabilities that constitute strategic assets. These assets, in turn, contribute to competitive advantage.[11] Barney (1986), Wernerfelt (1984), and Rumelt (1984), for example, suggest that firms use the resources and capabilities they possess in order to gain advantage over their competitors, thereby increasing profits.[12]

It is important to understand the extent to which this approach departs from prior research. The competitive strategy, industrial/organizational economics approach argues that profits come from the positioning of the firm in relation to outside markets, and complementary assets such as people are presumably matched to the competitive strategy; the resource-based perspective emphasizes advantages generated within the firm through preferential access to productive inputs or superior capabilities. Competitive strategy positions in the latter are presumably driven by advantages generated by resources and capabilities. Penrose's (1959) view of the firm as a bundle of assets provides the basis for this approach. By examining their assets, firms can determine their unique strengths, adjust their position with respect to the market, and generate higher profits.

At least part of the debate between the competitive strategy and resource views will eventually turn on an empirical matter: Is it easier to rearrange complementary assets/resources, given the choice of strategy, or to rearrange strategy, given the set of complementary assets? Most arguments in management strategy have assumed implicitly that the former is easier, although research on the difficulties of achieving organizational change/rearranging resources may suggest otherwise. Kogut (1991), for example, surveys the literature on the transfer of practices associated with competitive advantage and concludes that innovations in organizational and management practices diffuse more slowly than innovations in technology.

Following Williamson (1975), Barney (1991) proposes that in order to generate competitive advantage, firm resources should be valuable, scarce among competitors with few substitutes, and difficult to transfer or imitate.[13] Amit and Shoemaker (1990) argue that such resources produce competitive advantage by allowing firms to pursue strategies that competitors cannot.

Immobility of resources across firms is the largest change from standard economic theory, and developing the assumption behind immobile assets is central to establishing that strategic resources exist. Dierickx and Cool (1989) suggest, for example, that factor markets are far from complete. Wernerfelt (1984) describes the specificity of factors that results as "resource barriers," similar to entry barriers in the competitive forces approach, and they may lead to excess rents in the same way.

The crucial question for strategy is whether there is something that the firm itself can do to gain these resources and secure competitive advantage from them—what Teece, Pisano, and Shuen (1990) refer to as the "dynamics capabilities" approach. For our purposes, the issue is whether human resource policies and practices can contribute to, indeed create, those crucial assets and resources: Can firms manage their human resources in a way that creates a scarce capability, and is that technique one that competitors cannot easily copy?

Human Resource Barriers

Perhaps the place to begin thinking about the relationship between human resources and the resource-based view of the firm is with an "ideal type" firm whose capabilities by definition flow from its employees. Professional service firms are an ideal type in that the firm sells nothing but the services of its principals. Further, assume that there is some subset of these firms—law, accounting, and medicine in particular—where the skills are largely produced outside of the firm (that is, the firm effectively cannot produce the esources itself), where the principals are homogeneous, and where there are no resource barriers in that the skills are general and transfer almost perfectly across competitors.

The ideal type firm represents the most limited case for producing competitive advantage through human resources. But even in this case, HR practices can help create resource barriers that prevent the loss of valued employees. Thompson (1967), in a precursor to the competitive strategy literature, argued that firms could create buffers to protect their core technologies and competencies from the uncertainties of the outside environment. HR practices can essentially do the same thing, protecting the core resource of employees from competition in the outside labor market in much the same way that the competitive strategy perspective sees firms protecting themselves from product market competition.

Compensation systems that "backload" payments through pensions or other deferred compensation arrangements, sometimes referred to as bonding models (e.g., Lazear 1979), retain employees by making it costly to quit. Internal labor markets also make it difficult for employees to leave by creating better opportunities within the firm than employees are likely to find outside it. Firm-specific skills and promotion from within help create these opportunities. As Becker (1975) points out, moving one's firm to a geographic area where there are no competitors helps limit the mobility of labor by forcing employees who quit to relocate their home and family.

The firms themselves may effectively collude to help reduce the mobility of labor and create resource barriers. In the airline industry, for example, the fact that all carriers have pilot labor contracts with very steep seniority pay provisions means that senior pilots have so much to lose by changing carriers that they almost never do so.[14] Tournament promotion systems in law and accounting firms, where associates compete over a fixed time period for principal positions, make it difficult for employees to leave without having to start the tournament over at another firm. In Sweden, the employer's association requires that its members not advertise job openings for fear that doing so would simply lead to turnover (and higher wages) at other employers.

The synergies of teamwork are an aspect of firm-specific human resources that creates a resource barrier even in these ideal type conditions. The ability to create teams may in itself be an important source of competitive advantage, as the right configuration of employees may produce superior outputs that make possible higher pay. The team concept may be imitated by competitors, however. But once a team exists, it may create its own resource barrier because the entire team would have to leave in order to shift the resource elsewhere. Surgical teams or research laboratory groups do on occasion shift employers, but the logistics involved are daunting enough to reduce the frequency.

There are many more ways to create resource barriers once the assumption that employees are homogeneous is relaxed. The "match quality" argument in labor economics (Jovanovic 1979) suggests that the fit between employees and jobs is idiosyncratic. A good fit is hard to achieve but yields higher productivity and wages for the employee. A firm able to offer a different mix of terms and conditions may be able to make a better match with employees who have different preferences (e.g., a Colorado-based company may attract employees who like to ski even with a lower salary), and such employees will be reluctant to leave.

The ability to hold on to human resources by making it difficult for people to leave also has its drawbacks, however. There may be situations where it is desirable to get existing people out, either to downsize the organization or to replace them in order to facilitate organizational change. Internal labor markets and other buffers mean that voluntary turnover is sharply reduced, implying that the firm has to rely on more expensive measures, such as severance and early retirement packages, or options that may damage morale, such as layoffs. Firms that find turnover necessary (e.g., high tech firms concerned about engineering obsolescence) may find these buffers less useful.

Skills as a Resource

Relaxing the assumption that skills are produced outside the firm moves the discussion to how HR practices can help create resources. The most obvious employee resources are employees' knowledge, skills, and abilities. As Becker (1975) observed, employers are unlikely to provide general skills training, skills equally useful for all competitors for which the market wage must be paid, because there is no way to recoup the cost.[15] But they may provide a system where employees pay for the general skills themselves through lower wages during the training period. Not all firms are equally able to provide these apprentice-type arrangements; the scale economies associated with providing such training mean that large employers are much more likely to offer general training programs.

Firm-specific skills are perhaps the most obvious source of competitive advantage associated with employees. Employers must pay for the acquisition of those skills, but they recoup virtually all of the gains from them.[16] As Bishop's (1991) survey concludes, the highest economic returns come from on-the-job training, which is the most employer-specific type. There is also clear evidence of path dependence in firm-provided training. For example, employees with more education and more prior training are the most likely to receive additional training (see Bishop). This result is similar to the absorptive capacity (Cohen and Levinthal 1990) position that prior investment in research and development affects the ability of an organization to learn and then to innovate. As Bartel and Lichtenberg (1987) found earlier, firms whose employees had higher levels of skill were able to change and adapt to new technologies more quickly.

Equal in importance to programs that create skill are other human resource practices that can support the development of skill. Among the most significant of these is employment security. Because the returns to an investment in skill are paid out over time, employee turnover can destroy those returns and make investments in skill unprofitable. The kind of internal labor market practices noted earlier reduce voluntary turnover, but the firms also need to worry about involuntary turnover, especially layoffs of the kind that often accompany business cycles. Reducing these layoffs typically requires adjustments in business practices—taking on less cyclical business, for example—that not all firms are in a position to do.

Winter (1987) argues that despite extensive discussion of distinctive competencies within firm (Andrews 1971), not much work has been done in uncovering the conditions under which knowledge can be strategically valuable. He proposes four characteristics of knowledge that vary in their effect on strategic value: tacitness, teachability, observability, and complexity. He also notes variation in these characteristics by industry. The knowledge embedded in the work force is clearly an asset of the firm. Linking the characteristics of firm-specific knowledge with characteristics of the firm's human resource profile and its competitive position could be an important connection across fields of research.

One implication of the resource-based view concerns the extent of diversification. Wernerfelt (1984) suggests that if a firm has a strategic capability it should exploit that capability in other industries. Hitt and Ireland (1985) discuss functional capabilities that a firm may want to transfer to its other business units. Prahalad and Hamel's (1990) notion that a firm's "core competency" is its source of competitive advantage is similar.[17] Kogut (1991) argues that the relevant capability that drove expansion of U.S. firms into international markets was a human resource issue: superior systems for organizing work associated with scientific management.

The Difficulties of Imitating

Many desirable outcomes associated with employees and their management are difficult to achieve. For example, positive employee work attitudes are an important competitive advantage, especially in customer contact jobs, but even academic research has had relatively few lessons concerning how employers might improve work attitudes (see Cappelli and Sherer 1991). Securing workrule changes, for example, requires a series of conditions including the right combination of business strategy decisions and employment practices (see Cappelli and McKersie 1987).

Many human resource practices are known to produce relatively clear employee responses, especially in the area of compensation. And while these relationships are clearly imitable, it may not be in every firm's interest to adopt them. For example, firms offering above market wages may reduce turnover and secure superior performance even from current employees who fear losing their wage premium if they quit or were fired, the argument now known as "efficiency wages" in economics. A formal restaurant may find the cost of resource barriers worth the investment because a high-quality service team that develops personal relationships matters to their customers; a fast-food restaurant may find those barriers not worth the money because their low-price market niche is sustained by a lower-wage service team where turnover may not matter. Executive compensation programs that change how the CEO is rewarded have been shown to produce clear changes in characteristics of firm performance. These programs can also be easily imitated by competitors, but not all firms would find the same performance outcomes useful.

Even where given employee relations practices are useful for all competitors, it is not obvious that every competitor has the complementary assets necessary to introduce them. Lippman and Rumelt (1982) introduce the notion of "uncertain imitability" in strategic management, which argues that even well known practices can be a source of competitive advantage where special assets and capabilities are necessary to imitate them. For example, Continental Airlines adopted a low-fare business strategy that was based on low labor costs made possible by breaking its unions through bankruptcy proceedings following a 1983 strike. Although many carriers would like to have mimicked Continental's outcome, none had the circumstances (mainly unions in disarray) to do so. Similarly, General Motors was able to reduce its union work force (temporarily) and test out innovative, nonunion work practices in the 1970s by opening new, nonunion plants in the south, a strategy that competitors lacking both the scale and resources of GM could not follow. The more recent difficulty that GM has had in transferring the success of its work practices from NUMMI to the rest of its plants suggests how difficult such transfers are even within the same organization where barriers to information are relatively free.

Many programs have potentially important impacts on productivity and are relatively easy to introduce, but their impact is only achieved when combined with related programs. And introducing these complementary programs may be difficult. Gainsharing, for example, appears ineffective in securing productivity improvements unless linked to worker participation (see Levine and Strauss 1989). Participation is a much more difficult concept to introduce. Cutcher-Gershenfeld, Kochan, and Verma (in Gershenfeld 1987) argue, for example, that the successes of participation programs themselves only endure where there are "fundamental structural changes in the labor-management relationship." And these fundamental changes in structure are even more difficult to achieve than participation.

Further, programs that are easily imitated by themselves may be difficult to copy when combined into a package. Nordstrom's, for example, combines simple concepts such as tournament-based compensation and promotion systems, motivational training, and virtual complete employee autonomy to achieve sales service levels that, in turn, drive the company's business strategy and create its market. Yet, as their vice-president for human resources notes, competitors have been unable to duplicate Nordstrom's service level: "It's so simple, but they just can't put it together."

International Extension

The current public policy debate in the United States concerning national competitiveness is based on the view that human resources are in large part the factor that drives competitive advantage. Piore and Sabel (1984) argue that mass markets based on large production runs are increasingly dominated by low-skill, low-wage countries because the technology for such production (mainly automation) is easily transferable across national borders, and costs are therefore the only source of competitive advantage. Markets where high quality and innovation are valued, in contrast, must be met with production systems that are based less on mass production and assembly line technology and more on highly skilled, flexible work forces.

These debates begin with the argument that the success of our major competitors such as Japan and Germany results from manufacturing strategies made possible by their workers. In Japan, early skill shortages, Allied-imposed labor laws, and other historical baggage created an employment system characterized by low turnover, high investment in firm-specific skills, and job security; this system made possible products driven by rapid innovation and dictated a market share competitive strategy. The historically based apprenticeship system in Germany and welfare-state employment regulations created a high-cost, high-skill work force that virtually forced employers to target high-quality/high-margin sections of their product markets.

In the United States, in contrast, a number of reports have suggested that skill levels are related to competitiveness in foreign markets. Some argue that firms have had to de-skill jobs and reorganize the way they do business in order to match the lower skills of the incoming work force (National Center on Education and the Economy 1990); others suggest that U.S. manufacturing in particular is being forced out of the high-quality/innovative segments of markets because our low-skill systems of work organization cannot address them (Office of Technology Assessment 1990).

Conclusions

This discussion began with the arguments of human resource strategy, where the focus was on choosing employment policies and practices that reinforce business strategies. Research on the strategic perspective in industrial relations, on the other hand, focused on how management decisions, typically at the business strategy level, affect labor relations outcomes. We would like to stand these arguments on their respective heads and ask how employment practices—human resources and labor relations—affect competitive advantage and, ultimately, business strategy.

This point of view is distinct from prior research; it notes how employment policies and practices create resources and competencies that achieve competitive advantages. There are many well known examples of companies in which the characteristics of employees and work systems created business strategy, not simply reinforced it: at People Express, for example, where the low-fare and flexible scheduling strategy was created by a combination of human resource practices that produced low-cost, flexible systems of work organization; and at Lincoln Electric, where the high-quality and moderate-price product strategy is made possible by a highly skilled, productive, and committed work force. An employment system characterized by gainsharing, job security, participation programs, and a strong organizational culture made that possible.

The next step in this proposed research program would be to show how business strategies are adapted to fit the assets and resources created by these employment systems. At Hewlett-Packard, for example, the company routinely adjusts its business decisions in this manner; the company avoids proprietary contract work because the fluctuations in production entailed in such work would disrupt its job security and internal labor market programs.

Perhaps the most important element in the research program we propose is the perspective that competitive advantage arises from firm-specific, valuable resources that are difficult to imitate. With this perspective, an important research question relates to the role of human resource policies in the creation of valuable, firm-specific skills. A related question addresses the processes of diffusion or imitation of successful human resource practices across firms. A core agenda for the future is the development of an empirical base relating human resource policies to rent-generating resources of the firm. Such an empirical base will help develop more refined perspectives on human resource decisions that particularly impact long-term profits earned by the firm.

Endnotes

[1] In brief, he found that firms did not change their organizational structure unless faced with a crisis that demanded a new set of business goals (strategy), but when they did, the new structure was based upon the firm's new strategy.

[2] Schuler (1991) provides a thorough review of how a strategic perspective changes the human resource function.

[3] Other pressures that drove personnel toward a strategic perspective include general "open systems" critiques that research in the field was theoretically vacuous unless it was linked to some broader set of issues or context (Zedeck and Cascio 1984). But the move toward a strategic link was not empirically motivated, as opposed to that move in industrial relations (see later). That is, the academic development of strategic human resources was not designed to address academic problems. For example, there appears to have been little discussion or appreciation of the possibility that strategy could help explain the variance in human resource practices across firms. Only recently has this variance become a research topic, and so far it seems restricted to matters of compensation. Balkin and Gomez-Mejia (1984) and Gerhart and Milkovich (1990) consider explanations for why compensation practices differ, and Weber and Rynes (1991) examine how the variance in specific pay decisions can be traced to broader strategies of compensation. Instead, the move in personnel was normatively motivated: helping employers improve the performance of business strategy.

[4] Other studies had linked human resource practices to business goals (e.g., Fombrun 1982; Ellis 1982), but the concept of fit with union business strategies was generally ignored. Other studies set out frameworks for thinking about the fit between strategy and specific human resource practices such as management succession (Stumpf and Hanrahan 1984) and overall planning (Olian and Rynes 1984).

[5] Two interesting Ph.D. theses in progress—by Larry Hunter at MIT and Mark Usled at SUNY Buffalo—are also using survey data to examine issues of fit between human resource practices and business strategies.

[6] Coherence theories have historically been abandoned in most fields in favor of correspondence theories of truth, which judge the truth of an hypothesis based on its correspondence with reality—empirical tests.

[7] There is also the practical matter, as Venkatraman (1989) notes, that the word "fit" can be used to describe at least six different relationships, each with its own theoetical meaning and each requiring a different analytical approach to testing. Lack of care in differentiating the potential relationships associated with a fit hypothesis is an area for concern.

[8] In practice, of course, employers do not have complete control over personnel practices or employee responses. Outside factors such as employment law and markets provide constraints on their actions, and the general problems in securing organizational change make it difficult to introduce new policies or secure different responses from employees. It would be an interesting research question to evaluate the effects of these constraints on the fit between business strategies and human resource practices.

[9] For example, Lewin objects to Cappelli's (1985) argument that corporate decisions altering the wage-employment tradeoff for unions were strategic because "it appears to have occurred as a reaction to a key environmental change rather than in anticipation of or as a result of strategic planning for such a change" (p. 18). He later argues that all of the strategy research on collective bargaining "can just as readily be interpreted . . . (as) reacting to major environmental changes. . . ." (p. 22). When discussing innovations such as quality of worklife programs, he argues that "the parties are basically reacting to external environmental pressures" (p. 24) and that these innovations therefore cannot be strategic.

[10] One consequence of this peculiar view of strategy is that Lewin seems to demand that there must be one "strategic" option among any set of choices and a corresponding set of nonstrategic options, independent of context. For example, he objects to the fact that various union-management cooperation policies have been labelled strategic at different times: "Once more and lacking a sense of parsimony, it appears that every choice is labeled 'strategic'!" (p. 29). Following Schelling (1960) and all strategy research since, strategy is simply the decision process of trying to influence outcomes where there are competitors. Any tactic, therefore, can be strategic so long as the goal is to influence outcomes.

[11] Amit and Shoemaker (1990) suggest that resources are assets used as inputs—capital or patents—that could be transferred between competitors, while capabilities are more intangible assets specific to a given firm that constitute a kind of intermediate good, such as the capability to change products quickly.

[12] This work complements the earlier work of Porter (1980), which suggested that firms can create competitive advantage by tying their competitive strategies to the underlying economics of the industry.

[13] It is easy to see that the definition of resources currently in use in the early theoretical pieces are too broad. However, it is also clear that Barney's (1991) propositions are steps in the right direction, in that they attempt to specify conditions under which firm resources can contribute to competitive advantage. There is also a tautological quality to the definition of valuable resources, but this may be worked out over time by subsequent authors. The attempt to specify conditions under which firm resources are sources of competitive advantage is well conceived.

[14] Common union contracts provide the mechanism that enforces these steep seniority provisions, but these provisions do not appear to have been the result of union demands. Indeed, efforts to steepen the salary schedules in recent years have come from management (e.g., two-tier wage programs). There is no evidence of management initiatives to flatten salary schedules or to encourage mobility across carriers through other means.

[15] Given their opportunities in the market, employees must be paid the value of their marginal product—their market wage—and there is no surplus between wage and marginal product to recoup the employer's training costs.

[16] Following Becker (1975), there is no market for these skills, so the employee cannot necessarily secure any wage gain from them. For that reason, the employer has to pay to generate them. In practice, the situation is a bilateral monopoly, and the employer may share some of the gains from increased productivity to keep employees from leaving. Castanias and Helfat (1991) discuss managerial skill as a resource that leads to superior profits and follow Becker (1975) in noting that only firm-specific skills add value to the firm.

[17] Once a firm establishes that an asset is rare and difficult to imitate, one might expect corporations to operate in several different industries, deriving superior profits from that asset in each of them. The empirical evidence, however, does not bear this out. Schmanlensee (1985) did not find significant firm effects and Rumelt (1991) found that business-level effects produced the dominant difference. Perhaps if the capability is easy to transfer within the corporation, then it is also easily imitated.

References

Abowd, John M., and Joseph S. Tracey. "Market Structure, Strike Activity, and Union Wage Settlements." *Industrial Relations* 28 (Spring 1989), pp. 227-50.

Amit, Raphael, and Paul J. M. Shoemaker. "Key Success Factors: Their Nature and Determinants." Unpublished working paper, Northwestern University, January 1990.

Andrews, K. *The Concept of Corporate Strategy*. Homewood, IL: Richard D. Irwin, 1980 (1971).

Ansoff, Igor H. *Corporate Strategy*. New York: McGraw-Hill, 1965.

Arthur, Jeffrey B. "The Link Between Business Strategy and Industrial Relations Systems in American Steel Minimills." *Industrial and Labor Relations Review* 45 (April 1992), pp. 488-506.

Bain, J. S. *Industrial Organization*. New York: Wiley, 1959.

Balkin, D. B., and Luis R. Gomez-Mejia. "Determinants of R&D Compensation Strategy in High Tech Industry." *Personnel Psychology* 37, 4 (1984), pp. 635-50.

Bamberger, Peter, Samuel Bacharach, and Lee Dyer. "Human Resources Management and Organizational Effectiveness: High Technology Entrepreneurial Startup Firms in Israel." *Human Resource Management* 28 (Fall 1989), pp. 349-66.

Barney, J. B. "Strategic Factor Markets: Expectations, Luck, and Business Strategy." *Management Science* 32 (October 1986), pp. 1231-41.

________. "Firm Resources and the Theory of Competitive Advantage." *Journal of Management* 17 (1991), pp. 199-220.

Bartel, Ann P., and Frank R. Lichtenberg. "The Comparative Advantage of Educated Workers in Implementing New Technology." *Review of Economics and Statistics* 69 (February 1987), pp. 1-11.

Becker, Gary S. *Human Capital: A Theoretical and Empirical Analysis*. New York: Columbia University Press, 1975.

Bishop, John H. "The Impact of Previous Training in Schools and on Job on Productivity, Required OJT, and Turnover of New Hires." Unpublished manuscript, Center for Advanced Human Resource Studies, Cornell University, 1991.

Burack, Elmer H. "Linking Corporate Business and Human Resource Planning: Strategic Issues and Concerns." *Human Resource Planning* (1985), pp. 133-45.

Cappelli, Peter. "Plant-Level Concession Bargaining." *Industrial and Labor Relations Review* 39 (October 1985), pp. 90-104.

________. "Competitive Pressures and Labor Relations in the Airline Industry." *Industrial Relations* 24 (Fall 1985), pp. 316-38.

Cappelli, Peter, and John Chalykoff. "The Effects of Management Industrial Relations Strategy: Results of a Survey." *Proceedings of the 38th Annual Meeting, Industrial Relations Research Association*. Madison, WI: IRRA, 1986, pp. 171-78.

Cappelli, Peter, and Robert B. McKersie. "Management Strategies and the Redesign of Jobs," *Journal of Management Studies* 24 (September 1987), pp. 441-62.

Cappelli, Peter, and Peter D. Sherer. "The Missing Role of Context in Organizational Behavior Research: A Mexo-Approach." In *Research in Organizational Behavior*, eds. L. L. Cummings and Barry M. Staw. Greenwich, CT: JAI Press, 1991.

Castanias, R. E., and C. E. Helfat. "Managerial Resources and Rents." *Journal of Management* 17 (1991), pp. 155-72.

Caves, Richard E., and Michael Porter. "From Entry Barriers to Mobility Barriers: Conjectural Decisions and Contrived Deterrence to New Competition." *Quarterly Journal of Economics* 91 (1977), pp. 241-62.

Chandler, Alfred D. "Strategy and Structure." Cambridge, MA: MIT Press, 1962.

Cohen, Wesley M., and Daniel A. Levinthal. "Absorptive Capacity: A New Perspective on Learning and Innovation." *Administrative Science Quarterly* 35 (1990), pp. 128-52.

Commons, John R. "American Shoemakers, 1648-1895: A Sketch of Industrial Evolution." *Quarterly Journal of Economics* 24 (November 1919), pp. 39-84.

Cooke, William N. "Failure to Negotiate First Contracts: Determinants and Policy Implications." *Industrial and Labor Relations Review* 38 (January 1985), pp. 163-78.

Cooke, William N., and David G. Meyer. "Structural and Market Predictors of Corporate Labor Relations Strategies." *Industrial and Labor Relations Review* 43 (January 1990), pp. 280-93.

Craft, James A. "A Critical Perspective on Human Resources Planning." *Human Resource Planning* 3 (June 1980), pp. 39-52.

Dickens, William T. "Effects of Company Campaigns on Certification Elections: Law and Reality Once Again." *Industrial and Labor Relations Review* 36 (July 1983), pp. 560-75.

Dierickx, I., and K. Cool. "Asset Stock Accumulation and Sustainability of Competitive Advantage." *Management Science* 35 (December 1989), pp. 1504-11.

Dunlop, John T. *Industrial Relations Systems*. New York: Holt, 1957.
Dyer, Lee. "Strategic Human Resources Management and Planning." In *Research in Personnel and Human Resources Management*, ed. Kenneth Rowland. Greenwich, CT: JAI Press, 1984.
Ellis, R. J. "Improving Management Response in Turbulent Times." *Sloan Management Review* 23, 2 (1982), pp. 3-12.
Ferris, Gerald R., Gail S. Russ, Robert Albanese, and Joseph J. Martocchio. "Personnel/Human Resource Management, Unionization, and Strategy Determinants of Organizational Performance." *Human Resource Planning* 13, 3 (1990), pp. 215-27.
Fiorito, Jack, Christopher Lowman, and Forest B. Nelson. "The Impact of Human Resource Policies on Union Organizing." *Industrial Relations* 26 (Spring 1987), pp. 113-26.
Fombrun, C. "Environmental Trends Create New Pressures on Human Resources." *Journal of Business Strategy* 3, 1 (1982), pp. 61-9.
Galbraith, Jay, and Daniel Nathanson. *Strategy Implementation*. St. Paul, MN: West Publishing, 1978.
Gerhart, Barry, and George T. Milkovich. "Organizational Differences in Managerial Compensation and Financial Performance." *Academy of Management Journal* 33, 4 (1990), pp. 663-91.
Gershenfeld, Walter J. "Employee Participation in Firm Decisions." In *Human Resources and the Performance of the Firm*, eds. Morris M. Kleiner et al. Madison, WI: Industrial Relations Research Association, 1987.
Gospel, Howard, and Craig Littler. *Managerial Strategies and Industrial Relations*. London: Heineman, 1982.
Gupta, A. K., and V. Govindarajan. "Business Unit Strategy, Managerial Characteristics, and Business Unit Effectiveness at Strategy Implementation." *Academy of Management Journal* 9 (1984), pp. 25-41.
Hambrick, D. "High Profit Strategies in Mature Capital Goods Industries: A Contingency Approach." *Academy of Management Journal* 26, 2 (1983), pp. 687-707.
Harris, Howwell John. *The Right to Manage: Industrial Relations Policies of American Business in the 1940s*. Madison, WI: University of Wisconsin Press, 1982.
Hempel, C. G. "On the Logical Positivists' Theory of Truth." *Analysis* 2, 4 (1935), pp. 49-59.
Hendricks, Wallace. "Labor Market Structure and Union Wage Levels." *Economic Inquiry* 13 (September 1975), pp. 401-16.
Hitt, M. A., and R. D. Ireland. "Corporate Distinctive Competence, Strategy, Industry, and Performance." *Strategic Management Journal* 6 (1985), pp. 273-93.
Johnson, Nancy Brown, Rakesh B. Sambharya, and Philip Bobko. "Deregulation, Business Strategy, and Wages in the Airline Industry." *Industrial Relations* 28 (Fall 1989), pp. 419-30.
Jovanovic, Boyan. "Job Matching and the Theory of Turnover." *Journal of Political Economy* 87 (October 1979), pp. 972-90.
Kawla, Richard W. "Collective Bargaining in Steel: A Strategic Perspective." *Proceedings of the 39th Annual Meeting of the Industrial Relations Research Association*. Madison, WI: IRRA, 1987.
Kerr, J. L. "Diversification Strategies and Managerial Rewards: An Empirical Study." *Academy of Management Journal* 28 (1985), pp. 155-79.
Kobrin, Stephen J. "Multinational Strategy and International Human Resource Management Policy." Working paper of the Wharton School's Reginal Jones Center, Philadelphia, PA, 1992.
Kochan, Thomas A., and John Chalykoff. "The Effects of Corporate Strategy and Workplace Innovations on Union Representation." *Industrial and Labor Relations Review* 39 (July 1986), pp. 487-501.
Kochan, Thomas A., Harry C. Katz, and Robert B. McKersie. The Transformation of Industrial Relations. Boston: Basic Books, 1986.

Kochan, Thomas A., Robert B. McKersie, and Peter Cappelli. "Strategic Choice and Industrial Relations Theory." *Industrial Relations* 23 (Winter 1984), pp. 16-39.

Kogut, Bruce. "Country Capabilities and the Permeability of Borders." *Strategic Management Journal* 12, 3 (1991), pp. 33-47.

Lawler, John J. "The Influence of Management Consultants on the Outcome of Union Certification Elections." *Industrial and Labor Relations Review* 38 (October 1984), pp. 38-51.

Lawler, John J., and Robin West. "Impact of Union-Avoidance Strategy in Union Representation Elections." *Industrial Relations* 24 (Fall 1985), pp. 406-20.

Lazear, Edward. "Why Is There Mandatory Retirement?" *Journal of Political Economy* 87 (December 1979), pp. 261-84.

Levine, David I., and George Strauss. "Employee Participation and Involvement." In *Investing in People: A Strategy to Address America's Workforce Crisis. Background Papers, Vol. 1.* Washington, D.C.: U.S. Department of Labor, Commission on Workforce Quality and Labor Market Efficiency, 1989.

Lewin, David. "Industrial Relations as a Strategic Variable." In *Human Resources and Firm Performance*, eds. Morris M. Kleiner et al. Madison, WI: IRRA, 1987.

Lippman, S., and R. Rumelt. "Uncertain Imitability: An Analysis of Interfirm Difference In Efficiency Under Competition." *Bell Journal of Economics* 13 (1982), pp. 418-38.

Lorsch, Jay, and Stephen Allen. *Managing Diversity and Interdependence*. Boston, MA: Harvard Business School, 1973.

MacDuffie, John Paul. "Beyond Mass Production: Organizational Flexibility and Manufacturing Performance in the World Auto Industry." Unpublished manuscript, The Wharton School, 1992.

MacDuffie, John Paul, and Thomas A. Kochan. "Does the U.S. Underinvest in Training? Determinants of Training in the World Economy." Presentation at the Academy of Management Annual Meeting, 1991.

Marglin, Stephen. "What Do Bosses Do?" In *The Division of Labor*, ed. A. Gorz. Atlantic Highlands, NJ: Humanities Press, 1976.

Miles, Raymond E., and Charles C. Snow. *Organizational Strategy, Structure, and Process*. New York: McGraw-Hill, 1978.

Nathanson, Daniel, and James Cassano. "Organization Diversity and Performance." *The Wharton Magazine* (Summer 1982), pp. 18-26.

National Center on Education and the Economy. *America's Choice: High Skills or Low Wages?* Rochester, NY, 1990.

Nay, Leslie. "The Determinants of Concession Bargaining in the Airline Industry." *Industrial and Labor Relations Review* 44 (January 1991), pp. 307-23.

Nelson, Daniel. "Managers and Nonunion Workers in the Rubber Industry: Union Avoidance Strategies in the 1930s." *Industrial and Labor Relations Review* 43 (October 1989), pp. 41-52.

Office of Technology Assessment, U.S. Congress. *Manufacturing in the U.S.* Washington, D.C.: GPO, 1990.

Olian, J. D., and S. L. Rynes. "Organizational Staffing: Integrating Practice with Strategy." *Industrial Relations* 23, 2 (1984), pp. 170-83.

Penrose, E. *The Theory of the Growth of the Firm*. London: Basil Blackwell, 1959.

Piore, Michael J., and Charles Sabel. *The Second Industrial Divide*. Boston: Basic Books, 1984.

Porter, Michael E. *Competitive Strategy*. New York: Free Press, 1980.

Prahalad, C. K., and G. Hamel. "The Core Competence of the Corporation." *Harvard Business Review* (May-June 1990), pp. 79-91.

Purcell, John. "The Management of Industrial Relations in the Modern Corporation: Agenda for Research." *British Journal of Industrial Relations* 21 (March 1983), pp. 1-16.

Purcell, John, and Keith Sisson. "Strategies and Practices in the Management of Industrial Relations." In *Industrial Relations in Britain*, ed. G. S. Bain. Oxford: Basil Blackwell, 1983.

Quinn, J. B. "Strategic Change: Logical Incrementalism." *Sloan Management Review* 20 (1978), pp. 7-21.

Rumelt, R. P. "Towards a Strategic Theory of the Firm." In *Competitive Strategic Management*, ed. R. B. Lamb. Englewood Cliffs, NJ: Prentice-Hall, 1984.

________. "How Much Does Industry Matter?" *Strategic Management Journal* 12, 3 (1991), pp. 167-85.

Schelling, Thomas. *The Strategy of Conflict*. Cambridge, MA: Harvard University Press, 1960.

Schmalensee, Richard. "Do Markets Differ Much?" *American Economic Review* 75, 3 (1985), pp. 341-51.

Schuler, Randall S. "Strategic Human Resource Management: Linking the People with the Business at all Organizational Levels." Unpublished manuscript, New York University, 1991.

Schuler, Randall S., and Susan E. Jackson. "Determinants of Human Resource Management Priorities and Implications for Industrial Relations." *Journal of Management* 15, 1 (1989), pp. 89-99.

Schuler, Randall S., and James W. Walker. "Human Resources Strategy: Focusing on Issues and Actions." *Organizational Dynamics* 1, 18 (1990), pp. 5-19.

Smith, E. C. "Strategic Business Planning and Human Resources: Part I." *Personnel Journal* 61, 8 (1982), pp. 606-10.

Smith, D. S., and G. R. Ferris. "Strategic Human Resource Management and Firm Effectiveness in Industries Experiencing Decline." *Human Resource Management* 25 (1988), pp. 441-58.

Sorge, Arndt, and Wolfgang Streeck. "Industrial Relations and Technological Change." In *New Technology and Industrial Relations*, eds. Richard Hyman and Wolfgang Streeck. Oxford: Basil Blackwell, 1988.

Stratton, Kay, and Yonatan Reshef. "Private Sector Unions and Strategic Planning." *Relations Industrielles* 45, 1 (1990), pp. 76-93.

Stumpf, S. A., and N. M. Hanrahan. "Designing Organizational Career Management Practices to Fit the Strategic Management Objectives." In *Readings in Personnel and Human Resource Management*, eds. R. S. Schuler and S. A. Youngblood. St. Paul, MN: West Publishers, 1984.

Teece, David J., Gary Pisano, and Amy Shuen. "Firm Capabilities, Resources, and the Concept of Strategy: Four Paradigms of Strategic Management." Unpublished manuscript, University of California at Berkeley, December 1990.

Thompson, J. D. *Organizations in Action*. New York: McGraw-Hill, 1967.

Tichy, Noel M., Charles J. Fombrun, and Mary Anne Devanna. "Strategic Human Resource Management." *Sloan Management Review* 22 (Winter 1982), pp. 47-60.

Tosi, H. L., Jr., and J. W. Slocum, Jr. "Contingency Theory: Some Suggested Directions." *Journal of Management* 10, 3 (1984), pp. 9-26.

Van de Ven, A. H., and R. Drazin. "The Concept of Fit in Contingency Theory." In *Research in Organizational Behavior*, eds. L. L. Cummings and B. M. Staw. Greenwich, CT: JAI Press, 1985.

Venkatraman, N. "The Concept of Fit in Strategy Research: Toward Verbal and Statistical Correspondence." *Academy of Management Review* 14, 3 (1989), pp. 423-44.

Verma, Anil. "Relative Flow of Capital to Union and Nonunion Plants within the Same Firm." *Industrial Relations* 24 (Fall 1985), pp. 395-405.

Walker, James W. *Human Resource Planning*. New York: McGraw-Hill, 1980.

Weber, Caroline L., and Sara L. Rynes. "Effects of Compensation Strategy on Job Pay Decisions." *Academy of Management Journal* 34 (March 1991), pp. 86-109.

Wernerfelt, B. "A Resource-Based View of the Firm." *Strategic Management Journal* 5 (1984), pp. 171-80.

Whitaker, Alan. "Managerial Strategy and Industrial Relations: A Case Study of Plant Relocation." *Journal of Management Studies* 23 (November 1986), pp. 656-78.

Williamson, Oliver E. *Markets and Hierarchies*. New York: Free Press, 1975.

Winter, Sidney. "Knowledge and Competence as Strategic Assets." In *The Competitive Challenge*, ed. David J. Teece. Cambridge, MA: Ballinger, 1987.

Zedeck, Sheldon, and Wayne F. Cascio. "Psychological Issues in Personnel Decisions." *Annual Review of Psychology* 35 (1984), pp. 461-519.

CHAPTER 6

Pay, Performance, and Participation

BARRY GERHART, GEORGE T. MILKOVICH, AND BRIAN MURRAY
Cornell University

The employment relationship can be thought of as an exchange process where employees provide contributions such as skill and effort in return for various inducements from the employer (March and Simon 1958). This relationship has been conceived as a contract, either explicit (as in a written collective bargaining agreement) or implicit, that carries reciprocal obligations and returns for both parties (Barnard 1936; Simon 1951; Azariadis 1975; Williamson, Wachter, and Harris 1975; Rousseau 1990). Policies having to do with employee relations, employment security, and compensation that might otherwise be difficult to explain are sometimes more readily understood in this context.

The focus of this chapter is on pay or compensation (the terms are used interchangeably here), a key issue in most employment relationships. From the perspective of the employee, pay has an important influence on standard of living, status, and security. Less direct forms of compensation such as health care, pensions, and other benefits also have an important impact on employees' well-being. From the employer's point of view, compensation is both a major cost of doing business that needs to be controlled, and an investment that must generate adequate returns in terms of employee attitudes, skills, behaviors, and organization performance.

A major task from a human resource management and industrial relations perspective is to understand how to design and administer compensation policies that best meet the goals (partly overlapping, partly conflicting) of employers and employees in the employment exchange. As, however, the most recent review of compensation and performance published in an IRRA research volume noted, there have been significant gaps in the knowledge needed to do so: "Our survey of the literature on the relationship between the compensation policies a firm pursues and its economic performance leads us inevitably to the conclusion that we know very little about it" (Ehrenberg and Milkovich 1987, p. 113).

Although there remains, of course, a great deal to learn, some progress has been made in the years since the Ehrenberg and Milkovich review. In the present chapter, we survey some of the recent evidence on pay and performance. Another paper of ours (Gerhart and Milkovich 1992) provides a comprehensive review of the measurement, determinants, and consequences (including performance) of compensation decisions. We draw on that review to some extent here.

The present chapter focuses on three features. First, we emphasize that compensation decisions and employment contracts occur in the context of specific (and differing) organizations. This implies that organization differences in pay decisions should be an important focus of future research, as should the determinants and consequences of such differences. Empirically, this means that more data need to be collected using the organization as the sampling unit.

Moreover, because pay is multidimensional (Heneman and Schwab 1979; Heneman 1985; Ehrenberg and Milkovich 1987), breaking out into level, structure, individual pay determination, benefits, and administration issues, organization differences on each dimension need to be identified and evaluated in terms of their significance. To the degree that such differences are large, their determinants and consequences warrant study.

Second, to reinforce our points regarding the importance of organization differences and the need to look beyond pay level, we present new empirical evidence on organization differences in the market sensitivity of their internal pay structures.

A third and final focus is on the potential importance of process or administration issues in the success or failure of pay decisions (Gomez-Mejia and Balkin 1992; Gerhart and Milkovich 1992). Employee participation in decision making (PDM) receives the bulk of our attention in this area, partly because general PDM research is fairly extensive and partly because of the important role attached to it in a recent volume of review essays on pay and productivity (Blinder 1990). In addition, however, we discuss the potential importance of communication and fairness in the compensation area. The fact that employment relationships or contracts are often of a long-term nature reinforces the importance of such issues. In administration, as in the other areas of compensation, organization differences may be significant.

The chapter begins with a brief discussion of the general trend toward organization-level research in compensation. We then proceed to each dimension (i.e., pay level, pay mix, etc.) in turn, focusing, where available, on evidence regarding organization differences. Similarly, research on the performance consequences of such differences is covered to the extent such work exists. Because the bulk of this research has been conducted in the area of pay mix (or individual pay determination), a sizeable portion of the review is devoted to pay mix issues.

The Resurgence of Interest in Organization Differences

The growing recognition and consensus that compensation research needs to focus more on organizations and how they differ is, of course, consistent with the work conducted during the 1940s and 1950s by a group of economists that Segal (1986) has referred to as "post-institutionalists" (e.g., Lester 1946; Reynolds 1951; Dunlop 1957). Their focus was on the "actual operation of the labor market" (Segal, p. 389), which led to many of the assumptions of neoclassical economics being questioned. On both the supply and demand side, empirical observation identified factors that reduced the degree of pure competition, and thus, the extent to which firms' decisions were dictated by market forces. As a result, the post-institutionalist model emphasized that firms enjoyed a significant degree of discretion in choosing how much to pay their employees. However, with important exceptions (e.g., Doeringer and Piore 1971; Thurow 1975; Williamson 1975), this interest among economists in organizational differences seemed to have been relatively dormant during the 1960s and into the mid-1980s.

Among the recent developments are empirical studies by Groshen (1988; 1991), Leonard (1988), and Gerhart and Milkovich (1990) on organization differences in pay level and by Gerhart and Milkovich (1990) and Brown (1990) on organization differences in the extent to which variable pay systems are used. In addition, numerous special journal issues have appeared on compensation, often focusing on organization differences. Examples include: the "New Economics of Personnel" (*Journal of Labor Economics*, October 1987), "The Economics of Human Resource Management" (*Industrial Relations*, Spring 1990), and "Do Compensation Policies Matter?" (*Industrial and Labor Relations Review*, February 1990).

The Brookings Institution (Blinder 1990) recently published a series of papers by economists and other scholars that reviewed the effectiveness of pay programs such as profit sharing, employee ownership, and so forth. A report on pay for performance recently published by the National Academy of Sciences (Milkovich and Wigdor 1991) places a good deal of emphasis on the importance of organization differences in studying pay.

Sociologists too have called for researchers to "bring the firms back in" (Baron and Bielby 1980; Tolbert 1986). *Administrative Science Quarterly* recently issued a call for papers to be published in a special issue on the "Distribution of Rewards in Organizations." The desired emphasis was on "papers that examine reward-allocation processes or outcomes *within one or more organization contexts*" (1990, p. 391). In the comparable worth area, Hartmann, Roos, and Treiman's basic research agenda emphasized the "need to understand better how wages are set within enterprises" because "although many assumptions are made about the impact of market forces and competition . . . little research on wage determination within firms has been undertaken" (1985, p. 7). Thus, dominant models such as human capital in economics and status attainment and segmented labor markets in sociology may be giving way to a more organization-based research focus.

In contrast to some other fields, human resource management has traditionally worked under the assumption that organizations choose different employment policies and that the organization is the appropriate unit of analysis in empirical research. There is little debate about whether significant organization differences exist and little interest in showing that if such differences do exist, it must be for efficiency reasons. Instead, the focus is on developing and testing descriptive models in human resource strategy, including compensation strategy (Salter 1973; Foulkes 1980; Balkin and Gomez-Mejia 1987; Dyer and Holder 1988; Gomez-Mejia and Welbourne 1988; Milkovich 1988; Weber and Rynes 1991; Gomez-Mejia and Balkin 1992). A second focus is on using this work to build prescriptive models that will inform managers' employment policy decisions and implementation.

Organization Differences in Pay: Recognizing Multiple Dimensions

Although the bulk of theory and research has focused on organization differences in pay level, as discussed earlier, this is only one of several dimensions of compensation. Further, emerging evidence suggests that organization differences in pay level may be less pronounced than differences on some of the other dimensions.

For example, in the Gerhart and Milkovich (1990) study mentioned earlier, organization differences in pay mix were significantly larger and less well explained by industry, size, and financial performance differences than were differences in pay level. Why might this be the case? One explanation rests on the idea that there are important product market and labor market constraints on pay level, but not on pay mix. If an organization's labor costs are higher than those of its competitors, this may be reflected in higher product prices and, depending on demand elasticity, less ability to compete in the product market. In addition, there may be a floor below which labor costs cannot be driven without compromising the ability to hire and retain employees of adequate quality. Taken together, the organization's range of discretion may be relatively limited in setting pay level. On the other hand, at any particular pay level, an organization can deliver pay with any number of different programs (e.g., merit pay, team awards, profit sharing). Thus, pay mix decisions may not be subject to the same degree to product and labor market constraints.

Gerhart and Milkovich (1990) also found that organization differences in pay mix were related to subsequent differences in profitability. Specifically, organizations that relied more heavily on variable pay plans such as short-term bonuses and long-term incentives over a period of several years performed better than those relying more heavily on base pay. The relatively large organization differences, the theoretical flexibility in making pay mix decisions, and the consequences of such decisions for organizational performance all suggest that the real action in compensation research of the future will pertain to how pay is delivered (e.g., pay mix), not the amount of pay (pay level). More broadly, a focus on pay delivery (or form) suggests that organization differences in structure and benefits decisions should also provide fertile research ground.

We begin with a discussion of organization differences in pay level and then move on to the other dimensions.

Pay Level

Ehrenberg and Milkovich defined pay level as the "average

compensation paid by a firm relative to that paid by its competitors" (1987, p. 89). Pay level is a characteristic of the organization (e.g., Heneman and Schwab 1979; Mahoney 1979a). Conceptually, the term "compensation" includes any direct or indirect payments to employees, such as wages, bonuses, stock, and benefits. In most research, however, only the base wage or salary is typically measured.[1] Another limitation of most research is the use of cross-sectional data, which ignores the fact that organizations may differ in the timing of compensation payouts over employees' careers.

Traditionally, much of the literature on pay level has focused on industry differences (Krueger and Summers 1988), but more recent work has turned to an examination of organization differences. Although the findings are somewhat mixed, it seems fairly clear that there are often substantial differences in pay level between organizations within industries (Groshen 1986; 1988; 1991). The least supportive evidence for organization differences comes from a study by Leonard (1988) of one industry (California electronics firms). The highly competitive nature of this industry may have reduced organization differences. Groshen's research using other industries, however, suggests that organization differences in pay level are of a significant magnitude and persist over time. Leonard (1990), although not placing much importance on them, also found nontrivial organization differences in pay level in a sample of executives from a broad range of industries. Finally, Gerhart and Milkovich (1990), using the Cornell Center for Advanced Human Resource Studies (CAHRS) compensation data base, found significant and stable employer differences in pay level over a five-year period among 16,000 top and middle managers in over 200 organizations and many different industries.

Note that these findings do not indicate that market forces are unimportant. To the contrary, labor market and product market variables explain a substantial amount of the variance in individual pay (e.g., 78 percent in the Gerhart and Milkovich 1990 study).[2] However, the findings also strongly suggest that within the constraints imposed by market pressures, organizations have considerable discretion in choosing pay-level policies.

Why do employers exercise this discretion? A satisfactory answer must await the development of an accepted contingency theory. In lieu of this, we briefly describe two general frameworks that have received significant attention: efficiency wage and strategy models.

Efficiency Wages

The basic idea behind efficiency wages is that organizations may choose pay levels that exceed the market-clearing rate as a way of achieving greater efficiency. Four different variants (sorting, shirking, turnover, gift exchange) of the model explain how this might work (see Groshen 1988).

Sorting by ability (or adverse selection). Some employers may choose higher rates of pay as a means of hiring and retaining higher ability employees. At least two assumptions are required. First, the employee selection system must have sufficient validity. Second, of course, the gain in employee performance must exceed the added compensation cost. This might occur, for example, in an organization where technology or work design is especially sensitive to employee ability.

Shirking/monitoring and turnover. Because worker productivity is often difficult to measure, workers may have an incentive to "shirk." However, as a counterincentive, an organization can pay the worker more than can be obtained elsewhere, which should reduce shirking because the employee will not want to risk losing this premium wage (Shapiro and Stiglitz 1984; Yellen 1984). If all firms raise wages, job loss may further result in unemployment. In this sense, "unemployment plays a socially valuable role in creating work incentives" (Yellen 1984).[3]

Gift exchange/sociological morale. Social conventions are the driving force here (Yellen 1984). Akerlof's "partial gift exchange" model suggests that "some firms willingly pay workers in excess of the market-clearing wage; in return they expect workers to supply more effort" (1984, p. 79). Or, as Yellen describes it, firms pay "workers a gift of wages in excess of the minimum required, in return for their gift of effort above the minimum required" (1984, p. 204). Akerlof cites Adams' (1965) work on over-reward inequity as empirical support. He also notes, however, that "not all studies reproduce the result that 'overpaid' workers will produce more" (Akerlof 1984, p. 82).

We make the following observations on efficiency wage models. First, one interpretation of such models is that if organizations behave in a particular way, it must be for efficiency reasons. Because there is always the possibility that decision makers have access to information not available to the researcher, this will always be difficult to prove or disprove. However, we believe it is more useful to leave open the question of whether actions are necessarily efficient and let the data provide, to the extent possible, an empirical assessment of what is efficient and what is not. As the so-called post-institutionalists (Segal 1986) of the 1940s and 1950s demonstrated, it may be unrealistic to assume that efficiency, narrowly defined, is the only criterion used in making compensation decisions.

Second, empirical tests of efficiency wage theory remain few and far between. In designing empirical research, it will be particularly important to measure the key constructs of the theory to provide a valid test of the theory's predictions. Thus, the need for monitoring, the amount of monitoring, and the likely cost of job loss should be defined and measured.[4]

Although progress in this respect has been limited, there have been some interesting empirical studies beginning to appear. For example, Cappelli and Chauvin suggest that the basic efficiency wage hypothesis is that "a wage premium may change employee behavior in ways that benefit the firm" (1991, p. 6). They tested the hypothesis that unionized manufacturing employees would be less likely to resolve workplace problems or conflicts using methods that risked job loss when the costs of job loss were high. Specifically, the grievance procedure was expected to be used more, while absenteeism and shirking would decline. Cost of job loss was measured as the size of the wage premium (relative to the local market) and the magnitude of the local unemployment rate. Plants located in different geographic regions and local labor markets provided the variance in cost of job loss. Their hypothesis was supported. However, two issues should be noted. First, shirking was not directly measured. Instead, it was proxied by the percentage of workers dismissed for disciplinary reasons. Thus it is possible that employee behavior did not change, but managerial behavior did. The weak labor market may have led to management being more aggressive in terms of work rules, discipline, and so forth. If so, more use of the grievance system (as observed here) could have been an outcome. This suggests that measuring employee shirking directly would be desirable in future studies. Second, the study did not indicate whether the greater use of the grievance system in the presence of wage premiums and high unemployment rates was efficient in any sense.

Goshen and Krueger (1990) tested the idea that wage premiums would be larger in hospitals with fewer resources allocated to supervision (measured as the percentage of supervisors) because self-supervision (or self-monitoring) would be greater. In support of their hypothesis, wage level was indeed negatively related to amount of supervision. However, as they noted, other models could also account for this finding. For example, organizations that hire lower quality workers would pay them less and might need to compensate for their lack of ability by having more or closer supervision. Again, actual measurement of the central construct (self-monitoring) in future research would help clarify such results (e.g., Conlon and Parks 1990).

Although specific tests of the partial gift exchange form of efficiency wage theory have not been conducted, equity theory research is very relevant. Briefly, it suggests that paying employees more than they might initially think they deserve does not have much effect on long-term behavior. One reason is that people appear to be very adept at readjusting their self-assessments of worth (upwards, of course). Consequently, the feeling of over-reward inequity or guilt may often be transitory, as would any increase in effort to compensate for it (Miner 1980).

Strategy

The general idea behind the strategy perspective is that organizations facing similar internal and external environments have the discretion to choose different compensation policies (Gomez-Mejia and Welbourne 1988; Milkovich 1988; Lawler 1990; Weber and Rynes 1991). Moreover, pay level is only one of several pay dimensions on which important choices need to be made. Different pay strategies that vary along the level, mix, structure, and benefits dimensions are thought to be appropriate for different types of organizations. The main contingency approaches to date have focused on matching different pay strategies based on an organization's stage in the life cycle, e.g., Balkin and Gomez-Mejia (1987), or its pattern of diversification, e.g., Kerr (1985). (See Milkovich 1988; Gerhart and Milkovich 1992; and Gomez-Mejia and Balkin 1992, for reviews.) In contrast to an efficiency wage perspective, the focus is not limited to pay level, and there is no assumption that the current pay practices of organizations are necessarily efficient. Rather, it is viewed as an empirical question.

Unfortunately, as with the efficiency wage model literature, such evidence is rare. (See Gomez-Mejia 1992 for a recent exception.)

Although we are not yet at the point of being able to identify and measure all of the relevant contingency factors so we can enter them into our computerized expert system (along with a compensation strategy) and have the predicted consequences output to us, we can identify the other major compensation decision areas and some of the important issues that need to be addressed within each.

Pay Mix

Pay mix focuses on how rather than how much employees are paid. Programs such as merit pay, individual incentives, gainsharing, and profit sharing are some of the more common ("pay for performance") programs discussed in this context. Single rate systems and pay linked to seniority are other examples of relevant programs. The Gerhart and Milkovich (1990) study reviewed earlier suggests that organization differences in pay mix may be relatively large and important in influencing organization performance. Pay mix can have two general types of effects on employee and organization performance (Gerhart and Milkovich 1992). First, pay mix can provide incentives and reinforcements for particular behaviors among *current employees*. This tends to be the focus of psychological models such as expectancy theory and reinforcement theory, as well as of agency theory in the economics and finance literatures. Research on the effects of pay programs like merit pay, gainsharing, profit sharing, and the like typically work from this conceptual framework.

Nevertheless, pay mix also has the potential to influence the *composition* of the current work force, just as pay level is hypothesized to do under efficiency wage models. For example, an organization that links pay closely to individual or organization performance may send a different signal (Spence 1973) to applicants than one with a weaker pay-performance link (Rynes 1987; Bretz, Ash, and Dreher 1989; Lazear 1989; Brown 1990; Hannon and Milkovich 1992), resulting perhaps in the two organizations having different types of work forces in terms of ability, risk aversion, and so forth. Similarly, different pay systems may contribute to different types of employees being retained, e.g., Gerhart 1990.

Another issue that arises in examining the pay mix literature has to do with the appropriate degree of individual versus group emphasis in pay program design. Deming (1986) has been a vocal critic of pay programs that focus heavily on rewarding individual level goal achievement. Two of his criticisms are mentioned here. First, he believes that any individual's performance is largely a function of numerous "system" factors (e.g., management, supervision, technology) that tend to be beyond the individual's control. Thus, it is both unfair and unwise to evaluate individual performance. Second, an individual focus discourages teamwork. As he puts it, "Everyone propels himself forward, or tries to, for his own good, on his own life preserver. The organization is the loser" (p. 102).

Team- or group-based pay plans may increase in importance for a number of reasons. First, comparisons with Japanese organizations suggest that teams play a greater role in the production process. For example, the MIT study of the automobile industry (Womack, Jones, and Roos 1990) found that 69 to 70 percent of workers in Japanese plants in Japan and in North America worked in teams, compared with 17 percent in U.S.-owned plants in North America. The strong productivity growth of the Japanese economy and its well-publicized achievements in industries such as automobiles have contributed to an interest in team-based approaches in the United States. In addition, changes in manufacturing technology (e.g., advanced manufacturing technologies such as just-in-time, flexible manufacturing) have led to teams, interdependence, flexibility, and decentralization being more important. These factors may not fit well with the traditional focus on individual-based reward systems (Gerhart and Bretz, forthcoming).

A recent study by Dyer and Blancero (1992) provides some evidence for what the future may hold. They used a Delphi technique to obtain projections from 57 panelists on how the workplace of a hypothetical service company in the year 2000 would differ from today's workplace. Most respondents were corporate human resource executives (56 percent), academics (18 percent), or consultants (12 percent). For all employee groups, they found that the importance of individual merit in pay increase decisions was expected to decrease, while work group performance was expected to become more important (see Table 1). In addition, their results indicated a substantial shift toward the use of variable pay, especially plans that tie pay to firm and business unit results.

TABLE 1
Projections of the Basis of Pay

% Pay Increase Based On	Executives 1991	Executives 2000	Managers 1991	Managers 2000	Professional Technical 1991	Professional Technical 2000	Support Staff 1991	Support Staff 2000
Individual Merit	100%	83%	100%	80%	100%	72%	100%	71%
Individual Seniority	0	1	0	1	0	1	0	3
Pay for Knowledge	0	3	0	4	0	15	0	14
Work group Performance	0	13	0	15	0	12	0	12

Source: Dyer and Blancero 1992, p. 64.

Nevertheless, experience suggests the need for caution in evaluating such predictions. For example, in a related study of 12,000 experts worldwide conducted for IBM by Towers Perrin consulting, similar results were found in the U.S. sample. But, ironically, over 80 percent of the 300 Japanese respondents agreed that greater emphasis on individual merit pay was a strategy that would enhance their competitive advantage. As such, those wishing to emulate the Japanese are faced with something of a quandary.

Also, it would be unwise to ignore the fact that individuals differ in terms of their abilities and skills. When individual differences are not recognized, high performers may move to a situation where such differences are recognized (e.g., Weiss 1987; Gerhart 1990). In the world of sports, for example, there are numerous examples of a great individual performer who is much more highly paid than other team members. This does not preclude teamwork or success; rather, in many cases, teammates recognize that the team would not be nearly so successful if that person were to leave.[5] Both teamwork and individual performance probably need to be recognized.

Evidence on Specific Pay Mix Programs

Most empirical research has focused on the impact of pay programs on current employees. Several literature reviews of such programs have appeared since the Ehrenberg and Milkovich (1987) IRRA review chapter. We make use of these and the Gerhart and

Milkovich 1992 chapter to highlight the evidence regarding specific pay plans.

Merit Pay. Although basing the pay of managers and professionals on merit or performance is typically the stated policy in organizations (Bretz, Milkovich, and Read 1989), questions have been raised about the extent to which this policy is carried out in practice (Medoff and Abraham 1981; Teel 1986; Lawler 1989; Konrad and Pfeffer 1990). There has been no comprehensive study of a wide range of organizations that would provide the necessary evidence, but it may be safe to assume that organizations differ significantly in the degree to which pay and merit are closely linked. Moreover, in evaluating the research that is available, Gerhart and Milkovich (1992) suggested that much of it has approached the issue in a less than optimal fashion for two reasons. First, most of the studies have used cross-sectional data despite the fact that even small differences in pay can accumulate into large differences over a career (Gerhart and Milkovich 1989; Gerhart and Rynes 1991), and similarly, even "small" links between pay and performance can compound into significant links over several years (Gerhart and Milkovich 1992; Milkovich and Milkovich 1992). Second, performance can have substantial effects on lifetime earnings through its effect on promotion rates. When these factors are considered, the estimated link between pay and performance is usually significantly larger. However, we do not really have any good evidence on the extent to which employees evaluate pay packages in terms of career earnings.

Merit bonuses (not added into base pay), in contrast, are designed to more closely link current pay to current performance because an employee has to re-earn the bonus each year (Newman and Fisher 1992). This approach is sometimes suggested as a way to increase "pay for performance" and enhance motivation. Another suggested advantage is that fixed costs are kept lower and salary growth can be more readily controlled. Not surprisingly, however, employees typically do not react favorably to such plans, and it is not clear such an approach makes sense in the context of long-term employment relationships where employee commitment is a goal.

The empirical evidence on the consequences of merit pay is almost nonexistent (Milkovich and Wigdor 1991). An exception is a study of managers in a single organization by Kahn and Sherer

(1990). They found little effect of merit pay, per se, on subsequent performance, but did find that managers who had bonuses closely linked to their performance had higher subsequent performance levels. Obviously, more such work needs to be done.

Individual Incentives. There is plenty of evidence that individual incentives can have substantial effects on employee behaviors and attitudes. The problem, however, is that not all the effects are positive. Quantity of production can often be raised (for reviews see Locke, Feren, McCaleb, Shaw, and Denny 1980; Dyer and Schwab 1982) but may come at the expense of quality, a major problem, particularly in view of the current emphasis on "total quality management." Individual incentives also fit poorly with team-based production and are not applicable to most white collar jobs. Other common roadblocks stem from the difficulty in developing production standards and rates that are accepted as fair by both management and workers over the long run and the fear of job loss if productivity increases dramatically. Perhaps as a consequence, individual incentives have been used successfully in only a fairly small number of cases and their use continues to decline (Mitchell et al. 1990).

Profit sharing. Under profit sharing, payouts are based on organization-wide profits. The plan has two potential advantages. First, it may provide an incentive for employees to act in the best interests of the organization rather than pursue narrower goals. Second, by making a portion of compensation vary with organization profits, an organization can align its labor costs more closely with its ability to pay. Thus, during business downturns, it has fewer fixed labor costs.

Weitzman and Kruse (1990) have provided a comprehensive review of profit-sharing research. Based on previous attitude surveys, they concluded that both employees and employers believe that profit sharing has positive effects on organization performance. Further, they found consistent evidence of statistically significant and positive links between profit sharing and organization performance, usually defined as value added.

Nevertheless, Gerhart and Milkovich (1992) raised some issues that might temper the positive evaluation reached by Weitzman and Kruse. For example, the use of value added as a dependent variable carries potential risks because it is not a measure of physical productivity. Instead, it is defined as the degree to which the price of a product exceeds the cost of factor inputs (e.g., labor). Obviously, the price of a product can be influenced by factors other than productivity. Weitzman and Kruse seem to recognize this and other potential problems with the profit-sharing literature. They note that "a limitation of the econometric studies is that they shed little light on the mechanisms through which profit sharing may affect productivity" (1990, p. 139).

The reason for interpreting the profit-sharing research cautiously is that there are both conceptual problems and roadblocks that have arisen in practice. For example, from a motivational point of view, it is not clear that any single employee will see much link between his or her performance and the organization profits because of the large numbers of people and factors that influence profits (i.e., "line of sight" problem). This, together with the "free rider" problem, suggests that the motivational effect of such a plan may be limited. In addition, the attempt to make labor costs vary with business conditions has also not worked out in a number of cases (e.g., the DuPont Fibers unit case). Employees often think profit sharing is fine when profits are good because the profit-sharing payments are just "gravy." However, when profits go down and their pay goes down, serious opposition can arise and plans may be scrapped. It is also possible that the introduction of this sort of risk into employee pay packages may require a compensating wage differential (Abowd and Ashenfelter 1981). Otherwise, employees may gravitate toward organizations that do not require them to bear such risks. The "signalling" effects of these plans on applicants' attitudes and behaviors needs to be investigated.

Finally, whatever its performance consequences, we note that profit sharing has also been proposed as a means of enhancing employment stability (Weitzman 1984; 1985). The basic idea is that it provides a way for organizations to reduce labor costs during business downturns without necessarily reducing head count. The research to date seems to support this hypothesis (Chelius and Smith 1990; Gerhart 1991; Kruse 1991).

Employee Ownership

Stock Options. Stock options permit employees to purchase stock at a fixed price. In the past, they have been primarily reserved for executives, but some organizations like Pepsi-Cola now give them to all employees. If the stock price increases, the options can be exercised at the lower price, and the employee makes a profit upon selling the stock. Thus, like profit sharing, payouts are based on a measure of organization performance. The potential advantages and disadvantages are also similar. One additional aspect that deserves mention is the cost of stock options. Sometimes organizations seem to treat them as having no cost. In theory, however, they may dilute the value of existing stock or reduce the amount of earnings allocated to profits. In fact, the Financial Accounting Standards Board (FASB, overseen by the Securities and Exchange Commission) is currently looking into this issue (Cowan 1992). It is considering changing accounting rules so that options are charged to compensation expense like other forms of compensation.

ESOPs. Employee stock ownership plans (ESOPs) in the United States are defined in the Internal Revenue Code and the Employee Retirement Income Security Act and enjoy a number of tax/financing advantages (Conte and Svejnar 1990). They have also been used as a takeover defense under the assumption that the employee voting block will be supportive of the management team. ESOPs are unique in several respects, including the requirement that plan participants (i.e., employees) be permitted to vote their securities if they are registered on a national exchange (Conte and Svejnar 1990).

As with other organization-wide plans such as profit sharing and stock options, the motivational impact of stock ownership is open to question because the employee may see little connection between his or her own performance and the stock performance. Nevertheless, the research to date has been "encouraging" (Hammer 1988). As is probably the case with other plans (e.g., profit sharing), however, there is some concern about simultaneity—that actual or expected good stock performance may result in the establishment of ESOPs (Hammer 1988).

An important and recurring finding is that there are greater beneficial effects of ownership in cases where employees participate in decision making (Hammer 1988; Conte and Svejnar 1990). Similarly, Pierce, Rubenfeld, and Morgan (1991) suggest that employee ownership is most likely to influence motivation, attitudes, and behaviors when the "employee-owner comes to psychologically experience his/her ownership in the organization." Klein (1987) reports that employee satisfaction under ESOPs is related both to the monetary and participation components.

Areas of concern with ESOPs include (a) ownership stakes that do not translate into voting rights, (b) the difficulty in diversifying employee pay (or investment) risk, and (c) the cost to other stockholders that arises from the dilution of share value when ESOP shares are not purchased on the market ("Unseen Apples and Small Carrots" 1991).

Gainsharing. In contrast to the typical profit-sharing plan, gainsharing payouts are (a) typically linked to group or plant rather than organization-wide performance, (b) based on productivity rather than profits, and (c) distributed more frequently and not deferred. Taken together, these differences suggest a greater motivational impact for gainsharing because a payout criterion like group or plant productivity is likely to be seen as more controllable by employees than something like organization-wide profits. Not surprisingly, the evidence indicates that gainsharing has a positive impact on performance (Schuster 1984; Wagner, Rubin, and Callahan 1988; Hatcher and Ross 1991; Kaufman 1992).

Although gainsharing appears to have a positive influence on the performance of current employees, a potential concern stems from our earlier discussion regarding its effects on work force composition and some initial empirical evidence that high individual performers may not be more likely to leave under such plans (e.g., Weiss 1987). If this finding is replicated, research will be needed to evaluate the potential tradeoff between (negative) work force composition effects and (positive) effects on current (or remaining) employees. Alternatively, research might focus on the optimal blend of plans (e.g., merit pay, promotion) that rewards individual performance and the blend that rewards group performance (e.g., gainsharing).

Other research issues concern the conditions under which gainsharing is most effective. Gowen and Jennings (1991, p. 148) suggest that three "socio-psychological conditions—employee identification, ownership, and commitment" are important characteristics of effective gainsharing programs. Similarly, Hatcher, Ross, and Collins (1991) propose a model where "employee support for gainsharing" has three determinants: plan-instrumentality beliefs, affective organizational commitment, and trust. Such hypotheses again underscore the potential importance of noncompensation factors in determining the success of compensation programs, an issue we cover in more depth in a later section.

Pay Structure

Pay structures can be defined in terms of the "array of rates paid for different work within a single organization." In addition, they "focus attention on the levels, differentials, and criteria used to determine those pay rates" (Milkovich and Newman 1990, p. 31). To date, much of the empirical research has focused on relative pay (i.e., differentials), defined, for example, as the ratio of a position's pay to adjacent positions in the hierarchy (Jacques 1961; Mahoney 1979b) or to the average pay of other positions in the structure (Pfeffer and Davis-Blake 1987). As with pay mix, organizations may have considerable discretion in designing pay structures because many different structures are possible given a particular overall labor cost.

The evidence on organization differences in structure is sparse. However, a recent study by Pfeffer and Davis-Blake (1990) used a sample of colleges and universities to model the determinants of salary dispersion (coefficient of variation). Using roughly 20 predictors, including tenure dispersion, percent women, the distribution of jobs, and size, they obtained R^2s of .30 and .46, depending on the time period. By implication, there remain large unexplained organization differences in salary dispersion, especially compared to a pay dimension such as level, for which R^2s are typically considerably higher (e.g., Gerhart and Milkovich 1990).

Much of the literature on structures is based on the idea of an internal labor market (ILM). Work by Kerr (1954) and others "attacked the uncritical application of the textbook model of supply and demand to the ILM" (Wachter and Wright 1990, p. 241). Compared to the external labor market, an ILM allocates and prices labor (i.e., employees) on the basis of policy, rules, and procedures, and less on the basis of supply and demand. Market forces in an ILM are largely indirect, except for port of entry jobs. Although Doeringer and Piore (1971) incorporated both efficiency and institutional explanations for ILMs, most of the subsequent economic literature has stressed the efficiency advantages of ILMs (e.g., Becker 1964; Azariadis 1975; Williamson, Wachter, and Harris 1975; see Ehrenberg and Smith 1987 and Wachter and Wright 1990 for reviews). An important starting point for most such models is that employees and organizations "incur substantial sunk cost investments [which] are not easily portable across firms. Minimizing these sunk cost losses encourages the parties to maintain their ongoing relationship" (Wachter and Wright 1990, p. 243).

The existence of a long-term employment relationship means that structures must be designed not only with incentive effects in mind (e.g., Lazear and Rosen 1981), but also with the goal of achieving equity, fairness, and the favorable reputation that follows. Less complete information being held by one party than by the other (i.e., asymmetric information) might permit "strategic behavior" (i.e., not abiding by the implicit contract). Wachter and Wright suggest that "Perhaps the most important disincentive for strategic behavior is the repeated nature of the ILM relationship. Repeated transactions are less subject to opportunism than are short-run relationships" (1990, p. 253).

Although the preceding literature explains ILMs in terms of their efficiency advantages, little attention is given to how ILMs vary across organizations or what specific decisions are most consequential for organization performance. The administrative literature (Lawler 1980; Belcher and Atchison 1987; Wallace and Fay 1988; Milkovich and Newman 1990), for example, suggests that numerous specific decisions are required, including: using job- or skill-based structures, the number of separate structures, the number of steps or levels in a structure, the rate of progression through the structure, and the degree to which pay differentials represent the external market or use some other criterion (e.g., internal consistency). Little is known about organization differences in such decisions, let alone their potential implications for performance (Gerhart and Milkovich 1992).

New Evidence on Organization Differences: Market Sensitivity

To help remedy the lack of empirical evidence on organization differences in pay structures, we provide new results on organization differences relating to the market sensitivity of their pay structures. The compensation literature has long recognized the importance of both external competitiveness and internal consistency objectives. The former refers to comparisons between what the organization pays for a particular job or skill and what other organizations pay. Internal consistency, by comparison, focuses on within-organization comparisons of pay for different jobs or skills.

Although the two policies may go hand in hand, they may also conflict. For example, an internal consistency orientation might argue for vice presidents being paid the same, regardless of the labor market (e.g., finance, human resources, research and development) or product market (e.g., aerospace, consumer products). Such a policy may make the most sense in cases where the vice presidents make lateral moves across functional job areas or business units or where cooperation between vice presidents is important (Carroll 1987). However, if other organizations (the "market") tend to pay vice presidents in finance and/or consumer products more, there will be pressure to move away from internal consistency toward an external competitiveness focus. Otherwise, it may be difficult, for example, to attract and retain vice presidents of finance in the consumer products business. In such organizations, labor market and product market factors would play a more important role in pay setting.[6] In this sense, the pay structure would display more market sensitivity.

The empirical results reported here were obtained as part of the third author's Master's thesis (Murray 1992) and focus on the question of whether organizations differ significantly in the degree to which they pursue an external competitiveness or market sensitivity strategy, as is suggested by policy-capturing research of compensation professionals (Weber and Rynes 1991). If so, future research could try to ascertain the reasons for such differences and their possible consequences for organization performance.

The data are from the Cornell University Center for Advanced Human Resource Studies Compensation Database. There are 78,503 observations pooled across multiple years (1981 through 1985) on top- and middle-level managers in 282 firms. To be included in the sample, an organization had to report data on at least 75 employees in at least two different years.

The measure of market sensitivity was derived in two steps. First, a market-wide equation was estimated using cash compensation (base salary + short-term bonus) as the dependent variable. Second, for each organization, the predicted cash compensation from this general equation was matched with the actual cash compensation values to obtain an R^2 (or coefficient of determination). This, in turn, was used to measure the correspondence between an organization's pay structure and that of the market as a whole—in other words, its market sensitivity. To capture product market influences, the general equation included industry dummy variables, as well as size (sales, employees). Labor market influences were accounted for by including occupation dummy variables, level of responsibility, general and firm-specific experience, and years of education.

The results indicated that the mean of the market sensitivity index was .78 with a standard deviation of .08. With a normal distribution, the 95 percent confidence interval would run from .62 to .96, indicating a significant range in market sensitivity. An analysis of variance using organization dummies as the independent variables was statistically significant ($F_{281,78211} = 357.68$), reinforcing the finding of significant organization differences in market sensitivity.

An important criterion in assessing whether patterns are strategic is to examine their stability over time (Mintzberg 1987). To pursue this issue, market sensitivity indexes from 1981 and 1984 were used to obtain a measure of stability. The correlation between the two years was .44. Thus, organization differences in market sensitivity show some stability, but also significant change. However, it should be recognized that there is considerable movement of employees into and out of the organizations included in this sample. For example, using the same sample, Gerhart and Milkovich (1990) reported that about 50 percent of employees present in 1981 were not present as of 1985. Combined with the fact that the R^2s are based on modest sample sizes, there may be a fairly low ceiling on the amount of stability that could be found.[7] All things considered, we suggest that the results indicate significant and relatively stable organization differences in market sensitivity. Given the potential consequences of internal consistency and external competitiveness discussed above, this probably calls for work that explores the organization performance consequences of such differences.

Benefits

Employee benefits add an average of $.38 on top of every $1.00 of payroll (U.S. Chamber of Commerce 1991), accounting for about 28 percent of total compensation (EBRI 1992). Therefore, any discussion of organization differences in pay must consider differences in benefits. From publicly available data focusing primarily on industry differences, we know that spending for benefits is highest in manufacturing (31.9 percent) and lowest in retail trade (22.5 percent). However, as with pay structures, much of the evidence about organizational differences in benefit costs, forms, and levels of coverage, and their possible consequences, may only be available in the surveys conducted by private consulting firms. For example, Hewitt and Associates (1992) report that two-thirds of the manufacturers in their survey (approximately 200) provide comprehensive medical care with deductibles. Individual deductibles of $200 (23 percent of the plans) and $100 (29 percent of the plans) are most common. Family deductibles varied from $200 (12 percent of the plans) to $400 (12 percent of the plans). Employee monthly contributions for single coverage ranged from none (46 percent) to $50 and greater (12 percent).

Both level and growth of benefit costs are noteworthy. In 1935 benefits accounted for less than one percent of total compensation costs. By 1953 their share was 16 percent; by 1980 it was 27 percent. The types of coverage also changed. In 1960, employers spent 1.1 percent of total compensation on health care, 4.8 percent for retirement, and 2.1 percent on other forms. In contrast, in 1990 health care accounted for 6.4 percent, retirement 8.1 percent, and other forms 2.2 percent (EBRI 1992).

Although there is evidence of a recent slowdown in overall benefit growth relative to total compensation, even the most casual observer must be aware that health care costs are the notable exception. According to one survey, the cost of health care increased 21 percent (to $2,313 per employee in 1990, following increases of 20.4 percent and 17 percent in 1989 and 1988, respectively; Foster Higgins 1991). The United States spends about 12 percent of its gross domestic product on health care, the largest percentage amount of any developed country.

Despite this large and increasing expenditure of resources, there are 37 million U.S. citizens (14.8 percent of the population) who do not have public or private health care. Most conventional quality indices such as infant mortality (the United States ranks highest among developed countries), life expectancy (the United States ranks sixth out of six countries for men, fourth for women), and office waiting time per visit (14 minutes) raises questions about the return on the nation's investment in health care. Finally, according to public opinion polls, U.S. citizens are less satisfied with their health care system and more likely to say it needs fundamental change than citizens in other developed countries.

Public policy regarding employee benefits is beyond the editor's charge for our chapter. However, one only needs to consider the effects of changes in the tax code or of the wage and price controls in the 1940s and 1950s to realize that the current public policy debate on health care will shape the costs, forms, and levels of coverage of benefits offered employees. Further, the GAO recently noted that full taxation of benefits could raise $91 billion in new tax revenues and ". . . go a long way toward improving equity" between benefit recipients and nonrecipients (GAO 1992). They also noted that it may lead to fewer benefits provided by employers. However, given the virtual absence of research on organization differences, public policy formulation will not be well informed about the effects that differences in benefits have on employee behaviors or organization performance.

Employee Perceptions and Preferences

Evidence suggests that employees seriously underestimate the financial value of their benefits and in some cases are even unaware of their existence. In one study, employees were asked to recall which types of benefits they received; the average response was only about 15 percent of the total number of benefits (reported in Milkovich and Newman 1990).

The Wilson et al. (1985) study focused on employees' perceptions of their health care insurance benefits. Employees were knowledgeable about their own contributions, but not about those made by the employer. Over 90 percent of the employees underestimated both (a) the cost to the employer, and (b) what it would cost them to provide the benefits on their own. For example, for one health plan, employees estimated the employer cost to be $22 (the actual cost was $64) biweekly, and the market value to be $48 (the actual value was $169). In fact, some employees believed that the employer made no contribution at all to their health insurance coverage.

One interpretation of such findings is that employers may, to put it bluntly, be throwing away money on benefits. If employees do not know the benefits exist or fail to attach value to them, the benefits cannot influence their attitudes or behaviors in any positive fashion. As Lawler (1981) has suggested, any action that would enhance employee knowledge would help strengthen the impact of benefits. He advocated increasing employee choice (e.g., by using cafeteria or flexible benefits plans) as one approach. Organizations have in fact moved in this direction, with 61 percent now offering such plans, according to the Hewitt survey of 944 large organizations (Hewitt 1991). Preliminary evidence suggests that flexible benefits do positively influence benefits satisfaction (Barber, Dunham, and Formisano 1990). Other actions aimed at enhancing employee knowledge include greater use of copayments and deductibles. The effects of such approaches await evaluation.

There is longstanding evidence of significant employee differences in benefit preferences (Nealey 1963; Mahoney 1964; Nealey and Goodale 1967; Huseman, Hatfield, and Driver 1978; Davis, Giles, and Field 1985, 1988; Stonebraker 1985). Although interpreting these results is often complicated because of a lack of adequate controls (e.g., differences in the experience or use of different forms, employer differences in benefits packages and communication approaches), some findings seem robust (and perhaps even obvious to some): older workers tend to place more value on pensions, women tend to prefer more time off, and the number of dependents is related to the desire for health insurance.

Such employee differences, of course, lend greater weight to the need for offering employees a choice in the design of their benefits package. The increasing diversity of the work force further reinforces this suggestion. Employers hope that flexible benefits plans will help control costs and enhance employee satisfaction by increasing employee knowledge and improving the fit between employee preferences and benefits.

Survey and anecdotal evidence suggest that employee reactions to flexible plans are positive and that medical care costs are lower under such plans. However, little empirical research has taken advantage of the field opportunities offered by employers' shift to flexible plans (see Barber, Dunham, and Formisano 1990 for an exception). Little is known about why some employers shift and others do not. Even less is known about how employees make the choices that are so fundamental to such plans, or whether different choices are made (Barringer, Milkovich, and Mitchell 1991).

Barringer et al. (1991) studied the actual decisions made by employees (n = 1,500) among six health care options under a flexible benefit plan offered by a large manufacturing company. Employee choices were modelled as a function of employee and plan characteristics. Results indicated that employee decisions among multiple health plans were significantly influenced by option costs (i.e., premium, deductibles, and coinsurance amounts) and employee demographics (i.e., employees' age, income, marital status, and gender). As age and salary increased, the probability of selecting a reduced (less expensive) level of health care coverage decreased. The probability of selecting a lower cost alternative was greater among married employees and female employees.

Another study conducted by IBM reported that the selection of high coverage options did not drop when employee costs were raised, but employee satisfaction with their health care benefits actually increased. Simultaneously, the organization had launched a massive communication effort, including take-home videos. These findings suggest that employee expectations about their benefits are adaptive and communication efforts may have an influence. In addition, communication and employee involvement may be all the more important, since apparently employees underestimate the value and may not even be sensitive to organization differences in benefits. Increasing the knowledge through communication and involvement may increase benefit value to employees. In a recent study, knowledge and satisfaction with benefits increased for employees who used computer-based spreadsheets and an expert system compared to employees who did not have access to these decision aids (Hannon, Milkovich, and Sturman 1992).

Satisfaction, Attraction, and Retention

Benefits are believed to influence everything from employee satisfaction, health, and well-being to the decision to join and remain with an organization. Again, with some exceptions, research into the consequences of employee benefits is lacking.

Heneman and Schwab (1985) and others have found that satisfaction with benefits is a separate and independent dimension of pay satisfaction. Other findings suggest that benefit satisfaction increases with improved coverage and decreases with cost shifting to employees (Dreher, Ash, and Bretz 1988). A more complete review of this research is in Gerhart and Milkovich (1992).

Benefits are also believed to influence job choice decisions. The typical study involves asking graduate students to rank order the importance attached to various factors influencing their job choice (see Huseman, Hatfield, and Driver 1978). Benefits' last place rank is consistent with employees' tendency to underestimate their value (Mahoney 1964; Huseman, Hatfield, and Robinson 1978; Pergande

1988). In a recent Gallup poll, respondents claimed that they would require $5,000 more in extra pay to choose a job without pension, health, or life insurance.

There is increasing evidence that pensions and health care reduce voluntary turnover (Schiller and Weiss 1979; Mitchell 1982, 1983). Schiller and Weiss reported that turnover was not only influenced by the existence of pensions but also by vesting and employee contributions. Mitchell found that pensions were less likely to influence the turnover of women than men (1982). Luzadis and Mitchell (1991), using the longitudinal file of collectively bargained pension plans, reported that the nature of pension plans acts as an incentive to encourage workers with high tenure to retire. They suggested that employers, through the design of their pension and retirement incentives, can shape the demographic composition of their work force. However, a problem is that the optimal configuration (experience, age, etc.) is seldom attended to. Rather, the objective is more often simply to reduce labor costs (i.e., replacing older, more expensive employees with younger, less expensive ones). The effects on overall economic performance needs to be examined.

Explanation of Differences

The recurring theme of this chapter is to put the organization back into research on employee compensation. This is particularly important in the case of increasing our knowledge about employee benefits. Explanations of organizational differences in benefits can be derived from a number of different economic and organizational theories. Barringer and Milkovich (1992) examine how current theories drawn from economics and organizational behavior explain the observed patterns in the adoption and design of a specific benefit practice—decisions about flexible benefits.

Flexible benefits were offered by only 17 major U.S. employers in 1981, and only 99 in 1983, but by 1992 over 1,400 plans had been implemented. Survey evidence suggests that the incidence is highest in the service industry. Sixty-three percent of the top 100 commercial banks, 46 percent of the top 50 financial firms, and 46 percent of the top 50 utilities currently offer flexible plans (Hewitt 1992). This is also evidence of considerable variation in the design of these plans.

How do different theories account for this diffusion of flexible benefits? Barringer and Milkovich (1992) consider agency and transaction cost models from economics as well as institutional and resource dependency models from organization behavior. All rest on the premise that organization performance can depend on motivating important employee behaviors, and while they are not in complete agreement, all suggest that the ease of monitoring work effort is important. On the other hand, these theories disagree on the extent to which organization decisions are influenced by external versus internal conditions. The institutional model suggests that employment relationships are determined primarily by forces in the organization environment such as tax code changes, industry competitiveness, and labor market patterns. In contrast, the resource dependency, agency, and transaction cost perspectives all presume that internal conditions affecting contingencies in employment relationships primarily determine how an organization will design its compensation, including benefits.

Assumptions about the determinants of organization decisions about practices such as flexible benefits vary widely across models. Two conflicting themes emerge: decisions about the adoption and design of an innovation are rationally related to pressures in the environment; or organizations base their decisions on what others are doing (i.e., benchmarking) regardless of the effects on firm performance.

Consistent with the first theme, the resource dependence, agency, and transaction cost perspectives all imply that organizations can improve productivity by adopting practices that will motivate employees' work and attendance behaviors. Explanations of firms' decisions about flexible benefit plans thus require an examination of the factors related to the extent of organizations' reliance on and control or influence over these important behaviors. In contrast, the institutional perspective implies that organizations are less concerned with improving technical efficiency than with reaching an accommodation with their environment. This theory suggests that an organization's "field" as well as factors related to pressures to conform and organizations' immunities to these pressures can help explain decisions about flexible benefits plans.

None of the theories seem to offer a complete explanation of firms' decisions about flexible benefits plans. The institutional model does not consider "late adoption" decisions that may be related to rational considerations. Further, application of this model may be difficult because an organization's field is not easily identified, and because the criteria are unclear for determining when institutional forces begin to exert more influence than rational, performance-related considerations. The resource dependence, agency, and transaction cost perspectives seem to be more helpful in explaining the design than the incidence of flex plans, and each seems to focus narrowly on a single aspect of the employment relationship. Thus, for example, the transaction cost perspective focuses on the firm-specificity of work skills and the ease of monitoring productive efforts, and does not consider other factors (e.g., task uncertainty, task centrality) that would also make high turnover and low work motivation costly. If expanded, however, the transaction cost approach might prove to be the most parsimonious of all the models, since it recognizes not only the importance of efficiency as an important guiding force, but also the impact of environmental constraints beyond the organization's control. It could therefore incorporate the constraints imposed by institutional environments, as well as those imposed by contingencies in employment relationships that are implied by the resource dependence and agency models.

Benefits provide a unique context for testing a variety of economic and organization theories. Hypotheses about the determinants and consequences of organization differences in benefits can be derived. There is sufficient evidence that significant differences among organizations exist. Further, the dramatic changes currently underway in the benefits that organizations offer provide research opportunities. Their increasing cost only adds to the timeliness of benefits research.

So what are the potential barriers? First, the data requirements are considerable, since numerous variables are implied by the theories, and large longitudinal sample sizes are required. Moreover, testing hypotheses regarding organization differences requires data across several firms. Obtaining benefits data is proving to be a challenge because some firms consider it proprietary, and not all of it is well documented in existing information systems. Nevertheless, our survey of the research leads us to conclude that compared to the rest of compensation, we know very little about how employee benefits are determined or what their effects are. The opportunity to make a contribution by informing decision makers and adding to the body of knowledge is substantial.

Process Issues: Participation and Communication

Lawler (1980, p. 33) suggested that there was too often an assumption in employee compensation research and practice that "if the right technology can be developed, the right answers will be found." But, he argued, "there are no objectively right answers," and thus, process factors such as participation and communication are also important. The distinction between distributive equity and procedural equity (e.g., Greenberg 1986; Folger and Konovsky 1989) similarly suggests the need to treat outcomes and the process used to decide on (and administer) such outcomes as somewhat independent issues. Textbooks and chapters in the employee compensation field now regularly point to process issues as a key strategic decision area (Lawler 1980, 1990; Milkovich and Newman 1990; Gerhart and Milkovich 1992; Gomez-Mejia and Balkin 1992). Economists too have begun to focus more attention on the likely importance of process issues (Blinder 1990).

Consistent with our earlier discussion of compensation dimensions, there seem to be substantial differences in the decisions made regarding participation and communication both within (e.g., Cutcher-Gershenfeld 1991) and between organizations (Goll 1991). The latter study suggests that environmental conditions (e.g., foreign and domestic competition, deregulation, industry structure) are not very helpful in explaining differences between organizations in the degree of participative decision making. In contrast, top management ideology and values did explain a significant portion of such differences. Therefore, management may have considerable discretion in its decisions about employee participation in decision making and other aspects of general employee relations. (On this point, see also Kochan, Katz, and McKersie 1986; Lewin 1987; Kochan and Dyer 1992).

We focus on two process-related issues: participation in decision making and communication/information sharing.

Employee Participation in Decision Making

Levine and Tyson (1990) summarized two "economic" models of participation in decision making (PDM). The first is based on an agency theory approach. Delegation of decision making by a principal to an agent raises the question of how the principal can encourage the agent (whose interests differ to some degree) to act in the best interests of the principal (i.e., the agency problem). As the number of decision makers increase, so do monitoring costs (Jensen and Meckling 1979) and transaction costs (Williamson 1975). Thus, from this perspective, PDM would be inefficient. However, Levine and Tyson argue that both the agency and transactions costs frameworks can be extended to incorporate the fact that employees have knowledge about the workplace and behavior of fellow employees that managers do not, and that PDM may increase the communication of such information. The implication seems to be that employees will engage in self- and peer-monitoring.

But, as Levine and Tyson (1990) point out, there is the question of why employees would be motivated to share information and facilitate monitoring. Based on economic theory's focus on monetary incentives, the experiences of other industrialized nations (e.g., Japan), and psychological theories of PDM, they suggest that four factors are necessary for PDM to succeed: "gainsharing" (to provide a monetary incentive), and three actions geared toward building an environment that fosters trust and cooperation—long-term employment relations, measures to build group cohesiveness, and guaranteed individual rights for employees.

Perhaps the most influential psychological theory of PDM and its consequences is the Locke and Schweiger (1979) model, which is built around an expectancy theory perspective (Vroom 1964). PDM is hypothesized to increase productivity and quality by enhancing both employee ability and motivation. Ability effects occur through the greater sharing of information, which provides a better understanding of the job and a greater opportunity for employees to contribute ideas for improvement. Motivation is enhanced because of a greater sense of control, ego involvement, group pressure and support, and higher goals. These, in turn, reduce resistance to change and increase commitment to decisions and changes. Finally, there can also be positive effects on attitudes for those who value empowerment, respect, independence, and so forth. These effects may also contribute to lower levels of absenteeism, turnover, and conflict. (See Hammer 1988 for a related model in the context of gainsharing.)

Discussions of PDM in the compensation literature often take a relatively narrow focus, usually emphasizing employee involvement in the design and implementation of pay policies (Gomez-Mejia and Balkin 1992). Greater involvement has been linked to

higher pay and job satisfaction (Jenkins and Lawler 1981)
ably because employees have a better understanding of a
er commitment to the policy when they are involved (Gomez-Mejia and Balkin 1992).

More broadly, however, PDM may have important influences on effectiveness that go beyond its role in facilitating the success of pay programs. According to Blinder, for example (1990, pp. 12-13):

> Worker participation apparently helps make alternative compensation plans . . . work better—and also has beneficial effects of its own. It appears that changing the way workers are *treated* may boost productivity more than changing the way they are *paid*.

Looking beyond the compensation literature, there has been a substantial effort to document the effects of employee participation. Several literature reviews have examined the relationship between employee participation in decision making and outcomes such as performance and satisfaction (e.g., Locke and Schweiger 1979; Miller and Monge 1986; Gershenfeld 1987; Wagner and Gooding 1987; Cotton, Vollrath, Froggatt, Lengnick-Hall, and Jennings 1988; Levine and Tyson 1990). These reviews suggest several conclusions. First, participation seems to have a small to moderate positive relationship with both performance and satisfaction. Second, however, the magnitude of these relationships seems to vary significantly depending on how participation and the outcome variables are measured. When both are based on employee self-reports, the relationships with performance and satisfaction appear to be four times as large on average (Wagner and Gooding 1987). Thus, studies relying exclusively on self-report data need to be interpreted cautiously because they may significantly overestimate the strength of the participation effect.

A third conclusion, suggested by both Cotton et al. (1988) and Levine and Tyson (1990) is that different forms of participation may have very different effects. (See Leana, Locke, and Schweiger 1990 for a criticism of this conclusion and the rebuttal by Cotton et al. 1990). Both reviews include a number of types of participation studies such as Scanlon and employee ownership plans that were excluded in the aforementioned meta-analyses (because of the confound between participation and other factors like pay). For example, Levine and Tyson conclude that "participation is more likely to produce a significant, long-lasting increase in productivity when it involves decisions that extend to the shopfloor and when it involves substantive rather than consultative arrangements" (1990, p. 204).[8]

A recent study by Cutcher-Gershenfeld (1991) provides some interesting evidence on the effects of broad changes in workplace relations, which he defined in terms of conflict and conflict resolution, shopfloor cooperation, formal and informal autonomous worker activity, and information sharing. Using longitudinal data on 25 work areas at Xerox, he found that higher levels of these workplace relations variables were associated with lower costs as well as improvements in cost and quality.

Blinder's (1990) suggestion that employee PDM may have a greater impact on organization effectiveness than pay decisions, per se, raises the broader issue of the importance of pay decisions relative to other employee relations decisions such as broad PDM. In addressing this issue, it is useful to revisit the literature on gainsharing. In that context, the question has been raised about the degree to which it is the monetary component or the contextual conditions like participation that contribute to increased performance levels (Hammer 1988; Milkovich and Wigdor 1991; Mitchell, Lewin, and Lawler 1991).

Although it is difficult to find studies that disentangle pay and nonpay program effects, some evidence clearly supports the idea that pay is only one part of the story. For example, Pritchard, Jones, Roth, Stuebing, and Ekeberg (1988) conducted a 23-month study of the effect of gainsharing incentives, goal setting, and feedback in five separate organizational units at an air force base in the southwest United States. Although it is not completely clear from the article, the goals and feedback components appeared to include participative elements, in addition to information sharing. They used a baseline period of eight months, followed by five months of feedback only, five months of feedback + goal setting, and finally, five months of feedback + goal setting + incentives. They observed large increases in productivity due to feedback alone (50 percent over baseline), feedback + goal setting (75 percent over baseline), but little *additional* effect of incentives. Although it is probably incorrect to interpret the results as meaning that pay, *per se*, is not important (Pritchard et al. [1988] note the possibility of ceiling effects on performance and that incentives may have been necessary to sustain the substantial feedback and goal-setting effects over the longer run), the study does not reinforce the notion that pay is not the only means of influencing behavior.

That said, however, evidence (some of which was reviewed earlier) indicates that pay alone can have important effects on behavior. Schuster (1990) has argued that gainsharing plans have often worked well in cases where the main (or entire) focus was on the monetary aspect, unaccompanied by employee involvement or participation. Consistent with this argument, a recent literature review (Kaufman 1992) of several Improshare plans, which emphasize pay but not employee involvement (see Fein 1981 for a description of the program), found positive effects on employee performance.

Similarly, Wagner et al. (1988) studied the implementation of a nonmanagement group incentive payment plan that appeared to encompass little beyond changes on the monetary dimension and found a substantial increase in productivity, as well as significant declines in labor costs and grievances. They noted, however, that employees had positive experiences with incentive plans in other company plants, which may have generated greater trust in management and, in turn, more successful implementation of the new pay plan. In other words, we again see that both pay and the accompanying nonpay context may matter.

Gowen and Jennings argued that previous studies "have not examined the effects of participation independent of the effects of other pay plan attributes" (1991, p. 162). Their study of several departments in an automotive parts plant found that adding a participation component (monthly meetings with management to discuss the gainsharing plan and ways of increasing productivity) to a gainsharing pay incentive plan raised productivity.

Hatcher et al. (1991) note that many gainsharing plans (e.g., Scanlon) incorporate a formal employee suggestion system. Ideas for cutting costs, changing work methods, and so forth can be solicited and later evaluated by teams of management and nonmanagement employees for possible implementation. Hatcher et al. focused on identifying the factors that motivate employees to submit suggestions. An interesting finding was that the desire to earn a monetary bonus appeared to be much less important than a number of nonpay factors, particularly the desire for influence and control over how their work was done. They suggest that this finding "fails to support the position that gainsharing works by appealing exclusively to the financial interests of employees via the bonus" (p. 32).

Mitchell et al. (1990) examined the effects of what they termed economic participation (coverage by profit sharing, gainsharing, stock options, ESOPs, and production bonus or incentive plans) and noneconomic participation (i.e., of the type studied in the general participation literature) on productivity (net sales per employee) and profitability (return on investment and return on assets), using responses from 495 business units.[9] Cross-sectional regressions found support for positive effects of noneconomic participation on productivity, but not on profitability. Economic participation was not related to either profitability or productivity, although breaking out the separate programs provided some evidence of positive effects of profit sharing on each. Trend regressions, in comparison, provided consistent support for the effects of both types of participation on profitability and productivity. As such, the results again suggest the importance of both pay and accompanying process factors such as participation.

Communication and Information Sharing

Gerhart and Milkovich (1992) suggest that the way pay information is communicated to employees may have a significant effect on their attitudes and behaviors. Communication can pertain to either distributive or procedural aspects of compensation decisions. With respect to the former, for example, some organizations choose to carefully manage information regarding how pay compares with that of other relevant organizations. Employee reactions are likely to depend not only on their actual pay, but also on what comparisons they believe are relevant and the information that is available. Consequently, Cappelli and Sherer (1990) found, for example, that the lowest paid employees were actually the most satisfied with their pay because they used different comparisons.

Effective communication about procedural issues can also be important. A fairly dramatic example in this regard was provided by Greenberg (1990). He found that employee theft increased significantly after a 15 percent across-the-board pay cut was instituted. Most interesting, however, was that the manner of communicating the pay cut had a substantial impact on both pay equity perceptions and actual theft rates. With the "adequate explanation" experimental group, management provided a significant degree of information to explain the rationale behind the pay cut. It also made a point of expressing its remorse. The "inadequate explanation" group received much less information and no indication of remorse. The control group received no pay cut (and thus no explanation). Although the control group and two experimental groups began with the same theft rates and equity perceptions, after the pay cut, the theft rate was 54 percent higher in the adequate explanation group than in the control group. But, in the "inadequate explanation" condition, the theft rate was 141 percent greater than in the control group.

Two studies by Morishima examined the effects of information sharing on the wage negotiation process (1991a) and firm performance (1991b). Comparing his survey results from Japan to those of Kleiner and Bouillon (1988), who used U.S. data, revealed that information on firm profitability, employee productivity, and labor cost was much more likely to be shared with workers in Japan than in the United States. Morishima suggests that there are at least two potential effects of such information. One is that workers will use such information to make greater wage demands and obtain a greater share of the organization's profits. Alternatively, the sharing of information may engender greater goal alignment, trust, cooperation, and a reduction in the union's information disadvantage in negotiation. The result may be greater ability and motivation to perform effectively (see the Locke and Schweiger 1979 model above), as well as greater "responsibility" in terms of avoiding wage demands that could detract from the long-term viability of the organization. Of course, the greater commitment to employment security (i.e., the long-term relationship) in Japan would presumably play an important role here.

Morishima's (1991a; 1991b) findings generally support the notion that information sharing influences both wage negotiations and organization performance. Information sharing decreased (a) the length of negotiations, (b) the union's initial percentage wage increase demand, and (c) the final percentage wage increase settlement. In addition, there were improvements in labor cost, productivity, and profitability. Interestingly, the Kleiner and Bouillon (1988) study found that information sharing led to higher wages and benefits using U.S. data. Morishima suggests that the difference in results may be due to the fact that "other aspects" of industrial relations in many U.S. organizations does not include other aspects (e.g., employment security) of "the comprehensive labor relations strategy used by Japanese management" and that "a piecemeal application of Japanese industrial relations techniques" is not likely to be successful in the United States (1991b, p. 482).

A final note concerns the possibility of inconsistent trends in employee relations and the design of pay programs. There is much discussion of late around the idea of employee "empowerment"—giving employees the resources they need to make more key decisions. Recall that Levine and Tyson emphasized the importance of long-term employment relations, group cohesiveness, and individual rights for employees in building an environment conducive to PDM. Yet, the Dyer and Blancero (1992) Workplace 2000 study found an expectation among respondents of growth in the use of part-time, temporary, and fixed-term contract employees, especially at lower levels in the organization. A significantly smaller percentage of employees was expected to spend entire careers with the organization in the future.

At the same time, the Dyer and Blancero (1992) Workplace 2000 study found that HR experts anticipated greater use of variable pay and a shift to group and organization criteria in determining the payouts. A theme of the present paper has been that compensation operates in the context of a relatively long-term employment relationship or contract. In fact, this may be a precondition for employee acceptance of risk in their pay packages, their willingness to incorporate group and organization goals, and their active acceptance of participative arrangements. One interpretation of these trends is that as an employee, "your employment is more at risk and your pay is more at risk." At the same time organizations are purchasing this transfer of more risk to employees, organizations are trying to send the message that they "want dedication to the company with high levels of quality, quantity, innovation, speed, and adaptiveness." The bottom line is that there may be "an imbalance" (Dyer, cited in Bureau of National Affairs 1992).

Conclusions and Suggested Research Directions

Our review suggests that there has been a renewed emphasis on the importance of organization-based research on the determinants and consequences of employee compensation decisions. There has also been a good deal of recent empirical work as well as helpful literature reviews that have contributed significantly to our understanding of the consequences of specific pay for performance programs (e.g., profit sharing, gainsharing, etc.). In general, the research supports the effectiveness of such programs (relative to situations where pay is not linked to performance). However, there are several areas that require further study.

First, there is almost no research that compares the relative effects of different pay for performance programs (Milkovich and Wigdor 1991). Similarly, there has been little empirical research that identifies the conditions most conducive to the success of different programs (or combinations of programs). In other words, further development and testing of contingency theories is greatly needed (Gerhart and Milkovich 1992; Gomez-Mejia and Balkin 1992).

Second, the focus of the great majority of research (except in the pay-level area) has been on the effects of pay programs on the attitudes and behaviors of current employees. However, it is also quite possible that different pay programs have very different effects on self-selection by employees. Consequently, the composition of the work force (and its corresponding abilities, attitudes, etc.) may differ significantly across different pay programs.

Third, although there is now a substantial body of evidence regarding the importance of organization differences in pay level as well as a developing literature on pay mix differences, systematic examination of the magnitude of organization differences in pay structures and benefits is almost nonexistent. Consequently, evidence on the performance consequences of such differences is also quite limited.

Fourth, in designing empirical research on organization differences in pay decisions and their consequences, several factors should be kept in mind. For example, although we have focused on "organization" differences, substantial variation in pay decisions can exist within organizations as well. Groups, plants, and business units within a single organization can work under very different employment or compensation arrangements. There are also potential advantages in using within-organization designs (e.g., the ability to control for factors specific to the organization as a whole). In addition, to strengthen causal inferences, there is a need to study the process by which pay decisions influence distant outcomes such as organization performance. This means including potential mediating variables such as employee attitudes and behaviors as well as quality and productivity measures. Further, the use of longitudinal data is helpful in distinguishing between transitory and lasting effects of changes in compensation programs.

Fifth, there are many assumptions and beliefs regarding trends in the employment relationship and the design of compensation. For example, there is a good deal of discussion about the growth in team-based production, variable pay, and moving away from individual-level performance in making pay decisions. Down the road, evidence that documents or refutes past predictions would be useful in providing additional perspective on the accuracy of such predictions.

Sixth, based on both the literature and discussions with compensation professionals, it is clear that the monetary component of pay programs is only one part of what is important in influencing employee attitudes and behaviors and organization performance. Process issues such as participation in decision making and communication also appear to be critical in many cases. It would be useful to obtain a better understanding of the interplay between the process and monetary components. For example, to what extent are their effects additive or interactive?

Finally, we note that there are several areas not addressed in this chapter such as executive pay, international aspects of compensation, and equal employment opportunity issues. We refer readers to Gerhart and Milkovich (1992) for a discussion of these issues. That chapter also contains a heuristic model of the determinants and consequences of employee compensation decisions. Further information on other important aspects of compensation such as tournament models and agency theory is provided in companion chapters in this volume.

Endnotes

[1] There are other considerations in measuring pay level. Organizations often have multiple pay levels, varying across business units (product markets) and functional or skill groups (labor markets). Further, studying pay level with cross-sectional data may pose a problem if organizations differ in the sequencing of workers' pay (e.g., Lazear 1979; Ehrenberg and Smith 1988, p. 421; Wachter and Wright 1990). More broadly, money is only one of many aspects of an employment relation. Other relevant factors include security, challenge, coworkers, and so forth.

[2] Institutional theories (e.g., Zucker 1987) also emphasize the pressures (in this case, normative rather than market) on organizations to adopt policies that are similar to those of other organizations. Thus, it would seem to suggest relatively few differences in organization pay practices. As such, the findings regarding organization differences in pay level, and to a greater degree, pay mix (discussed above), are inconsistent with the theory.

[3] Many readers will note the resemblance of this idea to Marxist discussions of the role of the "reserve army."

[4] One possibility is to measure shirking using confidential self-assessments (e.g., Judge 1987) or peer assessments. Alternatively, laboratory experiments provide ample opportunity for measuring such constructs (e.g., Conlon and Parks 1990).

[5] Some examples include: Mark Messier and the New York Rangers (hockey), Michael Jordan and the Chicago Bulls (basketball), and Roger Clemens and the Boston Red Sox (baseball).

[6] Note that another possible outcome is that both internal equity and external equity (in a sense) are achieved by paying employees who command a premium in the market at the market rate and paying other employees at the same level (i.e., "overpaying them"). This, of course, could prove very costly and make it difficult to compete in the product market (Lawler 1986).

[7] The stability is less than that found by Gerhart and Milkovich (1990) for base pay and pay mix dimensions. However, they focused on organization averages, which are probably inherently more stable than an R^2-based index.

[8] Levine and Tyson (1990) define consultative arrangements as providing an opportunity for employees to express opinions, but management makes the decision. Quality circles are one common example. In contrast, substantive participation, although concentrating on the same types of issues, provides greater employee influence. An example would be formal work teams that are able to organize their work with minimal supervision.

[9] The final response rate for this data set was 6.5 percent and may raise concerns regarding selection bias (Ehrenberg 1990). Another concern raised by Ehrenberg is that the degree of economic and noneconomic participation may be endogenous. In the present study (and many others), this raises questions about the direction of causality.

References

Abowd, John M., and Orley Ashenfelter. "Anticipated Unemployment, Temporary Layoffs, and Compensating Wage Differentials." In *Studies in Labor Markets*, ed. S. Rosen. Chicago: University of Chicago Press, 1981.

Adams, J. Stacey. "Inequity in Social Exchange." In *Advances in Experimental Social Psychology*, ed. L. Berkowitz. New York: Academic Press, 1965.

Akerlof, George A. "Gift Exchange and Efficiency-Wage Theory: Four Views." *American Economic Review* 74 (1984), pp. 79-83.

Azariadis, Costas. "Implicit Contracts and Underemployment Equilibria." *Journal of Political Economy* 83 (1975), pp. 1183-1201.

Balkin, David B., and Luis R. Gomez-Mejia. "Toward a Contingent Theory of Compensation Strategy." *Strategic Management Journal* 8 (1987), pp. 169-82.

Barber, Alison E., Randall B. Dunham, and Roger A. Formisano. "The Impact of Flexible Benefits on Employee Benefit Satisfaction." Unpublished Manuscript, University of Wisconsin-Madison, 1990.

Barnard, Chester I. *The Functions of the Executive*. Cambridge: Harvard University Press, 1936.

Baron, James N., and William T. Bielby. "Bringing the Firms Back in: Stratification, Segmentation, and the Organization of Work." *American Sociological Review* 45 (1980), pp. 737-65.

Barringer, Melissa W., and George T. Milkovich. "A Theoretical Exploration of Firms' Decisions About Flexible Benefits Plans." Working Paper #92-17, Center for Advanced Human Resource Studies, Cornell University, 1992.

Barringer, Melissa W., George T. Milkovich, and Olivia Mitchell. "Predicting Employee Health Insurance Selections in a Flexible Benefits Environment." Working Paper 91-21, Center for Advanced Human Resource Studies, Cornell University, 1991.

Becker, Gary. *Human Capital: A Theoretical Analysis with Special Reference to Education*. New York: Columbia University Press, 1964.

Belcher, David, and Thomas Atchinson. *Compensation Administration*. Englewood Cliffs, NJ: Prentice-Hall, 1987.
Blinder, Alan S. *Paying for Productivity*. Washington, D.C.: The Brookings Institution, 1990.
Bretz, Robert D., Ronald A. Ash, and George F. Dreher. "Do People Make the Place? An Examination of the Attraction-Selection-Attrition Hypothesis." *Personnel Psychology* 42 (1989), pp. 561-81.
Bretz, Robert D., George T. Milkovich, and Walter Read. "The Current State of Performance Appraisal Research and Practice: Concerns, Directions, and Implications." Working Paper #89-17, Center for Advanced Human Resource Studies, Cornell University, 1989.
Brown, Charles. "Firms' Choice of Method of Pay." *Industrial and Labor Relations Review* 40 (1990), pp. 165S-82S.
Bureau of National Affairs, "Cornell Study." *Daily Labor Report* 45 (March 6, 1992), p. A-15.
Cappelli, Peter, and Keith Chauvin. "A Test of an Efficiency Wage Model of Grievance Activity." *Industrial and Labor Relations Review* 45 (1991), pp. 3-14.
Cappelli, Peter, and Peter D. Sherer. "Assessing Worker Attitudes under a Two-Tier Wage Plan." *Industrial and Labor Relations Review* 43 (1990), pp. 225-44.
Carroll, Stephen J. "Business Strategies and Compensation Systems." In *New Perspectives on Compensation*, eds. D. B. Balkin and Luis R. Gomez-Mejia. Englewood Cliffs, NJ: Prentice-Hall, 1987.
Chelius, James, and Robert S. Smith. "Profit Sharing and Employment Stability." *Industrial and Labor Relations Review* 43 (1990), pp. 256S-73S.
Conlon, Edward J., and Judi M. Parks. "Effects of Monitoring and Tradition on Compensation Arrangements: An Experiment with Principal-Agent Dyads." *Academy of Management Journal* 33 (1990), pp. 603-22.
Conte, Michael A., and Jan Svejnar. "The Performance Effects of Employee Ownership Plans." In *Paying for Productivity*, ed. A. S. Blinder. Washington, D.C.: The Brookings Institution, 1990.
Cotton, John L., David A. Vollrath, Kirk L. Froggatt, Mark L. Lengnick-Hall, and Kenneth R. Jennings. "Employee Participation: Diverse Forms and Diverse Outcomes." *Academy of Management Review* 13 (1988), pp. 8-22.
Cotton, John L., David A. Vollrath, Mark L. Lengnick-Hall, and Kirk L. Froggatt. "Fact: The Form of Participation Does Matter—A Rebuttal to Leana, Locke, and Schweiger." *Academy of Management Review* 15 (1990), pp. 147-53.
Cowan, Alison L. "Executive Stock Rule Considered." *New York Times* (January 22, 1992), pp. D1, D12.
Cutcher-Gershenfeld, Joel. "The Impact on Economic Performance of a Transformation in Workplace Relations." *Industrial and Labor Relations Review* 44 (1991), pp. 241-60.
Davis, Kermit R., William F. Giles, and Hubert S. Field. "Compensation and Fringe Benefits: How Recruiters View New College Graduate Preferences." *Personnel Administrator* (January 1985), pp. 43-50.
________. "Benefits Preferences of Recent College Graduates." Report 88-2, International Foundation of Employee Benefits Plans, Brookfield, WI, 1988.
Deming, W. Edwards. *Out of the Crisis*. Cambridge, MA: Center for Advanced Engineering Study, Massachusetts Institute of Technology, 1986.
Doeringer, Peter B., and Michael J. Piore. *Labor Markets and Manpower Analysis*. Lexington, MA: Heath, 1971.
Dreher, George F., Ronald A. Ash, and Robert D. Bretz. "Benefit Coverage and Employee Cost: Critical Factors in Explaining Compensation Satisfaction." *Personnel Psychology* 41 (1988), pp. 237-54.
Dunlop, John T. "Suggestions Toward a Reformulation of Wage Theory." Reprinted in *Compensation and Reward Perspectives*, ed. Thomas A. Mahoney. Homewood, IL: Richard D. Irwin, 1979 (1957).
Dyer, Lee, and Donna Blancero. "Workplace 2000: A Delphi Study." Working Paper #92-10, Center for Advanced Human Resource Studies, ILR, Cornell University, 1992.
Dyer, Lee, and Gerald W. Holder. "A Strategic Perspective of Human Resource Management." In *Human Resource Management—Evolving Roles and Responsibilities*. Volume 1, ed. Lee Dyer. Washington, D.C.: Bureau of National Affairs, 1988.

Dyer, Lee, and Donald P. Schwab. "Personnel/Human Resource Management Research." In *Industrial Relations Research in the 1970s: Review and Appraisal*, eds. Thomas A. Kochan, Daniel J.B. Mitchell, and Lee Dyer. Madison, WI: Industrial Relations Research Association, 1982.

EBRI. "Employee Benefit Notes." *EBRI Issue Brief* 13, 4 (1992), pp. 1-2.

Ehrenberg, Ronald G. "Comment." In *Paying for Productivity*, ed. Alan S. Blinder. Washington, D.C.: The Brookings Institution, 1990.

Ehrenberg, Ronald G., and George T. Milkovich. "Compensation and Firm Performance." In *Human Resources and the Performance of the Firm*, eds. Morris Kleiner et al. Madison, WI: Industrial Relations Research Association, 1987.

Ehrenberg, Ronald G., and Robert S. Smith. *Modern Labor Economics*. Glenview, IL: Scott, Foresman and Company, 1988.

Fein, Mitchell. *Improshare: An Alternative to Traditional Managing*. Norcross, GA: Institute of Industrial Engineers, 1981.

Folger, Robert, and Mary A. Konovsky. "Effects of Procedural and Distributive Justice on Reactions to Pay Raise Decisions." *Academy of Management Journal* 32 (1989), pp. 115-30.

Foster Higgins. "Flex Helps Control Health Plan Costs." *BeneNet Executive Summary* 1 (April 1991), p. 1.

Foulkes, Fred K. *Personnel Policies in Large Nonunion Companies*. Englewood Cliffs, NJ: Prentice-Hall, 1980.

GAO. *Implications of Taxation of Employer Provided Employee Benefits*. Washington, D.C.: U.S. General Accounting Office, 1992.

Gerhart, Barry. "Voluntary Turnover, Job Performance, Salary Growth, and Labor Market Conditions." Working Paper No. 90-12, Center for Advanced Human Resource Studies, Cornell University, 1990.

________. "Employment Stability Under Different Managerial Compensation Systems." Working Paper No. 91-02, Center for Advanced Human Resource Studies, Cornell University, 1991.

Gerhart, Barry, and Robert D. Bretz. "Employee Compensation in Advanced Manufacturing Technology." In *Human Factors in Advanced Manufacturing*, eds. W. Karwowski and G. Salvendy. New York: Wiley, forthcoming.

Gerhart, Barry, and George T. Milkovich. "Salaries, Salary Growth, and Promotions of Men and Women in a Large, Private Firm." In *Pay Equity: Empirical Inquiries*, eds. Robert Michael et al. Washington, D.C.: National Academy Press, 1989.

________. "Organization Differences in Managerial Compensation and Financial Performance." *Academy of Management Journal* 33 (1990), pp. 663-91.

________. "Employee Compensation: Research and Practice." In *Handbook of Industrial and Organizational Psychology*, Volume 3, Second Edition, eds. Marvin D. Dunnette and Leatta M. Hough. Palo Alto, CA: Consulting Psychologists Press, 1992.

Gerhart, Barry, and Sara Rynes. "Determinants and Consequences of Salary Negotiations by Graduating Male and Female MBAs." *Journal of Applied Psychology* 76, 2 (1991), pp. 256-62.

Gershenfeld, Walter J. "Employee Participation in Firm Decisions." In *Human Resources and the Performance of the Firm*, eds. Morris Kleiner et al. Madison, WI: IRRA, 1987.

Goll, Irene. "Environment, Corporate Ideology, and Involvement Programs." *Industrial Relations* 30 (1991), pp. 138-49.

Gomez-Mejia, Luis R. "Structure and Process of Diversification, Compensation Strategy, and Firm Performance." *Strategic Management Journal*, 1992, in press.

Gomez-Mejia, Luis R., and David B. Balkin. *Compensation, Organizational Strategy, and Firm Performance*. Cincinnati, OH: South-Western, 1992.

Gomez-Mejia, Luis R., and Theresa M. Welbourne. "Compensation Strategy: An Overview and Future Steps." *Human Resource Planning* 11 (1988), pp. 173-89.

Gowen, Charles R., III, and Sandra A. Jennings. "The Effects of Changes in Participation and Group Size on Gainsharing Success: A Case Study." *Journal of Organizational Behavior Management* 11 (1991), pp. 147-69.

Greenberg, Jerald. "Determinants of Perceived Fairness of Performance Evaluations." *Journal of Applied Psychology* 71 (1986), pp. 340-2.

________. "Theft as a Reaction to Underpayment Inequity: The Hidden Cost of Pay Cuts." *Journal of Applied Psychology* 75 (1990), pp. 561-8.

Groshen, Erica L. "Sources of Wage Dispersion: How Much do Employers Matter?" Unpublished Ph.D. Thesis, Harvard University, 1986.

________. "Why Do Wages Vary Among Employers?" *Economic Review* 24 (1988), pp. 19-38.

________. "Sources of Intra-Industry Wage Dispersion: How Much Do Employers Matter?" *Quarterly Journal of Economics* 106, 3 (1991), pp. 869-84.

Groshen, Erica L., and Alan B. Krueger. "The Structure of Supervision and Pay in Hospitals." *Industrial and Labor Relations* 43 (1990), pp. 134S-46S.

Hammer, Tove H. "New Developments in Profit Sharing, Gainsharing, and Employee Ownership." In *Productivity in Organizations*, eds. J.P. Campbell, R.J. Campbell, and Associates. San Francisco: Jossey-Bass, 1988.

Hannon, John, and George T. Milkovich. "Human Resource Reputation and Firm Performance." Working Paper, Center for Advanced Human Resource Studies, Cornell University, 1992.

Hannon, John, George T. Milkovich, and Michael Sturman. "The Effects of a Flexible Benefits Expert System or Employee Decisions and Satisfaction." Paper presented at the Academy of Management Meetings, Las Vegas, Nevada, August 1992.

Hartmann, Heidi I., Patricia A. Roos, and Donald J. Treiman. "An Agenda for Basic Research on Comparable Worth." In *Comparable Worth: New Directions for Research*, ed. Heidi I. Hartmann. Washington, D.C.: National Academy Press, 1985.

Hatcher, Larry, and Timothy L. Ross. "From Individual Incentives to an Organization-Wide Gainsharing Plan: Effects on Teamwork and Product Quality." *Journal of Organizational Behavior* 12 (1991), pp. 169-83.

Hatcher, Larry, Timothy L. Ross, and Denis Collins. "Attributions for Participation and Nonparticipation in Gainsharing-Plan Involvement Systems." *Group and Organization Studies* 16 (1991), pp. 25-43.

Heneman, Herbert G. III. "Pay Satisfaction." *Research in Personnel and Human Resource Management* 3 (1985), pp. 115-39.

Heneman, Herbert G. III., and Donald P. Schwab. "Work and Rewards Theory." In *ASPA Handbook of Personnel and Industrial Relations*, eds. D. Yoder and H.G. Heneman, Jr. Washington, D.C.: Bureau of National Affairs, 1979.

________. "Pay Satisfaction: Its Multidimensional Nature and Measurement." *International Journal of Psychology* 20 (1985), pp. 129-41.

Hewitt Associates. *Flexible Compensation Programs and Practices: 1990-91*. Lincolnshire, IL: Hewitt Associates, 1991.

________. *On Flexible Compensation*. Lincolnshire, IL: Hewitt Associates, 1992.

Huseman, Richard C., John D. Hatfield, and Russell Driver. "Getting Your Benefits Program Understood and Appreciated." *Personnel Journal* 57, 10 (1978), pp. 560-6.

Huseman, Richard C., John D. Hatfield, and Richard B. Robinson. "The MBA and Fringe Benefits." *Personnel Administrator* 23 (1978), pp. 57-60.

Jaques, Elliot. *Equitable Payment*. New York: Wiley, 1961.

Jenkins, G. Douglas, and Edward E. Lawler III. "Impact of Employee Participation in Pay Plan Development." *Organizational Behavior and Human Performance* 28 (1981), pp. 111-28.

Jensen, Michael C., and William H. Meckling. "Rights and Production Functions: An Application to Labor-Managed Firms and Codetermination." *Journal of Business* 52 (1979), pp. 469-506.

Judge, Timothy A. "The Dispositional Perspective in Human Resources Research." *Research in Personnel and Human Resource Management* 10 (1992), pp. 31-72.

Kahn, Lawrence M., and Peter D. Sherer. "Contingent Pay and Managerial Performance." *Industrial and Labor Relations Review* 43 (1990), pp. 107S-20S.

Kaufman, Roger T. "The Effects of Improshare on Productivity." *Industrial and Labor Relations Review* 45 (1992), pp. 311-22.

Kerr, Clark. "The Balkanization of Labor Markets." In *Labor Mobility and Economic Opportunity*, eds. E.W. Bakke et al. New York: Technology Press of MIT and John Wiley, 1954.

Kerr, Jeff. "Diversification Strategies and Managerial Rewards: An Empirical Study." *Academy of Management Journal* 28, 1 (1985), pp. 155-79

Klein, Katherine. "Employee Stock Ownership and Employee Attitudes: A Test of Three Models." *Journal of Applied Psychology* 72 (1987), pp. 319-32.

Kleiner, Morris M., and Marvin L. Bouillon. "Providing Business Information to Production Workers: Correlates of Compensation and Profitability." *Industrial and Labor Relations Review* 41 (1988), pp. 605-17.

Kochan, Thomas A., and Lee Dyer. "Managing Transformational Change: The Role of HR Professionals." Working Paper No. 92-06, Center for Advanced Human Resource Studies, Cornell University, 1992.

Kochan, Thomas A., Harry C. Katz, and Robert B. McKersie. *The Transformation of American Industrial Relations*. New York: Basic Books, 1986.

Konrad, Alison M., and Jeffrey Pfeffer. "Do You Get What You Deserve? Factors Affecting the Relationship Between Productivity and Pay." *Administrative Sciences Quarterly* 35 (1990), pp. 258-85.

Krueger, Alan B., and Lawrence H. Summers. "Efficiency Wages and the Inter-Industry Wage Structure." *Econometrica* 56 (1988), pp. 259-93.

Kruse, Douglas L. "Profit-Sharing and Employment Variability: Microeconomic Evidence on the Weitzman Theory." *Industrial and Labor Relations Review* 44 (1991), 437-53.

Lawler, Edward E. III. *Pay and Organization Development*. Reading, MA: Addison-Wesley, 1980.

________. *Pay and Organizational Effectiveness*. New York: McGraw-Hill, 1981.

________. "What's Wrong With Point Factor Job Evaluation." *Compensation and Benefits Review* 18, 2 (1986), pp. 20-8.

________. "Pay for Performance: A Strategic Analysis." In *Compensation and Benefits*, ed. Luis R. Gomez-Mejia. Washington, D.C.: Bureau of National Affairs, 1989.

________. *Strategic Pay*. San Francisco: Jossey-Bass, 1990.

Lazear, Edward. "Why is There Mandatory Retirement?" *Journal of Political Economy* 87 (1979), pp. 1261-84.

________."Pay Equality and Industrial Politics." *Journal of Political Economy* 97 (1989), pp. 561-81.

Lazear, Edward, and Sherwin Rosen. "Rank Order Tournaments as an Optimum Labor Contract." *Journal of Political Economy* 89 (1981), pp. 841-64.

Leana, Carrie R., Edwin A. Locke, and David M. Schweiger. "Fact and Fiction in Analyzing Research on Participative Decision Making: A Critique of Cotton, Vollrath, Froggatt, Lengnick-Hall, and Jennings." *Academy of Management Review* 15 (1990), pp. 137-46.

Leonard, J. S. "Wage Structure and Dynamics in the Electronics Industry." *Industrial Relations* 28 (1988), pp. 251-75.

________. "Executive Pay and Firm Performance." *Industrial and Labor Relations Review* 43 (1990), pp. 13S-29S.

Lester, R. A. "Wage Diversity and its Theoretical Consequences." *Review of Economics and Statistics* 28, 3 (1946), pp. 152-9.

Levine, David I., and Laura D. Tyson. "Participation, Productivity, and the Firm's Environment." In *Paying for Productivity*, ed. Alan S. Blinder. Washington, D.C.: Brookings Institution, 1990.

Lewin, David. (1987). "Industrial Relations as a Strategic Variable." In *Human Resources and the Performance of the Firm*, eds. Morris M. Kleiner et al. Madison, WI: IRRA, 1987.

Locke, Edwin A., D. B. Feren, V. M. McCaleb, K. N. Shaw, and A. T. Denny. "The Relative Effectiveness of Four Methods of Motivating Employee Performance." In *Changes in Working Life*, eds. K. D. Duncan et al. New York: John Wiley, 1980.

Locke, Edwin A., and David M. Schweiger. "Participation in Decision-Making: One More Look." In *Research in Organizational Behavior* 1 (1979), pp. 265-340.

Luzadis, Rebecca, and Olivia Mitchell. "Explaining Pension Dynamics." *Journal of Human Resources*, 26 (Fall 1991), pp. 679-703.
Mahoney, Thomas A. "Compensation Preferences of Managers." *Industrial Relations* 3, 3 (1964), pp. 135-44.
________. *Compensation and Reward Perspectives*. Homewood, IL: Irwin, 1979a.
________. "Organizational Hierarchy and Position Worth." *Academy of Management Journal* 22 (1979b), pp. 726-37.
March, James G., and Herbert A. Simon. *Organizations*. New York: Wiley, 1958.
Medoff, James L., and Katharine G. Abraham. "Are Those Paid More Really More Productive? The Case of Experience." *Journal of Human Resources* 16 (1981), pp. 186-216.
Milkovich, George T. "A Strategic Perspective on Compensation Management." *Research in Personnel and Human Resource Management* 6 (1988), pp. 263-88.
Milkovich, George T., and Carolyn Milkovich. "Strengthening the Pay-Performance Relationship: What Does the Research Say?" Center for Advanced Human Resource Studies Issue Paper, Cornell University, 1992.
Milkovich, George T., and Jerry Newman. *Compensation*. Homewood, IL: BPI/ Irwin, 1990.
Milkovich, George T., and Alexandra K. Wigdor. *Pay for Performance*. Washington, D.C.: National Academy Press, 1991.
Miller, Katherine I., and Peter R. Monge. "Participation, Satisfaction, and Productivity: A Meta-Analytic Review." *Academy of Management Journal* 29 (1986), pp. 727-53.
Miner, John B. *Theories of Organizational Behavior*. Hinsdale, IL: Dryden Press, 1980.
Mintzberg, Henry. "Crafting Strategy." *Harvard Business Review* 65 (July-August 1987), pp. 66-75.
Mitchell, Daniel J.B., David Lewin, and Edward E. Lawler III. "Alternative Pay Systems, Firm Performance and Productivity." In *Paying for Productivity*, ed. Alan S. Blinder. Washington, D.C.: Brookings Institution, 1990.
Mitchell, Olivia S. "Fringe Benefits and Labor Mobility." *Journal of Human Resources* 17 (1982), pp. 286-98.
________. "Fringe Benefits and the Cost of Changing Jobs." *Industrial and Labor Relations Review* 37 (1983), pp. 70-8.
Morishima, Motohiro. "Information Sharing and Firm Performance in Japan." *Industrial Relations* 30 (1991a), pp. 37-61.
________. "Information Sharing and Collective Bargaining in Japan: Effects on Wage Negotiation." *Industrial and Labor Relations Review* 44 (1991b), pp. 469-85.
Murray, Brian. "External Competitiveness Versus Internal Consistency in Pay-Setting: Consequences for Organization Performance." Unpublished Master's Thesis, Cornell University, 1992.
Nealey, Stanley T. "Pay and Benefits Preferences." *Industrial Relations* (October 1963), pp. 17-28.
Nealey, Stanley T., and J. Goodale. "Worker Preferences Among Time and Benefits of Pay." *Journal of Applied Psychology* 51 (1967), pp. 357-61.
Newman, Jerry, and D. Fisher. "Strategic Impact of Merit Pay." *Compensation and Benefits Review* 24 (July-August 1992), p. 4.
Pergande, Jill M. "Organization Choice: The Role of Job Characteristics." Report 88-2, International Foundation of Employee Benefit Plans, Brookfield, WI, 1988.
Pfeffer, Jeffrey, and Alison Davis-Blake. "Understanding Organizational Wage Structures: A Resource Dependence Approach." *Academy of Management Journal* 30 (1987), pp. 437-55.
________. "Determinants of Salary Dispersion in Organizations." *Industrial Relations* 29 (1990), pp. 38-57.
Pierce, Jon, Stephen Rubenfeld, and Susan Morgan (1991). "Employee Ownership: A Conceptual Model of Process and Effects," *Academy of Management Review* 16, 1 (1991), pp. 121-44.
Pritchard, Robert D., Steven D. Jones, Philip L. Roth, Karla K. Stuebing, and Steven E. Ekeberg. "Effects of Group Feedback, Goal Setting, and Incentives on Organizational Productivity." *Journal of Applied Psychology* 73 (1988), pp. 337-58.

Reynolds, Lloyd G. *The Structure of Labor Markets: Wages and Labor Mobility in Theory and Practice*. New York: Harper and Brothers, 1951.
Rousseau, Diane M. "New Hire Perceptions of Their Own and Their Employer's Obligations: A Study of Psychological Contracts." *Journal of Organizational Behavior* 11 (1990), pp. 389-400.
Rynes, Sara L. "Compensation Strategies for Recruiting." *Topics in Total Compensation* 2 (1987), pp. 185-96.
Salter, Malcolm S. "Tailor Incentive Compensation to Strategy." *Harvard Business Review* 51, 2 (1973), pp. 94-102.
Schiller, Bradley R., and Randall D. Weiss. "The Impact of Private Pensions on Firm Attachment." *Review of Economics and Statistics* 61 (1979), pp. 369-80.
Schuster, Michael H. "The Scanlon Plan: A Longitudinal Analysis." *Journal of Applied Behavioral Science* 20 (1984), pp. 23-8.
________. "Gainsharing: Current Issues and Research Needs." Workshop, School of Industrial and Labor Relations, Cornell University, March 1990.
Segal, Martin. "Post-Institutionalism in Labor Economics: The Forties and Fifties Revisited." *Industrial and Labor Relations Review* 39 (1986), pp. 388-403.
Shapiro, Carl, and Joseph E. Stiglitz. "Equilibrium Unemployment as a Worker Discipline Device." *American Economic Review* 74 (1984), pp. 433-44.
Simon, Herbert A. "A Formal Theory of the Employment Relationship." *Econometrica* 19 (1951), pp. 293-305.
Spence, Michael A. "Job Market Signalling." *Quarterly Journal of Economics* 87 (1973), pp. 355-74.
Stonebraker, Peter W. "Flexibility and Incentive Benefits: A Guide to Program Development." *Compensation Review* 17, 2 (1985), pp. 40-53.
Teel, Kenneth S. "Are Merit Raises Really Based on Merit?" *Personnel Journal* 65, 3 (1986), pp. 88-95.
Thurow, Lester. *Generating Inequality*. New York: Basic Books, 1975.
Tolbert, Pamela S. "Organizations and Inequality: Sources of Earnings Differences Between Male and Female Faculty." *Sociology of Education* 59 (1986), 227-35.
"Unseen Apples and Small Carrots." *Economist* 319, 7702 (April 13, 1991), p. 75.
U.S. Chamber of Commerce. *Employee Benefits 1990*. Washington, D.C.: U.S. Chamber of Commerce, 1991.
Vroom, Victor H. *Work and Motivation*. New York: Wiley, 1964.
Wachter, Michael L., and Randall D. Wright (1990). "The Economics of Internal Labor Markets." *Industrial Relations* 29 (1990), pp. 240-62.
Wagner, John A. III, and Richard Z. Gooding. "Shared Influence and Organizational Behavior: A Meta-analysis of Situational Variables Expected to Moderate Participation-Outcome Relationships." *Academy of Management Journal* 30 (1987), pp. 524-41.
Wagner, John A. III, Paul Rubin, and Thomas J. Callahan. "Incentive Payment and Nonmanagerial Productivity: An Interrupted Time Series Analysis of Magnitude and Trend." *Organizational Behavior and Human Decision Processes* 42 (1988), pp. 47-74.
Wallace, Marc J., Jr., and Charles H. Fay. *Compensation Theory and Practice*. Boston: PWS-Kent, 1988.
Weber, Caroline, and Sara Rynes. "Effects of Compensation Strategy on Job Pay Decisions." *Academy of Management Journal* 34, 1 (1991), pp. 86-109.
Weiss, Andrew. "Incentives and Worker Behavior: Some Evidence." In *Incentives, Cooperation, and Risk Taking*, ed. H. R. Nalbantian. Totowa, NJ: Rowman and Littlefield, 1987.
Weitzman, Martin L. *The Share Economy*. Cambridge, MA: Harvard University Press, 1984.
________. "The Simple Macroeconomics of Profit Sharing." *American Economic Review* 75 (1985), pp. 937-53.
Weitzman, Martin L., and Douglas L. Kruse. "Profit Sharing and Productivity." In *Paying for Productivity*, ed. Alan S. Blinder. Washington, D.C.: The Brookings Institution, 1990.
Williamson, Oliver E. *Markets and Hierarchies*. New York: Free Press, 1975.

Williamson, Oliver E., Michael L. Wachter, and Jeffrey E. Harris. "Understanding the Employment Relation: The Analysis of Idiosyncratic Exchange." *Bell Journal of Economics* 6 (1975), pp. 250-78.
Wilson, Marie, Gregory B. Northcraft, and Margaret A. Neale. "The Perceived Value of Fringe Benefits." *Personnel Psychology* 38 (1985), pp. 309-20.
Womack, James P., Daniel T. Jones, and David Roos. *The Machine That Changed the World*. New York: MacMillan, 1990.
Yellen, Janet L. "Efficiency Wage Models of Unemployment." *American Economic Review* 74 (1984), pp. 200-5.
Zucker, Lynne G. "Institutional Theories of Organization." *American Review of Sociology* 13 (1987), pp. 443-64.

CHAPTER 7

Human Resource Practices and Productive Labor-Management Relations

CASEY ICHNIOWSKI
Columbia University and
National Bureau of Economic Research

How are "good" labor-management relations created? This may be one of the most important questions facing workers, union representatives, and managers in today's competitive environment. One of the first studies ever to try to relate establishment-level labor relations environments to performance found that in plants where workers and managers rated the labor relations environment as good, output per worker and other measures of economic performance were higher than in plants with worse ratings of the labor relations environment (Katz, Kochan, and Gobeille 1983). A number of other recent studies have come to similar conclusions (for reviews, see Freeman and Medoff 1984, 176-9; and Belman 1990, 32-38). If high-quality labor relations do promote productivity, then the question of how to create "good" labor relations is indeed critical. While several studies now provide support for the proposition that good labor relations coincide with higher productivity, these studies have not been able to answer the question of how to establish good labor-management relations.

Human resource (HR) policies and practices define many aspects of the relationship between labor and management. Differences in HR policies and practices might therefore be responsible for differences in the quality of labor-management relations and also for differences in economic performance across firms. The relationship between HR policies and firm performance was the focus of the 1987 Industrial Relations Research Association (IRRA) research volume *Human Resources and the Performance of the Firm*. Extensive literature reviews in the 1987 volume considered the links between economic performance and HR policies in diverse areas including compensation and pensions, recruiting and selection, employee involvement, grievance procedures, and employment security. These reviews typically concluded that "we know very little" about the relationship between fundamental HR policies that a firm pursues and its economic performance (see as examples Ehrenberg and Milkovich 1987, 113; Ichniowski and Lewin 1987, 189).

While several recent studies have helped to temper the blunt conclusions of the 1987 IRRA volume, particularly with regard to the link between compensation policies and performance (see Ehrenberg 1990 for a summary), it is inevitable that in the short space of a few years the general conclusions of the 1987 IRRA research volume have not changed much. Empirical tests of the links among HR practices and measures of competitive performance are still very rare.

With only limited new empirical evidence to review on this topic, this chapter takes a somewhat different approach than a review of the literature. The paper focuses on HR policies and issues that are commanding a great deal of attention in current management literature and the popular business press—work force "flexibility," employment security, and workplace norms or "culture." The first section presents a longitudinal case study of the experience of one facility that provides detailed evidence on how HR practices in these three areas helped to change the facility's labor relations environment and its economic performance. The next section selectively reviews recent theoretical models of worker and management behavior in the face of "agency problems." This section focuses specifically on models which consider the possible competitive rationales for HR policies that increase work force flexibility, enhance employment security, and help establish the norm or "culture" of worker commitment to the performance goals of an organization—HR policies which seem to have been instrumental in stimulating superior performance in the case study. The third section discusses how the case study may help provide a richer understanding of the empirical link between "good labor-management relations" and economic performance. A final section discusses methodological features that would be desirable in future empirical studies of the relationship among HR practices, labor-management relations, and competitive performance.

An Illustrative Case Study: HR Practices Can Matter

In the early 1980s I conducted a study of eleven North American paper-making facilities to investigate the relationship between plant-level industrial relations environments and productivity. My study which documents an inverse relationship between grievance activity and productivity in this sample is one of the pieces of evidence supporting the general conclusion that the quality of an establishment's labor-management relations affects economic performance (Ichniowski 1986). However, as in other studies, factors that caused the high grievance rates and determined the "quality" of the labor-management environment could not convincingly be detected.

That study analyzed the experience of the paper mills over the six-year period from 1976 through mid-1982. In late 1983, the mill with perhaps the most adversarial labor-management relations and the highest grievance rates embarked on a radical series of changes in its fundamental HR practices in an attempt to change its labor relations environment and to improve the poor economic performance of the mill. This section summarizes those HR changes and the impacts of those changes on economic performance and industrial relations outcomes in the paper mill.

Employment Practices and Declining Mill Performance

The paper mill investigated in this case study began operating in the late 1960s. During the last half of the 1970s, the mill experienced a dramatic decline in performance. In 1975 the annual rate of return on the capital stock, as measured by the ratio of operating income to total capital investment at the mill, was 37.8 percent. By 1980 this rate of return had fallen to just 4.7 percent—an unacceptably low level of profitability according to mill managers. With the relatively modern paper-making technology in the mill, management expected and required much higher operating incomes and rates of return for this mill.

The mill's capital and technology remained essentially unchanged during this period, so changes in the stock of capital were not responsible for the declining performance. Cyclical effects on prices of the mill's paper were also not to blame for the declining performance between 1975 and 1980. Another of this company's mills that produced similar paper products experienced an increase in its rate of return over this period, with no adverse effects from any decline in paper prices in this six-year period.

Rather the decline in profitability could be traced to a consistent and marked increase in manning levels. Between 1975 and 1980 the production work force grew from 375 to 474 employees. Because of the high level of capital intensity and the high costs of lost production from shutdowns and startups, this mill, like other paper mills, operated seven days a week, twenty-four hours a day. Over the 1975-1980 period, output levels were fairly constant at about 1450 tons per day, but by 1980 it was taking 25 percent more workers than it had just a few years earlier to produce the same level of output in this mill's round-the-clock operations.

An Adversarial Labor Relations Environment

While the manning increases were the proximate reason for a decline in mill productivity and profitability, the underlying causes for the manning increases were more complex. The mill experienced two long strikes in negotiating a labor contract with two United Paperworkers International Union (UPIU) locals at the mill in 1971 and in 1974. These strikes were very costly for the company, as expensive capital remained idle for months in both strikes. While the 1977 and 1980 contracts were renegotiated without strikes, the evolution of the formal labor contract, as well as associated sidebar agreements and unwritten past practices, help explain the manning increases in the mill during the late 1970s.

Between 1970 and 1982 the mill had seven different top managers. Managers of various functional areas in the mill also turned over relatively frequently. In contrast the production work force tended to be long-tenure employees, since the mill was by far the high-wage employer in this mill town.

With little top management continuity, supervisors had assumed wide latitude in making agreements with employees and union representatives on the mill floor. Often these agreements were specified in memoranda. According to one manager, "Most of the contract wasn't even in the contract anymore." Many memoranda and sidebar agreements were inconsistent with one another. The union locals had detailed records on the individual agreements, while the high levels of management turnover resulted in inconsistent and incomplete records.

The union controlled the interpretation of the work rules and practices through the grievance procedure with better evidence on the relevant past practices ready for any arbitration hearing. By 1983, the mill's work force of about 485 employees was filing an average of 80 grievances each month. The number of job classifications had grown to 94. Each of the three daily shifts had approximately 160 workers, so that by 1983 there were only one or two workers per job classification.

After a lengthy research and planning process, management was preparing to insist upon sweeping changes in the mill's HR practices in the 1983 contract negotiations. In late 1983, after a two and one-half month strike over management's proposed changes, the mill's two UPIU locals signed the new collective bargaining agreement. With over a decade-long history of adversarial labor-management relations, high levels of grievance activity, several bitter strikes including a long strike over the previous two and one-half months, the term of the 1983 contract—the "team concept" contract—took effect.

The Terms of the "Team Concept" Agreement

The "team concept" contract specified sweeping changes in the mill's HR practices. Key changes in the HR policy areas of job design, compensation, training, performance evaluation, and communication are noted here.

Broad, flexible job design. The ninety-four job classifications were reduced to four operator classifications—or "job clusters." In one paper machine department, for example, the fourth, fifth, sixth, and seventh hands—the paper tester, refiner hand, and utility man—were redesignated as "C operators."

Employees were given the opportunity to rotate to other new tasks in the broader "job clusters." Along with the more broadly defined job clusters, management was granted greater flexibility in job assignment. The first page of the new agreement clearly stated that the goal of team concept:

> . . . was to improve the efficiency and competitive position of the mill providing for the flexible utilization of

> . . . personnel . . . Team Concept means that the company has flexibility in how it assigns employees.

Compensation. Pay rates were increased by 6 percent, 5 percent, and 5 percent on the anniversary dates of the implementation of the contract. In an era when concession agreements were negotiated in many industries, this was not a concession agreement.

More importantly, these percentage increases were actually the minimum increases employees would obtain. Upon return from the strike, the pay of all employees in a given operator cluster was calculated as 6 percent above the highest pay rate of any of the old classifications now in that cluster. In the case of the C operator cluster described above, fourth hands received a 6 percent wage increase, while utility hands who were formerly the lowest paid employees among the new C operators received a 52 percent wage increase.

Training and development. Training procedures were implemented to help ensure employees were acquiring the skills necessary for the more broadly defined job clusters. Mastery of new skills required in the new broader job clusters was evaluated with a new performance monitoring system. Under "team concept," production workers also received training in the form of visits to sites of customers. Workers returned with knowledge about the types of quality imperfections that were particularly problematic for different customers.

Communication and dispute resolution. The structure of the grievance procedure was left intact. However, one of the most important changes of the team concept contract, from management's perspective, was the elimination of the precedents contained in past practices and memoranda of understanding, many of which remained unknown to current managers. The new contract specified:

> The elements of Team Concept supersede all conflicting limitations on management rights provided in the labor agreement, and all pre-existing rules, commitments, understandings, work practices, past practices, grievance settlements, arbitrations or side agreements written or unwritten.

While the contract left the grievance procedure in place, it dramatically altered the substance of the work rules and conditions over which grievances could be filed.

New communication procedures supplemented the historically adversarial grievance procedure. Attitude surveys were to be conducted on a regular basis. In addition, the mill manager and senior HR manager conducted "listening sessions" with a different shift of a given department each month. The sessions had the double purpose of identifying worker complaints and eliciting suggestions on ways to improve work life and mill performance. Neither the attitude surveys nor the monthly listening sessions were contractually required.

Employment security. Finally, along with these sweeping changes in HR practices, the team concept contract also included a bold job security pledge on the first page of the new labor agreement:

> No current employee will lose his employment or suffer a reduction in his wage rate due to the implementation of the Team Concept.

While this pledge was explicit, it was nevertheless conditional. In particular, management reserved the right to reduce the work force in the event of declines in product demand. Still the new agreement pledged job security to the existing work force despite the dramatic employment increases in the late 1970s and 1980s that contributed to the decline in productivity and profitability.

The Impact of Team Concept

Economic outcomes. The terms of the team concept labor agreement directly determined many aspects of the competitive performance of the mill after 1983. First, mill management honored the job security pledge. The number of full-time employees in 1983 before team concept was 485. In the first two years of team concept, it remained at 485 to 486 employees.

The work force enjoyed large increases in compensation. In the last year before team concept, total monthly labor costs averaged $1.8 million. Average monthly labor costs in years one and two of team concept were $2.6 million and $2.4 million respectively—or about 44 percent and 33 percent higher than in 1983.

Average daily production in the last year before team concept was 1744 tons. In the first twelve months, output declined to 1703 tons per day. Year two of team concept, however, marked the beginning of a performance renaissance at the mill. Output increased, on average, by 86 tons per day over its pre-team concept level to 1830 tons per day. The 86 ton per day increase corresponds to a revenue increase of $831,000 per month when the production increase is evaluated at relatively low 1985 paper prices for the mill. This conservative estimate of the revenue increase associated with the productivity improvement between 1983 and 1985 more than offset the $600,000 increase in average monthly labor costs between 1983 and 1985. Moreover, with additional significant improvements in the efficiency of the utilization of other nonlabor inputs, monthly operating profits increased from $.89 million in 1984 to $2.75 million in 1985.

There were many specific causes for the production increases and associated increases in profitability. At the heart of all of these specific reasons were workers' ideas for improving operations that workers had never before offered. Downtime was dramatically reduced. One of the two annual shutdowns for major maintenance, the standard practice for the industry, was eliminated in year two. Most importantly, the worker-generated suggestions and modifications simply increased the speed and efficiency of the machinery.

Industrial relations outcomes. Indicators of the industrial relations environment on the mill floor also exhibited changes in the first two years of team concept. With the elimination of the power of precedent for past practices and side agreements, grievances dropped from about 80 per month in 1983 to four per month in 1984. Year two of team concept saw an additional drop in grievances to 1.6 per month.

Average monthly recordable accidents were comparable in the year before and after the adoption of team concept at about 4.0 per month. In year two of team concept, this accident statistic dropped to 1.4 accidents per month. The ratio of absentee hours to the planned number of production hours declined from 2.1 percent in 1983 to 1.6 percent in 1984, and then to 1.0 percent in 1985.

After 1985. The worker-generated production increases in 1985 were the key to improving the competitive performance of the mill. The key to continued success was the continuation of the unprecedented level of production in 1985 when output totaled 658,000 tons. Through the same worker-led efforts to improve the speed and efficiency of the machines, mill production increased steadily after 1985 to approximately 800,000 tons in 1990. The team concept contract has been voluntarily extended three times in peaceful, out-of-phase negotiations since the original 1983 agreement. Each of these contracts substantially increased the pay rates of the operator clusters and were the negotiated means by which the benefits of the productivity improvements were shared with the work force. The mill by 1990 was the most productive in North America, manned by the highest paid paperworkers, and operating at levels of profitability never previously attained.

Theoretical Perspectives on the Competitive Consequences of Multiskilling, Employment Security, and Workplace Norms

The case study of the paper mill is unique for the richness of data on productivity and profitability, compensation and staffing patterns, labor relations outcomes, and HR practices. It provides striking evidence that HR policies and practices can affect indicators of an establishment's labor relations environment as well as its economic performance. In the longitudinal case study, it is almost impossible to believe that the worker-generated improvements in the paper machines' speed and efficiency would have occurred in the earlier era of distrust and adversarial relations. The dramatic increase in productivity yielded levels of production that today far exceed the original engineering estimates of the paper machines' capacities and also exceed the levels of labor productivity in similar North American mills. A productivity decline that was produced in large part by increases in manning was reversed by dramatic increases in production levels while freezing manning levels in accordance with a job security pledge.

The improvement in economic performance also coincides with a striking shift from conflict to cooperation in labor-management relations at one workplace with a fixed complement of workers. An era of lengthy violent strikes, frequent grievance filings, and reductions in the tasks within the scope of a given job was replaced by an era of peaceful extensions of labor contracts, the near elimination of grievances, and valuable voluntary contributions of productivity-enhancing ideas by employees.

Still the case study describes the history of only one plant. It provides no direct information on whether the team concept approach could yield similar results in other settings. It provides no way to identify whether certain important preconditions were present in the paper mill that made team concept an appropriate choice for that particular facility or whether labor-management cooperation would be associated with superior economic performance in other types of firms or workplaces.

To provide a broader context for considering the performance turnaround in the paper mill, I summarize the main arguments from several theoretical models which focus specifically on multiskilling, employment security, and workplace norms and culture as possible determinants of economic performance. While convincing empirical studies of the relation between HR practices and firm performance are rare, the 1980s witnessed dramatic growth in theoretical studies that sought to model rigorously the possible economic rationales for various HR practices. These studies view HR practices as formal or informal arrangements between labor and management that attempt to overcome inherent "agency problems" between workers and managers.

The Basic Structure of Agency Problems in the Employment Relationship

Before reviewing several theoretical studies that may provide insight into the paper mill case study, it is useful to review the basic structure shared by many models that address agency problems in employment relationships. An agency problem exists when some individual (the principal) contracts with another (the agent) to act on his or her behalf. In the modern business firm, shareholders are ultimately the principals. One set of agency problems exists between shareholders and managers, and various studies of executive compensation address the kinds of contracts that might best assure that managers operate in shareholders' interests (see for example, Leonard 1990; Gibbons and Murphy 1990; Abowd 1990). A second set of agency problems exists between management as principals and the nonsupervisory work force as agents.

Many models of workplace arrangements designed to overcome agency problems often contain several similar structural elements. First, these models acknowledge that a given worker is capable of different levels of performance. There is no competitive challenge in designing more effective workplace arrangements if each worker is capable of only one invariant level of performance under all arrangements. In models addressing agency problems in the workplace, an individual worker is capable of higher or lower levels of contribution of "effort" (e_i). Extra effort in these models corresponds to valuable worker behavior that is hard for management to observe or otherwise collect evidence about, such as attentiveness on the production line, courteous treatment of customers, ideas from workers to improve business operations, or assistance to co-workers.

Second, management and labor have different underlying objectives. Management wants to maximize profits. The firm's output (Q) depends on the variable worker effort (i.e., $Q = Q(e)$) with higher effort yielding higher output. Letting p represent the market price of firm's output and w the wage paid to the work force of N employees, management tries to maximize:

$$p * Q(N,e_i) - wN . \quad (1)$$

Third, workers maximize their utility. Worker utility increases with their pay. However, at some point, their variable effort or contribution begins to reduce the worker's utility. Letting C represent the cost to a given worker of providing effort, where C increases with e, workers try to maximize:

$$w - C(e_i) . \quad (2)$$

While the underlying objectives of management and labor are different, this difference does not necessarily have to produce conflict in the behavioral interactions between labor and management. Rather, HR policies and practices may be devised that provide a motivation for workers to engage in activities that are consistent with the management's interests in higher profitability.

The paper mill case might be usefully viewed from the perspective of various models that are built on this basic framework. Certainly, a model that tries to explain the changes in behavior and performance after the implementation of team concept must allow for different levels of performance from the same work force with the same capital equipment. The key component of the valuable worker "effort" in the case study appears to be their participation in offering and implementing important productivity-enhancing ideas. Under the old, pre-team concept HR practices, employees sought opportunities to gain interpretations of the labor contract that eliminated tasks and responsibilities and narrowed job specifications while still maintaining contractually specified wage rates. In contrast, after 1983, team concept seems to have been successful in eliciting valuable worker ideas. However, the workers' productivity-enhancing ideas could also be costly to employees. Worker ideas are probably not costly so much in terms of requiring extra mental or physical effort. Rather, workers will not inherently act in management's interests due to the potential costs of employment losses to themselves or coworkers when they offer or support productivity-enhancing ideas.

Many theoretical studies elaborate on the basic agency problem framework to consider the possible competitive rationale for many different HR employment policies. Elsewhere in this volume, Lazear provides a broader review of recent contributions to the theoretical literature on employment practices and agency problems. From the many theoretical studies that discuss ways to overcome agency problems in employment relationships, this section will focus on a few specific models that consider these HR practices that seem so central to the paper mill case study—flexibility, employment security, and norms or "culture" of a workplace.

This chapter's selective review will necessarily omit several prominent categories of models in this broad area of theoretical research. For example, in a basic "efficiency wage" model, employees provide higher effort when employers offer higher than market wages, because they are afraid that failing to do so will cause them to lose their jobs and force them to spend time either unemployed or in a lower paying secondary labor market job. (See Carmichael [1990] for a review of this set of models.) Instead of providing a broad review of this theoretical literature, the paper concentrates on models that specifically address work force flexibility, employment security, and norms and culture of the workplace.

A simple solution. HR compensation policies theoretically can solve the basic agency problem very directly. Management could set up a "pay-for-performance" compensation scheme that directly rewards workers for the valuable output they create or for their productivity-enhancing effort input. Why might this relatively direct approach of paying workers directly in proportion to their output or in proportion to their productivity-enhancing ideas have been unsuccessful in improving productivity and performance?

The approach of implementing an output-based, pay-for-performance scheme in the paper mill would probably be problematic because of difficulties in linking useful measures of output to the workers. First, quality and quantity of output were both valuable dimensions of the output. While tons of output may be measurable, quality dimensions may be more difficult to measure. Even if both quantity and quality of output for the mill or departments of the mill are measurable, differences in various individuals' contributions to that group output may not. This difficulty may have been an especially important limitation on the usefulness of this kind of pay-for-performance scheme.

Alternatively, management could have tried to reward directly those workers who most successfully generated productivity-improving ideas. This "pay-for-effort" compensation scheme might also be problematic. Employees' suggestions, once revealed, are public knowledge and management may have an incentive to renege on any promised rewards. Even if the prospect of even more suggestions in the future overcomes this difficulty, evaluating the payoff of a suggestion may be difficult.

Furthermore, the 1983 labor contract is explicitly based on a team concept in work organization. Part of the reason for this form of work organization may be that higher quality ideas are generated through sharing ideas and working together with other workers on solving productivity problems in a cooperative team environment. If team work is important in this way, a reward structure that offers higher pay or some form of employment security only to a certain percentage of the more successful workers while eliminating jobs of the other less successful workers could undermine the cooperative team spirit needed to develop significant productivity-advancing ideas (Lazear and Rosen 1981).

More generally, relatively straightforward pay-for-performance solutions are untenable in the recent theoretical literature on agency problems in employment relationships because of these kinds of presumably common difficulties in measuring or observing employee "effort" and in measuring all valued dimensions of output. In any case, this direct pay-for-performance approach was not in evidence in the paper mill. How did the HR practices that were a part of team concept help stimulate more productive behavior and superior performance outcomes in the mill?

Flexibility and Employment Security

Prominent among the HR changes in the paper mill case were the dramatic reduction in job classifications, the related increases in flexibility and multiskilling, and the bold pledge of employment security. Aoki (1988, 174-203; 1986), and more recently Carmichael and MacLeod (1991), develop models that consider the possible competitive rationales for multiskilling and employment security. The models of both authors are complementary, emphasizing different reasons why multiskilling might make competitive sense.

Multiskilling as employment security. The Carmichael-MacLeod (C-M) model explicitly addresses the question of how the HR practice of multiskilling can help secure workers' cooperation in supporting and offering productivity-enhancing ideas—ideas that if implemented could threaten the workers' jobs. Management's objective in the C-M model is essentially the equation (1) profitability equation. However, the employees' utility calculations are more involved than is implied by the equation (2) utility function, because the changes in employment and wage levels that occur after an increase in productivity do not fall squarely within the framework of a simple wage-effort calculation. Still, employees control the productivity-enhancing ideas and this valuable "effort" is costly to workers because of potential job loss that a productivity improvement could produce.

C-M review the likely problems with a more direct "pay-for-suggestions" compensation scheme and consider other HR policies that might elicit worker ideas. C-M argue that one possible solution would be for management to invest in training workers in skills needed in other jobs before workers have offered any valuable ideas. This precommitment to multiskilling workers for the requirements of other jobs alters management's incentives to lay workers off after any worker-generated productivity improvements. If a certain number of the workers' jobs are no longer necessary, the displaced workers can be shifted to other jobs still in demand. Ultimately the C-M model argues that multiskilling can itself be a guarantee of job security.

In the case of the paper mill, the 1983 team concept contract simultaneously provided for multiskilling, the training to achieve the multiskilling, and an employment security pledge. The investment in multiskilling also predated any of the productivity improvements. According to the C-M model, the employment security pledge need not be explicitly stated as it was in the 1983 team concept contract. However, if multiskilling does make employees' jobs more secure, there is no harm in making the employment security pledge explicit and probably some benefit in allaying worker fears about job loss.

The C-M model therefore seems consistent in some ways with the experience in the paper mill. However, the C-M model elaborates more specifically on the conditions when multiskilling by itself will help guarantee employment security. In particular, the impact of technological change on employment levels in different job classes is a critical determinant of whether multiskilling by itself will produce employment security. If the technological change is likely to reduce employment in all job classes, multiskilling will not in and of itself provide employment security. Multiskilling is more likely to guarantee employment security when the technological change displaces one job class in favor of another, so that the multiskilled workers can be employed in the expanding job classes. In this case, multiskilling will be more likely to succeed in eliciting workers' productivity-improving ideas. When job loss is likely to be more pervasive across job categories, additional contractual guarantees of employment security may be necessary to allay worker fears about job loss and secure the benefits of their productivity improvements.

In the case of the paper mill, it seems reasonable to suspect that multiskilling would not have allayed worker fears about job loss without the more direct pledge of employment security. In particular, the mill had previously operated in the early 1970s with many fewer workers, and with the protection of past practices and narrow job classifications no longer available under the 1983 contract, fear of job loss would seem natural. The pledge of employment security in the paper mill extended to all production workers, which differs from the kind of employment security that only a portion of the work force enjoys under multiskilling in the C-M model.

The up-front commitment to multiskilling in the paper mill may still have altered management's incentives to lay off workers. But, by itself, multiskilling probably did not eliminate incentives for management to reduce the size of its work force. These remaining fears of job loss may have made it necessary to offer workers a more expansive and explicit job security pledge than was provided by multiskilling.

Direct benefits of employment security. If the explicit, yet conditional, pledge of employment security somehow provided more expansive protection than multiskilling would provide, then the pledge of employment security arguably could have been enough to elicit workers' productivity-improving ideas. If so, there would also need to be additional reasons for management to invest in multiskilling, since employment security would, by itself, secure worker cooperation in efforts to improve productivity. In his studies of the employment practices in Japanese firms, Aoki develops models that suggest somewhat more separate reasons for adopting policies of employment security and multiskilling.

With regard to employment security, Aoki (1988, 174-203) evaluates the possibility that management and labor can commit themselves to a more direct exchange of conditional employment security from management for higher effort from the work force. An unconditional, iron-clad guarantee of employment security would certainly eliminate workers' fear of job loss that might result from offering and supporting productivity-improving ideas. However, a complete and unconditional guarantee of employment security may be too costly because of the possibility of declines in demand for the firm's goods and services that are beyond management's control. While management may want to assure workers that any worker-generated productivity enhancements will not lead to job loss, management also would like to retain some ability to adjust the size of the work force when demand for the firm's goods and services declines significantly. This is precisely the condition on the employment security pledge in the paper mill case study.

The conditional nature of the employment security pledge may lead workers to believe that the pledge is not credible, thereby rendering it ineffective as a means of eliciting worker effort and ideas. If management were to reduce employment, workers would have difficulty distinguishing between different possible reasons for the manpower reductions. Management would have difficulty proving that declines in demand for the product, rather than worker-generated improvements in efficiency of the firm's operations, were the cause of layoffs. In the case of the paper mill, it seems likely that the long history of adversarial relations would have made the union locals and the work force very suspicious of the condition on the pledge of employment security.

Aoki argues that the workers' difficulties in distinguishing management's motivations for reducing employment were a layoff to occur, together with management's difficulties in measuring and evaluating workers' variable "effort," make an exchange of conditional job security in return for higher effort very difficult to enforce—even when such an exchange is explicitly contained in a labor agreement. According to Aoki (1988), management's commitment to a conditional employment security pledge is only credible if it is the least expensive way to elicit higher effort levels from workers. Aoki describes situations in which there are other, less costly, ways to elicit worker effort. In particular, when workers' fear of unemployment is relatively high, workers would already have a motivation for working at higher effort levels without a pledge of employment security (Aoki 1988, 176).

Is it possible that the conditional employment security pledge in the paper mill was simply not credible, and higher worker effort was motivated by fear of job loss? At the start of the paper mill's team concept contract, the precedents contained in past practices and the protection from job loss that these precedents provided were completely eliminated. Furthermore, since the mill was the high-wage employer in the town, job loss would be very costly to any workers that would be laid off. While it seems reasonable to suspect that fear of unemployment might have been considerable at the start of the 1983 contract in the paper mill, this fear still does not appear to have been the cause of the improved performance. The productivity improvements did not begin for some two years after the past practices were eliminated. The timing of the productivity improvements suggests that fear of job loss was not the stimulus for eliciting worker ideas.

At the same time, the lag between the start of the team concept contract and the productivity improvements suggests that workers also did not respond immediately to the conditional employment security pledge. This brings into focus one of the most difficult, yet most important, questions to address in the paper mill. Why and when did workers begin to trust management and offer their productivity-enhancing ideas? Without trust, employees will always be concerned that, in the future, management will not honor pledges of job security that are not completely unconditional.

In the paper mill, management maintained employment at its pre-team concept level for some two years before worker-generated productivity improvements began to pay off. This suggests that a long and expensive process may be required to establish trust. Furthermore, the expected payoff from worker ideas would therefore have to be significant, as in the case of the paper mill, for management to pursue these expensive policies. While the workers' inability to verify management's commitment to a conditional job security pledge may be a critical impediment to the development of trust, another impediment to the development of mutual cooperation at the workplace could also be that management is simply unsure about whether or not worker ideas will have the kind of payoff they did in the paper mill case study.

More research on how trust evolves would be useful in this regard. (For useful analysis of the importance of trust and cooperation, see Axelrod 1984.) In addition, empirical analyses of the economic performance of firms that undertake cooperative "ideas-for-employment security" exchanges relative to other firms that adhere to noncooperative behavior would be beneficial in this regard. For the present, we must rely on an occasional opportunistic case study for our evidence on the possible benefits of these different approaches to HR.

Direct benefits of multiskilling. While certain aspects of Aoki's "employment security-for-effort" model may not completely capture the experience of the paper mill, it does seem reasonable to suspect that the pledge of employment security, though less than complete, was required to make workers willing to offer their productivity-improving ideas. This raises an additional question about the investment in multiskilling. If the direct pledge of job security was responsible for making workers willing to offer their productivity-improving ideas, management could have made this pledge and secured workers' ideas without relying on multiskilling. Were there other competitive rationales for developing a multiskilled, flexible work force beyond the benefits suggested in the C-M model?

In further work on the employment practices of Japanese firms, Aoki argues that other benefits of "flexibility," beyond any job security that multiskilling might imply, are also important. According to Aoki (1986), additional efficiency gains from a more flexible, multiskilled work force arise from potentially superior information processing and decision making by workers on the shop floor.

In particular, many technologically complex production processes are subject to high degrees of uncertainty in operations. Some changes in operations may be needed in the future when changes in customers' preferences call for accommodating adaptations to the production process. Similarly, unforeseen problems may arise in technologically complex production processes that require the attention of either supervisory or nonsupervisory employees. Aoki (1986) argues that when these kinds of uncertainties in production processes are more common, and when employees are closer to operations than managers, it may make competitive sense to employ a higher-paid, multiskilled work force. Such a work force would have greater ability to process production-related information efficiently and could respond more quickly and efficiently to any unforeseen developments.

Multiskilling in this model is not a solution to a fundamental principal-agent problem. Rather, Aoki argues that multiskilling also makes sense in situations where information flows among multiskilled workers are needed to respond efficiently to unexpected problems and modifications in technologically complex production processes.

These types of benefits of multiskilling and flexibility also seem to be in evidence in the paper mill case. For example, some of the training the workers received was in the form of visits to customers' operations to understand quality imperfections that were particularly costly for these customers. This type of training presumably made workers better able to detect and respond quickly to such quality problems.

The models of Carmichael and MacLeod, and Aoki differ in several respects and emphasize different benefits of employment security and multiskilling. At the same time, these models focus attention on the ultimate source of economic improvement in the paper mill—workers' commitment to "constant productivity improvement" or *kaisen*—as a potentially important source of competitive advantage.

A simpler argument in favor of "flexibility" is that multiskilling would ultimately allow managers to reduce labor costs through reductions in manning. A smaller number of somewhat more highly paid workers may be a more cost efficient way to run an operation. In the paper mill, this argument does not capture the benefit of flexibility since employment levels were maintained.

Another traditional argument about the benefits of "flexibility" is that broader job classifications will eliminate payments to workers who would be idle under narrower job definitions. In the paper mill, management tracked monthly statistics on "pay for time not worked" before and after team concept. This dimension of labor costs declined by 82 percent from the year before to the year after the implementation of team concept. However, the total savings in this component of labor costs was only $12,025 per month—$14,695 before team concept versus $2,670 after team concept. For a mill with monthly labor costs of $2 million, this was only a minor source of improved profitability. This was not the key source of improved profitability in the paper mill. The theoretical models and the case study stress a different source of increased profitability—worker support for and generation of productivity-enhancing improvements.

In the context of the paper mill, these productivity improvements were so valuable they more than offset any inefficiency associated with levels of employment that were above the minimum necessary to run the mill. Related bargaining models that emphasize the potential importance of worker ideas make the same point. For example, Farrell and Gibbons (1991) demonstrate that management may have to consider organizational designs that may sacrifice efficiency along some dimensions (e.g., "inefficient" employment levels) to get potentially greater benefits associated with "worker-owned" ideas on how to improve operations.

Overall, several broad themes emerge from the existing models on multiskilling and employment security. First, the productivity-enhancing benefits of work force flexibility or job security only accrue over time in a dynamic context. C-M emphasize the dynamic process of implementing technological changes. Aoki (1986) emphasizes the greater abilities of multiskilled workers to respond to unforeseen occurrences on the shop floor and to accumulate and process valuable production information. The benefits of multiskilling and employment security should therefore accrue over time. Cross-section comparisons of otherwise comparable firms with more and less flexible organizational designs will reflect only those productivity and performance differences that have accrued up to that time. Productivity growth models of more and less "flexible" operations are also needed to test the hypotheses developed in these theoretical models.

Second, multiskilling may not necessarily be an HR policy that can be implemented "at the margin." The flexibility associated with multiskilling obviously implies a simultaneous implementation of employee training. But, it may also be misleading to separate the effects of multiskilling from policies of employment security.

Team Work, Free Riders, and the Norms and Culture of the Workplace

Multiskilling, flexibility, and employment security were all part of the HR policy changes that helped produce the changes in the paper mill's labor-management relations and in its economic performance. However, these HR policy changes do not seem sufficient by themselves to create a set of incentives that overcome all potential agency problems in the paper mill. Output and productivity are still most easily measured for the mill as a whole. It is more difficult to measure performance for individual departments or workers in this continuous flow production process. Presumably the value of the specific suggestions from individual workers was still difficult to measure, even though the cumulative impact of these ideas was ultimately responsible for much of the performance improvement in the mill. Perhaps because of the difficulties in obtaining accurate individual or work group performance measures, the method of pay in the mill remained a wage-rate-based system (Lazear 1986).

Furthermore, productivity began to improve in the last year of the 1983 team concept contract before the relatively large increases in pay of the next contract were negotiated. Worker-generated productivity improvements began while wage rates were contractually fixed. The link between improved performance in the mill and worker wages was at best still very indirect.

Given these difficulties in measuring individual or work group performance in a paper mill of nearly 500 production workers, an additional incentive problem remained unaddressed by HR policies such as employment security and multiskilling. Workers in the paper mill may still have incentives to free ride on the work and ideas of other employees. Even if workers trusted management sufficiently to believe that subsequently negotiated pay rates in the operator clusters would increase in response to improved mill performance, the valuable contribution of one worker in a 500-employee work force would ultimately be shared with 499 coworkers. Any incentive to contribute ideas would be diluted even further by the wage-rate pay scheme that at best provides only an indirect link between improved performance and increased wages for individual workers. Why did workers provide their ideas given the incentives they faced?

One simple answer within the structure of the basic agency problem framework may help explain this change in employee behavior. The impediment to extra "effort" from workers in the agency problem framework is $C(e)$—the cost of effort function. Perhaps developing and revealing productivity-enhancing ideas imposed relatively little cost on workers—particularly once the job security pledge seemed credible.

Another possibility that may also have been at work in the paper mill is that, after the implementation of team concept, psychological and sociological forces imposed positive costs on workers who did *not* offer ideas. In particular, several contracting studies have begun to specify more detailed components of the "cost-of-effort" function, and acknowledge the importance of psychological and sociological factors as potential determinants of worker behavior and ultimately competitive performance.

As an example, in their theoretical analysis of partnerships and profit sharing, Kandel and Lazear (1991) consider several more detailed specifications that a cost-of-effort function may take. Unlike the simplest agency problem framework described above, Kandel and Lazear (K-L) consider the possibility that the cost of effort to a worker may often be determined by more than just the individual worker's own effort (e_i). The costs a worker experiences can also be affected by the relative effort levels of other workers ($e_j, \ldots e_n$), by other activities of the individual worker (a_i), and by other activities of coworkers ($a_j, \ldots a_n$). These other activities of the individual worker and his or her coworkers are ones that do not directly affect the firm's output but which still can influence the individual worker's effort, such as the time and energy workers take to observe other workers' behavior and to make other workers comfortable or uncomfortable about their behavior.

K-L introduce these elaborations by including a "peer pressure" cost function as an additional source of the costs that workers face when deciding their effort levels. Unlike the simpler formulation of the cost-of-effort function in which higher effort levels necessarily impose costs on the worker, peer pressure costs can be lower when workers put forth more effort. In K-L's formulation, the cost-of-effort function has two main components. Effort will increase one component of costs (*C*) as in the simpler formulation, but the peer pressure component of costs (*P*) can decrease as workers put forth more effort. Workers therefore want to maximize:

$$w - C(e_i, a_i) - P(e_i, e_j, \ldots e_n; a_i, a_j, \ldots a_n) . \tag{3}$$

These simple elaborations to the cost-of-effort function allow for a richer set of theoretical possibilities for how HR policies might affect the behavior of labor and management and ultimately economic performance.

To illustrate how sociological effects of HR policies could alter economic performance, consider one of the specific formulations that the peer pressure function may take in K-L's study. Some workplaces or work groups may develop "norms" of effort, represented by $\bar{e}$. Peer pressure (*P*) in equation (3) may be determined by deviations from this behavioral norm, so that:

$$P = \alpha * (e_i - \bar{e}) , \tag{4}$$

where α measures the penalty or reward experienced by the worker for exceeding or falling below the norm. When peer pressure exists (*P* is positive), workers are worse off. This occurs when α is positive. In this case, workers are penalized for exceeding the norm. For example, "rate busters" can be ostracized by coworkers under traditional piece-rate systems that are based on production of physical units of output (Gibbons 1987; Kanemoto and MacLeod 1992).

Conversely, when α is negative, there are "negative peer pressure costs" or support from coworkers. In this case, workers are rewarded for exceeding the norm. For example, profit sharing would give workers an incentive to support coworkers who exceed the norm. Other more complex specifications of α and the peer pressure function are of course possible.

While K-L develop their model to explain HR policies of profit sharing and partnerships that are not in evidence in the case study, some of the implications of their model do seem applicable to the paper mill case study. In particular, one feature of peer pressure in K-L's formulation is that it can be manipulated by managers, workers, and HR policies. If line managers or coworkers have difficulty measuring or observing an individual worker's contribution and effort, then in work situations where effort "norms" ($\bar{e}$) are important, HR policies or other methods that raise $\bar{e}$ will improve economic performance.

Even in the absence of sociological norms of effort within a work group, it may still make competitive sense to devote resources to develop a sense of "team spirit" and loyalty among coworkers. Such indoctrination efforts could make workers feel guilty when they withhold effort and let their coworkers down even if they are never observed or caught shirking on their expected duties. More specifically, even in the absence of norms or of mutual monitoring among coworkers, a sense of loyalty could make $P(e_i)$ smaller as e_i increases in equation (3). HR policies that help instill workers with a sense of loyalty and team spirit would therefore help elicit more effort from workers.

According to interviews with managers in the paper mill, efforts to alter norms of behavior seem to have been an important element in the implementation of team concept. One of the most interesting HR policy decisions in the team concept contract was the uneven wage increase ranging from 6 percent to 52 percent after workers returned from the 1983 strike. In interviews managers reported that this was the most controversial and difficult decision about team concept. Managers acknowledged the potential negative consequences of 30 percent to 40 percent increases in labor costs that the terms of team concept would produce as well as the negative reactions of workers who were receiving the relatively smaller wage increases. However, managers ultimately decided that "something this dramatic had to be done to change the norms and culture around here." The face-to-face, department-by-department listening sessions may also have been instrumental in communicating and establishing new expectations about new "norms" under team concept.

While K-L provide one of the more specific and rigorous treatments of the theoretical routes through which psychological and sociological forces determine worker and firm performance, the role of sociological norms is emerging as an important theme in several contracting models (Akerlof 1982; MacLeod 1987; 1988). In one of the first formal models of workers' decisions to work hard in situations where team work is important, Holmstrom (1982) argues that free rider problems would ultimately keep effort levels undesirably low. In subsequent theoretical work, MacLeod (1987; 1988) demonstrates how norms of behavior might overcome free rider problems in worker cooperatives or other profit sharing situations where teamwork is important. MacLeod's (1987) formal model of social norms demonstrates the importance of workers understanding and agreeing on the norm of mutual cooperation. Without this agreement, the resulting performance of the work organization can be very inefficient.

It is far from a novel notion that fundamental sociological constructs like norms of work group behavior or psychological constructs like feelings of guilt provide a richer and more complete understanding of employee behavior in the workplace. However, the incorporation of these constructs into theoretical models that focus explicitly on the economic efficiency of various workplace practices is a relatively recent development that may ultimately lead to a better understanding of the causes and consequences of HR practices.

The Case Study and Empirical Studies of Labor Relations and Productivity

The models and constructs reviewed in the previous section offer several interesting ideas and interpretations about the theoretical mechanisms responsible for the changes in behavior in the paper mill case study. At the same time, the case study may help provide a richer understanding of the mechanisms that have generated the empirical pattern documented in several previous studies that "good" labor-management relations promote productivity.

The few studies that have estimated the empirical relationship between quality of labor relations environment and direct measures of business performance have often included an establishment's grievance rate as part of the measure of the labor relations environment. Typically, lower grievance rates are associated with higher levels of at least some productivity or quality performance measure (for a review, see Ichniowski and Lewin 1987).

Still, a careful review of these studies suggests that this finding has been documented in only two industry settings—automobile manufacturing (Katz, Kochan, and Gobeille 1983; Katz, Kochan, and Weber 1985; Norsworthy and Zabala 1985) and paper manufacturing (Ichniowski 1986). It is possible that patterns observed in these two industry settings may not apply to the experience of other industries. However, the pattern of higher grievance rates and lower productivity documented in my 1986 study should be a pattern that applies to the paper mill in the case study, since that mill was included in the sample of my 1986 study. The prediction that lower grievance rates would coincide with higher labor productivity is generally borne out in the case study. By 1983 labor productivity in the mill was at all time lows, while grievance rates had escalated to all time highs. The record-setting productivity levels from 1985 and after coincided with a nearly grievance-free work environment.

However, a thoughtful consideration of the case study and the reasons why declines in grievance rates did not move in lock step with increases in productivity can provide a deeper understanding of why lower grievance rates would tend to be inversely related to productivity. The case study seems to provide considerable support for the argument that low productivity and high grievance rates were simultaneously caused by subtler factors not included in the statistical models in my 1986 study.

In particular, HR practices, especially the rules and interpretations that defined job duties, were frequently the source of disputes in pre-team concept grievances. The existence of conflicting interpretations of work practices that were often not known by managers seems to have been responsible for the exceptionally high levels of grievances relative to other mills. The elimination of work rules and past practices in the 1983 contract were clearly the proximate cause of the reduction in grievance rates.

Furthermore, the reduction in grievances that occurred with the implementation of the 1983 contract did not immediately bring about an increase in productivity. There was clearly a lag before performance improved. Interviews with managers also suggest that neither they nor the production workers would have rated the labor relations environment in the first year of team concept as "good" even though grievance rates had dropped substantially.

The improvement in both the "quality" of the labor relations environment and in mill productivity occurred only after time had passed for workers to acquire a new, broader set of skills. Time also had to pass for workers to develop trust that managers would honor the pledge of job security—a pledge that still allowed managers the ability to lay off workers under certain conditions. Time had to pass before more extensive communication efforts in the form of attitude surveys and listening sessions could reshape norms of behavior in work groups. Even more time had to pass before workers would observe different management behavior in contract negotiations that would ultimately reward the more productive work force with much higher pay. Only after these dynamics had taken place would "good labor relations" and high productivity be simultaneously established.

It would seem incorrect to interpret the decline in grievance activity as a cause of improved productivity. Reductions in job categories and the elimination of past practices reduced grievance filings. These specific policy changes were directly responsible for reductions in grievances.

In contrast, the improvement in economic performance seems to have been the result of the overall system of new HR policies implemented in the 1983 team concept contract even if it took time for this set of policy changes to affect worker behavior and economic performance. Employment security allayed workers' fears about displacement should they offer productivity-enhancing, yet laborsaving, ideas. Multiskilling in many tasks and training at the site of key customers enhanced the workers' abilities to identify ways to improve performance. Changes in the nature of the reward structure and constant face-to-face communications may have substantially altered the sociology of the workplace relations in ways that elicited higher performance levels. A careful review of the case study suggests complex human dynamics that allowed changes in HR policies to lead to superior competitive performance.

Desirable Features for Future Studies

I began this paper by presenting a longitudinal case study in which a new set of HR practices helped to improve labor-management relations and competitive performance. I then proceeded to review several theoretical models and constructs that might help explain why these HR policies could have the effects on worker behavior and economic performance observed in the case study. The theoretical studies considered are but a small portion of the very large number of "implicit contract" type models that have recently been offered in the literature. At this point, in the broad area of research concerned with HR practices, labor-management relations, and economic performance, convincing empirical analyses that seek to estimate the links between HR practices or industrial relations environments on the one hand and economic outcomes on the other would clearly be "frontier" research for industrial relations scholars. How might researchers approach this frontier?

Determinants of HR Policies

Clearly more primary source data collection will be required to execute an empirical research agenda on these important topics. But more specifically, the sample design will be a critical determinant of the types of primary data that would need to be collected. A broad-based sample covering establishments in many different industries will require the analyst to collect data not only on HR practices, industrial relations outcomes, and performance measures, but data on the underlying determinants of the choice of HR policies as well.

In particular, the theoretical studies reviewed earlier in this paper suggest that HR policies like multiskilling, job security guarantees, and specific compensation strategies can stimulate competitive performance, but only in the appropriate settings. The advantages of multiskilling and employment security should be determined by whether or not worker suggested improvements are a relatively important source of productivity improvements. The success of these HR policies may also be determined by how technologically complex the production process is and how often the production process has to be adapted to changing consumer preferences. Therefore, it may be the case that HR policies like multiskilling and employment security have their biggest performance effects in technologically advanced, capital intensive manufacturing industries.

Unfortunately, it is difficult to develop measures of the underlying constructs that these models suggest are the ultimate determinants of various HR policies. Some of the factors that favor the use of the kinds of HR practices used in the paper mill case study include: the relative importance of suggestions to improve the production process, whether workers are more likely than managers to be the source of these suggestions, and the importance of information flows from management to labor relative to that of information flows among workers as determinants of performance.

While these constructs are difficult to measure, creative efforts at developing measures of these constructs may be possible. For example, Hutchens (1987) measures the relative ease of making direct observations on worker "effort or contribution" and provides a revealing empirical study of the occupational locus of pay-for-performance schemes. The general point here is that a broad-based, multi-industry study of HR practices and firm performance would require an explicit analysis of the factors that lead some businesses to adopt certain HR policies and of the settings in which these HR policies improve economic performance. Furthermore, if the factors which determine a firm's choice of HR policies are not easy to measure, then research strategies other than a survey of firms and businesses may be required.

An alternative approach would be to investigate a more specific, narrowly defined sample of similar businesses. A more narrowly defined sample of businesses should limit the variation in factors that favor one set of HR policies over another. If, in fact, certain HR policies are more efficient than others within a given, narrowly defined setting, and if different businesses in a given setting adopt different HR policies, a reasonable case could be made that HR policies are responsible for any performance differences that are systematically related to the HR policies. This research strategy could only be successful if the economic environment was forgiving enough to allow, at least temporarily, the adoption of more and less efficient HR policies.

Performance Measures and Level of Analysis

Convincing measures of economic performance across businesses are a necessary part of any future empirical study of HR practices and competitive performance. Ultimately, capital market performance provides the most compelling measure of economic performance. Stock market performance measures probably make sense for studying the impacts of HR policies in the area of compensation packages for top corporate executives. There is only one chief executive officer per company subject to only one compensation package at any given time. CEO decisions affecting the broad direction of the corporation's activities are important enough to affect overall shareholder wealth.

However, there will often be substantial variation across occupations, divisions, product lines, and work sites for the vast array of other HR policies. It may be impossible to isolate empirically the stock market impact of differences in specific HR practices that apply to only a portion of a given corporation's work force. An ambitious attempt to isolate changes in corporate stock market performance from immediately before to immediately after various HR policy changes revealed little impact of the HR events (Abowd, Milkovich, and Hannon 1990).

Therefore, it may be preferable to measure performance and the performance effects of HR policies at the level of individual work sites or facilities where HR policies are implemented. This strategy would again seem to favor a focus on a narrowly defined industry sample to ensure greater comparability of the performance measures. In this vein, Shuster (1983) presents a series of nine plant-specific case studies, before and after the introduction of a worker participation effort that included some kind of gainsharing-type compensation plan.

In pursuing this research strategy, it is desirable to collect data on both productivity-type measures and labor cost measures as in the paper mill case study. The contracting models considered in this study uniformly predict that higher levels of worker effort and contribution imply higher wages for workers. Therefore, the researcher needs to identify productivity differences and whether labor cost differences offset any differences in revenues due to the productivity differences.

Understanding Workers' Contributions

One of the more convincing pieces of evidence in the paper mill study that helps buttress the conclusion that the HR policy changes helped improve performance was the direct evidence on changes in worker behavior. If some future investigation of a carefully crafted sample of comparable businesses did reveal HR-related performance differences, it would be especially helpful to include at least some qualitative evidence on underlying differences in worker behavior to help explain the performance differences. One empirical case study that provides some of this kind of evidence is Rosenberg and Rosenstein's longitudinal study (1980) of economic performance and employee participation in one foundry which includes detailed information on participation meetings and the substance of the issues discussed by the employee participation groups.

Field Research

Very subtle human forces may ultimately prove to be links among HR practices, worker motivation and behavior, improved relations between labor and management, and economic performance. Precisely because human aspects in work organization cannot be mechanically controlled, managers in the paper mill indicated in interviews that they were not at all confident that the three-year duration of the original team concept contract would provide sufficient time to improve the performance of the mill. It may therefore be quite possible that the exact same set of HR policies that comprised team concept in the paper mill case study would not produce the performance effects in another comparable facility. Perhaps a subtler feel for how the implementation process shaped critical factors like norms of workplace behavior are critical to our understanding of how HR policies impact performance. If so, large scale survey research may not be accurate enough to capture the subtle yet important forces at work. Ethnographic studies of workplace norms and culture based on extensive contact with workers may prove to be the most effective and convincing way to develop evidence on whether these subtle forces shape the relationship between HR practices and economic performance.

The research strategy I have advocated in this concluding section has been exceedingly rare in recent years. It requires a high degree of access to and cooperation from labor and management practitioners in different firms and a detailed understanding of some specific industry setting. This research will take great patience and time. It would benefit from scholars in different discipline bases as it investigates the effects of psychological and sociological factors in the workplace on a firm's economic efficiency. While this type of study is relatively uncommon today, it is precisely in the long-standing, interdisciplinary, hands-on, field research tradition of industrial relations.

Acknowledgments

The author thanks Ann Bartel, David Lewin, Bentley MacLeod, Giovanna Prennushi, John Roberts, and Peter Sherer for comments.

References

Abowd, John M. "Does Performance-Based Managerial Compensation Affect Corporate Performance?" *Industrial and Labor Relations Review* 43 (1990), pp. 52S-73S.

Abowd, John M., George T. Milkovich, and John M. Hannon. "The Effects of Human Resource Management Decisions on Shareholder Value." *Industrial and Labor Relations Review* 43 (1990), pp. 203S-36S.

Akerlof, George A. "Labor Contracts as Partial Gift Exchange." *Quarterly Journal of Economics* 97 (1982), pp. 543-69.

Aoki, Masahiko. "Horizontal vs. Vertical Information Structure of the Firm." *American Economic Review* 76 (1986), pp. 971-83.

________. *Information, Incentives, and Bargaining in the Japanese Economy*. New York: Cambridge University Press, 1988.

Axelrod, Robert M. *The Evolution of Cooperation*. New York: Basic Books, 1984.

Belman, Dale. "Unions, the Quality of Labor Relations, and Firm Performance." Manuscript, 1990.

Carmichael, H. Lorne. "Efficiency Wage Models of Unemployment—One View." *Economic Inquiry* 28 (1990), pp. 269-95.

Carmichael, H. Lorne, and W. Bentley MacLeod. "Multiskilling, Technical Change, and the Japanese Firm." Discussion paper no. 9112, Department of Economics, University of Montreal, 1991.

Ehrenberg, Ronald G., and George T. Milkovich. "Compensation and Firm Performance." In *Human Resources and the Performance of the Firm*, eds. Morris M. Kleiner, Richard N. Block, Myron Roomkin, and Sidney W. Salsburg. Madison, WI: Industrial Relations Research Association, 1987.

Ehrenberg, Ronald G. "Introduction: Do Compensation Policies Matter?" *Industrial and Labor Relations Review* 43 (1990), pp. 3S-12S.

Farrell, Joseph, and Robert Gibbons. "Bargaining Power and Voice in Organizations." Manuscript, 1991.

Freeman, Richard B., and James L. Medoff. *What Do Unions Do?* New York: Basic Books, 1984.

Gibbons, Robert. "Piece-Rate Incentive Schemes." *Journal of Labor Economics* 5 (1987), pp. 413-29.

Gibbons, Robert, and Kevin J. Murphy. "Relative Performance Evaluation for Chief Executive Officers." *Industrial and Labor Relations Review* 43 (1990), pp. 30S-51S.

Holmstrom, Bengt. "Moral Hazard in Teams." *Bell Journal of Economics* 13 (1982), pp. 324-40.

Hutchens, Robert. "A Test of Lazear's Theory of Delayed Payment Contracts." *Journal of Labor Economics* 5 (1987), pp. 153S-70S.

Ichniowski, Casey. "The Effects of Grievance Activity on Productivity." *Industrial and Labor Relations Review* 40 (1986), pp. 75-89.

Ichniowski, Casey, and David Lewin. "Grievance Procedures and Firm Performance." In *Human Resources and the Performance of the Firm*, eds. Morris M. Kleiner, Richard N. Block, Myron Roomkin, and Sidney W. Salsburg. Madison, WI: Industrial Relations Research Association, 1987.

Kandel, Eugene, and Edward Lazear. "Peer Pressure and Partnerships." Manuscript, 1991.

Kanemoto, Yoshitsugu, and W. Bentley MacLeod. "The Ratchet Effect and the Market for Second-Hand Workers." *Journal of Labor Economics* 10 (1992), pp. 85-98.

Katz, Harry C., Thomas A. Kochan, and Kenneth Gobeille. "Industrial Relations Performance, Economic Performance, and Quality of Working Life Efforts: An Interplant Analysis." *Industrial and Labor Relations Review* 37 (1983), pp. 3-17.

Katz, Harry C., Thomas A. Kochan, and Mark Weber. "Assessing the Effects of Industrial Relations Systems and Efforts to Improve the Quality of Working Life on Organizational Effectiveness." *Academy of Management Journal* 28 (1985), pp. 509-26.
Lazear, Edward. "Salaries and Piece Rates." *Journal of Business* 59 (1986), pp. 405-31.
Lazear, Edward, and Sherwin Rosen. "Rank-Order Tournaments as Optimum Labor Contracts." *Journal of Political Economy* 89 (1981), pp. 841-64.
Leonard, Jonathan. "Executive Pay and Firm Performance." *Industrial and Labor Relations Review* 43 (1990), pp. 13S-29S.
________. "Equity, Efficiency, and Incentives in Cooperative Teams." In *Advances in the Economic Analysis of Participatory and Labor Managed Firms* 3 (1988), pp. 5-23.
Norsworthy, J.R., and Craig A. Zabala. "Worker Attitudes, Worker Behavior, and Productivity in the U.S. Automobile Industry, 1959-1976." *Industrial and Labor Relations Review* 38 (1985), pp. 544-57.
Rosenberg, Richard D., and Eliezer Rosenstein. "Participation and Productivity: An Empirical Study." *Industrial and Labor Relations Review* 33 (1980), pp. 355-67.
Shuster, Michael. "The Impact of Union-Management Cooperation on Productivity and Employment." *Industrial and Labor Relations Review* 36 (1983), pp. 415-30.

CHAPTER 8

Internal Labor Markets in a Changing Environment: Models and Evidence

PAUL OSTERMAN
Massachusetts Institute of Technology

It is by now apparent to even the most market-oriented economist that many of the rules which determine economic outcomes and social welfare originate within the firm and are in a nontrivial sense chosen by the firm. Because many workers spend long stretches of their careers within the shelter of enterprises, understanding these rules is very important. These rules have come to be characterized as the *internal labor market* (ILM).

The central idea of ILMs was set forth by Kerr (1954) in his description of "institutional labor markets." Kerr argued that these labor markets created noncompeting groups and that one of the central boundaries was between the firm and the external labor market. Kerr identified "ports of entry" as the link between the inside and outside and described the implications for labor mobility of the boundaries and rules. Dunlop (1966) coined the term "internal labor markets" and provided a description of one of the central rules, those concerning job ladders. In the 1970s Doeringer and Piore (1971) provided a full description of the rules of blue-collar ILMs as well as the tradeoffs among the rules (for example between hiring criteria and training procedures). Doeringer and Piore also began the process of linking analysis of ILMs back to mainstream labor economics through their discussion of how specific human capital helps cement employee attachment to firms.

These ILM "classics" set the stage for later work in several ways. First, while all of the original authors recognized that there are a variety of alternatives for organizing work, each emphasized, almost exclusively, blue-collar industrial models and within these the traditional unionized pattern (which might then have been the central tendency even in the nonunion sector). Much of the recent work on ILMs has focused upon variation both within the blue-collar world and between blue-collar and other types of employment.

Second, none of the classics developed well-structured explanations of why ILMs arise and the need to do so has invited a wide range of theoretical efforts. This has led to development of elaborate microeconomic models of long-term employment relationships as well as efforts by sociologists to explain these institutions in noneconomic terms. To date these efforts have not been integrated, but this essay will attempt to provide a framework which encompasses several approaches.

Internal labor markets attract scholars of divergent bents. For mainstream economists, the challenge is to explain these rules in a framework which preserves the core ideas of maximization and efficiency. Institutional economists do not deny the impact of standard economic considerations, but they emphasize the interplay of economic, political, and social forces. This orientation has been reenforced by recent interest in international comparisons. There is also a vibrant sociology literature, albeit one which has not been fully incorporated into the discourse within economics. Since stable work groups lead to the formation of norms, customs, and interpersonal comparisons, ILMs provide sociologists with an opportunity to illustrate and explore the importance of these phenomena. In addition, variation across enterprises in extent and content of rules suggests that sociological models which focus on the diffusion and adoption of institutional practices independently of their efficiency properties (for example the search for legitimacy via mimicry) can be fruitfully applied to ILMs.

The nature of research on ILMs has also expanded. The initial investigations were largely field based and the ideas rested upon interviews with firms and unions. The power of this approach is demonstrated by the fact that many of the insights developed in this manner have survived. Our confidence in these observations has, however, been strengthened by studies based upon representative samples of firms (Baron and Bielby 1986; Pfeffer and Cohen 1984; Delaney, Lewin, and Ichniowski 1989; Osterman 1984) as well as more thorough examinations of particular practices such as firm-based wage setting (Groshen 1991), long-term tenure (Abraham and

Medoff 1984), or part-time work (Rebitzer and Taylor 1991). In the course of this research the original concept, while generally affirmed, has been modified in important ways. For example, there is heightened sensitivity to the fact that a firm is not a unitary employment system but rather consists of a set of ILM subsystems which may operate on quite different principles (Osterman 1984, 1987). It also seems apparent that the correlates of ILM practices include a mixture of technical, economic, and social considerations (Bielby and Baron 1983).

In surveying this rich line of research there appear to be two useful questions which an essay such as this might address. The first is to sort out the alternative theories which have been generated to explain ILMs. The second is to understand how ILMs have changed in the past 20 years.

Sorting out theory is important, but if done in isolation the exercise is likely to be both arid and inconclusive. It would be arid because, unless grounded in data and specific cases, it would be difficult to keep in mind just what it is we are trying to explain. The results would be inconclusive because of the obvious fact that no single model is likely to be completely satisfactory and also because most models are sufficiently elastic that they can be made (to appear) to cover more than originally intended.

A better strategy is to begin with the data; and in this case the data are the substantial shifts which seem to have transpired in work organization. These shifts render the traditional image of ILMs at least partially obsolete and are important to document in their own terms. In addition they provide a handle on the various models because, after describing the shifts, we can ask which theories are best able to explain what occurred. Thus, rather than argue in the abstract about models, and rather than applying the models to a static description, we can treat recent changes as data to be explained and search for the theory with the best "fit."

Before turning to recent shifts in the organization of work, there is one definitional issue to clear up. The Doeringer and Piore description of ILMs focused upon closed job ladders and ports of entry and this has tended to stick in people's minds as the central defining characteristic of ILMs (for example, Althauser and Kalleberg 1981). I think that a more expansive definition—which includes wage systems, job classifications, rules regarding the deployment of labor, and rules regarding employment security—is more helpful.

The point is that these various categories of rules fit together in a logical system and it does not make sense to isolate one rule and ignore the others. For example, narrow job classifications, wages attached to the job, few restrictions on the ability of the firm to lay off workers, and strict seniority are a mutually reenforcing set of practices; while broad classifications, wages attached to individuals rather than jobs, ease of deployment, and high levels of job security constitute another logical cluster. Anyone familiar with the literature will recognize the first cluster as the traditional American model, while the second is a model associated (at least until recently) with leading edge American firms and with the Japanese.

It is much more helpful to think in these terms rather than focusing on any particular rule such as the presence or absence of job ladders. The idea of a system of rules which fit logically together enables us to make sense of broader differences in ILMs. Thus, for example, both Japanese and traditionally organized American automobile firms have closed job ladders, yet there are very substantial differences along other dimensions which add up to quite distinct ILM arrangements. ILMs conceived in these broader terms come to represent the overall human resource management strategy of an enterprise, and by thinking of ILMs in this way we can ask more ambitious questions. This more expansive perspective, however, introduces difficulties for theoretical models which purport to explain one rule (for example, wage premiums above market levels) but which appear ignorant of the fact that said rule is part of a larger system.

The Evolution of Internal Labor Markets

The stylized facts concerning the evolution of internal labor markets in the United States would go as follows. Prior to the Depression and World War II, large industrial firms gyrated between several strategies of organizing work including the foreman-centered "drive system," with few rules and arbitrary management authority, and the "American plan" with its emphasis on paternalism, welfare benefits, and more regularized employment relationships. The great unionizing drives of the Depression, combined with the diffusion of standardized union practices by the War Labor Board, decisively led to the triumph of the standard union model (with strict job classifications, seniority, grievance procedures, etc.) over its alternatives (the most complete history of these alternatives is found in Jacoby [1985]).

From the mid-1940s to the mid-1970s, this model—which is essentially what Doeringer and Piore described—dominated both in the union sector and in largely imitative nonunion firms. Towards the end of this era a competing model emerged, one which placed much greater emphasis upon direct communication with workers and upon innovations such as team production and quality circles (Kochan, Katz, and McKersie 1986). This structure was motivated in part by its superior performance and in part by its ability to keep unions at bay. It emerged in a progressive segment of the American nonunion sector (e.g., IBM), but it also gained momentum from the spread of Japanese transplants, such as the Honda factory in Ohio, which organized work along the Japanese model. The more traditional sector, union and nonunion, was torn between adoption of the new (often called "transformed" or "salaried") model and defense of old structures. The playing out and resolving of this tension is the current ILM "story" of greatest interest and importance.

Adding to the turmoil and uncertainty are broader shifts in the economy which undermine standard assumptions. These shifts include heightened economic volatility, which threatens the job security implicit for high-tenure workers in the traditional system. In addition, the combination of technical change and increased education levels of the labor force may alter firms' calculation of the best locus of training and undermine the traditional reliance on job ladders and closed internal markets. Both of these macro shifts make employment unstable and reduce long-term employment within an enterprise. Indeed, many commentators now assert that workers must expect to change jobs far more frequently than in the past. Implicit in this assertion is that the closed traditional ILM is of declining importance.

The foregoing represents an amalgam of various views about recent trends, but if there is such a thing as a consensus, this would be it. It remains to be seen, of course, just how much evidence there is to support the various assertions.

Recent Changes in Internal Labor Markets

In this section I will address three questions concerning the evolution of ILMs: (1) are ILMs still important or are they dissolving,

(2) is the character of ILMs changing, and (3) how much international variation is there in the structure of ILMs in similar industries. Taken together these seem to be the three questions which emerge naturally from the above narrative and which are likely to have the most important implications for theories of ILMs.

Are ILMs Still Important?

Do people still spend long periods of their careers within the shelter of a single employer? The extreme alternative is a return to a high turnover spot market in which at least one side of the market, either employers or employees, sees little advantage in maintaining stable employment.

There are several commonly remarked upon trends which suggest that ILMs are of diminishing relevance. These include growing white-collar and managerial layoffs which erode stability in what has hitherto been the most secure segment of the labor market, the rise of contingent or temporary employment arrangements, an alleged growing reliance upon educational institutions rather than firms for training, and the emergence of regional networks as the locus of careers rather than single organizations.

Any of these developments, if important, would reduce the amount of time a person works with a single employer. A relatively straightforward test is to ask whether the distribution of worker tenure has changed over time. If ILMs are becoming less important, then this should be picked up in surveys which ask employees how long they have worked for their current employer.

The May 1979 and May 1988 Current Population Surveys asked respondents how long they had worked for their current employer. The top panel in Table 1 shows the job tenure distribution for all employed workers in those two years and it is apparent that there is no change in the distribution. The second panel breaks the sample out by sex, and the conclusion of stable tenure distributions remains. However, these findings may be deceptive since the age distribution of the labor force changed between the two periods (the labor force in 1988 was slightly older). Furthermore, we would expect that the impact of ILMs on tenure would show up most strongly in middle age workers who have passed the period of high turnover and exploration which characterizes younger employees.

Table 2 is limited to employees in two age categories: 35 through 44 and 45 through 60. Among these groups there is some reduction

TABLE 1
Job Tenure 1979 and 1988: All Age Groups
(in percent)

A.

Years With Current Employer	1979	1988
0-2	46.4	44.4
3-5	18.1	19.2
6-10	15.2	15.9
11-15	8.1	8.3
16+	12.0	12.0

B.

	Men		Women	
	1979	1988	1979	1988
0-2	41.9	40.4	52.4	48.9
3-5	17.0	19.0	19.5	19.4
6-10	15.8	15.9	14.3	15.9
11-15	9.3	8.8	6.4	7.1
16+	15.7	15.7	7.2	7.8

Source: Current Population Survey.

of job tenure which is limited entirely to males. For men in both age groups there is a lower share of employees in the top two tenure groups, with the drop being as large as 5.6 percentage points for the oldest group of men. By contrast, for women in the 35- to 44-year-old group there is an increased share in the high-tenure categories, and the proportions remain constant for the older group of women. These patterns remain unchanged when the data are broken down by educational group, suggesting that the findings are not limited to any single occupational subgroup.

Taken as a whole, these data show that long-term employment relationships retain their centrality for men and, indeed, are of increasing importance for women.[1] If one had to draw only one conclusion from these data, it would be the ongoing importance of long-term relationships. The more extreme statements about the demise of ILMs or the substantial restructuring of career patterns are not true.[2] However, for men there is a deterioration, with a clear and nontrivial drop in the fraction of middle-age workers in stable employment relationships. Furthermore, this decline occurred in the 1980s, a period of sustained growth in jobs and declining

TABLE 2
Job Tenure 1979 and 1988: 35-60 Year Olds
(in percent)

Men	35-44 Years Old		45-60 Years Old	
	1979	1988	1979	1988
0-2	27.7	28.2	17.4	21.7
3-5	15.9	18.0	10.9	12.7
6-10	20.4	19.4	13.9	13.3
11-15	20.5	15.1	12.9	10.3
16+	15.3	18.6	44.7	41.7

Women	35-44 Years Old		45-60 Years Old	
	1979	1988	1979	1988
0-2	44.8	39.3	26.7	28.5
3-5	22.1	20.6	18.2	17.4
6-10	17.2	20.1	21.0	19.9
11-15	9.6	11.2	13.2	13.3
16+	6.1	8.7	20.6	20.7

Source: Current Population Survey.

unemployment rates. It is apparent, then, that a portion of our discussion of ILMs must seek to explain this fraying around the edges of the standard pattern for men.

Contingent Employment

One commonly noted pattern, which might underlie some of these developments, is the increased use of contingent workers. This is a complicated issue to sort out because several forces are at play. In part, growing use of contingent employees may reflect the disassembling of ILMs as firms seek to reduce job security and implied commitments to incumbent employees. On the other hand, the transformed model requires increased employment security and one way in which firms may attempt to provide this is to surround a core labor force, which receives the security, with a buffer of peripheral employees. For example, the Saturn contract (an exemplar of the transformed model) permits General Motors to staff 20 percent of the labor force with workers who are not covered by security pledges.

Interviews with large, white-collar employers show them to be increasingly employing temporary help staff, outside consultants, contract workers, and the like. These employees work at all skill levels:[3] the use of such temporaries is not limited to clerical workers, but includes occupations such as engineers, computer programmers, and draftsmen (Applebaum 1989; Mangum, Mayhill, and Nelson 1985; Osterman 1984).

Data on the increase in temporary help agency employment are also suggestive. Figures supplied by the employers' association, The National Association of Temporary Services, Inc., show payroll increasing from $3 billion in 1980 to $6 billion in 1985 (*New York Times*, October 24, 1985). Hartmann and Lapidus (1989) report that the constant dollar payroll of temporary help firms grew by 754 percent in the 1970s and 236 percent in the 1980s.

The use of formal temporary help agencies is, in fact, an understatement of the extent of this practice. It is common for companies to establish in-house temporary pools, internalizing the advantages and avoiding fees. The best available survey (a national probability sample of 1,200 firms in six industries—health, business service, finance and insurance, retail, transportation, and manufacturing—found that between 25 and 35 percent of firms with over 250 employees had established such internal pools (Mangum, Mayhill, and Nelson 1985).

It does not necessarily follow that the growing use of contingent employees shifts the job tenure distribution towards the lower end. One possibility is for firms to externalize functions by shifting employment to outside contractors, and at the same time workers develop stable employment relationships with those contractors. An example would be an increase in the amount of legal work corporations delegate to law firms where the partners and associates have long-term (or at least not shorter-term) employment. One might also speculate that employees in temporary help firms tend to be new labor market entrants who in different circumstances would have exhibited other forms of unstable work attachment.

While there is certainly some truth to these arguments, they do not seem fully convincing. First, with regard to the example of the law firms, it must also be true that the lawyers who used to do legal work in-house and whose business has been externalized have therefore lost their jobs. This should show up in the data. Second, the spirit of much of the discussion of contingent employment, and the observations of temporary help firms, suggest that these jobs are inherently less stable than the work they replace.

Another paradox lies in the gender patterns. Many employees of temporary help firms are women, yet, as just noted, female tenure is increasing.[4] One possibility, therefore, is that women who work in temporary help firms are being used to substitute for men in previously long-term jobs. The other possibility is that the decline of male tenure is due to the spread of contracts (explicit or implicit) such as the Saturn contract. This agreement creates a buffer or contingent group of workers whose occupation/industry assignment remains with the original firm, not with a temporary help employer, yet whose employment security is more tenuous than that of regular employees.

In the end we are left with a substantial dollop of speculation. We know there is a slight deterioration in the extent of long-term employment relationships among middle-aged men, and we also know there is an increase in various forms of contingent employment relationships. However, only guesswork connects these two developments. Furthermore, there is no systematic evidence concerning other explanations for the dip in male tenure. Clearly more work is necessary to elucidate shifting tenure patterns.

Has the Character of ILMs Changed?

The foregoing evidence suggests that ILMs remain important, albeit with some fraying around the edges. There remains the important question of whether their character is changing in other respects. Is the transformed model capturing the field?

There are two kinds of evidence on this question: anecdotal and survey based. The former is widely available and suggestive but is, of course, subject to numerous caveats. The latter is extremely uneven. In this section, data of both kinds will be presented, but in the end the portrait will be fuzzy and incomplete. There are simply not adequate data to permit a definitive judgment about the distribution of ILM practices or the trend.

If we had asked several years ago whether the transformed model was making progress on its march through American firms, the answer would clearly have been yes. Three of the most widely cited examples concern the Saturn program at General Motors, Corning, and Xerox.

Corning,[5] with its headquarters in upstate New York, had closed nearly 35 plants in the 1970s and 1980s with no end in sight. In 1986, however, the firm decided to reverse its decline in manufacturing by dramatically altering work systems and ILM rules. It built two greenfield factories, one in West Virginia and one in New York, which were organized around "high-performance work systems." These proved successful enough that the company began retrofitting existing plants. The retrofitting process typically involves establishing a joint union-management team which visits other companies, attends workshops, and develops a common vision of what new work systems might look like. This is followed by an "awareness program" in which all employees in the plant attend workshops. Subsequently, joint design teams, working with consultants, reorganize work flows, change job descriptions, organize and attend training, and establish training programs for the work force. A typical result is a reduced number of job classifications and team production. These shifts in work rules and work flow are also linked to a new compensation system which puts substantial emphasis on performance pay. The performance targets are established by a joint union/management committee. Employees are promised that no layoffs will be implemented as a result of the reorganizations; however, the firm retains the right to implement layoffs due to product market developments.

At Xerox Corporation, early experiments with Quality of Work Life programs evolved into far-reaching changes in work organization (Cutcher-Gershenfeld 1989). This process, which began in 1980 in the Webster, New York manufacturing facility, had as its initial impetus the loss of low-end market share to the Japanese. The initial and halting QWL experiments led eventually to employee involvement in a wide range of previously managerial decisions (such as out-sourcing), problem-solving teams aimed at specific issues, the creation of work teams for normal production, management agreement to no-layoff pledges, much broadened job assignments with new classifications, and experiments with gainsharing pay systems. The ILM of the manufacturing system clearly became very close to the ideal of the transformed or salaried model.

Events in some automobile industry plants are by now widely known. The most far-reaching is the General Motors Saturn plant, in which the union and management jointly designed the production system and the product, and in which job classifications have nearly been eliminated and job security is essentially guaranteed. However, similar initiatives have occurred in many other auto plants, albeit in less dramatic circumstances (Katz 1985).

These shifts in ILM systems are not limited to the union sector in heavy industry. Kochan, Katz, and McKersie (1986) report numerous examples of nonunion firms which have opened new plants along the lines of the transformed model or altered the ILM of existing plants. They also describe partially unionized firms whose nonunion plants are consciously intended to provide a transformed counterweight to the more traditional union work settings. Typical is the electronic cable plant of TRW which employs an all salaried work force, a pay-for-knowledge compensation system, nine job classifications, and team production (Kochan, Katz, and McKersie 1986, 96). Anil Verma, whose research provided the details of the TRW case, provides data on a multiplant firm which includes new nonunion, old nonunion, and old union plants. The new nonunion plants have an average of six job classifications compared to an average of 65 in the old nonunion and 96 in the old union plants (Verma 1983). In a twist on this theme, Cappelli and Sherer (1989) describe a very interesting experiment at Cummings Engine in which ILMs were redesigned to permit employees to remain within the union bargaining unit but work according to the ILM rules which applied to nonunion supervisors.

In these examples the ILM rules have changed substantially and in a reasonably similar direction. This direction might be taken to represent the path along which American firms are moving as they restructure their internal labor markets. It is apparent that the ideas or inspiration underlying all three come from the observation of Japanese firms and from ideas taken from leading American nonunion firms such as IBM. Is it correct to believe that this transformed model is winning out?

The recent experiences of two leading U.S. nonunion "transformed" firms—IBM and Digital Equipment Corporation—raise warning flags. Both IBM and DEC are companies that most observers believed to be the closest American equivalents to the Japanese model of commitment, lifetime employment, extensive training, and so forth. Yet recently, both companies retreated from this model. Digital laid off, for the first time in its history, several thousand employees. IBM implemented a number of financial incentives which, when combined with increasingly strict performance standards, are designed to force employees to leave. Indeed, the firm recently enacted a strict new performance review system under which the bottom 10 percent of workers will come under pressure to resign. By all accounts the atmosphere in both companies has changed dramatically.

Observers in a wide range of other companies report that efforts to reorganize or "transform" ILMs, via introduction of teams, expansion of training, or provision of job protections, are surprisingly slow. Boeing Aircraft included a number of provisions in recent contracts aimed at involving employees more fully in decisions about work organization and technology, but these have not been implemented nor have the company and union been able to agree upon how to organize a joint training fund which they established. In the nonunion sector Eastman Kodak has repeatedly swung back and forth between a strategy of building commitment and employee participation and widespread layoffs which undermined the other efforts.

The war of the anecdotes leads to an inconclusive result but at the minimum does cast doubt on the view that the transformed model is triumphing. Unfortunately, there are no survey data which shed brighter light. An ideal data set would measure a wide range of ILM rules for a panel of firms over time. With such data we could classify the firms into types and see how the distribution of those types was changing. The closest such data are found in the Columbia University survey of firms (Delaney, Lewin, and Ichniowski 1989), based upon a sample taken from the Compustat II files. However, these data are cross-sectional and hence cannot be employed to examine the evolution of ILMs. They are, however, potentially helpful in describing the current distribution of ILM practices.[6]

Ichniowski (1990) classified firms into nine clusters according to the content of their ILM rules. These clusters included typical union firms (with, for example, strict seniority and grievance procedures), transformed firms (with flexible job design, high levels of communication between management and workers, and substantial training), and a range of intermediate forms. There were also a substantial number of firms whose rules fell into no discernable pattern. The most traditional firms constituted 13 percent of the sample, the most transformed 13 percent, 46 percent fell between these extremes, and 28 percent were unclassifiable (Ichniowski 1990, 15). What is most striking in this study is the range of alternative systems and their relatively even distribution.[7]

Another approach is to ask about the diffusion of specific practices. When transformed ILM systems are implemented, important elements often include movements towards incentive-based pay systems and implementation of quality circles of one sort or another. There is some evidence available on the spread of both of these innovations.

Up until the late 1970s or early 1980s, the only important groups paid by other than straight time were sales workers and senior managers, but this began to change as firms reconsidered compensation arrangements. A sense of how widespread new compensation systems are can be gained from a 1987 survey conducted by the American Productivity Center. They found that 32 percent of responding firms reported having profit-sharing arrangements, 28 percent reported having individual incentives, 14 percent had small group incentives, and 13 percent had gainsharing (Mitchell, Lewin, and Lawler 1990, 23).

Turning to teams and QWL, the Work In America Institute estimates that about 25 percent of U.S. workers are covered by some form of employee involvement program, although the depth and quality of these programs vary considerably (Gershenfeld 1987, 131). However, this estimate is very much on the high side of the literature. A 1982 survey of firms with over 500 employees, which was conducted by the New York Stock Exchange, estimated that 14 percent of all firms and 52 percent of manufacturing firms had quality circles, and that 20 percent of all firms and 59 percent of manufacturing firms had either teams or other forms of work redesign. However, only a relatively small fraction (perhaps a quarter) of employees at firms which had such programs in fact participated in them (Russell 1988).

An additional and very provocative source of data about trends in ILM systems comes from examining the practices of Japanese transplants in the United States. These transplants are important because they provide American firms with examples or illustrations of alternative practices; I will discuss this role later in this essay. For now, we can simply ask whether we know what these firms are doing.

The best publicized of the transplants are the large automobile assembly factories—Honda, Mazda, NUMMI, and so on—and all reports suggest that these firms are organized along the lines of the transformed model (see Brown, Reich, and Stern 1991; Shimada and MacDuffie 1987; Adler 1991). However, these enterprises may not be typical of the much larger number of Japanese-owned companies which have emerged in recent years. As in the earlier discussion, what evidence we have on these firms suggests considerable diversity.

One striking study, by Ruth Milkman (1991), surveyed 50 Japanese-owned electronic assembly plants with over one hundred employees in California. She collected data on ILM rules and found that

> . . . the Japanese owned plants in California bear little resemblance to the Japanese management model. Relatively few have quality circles or the equivalent; flexible teams are even more exceptional; and most of the managers we interviewed laughed outright when asked about just-in-time delivery or the like. One "Japanese practice" is more typical of these plants, however; most are committed, in principle, to avoiding layoffs. However, even this is tempered by the fact that these plants typically have high turnover rates. . . . (pp. 79-80)

These findings are provocative because one surely cannot argue that the owners of these firms were not aware of, and not accustomed to, alternative models and their presumed productivity advantages.

There is, however, counterevidence. Florida and Kenny (1991) surveyed Japanese transplants which supply parts to the large Japanese automobile assemblers. They found a very high adoption rate of transformed practices: for example, 76 percent of the suppliers use work teams and 79 percent have workers maintain their own machines. They also found substantial union avoidance (Milkman also observed this) and considerable use of contingent or temporary workers. This pattern of supply firms adopting transformed practices at the behest of their customers is informally confirmed by anecdotal evidence I collected of midwestern supplier networks which implemented a range of transformed practices in response to their customers' demands for innovations such as statistical process control.

In short, just as American firms seem torn between alternative ILM systems, so do Japanese-owned firms that are located in America. There is obviously movement away from the traditional model, as it was developed in the 1940s through the 1960s, but it is not clear how far this shift has gone.

International Variation

The final element of "data" is the very substantial variation across nations in how ILMs are organized to produce similar products. While some years ago this point might have been controversial, by now it is almost commonplace in the discussion of international competitiveness, although it has yet to be incorporated fully in the ILM literature. At least since Ronald Dore's *British Factory, Japanese Factory* (1973) we have known that Japanese ILMs differ in many important respects from comparable American ones on dimensions such as wage ratios (Japanese pay their managers many fewer multiples of worker wages than do Americans), job security (the core workers of large Japanese firms are protected from layoffs), job rotation and training (there is much more of both in Japan), and career paths (movements from blue- to white-collar ranks are more common in Japan).

While the Japanese comparison is by now well known, it is often not understood that other nations also differ from our patterns. For example, in German firms job security is also stronger, employees are involved in personnel decisions via their participation in works councils, there appear to be lower ratios of supervisors to front-line employees, and there is much greater emphasis on formal skill-based training systems as a gateway to promotions.

The point of these international comparisons is that they create problems for arguments which make technology and product markets the central determinants of ILM structure. It may still be the case that product markets and technology are important in the sense of restricting the range of alternatives[8] or by altering the relative costs and benefits of various ILM systems. However, the international evidence makes clear that there must be more to the story.

In summary, these are the conclusions from the review of recent developments in ILMs:

1. As judged by data on job tenure, long-term employment in ILMs remains important. In fact, it is of growing relevance for

women. Among middle-age men there is a noticeable decline in the fraction in extended employment relationships, but the dominant pattern remains lengthy spells in ILMs.

2. Although the central tendency is clearly stability, the evidence on the growth of contingent employment relationships also suggests there is some slippage around the edges. Some firms are seeking to establish looser relationships with a portion of their labor force. It will take further research to determine whether this development can explain the tenure patterns noted above.

3. Many firms are seeking to implement significant shifts in the organization of their ILMs. These shifts typically involve more flexible job boundaries, greater attention to training, more communications with the labor force, movements toward performance-based pay systems, and—at least in some cases—enhanced job security. At the same time, these transformations are not diffusing as rapidly as might have been predicted some years ago and there appear to be important obstacles. While it is hard to know which way the balance will tilt, it does seem fair to conclude that the rules regarding ILMs are a much more open question than in the past. Both the changes and the barriers are important "facts" which can be brought to bear upon theory.

4. There is considerable international variation in the organization of ILMs in firms which operate in similar product markets using similar technology.

Understanding How Internal Labor Markets Evolve

The foregoing material can be thought of as the data against which we will try to develop a credible theory of the development of ILMs. In making this effort we of course have a great deal of prior research and theorizing with which to work, but this doesn't necessarily make the task easier. A nice way of illustrating the problem is to consider the following two quotations which describe the same ILM phenomena, the determinants of the careers of senior executives in large corporations. The first quotation is from Robert Jackall's (1988) ethnographic study of three large firms and the second is from Sherwin Rosen's (1990) review article of the economic literature concerning the market for executives:

> . . . more frequent is the case where those with the power to do so foist or allow blame to fall on the unwary or

> inexperienced underlings . . . the most feared situation is to end up inadvertently in the wrong place at the wrong time. Yet this is exactly what happens in a structure that systematically diffuses responsibility . . . big corporations implicitly encourage scapegoating by their complete lack of any tracking system to trace responsibility . . . managers see [what happens] as completely capricious but completely understandable . . . what does matter when things go wrong is agility and political connections . . . most important they can "outrun their mistakes" so that when blame time arrives the burden will fall on someone else. At the institutional level, the absence of tracking responsibility becomes crucial. . . . (pp. 85-90)

> How a career develops depends upon the quality of the person's previous work, what talents were demonstrated at lower positions, and the talent of other people available to be selected . . . this process can be modeled as a tournament. Competitors with the highest score on some performance criteria are declared winners and get promoted to a better job . . . within firm competition can sometimes be structured to approximate socially optimum incentives by adjusting the wage structure across ranks . . . competition generated by these kinds of relative performance evaluation can lead to moral hazard problems. (pp. 33-39)

In Jackall's world (and the generalizations are supported by numerous anecdotes in the three firms), moral hazard is everything and efficiency an afterthought if that. In Rosen's world (which is supported by data on wage structures derived from several firm surveys), efficiency is at the core of firm structure and moral hazard is a troublesome side issue but not one which undermines the basic model or which suggests that the models are on the wrong track. Both purport to be representations of the rules governing careers in large private enterprises.

It is perhaps discouraging that two scholars can have such radically different views of the same question, each relegating the other's to an afterthought; but if the question were this constrained, it would not be too difficult to make progress. Choosing from between two such views is difficult but perhaps easier—given the sharp differences—than the broader and fuzzier question of why National Steel has transformed its ILM while U.S. Steel has

remained traditional. What combination of economic, polit
social factors explain these divergent outcomes? When ı
differences are added the problem becomes even harder.

To make progress I will first identify the core ideas of the competing models and then try to show how they can be fit together to provide a coherent explanation of the patterns.

Performance

One set of ideas suggests that ILM structure is determined by performance considerations. Employment rules are determined by the firm's calculation of which configuration will produce the most output given the environment (chiefly product markets, technology, and labor force characteristics). This is a view traditionally associated with economic models, although I will add additional elements to it.

The most longstanding explanation of why ILMs improve performance is that they reduce the costs for firms of training the work force and retaining skilled labor. By creating incentives for people to remain with the employer (e.g., compensation schemes which are "back-loaded") and disincentives for them to move (e.g., other firms force movers to start at the bottom of a job ladder), ILMs help resolve the bargaining problems inherent in the provision of specific human capital.[9] The evidence on this general point has always been the wage returns to job tenure, and although there have been several recent papers which argue that this is not as high as sometimes assumed (Abraham and Farber 1987), the evidence is still strong that these returns are substantial (Topel 1990).

More recently, economic theorists have emphasized new explanations of why long-term employment relationships enhance efficiency and hence performance. These explanations include minimizing transactions costs, helping resolve principal-agent problems, or job stability flowing from above-market-clearing efficiency wages (Wachter and Wright 1990; Williamson, Wachter, and Harris 1975; Akerlof 1984). Although models based on each of these ideas have been developed independently, I think it is best to think of them as part of a more general class of explanations which emphasize the issue of *control*. The firm is seen as having to solve the problem of how best to elicit effort from its labor force while minimizing the ability of employees to act in their personal interest rather than in the firm's interest.[10] These problems are especially serious when complexity or size render direct supervision of employees difficult. ILMs help resolve the problem by providing long-term opportunities to observe employees' behavior (the transactions cost argument), by creating sunk employee investment in the firm and hence raising the costs of cheating or poor effort (the bonding and implicit contract models), and by establishing an employment framework which permits development of wage systems which harmonize agent and principal interests (principal-agent and efficiency wage explanations).

The two foregoing groups of performance-based explanations of ILMs flow largely from the economics literature. There is, however, a third class of performance-centered explanations whose origin lies more in the industrial relations, human resource management, and organizational sociology fields. Particular ILM configurations may induce greater employee commitment not because of fear of unemployment or loss of wage premiums, as is posited by the economic models, but because of increased identification with the goals of the organization. This heightened commitment may in turn lead to more effort, more attention to quality, lower turnover rates, and other behaviors which enhance productivity.

The most commonly cited example of the relationship between ILM structure and commitment is Japan. Most casual observers believe that Japanese employees are more committed to their employer and that this does in fact lead to the performance enhancing behaviors listed above. In a recent important study, Lincoln and Kalleberg (1990) analyzed a sample of workers drawn from manufacturing firms in Japan and America. Surprisingly they did not find higher average levels of commitment in Japan than in the United States.[11] However, they did find that in both Japan and the United States some aspects of ILMs, particularly employee welfare programs and employee participation in quality circles and other forms of joint decision making, were associated with heightened commitment.[12] Assuming that this commitment improves performance—an assumption I will examine below—this line of thought suggests a different performance-based rationale for some types of ILM systems.

It is important to understand that the salience of each variant of performance-based explanation is conditioned upon external conditions or constraints. One obvious example is technology. The nature of the technology has a significant impact upon the relative

importance of specific skills in the production process. Techno
also plays a role in determining the ease or difficulty of dire
monitoring employee performance. Other external constraints include the skills which the labor force brings to the firm (and hence the nature of the education system) and the characteristics of product markets (high volatility and consequent frequent shifts in product characteristics affect optimal supervision practices).[13]

Customs, Norms, and Political Contests

An alternative perspective, quite different in spirit from performance-based explanations, interprets ILMs as work rules which represent the outcome of social processes within organizations. These social processes may be the relatively invisible, inertial impact of norms and custom enforced through employee pressure or they may be the result of active power struggles.

Custom and norms emerge naturally out of the fact that when groups exist for extended periods they develop a history and a sense of what is appropriate and inappropriate. These norms include rules regarding output (Roethlisberger and Dickson 1939; Roy 1954) but also job demarcations, promotion procedures, and the like.

More active contests among factions within an organization can also shape the ILM rules. In the course of such struggles the kinds of performance considerations discussed earlier may underlie management motives, but even this is not necessarily true. Management itself may be driven by self-interest or ideology to retain certain powers or structures which bear little direct relationship to productivity.

The literature is replete with illustrations of these points. Jacoby (1985) describes the struggles of personnel staff against foremen, with the personnel department seeking to establish a legitimate role for itself. Various ILM rules such as job posting resulted from this conflict. This phenomenon continues: Baron, Davis-Blake, and Bielby (1986) show that job titles tend to proliferate in organizations which employ relatively large proportions of personnel specialists.[14] Elbaum (1984), in his discussion of wages in the steel industry, documents how the modern wage structure reflects long ago political struggles among different factions of the steel union. Indeed, the persistence of customary wage differentials in the face of shifting market conditions has long been observed by industrial relations scholars. Middle managers and foremen have resisted shifts in ILMs which transfer power to employees; and the resulting structures represent a compromise (Klein 1989).

The External Environment: Constraints and Guidance

Along some dimensions the impact of the external environment upon ILM structure is so obvious as to not require much comment. Government regulations regarding wages or equal employment opportunity are clearly reflected in organizational rules regarding such matters. Another example is that during World War II the War Labor Board, in an effort to maintain labor peace, implanted personnel practices within firms and these practices remained in place long after the war ended. The government was also influential in establishing ILM rules in railroads and airlines.

There are, however, more subtle channels of external influence. Maurice, Sellier, and Silvestre (1986) show how the differing educational systems of France and Germany are reflected in organizational rules within firms. Because German schools imbue both more skill and respect for authority flowing from formal credentials than does France, the ratio of supervisors to workers is much lower and promotion paths between high-level blue-collar jobs and low-level supervisors are more open. The extensive debate about the role of Japanese culture in supporting the supposedly distinctive characteristics of the Japanese ILM is another illustration of the impact of the external environment. (Dore 1973; Lincoln and Kalleberg 1990). There are also international differences in norms governing appropriate pay differentials across levels within an organization and these differences do not appear to be related to corresponding variation in labor supply or demand.

The external environment also acts upon firm decisions through the coercive channels of imitation. The sociological literature on institutionalism or isomorphism (e.g., DiMaggio and Powell 1983) argues that institutions seek legitimacy by imitating powerful actors in their environment. Hence Pfeffer and Cohen (1984) find that organizations which are regulated by government agencies are more likely to adopt particular formalized internal employment rules than are other organizations. Baron, Jennings, and Dobbin (1986) describe how professional personnel organizations diffused particular practices after World War II in an effort to maintain and expand their status within firms. One can surely speculate that there is a substantial element of mimicry in the spread of "transformed" ILM models today.[15]

Explaining the Data

How well do the alternative perspectives described above explain the ILM patterns in the 1980s? As a first step, consider the following analogy: what leads to a change in relative wages across occupations? It is helpful to think of the process as a set of three rings.

Within the first ring, the impetus for such a shift comes from supply and demand developments, for example a technological shift which might increase the demand for a particular skill. This impetus is analogous to the performance considerations cited above and sets off a series of reactions. In a frictionless universe, the outward shift in the demand curve would yield a temporarily higher wage which, over time, would be gradually offset by appropriate supply responses. In at least the short run, the wage structure would shift.[16]

If in the inner ring performance considerations started the process in motion, how it actually plays out is modified in the second and third rings. Internal firm customs, norms, and politics modify the thrust of market forces. Historical differentials, the problems of dramatically increasing the wages of one group within an organization, fears of compression if the wages of entry employees rise sharply relative to incumbents, the competing demands of managers elsewhere for resources, and fears of wage inflation as other groups seek to maintain their customary relative standing, all taken together, influence the outcome. None of this is to say that the relative wages of the affected group do not rise; the performance considerations are indeed powerful. However it is easy to imagine a vice-president for human resources limiting the size and timing of the wage increase for the reasons just cited.[17] Hence the impact of performance concerns is refracted and modified to an important extent by the considerations in the second ring.

In the United States the third ring—the external environment—is less important in understanding wage changes. At the bottom of the labor market the minimum wage and the "social wage"—welfare and other benefits—influence the wage structure, but these are much less important further up. Wage and hours legislation—the requirement that time and a half be paid for overtime—may be important and so may equal employment opportunity considerations. Even mimicry can be important if, for example, a portion of the wage increase takes the form of performance pay, an innovation which has been spread via the business press. All in all, however, this third ring probably would exert a much weaker effect than the other two.

It should be apparent that explaining the evolution of the wage structure is complicated and that all three rings play some role.[18] Yet wages are a single measurable variable. Understanding the evolution of work organization, with its many dimensions and tradeoffs among these dimensions, must be even more difficult. This said, how can we apply the models to recent ILM shifts?

It is evident that transformations, and attempted transformations, in ILM structure were initiated by performance considerations. In some industries, American firms appeared to be less productive than their foreign competitors and the organization of work was apparently the culprit.[19] It is clear that performance concerns drove the adoption of innovations such as team production, quality circles, cross-training, and so on. These ideas had been around for a long time and received considerable academic discussion, and even press attention, under the rubric of the movements to humanize work. The federal government's 1972 report, *Work in America*, exemplified these interests. However, the innovations did not penetrate until they were perceived to be tied to performance, and this happened when the workplace innovations were incorporated into the overall production system and when competitors showed the payoffs to such efforts.

In thinking about the nature of the performance considerations behind ILM shifts, economic explanations centering on control do not, at first blush, seem adequate. It is certainly plausible that efforts to improve quality, for example, may lead employers to improve control of the labor force. However, most observers of foreign ILM models tend to emphasize employee cooperation and commitment more than control, at least as control is normally understood. That is, the control models in the economics literature, with their emphasis on monitoring, wage profiles, and optimal incentive structures do not seem to capture what underlies the gains made in transformed ILMs.

However, even if control as it is typically described is not what explains recent changes, it may nonetheless be true that commitment is simply a more subtle form of control, one which is grounded in social psychology rather than economic principles. Put differently, do these new production systems succeed simply because they are a cleverer way of controlling the work force and eliciting effort, for example by using work teams to monitor the performance of peers? Japanese firms refer to their employees as "members." Does this capture a distinctive reality or is it a mask for control?

The best available American evidence on this question comes from the experience of automobile firms that have adopted transformed ILM systems (these provide the best evidence simply because they have been studied most closely). My reading of this research is that while control considerations remain important—and may be accomplished more effectively in transformed systems—the dimension of commitment is in fact real and distinctive.

Paul Adler (1991) conducted a series of intensive interviews in the General Motors-Toyota NUMMI plant in California. This plant implemented the Toyota system of team work, just-in-time inventories, continuous improvement, and employee responsibility for quality along the line. Taken together these constitute a new production system. These production changes alone do not necessarily buy commitment, as Mazda learned in Flat Rock, Michigan.[20] However at NUMMI the new system was combined with management behavior shifts. For example, one of Adler's interviewees says

> NUMMI's managers are generally pretty good at considering suggestions when workers make them. They respect workers' ideas. NUMMI's managers always get back with: "It's a great idea" or "It's a good idea but . . ." This is what we like to see. At GM, you were lucky if they wrote the idea down; as soon as you left the room you knew the idea was headed for the garbage can.

NUMMI was also explicit in offering strong job security pledges and in respecting worker power along the assembly line (in terms of ability to stop the line to correct quality problems). The consequence of all of this is that NUMMI is judged to have made tremendous gains on productivity and quality (MacDuffie and Krafcik

1992), but the point here is that these gains are not ones which can be easily attributed to control, at least as traditionally understood.

Adler (1991) provides numerous examples of workers making small suggestions which cumulate into substantial savings (such as color coding of circuit breakers or replacing chrome water fountains with metal), as well as such behavior as voluntarily picking up cigarette butts from the floor in the work area. Shimada and MacDuffie (1987) use the phrase "giving knowledge to the machine" to characterize employee contributions in transformed systems. Control models focus on shirking, cheating, misreporting, absenteeism, and the like. They do not satisfactorily explain *positive* voluntary behaviors such as these. Nor do they explain what Adler's quotes show is the explicit *reciprocal* nature of these actions: they are in response to management demonstrations of commitment to the labor force (which take the form of job security, concern with health and safety, respect for suggestions, etc.).

There are also elements of control in these transformed systems. As Adler points out, the absence of buffers makes errors and problems along the line much more visible to supervisors. Teams do put pressure on peers with respect to absenteeism. Most dramatically, at least at NUMMI, is the heavy use of time and motion studies to decrease cycle time and hence to reduce employee discretion over their behavior along the assembly line.

In short, it does appear that commitment is a genuinely distinctive dimension of performance, distinct from control. At the core of the difference is the idea of reciprocity. Management in fact gives up something significant—it transfers power—in order to gain commitment. This suggests that there is a tradeoff between control and commitment, and delineating the nature of that tradeoff is an important theme for future work.

At the same time, the line between control and commitment is not always clear and transformed ILM systems may achieve higher performance via gains on both dimensions. This explains the dilemma facing unions in such settings as they seek to protect employees from intensified control, yet need to avoid challenging the gains from commitment.

Traditional economic considerations can more successfully explain development of core-periphery employment patterns. Moving to high commitment ILMs is costly because of the heightened job security implicit in such arrangements. To reduce costs, management excludes as many employees as possible from the core. How far one can go along these lines is determined by how deeply into an organization contingent employment can penetrate before it has adverse performance impacts[21] and by the supply of willing contingent employees. For firms that adopt contingent employment relationships without ILM transformations, cost considerations alone seem to dominate.[22]

If performance explains the emergence of new forms of ILM in the United States, what can explain their halting progress? In part the answer again is performance. It would appear that there are many circumstances in which the traditional mode of organizing work is superior (or at least as good) and probably cheaper. One important clue here is the transplanted Japanese electronic assemblers cited earlier. There is no obstacle which one can plausibly cite other than that they believe that traditional work organization is the most profitable given their market and technology.[23]

The impetus given to transforming ILM systems by performance considerations has also been refracted by the customs, norms, and politics of organizations. One perspective on the union sector is to note that it has taken some time for many unions to believe, or at least grudgingly accept, that work rule changes are the price for remaining in business. The time this has taken and the compromises which have been reached are reflected in ILM outcomes.

Performance pressures are also filtered through managerial politics and custom. As I have already noted, transformed work systems are often a direct threat to first-line supervisors and these concerns can be an obstacle to change. Considerable anecdotal evidence also suggests that middle managers find the devolution of authority inherent in transformed systems to be a threat, or a violation of norms, and often resist. It is easy to understand why a traditionally trained manager would find it difficult to pay close attention to employee suggestions. There are also barriers at the more senior management level. Full implementation of the transformed system requires expenditure of resources on large commitments (employment continuity) as well as small ones (consistent responses to employee suggestions for improvements related to comfort and safety). Where a union is present, senior management may find it difficult to accept the degree of cooperation that is typically necessary. In the absence of a union, management is likely to fear that empowering the labor force is the first step towards unionization. Taken together, these concerns are often enough to block adoption of the transformed ILM system.[24]

The best evidence of the importance of the third ring—the external environment—comes from international comparisons. One example is skill: the United States lacks the deep vocational training of Germany that can ease the introduction of new work systems.[25] In addition, U.S. managerial culture is hostile to the transformed model by virtue of its restriction of legitimate goals to maximizing stockholder interests. This stands in contrast to the broader stakeholder perspective of both Japan and Germany. In addition to the bias inherent in a stockholder versus stakeholder perspective, the problem is exacerbated by an emphasis on short-term gains. This bias is not a logical part of stockholder systems but it does appear to be characteristic of the American managerial system and it makes it more difficult to justify long-term investments in training and enhanced employment security. In both Germany and Japan, legal restrictions and national culture lead firms to be much more reluctant to follow a hire/fire strategy and to adopt the ILM associated with such a policy.[26]

To summarize, what do recent events tell us about the merits of alternative ILM theories? In some sense I have ducked the question by arguing, via the analogy of the three rings, that no single model is adequate and that many of the contenders have a role in the story. This may not seem clean, but it fairly reflects a complex world. However, we have made some additional progress. I have argued that performance-based models are central in explaining the recent drive for change in ILMs and that the norms/customs/politics/mimicry models shape the actual outcome which results from the initial performance impulse. These performance models are contingent upon a variety of considerations, such as technology and product markets, and also upon the external environment in which the firm finds itself.

I also argued that we need to work with a broader view of performance models than is typically permitted in the economics literature. Economics stresses control, but recent events seem equally, if not more, driven by efforts to obtain commitment. Central to commitment is reciprocity, i.e., managers giving up control. When reciprocity is added, commitment becomes more than a new and sly way of obtaining control. Nonetheless, the line between commitment and control is not always clear.

Finally, the reader may be troubled by the ring analogy because it implies a series of sequential, not simultaneous, steps and because it appears to give primacy to performance. The sequential structure is simply a conceit intended to indicate which factor is most important and to permit clear exposition. In reality all factors may be in play at once. Giving primacy to performance is, I think, historically contingent but accurate for the current period. By contrast, when the War Labor Board essentially imposed ILM patterns in a variety of industries, or when personnel staff diffused them through professional associations, other rings may have claimed center stage. Furthermore, although the impetus for change comes from performance, researchers may be more struck, and more interested, in why transformations occur so haltingly. In that case the other rings should occupy their attention.

Conclusion

There has been a great deal of useful and important research on ILMs and our understanding of these institutions has progressed a great deal. However, an obvious research task is to collect nationally representative data on the distribution of ILM types and on the change in that distribution over time. As the reader no doubt has noticed, much of the evidence deployed here is anecdotal and impressionistic and there is no good reason to permit that to continue.

There are, in addition, several themes which have been insufficiently addressed in the literature. The first is white-collar or managerial ILMs and the second concerns placing ILMs in a broader context.

Any casual reader of the ILM literature will immediately observe that most of the material is drawn from the blue-collar manufacturing world. Whether the central models and descriptions are equally valid for managerial ILMs or in the service sector more generally is an open question. On the one hand, the core constructs (e.g., control or commitment) must be important in other settings. However, the context in which these ideas are set may be quite different.[27]

In addition there is a great deal of talk in the business press about the flattening of organizational hierarchies, white-collar job insecurity, and the impact of technical change on white-collar skills and tasks. Other work suggests that new work forms, such as ad hoc teams for product development, are increasingly important (Ancona and Caldwell 1987). Some observers speak of the Taylorization of service work, while others emphasize that quality is key in the service sector and hence high commitment systems are important there also. All of these developments, or alleged developments, can be systematically examined in the context of ILMs.

Some of the economics literature on principal-agent issues, compensation models, and tournament mobility have managers as their focus, but the empirical evidence is slim relative to the theories. There is also a large "careers" literature which is most closely associated with human resource management as taught in business schools. Much of this literature is very prescriptive and managerial, and when it is more academic it tends to be grounded in the psychology or ethnography literatures. It rarely asks about explanations for variation across organizations nor does it seek general explanatory models. Finally, there is very little work of any kind concerning employment patterns in the service sector. Clearly, expanding the ambit of ILM research beyond blue-collar employment represents a major challenge.

An additional challenge to future ILM research is embedding ILMs in a framework which is broader than the terms in which they have been typically conceived. As I noted in the introduction, the early ILM researchers took public policy and the firm's competitive strategy as given and focused on the labor market implications of ILM institutions. However, ILMs are important because they have substantial impacts upon the welfare of individuals (along the dimensions of pay, job security, skill acquisition, and so on) and upon the competitiveness of firms and of the economy. This suggests that it is important to place ILMs firmly in both a public policy and a business strategy perspective.

We currently have a very poor understanding of how to deploy policy levers to influence ILMs. If, for example, we wished as a matter of policy to encourage the diffusion of the transformed ILM model, we would not know where to start. As already indicated, the simple prescription of more training is not convincing. Some experience suggests that interventions in firms around a particular issue (for example, the introduction of Statistical Process Control) can lead to broader changes as the firm trains its labor force and reorganizes work (Batt and Osterman 1991). However, there has been very little systematic research along these lines and almost none on the broader question of how (or whether) to attempt transformations in the external environment which would in turn induce firms to shift ILM patterns.

In a similar vein only recently has research begun to place ILMs in the context of competitive strategy. The productivity consequences of alternative ILM patterns are poorly understood. How work organization fits with market strategy (e.g., variety or quality) is not well developed. In these and other ways, the firm's employment system should be more systematically linked to other aspects of its strategy and structure.

These limitations aside, it is apparent that ILMs provide a fruitful research arena for a variety of disciplines and intellectual perspectives. This will doubtlessly continue to be true. Whether ILMs will also be an arena in which the disciplines and perspectives can reach a mutually rewarding accommodation remains to be seen.

Acknowledgments

I am grateful for comments to Rosemary Batt, Peter Cappelli, Thomas Kochan, James Rebitzer, Peter Sherer, and Maureen Scully. Research support was provided by the Spencer Foundation.

Endnotes

[1] It is important to remember that many individuals in the lower tenure categories in the foregoing tables are in the early stages of a long-term employment relationship and hence the fraction of the labor force which is ever in a long-term employment relationship is larger than the proportion in such a relationship at any cross-section. See Hall (1982) for a discussion of this.

[2] I have in mind the commonly heard assertions that the average worker will have to change his/her employer many more times than in the past.

[3] Hartmann and Lapidus (1989, 1567) report that 45 percent of workers employed by temporary help services are clerical, 20 percent are in blue-collar manufacturing jobs, and 15 percent are in technical/professional specialties. A survey by Mangum, Mayhill, and Nelson (1985) showed that 62 percent of respondents used temporary workers in clerical jobs, 43 percent used temporaries for production jobs, 46 percent used temporary professional workers, and 41 percent used temporary service workers.

[4] The increase in female tenure is influenced by supply developments as well as the demand-side factors emphasized here.

[5] The material on Corning which follows is taken from interviews I conducted in the company. Similar information has been widely reported in the business press.

[6] A great deal of effort and imagination went into the collection of these data. Unfortunately, the response rate was only 6.5 percent and hence it is not entirely clear what we should make of any findings.

[7] There is a question, however, about the extent to which these clusters represent theoretically distinct groupings as opposed to artifacts of the particular statistical procedure.

[8] The classic example is that the dispersed character of construction, particularly home construction, discourages formation of firm based ILMs.

[9] ILMs also make it safe for senior workers to pass on skills since they are protected, by virtue of job ladders, from competition from their "students."

[10] The more power workers have, the more serious is the firm's control problem. This power can take various forms, including knowledge in the minds of workers but not managers and ability to affect production at key "choke points."

[11] When they manipulated the data by estimating commitment levels via a two-stage instruments procedure, they did find higher levels of commitment in Japan.

[12] This supports the argument developed in Cappelli and Sherer (1991) that ILMs represent an important link in the organizational behavior literature between individual behavior (in this case commitment) and context.

[13] For a more extended discussion of the interaction between performance based objectives of the firm and external constraints in the establishment of ILM patterns, see Osterman (1987). This paper does not, however, discuss the theme of commitment.

[14] Of course, there is a question about direction of causality. Complex organizations may require personnel specialists.

[15] The mimicry models are convincing in a number of respects and certainly in my own interviews with managers I have been struck by the frequency with which they explain their own policies by reference to practices they have heard of at other firms. However, copying may simply be a cheap form of economic search. The mimicry models also tend to leave open the question of where the initial ideas come from and, more troubling, what role is played by performance in determining which models are ultimately selected and survive.

[16] In the textbook world, in the long run the former structure would reemerge as the supply responses reached completion.

[17] In response to the objection that "market discipline" (e.g., quit rates or difficulty in recruitment) would thwart such administrative action, one can point to the substantial variation within a geographical area of wages for comparable jobs (Groshen 1991; Dunlop 1957). Doeringer and Piore (1971) discuss a number of adjustment mechanisms which firms can use in lieu of wage increase to adjust the size and quality of their labor force.

[18] In a recent paper Groshen (1991) reviews various theories for why wages for comparable skills and occupations vary by firm. She rejects most standard neoclassical models and instead places greatest emphasis on efficiency wage and rent sharing explanations. However, she notes that the direct evidence on these models is very weak and one is left with the view that even after many years of research on wages we still cannot develop a convincing explanation for variation across enterprises.

[19] In other industries, American firms seem to more than hold their own in international competition. The relationship of this success to ILM structure is less well understood since much research has (unfortunately in my view) been concentrated in declining industries.

[20] At the Mazda plant in Flat Rock, Michigan, a production system and ILM which initially appeared to have the same characteristics as at NUMMI broke down under employee complaints about work pace and health and safety. A difficult industrial relations climate emerged, culminating in the election of a dissident union group and challenges to company policy. See Fucini and Fucini (1990).

[21] Rebitzer (1991) shows that in the petroleum refining industry heavy use of contingent employees is associated with increased risks of accidents.

[22] For a more subtle view of core-periphery patterns, which sees them as a point on a continuum of nontraditional employment forms, see Sherer and Lee (1992).

[23] The contingency of the performance gains probably helps explain the mixed findings in the literature seeking to establish a link between work organization and outcomes such as productivity. There are investigations which suggest such links (MacDuffie 1991; Cutcher-Gershenfeld 1991), but there is also quality research whose findings are much more on the neutral or negative side (for example, Wall, Kemp, Jackson, and Klegg 1986). If one had to make a bet, the safer one, given the research and given the international evidence, would be that transformed systems do provide a performance boost. However, the mixed findings in the research give pause as do the serious methodological problems which characterize this line of work. The greatest methodological problem is that much of the research consists of studies of "best practice," i.e., settings in which the researcher knows in advance that there was some success. It is not at all clear from this style of research what would happen were the "treatment" administered to a random firm. Given the possible costs of making the transition, it is evident why caution is a reasonable strategy.

[24] The survival rate of QWL plans is low. According to Goodman (1980), of the plans established in the 1970s only 25 percent managed to last for five years. It is not clear whether programs in the 1980s had better prospects.

[25] However, skill alone is not the explanation, since Japan provides relatively little school-based vocational training; firms instead train intensively in the context of ILMs. American firms could follow a similar strategy should they wish.

[26] Levine and Tyson (1990) point to another external environment issue. When only a few firms implement transformed systems, with their heightened commitment to employment security, this may have an adverse selection effect as employees who would be fired in other environments gravitate to the transformed firms. It is hard to assess how important this is, although it may help explain some of the extensive investment in selection and hiring which characterizes some of the start-up transformed firms.

[27] Kanter (1977, 132) wrote of a group of managers: "People in the same position disagreed among themselves about its place in the organizational career map. Twenty distribution managers identified seven routes to their jobs . . . and they imagined that there were three likely and seven rare moves from their job." A description of a traditional blue-collar job ladder would be quite different.

References

Abraham, Katherine, and Henry Farber. "Job Duration, Seniority, and Earnings." *American Economic Review* 77 (June 1987), pp. 278-97.

Abraham, Katherine, and James Medoff. "Length of Service and Layoffs in Union and Non-Union Groups," *Industrial and Labor Relations Review* 38 (October 1984), pp. 87-97.

Adler, Paul. "The New 'Learning Bureaucracy': New United Motor Manufacturing, Inc." Mimeo, University of Southern California, October 1991.

Akerlof, George. "Gift Exchange and Efficiency Wages." *American Economic Review* 74 (May 1984), pp. 79-83.

Althauser, Robert, and Arne Kalleberg. "Firms, Occupations, and the Structure of Labor Markets." In *Sociological Perspectives on Labor Markets*, ed. Ivan Berg. New York: Academic Press, 1981, pp. 119-45.

Ancona, Deborah, and David Caldwell. "Management Issues in New Product Teams in High Technology Companies." In *Advances in Industrial Relations*. Greenwich, CT: JAI Press, 1987.

Applebaum, Eileen. "The Growth of the U.S. Contingent Labor Force." In *Microeconomic Issues in Labor Economics*, eds. Robert Drago and Richard Perlman. New York: Harvester Wheatsheaf, 1989.

Baron, James, and William Bielby. "The Proliferation of Job Titles in Organizations." *Administration Science Quarterly* 31 (December 1986), pp. 561-86.

Baron, James, Alison Davis-Blake, and William Bielby. "The Structure of Opportunity: How Promotion Ladders Vary Within and Among Organizations." *Administrative Science Quarterly* 31 (June 1986), pp. 248-73.

Baron, James, P. Devereaus Jennings, and Frank Dobbin. "Mission Control? The Development of Personnel Systems in U.S. Industry." *American Sociological Review* 53 (August 1988), pp. 497-514.

Batt, Rose, and Paul Osterman. *A National Framework for Employment and Training Policy: Lessons from Local Initiatives*. Washington, D.C.: Economic Policy Institute, 1991.

Bielby, William, and James Baron. "Organization, Technology, and Worker Attachment to the Firm." *Research In Social Mobility*, eds. Donald Treiman and Robert Robertson. Greenwich, CT: JAI Press, 1983.

Brown, Clair, Michael Reich, and David Stern. "Skills and Security in Evolving Employment Systems; Observations from Case Studies." Mimeo, U.C. Berkeley, Institute of Industrial Relations, 1991.

Cappelli, Peter, and Peter Sherer. "The Missing Role of Context in OB: The Need for a Meso-Level Approach." In *Research in Organizational Behavior* 13, eds. L. L. Cummings and Barry Staw. Greenwich, CT: JAI Press, 1991.

________. "Spanning the Union/Nonunion Boundary." *Industrial Relations* 28 (Spring 1989), pp. 188-205.

Cutcher-Gershenfeld, Joel. "The Impact on Economic Performance of a Transformation in Workplace Relations." *Industrial and Labor Relations Review* 44 (January 1991), pp. 241-60.

________. "The Institutionalization of Organizational Change: A Case Study of Xerox and the ACTWU." In *Human Resource Management: Text and Cases*, Second Edition, ed. Fred Foulkes. Englewood Cliffs, NJ: Prentice-Hall, 1989.

Delaney, John, David Lewin, and Casey Ichniowski. *Human Resource Policies and Practices in American Firms*, BLMR Report No. 137. Washington, D.C.: U.S. Department of Labor, 1989.

DiMaggio, Paul, and Walter Powell. "The Iron Cage Revisited: Institutional Isomorphism and Collective Rationality in Organizational Fields." *American Sociological Review* 48 (1983), pp. 147-60.

Doeringer, Peter, and Michael Piore. *Internal Labor Markets*. Lexington: D. C. Heath, 1971.

Dore, Ronald. *British Factory, Japanese Factory*. Berkeley: University of California Press, 1973.

Dunlop, John. "Job Vacancy Measures and Economic Analysis." In *The Measurement and Interpretation of Job Vacancies: A Conference Report*. National Bureau of Economic Research. New York: Columbia University Press, 1966.

________. "The Task of Contemporary Wage Theory." In *New Concepts In Wage Determination*, eds. G. Taylor and F. Pierson. New York: McGraw Hill, 1957.

Elbaum, Bernard. "The Making and Shaping of Job and Pay Structures in the Iron and Steel Industry." In *Internal Labor Markets*, ed. Paul Osterman. Cambridge, MA: MIT Press, 1984.

Florida, Richard, and Martin Kenney. "The Transfer of Japanese Industrial Organization to the U.S." *American Sociological Review* 56 (June 1991), pp. 381-98.

Fucini, J., and S. Fucini. *Working for the Japanese*. New York: Free Press, 1990.

Gershenfeld, Walter. "Employee Participation in Firm Decisions." In *I Resources and the Performance of the Firm*, eds. Morris Kleiner, Richard Block, Myron Roomkin, and Sidney W. Salsburg. Madison, WI: Industrial Relations Research Association, 1987.

Goodman, Paul. "Realities of Improving Quality Work Life." *Labor Law Journal* 31 (August 1980), pp. 487-94.

Groshen, Erica L. "Sources of Intra-Industry Wage Dispersion: How Much Do Employers Matter?" *Quarterly Journal of Economics* 106 (August 1991), pp. 869-85.

Hall, Robert. "The Importance of Lifetime Jobs in the U.S. Economy." *American Economic Review* 72 (September 1982), pp. 716-24.

Hartmann, Heidi, and June Lapidus. "Temporary Work." In *Commission on Workforce Quality, Investing in People*. Washington, D.C.: U.S. Department of Labor, 1989.

Ichniowski, Casey. "Human Resource Management Systems and the Performance of U.S. Manufacturing Business." NBER Working Paper No. 3449, September 1990.

Jackall, Robert. *Moral Mazes: The World of Corporate Managers*. New York: Oxford University Press, 1988.

Jacoby, Sanford. *Employing Bureaucracy*. New York: Columbia University Press, 1985.

Kanter, Rosabeth Moss. *Men and Women of the Corporation*. New York: Basic Books, 1977.

Katz, Harry. *Shifting Gears: Changing Labor Relations in the U.S. Auto Industry*. Cambridge, MA: MIT Press, 1985.

Kerr, Clark. "The Balkanization of Labor Markets." In *Labor Mobility and Economic Opportunity*, ed. E. Wright Bakke. Cambridge, MA: MIT Press, 1954.

Klein, Janice. "Why Supervisors Resist Employee Involvement." *Harvard Business Review* 62 (September-October 1989), pp. 87-95.

Kochan, Thomas, Harry Katz, and Robert McKersie. *The Transformation of American Industrial Relations*. New York: Basic Books, 1986.

Levine, David, and Laura D'Andrea Tyson. "Participation, Productivity, and the Firm's Environment." In *Paying for Productivity*, ed. Alan Blinder. Washington, D.C.: The Brookings Institution, 1990.

Lincoln, James, and Arne Kalleberg. *Culture, Control, and Commitment: A Study of Work Organization and Work Artifacts in the United States and Japan*. Cambridge: Cambridge University Press, 1990.

MacDuffie, John Paul. *Beyond Mass Production, Flexible Production Systems and Manufacturing Performance in the World Auto Industry*. Ph.D. dissertation, MIT Sloan School of Management, 1991.

MacDuffie, John Paul, and John Krafcik. "Integrating Technology and Human Resources for High Performance Manufacturing: Evidence from the International Auto Industry." In *Transforming Organizations*, eds. Thomas A. Kochan and Michael Useem. New York: Oxford University Press, forthcoming, 1992.

Mangum, Garth, Donald Mayhill, and Kristin Nelson. "The Temporary Help Market: A Response to the Dual Internal Labor Market." *Industrial and Labor Relations Review* 38 (July 1985), pp. 599-611.

Maurice, Marc, Francois Sellier, and Jean-Jacques Silvestre. *The Social Foundations of Industrial Power*. Cambridge, MA: MIT Press, 1986.

Milkman, Ruth. *Japan's California Factories: Labor Relations and Economic Globalization*. Los Angeles, UCLA Institute of Industrial Relations, 1991.

Mitchell, Daniel J.B., David Lewin, and Edward Lawler. "Alternative Pay Systems, Firm Performance, and Productivity." In *Paying for Productivity*, ed. Alan Blinder. Washington, D.C.: The Brookings Institution, 1990.

New York Stock Exchange. *People and Productivity: A Challenge to Corporate America*. New York, 1982.

Osterman, Paul. "Choice Among Alternative Internal Labor Market Systems." *Industrial Relations* (February 1987), pp. 46-67.

Osterman, Paul, ed. *Internal Labor Markets*. Cambridge, MA: MIT Press, 1984.

Osterman, Paul. "Turnover and the Performance of the Firm." In *Human Resources and the Performance of the Firm*, eds. Morris Kleiner, Richard Block, Myron Roomkin, and Sidney W. Salsburg. Madison, WI: IRRA, 1987.

_______. "White Collar Internal Labor Markets." In *Internal Labor Markets*, ed. Paul Osterman. Cambridge, MA: MIT Press, 1984.

Pfeffer, Jeffrey, and Yinon Cohen. "Determinants of Internal Labor Markets in Organizations." *Administrative Science Quarterly* 29 (1984), pp. 550-72.

Rebitzer, James. "Short-Term Employment Relations and Labor Market Outcomes: Contract Workers in the U.S. Petrochemical Industry." Mimeo, MIT Sloan School of Management, 1991.

Rebitzer, James, and Lowell Taylor. "Do Labor Markets Provide Enough Short Hour Jobs? An Analysis of Work Hours and Work Incentives." Mimeo, MIT Sloan School of Management, 1991.

Roethlisberger, F. J., and William Dickson. *Management and the Worker*. Cambridge, MA: Harvard University Press, 1939.

Rosen, Sherwin. "Contracts and the Markets for Executives." NBER Working Paper No. 3542, December 1990.

Roy, Donald. "Quota Restriction and Goldbricking in a Machine Shop." *American Journal of Sociology* 60 (1954), pp. 255-66.

Russell, Raymond. "Forms and Extent of Employee Participation in the Contemporary United States." *Work and Occupations* 15 (1988), pp. 374-95.

Sherer, Peter, and Kyungmook Lee. "Core, Peripheries and More and Less: Mixes of Labor Relationships in Firms." Paper presented at the 1992 meetings of the Industrial Relations Research Association.

Shimada, Haruo, and John Paul MacDuffie. "Industrial Relations and Humanware: Japanese Investments in Automobile Manufacturing in the United States." Working Paper, MIT Sloan School of Management, 1987.

Topel, Robert. "Specific Capital, Mobility, and Wages: Wages Rise with Job Seniority." NBER Working Paper No. 3294, March 1990.

U.S. Department of Health, Education and Welfare. *Work in America*. Washington, DC, 1972.

Verma, Anil. "Union and Non-Union Industrial Relations at the Plant Level." Ph.D. dissertation, MIT Sloan School of Management, 1983.

Wachter, Michael, and Richard Wright. "The Economics of Internal Labor Markets." *Industrial Relations* 29 (Spring 1990), pp. 240-62.

Wall, Toby, Nigel Kemp, Paul Jackson, and Chris Clegg. "Outcomes of Autonomous Work Groups: A Long Term Field Experiment." *Academy of Management Journal* 29 (1986), pp. 280-304.

Williamson, Oliver, Michael Wachter, and Jeffrey Harris. "Understanding the Employment Relation: The Analysis of Idiosyncratic Exchange." *Bell Journal of Economics* 6 (Spring 1975), pp. 250-80.

CHAPTER 9

International Human Resource Studies: A Framework for Future Research

THOMAS A. KOCHAN AND ROSEMARY BATT
Massachusetts Institute of Technology

LEE DYER
Cornell University

The purpose of this chapter is to develop a theoretical framework for research in a broadened and redefined field of international human resource studies. Interest in international aspects of human resource management (HRM) and policy has increased markedly in recent years. This should not be surprising, given the growing importance of international economic activity in general, and the increased mobility of technology, capital, and human resources across national boundaries in particular. We are concerned that current research falling under this label is not only too narrowly conceived, but ignores important work from allied areas and disciplines. We also believe that the theoretical appeal and practical value of this work would be strengthened by including contributions from a broader array of scholars, policymakers, and practitioners who share interests in employment and industrial relations (IR) issues.

Limitations of Contemporary International HRM Research

To date, the majority of international HRM research has focused on providing insights and advice to firms on how to select and manage expatriate managers in international job assignments (Zeira and Banai 1984; Mendenhall, Dunbar, and Oddou 1987; Tung 1988; Dowling and Schuler 1990; Napier 1991; Von Glinow 1991). A second, parallel body of work addresses the challenges to firms of developing managers with international exposure, experience, and understanding (Mendenhall and Oddou 1985; Doz and Prahalad 1986; Galbraith and Kazanjian 1986; Evans, Doz, and Laurent 1989; Black and Mendenhall 1990). While these issues are of practical importance to personnel managers, this work suffers from the same conceptual and normative limitations of much of the traditional domestic personnel research that recent human resource scholars have been attempting to overcome: it focuses too narrowly on functional activities and lacks a deep theoretical structure. Thus the work is largely an extension of the field of personnel and human resource management designed to speak to the needs of multinational or transnational firms. Much of the literature also continues to be written from an American rather than an international perspective (Boyacigiller and Adler 1991).

A third, more theoretically driven body of work challenges the concept of convergence on an American model of HRM, but tends to focus on cultural explanations to the exclusion of the political, economic, institutional, and strategic contexts in which multinational firms operate (Hofstede 1980; Adler 1982, 1983, 1986; Laurent 1986; Ronen 1986; Adler and Ghadar 1990; Hofstede et al. 1990). As in the case of the literature described earlier, this work is also oriented toward providing advice to improve the performance of individual firms and managers.

In brief, the current literature in international HRM defines the field too narrowly. As a result, it ignores many of the most challenging questions and theoretical implications for modern employment relations that flow from the expansion of international economic, political, technical, and organizational interdependence. Moreover, it is heavily dominated by a discussion of concepts and issues with little or no backing in systematic empirical research.

As we will outline, it is around a broader set of questions that a field of international human resource studies should be built. This broader set of questions requires an interdisciplinary framework. Understanding, for example, how employment relationships are affected by the internationalization of capital, labor, technology, and product markets requires scholars to consider research from the fields of political economy, the economics of human resources and internal labor markets, industrial relations, and international human resource management. Similarly, explaining variations in human resource practices and employment relations within and across industries and nations requires researchers to combine micro (firm and below) and macro (regional, national, and international) levels of analysis.

Furthermore, if we are to be true to the perspective of industrial relations as well as the broader concerns of social science, we need to go beyond the boundaries and normative frame of reference of multinational firm managers and the tasks they face in structuring employment relationships for their international (expatriate and foreign) managers and professionals. A broader field of human resource studies consider the lessons and outcomes for all types of employers and employees (not just multinational firms and their managers), as well as for labor organizations and public policy-makers. This new definition of the field should allow researchers to take advantage of the learning opportunities offered by the diverse natural experiments in human resource practices and innovations that are occurring around the world.

Key Questions for International Human Resource Studies

Given these critiques, what then might serve as a broader and deeper set of questions for constructing this new field? Consistent with our earlier efforts to add a more strategic orientation to HRM and IR research (Dyer 1984; Kochan, Katz, and McKersie 1986), we rely heavily on a framework that seeks to understand the factors in a firm's external environment and/or its governance structure that influence the choice and consequences of human resource strategies for the different stakeholders involved. We then propose examining how these strategies affect critical economic and social outcomes of interest to the firm, its employees, and the larger society and economy.

Extending this perspective to the international arena, however, provides an opportunity to explore more fully the basic question of whether, or how, human resources contribute to the competitive advantage of individual firms and national economies.[1] Moreover, by embedding the choices of individual firms in their national settings we believe a deeper understanding will be achieved of the extent to which human resource strategies that have proven useful for producing competitive advantage are diffused across an economy. Finally, we believe that one of the unique contributions of an international perspective is the opportunity to learn from practices developed in different national and cultural settings and to assess their transferability to other national settings.

Specifically, we suggest that the following questions might provide a starting point for analysis in this field of study:

1. What factors influence whether human resources serve as a source of competitive advantage to individual firms and the national economies in which they are located?

2. How do different countries and firms go about efforts to gain competitive advantage from their human resources? What mix of HR strategies and policies are critical to such efforts? How and at what levels do different parties to the employment relationship (government, employers, workers and their representatives) individually and jointly influence human resource strategies and policies?

3. What are the effects on the key outcomes of interest to the different stakeholders in employment relationships? While the competitive advantage and much of the strategic HRM literatures have focused on the performance of individual firms, we believe the outcomes examined need to capture the interests of employees and other stakeholders as well. Indeed, stated most broadly, we see the critical research and policy question as being: What are the effects of alternative human resource strategies on the twin objectives of economic performance (competitiveness) and social welfare?

4. How widely are practices that achieve competitive advantage diffused within a country and what factors influence the rate and process of diffusion?

5. To what extent are practices that perform well in one setting transferable across national boundaries to perform equally well elsewhere?

We believe these questions can and should be studied at various levels of analysis ranging from the nation state (where political literatures tend to focus) to the level of the firm (where the labor economics and human resource management literatures focus). Whatever level of analysis is chosen, however, we argue that it is important to examine the interrelationship among human resource policies and practices. In this sense we adopt the approach of industrial relations (Dunlop 1958; Kochan, Katz, and McKersie 1986) and internal labor market theorists (Doeringer and Piore 1971; Osterman 1984). But consistent with other aspects of industrial relations or

internal labor markets, the economic or market forces that
institutional, firm, and individual behavior need to serve as
ing point for analyzing these questions. Thus, classical and ne
sical economic models and their modern derivatives often ser as
the starting point for answering these questions.

Human Resources and Competitive Advantage

Human Resources as a Source of Competitive Advantage

Classical and neoclassical economics provide a parsimonious model for answering the question of how human resources serve as a source of competitive advantage to an individual firm or a nation. The most elementary model assumes that firms exist to maximize shareholder value and compete only on the basis of price. As a factor of production, labor is a cost to be minimized. An abundant supply of cheap labor provides firms and nations with a natural basis for using human resources for competitive advantage. Relative labor costs determine the international division of labor: firms locate production within and across countries wherever the costs of workers with the requisite skills are lowest. Following Smith and Marx, modern development economists have viewed economic growth as depending on the extension of the market through continual increases in the division of labor; skill specialization enhances the ability of employees to increase productivity, and economies of scale lead to cost reductions. Although the incorporation of human capital theory into labor economics in the 1960s changed the conception of labor from strictly a cost to a quasi-fixed capital asset (Oi 1962; Becker 1964), the neoclassical approach to human resources largely continues to treat labor as a cost to be minimized, with the recognition that cost varies according to the skill and productivity of workers.

More recently, however, scholars across a number of fields have argued that in addition to price competition, firms compete on the basis of quality, product differentiation, technological innovation, and speed to market. Moreover, there is growing recognition among both scholars and public policy groups that for enterprises in advanced industrialized societies to achieve the twin objectives of being competitive at high standards of living for employees they must fully develop and utilize the skills, motivation, and analytical problem-solving potential of their human resources. That is, human resources need to serve as a source of strategic or competitive advantage. Over the last decade, the argument has developed along parallel lines in three sets of literature: flexible specialization (Brusco 1982; Piore and Sabel 1984; Best 1990; Pyke, Becattini, and Sengenberger 1990), strategic human resource management (Tichy, Fombrun, and Devanna 1982; Beer et al. 1985; Dyer 1988), and strategic industrial relations (Kochan, Katz, and McKersie 1986).

The argument generally runs along the following lines: the inability to compete on the basis of low factor costs leads firms in advanced industrial societies to compete on the basis of high product quality, differentiation, innovation, and advances in technology. To do so, however, requires that firms develop particular types of high productivity human resource systems—often referred to in the U.S. literature as high- or mutual-commitment systems—which include policies to attract, motivate, and gain the commitment of highly skilled and flexible workers (Walton 1985; Kochan and Dyer 1991).

Although this argument has gained some empirical support (Blinder 1990; Levine and D'Andrea Tyson 1990; MacDuffie and Krafcik 1992) and increasing acceptance in both the research and policymaking communities, as yet we have not fully explored the extent to which human resources do in fact serve as a source of competitive advantage for individual firms and/or nations. This, therefore, serves as the first building block or question for this field to address on both a clear theoretical level and with empirical evidence.

Disagreement in the literature also exists over the extent to which differentiated markets and new (more flexible) technologies are more or less determinative of human resource policies, although there is increasing agreement that new flexible technologies are more permissive than determinative. In the former view, product markets and technology drive firms to adapt their labor and human resource practices in particular ways that achieve high productivity outcomes (Kern and Schumann 1984; Piore and Sabel 1984). An alternative but equally deterministic view links new technologies to the de-skilling of workers (Shaiken, Herzenberg, and Kuhn 1986; Noble 1987).

Other models are less deterministic. There are various ways of achieving technological flexibility (Suarez, Cusamano, and Fine 1991). Because new technologies are more permissive than dedicated machinery, employer strategies play a more significant role than they did in the past. Those that take a strategic human resource management approach, for example, argue that the choice of a competitive business strategy will determine the human resource policies of the firm or its business unit (Dyer 1988; Schuler 1992). That is, firms can choose along a continuum of competing primarily on the basis of price or quality, and this choice will determine whether the firm requires high skills or low wages as its primary human resource attribute.

Other researchers in political economy and industrial relations expand the range of variation, arguing that firms may choose along a continuum of high and low volume as well as price and quality—a two-by-two matrix of alternative production strategies that imply alternative human resource strategies as well (Sorge and Streeck 1988). A growing body of empirical research does suggest that the relationship between technology and human resource policies is indeterminate (Kelley 1986; Hyman and Streeck 1988; Zuboff 1988; Keefe 1991; Thomas 1991) and depends largely on the choices made by employers and employees.

If there is debate over the relationship between technology and human resource policies, there is also debate over what determines employer choices. Most neoclassical economic and game-theoretic models focus on the role of product markets and the strategies of competitors in shaping employer strategies. The business strategy literature likewise emphasizes the importance of product markets and competitors (Porter 1980, 1985), as does the strategic human resource management perspective (Dyer 1988).

Traditional industrial relations theory (Commons 1919), by contrast, argues that organized labor would constrain employer choices and managerial discretion: as product markets expanded, institutions such as national unions and government standards would "take wages out of competition" and thereby limit the ability of wage competition to drive down labor standards. Similarly, some branches of political economy argue that regional, sectoral, and national institutions and politics influence or constrain firm-level strategic choices; thus, they place priority on the role of the state and institutions of interest intermediation as key determinants of the human resource policies open to the firm and, therefore, of the competitive strategies that are viable in a given environment (Goldthorpe 1984; Cawson 1985; Streeck and Schmitter 1985). Those countries with more corporatist arrangements are seen as able to build cooperation and communication between employers and labor at both firm and extra-firm levels of policy making, thereby facilitating the coordination of policy implementation (Scharpf 1984).

Still others give more weight to the role of capital markets and financial institutions (Zysman 1983). Some of this work develops a stakeholder conception of the firm in which the governance structure and nature of the firm itself are endogenous rather than fixed by market forces. Aoki (1988), for example, argues that Japanese firms should be conceptualized as coalitions between shareholders and employees rather than as instruments that exist solely to maximize shareholder wealth. Wever and Allen (1992) make a similar argument about Germany.

This emerging body of research therefore suggests that nations such as Japan and Germany with financial institutions and investors who share long-term time horizons with corporate decisionmakers are expected to have human resource systems or internal labor markets that likewise emphasize long-term employment relationships, high levels of investment in human capital, compensation systems that reward long tenure and internal promotions, and a more cooperative corporate culture. These firms, in turn, are expected to respond to exogenous demand shocks or make structural adjustments in ways that better accommodate employee and employer interests than has been the case with the forms of corporate restructuring experienced in the United States in the 1980s (Dore 1986; Reich 1988; Abraham and Houseman 1992; Locke 1992), where capital markets and the governance structures of firms require firms to give greater emphasis to maximizing shareholder wealth and pursuing more short-term profits. To the extent that mutual commitment human resource policies require firms to make long-term investments in human resources, nations with patient capital markets, financial institutions, and governance structures may therefore be better positioned to gain competitive advantage from their human resources.

We see this as a very promising and pivotal hypothesis. Thus, while still in the very early stages of development, comparative analysis of the relationships among the sources of capital, the structure and time horizons of financial institutions, the governance structure of the corporation, and human resource practices would appear to be an intriguing and potentially rich area of research.

In summary, while there is general agreement now about the potential strategic value of human resources for achieving competitive advantage at the firm and national levels, there is a lack of agreement concerning the relative importance of human resources and other factors such as technology, the role and determinants of employer choice, the relative importance of particular human resource policies, the relationship between firm- and state-level policies, and the role played by financial markets and institutions that shape the governance structures of firms. All this suggests, however, that researchers should be careful not to assume that an invisible hand of the market shapes the nature and goals of corporations or the strategies they choose to pursue these goals. The extent to which human resources serve as a source of competitive advantage may reflect the goals nations set and the way they define the firm and its governance structure.

How Competitive Advantage is Created Through Human Resources

A second key question for research in this field concerns understanding *how* firms and/or nations go about the task of gaining competitive advantage through human resources. Human capital theory provides the standard economic answer to this question by focusing on the supply side of the labor market. Since workers are paid their marginal product, and their productivity is a function of their general education and skills plus the specific skills required by a particular firm, it is the stock of general and specific training that influences the quality of the labor force and its relative productivity. Human capital theory further specifies the relative responsibilities of individual firms and the general society for providing training. Individual firms will provide firm-specific training that develops skills unique to its production system or organizational environment for three reasons: (1) no other entity will supply this training, (2) it does not make workers more competitive in the external labor market, and therefore, (3) it can be appropriated by the firm over time—assuming the worker remains with the firm. Consistent with theories of market failure (Arrow 1974), however, general training will be underprovided if left to individual firms since it is portable and therefore not likely to be fully appropriable by the firm. Comparative research on the United States and other countries generally supports this proposition (Kochan and Osterman 1991).

While human capital theory only generally links investments in human resources to skill, productivity, and wages, it provides little guidance for purposes of strategic human resource management. Moreover, although intended to be universally applicable, its assumptions grow out of the context of American labor markets and mass-production industries in a particular historical period. The dichotomy between general and specific skills, for example, has been much more salient in U.S. mass production industries than, for example, Japanese-style human resource systems. Similarly, the theory conceives of training as a narrow skill formation process rather than, more broadly, a learning process that evolves out of the structure of jobs and career ladders (Koike and Inoki 1990) and includes the social and psychological experience of workers in an organizational environment (Cole 1989). Finally, human capital theory has nothing to say about what, if any, human resource policies should accompany the training in order for it to be effective or how production must be organized in order to take advantage of training. In other words, it does not link the argument for investment in human resources to business strategy, a theory of the firm, or an understanding of the relationship between the firm and its external environment.

Recently a stream of economic analysis described as the "new economics of personnel" has sought to go beyond human capital theory by linking productivity to the strategic use of incentive policies (Ehrenberg 1990; Mitchell and Zaidi 1990). This work builds on the rapidly expanding literature on the economics of industrial organization (Coase 1937; Alchien and Demsetz 1972; Williamson 1975; Putterman 1986; Simon 1991; Stiglitz 1991) that takes as its basic theoretical task the explanation of why firms, and by extension, employment contracts of different durations and structures, exist at all in market economies. These models are extended to the study of human resource policy by the derived proposition that firms will internalize labor contracts to coordinate, monitor, and motivate employees (rather than simply depend on the market to structure the employment contract) whenever the collective efforts of "teams" of employees can be more productive than the efforts of individuals working separately in the external labor market. Where coordination (organizations) can be more efficient, the task then turns to the appropriate human resource policies (or the incentive structures of the contract) to achieve these efficiencies. Agency theory (Berle and Means 1933; Jensen and Meckling 1976), for example, seeks to remedy conflicts of interest between the organization and the individual by constructing market-like incentive contracts such as employee stock ownership plans (ESOPs) and contingent pay schemes.

Researchers have also extended these models to explain the relationship between efficiency wages and other personnel policies such as employment security, closeness of monitoring and supervision, and employee discipline. By attempting to examine the interrelationships among different personnel policies rather than treat each as an isolated or independent choice, this work takes an important step forward. Yet in some ways these perspectives are merely catching up with literatures on internal labor markets (Kerr 1954; Doeringer and Piore 1971; Osterman 1984, 1988) that have long argued that personnel policies must be seen as linked together in a coherent fashion to the competitive strategies and governance structures of the firm. We will now turn to an examination of the propositions that these literatures suggest for how firms gain strategic advantage from their human resource policies.

Internal labor market and industrial relations researchers contribute to the study of human resource management in at least two important ways. First, as noted earlier, they view the choice of the full range of personnel policies and practices as interrelated and mutually reinforcing. Thus, changes in one personnel policy area must be accompanied by changes in other areas if the overall human resource strategy of a firm is to achieve its maximum desired effect on organizational performance. Second, they see these choices as not uniquely determined by efficiency considerations. Rather, firm choices related to personnel and other policies are embedded in a social, political, and institutional context and are therefore influenced by the ideologies or beliefs, interests, power relations, and historical experiences of those who participate in setting these policies. This perspective, we will argue, is essential for any theory of the competitive advantage of human resource policies, but it takes on even greater importance as we seek to explain how human resource practices and their effects on performance vary in different international and cultural settings.

Osterman (1984, 1987, 1988), for example, goes considerably beyond economic perspectives of internal labor markets that emphasize efficiency (e.g., Williamson 1985) as well as sociological perspectives that focus on promotion rules and career development (Baron 1984; Arthur, Hall, and Lawrence 1989). Rather, employers create different types of employment subsystems for different labor markets, and each subsystem is characterized by an interrelated set of policies governing training, job design, promotion, employment security, and compensation policies. Kochan, Katz, and McKersie's (1986) industrial relations model additionally suggests that three tiers of organizational policies are interrelated: workplace practices (involving labor management relations, work organization, and employee participation); personnel-level policies (of compensation, training, and employment security); and corporate strategy issues involving the choice of a competitive strategy, the level of involvement of labor representatives and/or human resource professionals in strategic decisions and governance processes, and the basic values or beliefs that influence those who participate in these broad firm decisions and long-run strategies.

Empirical research supports this perspective. For example, union representation on boards of directors in U.S. corporations or under German codetermination does not in and of itself substantially affect productivity levels (Svejnar 1982). Similarly, Levine and D'Andrea Tyson compare the arrangements for, and impacts of, employee participation in producer cooperatives in Mondragon, Spain and other parts of Europe as well as large Swedish, Japanese, and U.S. firms with "high-commitment" work relations. They find that the relationship between participation and productivity is shaped by four factors: "gain sharing, long-term employment relations, measures to build group cohesiveness, and guaranteed individual rights for employees" (1990, p. 184).

MacDuffie and Krafcik (1992) reach comparable results based on the comparative evidence of 70 automotive assembly plants in 17 countries. For firms to be "world-class competitors," they must adopt a combined human resource/flexible technology production strategy. The human resource practices associated with high performance include: multi-skilling, extensive off- and on-the-job training, work teams, job rotation, worker participation in problem solving and production decisions, and mutual commitment incentive structures (employment security; compensation that is partially contingent on corporate, plant, and/or individual performance; and low status barriers between management and workers).

As noted earlier, political economists and industrial relations scholars contribute to a fuller understanding of human resource policies by noting that the discretion over the choice of an internal labor market system or human resource strategy may be only partly left to decision making at the firm level. Employers and unions may influence public policy, which in turn shapes market conditions for all firms. Research over the last decade, for example, has demonstrated the role of employers' associations in shaping state industrial and labor policy (Vogel 1978; Harris 1982; Gospel and Littler 1983; Windmuller and Gladstone 1984; Jacoby 1985, 1991; Sisson 1987; Tolliday and Zeitlin 1991). Similarly, as indicated earlier, research on corporatist interest representation identifies the importance of variation in labor union strategies beyond the firm level for shaping employment conditions on a regional, sectoral, or national level. State policies, industry associations, and/or the power of unions can all shape and constrain firm discretion and set standards that reverse the causal arrow—in this case the constraints of labor standards limit the types of competitive strategies that are viable. Thus, human resource policies drive competitive strategies and, over time, influence managerial values and attitudes.

Some international research supports this view. In a comparative study of the German and U.S. auto industries, for example, Streeck (1987) found that in contrast to the U.S. experience, the powerful IG Metall union constrained German employers' ability to compete on the basis of wage and employment cuts, thereby providing an incentive for employers to compete on product quality and to internally reorganize production to achieve higher levels of productivity. In a comparable study, Turner (1990) reaches a similar conclusion. In addition, based on interviews conducted outside of the metalworking sector, Wever (1992) reports that works councils are not only widely accepted but viewed as positive institutions by German managers. Thus, state-mandated institutions of worker representation not only influence managerial behavior but also, over time, apparently induce shifts in attitudes as well.

Some political economists and industrial relations scholars further argue that the extent to which cooperation and coordination of policy occurs between firms, unions, and the state determines the competitive advantage of firms and nations in confronting the international economy. Unions may play a positive role in economic stabilization (Flanagan, Soskice, and Ulman 1983). The argument is that coordinated and negotiated interest representation, or corporatism, allows firms and nations to respond better to exogenous shocks and market uncertainties and achieve lower unemployment levels. Governments are freer to use expansionary monetary and fiscal policy when centralized collective bargaining can be relied on to guarantee wage restraint (Scharpf 1984). Newell and Symons (1985) review the wage-employment relationship in five countries—Sweden, Germany, Britain, Japan, and the United States—in decreasing order of corporatism; they find that more corporatist economies respond better to exogenous shocks. Moreover, correlating unemployment levels with corporatist and noncorporatist episodes within each country, they show that external shocks result in far more unemployment when countries are pursuing noncorporatist policies—twice as much in Germany, three times as much in Japan, and six times as much in the United Kingdom. Others find that countries with highly centralized (Sweden and Austria) and highly decentralized (the United States, Japan, and Switzerland) bargaining arrangements have lower unemployment rates, but note that whereas centralized bargaining also produces wage compression, decentralized arrangements produce high wage dispersion and low wage levels on average (Calmfors and Driffill 1988; Freeman 1988). The internationalization of the economy in the last two decades, however, has put intense pressure on corporatist arrangements, decreasing the ability of unions to take wages out of competition, and it is unclear whether such arrangements will continue to play the role they have played in the past (Boyer 1988).

In summary, there are a number of points of agreement among these literatures on the question of how firms and/or nations develop human resources for competitive advantage. First, all of these literatures accept and build on human capital theory by noting that a well-educated and trained labor force is the key supply side characteristic needed if firms are to compete on any basis other than minimizing factor (labor) costs and prices. Second, researchers generally agree that labor force skills and quality must be matched with a series of other human resource policies that reinforce and utilize these skills in the production process. Thus, the interdependence of human resource policies and technology or production strategies and the complementary nature of technology and production strategies are recognized. Third, the interrelated nature of human resource policies is gaining acceptance among both the new economics and the traditional personnel/human resource management literatures. Training, compensation, employment staffing and security, work organization, trust, and employee relations are more widely recognized as an interdependent bundle of practices rather than as a menu of isolated functional activities from which firms can make independent choices. Fourth, there is growing recognition that these policies are closely linked to competitive strategies of the firm, although as we will note later the causal nature of these relationships remains in some dispute among the different approaches to the field. Fifth, organizational economists, industrial relations, and political economists all share an interest in the governance structure of the firm and recognize, for different reasons, that the nature of organizational governance will influence the nature of the employment contract and human resource policies.

Yet despite these areas of convergence and consensus among the different schools of thought, there remains considerable theoretical debate over issues like whether human resource policies are driven by factors beyond efficiency; how important it is to have formal voice or representation for workers in strategy making and organizational governance or whether human resource professionals can and do serve this role as agents for employee interests; how important it is take into account the social and institutional embeddedness of organizational decision making; and what the future role of national-level institutions governing the employment relation will be. These areas of debate will become more important as we explore the next issue that we see as critical to this field of inquiry—namely, how human resource strategies affect worker standards of living and other equity interests of society.

Human Resource Strategies and Employee Interests

The field of human resource studies must not only be concerned with how human resource management policies affect the economic performance of individual enterprises or national economies. It must also examine the other half of the twin objectives noted at the outset of this paper—namely, the effects of different employment policies and practices on employee interests and social welfare.

Neoclassical economics answers this distributional question quite clearly. Social welfare is maximized when employees' wages equal their marginal products regardless of competitive strategies or governance arrangements. Those policies that increase productivity and firm performance will as a natural by-product improve real incomes and the standards of living in society. Spending on personnel policies over and beyond the marginal products of a firm's labor force results in rents that produce inefficient resource allocations and economic inequality.

Industrial relations theorists have historically challenged this perspective by arguing that productivity improvements are a necessary but not sufficient condition to insure the equitable distribution of productivity gains with employees and in society. This may be most visible when countries are in the early stages of industrialization. Currently, for example, in newly industrializing countries such as Korea, governments have followed a development strategy of "growth first, share later" (Kim 1990), and thus worker incomes have lagged considerably behind the rates of productivity and economic growth experienced in that country between 1960 and 1985. Labor movements have historically arisen to respond to such a lack of equitable gainsharing. Thus, industrial relations scholars view unregulated labor market competition as a threat to worker standards because of the unequal balance of power that often characterizes employment relationships. The role of unions, labor standards legislation, and institutions such as collective bargaining, works councils, codetermination, or other forums for employee voice has been to create protected or "internal labor markets" and to "take wages out of competition"—that is, to limit management's ability to compete on the basis of low labor costs. By driving up wages and improving other labor standards, unions have pushed employers to search for offsetting productivity gains and/or other improved competitive strategies that would allow them to survive as high-wage employers. Unions have also sought to further stabilize employment conditions and reduce management resistance to improvements by standardizing conditions across the product and labor markets in which the firm competed, thereby completing the process of "taking wages out of competition."

According to this perspective, then, to the extent that unions succeed in expanding their scope of influence over regional, sectoral, and national markets, they represent a force for greater social and economic equality in the society as a whole. Unions, for example, have a net positive effect on wage compression (Freeman and Medoff 1984), a factor also associated with increased cooperation and productivity in the literature on incentive contracts reviewed earlier. Unions may improve equality in a number of ways: by extending collective bargaining to larger numbers of workers, by negotiating in key firms or sectors and pushing the government to extend wage bargains to nonunion workplaces, or by influencing social and labor legislation applicable to all employers and workers.

Political economists in the corporatist tradition further argue that trade unions that are centralized and adopt inclusive political strategies are likely to have a greater positive impact on social and economic equality (e.g., Goldthorpe 1984). Thus, researchers generally find higher levels of wage compression in more centralized or corporatist economies (Calmfors and Driffill 1988; Freeman 1988). Where labor movements are more fragmented, as in the United States, they are less likely to be able to offset the labor market segmentation arising from business cycles and differences in product markets, technology, and ownership structures (Piore 1975; Gordon, Edwards, and Reich 1975, 1982). A significant body of empirical research supports the theories of labor market segmentation as applied to the United States (Dickens and Lang 1985; Bulow and Summers 1986; Dickens and Katz 1987; Krueger and Summers 1988).

Despite higher levels of unionization and corporatism, however, labor markets in Western Europe and Japan have also been characterized by dualism (Berger and Piore 1980), with "insiders" enjoying substantial employment security and "outsiders" enduring long-term unemployment (Blanchard and Summers 1986). Japanese labor markets have been characterized as providing lifetime security for a core of workers in large corporations while a periphery of workers in temporary jobs or in smaller independent enterprises absorb demand fluctuations (Dore 1986). Aoki (1988) notes that this is one expected outcome of the governance structure of Japanese firms.

More recently, labor market analysts have suggested that the restructuring of internal labor markets in the United States and Western Europe is resegmenting the work force along such core/periphery dimensions within firms (Osterman 1988; Pfeffer and Baron 1988). The increased use of less secure, nonregular forms of labor contracts (part-time, temporary, contingent) has been observed cross-nationally (Applebaum 1989; Casey et al. 1989; Standing 1991). Moreover, in most instances cross-nationally, women, minorities, immigrants, and older workers bear a disproportionate share of the costs of cyclical and structural adjustment (Henwood and Wyatt 1987; Christopherson 1988; Standing 1991).

If the effect of unionization is to improve social and economic equality, then the relative decline in unions cross-nationally in the last decade as well as the shift to more decentralized bargaining structures (Edwards, Garonna, and Todtling 1986; Gourevitch 1989; Blanchflower and Freeman 1990; Visser 1991) increases the likelihood of greater wage inequality in advanced industrial nations. While union structure and density only partially determine wages, it is noteworthy that cross-national studies of changes in the structure of wages find increasing within-group inequality in some countries—U.S., U.K.—but not others—France, Japan (Katz and Revenga 1989; Katz and Loveman 1991). Clearly, this is an area in which further empirical research is needed.

To summarize our argument, the clearest proposition to flow from combining the competitive strategy and industrial relations perspectives is that competitive strategies that emphasize high quality, differentiation, and innovation are necessary conditions for producing human resource policies and practices that result in high standards of living for employees. The industrial relations scholars would further argue that employee voice or strong human resource management participation in these policies is necessary for maintaining high standards and translating these competitive strategies into profitable outcomes that are equitably shared between employees and shareholders. Political economists add that the level of society-wide equality depends upon union organization and the more or less inclusive strategies that unions undertake.

Moreover, there remains an empirical question separating the human resource management researchers from those in the industrial relations tradition—namely, whether the commitment of top managers and the integration of human resource executives within the top decision-making structure of firms serve as a vehicle for employee voice as effectively as other independent and legally sanctioned mechanisms such as collective bargaining, codetermination, consultation, and works councils.

Another proposition challenges the strategic human resource management literature to go beyond the boundaries of the individual firm to assess how the broader society and employee population is affected by the combination of firm-specific and state-directed (required and encouraged) human resource policies.

Leaving all policies to the firm is expected to produce inequality in labor market outcomes and economic welfare since those on the "inside" of corporate standards will receive significant welfare advantages compared to those who remain in peripheral jobs and labor market statuses. This again argues for supplementing micro or firm-specific models of human resource policy with a broader model that considers the effects of different institutional and social policy arrangements on the labor force in its entirety. The key question here becomes how wide the coverage of human resource policies and practices is that achieves both high levels of competitiveness and high standards of living. We now turn to a more direct examination of this question.

Diffusion of Human Resource Strategies

The diffusion of human resource strategies that enables firms and societies to gain strategic advantage is not only, as suggested earlier, important from a distributional or social welfare perspective. It has economic implications as well. To the extent that the strategic choices of firms are interdependent, absent some broader collective coordination or requirement to comply, a market failure will occur that produces an underinvestment in these policies (Arrow 1974). Neoclassical theory would respond that if practices improve productivity and economic efficiency for an individual firm, the practice will spread naturally via market forces. But in the case of investments in highly portable training and human resources, the market is unlikely to be sufficient because no individual firm can capture the full return on its investment (Kochan and Osterman 1991). Case studies suggest that those firms that have tried on their own to invest more heavily in long-term human resource strategies have been unable to sustain them (Kochan, MacDuffie, and Osterman 1988).

Others recognize that there are systemic social and political barriers to diffusion of new human resource strategies both within corporations and across society. Industrial relations and internal labor market researchers who conceptualize strategic decision making and organizational governance as a political process involving contests among competing interests for scarce resources recognize that deep seated values, ideologies, and considerations of power and control all influence the extent to which firms are willing to commit to a human resource strategy that increases costs with the promise of future competitive advantage.

The role of institutions outside or beyond the level of the firm becomes central to debates over the diffusion of human resource strategies and practices. Industrial relations and political economists would generally agree with the proposition introduced earlier that the more centralized the structure of bargaining, the more economic policy making is conducted through corporatist structures, and the broader the scope of union coverage, the more widely diffused human resource strategies and practices that are capable of achieving the twin goals of competitiveness and high standards of living will be. The common characteristic of these institutional arrangements is that they take some of the range of choice or discretion over both competitive strategies and labor standards away from individual firms.

The specific strategies, policies, or institutional arrangements used to diffuse human resource practices, and their relative effectiveness, vary across countries and continue to be the subject of considerable debate. Recent research has, for example, documented the decline of the formal, highly centralized, European-style, corporatist structures that were popular in the 1950s through the 1970s (Boyer 1988; Swenson 1989; Martin 1991). State-directed corporatism without strong inputs from labor as found in Japan (Sharai 1983) and Korea (Im 1990) has also been criticized for emphasizing competitiveness over living standards (i.e., the growth first, share later strategy). Australia has recently been described as a nation that is moving from a highly centralized and rigid system of national industrial relations to one that is following a labor-initiated and labor-led strategy of economic restructuring designed to promote greater efficiency and competitiveness through reforms in work organization, skill enhancement, and compensation at the individual firm level. In Canada, various tripartite labor market and training institutions have been put in place and a number of key labor unions are now urging firms and policymakers to adopt a high-skills strategy in an effort to avoid what they fear would otherwise be an Americanization of industrial relations and human resource standards as a result of the recent Canada-U.S. Free Trade Agreement. Whether the Canadian labor movement can translate its emerging views on this issue into firm-level strategies capable of sustaining high labor standards and competitive industries and firms in its increasingly open economy is both an open question and a golden opportunity for future research. Finally, countries such as the United States and Britain provide an opportunity to observe the rate of diffusion in more unregulated environments—environments in which unions have lost political power in the 1980s; where few, if any, significant macro or cross-firm institutional structures for promoting diffusion exist; and where economic policymakers have yet to accept the argument that state policy has an important role to play in diffusing standards and practices if a nation is to gain competitive advantage from its human resources. Thus, this is perhaps an area where theory is still rather weak but where opportunities for cross-national comparative research are readily available.

Even if some corporations succeed in achieving high-quality, high-commitment human resource systems, two other questions remain open for debate over diffusion. First, if diffusion depends on the extent of demand for high-quality differentiated goods, can all firms compete in these markets, or will unregulated international competition drive down prices and erode the ability of firms and nations to support costly human resource systems on a wide scale? In the United States, for example, even the most successful firms with high commitment systems have had to cut back on human resource costs and employment security pledges. Second, do high-commitment production systems depend upon the simultaneous existence of secondary firms that absorb demand fluctuations or produce low-cost inputs? If so, then the location of these enterprises will depend heavily on national policies governing the flow of capital, labor, and products across national boundaries. All these are questions that need further investigation in the broader domain of international human resource studies we are advocating here.

Transferring Human Resource Practices Across National Borders

Since the 1960s and the landmark international industrial relations project by Kerr et al. (1960), scholars have debated the question of whether human resource management and industrial relations systems were converging toward a single, common model driven largely by the pressures of industrialization. The convergence hypothesis has fallen out of favor in recent years with studies that have demonstrated the diversity of practices among and within national systems (Dore 1973; Maurice, Sellier, and Silvestre 1986). Yet in the 1980s considerable interest has been rekindled in the more narrow question of the extent to which practices that work effectively in one country and culture can be exported to others. This issue is central, for example, to most of the international human resource management research dealing with questions of degree of centralized versus decentralized policies; local control and discretion; and the type of training, management development, and local staffing firms need to use in managing international subsidiaries and global operations.

Neoclassical theory would answer this question quite simply: if a practice has demonstrated ability to improve productivity it will spread as fast as the information about it crosses national boundaries. Others disagree, especially those who view employment relationships as embedded deep within the culture and social structure of a society. At the extreme, organizational culture theorists (Schein 1985) would argue that no two organizations, let alone societies, will replicate the effects of a given practice in equivalent fashion: the cultures are too impenetrable. Yet clearly, the transfer of knowledge and technology does occur across national boundaries.

A position that builds on the recognition of ongoing international borrowing draws on institutional industrial relations and internal labor market traditions: single practices cannot be transplanted with equivalent effects unless the broader institutional and/or organizational practices in which they are embedded are likewise carried over and adapted to the new setting.

Based on her historical examination of Japanese organizations, Westney (1987) adds a further proposition: practices can be imported from other cultures but do not result in straight imitation. Instead, the process of introducing new practices itself results in institutional innovations that over time create a new practice out of the one being borrowed from abroad. Thus the process of borrowing from other countries is not one that produces convergence through imitation but one that produces innovation from institutional adaptation. As in the case of the issues involving diffusion, this is an area where theory and careful empirical analysis have yet to catch up to speculation, prescriptive writing, and practical experimentation by firms faced with the pragmatic challenges of managing global operations. We expect this set of issues to play a prominent role in future research in this field.

Implications for Policy and Research

Implications for Policy and Practice

A central argument of this chapter is that by expanding and deepening the range of questions and theoretical literatures brought to bear on international human resource studies, new and richer insights could be offered toward a broader range of options for practitioners and policymakers than has been generated by prior approaches to this subject. For employers (especially human resource management professionals), the central insight that we see flowing from this broader, more integrated perspective is that their ability to promote and sustain a high standard of human resource policies and practices depends not only on their own power and status within their individual firm but also on the power and status of other human resource and labor professionals and institutions (such as unions and government regulations) in their society. In another paper (Kochan and Dyer 1991), we argue that this recognition challenges human resource professionals to modify the strategy for change they have emphasized in the 1980s from one dominated by the need to form partnerships with line managers and senior corporate executives to a broader coalitional model that includes the external groups, interests, and institutional agents.

For labor representatives, we see this broadened focus opening up their strategic options for influencing human resource choices. This is an especially important challenge for union leaders, given the internationalization of capital, technology, and product markets. If labor has any hope for reversing its declining power and membership in advanced industrialized economies, it must find ways to go beyond traditional national-based strategies for taking wages out of competition. It will need to find ways to participate at many levels of the economy, from participation in formulating competitive strategies at the firm level to regional and national coalition building with other social movements.

For government policymakers the message is equally clear. No longer can labor and human resource policies be effectively separated from macroeconomic policies regulating interest rates, financial markets, trade, and public and private investment. All of these are tightly interrelated and affect the extent to which human resources can be developed and fully utilized to achieve the twin objectives of competitiveness and high living standards.

Finally, for international agencies such as the ILO, this perspective provides a new way of thinking about how to approach its technical assistance to individual countries and its assessment of the extent to which country practices are in compliance with ILO principles and conventions in a world where national boundaries have lost some of their significance. Specifically, this perspective suggests that the ILO would benefit from a closer examination of firm-specific human resource policies, but in so doing needs to keep in mind the interrelationships between individual firms and broader state and labor institutions and policies.

Implications for Future Research

Clearly, the dominant implication for research that flows from this chapter is that it is time to rekindle interest in comparative human resource research, and to do so in a fashion that overcomes the narrow prescriptive approaches that dominate much of the existing HRM and IR research that seldom goes beyond the stage of describing broad features of national systems or institutional patterns. By building on the insights of economics, political economy, internal labor markets, industrial relations, and strategic human resource management, we believe a new, more theoretically rich, and empirically informative body of research can be developed and sustained in the years ahead.

Endnotes

[1] We use the term competitive advantage here to refer to both competitive and comparative advantage as previously defined in the business strategy (Porter 1980, 1985, 1990) and the international economics literatures (Krugman 1986; Spence and Hazard 1988). In this way we can continue to move across levels of analysis from the firm to the nation state.

References

Abraham, Katherine, and Susan Houseman. "Job Security Regulation and the Accommodation of Economic Flux." Unpublished manuscript, University of Maryland, Department of Economics, 1992.

Adler, Nancy, ed. "Special Issue: Cross-Cultural Management: Conceptual Analyses." *International Studies of Management and Organization* 12, 4 (1982-3).

________, ed. "Special Issue: Cross-Cultural Management: Empirical Studies." *International Studies of Management and Organization* 13, 1-2 (1983).

________. *International Dimensions of Organizational Behavior*. Boston: Kent, 1986.

Adler, Nancy, and Fariborz Ghadar. "Strategic Human Resource Management: A Global Perspective." In *Human Resource Management: An International Comparison*, ed. Rudiger Pieper. Berlin: Walter De Gruyter, 1990.

Alchien, Armen, and Harold Demsetz. "Production, Information Costs, and Economic Organization." *American Economic Review* 62 (1972), pp. 777-95.

Aoki, Masahiko. "Toward an Economic Model of the Japanese Firm." *Journal of Economic Literature* 28 (1990), pp. 1-27.

Appelbaum, Eileen. "The Growth of the U.S. Contingent Labor Force." In *Microeconomic Issues in Labor Economics*, eds. Robert Drago and Richard Perlman. New York: Harvester Wheatsheaf, 1989.

Arrow, Kenneth. *Limits of Organization*. New York: Norton, 1974.

Arthur, Michael, Douglas Hall, and Barbara Lawrence, eds. *Handbook of Career Theory*. Cambridge, England: Cambridge University Press, 1989.

Baron, James. "Organizational Perspectives on Stratification." *Annual Review of Sociology* 10 (1984), pp. 37-69.
Becker, Gary. *Human Capital: A Theoretical and Empirical Analysis with Special Reference to Education*. New York: NBER, 1964.
Beer, M., B. Spector, P. Lawrence, D. Mills, and R. Walton. *Managing Human Assets*. New York: Free Press, 1985.
Berle, Adolfe, and Gardiner Means. *The Modern Corporation and Private Property*. New York: MacMillan, 1933.
Best, Michael. *The New Competition: Institutions of Industrial Restructuring*. Cambridge, MA: Harvard University Press, 1990.
Black, Stewart, and Mark Mendenhall. "Cross-Cultural Training Effectiveness: A Review and a Theoretical Framework for Future Research." *Academy of Management Review* 15, 1 (1990), pp. 113-36.
Blanchard, Olivier, and Lawrence Summers. "Hysteresis and the European Unemployment Problem." NBER Working Paper No. 1950. Cambridge, MA: National Bureau of Economic Research, 1986.
Blanchflower, David, and Richard Freeman. "Going Different Ways: Unionism in the U.S. and Other Advanced O.E.C.D. Countries." NBER Working Paper 3342. Cambridge, MA: National Bureau of Economic Research, April 1990.
Blinder, Alan, ed. *Paying for Productivity*. Washington, D.C.: The Brookings Institution, 1990.
Boyer, Robert, ed. *The Search for Labor Market Flexibility: The European Economies in Transition*. Oxford: Clarendon Press, 1988.
Boyacigiller, Nakiye, and Nancy Adler. "The Parochial Dinosaur: Organizational Science in a Global Context." *Academy of Management Review* 16, 2 (1991), pp. 262-90.
Brusco, S. "Small Firms and Industrial Districts: the Experience of Italy." In *New Firms and Regional Development*, eds. D. Keeble and F. Weever. London: Croom Helm, 1982.
Bulow, Jeremy, and Lawrence Summers. "A Theory of Dual Labor Markets with Application to Industrial Policy, Discrimination, and Keynesian Unemployment." *Journal of Labor Economics* 4, 3 (1986), pp. 376-414.
Calmfors, Lars, and John Driffill. "Bargaining Structure, Corporatism, and Macroeconomic Performance." *Economic Review* 6 (Spring 1988), pp. 13-62.
Casey, Bernard, Rudiger Dragendorf, Walter Heering, and Gunnar John. "Temporary Employment in Great Britain and the Federal Republic of Germany: An Overview." *International Labor Review* 128, 4 (1989), pp. 449-64.
Cawson, Alan, ed. *Organizational Interests and the State: Studies in Meso-Corporatism*. London: SAGE, 1985.
Christopherson, Susan. "Labor Flexibility: Implications for Women Workers." Paper Presented at the Annual Conference of the Institute of British Geographers, Loughborough, England, January 1988.
Coase, Ronald. "The Nature of the Firm." *Economica* 4 (1937), pp. 386-405.
Cole, Robert. *Strategies for Learning: Small-Group Activities in American, Japanese, and Swedish Industry*. Berkeley: University of California Press, 1989.
Commons, John. "American Shoemakers, 1648-1895: A Sketch of Industrial Evolution." *The Quarterly Journal of Economics* 24 (November 1920), pp. 39-81.
Dickens, William, and Lawrence Katz. "Interindustry Wage Differences and Industry Characteristics." NBER Working Paper No. 2014. Cambridge, MA: National Bureau of Economic Research, September 1986.
Dickens, William, and Kevin Lang. "A Test of the Dual Labor Market Theory." *American Economic Review* 75, 4 (1985), pp. 792-805.
Doeringer, Peter, and Michael Piore. *Internal Labor Markets and Manpower Analysis*. Lexington, MA: D.C. Heath, 1971.
Dore, Ronald. *British Factory - Japanese Factory: The Origins of National Diversity in Industrial Relations*. Berkeley: University of California Press, 1973.
________. *Flexible Rigidities: Industrial Policy and Stuctural Adjustment in the Japanese Economy, 1970-80*. Stanford, CA: Stanford University Press, 1986.
Dowling, Peter, and Randall Schuler. *International Dimensions of Human Resource Management*. Boston, MA: PWS-Kent, 1990.

Doz, Yves, and C. K. Prahalad. "Controlled Variety: A Challenge for Human Resource Management in the MNC." *Human Resource Management* 25, 1 (1986), pp. 55-72.
Dunlop, John. *Industrial Relations Systems.* New York: Holt, Reinhardt, and Winston, 1958.
Dyer, Lee. "Strategic Human Resource Management Research." *Industrial Relations* 23, 2 (1984), pp. 156-69.
________, ed. *Human Resource Management: Evolving Roles and Responsibilities.* Washington, D.C.: BNA Books, 1988.
Edwards, Richard, Paolo Garonna, and Franz Todtling, eds. *Unions in Crisis and Beyond.* Dover, MA: Auburn House, 1986.
Ehrenberg, Ronald, ed. "Special Issue: Do Compensation Policies Matter?" *Industrial and Labor Relations Review* 43, 3 (1990).
Evans, Paul, Yves Doz, and A. Laurent. *Human Resource Management in International Firms.* London: Macmillan, 1989.
Flanagan, Robert, David Soskice, and Lloyd Ulman. *Unionism, Economic Stabilization, and Incomes Policies: European Experience.* Washington, D.C.: The Brookings Institution, 1983.
Freeman, Richard. "Labor Market Institutions and Economic Performance." *Economic Policy* 6 (Spring 1988), pp. 63-80.
Freeman, Richard, and James Medoff. *What Do Unions Do?* New York: Basic Books, 1984.
Goldthorpe, John, ed. *Order and Conflict in Contemporary Capitalism.* London: Oxford University Press, 1984.
Galbraith, Jay, and Robert Kazanjian. "Organizing to Implement Strategies of Diversity and Globalization: The Role of Matrix Designs." *Human Resource Management* 25, 1 (1986), pp. 37-54.
Gordon, David, Richard Edwards, and Michael Reich. *Labor Market Segmentation.* Lexington, MA: Heath, 1975.
________. *Segmented Work, Divided Workers.* Cambridge, MA: Cambridge University Press, 1982.
Gospel, Howard, and Craig Littler, eds. *Managerial Strategies and Industrial Relations: An Historical and Comparative Study.* London: Heinemann Educational Books, 1983.
Gourevitch, Peter, et al. *Unions and Economic Crisis: Britain, West Germany, and Sweden.* London: Allen and Unwin, 1989.
Harris, Howell John. *The Right to Manage: Industrial Policies of American Business in the 1940s.* Madison, WI: University of Wisconsin Press, 1982.
Henwood, Felicity, and Sally Wyatt. "Managing Technological Change: Responses of Government, Employers, and Trade Unions in Western Europe and Canada." In *Computer Chips and Paper Clips*, Vol. 2, ed. Heidi Hartmann. Washington, D.C.: National Research Council, 1987.
Hofstede, Geert. *Culture's Consequences: International Difference in Work Related Values.* Beverly Hills: Sage, 1980.
Hofstede, Geert, Bram Neuijen, Denise Daval Ohayv, and Geert Sanders. "Measuring Organizational Cultures: A Qualitative and Quantitative Study across Twenty Cases." *Administrative Science Quarterly* 35 (1990), pp. 286-316.
Hyman, Richard, and Wolfgang Streeck. *New Technology and Industrial Relations* London: Blackwell, 1988.
Im, Hyug Bueg. "State, Labor, and Capital in the Consolidation of Democracy." Unpublished manuscript, Seoul National University, Seoul, Korea, 1990.
Jacoby, Sanford. *Employing Bureaucracy: Managers, Unions, and the Transformation of Work in American Industry, 1900-1945.* New York: Columbia University Press, 1985.
________, ed. *From Masters to Managers: Historical and Comparative Perspectives on American Employers.* New York: Columbia University Press, 1991.
Jensen, Michael, and William Meckling. "Theory of the Firm: Managerial Behavior, Agency Costs, and Ownership Structure." *Journal of Financial Economics* 3 (October 1976), pp. 305-60.

Katz, Lawrence, and Gary Loveman. "An International Comparison of Changes in the Structure of Wages: France, the United Kingdom, and the United States." Mimeo, Harvard University, January 1991.

Katz, Lawrence, and Ana Revenga. "Changes in the Structure of Wages: The U.S. versus Japan." NBER Working Paper No. 3021. Cambridge, MA: National Bureau of Economic Research, July 1989.

Keefe, Jeffrey. "Numerically Controlled Machine Tools and Worker Skills." *Industrial and Labor Relations Review* 44, 3 (1991), pp. 503-19.

Kelley, Maryellen. "Programmable Automation and the Skill Question: A Reinterpretation of the Cross-National Evidence." *Human Systems Management* (Fall 1986), pp. 223-42.

Kern, Horst, and Michael Schumann. *Das Ende de Arbeitsteilung*? Munchen: Verlag C.H. Beck, 4 Auflage, 1984.

Kerr, Clark. "The Balkanization of Labor Markets." In *Labor Mobility and Economic Opportunity*, ed. E. Wight Bakke. Cambridge, MA: MIT Press, 1954.

Kerr, Clark, John Dunlop, Frederick Harbison, and Charles Myers. *Industrialism and Industrial Man*. Cambridge: Harvard University Press, 1960.

Kim Sookon. "Labor Management Relations: Past, Present, and Future." Mimeo, East-West Center, Honolulu, Hawaii, 1990.

Kochan, Thomas, and Lee Dyer. "Managing Transformational Change: The Role of Human Resource Professionals." Working Paper, MIT, 1991.

Kochan, Thomas, Harry Katz, and Robert McKersie. *The Transformation of American Industrial Relations*. New York: Basic Books, 1986.

Kochan, Thomas, John Paul MacDuffie, and Paul Osterman. "Employment Security at DEC: Sustaining Values Amid Environmental Change." MIT Sloan School of Management Working Papers Series, Report No. 2054, June 1988.

Kochan, Thomas, and Paul Osterman. "Human Resource Development and Utilization: Is There Too Little in the U.S.?" Unpublished manuscript, MIT, February 1991.

Koike, Kazuo, and Takehori Inoki. *Skill Formation in Japan and Southeast Asia*. Tokoyo: University of Tokyo, 1990.

Krueger, Alan, and Lawrence Summers. "Efficiency Wages and the Inter-Industry Wage Structure." *Econometrica* 56, 2 (1988), pp. 259-93.

Krugman, Paul, ed. *Strategic Trade Policy and the New International Economics*. Cambridge, MA: MIT Press, 1986.

Laurent, A. "The Cross-Cultural Puzzle of International Human Resource Management." *Human Resource Management* 25, 1 (1986), pp. 91-102.

Levine, David, and Laura D'Andrea Tyson. "Participation, Productivity, and the Firm's Environment." In *Paying for Productivity*, ed. Alan Blinder. Washington, D.C.: The Brookings Institution, 1990.

Locke, Richard. "The Political Embeddedness of Industrial Change: Corporate Restructuring and Local Politics in Contemporary Italy." In *Transforming Organizations*, eds. Thomas A. Kochan and Michael Useem. New York: Oxford University Press, 1992.

MacDuffie, John Paul, and John Krafcik. "Integrating Technology and Human Resources for High Performance Manufacturing: Evidence from the International Auto Industry." In *Transforming Organizations*, eds. Thomas A. Kochan and Michael Useem. New York: Oxford University Press, 1992.

Martin, Andrew. "Wage Bargaining and Swedish Politics: The Political Implications of the End of Central Negotiations." Manuscript prepared for the Study of Power and Democracy in Sweden, 1991.

Maurice, Marc, Francois Sellier, and Jean-Jacques Silvestre. *The Social Foundations of Industrial Power: A Comparison of France and Germany*, ed. Arthur Goldhammer. Cambridge, MA: MIT Press, 1986.

Mendenhall, Mark, and Gary Oddou. "The Dimensions of Expatriate Acculturation: A Review." *Academy of Management Review* 10 (1985), pp. 39-47.

Mendenhall, Mark, Edward Dunbar, and Gary Oddou. "Expatriate Selection, Training, and Career-Pathing: A Review and Critique." *Human Resource Management* 26, 3 (1987), pp. 331-46.

Mitchell, Daniel, and Mahmood Zaidi. "Introduction to A Symposium: The Economics of Human Resource Management." *Industrial Relations* 29, 2 (1990), pp. 155-63.
Napier, Nancy, ed. "Special Issue—International Human Resource Management." *Human Resource Planning* 14, 1 (1991).
Newell, A., and J. Symons. "Wages and Employment in the OECD Countries." London School of Economics Centre for Labour Economics Discussion Paper 219, May 1985.
Noble, David. *America By design: Science, Technology, and the Rise of Corporate Capitalism*. Oxford: Oxford University Press, 1977.
Oi, Walter. "Labor as a Quasi-Fixed Factor." *Journal of Political Economy* 70 (December 1962), pp. 538-55.
Osterman, Paul. "White Collar Internal Labor Markets." In *Internal Labor Markets*, ed. Paul Osterman. Cambridge, MA: MIT Press, 1984.
________. "Choice of Employment Systems in Internal Labor Markets." *Industrial Relations* 26, 1 (1987), pp. 46-67.
________. *Employment Futures: Reorganization, Dislocation, and Public Policy*. New York and Oxford: Oxford University Press, 1988.
Pfeffer, Jeffrey, and James Baron. "Taking the Workers Back Out: Recent Trends in the Structuring of Employment." In *Research in Organizational Behavior*, eds. Barry Staw and L.L. Cummings. Greenwich, CT: JAI Press, 1988.
Piore, Michael. "Notes for a Theory of Labor Market Stratification." In *Labor Market Segmentation*, eds. Richard Edwards, Michael Reich, and David Gordon. Lexington, MA: D.C. Heath, 1975.
Piore, Michael, and Charles Sabel. *The Second Industrial Divide*. New York: Basic Books, 1984.
Porter, Michael. *Competitive Strategy: Techniques for Analyzing Industries and Competitors*. New York: Free Press, 1980.
________. *Competitive Advantage: Creating and Sustaining Superior Performance*. New York: Free Press, 1985.
________. *The Competitive Advantage of Nations*. New York: Free Press, 1990.
Putterman, Louis, ed. *The Economic Nature of the Firm: A Reader*. Cambridge, MA: Cambridge University Press, 1986.
Pyke, Frank, Giacomo Becattini, and Werner Sengenberger. *Industrial Districts and Interfirm Cooperation in Italy*. Geneva, Switzerland: International Institute for Labour Studies, International Labour Organisation, 1990.
Reich, Robert. "Bailout: A Comparative Study in Law and Industrial Structure." In *International Competitiveness*, eds. Michael Spence and Heather Hazard. Lexington, MA: Ballinger Press, 1988.
Ronen, S. *Comparative and Multinational Management*. New York: John Wiley, 1986.
Scharpf, Fritz. "Economic and Institutional Constraints of Full-Employment Strategies: Sweden, Austria, and Western Germany, 1973-1982." In *Order and Conflict in Contemporary Capitalism*, ed. John Goldthorpe. London: Clarendon/Oxford Press, 1984.
Schein, Edgar. *Organizational Culture and Leadership*. San Francisco, CA: Jossey-Bass, 1985.
Schuler, Randall. *World Class HR Departments: Six Critical Issues*. Report Prepared for IBM, New York University, 1992.
Shaiken, S., S. Herzenberg, and S. Kuhn. "The Work Process Under More Flexible Production." *Industrial Relations* 25, 2 (1986), pp. 167-83.
Shirai, Taishiro. "A Supplement: Characteristics of Japanese Management and Personnel Policies." In *Contemporary Industrial Relations in Japan*, ed. Taishiro Shirai. Madison, WI: University of Wisconsin Press, 1983.
Simon, Herbert. "Organizations and Markets." *Journal of Economic Perspectives* 5, 2 (1991), pp. 25-44.
Sisson, Keith. *The Management of Collective Bargaining: An International Comparison*. Oxford: Basil Blackwell, 1987.
Sorge, Arndt, and Wolfgang Streeck. "Industrial Relations and Technical Change: The Case for an Extended Perspective." In *New Technology and Industrial Relations*, eds. Richard Hyman and Wolfgang Streeck. London: Blackwell, 1988.

Spence, Michael, and Heather Hazard, eds. *International Competitiveness*. Cambridge, MA: Ballinger, 1988.
Standing, Guy. "Labour Insecurity Through Market Regulation: Legacy of the 1980s, Challenge for the 1990s." Paper prepared as part of a research project of the Joint Center for Political and Economic Studies, 1991.
Stiglitz, Joseph. "Symposium on Organizations and Economics." *Journal of Economic Perspectives* 5, 2 (1991), pp. 15-24.
Streeck, Wolfgang, "Industrial Relations and Industrial Change: The Restructuring of the World Automobile Industry in the 1970s and 1980s." *Economic and Industrial Democracy* 8 (1987), pp. 437-62.
Streeck, Wolfgang, and Philippe Schmitter, eds. *Private Interest Government: Beyond Market and State*. London: SAGE, 1985.
Suarez, Fernando, Michael Cusamano, and Charles Fine. "Flexibility and Performance: A Literature Critique and Strategic Framework." Working Paper No. 3298-921-BPS, MIT Sloan School of Management, 1991.
Swenson, Peter. *Fair Shares: Unions, Pay, and Politics in Sweden and West Germany*. Ithaca, NY: Cornell University Press, 1989.
Svejnar, Jan. "Codetermination and Productivity: Empirical Evidence from the Federal Republic of Germany." In *Participatory and Self-Managed Firms: Evaluating Economic Performance*, eds. Derek Jones and Jan Svejnar. Lexington, MA: Lexington Books, 1982.
Thomas, Robert. *What Machines Can't Do: Politics and Technology in the Industrial Enterprise*. Berkeley: University of California Press, 1991.
Tichy, N., C. Fombrun, and M. Devanna. "Strategic Human Resource Management." *Sloan Management Review* 2 (1982), pp. 47-61.
Tolliday, Steven, and Jonathon Zeitlin. The Power to Manage? Employers and Industrial Relations in Comparative Historical Perspective. London: Routledge, 1991.
Tung, Rosalie. *The New Expatriates*. Cambridge, MA: Ballinger, 1988.
Turner, Lowell. *Democracy at Work? Labor and the Politics of New Work Organization*. Ithaca, NY: Cornell University Press, 1990.
Visser, Jelle. "Recent Trends in Unionisation in OECD Countries." A report prepared for the Organisation of Economic Cooperation and Development, Social Affairs and Industrial Relations Division, 1991.
Vogel, David. "Why Businessmen Distrust Their State: The Polirical Consciousness of American Corporate Executives." *British Journal of Political Science* 8 (January 1978), p. 63.
Von Glinow, Mary Anne. "Bibliography on International Human Resource Management." Unpublished manuscript, University of Southern California, 1991.
Walton, Richard. "From Control to Commitment in the Workplace." *Harvard Business Review* (March-April 1985), pp. 77-84.
Westney, Eleanor. *Imitation and Innovation: Transfer of Western Organizational Patterns to Meiji, Japan*. Cambridge, MA: Harvard University Press, 1987.
Wever, Kirsten. "German Managerial Ideology." Unpublished manuscript, Northeastern University School of Management, 1992.
Wever, Kirsten, and Christopher Allen. "German and American Financial Institutions and Industrial Relations." Unpublished manuscript, Northeastern University School of Management, 1992.
Williamson, Oliver. *Markets, Hierarchies: Analysis and Anti-trust Implications—A Study in the Economics of Internal Organization*. New York: Free Press, 1975.
________. *The Economic Institutions of Capitalism*. New York: Free Press, 1985.
Windmuller, John, and Alan Gladstone. *Employers Associations and Industrial Relations: A Comparative Study*. Oxford: Oxford University Press, 1984.
Zeira, Y., and M. Banai. "Present and Desired Methods of Selecting Expatriate Managers for International Assignments." *Personnel Review* 13, 3 (1984), pp. 29-35.
Zuboff, Shoshana. *In the Age of the Smart Machine*. Cambridge, MA: Harvard University Press, 1988.
Zysman, John. *Governments, Markets, and Growth*. Ithaca, NY: Cornell University Press, 1983.

Part III

Labor Markets

CHAPTER 10

Compensation, Productivity and the New Economics of Personnel

EDWARD P. LAZEAR
University of Chicago and Hoover Institution

Much has occurred during the last decade to alter the nature of personnel science. While still largely in the domain of the industrial psychologist, personnel issues are of growing interest to economists. As a result, the analyses have become more technical and have had a somewhat different focus. A large part of the new work has focused specifically on pay and its various forms. But other parts of the literature examine non-pay issues, such as up-or-out promotion schemes and the hierarchical structure of the organization.

Virtually all of the new economics of personnel place heavy emphasis on two features: the provision of incentives and the allocation of risk bearing. In this essay, I discuss how these factors have reshaped thinking in the personnel area.

New Analyses of Compensation Practices

Because so much of the focus is on compensation, it is natural to start here. Concurrent with the economic interest is increasing interest by practitioners and consultants in innovative pay structures. Variable pay has become the new buzzword of the compensation consulting industry. There is good reason. Compensation that is linked to productivity has been championed by individuals at all ends of the political spectrum. Liberals feel that workers should be entitled to share in the profits of the enterprise. Implicit is the belief that labor is in large part responsible for the wealth that the firm creates. Conservatives like the idea because they believe inherently that pay should be based on performance rather than on broader social goals. Thus, workers who perform well should be rewarded and those who do not perform should be punished.

Proponents of variable pay generally have output measures in mind, but the quantification of performance is left somewhat vague. There is no necessity from an efficiency point of view that compensation even be based on output. If a perfect measure of effort were available, paying on the basis of the effort measure could provide appropriate incentives. Even better, if workers are more sensitive to risk than capital owners, paying on the basis of effort provides incentives without forcing workers to bear the risk inherent in output variations.

Of course, effort or input measures are not very easy to obtain in most activities, which has led most practitioners to focus on output measures. In what follows, various theories of variable pay are presented and some evidence is discussed.

Piece Rates

The most fundamental of all pay for performance contracts is the piece rate. The simplest form of piece rate contract is

$$\text{Pay} = s + r\,Q, \tag{1}$$

where Q is some measure of output.[1] The worker receives (or pays) a base amount s plus a commission of r for each unit or dollar of output.

The classic piece rate is generally applied to workers who produce some easily measured physical good. For example, farm workers are often paid a piece rate, with earnings being proportionately related to the number of vegetables they pick. Garment workers were sometimes paid piece rates because the amount produced could be measured with little cost.

The measure of output need not and in general should not be in physical units. Such is especially the case when the piece rate is applied to salespeople. Commission sales people are paid a piece rate, where r is the commission rate and s the fixed component of salary that does not depend on output. Since the firm cares about profit, not physical units produced, Q is generally expressed in terms of some profit measure. Often, profit is not easily identified and so it must be measured by some proxy, like sales.

The choice of s and r reflects market conditions, effort elasticity, measurement cost, and risk preferences. At one extreme, suppose that workers are risk neutral and that Q is a perfect measure of the difference between revenue and all cost other than the labor by the individual in question. Then $r = 1$. By setting $r = 1$ two goals are achieved: The worker puts forth efficient effort and the right workers are attracted to the firm. Let us consider each in turn.

The salesperson wants to maximize income for the minimum amount of pain. But there is a positive relation of sales made to effort. Thus, defining E as effort,

$$Q = E + u, \tag{2}$$

where u is luck, reflecting market conditions or other factors over which the salesperson has no control. E reflects some total effort equaling the amount of effort per hour times the number of hours worked. In (2), E is normalized and effort is defined such that one unit of effort produces one unit of output. If effort per hour were invariant, then E would simply be a measure of hours worked.

Effort is painful and the pain associated with the effort can be measured as

$$\text{Pain} = C(E) \tag{3}$$

where C has the usual properties.[2] The worker's problem is to maximize his income, net of pain or

$$\max_{E} \ (\text{Pay}) - C(E). \tag{4}$$

If pay is given by (1), then using (2), (4) becomes

$$\max_{E} \ s + r[E + u] - C(E),$$

or, since the worker is risk neutral,

$$\max_{E} \ s + rE - C(E). \tag{5}$$

The first-order condition for a maximum involves equating the marginal cost of effort with the marginal effect of effort on compensation:

$$r - C'(E) = 0 \tag{6}$$

Eq. (6) is a labor supply function. If solved out for E, it relates the amount of effort (or hours if effort-per-hour were fixed) that an individual is willing to supply. The supply depends on r, the price that the firm pays to the worker per unit of effort.

The firm's problem is to maximize profit on the worker. Profit is measured as

$$Q - \text{Pay}$$

or as

$$Q - s - rQ.$$

Substitution of (2) into the profit definition means that the firm's problem is to choose s and r to maximize

$$\max_{E} E - s - rE \tag{7}$$

The first-order condition to (7) is

$$(1 - \text{r})\frac{\partial E}{\partial r} = 0 \tag{8}$$

since E is a function of r through the labor supply condition, (6). The solution to (8) is to set $r = 1$, i.e., to pay a 100 percent commission rate on profit.

The logic is that each unit of effort produces a certain amount of output which the firm can sell. The firm wants to induce the worker to put forth a dollar's worth of effort when the fruits of the effort produce at least one dollar. Anything short of that means that profits are being sacrificed. By implicitly paying the worker a dollar for every dollar that he produces, the worker will always produce a dollar as long as the pain cost to him is less than a dollar.

How does the firm make money? The firm extracts payment from the worker by setting s so that the worker is just indifferent between working here or elsewhere.[3] The firm gets back its profit by "charging" the worker s to have the right to engage in this activity.

Taxicab drivers are paid according to this scheme. A cab driver rents his cab from the company, paying $-s$ up front (i.e., s is a negative number). He is then entitled to 100 percent of the revenue that he collects from passengers. Under this scheme, drivers have incentives to use the cab efficiently and the cab company can charge higher rent on the cab because it is a more valuable asset. Less would be collected if the driver were to share the proceeds with the firm. Drivers would not work as hard and total revenue collected from any given cab would be lower.

While 100 percent commission rates are not unheard of, they are unusual. The taxicab example is the exception rather than the rule.

But a 100 percent commission rate on profit is not the same as a 100 percent commission rate. Rates are usually stated as a function of sales rather than profit because sales are easier to measure and less easy to manipulate. So if profit were 10 percent of sales, and if the commission rate were 10 percent on sales, the salesperson would implicitly be paid a 100 percent commission on profit as the solution above dictates. The 100 percent commission rate may not be as rare as it appears at the most naive level.

There is another reason for using a 100 percent commission rate. The best workers are attracted by it, especially when capital or brand name is an important component of production. Suppose, for example, that the cost of renting a machine which is necessary for worker output is k. Suppose further that workers have abilities or effort levels that are not the same. Let us abstract from effort for now and let ability, q, vary. Replacing E in (2) with q, per-worker profit depends directly on q as

$$\text{Profit} = q - \text{pay}.$$

If pay equals $(s + rq)$ as above, then compensation is shown in Figure 1 as a function of q.

Suppose that $r = 1$ *and* $s = -k$. Then $s + rq$ becomes $q - k$. Alternatively, consider another payment structure where the implicit fee s' is less than s (so $s\partial > s$) and where $r < 1$ to make up for the lower fee, also shown in Figure 1. All workers with $q > q^*$ prefer the $q - k$ scheme and all workers with $q < q^*$ prefer the $s' + r'q$ scheme. Thus, the higher commission rate structure attracts the better workers.

But things are even worse. The firm that pays $s' + r'q$ can only suffer losses. The revenue generated by any worker at that firm is

$$\text{Profit} = q - k - s' - r'q.$$

But since $s' + r'q^* = q^* - \text{k}$, profit on a worker of type q^* is

$$q^* - \text{k} - \text{q}^* - k = 0.$$

For any worker with $q < q^*$, $\text{q} - k < s' - r'q$ (see Figure 1). Thus, the firm suffers losses on all workers that it succeeds in attracting.

It would be equally unprofitable to pay $r > 1$. Then all high-ability workers would be attracted to the firm, but the firm would suffer losses on those individuals. The only rational choice in a

FIGURE 1

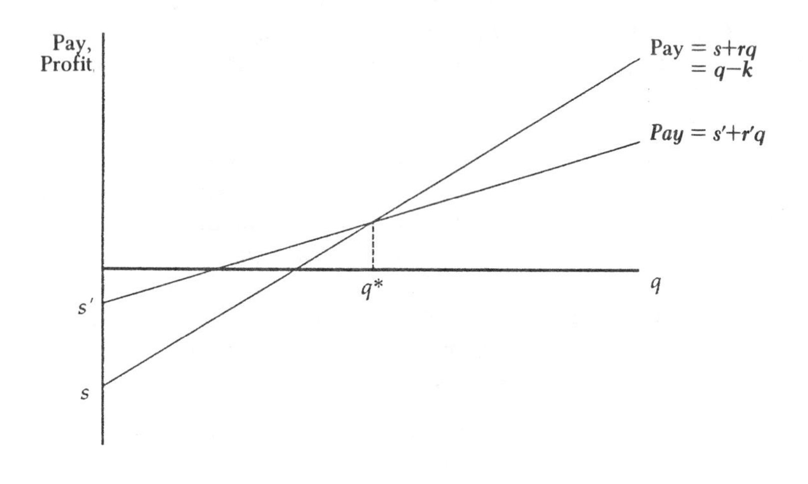

competitive labor market is to pay a commission rate of 100 percent.

The argument for a 100 percent commission rate seems too strong and indeed it is. At the outset, two important assumptions were made. First, it was assumed that workers were risk neutral. Second, it was assumed that the costs of measurement were zero or low. In reality, neither is likely to hold.

Much of the literature on optimal contracts revolves around what can be done when risk considerations are important.[4] The general result is that s must be larger (often a positive number) and r must be reduced. The reason is straightforward. Risk neutrality allowed us to write the worker's objective function as (5). But if workers dislike risk, then it is not merely expected compensation that they care about. They dislike being in situations where output and therefore compensation is low because luck was bad, causing u to be a large negative number. Workers would prefer to be insured to some extent. When output is high, they do not receive the full value of the output, but when output is low, they are not penalized to the full extent of the decrease. Using a commission scheme with

$r < 1$ has a number of implications. First, effort is sacrificed when the low commission rate is used. One of the disadvantages of an insurance scheme is that the worker does not receive the full fruits of his effort. When $r < 1$, a dollar's worth of effort generates less than a dollar of revenue to the worker. As a result, the worker is inclined to put less into the activity. This is analogous to the moral hazard problem implicit in any insurance scheme; if an automobile owner is insured against theft, he is less likely to lock his car. Second, risk averse workers are attracted to the firm that implicitly insures its employees. Risk neutral workers (or those with a preference for risk) gravitate to firms with large implicit fees but high commission rates. Third, while risk averse workers are better off as a result of the insurance scheme, paying $r < 1$ results in lower expected income. Since effort is sacrificed, total output is lower, which, in a competitive labor market, must imply lower expected earnings.

A. Bergson (1978) was among the first to understand the interaction between risk and incentives. He points out that if individuals are risk averse, they must be rewarded along a convex payoff function. The logic is that since a dollar does not mean as much to an individual when his income is high, he must receive more dollars as reward to induce the same effort. One dollar may motivate a poor man, but it may take $10 to elicit the same effort from a rich man.

Similarly, costs of measurement tend to lower the commission rate.[5] The essence of the agency problem as first laid out by Ross (1973) is that an agent's actions are not fully observable and the agent does not generally have the principal's interests at heart. Even if risk were not an issue, the costs of monitoring a worker's output may prevent payment of a 100 percent commission rate.

At one extreme, suppose that workers are risk neutral, but that measuring their individual output is prohibitively expensive. Attempting to pay workers on the basis of q imposes measurement costs that eat up all profits. Workers must then be paid on the basis of input, like some measure of hours worked, or perhaps on the basis of an annual salary.[6] In the case of, say, a middle-level manager, output is difficult to define and measure. Commission is zero and the worker is paid a given amount per month to show up. Even hours are not monitored closely because there is only a very rough relation of output to hours worked for these individuals.

In the real world, monitoring costs and risk are real problems. The taxicab example above is really one where the driver is self-employed as a way to get around the measurement cost issue. Yellow Cab can attempt to monitor output by reading sales off the meter. But drivers can cheat by negotiating fixed fares with passengers and leaving the meter off. The easiest way around the problem is to rent the cab to the employee, making him not only agent, but residual claimant. Then the only problem is that the driver does not care for the rented cab appropriately because he neither bears the costs of repair nor reaps the benefit from high resale value.

In football, some have alleged that the ability of players to become free agents has resulted in more injuries. Since owners cannot capture the full return to the player, they have less incentive to treat him well, forcing him to play when injured despite long-term consequences. If the team owned the rights to the player, it is argued, they would protect their investment more carefully.[7]

There are other contractual arrangements that are like piece rate pay. Sharecropping is one.[8] In sharecropping, the measurement problem is not avoided (because the owner of the land must determine output to receive his share), but risk and effort are traded off by selecting a commission rate less than 100 percent. Sharecropping is somewhat different from other partnership arrangements since observability is asymmetric in sharecropping. The tenant can observe output perfectly, but the owner cannot. In most partnerships, all parties can observe total output of the firm, but individual contribution is more difficult to assess.

Piece rate pay presents other problems. It is often argued that workers who are paid piece rates focus too strongly on quantity and not enough on quality. While perhaps true, overweighting quantity is not a necessary consequence of paying a piece rate. For example, a typist who is paid per page will type too fast and make too many errors. But a typist who is penalized substantially for each error may actually type too slowly and make too few errors, given the amount that consumers are willing to pay for high-quality typing. In theory, a piece rate can be gauged to quality or quantity and there is no necessity that one be emphasized over the other. In practice, quality may be more difficult to observe than quantity, causing workers to produce too many shoddy products.[9]

Similarly, paying on the basis of output may induce workers to place their effort on the measured components of output while sacrificing unmeasured components.[10] For example, a salesperson may spend all of his time attempting to make the sale without worrying about teaching the consumer to use the product. Life insurance salespeople often induce their customers to switch policies because their commissions are higher on initial sales than on renewals.

Baker (1992) has analyzed the optimum compensation scheme, taking into account that output cannot be measured perfectly. He shows that the stronger is the correlation between the measure of performance and effort, the closer to 1 is the optimal piece rate. If there is only a weak correlation between effort and the measure of performance, a small weight should be attached to the measure. Otherwise individuals choose the wrong level of effort, which is costly, and must be compensated. Thus, using incentive pay induces employees to take unproductive actions when the measure of performance is a poor indicator of effort.

Milgrom (1988) makes a similar argument. He suggests that employees can take two kinds of actions: those that actually do increase output and those that only mislead the supervisor into thinking that output has been increased. If performance is weighted too heavily, workers spend too much time trying to convince their supervisors that what they are doing is productive. As a result, r is reduced with two effects. The benefit is that unproductive effort is cut, but the cost is that productive effort is reduced. The tradeoff yields an optimal piece rate.

A final problem with using a piece rate is the "ratchet effect." If a worker does well, he tips off the supervisor that the job may not be as difficult as thought. A multi-period compensation scheme can eliminate or at least reduce the importance of the problem, as shown in Lazear (1986) and Gibbons (1987). Ickes and Samuelson (1987) argue that changing jobs breaks the link between current performance and future incentive schemes, thereby eliminating the ratchet effect.[11]

Upward Sloping Age-Earnings Profiles

Piece rates are one way to motivate workers, but they are not the only way. Using a piece rate requires frequent monitoring of worker output, which may be extremely costly. When measurement is expensive, an alternative is to use a sampling scheme that punishes workers sufficiently for observed deviations from the standard. Becker and Stigler (1974) first made this argument in the context of law enforcement. When individuals are entrusted with a task such as law enforcement where criminals may bribe the enforcers to shirk, one solution is to require that an enforcer post a bond. If he is caught being dishonest, he forfeits the bond. A judiciously chosen bond structure prevents the enforcer from behaving dishonestly and raises output.

The theory has been extended in Lazear (1979, 1981) to argue that an upward sloping age-earnings profile can induce workers to put forth effort, even when their output cannot be observed on a frequent basis. Young workers are paid less than they are worth with the promise that they will receive more than they are worth when old. Workers continue to put forth effort because they do not want to risk termination that would imply losing the high wages later on. The worker is like a bond holder because he implicitly lends to the firm when young by accepting a wage that falls short of output. When the worker is older, he receives the principal plus interest back in the form of wages that exceed his output.[12] Lee and Png (1990) have extended this notion to argue that installment payments, which are like deferred compensation, induce higher effort in the first stage by holding off payment until later.

Upward sloping age-earnings profiles eliminate the need to observe output at each point in time. Occasionally, a reading must be made or the threat of termination based on poor performance would be vacuous. (Random termination has no effect on effort.) But because a great deal is at stake, workers are reluctant to reduce their effort too much.

One consequence of the upward sloping age-earnings profile is the need for mandatory retirement or some buyout scheme. Since older workers are overpaid relative to their productivity, their incentives to retire are distorted. A prospective retiree compares his wage to the value of his leisure and leaves when the latter exceeds the former. Since the wage exceeds productivity, the worker will not want to leave efficiently, when the value of his leisure exceeds the value of his output. Some push is therefore necessary. Mandatory retirement is one such mechanism. Strategically chosen compulsory retirement dates can remove the labor supply distortion, while at the same time taking advantage of incentives generated by the upward sloping age-earnings profile.

Mandatory retirement is not the only solution to the problem. Implicit in virtually all defined benefit pension schemes is a buyout.[13] Consider, for example, a pattern plan, where a worker receives, say, $500 a year during retirement for each year of service that he completes before retirement. Thus, a worker who retires at age 65 with 30 years of service receives $15,000 per year in pension for each year between age 65 and 90, when he dies.

The expected present value of pension benefits as a function of age of retirement is shown in Figure 2. Individuals who "retired" at age 40 would receive very little in pension because they would only have accumulated five years of service and would not begin to receive the pension until the normal retirement age. Individuals who retire at age 63 receive a substantial pension. But those who retired at age 89 would receive a large per year pension ($27,000 per year), but would receive it for only one year. Thus, the value of the pension first rises with age of retirement and then falls. The result is

FIGURE 2

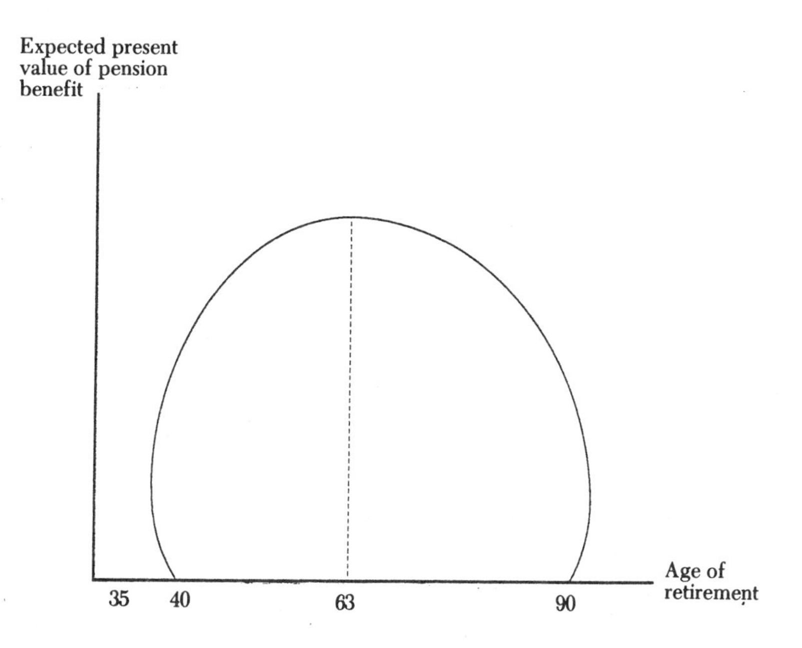

that a worker who continues to work beyond age 63 in this example gives up pension value for each year of continued work. Thus, the firm is implicitly paying him not to postpone retirement. The implicit payment can be quite substantial, depending on the pension formula, and this is sometimes coupled with explicit pension payments as well.

The distortions of inefficient separation have been analyzed by other researchers in contexts other than retirement. Parsons (1972) was the first to look at the effects of specific human capital on turnover rates. Kennan (1979) discusses the general problem of distorted separation decisions when each side owns part of the (human) capital, but does not have rights to receive the full return to it. An ingenious graphical treatment of separation distortions is presented by Hashimoto and Yu (1980) also in the context of specific human capital. Finally, a more general treatment of the labor contracting problem is given by Hall and Lazear (1984), who analyze a variety of different contracting methods and their implications for investment in human capital and separation efficiency. Johnson (1985) argues that decision costs may push firms toward a fixed wage contract that would otherwise appear inefficient.

Further, the pension solution to the mandatory retirement problem led this author to think about pensions in a somewhat different way.[14] While it is intuitive that pension formulas can affect turnover decisions, the exact nature of the mechanism is far from clear. The problem can best be understood by considering the military pension plan. Soldiers who retire with less than 20 years of service receive no pension at all, whereas those with 20 years or more receive quite a generous pension. Correspondingly, once an individual has served for eight to ten years, he is very unlikely to leave before serving twenty. But at the simple level, pension accrual for years 0 through 19 is 0, while pension accrual during the twentieth year is huge. A regression of turnover rates on accrual defined in this way would not explain the very low turnover rates during years ten through 19.

A better way to think about the problem is to recognize that serving the ninth year gives a soldier the option to serve the tenth year, which gives him the option to serve the eleventh, and so forth. Thus, the pension accrual during the tenth year is not zero, but instead the option value associated with serving that year. A simple formula computes option value recursively for each year of service. This method can explain turnover rates much more effectively than the naive approach where independent variables are observed rather than option accrual.

Stock and Wise (1990) have modified the approach and have used it successfully to explain turnover behavior using data from particular companies. What is most impressive about their work is the ability to fit the discontinuities associated with early retirement and other provisions as well as the continuous pension accrual dates. Their paper along with extensions of it is a superb example of using theory based on the "new economics of personnel" to explain behavior in the real world. Ippolito (1987) has found that for federal workers, the pension formula imposes penalties on workers who quit early, leading to low turnover rates.[15]

The previous discussion of upward sloping age-earnings profiles and the slight digression to pension analysis was motivated by effort considerations. But there are other explanations of upward sloping age-earnings profiles that do not rely on effort. One of the most interesting is presented by Harris and Hölmstrom (1982), who argue that an upward sloping age-earnings profile is essentially an insurance policy against low ability. A simplified version of their model follows.

Suppose that young workers are either high ability or low ability, but neither worker nor firm knows a worker's type at the outset. Suppose further that high-ability workers produce 1 and low-ability workers produce 0 and that workers live two periods. Let there be, say, 75 percent high-ability and 25 percent low-ability workers (the proportions are unimportant). Then a young worker's expected output is .75. After one period, ability is learned by all. Competition pushes the wage of high-ability workers up to 1, whereas low-ability workers would earn 0 in a competitive market.

If workers are risk averse, they prefer another payment scheme. All workers are paid .5 when young and 1 when old. The firm breaks even because two period output is 1.5 on average. Workers are better off because every worker is fully insured, receiving exactly 1.5 over his lifetime irrespective of ability. Since workers are risk averse, this scheme dominates the per period competitive equilibrium, which would pay all workers .75 when young, low-ability workers 0, and high-ability workers 1 when old.[16]

There is some evidence on upward sloping age-earnings profiles. Robert Hutchens has done the most extensive analysis of these issues. In one of his earlier papers (1987), he shows that upward sloping profiles are more likely to be used in jobs that do not lend themselves well to measurement of output by piece. He takes this as evidence that upward sloping age-earnings profiles are a way to motivate workers. Two good and deeper discussions of the issues introduced above are provided by Carmichael (1989) and Hutchens (1989). Gordon (1990) documents the rise in supervisory personnel and links it to incentive and efficiency wage theory. Goldin (1986) shows that women who had less permanent attachments to jobs, and for whom upward sloping age-earnings profiles were less effective, were more likely to be paid piece rates than were men.

Finally, Fama (1980) argues that workers need not be paid their output on their current job to induce them to put forth appropriate levels of effort. He points out that the discipline of the external labor market can provide incentives for workers. Fama invokes the notion of "*ex post* settling up." In a nutshell, the idea is that new, prospective employers derive information about an individual from his performance on the current job. If he does well, other firms will infer that the worker is energetic or able and will bid accordingly. As a result, the current firm is forced to raise the worker's wage to meet market pressure so the worker is compensated *ex post* for effort undertaken today.

Whether upward sloping age-earnings profiles or piece rates are used to motivate workers is really a question of how often and when to measure a worker's output. An upward sloping profile is associated with infrequent and random measurement of output whereas a piece rate is associated with frequent and predictable measurement of output. Lazear (1990) analyzes the details of when, how often and how predictably worker output should be measured. Among other points, the analysis implies that workers with more specific human capital should be evaluated less frequently, that older workers should be evaluated less often than young workers, and that evaluation should be more common in firms where the probability of failure and turnover is high and where performance is highly correlated over time.

Payment by Relative Performance

Piece rate compensation elicits effort by compensating a worker on the basis of his absolute performance, irrespective of the performance of other workers in the firm. If all workers produce very high levels of output, then all workers receive high levels of pay. If all workers produce low levels of output, then all workers receive low pay.

A relative compensation scheme rewards on the basis of relative, rather than absolute performance. It, too, if set up properly, can induce workers to perform efficiently.

The most frequently discussed relative compensation scheme is a tournament, where workers implicitly (or sometimes explicitly) compete with one another for positions in the organization.[17] Higher positions carry with them higher wages as reward for winning the tournament. Individuals are assigned to jobs based on their relative performance, rather than on their absolute performance. The metaphor of a tennis match is useful.

At Wimbledon, prizes are fixed in advance and are independent of absolute performance. The match may be superb, but the winner's and loser's prizes are not altered to reflect the superior quality of play.

Further, whether a player receives the winner's prize or loser's prize depends on his performance relative to the other player, not on absolute performance. Edberg wins by being better than Becker, not by being good. It is the comparison that is crucial.

Finally, the spread between winner's prize and loser's prize affects effort. If the prize is $500,000, winner-take-all, the contestants will be quite motivated to play hard to capture the prize. But if the prize money were split evenly between winner and loser, neither player would care as much about the victory. So effort increases in spread. But if the spread is too large, players will not want to compete because the equilibrium level of effort will be too large to compensate for the pain of having to earn it.

Compensation in a firm can be thought of in a similar fashion. Salaries may be attached to jobs so that the president earns $500,000, the vice-presidents earn $200,000, and so forth. Furthermore, these salaries may, to a first approximation, be said to be fixed and independent of absolute performance.

An individual becomes president by being the best among the vice-presidents. The losers, i.e., those who remain vice-president, are not poor performers, but are simply inferior to the individual who is selected for the president's job. Thus, selection, and therefore compensation, are relative.

Finally, the larger is the difference between the wage[18] of the president and the wage of the vice-president, the larger the amount of effort that each vice-president will exert to win the president's job.[19]

The basic tournament model can be written as follows:

There are two workers, j and k. Each produces output according to

$$q_i = E_i + u_i\ , \qquad i = j,\ k, \tag{9}$$

where q is output, E is effort, and u is a random variable which we think of as luck. As before, it is painful to put forth effort and the pain is given by $C(E)$.

Two wages are paid. The winner receives W_1 and the loser receives W_2. Workers are risk neutral. Winning means obtaining a q that exceeds that of one's rival. Thus, worker j's problem is to choose effort to maximize wealth:

$$\max_{E_j} W_1 P + W_2(1-P) - C(E_j), \tag{10}$$

where P, the probability of winning, is

$$P = \text{Prob}(q_j > q_k)$$

$$= \text{Prob}(E_j - E_k > u_k - u_j).$$

If $u_k - u_j$ is a random variable with distribution function G, then

$$P = G(E_j - E_k).$$

The first-order condition is

$$(W_1 - W_2)\frac{\partial P}{\partial E_j} = C'(E_j) \tag{11}$$

or

$$(W_1 - W_2)g(E_j - E_k) = C'(E_j).$$

Since k's problem is symmetric, $E_j = E_k$ in equilibrium so (11) can be rewritten as

$$(W_1 - W_2)g(0) = C'(E_j). \tag{12}$$

The intuition behind (11) is straightforward. It says that j should exert effort up to the point where the marginal cost of effort equals its marginal return. The left-hand side is the marginal return to effort because $W_1 - W_2$ is what the player nets from winning and $\partial P/\partial E_j$ is the change in the probability of winning associated with an additional unit of effort.

Equation (12) has two important implications. First, as the tennis match story implied, the larger is the spread, the larger is the effort. Larger spreads mean an increase in the marginal return to effort which induces workers to put forth more effort, even at a higher marginal cost. Second, as $g(0)$ decreases, effort decreases. What is $g(0)$? Technically, it is the height of the density function at 0 (its mode and mean), but it can be thought of intuitively as the importance of luck in the contest. If luck were totally unimportant, both u's would always equal zero. The density function would be degenerate at 0 with a value of infinity. If luck were very important, the density would have fat tails, implying that there was a good chance of drawing very large or very small u_j and u_k. Under these circumstances, $g(0)$ would be very small. Thus, $g(0)$ is inversely related to the importance of luck.

As luck becomes more important, effort falls. If luck is paramount so that a player's effort has little effect on the outcome of the game, he loses his incentive to try. A worker with a completely capricious supervisor is less inclined to work hard because he knows that it will have little impact on the supervisor's evaluation of him. Similarly, if output determined primarily by other factors such as business cycle conditions or the weather, the worker is less inclined to exert effort because it can have little effect on measured performance.

There is an immediate solution. The firm should offset the decreased effort by increasing the prize spread. This implies that earnings should be more skewed in activities where luck is more important. When the choice of the president depends mostly on luck, it is important to make the value of being president high so that the vice-presidents will try hard to win the job.

The mathematics above present only half of the problem. Workers behave according to (12), but the firm has to choose W_1 and W_2. This involves solving a profit maximization problem subject to the constraint that workers' labor or effort supply depends on wages according to (12) and subject to the constraint that the average wage must be high enough to cover the pain from work in the first place. The solution boils down to inducing workers to put forth effort until its marginal cost exactly equals the profit associated with it. Thus, the solution is efficient and equivalent to the one obtained by paying a piece rate with $r = 1$. This is an important result because it implies that relative compensation is just as effective as absolute compensation in eliciting effort. What are the advantages of each scheme?

There are two major advantages to using tournaments. The first is that tournaments "difference out common noise." For example, two salespersons on 100 percent commission may encounter a good or bad economy, conditions over which they have no control. If the economy is bad, their wages will be low, even if effort was high. Risk averse workers dislike random income variation and it can be eliminated by using a tournament. If the salespersons are compensated on the basis of their relative performance, rather than their absolute performance, then the bad economy which affects both similarly has no adverse consequences for salary.

It is unnecessary to use a tournament to get rid of common noise. As Hölmstrom (1979) has shown, performance can be made relative to some group statistic. For example, an individual can be paid on the difference between his performance and the group average. The way in which group is defined is important here, but the general point, that common noise can be reduced or eliminated, is valid in the Hölmstrom set-up.

Second, risk issues aside, it may simply be cheaper to observe rank than it is to observe absolute levels of output. In academics, it is difficult to define, let alone measure, output in a clear way. But we often feel quite confident about ranking one individual relative to another, even though we cannot easily describe the dimensions on which we are judging.

Carmichael (1983) suggests another advantage to using tournaments. When firms pay on the basis of absolute performance, they can lie about worker performance, claiming that productivity is low so wages must be low. But with a tournament structure, a fixed number of high-paying and low-paying jobs are assigned so firms are less able to cheat their workers. Thus, tournaments make the firm's promises more credible with corresponding improvements in efficiency.

There are two major disadvantages with tournaments. The first is that tournaments provide incentives for collusion.[20] Since total compensation is not dependent on the level of effort, j and k have an incentive to get together and agree to split the prize at very low levels of effort. No such incentive exists when each worker is paid on the basis of his absolute performance.

Second, at the other extreme, tournaments foster unhealthy competition as well as healthy competition. Player j benefits not only when his output is high, but also when k's output is low. As a result, he may attempt to harm his rival. At a minimum, he will be unwilling to cooperate in a way that improves k's relative position. Cooperation may be important to the firm, but a tournament structure discourages it.[21] The negative effects can be mitigated in two ways. First, the prize spread can be reduced somewhat with the negative consequence of discouraging effort, but with the positive effect of reducing uncooperative behavior. Second, individuals who need to cooperate with one another should not be grouped into the same tournament. They should compete against individuals whose cooperation is unimportant for output, either because they are in separate locations or separate activities.

There is empirical evidence on the effectiveness of tournaments as incentive mechanisms. Bull, Schotter, and Weigelt (1987) use experimental techniques to show that individuals who are faced with a tournament of the type described in Lazear and Rosen behave very much as the theoretical model would predict. Specifically, they move quickly to the Nash equilibrium level of effort as described in eq. (12) above.

Real world evidence comes from two sources. First, it has been found that chicken breeders are paid on the basis of relative performance to difference out the effects of the weather on their output. Rank among chicken breeders, rather than the number of chickens produced, determines compensation.[22] Second, and more surprising, Ehrenberg and Bognanno (1990) look at golf scores in PGA tournaments. They find that the structure of the prize money, in particular the spread associated with winning or losing in the final round, affects performance in the contest. Scores are actually lower when prizes are more skewed, just as eq. (12) predicts.

Profit Sharing, Partnerships, and Team Incentives

The cliché in comparative industrial relations is that Americans work as individuals whereas the Japanese work as teams. Because of high growth rates in Japan in the recent past, the implication is that teamwork is better than individual performance.[23]

A major issue involves motivation and the free rider problem. Japanese workers are profit sharers, but their compensation is related to the profits of a very large group, not generally the immediate group of individuals with whom they work. Why should an individual worker put forth effort when the fruits of it are split among 100,000 other workers, most of whom he does not even know? There are two possible explanations.[24]

First, the worker may derive some direct benefit from putting forth effort beyond that of pecuniary compensation. For example, the worker may feel altruism toward his coworkers. Harming them may also harm him. In order for this mechanism to be effective, it is necessary that coworkers share in profits. Otherwise, any action to reduce the output of the firm would harm holders of the firm's capital, not its work force. Thus, workers must empathize more with workers whom they do not know than with shareholders. Empathy, shame, and guilt, and their implications for behavior, have been analyzed by sociologists. The economic approach has made more rigorous the notion of norms and how they develop within a corporation.[25]

Second, mutual monitoring may prevent workers from shirking. In order for workers to monitor one another, they must have some incentive to do so. Again, without profit sharing of some sort, it is difficult to imagine why any worker would bear the costs of chastising a coworker for his reduced output. After all, in the absence of profit sharing, another worker's shirking has little effect on any given worker.[26]

One possibility is that work sharing substitutes for profit sharing as the motivation for mutual monitoring. In Hölmstrom (1982) workers may be assigned a task and compensation is denied if the task is not completed. If one worker shirks, then another must put forth additional effort to compensate for it. Under these circumstances, it is reasonable that workers would resent coworkers who do not carry their own weight.[27]

Partnerships as a form of economic organization have been analyzed recently. Farrell and Scotchmer (1988) show that the equal sharing rule inefficiently limits the size of partnerships and they apply their model to the salmon fishing industry. Some interesting empirical evidence comes from Gilson and Mnookin (1985) who examine law firms. They find that compensation is not the same among partners, but that there is compression in earnings; partners' earnings are not as different as their contributions to total output.

Gaynor and Pauly (1990) find that incentives get diluted and productivity falls when group size rises in medical group practices. Benelli, Loderer, and Lys (1987) find that worker participation in firm decision making has little, if any effect on corporate operations and performance.

Pay Equality

Personnel departments often speak vaguely, but forcefully, about the need to ensure that salaries are not too disparate. Internal harmony will be affected by a pay structure that rewards people too differently, it is argued. Some economists have taken this claim seriously and have discussed models in which that statement can be true.

One of the earliest with this implication is Frank (1985). He suggests that people have tastes for being the best in an organization. As a result, they are willing to accept less to work in an organization in which they are the highest quality worker. At the other end, workers who are low quality must be compensated for being in an organization where they are at the bottom. Both forces push wages toward equality so that resulting compensation is not as different as productivity within the organization.

Frank's explanation is clever and well presented, but may be dominated by two forces which work in the opposite direction. First, workers may actually pay to be in better firms because they can acquire skills from other workers. For example, a young assistant professor would accept a lower salary from a top-five school than he would from some community college because the former puts him on a better career path than the latter. Second, to the extent that institutional brand name carries over to an individual, workers benefit from being associated with better organizations. Again, assistant professors like to be associated with good research universities because outsiders infer that the assistant professor must be high quality to have been hired by the prestige department. Both forces work to exacerbate, rather than mitigate, pay differences.

Another mechanism is suggested by Lazear (1989) which was discussed briefly above. When compensation is based at least in part on relative performance, a large spread in pay discourages cooperation among workers. Compressing the pay structure does not impede cooperation. This comes close to the personnel manager's concern over harmony within the organization.

Pay and Performance

There is a growing literature that relates compensation practices to performance. There are two questions here. The first relates to the compensation formula. Do workers suffer when company profits fall and do they benefit when firm profits rise? The second relates to the effect of the compensation scheme on company performance. Do companies that, say, pay managers on the basis of output, obtain higher profits?

The first question has a long history. Workers can share in the prosperity of the firm through their wages or through their employment. The second is more obvious and quite industry specific. Production workers are more likely to suffer layoffs during downturns than during good periods. Since both the sensitivity of industry demand and the fixed costs of hiring workers are industry specific, some industries pass more employment risk on to their workers than others. Durable goods manufacturing and construction are among the most volatile industries, whereas service sector jobs, e.g., in health and education, are much less uncertain. Abowd and Ashenfelter (1981) have shown that industries with a great deal of layoff risk must pay a large premium (up to 25 percent) to compensate for working in uncertain conditions.

Less straightforward is the relation of wages to performance. Early studies (e.g., see Weiss 1966) have demonstrated the relation of worker wages to company profits and industry structure. More recently (Pergamit 1983), the analysis has been used to examine the relation of wages to regulatory structure. But most interest in empirical personnel economics has centered on executive compensation and performance.

Jensen and Murphy (1990) find that there is a clear relation of executive compensation to company performance. When firm profits, measured in a variety of ways, rise, executive salaries also rise. But while the effect is clearly statistically significant, it is also quite small in magnitude. The upper boundary on one estimate is a $2 increase in compensation of the CEO for a $1,000 increase in equity value. Using a somewhat broader definition of manager, Leonard (1989) finds that base and bonus pay of managers responds very little to changes in corporate sales or profits or to unit sales. Of course, the seemingly small number may be very large in terms of its impact on the CEO's wealth so incentives may still be well served. Deckop (1988) shows that CEO compensation is positively related to profit as a percentage of sales. Kostiuk (1990) finds that there is a stable, positive relation of executive earnings to firm size. These results raise the second question.

Do firms that pay on the basis of performance do better? The evidence here is more difficult to obtain, but there is some. Leonard (1990) finds that companies with long-term incentive plans enjoy significantly greater increase in returns on earnings, at least during the period of the early 1980s. But he also finds that "corporations appear able to succeed with a variety of internal pay and promotion practices" and the degree of equity in executive pay does not correlate well with company performance. Abowd (1990) obtains somewhat asymmetric results. He finds that companies that give bonuses for good current performance enjoy improved future performance. But companies that penalize poor current performance do not seem to receive this productivity boost. The result is somewhat puzzling since bonuses and penalties are formally equivalent and calling a scheme a bonus or a penalty is somewhat arbitrary.[28]

An extension of the question relates to relative performance. As mentioned earlier, risk averse workers prefer compensation schemes that difference out common noise. One obvious way to do this is to condition compensation on deviations from some norm. Antle and Smith (1986) find weak support for the proposition that executive compensation depends on how his/her firm does relative to others in the industry. Other authors, most notably Jensen and Murphy (1990) and Gibbons and Murphy (1990), obtain conflicting results, sometimes finding that industry effects matter, other times finding that they do not.[29]

Tax considerations may make difficult disentangling the empirical validity of some of the theories. For example, it may be that upward sloping age-earnings profiles serve as an important motivator, but the additional tax that must be paid in a progressive tax structure may hinder its use. Or it might go the other way. Since investments in one's own firm that show up as higher earnings later on accumulate at a before tax rate, there may be incentives to tilt the profile simply to take advantage of tax savings. Miller and Scholes (1982) analyze this issue and conclude that there are incentive reasons for upward sloping age-earnings profiles. More recently Scholes and Wolfson (1992) have examined the interrelation of taxes, incentives, and other concerns within the organization.

Some Specific Compensation Questions

While the foregoing discussion deals with specific compensation issues, many of the points above may still strike the practitioner as somewhat abstract. To illustrate how these points can be applied to real world situations, a couple of specific issues are delineated.

Stock and stock options are among the most common compensation devices used for incentive purposes. Indeed, when personnel people talk about incentive pay for high-level managers, they often have in mind only stock and stock option programs. To be sure, stock options are an important type of performance pay, but as the previous discussion should have made clear, stock and stock options are far from the only type of incentive pay. Bonuses that depend on performance, upward sloping age-earnings profiles, and raises associated with promotions based on relative performance can all be thought of as incentive pay. In effect, they are substitute methods for motivating the worker.

Jackson and Lazear (1991) analyze the advantages of using one scheme over another. But in this section, only results that relate specifically to the kinds of tradeoffs implicit in using options will be discussed. Let us ignore risk considerations and imagine that an executive is to receive an option that has expected value of $1,000. There are an infinite number of ways to produce an option, the expected value of which is $1,000. One way is to set a very low exercise price, say, zero. Under these conditions, the option is always in the money (i.e., it will be exercised with certainty, so this is like giving the worker stock). Alternatively, the exercise price can be set at twice the market value. The chances that the stock will be in the money are now much lower, so a larger number of options must be given to produce the same expected value of $1,000.

While the expected value is the same, the incentive effects of the various schemes are very different. A couple of points are worth making. A disadvantage of using a high exercise price with the right to buy many shares is that once it becomes clear that the option is out of the money, all incentive effects are lost. For example, suppose that the stock price falls to half its initial market value. The chances that it will exceed the exercise price of twice the initial market value are remote. To the extent that the option produced any incentives at all, those incentives are lost. This suggests that a low exercise price is preferable. But there may be some negative consequences of using a low exercise price as well.

It is well known that the value of an option increases in variance. If the exercise price is high, a manager would like to take chances that will give the firm a reasonable chance of putting his/her option in the money. The higher the exercise price, the more desire for risky projects. Conversely, a low exercise price pushes in the direction of safer projects. It is often alleged that managers tend to be overly conservative, adopting strategies that may not move the firm ahead, but are very unlikely to get them fired. In order to undo this overly conservative tendency, the manager can be given options with high exercise prices.

Finally, the same logic explains why managers are long call options rather than short put options. This is analogous to the question of using bonuses or penalties. In theory, a manager could be paid to be at the short end of a put option so that if the value of the firm falls, owners would exercise their put and punish the manager. But the reverse pattern is always used. One reason is that making managers short on puts induces them to take very safe strategies that will neither lower nor raise the value of the stock too much. A manager who is at the short end of a put fears a large downturn in the value of the stock, which would have significant negative consequences for his wealth.

Stocks and options have been analyzed by Nitzan and Pakes (1983) in a somewhat different context. They are concerned with the problem of inventors who work for an organization and then spin off from the parent organization, taking their invention with them. Society may benefit as a monopoly becomes a duopoly, but the original firm loses monopoly profits and would like to prevent the departure. The solution, they argue, is to tie inventor compensation to the future of the enterprise by paying the inventor in the form of options. This is analogous to the problem of specific human capital, where avoiding separation can make both parties better off, but contracting problems induce separation. Options are one form of compensation that operates as a golden handcuff, but there are many others. Any type of deferred compensation, i.e., through upward sloping age-earnings profiles, also locks the worker into the job. The difference rests primarily on risk considerations. Upward sloping age-earnings profiles are closer to debt, whereas options are equity.

Efficiency Wages

The theory of efficiency wages, first proposed by Robert Solow, has received a great deal of attention in recent years. Laid out formally by Shapiro and Stiglitz (1984), the model has intrigued economists for two reasons.[30] First, as the Keynesian framework fell out of fashion, efficiency wage stories provided an alternative explanation of involuntary unemployment in the spirit of Keynes. Second, the intuition struck many as plausible, with high wages serving as a motivator. As the previous discussion should have made clear, incentives do not necessarily imply involuntary unemployment.

In fact, the two are not very closely linked. The point of my first paper on incentives was that efficient separation in the context of the retirement decision could be achieved even when high wages were paid.[31] What has captured most fans of efficiency wages is the theory of labor supply in disguise. The standard model of labor supply suggests that at least in some range, the more workers are paid, the more hours or effort they will supply. This seems quite intuitive and squares with ideas most of us have about paying child-care and other domestic workers more to ensure high-quality work.

Involuntary unemployment results only when there is a sticky price in the system. The difference between incentives and sticky prices can best be understood in the original formulation, attributed to Solow's lectures at MIT. Solow expresses effort as a function of the wage. He shows that the equilibrium is one where the wage that will be chosen by the profit-maximizing firm exceeds the wage that will clear the market. But if the wage could have two components, the market would clear. Instead of paying on the basis of effort, only the wage could have a fixed (negative) component and a marginal component. Thus, instead of paying

$$\text{Wage} = b \text{ Effort},$$

pay

$$\text{Wage} = z + b \text{ Effort}.$$

The choice of b can be made to obtain efficiency on effort and the market can be cleared by choosing z appropriately so that individuals are indifferent between this job and any other job.

Put in other terms, if the optimal choice of the effort premium results in too many applicants, the firm should "charge" an entry fee for the job. A negative z above accomplishes this task.

The unemployment equilibrium results not because wages induce effort, but because one price in this system, in this case z, has been frozen at zero. If z were a free parameter, efficiency would be obtained and the market would clear. The unemployment equilibrium is generated as it is in the standard Keynesian framework by a rigid wage that does not adjust.

All efficiency wage stories do not suffer from the same criticism. For example, it is possible to argue that a psychological effect makes workers put forth more effort when their total wage (not just the effort-related component) is high. But the story that has captured the hearts of many economists is the one that ties wage to effort. And the unemployment equilibrium which results from that story depends on a rigid price, which results from restricting the compensation formula arbitrarily, not from the fact that higher wages induce more effort. The latter is completely consistent with a market clearing theory of labor supply.

Efficiency wages are related to the topic of this essay because they do emphasize the role of effort in determining the compensation formula. But this is not the place to discuss the details of what has grown to be a large literature. Some important critical reviews of the efficiency wage literature are Carmichael (1985) and MacLeod and Malcomson (1988). An excellent and more sympathetic analysis of efficiency wages is presented by A. Weiss (1990). The empirical evidence on efficiency wage theory is limited. One of the more interesting papers is historical, by Raff and Summers (1987). To show that efficiency wages are paid, three points must be established. The first requirement is that high wages affect performance positively. But this is consistent with any market clearing theory of labor supply, so it is not sufficient. Second, the high wages must result in queues for jobs. But even competitive firms that pay more than the market wage will induce workers to queue for jobs. Thus, third, it is necessary that the high-wage policy not be a mistake, i.e., profits must be higher with the high wages than they are with the low wages. Raff and Summers provide some evidence that Henry Ford's automobile plant raised wages and all three conditions held. Key is that profits are higher after because the fact that Ford had a before-and-after wage policy implies that at least one wage was not profit maximizing.[32]

Other Personnel Issues

The focus of this essay is compensation and its effects on productivity. But there are a number of tangentially related topics (as already discussed efficiency wages) where the choice of compensation formula is crucial. In the next section, a subset of the issues will be sketched.

Up-or-out Promotion Rules

Up-or-out is a perplexing phenomenon. Much like mandatory retirement, the question is why force some workers out of the firm, rather than simply adjusting their wage rate? There is some price at which the firm would be happy to keep the worker. Why not make the offer and allow the worker to decide? With up-or-out, a worker is not given a choice. If he cannot make the cut, he is terminated. Continued employment at a lower wage rate is not one of the options.

Kahn and Huberman (1988) offer an explanation. They argue that up-or-out assists in guaranteeing that firms behave honestly. As a result, credible contracts, which could not otherwise be written, are feasible. Suppose that instead of up-or-out a firm would take a reading on a worker's productivity and announce a wage offer. To the extent that workers are locked into the firm at all, either because of specific human capital or mobility costs, a firm could behave opportunistically, telling workers that they are lower quality than in fact they are. Workers would not necessarily leave because even the lower wage that they receive might exceed their best offer from another firm.[33]

Up-or-out prevents this type of opportunistic behavior. If the firm wants to claim that a worker has low productivity, it must fire the worker, losing any of the benefits that would derive from lying about productivity. Thus, up-or-out assists in truth telling. Workers who know this prefer firms with up-or-out because they are less likely to be exploited. Up-or-out may even improve their incentives for investment in human capital.

Tenure

Academic tenure is another curious phenomenon. While it generally is coupled with up-or-out practices, the two are distinct. Tenure could be granted to selected employees, and the others could be retained on a term basis.[34] Alternatively, up-or-out need not result in tenure. Those who are retained could simply make it to the next level, where they would be reevaluated. No guarantee of future employment need be associated with up-or-out.[35]

Carmichael (1988) offers an explanation of tenure based on relative performance. If an individual's compensation is based even in part on his relative position in the firm, and if that individual has some control over hiring, he has an incentive to hire workers who are inferior to himself. The quality of an organization would be hurt by individuals who behaved in a self-serving fashion. Tenure helps insulate workers who also make hiring decisions from these kinds of incentives.

If a worker's salary and security with the firm did not depend on relative performance, then he would have no incentive to select low-quality peers. In fact, if compensation were tied in part to total output of the firm, incentives would be provided to select better workers. Thus, the problem is one of choosing appropriate weights for relative performance versus aggregate output in determining the compensation of one individual. Tenure is an institution that deemphasizes relative performance. But even in the absence of tenure, a compensation scheme that weighted aggregate output sufficiently could overcome some of the hiring selection problems that Carmichael focuses on in his explanation.[36]

Supervision and Hierarchical Structures

Supervisors perform a number of roles. Among the most important are setting salary, instruction, monitoring, selecting individuals for promotion, and approving projects. A number of models of supervision have been presented in recent years. They fall into two categories. The premise of the first is that supervision affects the output of the entire firm because supervisors pass on their skills to those whom they supervise. This literature was begun by Mayer (1960) and includes Rosen (1982, 1986) and Miller (1982).[37] The essence of their model is that a supervisor has a span of control and that his quality affects the performance of all of his subordinates. By placing the highest quality individual at the top of the corporation, the largest number of individuals can be positively affected. This also means that the most able people will be sorted to the largest organizations, where their skills can have the greatest effect on others.

The other strain of the literature is best represented by Sah and Stiglitz (1986). Their supervisors are not salary setters or trainers, but instead merely screen and approve or disapprove projects. The hierarchy of the organization is determined statistically. Some structures lead to more errors of one type or another being made.

Whereas compensation is essential to the first set of models, it is unimportant in the second. In the first group of papers, compensation is the key determinant of sorting, which moves workers to their most productive use.

Wages and Separation

What is the relation of wage policy to turnover? The theory of specific human capital (Becker 1962; Oi 1962) establishes one mechanism for thinking about the issue. Another, different approach comes from the information literature. In papers by Greenwald (1986), Waldman (1984), Lazear (1986b), and Gibbons and Katz (1991), the adverse selection problem is analyzed.

For example, Greenwald extends Akerlof's (1970) lemons model to the labor market, arguing that individuals who are in the pool of unemployed are lower quality on average because they got there either by bad luck, or by being bad workers. Gibbons and Katz (1991) are in the same spirit.

Lazear examines turnover that does not transit through unemployment. Many workers have another job lined up before they leave the first. It is shown that turnover of this sort will be concentrated among the higher quality workers who have a comparative advantage at the new firm. Because of the raider's fear of the winner's curse (i.e., only succeeding in getting those workers who turn out to be low quality), outside firms raid only when they have information about a worker's superior fit in the raiding firm.

Waldman (1990) and Milgrom and Oster (1987) push the argument that promotions and job descriptions may provide outsiders with information that could lead to cherry picking. As a result, workers are assigned inefficiently to lower job titles to reduce the likelihood of a raid by outside firms.

Jobs

What is a job and what role does it play in economic analyses of the labor market? The idea of a job is absent from standard production theory, but some of the newer theories have given specific content to what most personnel people think of as a fundamental unit of analysis.[38]

The traditional, more institutional view emphasizes the job as the unit of analysis. Although there is some recognition that skills affect the placement of an employee in a particular slot, this view tends to assert that workers can be substituted for one another and that the allocation of individuals to jobs generally reflects luck or other factors.[39] The literature that most forcefully advances this view deals with internal labor markets.[40]

The other view, dominant since the 1960s, derives from the theory of human capital.[41] This view focuses on the supply-side approach, arguing that workers invest in productivity-enhancing skills, which they bring into the labor market. The job is unimportant. Wages and lifetime wealth are determined primarily by the individual's stock of human capital, although psychic aspects of the job (e.g., danger, dirtiness, undesirable work hours) are also admitted to affect monetary compensation. Occupation and industry variables play a secondary role in this theory. There is evidence to suggest that jobs are often tailored to the individual at high levels in the firm's hierarchy. Jobs are created, for example, to accommodate former CEOs when a new person steps into the job.[42]

The new theories do prescribe roles for jobs. In the tournament model, a job is a name for a wage category. Wages are assigned to the slots, not to the individuals. The reason for doing this is that appropriate incentive effects are generated by relative comparisons.

Indeed, it is the existence of fixed slots that distinguishes tournament incentive structures from others based on relative performance. One reason for using a tournament is to difference out random factors or common noise. But tournaments are not the only way to eliminate the effects of common noise. For example, paying workers on the basis of their performance relative to the group mean eliminates common noise. This scheme differs from the tournament, however, in that tournaments imply slots, whereas relative pay by itself does not. With tournaments, only one individual gets the first prize or top job. One and only one gets the second prize or second-best job, and so forth. With relative compensation, the structure of wages and positions evolves *ex post*, rather than *ex ante*. Tournament models emphasize relative performance, but also rely on jobs per se.

Jobs are at the center of any discussion of insurance and worksharing. Firms may reduce hours during downturns without eliminating jobs (if only through variations in overtime), but layoffs are still an accepted part of the American work environment. Thus, a job may be defined as the right to work in a given state of the economy. Reducing employment by reducing the number of heads means that there must be a fixed cost, either in production or in leisure, that makes it preferable to set up jobs of fixed length and vary the number of them according to the state of the economy. This means that although the number of slots varies with economic conditions, slots have a well-defined meaning.

The literature on hierarchies and on the structure of control in organizations is inherently cast in terms of jobs. The hierarchy analyses are explicit in their use of jobs. Most assume that each position has a span of control over a fixed number of other positions. Thus, the shape of the pyramid is determined *ex ante*, although the size of the firm, the number of levels, and the quality of the work force are endogenous.

Contemporary theories of control in organizations also assume that slots are crucial. Here the question is whether projects should be evaluated in a vertical or horizontal manner. In a vertical organization, only projects accepted at lower levels are evaluated by more senior individuals. But seniority implies that the job, rather than the incumbent, defines the activity.

Hedonic wage analysis also dignifies the concept of jobs.[43] Proponents of this school of thought have emphasized the importance of the characteristics of the job. The focus is not on the skills or attributes of the individual, but rather on the attributes of the position itself. For example, some jobs have more variable employment schedules than others. It is well known that durables manufacturing is more procyclic than health care. Layoffs are not high in manufacturing because the individuals who work there enjoy losing their jobs. Layoff rates are high as a result of demand conditions that pertain to the industry and that consequently dictate the duration of jobs in the industry.

Similarly, jobs with significant safety hazards tend to pay higher wages as a compensation differential.[44] The higher wages are attached to the jobs because the jobs themselves are risky, not because the workers who hold them are clumsy. The hedonic wage literature is thus the best example of empirical analysis that focuses on the characteristics of jobs rather than workers.

This approach has permeated the business community as well. Some consulting firms place a great deal of emphasis on jobs and their characteristics. Their surveys and resulting salary recommendations adjust for the skill requirements, technical know-how, accountability, and pleasantness of work associated with a given job. Although the incumbent may help to define the job, such analyses are targeted at deciding the salary appropriate to the position, rather than to the individual who holds it.

Even human capital theory offers a role for the concept of a job. Some jobs offer more opportunity for advancement than others. In some fields, young workers spend a great deal of time and effort acquiring human capital, which makes them more productive in later work years. In other fields, human capital is less important. One way to define jobs is by the technological investment opportunities available to workers. There are different career paths, but the opportunity for investment is fixed in advance, with the workers assigned to those paths determined in some maximizing fashion.[45] Unlike other theories that deal with job structures, human capital theory does not assert that the number of slots must be fixed in advance. If more investors show up at the door during any given period, this theory assumes that the firm can accommodate them by creating more investment-type positions. Jobs dictate, *ex ante*, the amount of investment that the incumbent undertakes. Individuals can choose the amount that they invest only by choosing the appropriate job.

One interpretation is that the human-capital investment opportunity is one of the characteristics of the job that enter the hedonic wage function. An alternative view is that jobs are unimportant in determining how much investment occurs. Workers simply alter the amount of time that they spend investing and working to suit their optimal investment profile, irrespective of job assignment.

The final interpretation of a job is the most traditional one. A job can be defined as a collection of tasks. The tasks need not be hierarchical, nor need they be compensated in any particular way. In this sense, a job is defined as a partition of the firm's technology. Recently, Hölmstrom and Milgrom (1990) have attempted to make endogenous the tasks associated with a particular job.

Conclusion

Personnel analysts have a great deal to say about turnover, wage setting, incentives, organizational structure, and other issues that involve the internal labor market. But economists have contributed in a fundamental and new way to the literature and are beginning to alter the way that practitioners think about these problems. The older approaches probably lend themselves better to description and taxonomy. The new economics of personnel is rougher as a descriptive tool, but probably better as a rigorous conceptual framework on which prediction and normative prescription can be based. There is no reason why the two literatures cannot complement one another.

Acknowledgments

This work was supported in part by the National Science Foundation. Research assistance by Edward Glaeser and Katherine Ierulli is gratefully acknowledged.

Endnotes

[1] Much of what follows is based on Lazear (1986).

[2] I.e., $C', C'' > 0$.

[3] Whether the firm gets all the rent, as it would were it to set s to make the worker indifferent, or whether the worker gets the rent depends on whether there is a perfectly elastic supply of workers or of firms.

[4] See Hölmstrom (1979) and Stiglitz (1975).

[5] Alchian and Demsetz (1972) were among the first to discuss the effect of monitoring costs on the organization of the firm and its compensation structure.

[6] See Fama (1991) for a discussion of the difference between hourly wages and weekly, monthly or annual salaries.

[7] Fogel and Engerman (1989) make the same argument with respect to slaves in their controversial book.

[8] See Johnson (1950) and Cheung (1969) for an analysis of sharecropping and the effort issues involved.

[9] See Lazear (1986a).

[10] See Baker, Jensen, and Murphy (1988a).

[11] See also Dearden, Ickes, and Samuelson (1990).

[12] Akerlof and Katz (1989) examine the difference between upward sloping age-earnings profiles and a formal up-front bond. In the absence of an up-front bond, they argue that some efficiency-wage-style unemployment is associated with the second-best compensation profile.

[13] See Lazear (1983).

[14] See Lazear and Moore (1988).

[15] In the military context, Lakhani (1988) finds that departure rates were affected by the pay level and the size of the reenlistment bonus offered.

[16] One other explanation of upward sloping age-earnings profiles has been offered by Loewenstein and Sicherman (1991). They argue that individuals have a preference for delayed gratification in a work environment. This runs counter to general notions of positive time preference. They provide some experimental evidence for their claim.

[17] There is now an extensive literature on tournaments. The model was first presented in Lazear and Rosen (1981) and was extended by Nalebuff and Stiglitz (1983) to consider more general production functions and to delineate some of the advantages of using tournaments over piece rates. Green and Stokey (1983) show the dominance of nonlinear price rate schemes when risk aversion is the primary consideration. O'Keeffe, Viscusi, and Zeckhauser (1984) argue that it is sometimes helpful to change the noise associated with a contest.

[18] In reality, it is total compensation, including nonpecuniary components, that is relevant for this calculation.

[19] O'Reilly, Main, and Crystal (1988) test the theory using data from major corporations. Their findings are somewhat mixed.

[20] See Dye (1984).

[21] See Lazear (1989).

[22] See Knoeber (1989).

[23] Varian (1990) argues that Japanese society traditionally had very strong clan links which may be useful in creating team spirit.

[24] Much of this material derives from Kandel and Lazear (1992).

[25] In addition to Kandel and Lazear (1992), Hollander (1990) speaks to this set of issues. Jones (1984) invokes an asymmetry in order to explain why there is pressure to conform. Low-effort workers depress the size of the pie, but have little effect on the compensation schedule. High-effort workers have a greater effect on the standard by which the wage is set. There is pressure, therefore, to avoid working too hard. More recently Bernheim (1991) models conformism as analogous to altruism. In altruism, an individual cares about other individuals. With conformism, an individual cares about how he enters others' utility function.

[26] Arnott and Stiglitz (1991) emphasize the potential role that peer relationships can play in mutual monitoring. But as Kandel and Lazear (1992) argue, the conditions under which incentives for mutual monitoring are effective may not be present in many organizations.

[27] The injustice that a worker feels when others shirk is described by Frey (1991) and is quite close to the Hölmstrom (1982) mechanism.

[28] See Lazear (1991).

[29] Lambert and Larcker (1987) focus on differences between the relation of executive compensation to accounting versus market measures of performance.

[30] Akerlof (1984) discusses a number of reasons why firms may pay efficiency wages. Some, although not all, rely on incentives. The following discussion pertains more closely to those that focus on incentives. Bulow and Summers (1986) have a later paper that draws out a number of implications from the initial model.

[31] Lazear (1979).

[32] This ignores the unlikely situation of multiple optima.

[33] Waldman (1990) modifies their model to examine up-or-out even when specific human capital is not present. His explanation relies on information that is conveyed to other employers through the up-or-out decision.

[34] One of the author's employers, the Hoover Institution, does exactly that. But Hoover's practices are rare in academics and in other fields as well. Generally law firms that have up-or-out promotion also grant "tenure" to those who make it to partner. In recent years, this is somewhat less true.

[35] The U.S. military has up-or-out without tenure. Soldiers who do not get promoted are forced to leave, but those who do get promoted are not guaranteed lifetime or even long-term employment.

[36] A Groves (1973) scheme, which makes all workers residual claimants, would provide appropriate incentives to select high-quality employees, even in the absence of tenure.

[37] Calvo and Wellisz (1978), who emphasize the monitoring role of supervisors and the span of control, also fit into this literature.

[38] The next section is taken almost directly from Lazear (1992).

[39] These factors may include race, sex, ethnic background, and family ties.

[40] See, for example, Doeringer and Piore (1971), Thurow (1972), and Reder (1955).

[41] The major references here are Becker (1962, 1975) and Mincer (1962).

[42] See Murphy (1985).

[43] Rosen (1974).

[44] See Antos and Rosen (1975).

[45] This is the approach used in Lazear and Rosen (1990) to examine male-female wage differences. There, the investment profiles of jobs are determined *ex ante*, although the number of individuals assigned to each type is endogenous.

References

Abowd, John M. "Does Performance-Based Compensation Affect Subsequent Corporate Performance?" ILR-Cornell Research Conference on Compensation Policies, May 1989. ILRR 43 (February 1990), pp. 52s-73s.

Abowd, John, and Orley Ashenfelter. "Anticipated Unemployment, Temporary Layoffs, and Compensating Wage Differentials." In *Studies in Labor Markets*, ed. Sherwin Rosen. Chicago: University of Chicago Press for NBER, 1981.

Akerlof, George. "The Market for 'Lemons': Quality Uncertainty and the Market Mechanism," *Quarterly Journal of Economics* 84 (August 1970), pp. 488-500.

________. "Gift Exchange and Efficiency Wage Theory: Four Views." *American Economic Review* 74 (May 1984), pp. 79-83.

Akerlof, George A., and Lawrence F. Katz. "Workers' Trust Funds and the Logic of Wage Profiles." *Quarterly Journal of Economics* 104 (August 1987), pp. 525-36.

Alchian, Armen A., and Harold Demsetz. "Production, Information Costs, and Economic Organization." *American Economic Review* 62 (December 1972), pp. 777-95.

Antle, Rick, and Abbie Smith. "An Empirical Investigation into the Relative Performance Evaluation of Corporate Executives." *Journal of Accounting Research* 24 (Spring 1986), pp. 1-39.

Antos, Joseph R., and Sherwin Rosen. "Discrimination in the Market for Public School Teachers." *Journal of Econometrics* 3 (May 1975), pp. 123-50.

Arnot, Richard, and Joseph E. Stiglitz. "Moral Hazard and Nonmarket Institutions: Dysfunctional Crowding Out or Peer Monitoring." *American Economic Review* 81 (March 1991), pp. 179-90.

Baker, George. "Incentive Contracts and Performance Measurement." *Journal of Political Economy* 100, 3 (June 1992), pp. 598-614.

Baker, George P., Michael C. Jensen, and Kevin J. Murphy. "Compensation and Incentives: Practice vs. Theory." *Journal of Finance* 43 (July 1988), pp. 593-616.

Becker, Gary S. "Investment in Human Capital: A Theoretical Analysis." *Journal of Political Economy* 70 (October 1962), pp. 9-49.

________. *Human Capital: A Theoretical and Empirical Analysis, with Special Reference to Education*, 2nd ed. New York: Columbia University Press for National Bureau of Economic Research, 1975.

Becker, Gary S., and George J. Stigler. "Law Enforcement, Malfeasance, and Compensation of Enforcers." *Journal of Legal Studies* 3 (January 1974), pp. 1-18.

Benelli, Giuseppe, Claudio Loderer, and Thomas Lys. "Labor Participation in Corporate Policymaking Decisions: West Germany's Experience with Codetermination." *Journal of Business* 60 (October 1987), pp. 553-75.

Bergson, Abram. "Managerial Risks and Rewards in Public Enterprises." *Journal of Comparative Economics* 2 (September 1978), pp. 211-25.

Bernheim, B. Douglas. "A Theory of Conformity." Princeton University, July 1991.

Bull, Clive, Andrew Schotter, and Keith Weigelt. "Tournaments and Piece Rates: An Experimental Study." *Journal of Political Economy* 95 (February 1987), pp. 1-33.

Bulow, Jeremy I., and Lawrence H. Summers. "A Theory of Dual Labor Markets with Application to Industry Policy, Discrimination, and Keynesian Unemployment." *Journal of Labor Economics* 4 (July 1986), pp. 376-414.

Calvo, Guillermo, and Stanislaw Wellisz. "Supervision, Loss of Control, and Optimum Size of the Firm." *Journal of Political Economy* 86 (October 1978), pp. 943-52.

Carmichael, H. Lorne. "Firm Specific Human Capital and Promotion Ladders." *Bell's Journal of Economics* 14 (Spring 1983), pp. 251-8.

________. "Can Unemployment Be Involuntary?: Comment." *American Economic Review* 75 (December 1985), pp. 1213-14.

________. "Incentives in Academics: Why Is There Tenure?" *Journal of Political Economy* 96 (June 1988), pp. 453-72.

________. "Self-Enforcing Contracts, Shirking, and Life Cycle Incentives." *Journal of Economic Perspectives* 3 (Fall 1989), pp. 65-83.

Cheung, Steven N. S. *The Theory of Share Tenancy: With Special Application to Asian Agriculture and the First Phase of Taiwan Land Reform*. Chicago: University of Chicago Press, 1969.

Deardon, James, Barry W. Ickes, and Larry W. Samuelson. "To Innovate or Not To Innovate: Incentives and Innovation in Hierarchies." *American Economic Review* 80 (December 1990), pp. 1105-24.

Deckop, John R. "Determinants of Chief Executive Officer Compensation." *Industrial and Labor Relations Review* 41 (January 1988), pp. 215-26.

Doeringer, Peter, and Michael Piore. *Internal Labor Markets and Manpower Analysis*. Lexington, MA: D.C. Heath, 1971.

Dye, Ronald. "The Trouble with Tournaments." *Economic Inquiry* 22 (January 1984), pp. 147-9.

Ehrenberg, Ronald G., and Michael L. Bognanno. "Do Tournaments Have Incentive Effects?" *Journal of Political Economy* 98 (December 1990), pp. 1307-24.

Fama, Eugene F. "Agency Problems and the Theory of the Firm." *Journal of Political Economy* (April 1980), pp. 288-307.

________. "Time, Salary, and Incentive Payoffs in Labor Contracts." *Journal of Labor Economics* 9 (January 1991), pp. 25-44.

Farrell, Joseph, and Suzanne Scotchmer. "Partnerships." *Quarterly Journal of Economics* 103 (May 1988), pp. 279-97.

Fogel, Robert William, and Stanley L. Engerman. *Time on the Cross: The Economics of American Negro Slavery*. New York: W. W. Norton, 1989.

Frank, Robert H. *Choosing the Right Pond: The Economics and Politics of the Quest for Status*. New York: Oxford University Press, 1985.

Frey, Bruno. "Monitoring and Crowding Out Work Morale." University of Chicago, 1991.

Gaynor, Martin, and Mark V. Pauly. "Compensation and Productive Efficiency in Partnerships: Evidence from Medical Group Practice." *Journal of Political Economy* 98 (June 1990), pp. 544-73.

Gibbons, Robert. "Piece-Rate Incentive Schemes." *Journal of Labor Economics* 5 (October 1987), pp. 413-29.

Gibbons, Robert, and Lawrence F. Katz. "Layoffs and Lemons." *Journal of Labor Economics* 9 (October 1991), pp. 351-80.

Gibbons, Robert, and Kevin J. Murphy. "Relative Performance Evaluation for Chief Executive Officers." *Industrial and Labor Relations Review* 43 (February 1990), pp. 30S-51S.

Gilson, R., and R. Mnookin. "Sharing among the Human Capitalists: An Economic Inquiry into the Corporate Law Firm and How Partners Split Profits." *Stanford Law Review* 37 (January 1985), pp. 313-97.
Goldin, Claudia. "Monitoring Costs and Occupational Segregation by Sex: A Historical Analysis." *Journal of Labor Economics* 4 (January 1986), pp. 1-27.
Gordon, David M. "Who Bosses Whom? The Intensity of Supervision and the Discipline of Labor." *American Economic Review* 80 (May 1990), pp. 28-32.
Green, Jerry R., and Nancy L. Stokey. "A Comparison of Tournaments and Contracts." *Journal of Political Economy* 91 (June 1983), pp. 349-64.
Greenwald, Bruce C. "Adverse Selection in the Labor Market." *Review of Economic Studies* 53 (July 1986), pp. 325-47.
Groves, Theodore. "Incentives in Teams." *Econometrica* 41 (May 1973), pp. 617-31.
Hall, Robert E., and Edward Lazear. "The Excess Sensitivity of Layoffs and Quits to Demand." *Journal of Labor Economics* 2 (April 1984), pp. 233-57.
Harris, Milton, and Bengt Hölmstrom. "A Theory of Wage Dynamics." *Review of Economic Studies* 49 (July 1982), pp. 315-33.
Hashimoto, Masanori, and Ben Yu. "Specific Capital, Employment Contracts, and Wage Rigidity." *Bell Journal of Economics* (Autumn 1980), pp. 536-49.
Hollander, Heinz. "A Social Exchange Approach to Voluntary Cooperation." *American Economic Review* 80 (December 1990), pp. 1157-67.
Hölmstrom, Bengt. "Moral Hazard and Observability." *Bell Journal of Economics* 10 (Spring 1979), pp. 74-91.
________. "Moral Hazard in Teams." *Bell Journal of Economics* 13 (Autumn 1982), pp. 324-40.
Hölmstrom, Bengt, and Paul Milgrom. "Multi-Task Principal-Agent Problems Analyses." Yale School of Organization and Management, Series D, Working Paper 45, May 1990.
Hutchens, Robert M. "A Test of Lazear's Theory of Delayed Payment Contracts." *Journal of Labor Economics* 5 (October 1987), pp. S153-S170.
________. "Seniority, Wages and Productivity: A Turbulent Decade." *Journal of Economic Perspectives* 3 (Fall 1989), pp. 49-64.
Ickes, Barry W., and Larry Samuelson. "Job Transfers and Incentives in Complex Organizations: Thwarting the Ratchet Effect." *RAND Journal of Economics* 18 (Summer 1987), pp. 275-86.
Ippolito, Richard A. "Why Federal Workers Don't Quit." *Journal of Human Resources* 22 (Spring 1987), pp. 281-89.
Jackson, Matthew, and Edward P. Lazear. "Stock, Options, and Deferred Compensation." *Research in Labor Economics*, vol. 12, ed. Ron Ehrenberg, Greenwich, CT: JAI Press, 1991, pp. 41-62.
Jensen, Michael C., and Kevin J. Murphy. "Performance Pay and Top-Management Incentives." *Journal of Political Economy* 98 (April 1990), pp. 225-64.
Johnson, D. Gale. "Resource Allocation Under Share Contracts." *Journal of Political Economy* 58 (1950), pp. 111-23.
Johnson, William R. "The Social Efficiency of Fixed Wages." *Quarterly Journal of Economics* 100 (February 1985), pp. 101-18.
Jones, Stephen R. G. *The Economics of Conformism*. Oxford: Basil Blackwell, 1984.
Kahn, Charles, and Gur Huberman. "Two-sided Uncertainty and 'Up-or-Out' Contracts." *Journal of Labor Economics* 6 (October 1988), pp. 423-45.
Kandel, Eugene, and Edward P. Lazear. "Peer Pressure and Partnerships." *Journal of Political Economy*, 100 (August 1992), pp. 801-17.
Kennan, John. "Bonding and the Enforcement of Labor Contracts." *Economics Letters* 3 (1979), pp. 61-66.
Knoeber, Charles R. "A Real Game of Chicken: Contracts, Tournaments, and the Production of Broilers." *Journal of Law, Economics & Organization* 5 (Fall 1989), pp. 271-92.
Kostiuk, Peter F. "Firm Size and Executive Compensation." *Journal of Human Resources* 25 (Winter 1990), pp. 90-105.
Lakhani, Hyder. "The Effect of Pay and Retention Bonuses on Quit Rates in the U.S. Army." *Industrial and Labor Relations Review* 41 (April 1988), pp. 430-38.

Lambert, Richard A., and David F. Larcker. "An Analysis of the Use of Accounting and Market Measures of Performance in Executive Compensation Contracts." *Journal of Accounting Research* 25 (Supplement, 1987), pp. 85-125.
Lazear, Edward P. "Why Is There Mandatory Retirement?" *Journal of Political Economy* 87 (December 1979), pp. 1261-64.
________. "Agency, Earnings Profiles, Productivity, and Hours Restrictions." *American Economic Review* 71 (September 1981), pp. 606-20.
________. "Pensions as Severance Pay." In *Financial Aspects of the U.S. Pension System*, a National Bureau of Economic Research Project Report, eds. Zvi Bodie and John Shoven, Chicago: University of Chicago Press, 1983.
________. "Salaries and Piece Rates." *Journal of Business* 59 (July 1986a), pp. 405-31.
________. "Raids and Offer-Matching." In *Research in Labor Economics* Vol. 8, ed. Ron Ehrenberg, Greenwich, CT: JAI Press, 1986b.
________. "Pay Equality and Industrial Politics." *Journal of Political Economy* 97 (June 1989), pp. 561-80.
________. "The Timing of Raises and Other Payments." *Carnegie-Rochester Conference Series on Public Policy* 33 (Autumn 1990), pp. 13-48.
________. "Labor Economics and the Psychology of Organizations." *Journal of Economic Perspectives* 5 (Spring 1991), pp. 89-110.
________. "The Job as a Concept." In *Performance Measurement and Incentive Compensation*, ed. William J. Bruns, Jr. Cambridge: Harvard Business School Press, 1992.
Lazear, Edward P., and Robert L. Moore. "Pensions and Turnover." In *Issues in Pension Economics*, eds. J. Shoven, Z. Bodie, and D. Wise. Chicago: University of Chicago Press for NBER, 1988.
Lazear, Edward P., and Sherwin Rosen. "Male-Female Wage Differentials in Job Ladders." *Journal of Labor Economics* 8 (part 2, January 1990), pp. S106-S123.
________. "Rank-Order Tournaments as Optimum Labor Contracts." *Journal of Political Economy* 89 (October 1981), pp. 841-64.
Lee, Tom K., and I.P.L. Png. "The Role of Installment Payments in Contracts for Services." *RAND Journal of Economics* 21 (Spring 1990), pp. 83-99.
Leonard, Jonathan S. "Executive Pay and Firm Performance." *Industrial and Labor Relations Review* 43 (Special Issue, February 1990), pp. 13s-29s.
Loewenstein, George, and Nachum Sicherman. "Do Workers Prefer Increasing Wage Profiles?" *Journal of Labor Economics* 9 (January 1991), pp. 67-84.
MacLeod, Bentley, and James M. Malcomson. "Reputation and Hierarchy in Dynamic Models of Employment." *Journal of Political Economy* 96 (August 1988), pp. 832-58.
Mayer, Thomas. "The Distribution of Ability and Earnings." *Review of Economics and Statistics* 62 (February 1960), pp. 189-95.
Milgrom, Paul R. "Employment Contracts, Influence Activities, and Efficient Organization Design." *Journal of Political Economy* 96 (February 1988), pp. 42-60.
Milgrom, Paul, and Oster, Sharon. "Job Discrimination, Market Forces, and the Invisibility Hypothesis." *Quarterly Journal of Economics* 102 (August 1987), pp. 453-76.
Miller, Frederick H. "Wages and Establishment Sizes." Ph.D. dissertation, University of Chicago, 1982.
Miller, Merton, and Myron Scholes. "Executive Compensation, Taxes and Incentives." In *Financial Economics: Essays in Honor of Paul Cottner*, eds. William F. Sharpe and Cathryn M. Cottner. Englewood Cliffs, NJ: Prentice-Hall, 1982.
Mincer, Jacob. "On-the-Job Training: Costs, Returns, and Some Implications." *Journal of Political Economy* 70 (October 1962), pp. S50-S79.
Murphy, Kevin J. "Corporate Performance and Managerial Remuneration: An Empirical Analysis." *Journal of Accounting and Economics* 7 (April 1985), pp. 11-42.
Nalebuff, Barry J., and Joseph E. Stiglitz. "Prizes and Incentives: Toward a General Theory of Compensation and Competition." *Bell Journal of Economics* 14 (Spring 1983), pp. 21-43.

Nitzan, Shmuel, and Ariel Pakes. "Optimum Contracts for Research Personnel, Research Employment, and the Establishment of Rival Enterprises." *Journal of Labor Economics* 1 (October 1983), pp. 345-65.

Oi, Walter Y. "Labor as a Quasi-fixed Factor." *Journal of Political Economy* 70 (1962), pp. 538-56.

O'Keeffe, Mary, W. Kip Viscusi, and Richard J. Zeckhauser. "Economic Contests: Comparative Reward Schemes." *Journal of Labor Economics* 2 (January 1984), pp. 27-56.

O'Reilly, Charles, Brian Main, and Graef Crystal. "CEO Compensation as Tournament and Social Comparison: A Tale of Two Theories." *Administrative Science Quarterly* 33 (June 1988), pp. 257-74.

Parsons, Donald. "Specific Human Capital: Layoffs and Quits." *Journal of Political Economy* 80 (November 1972), pp. 1120-43.

Pergamit, Michael. "Wages and Employment in Regulated Industries." Ph.D. dissertation, University of Chicago, 1983.

Raff, Daniel M. G., and Lawrence H. Summers. "Did Henry Ford Pay Efficiency Wages?" *Journal of Labor Economics* 5 (October 1987), pp. S57-D86.

Reder, Melvin W. "Theory of Occupational Wage Differentials." *American Economic Review* 45 (December 1955), pp. 833-52.

Rosen, Sherwin. "Hedonic Prices and Implicit Markets: Product Differentiation in Pure Competition." *Journal of Political Economy* 82 (January/February 1974), pp. 34-55.

________. "Authority, Control, and the Distribution of Earnings." *Bell Journal of Economics* 13 (October 1982), pp. 311-23.

________. "Prizes and Incentives in Elimination Tournaments." *American Economic Review* 76 (September 1986), pp. 701-15.

Ross, Stephen A. "The Economic Theory of Agency: The Principal's Problem." *American Economic Review* 63 (May 1973), pp. 134-39.

Sah, Raaj Kumar, and Joseph E. Stiglitz."The Architecture of Economic Systems: Hierarchies and Polyarchies." *American Economic Review* 76 (September 1986), pp. 716-27.

Scholes, Myron, and Mark Wolfson. *Taxes and Business Strategy: A Planning Approach*. Englewood Cliffs, NJ: Prentice-Hall, 1992.

Shapiro, Carl, and Joseph E. Stiglitz. "Equilibrium Unemployment as a Worker Discipline Device." *American Economic Review* 74 (1984), pp. 433-44.

Stiglitz, Joseph E. "The Theory of 'Screening', Education, and the Distribution of Income." *American Economic Review* 65 (June 1975), pp. 283-300.

Stock, James H., and David A. Wise. "Pension, the Option Value of Work, and Retirement." *Econometrica* 58 (September 1990), pp. 1151-80.

Thurow, Lester. "Education and Economic Equality." *Public Interest* 28 (Summer 1972), pp. 66-81.

Varian, Hal R. "Monitoring Agents with Other Agents." *Journal of Institutional and Theoretical Economics* 146 (March 1990), pp. 153-74.

Waldman, Michael. "Job Assignments, Signalling, and Efficiency." *RAND Journal of Economics* 15 (Summer 1984), pp. 255-67.

________. "Up-or-Out Contracts: A Signaling Perspective." *Journal of Labor Economics* 8 (April 1990), pp. 230-50.

Weiss, Andrew. *Efficiency Wages: Models of Unemployment, Layoffs, and Wage Dispersion*. Princeton: Princeton University Press, 1990.

Weiss, Leonard. "Concentration and Labor Earnings." *American Economic Review* (March 1966), pp. 96-117.

CHAPTER 11

Race and Gender Pay Differentials

FRANCINE D. BLAU
University of Illinois and NBER

LAWRENCE M. KAHN
University of Illinois

In the 1980s, trends in race and gender pay differentials in the United States diverged notably from previous patterns. This is illustrated in Figures 1 and 2 which show respectively race and gender ratios in weekly earnings for full-time wage and salary workers for the 1967-90 period. The story told by these figures is striking. Specifically, after a steady reduction of racial pay differences from the passage of the Civil Rights Act of 1964 through the late 1970s, black-white wage differentials stopped narrowing and have even widened in some instances.[1] On the other hand, after decades of near constancy at about 60 percent through the 1970s, the female-male pay ratio began to rise at the end of the decade.

Explaining these new trends has been an important focus of research on race and gender pay differentials in the 1980s and early 1990s. The analysis of competing explanations for these trends in the 1980s is the unifying theme of our review of recent industrial relations research in this field. In our survey of this work, we have found several areas where researchers have focused their efforts.

First, an innovative feature of recent research has been to integrate the analysis of race and gender pay gaps into the study of the wage structure in general. Much of this work finds increasing overall wage inequality in the 1980s, and many of the reasons for this trend also affect race and gender wage differentials.[2] In such work researchers have often studied supply and demand factors as potential explanations of changing pay gaps. In addition, institutional changes such as the decline in unionism have been proposed as important causes of relative wage trends.

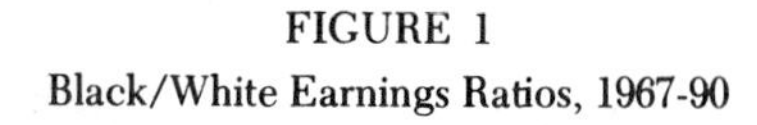

FIGURE 1
Black/White Earnings Ratios, 1967-90

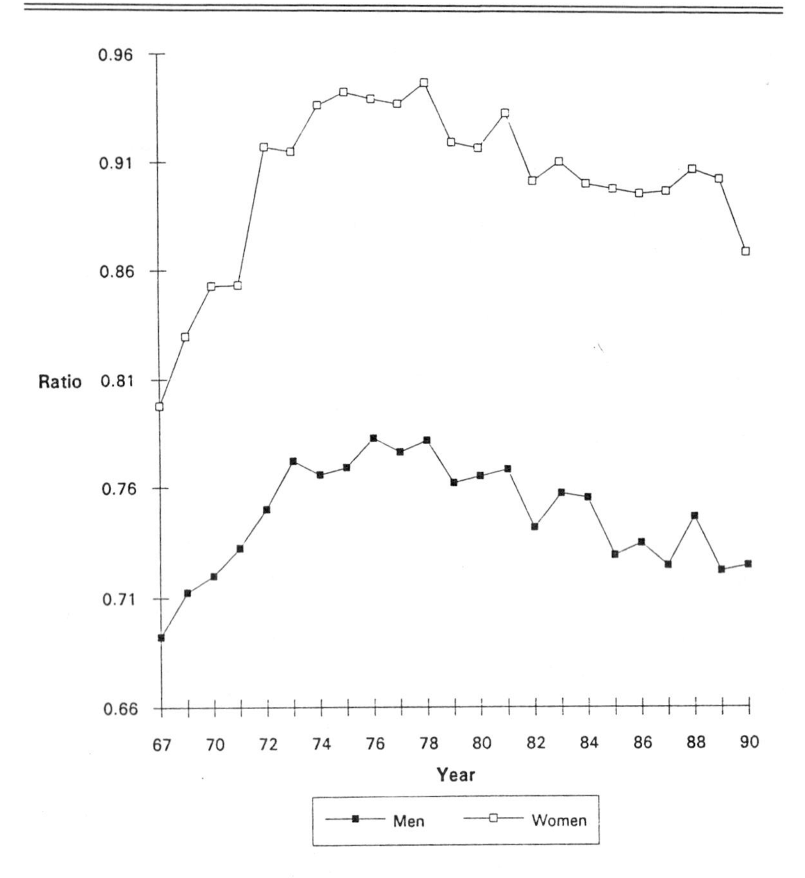

Second, changes in the composition of the labor force have been a focus of several papers. In this regard researchers have attempted to gauge changes in the relative productivity of labor market participants from various groups.

Third, a large body of literature has examined the impact of government policy on pay gaps. Such policies range from the enforcement of equal employment opportunity laws and affirmative action requirements for government contractors to the implementation of comparable worth-based pay adjustments. International comparisons in such analyses are particularly useful since labor market policies differ substantially across countries.

FIGURE 2
Male/Female Earnings Ratios, 1967-90

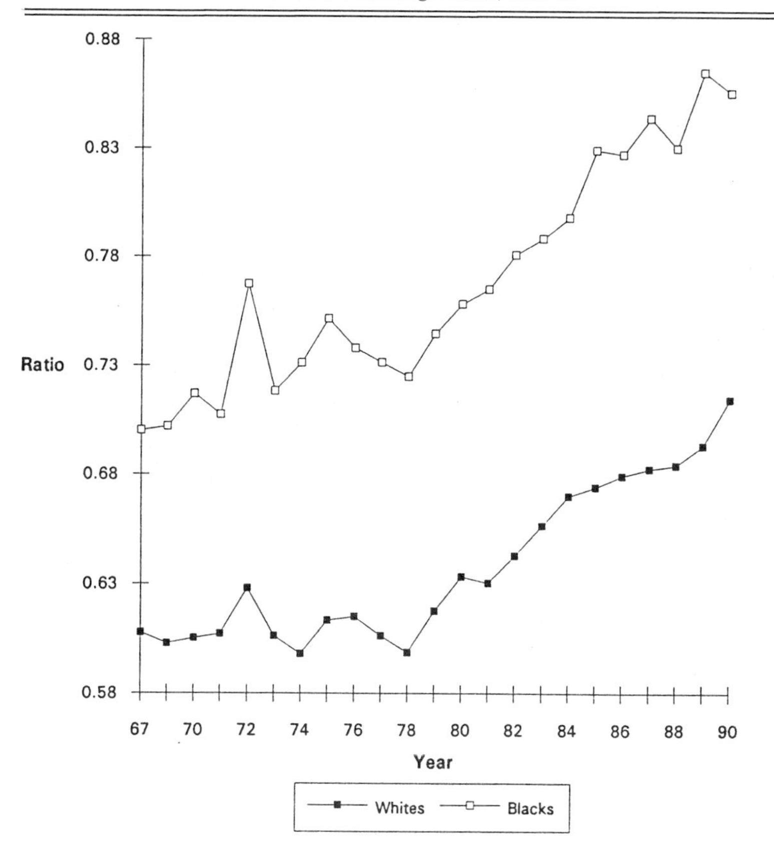

While much of the industrial relations research on race and gender in the 1980s and early 1990s has concentrated on these substantive, empirical issues, theoretical and methodological concerns have also received some attention. In particular Becker's (1957) seminal theory of labor market discrimination has been refined in several ways, as economists have examined the issue of the persistence of discrimination. Further, the problem of measuring workers' productivity-related characteristics has important implications for the interpretation of race and gender wage differentials. Much empirical work in this area has found improved productivity measures, and some statistical research has proposed methods to use when such measures are lacking.[3] In this chapter we first briefly summarize these developments and then turn to our major focus, a review of empirical work aimed at explaining the recent trends in race and gender differentials.

After reviewing these themes of research in the 1980s and early 1990s and presenting some data that bear on specific unanswered questions, we offer suggestions for future work on race and gender differences in labor market outcomes. Some of our prescriptions are primarily methodological, while others call for better integration of race and gender research with recent developments in the analysis of labor markets.

Theoretical and Econometric Advances in the Analysis of Discrimination

Becker's (1957) model of discrimination predicted that competition would erode many forms of discrimination. For example, suppose that employers or coworkers were prejudiced against blacks. If there were some nondiscriminating firms, free entry, and constant returns to scale, then competition would undermine the position of firms paying whites a wage premium. The nondiscriminators would have lower costs and would thus increase their market shares. This competitive pressure would either drive the discriminators out of business or force them to maximize profits by ending their discriminatory practices. This reasoning would imply that under competition, observed race or gender wage differentials could not be due to discrimination. A corollary of this analysis is that discrimination should be less prevalent in competitive than in monopolistic or oligopolistic markets.[4]

Some research in the 1980s has attempted to devise models in which discrimination can persist even under competition. The implication of such models is that race and gender wage differentials could still at least in part reflect discrimination even if there were competition. We thus cannot rely on competition to eliminate the effects of prejudice.

First, Goldberg (1982) argues that prejudice may result from a positive preference for whites or men rather than an aversion to women or minorities. If this is true, then discriminating firms willingly earn below normal profits and are compensated by employing members of their favored groups. Prejudiced and nonprejudiced firms can coexist even with competition.

Second, Lundberg and Startz (1983) extend an imperfect information model first introduced by Aigner and Cain (1977). In this model, firms can more easily predict the performance of whites or men than of minorities or women. In such a world, firms offer different wage schedules to, say, whites and blacks: the white wage-education schedule is steeper, reflecting the more accurate predictions of productivity for this group.[5] Workers then respond to their own wage schedule: whites invest more in education than blacks. Thus, differential treatment results in differential investment in a self-fulfilling prophecy.[6] In Lundberg and Startz's (1983) view, only a government policy outlawing the separate wage schedules can eliminate the pay gap. Competition will not suffice.

Third, some authors have focused on the idea of customer prejudice as leading to discrimination that will not be eroded by competition. Customer prejudice differs from firm or coworker prejudice in that the buyer places a different valuation on the identical output of, say, whites and minorities. Cain (1986) questions the argument that customer discrimination will result in pay differentials. In his view, if there is customer discrimination, then blacks will only take jobs in the sector with no producer-consumer contact; occupational differences will result, but not a pay gap.

However, Borjas and Bronars (1989) show that in a world with imperfect information and search costs, customer prejudice can lead to long-run, discriminatory wage gaps. Evidence from the incomes of the self-employed (who must necessarily deal directly with consumers) is consistent with this model of customer discrimination (Borjas and Bronars 1989). Further, Kahn (1991a) argues that customer prejudice can lead to discriminatory wage gaps if the customer-prejudice sector is large or if minorities have a comparative advantage in such sectors. Evidence from a variety of professional sports confirms the presence of customer discrimination in that sector of the entertainment industry (Kahn 1991b).

While the continued existence of race and gender earnings gaps has prompted some interesting new models seeking to explain how discrimination can persist in the face of competitive pressures, other theoretical developments have taken a different tack, seeking to explain why men and women with similar measured characteristics might not in fact be perfect substitutes. In particular, two recent papers have focused on the division of labor within the family, originally identified by Mincer and Polachek (1974) as an important factor in influencing male-female differences in human capital investments. Becker (1985) developed a model in which married women's lower pay and occupational attainment are due to the lesser effort they expend on their jobs due to their responsibility for child care and housework. Similarly, in a variant of statistical discrimination models, Lazear and Rosen (1990) suggest that women are less likely to be promoted than men of similar ability due to their higher expected separation rate, where this higher separation rate is again due to the division of labor in the family.[7]

These papers present cogent arguments regarding the impact of gender roles within the family for sex differences in economic outcomes. However, it is important to bear in mind that, as suggested by our discussion of Lundberg and Startz's (1983) paper above, the division of labor within the family may be affected by gender pay gaps caused by labor market discrimination. Such feedback effects of gender discrimination have been emphasized by a variety of scholars (e.g., Arrow 1973, 1976; Blau 1984; Blau and Ferber 1986, 1992; Weiss and Gronau 1981; Gronau 1988).

As the theoretical analysis of race and gender differentials has been refined in the 1980s, so have empirical techniques for measuring the causes of these pay gaps. One issue of some concern in this regard has been sample selection bias. To compare differences in wage offers, we need to look at more than just the set of employed workers, if the nonemployed differ in ways not directly measurable.

Two approaches have been used to deal with the problem of sample selectivity. First, Heckman (1976, 1979) has devised models which pose a specific selection mechanism: with distributional assumptions about the unobserved variables that influence employment and wages, these models lead to particular econometric specifications for the wage equations of interest. In addition, using this approach, the extent of the selectivity bias can be directly estimated (and therefore eliminated).[8] On the other hand, such models have been criticized because they depend on specific distributional assumptions for their identification and because their results tend to be very sensitive to the choice of variables in the selection equation (Lewis 1986; Freeman and Medoff 1982; Manski 1989).

A second method for dealing with selectivity is more modest. Some authors have made alternative assumptions about the relative productivity of those not employed and tested the sensitivity of results with respect to these assumptions (Smith and Welch 1989; Blau and Beller 1992). In such analyses, one can compute reasonable bounds for the impact of selectivity on measured wage differentials.

An additional problem of importance in studying race and gender discrimination is the issue of omitted variables. For example, if, even controlling for the usual explanatory variables, men have higher unmeasured productivity than women, then *ceteris paribus* wage gaps may in part reflect unmeasured skills rather than discrimination. Of course, if women have higher unmeasured productivity than men, then conventional estimates (i.e., the *ceteris paribus* wage gap) will understate discrimination. In the early 1980s, a technique was proposed by Roberts (1980) to solve the omitted variable problem in estimating discrimination.

The new technique, termed reverse regression, involves regressing qualifications on wages and race or gender. Roberts (1980) showed that under some circumstances this technique could give an unbiased estimate of discrimination. We ask, in effect, whether to achieve the same pay level, women or minorities need to possess higher levels of labor market skills. In some instances, use of this method led to much lower estimates of labor market discrimination than the conventional direct regression techniques (i.e., with log of wages as dependent variable); however, in others the technique led to higher estimates.[9]

While reverse regression held some early promise as a method for solving the omitted variables problem, Goldberger (1984) showed that the technique was, in general, no more likely to result in unbiased estimates than the direct regression method. Only by chance could reverse regression lead to unbiased estimates. Thus, the problem of omitted variable bias remains a potentially serious one for those interested in estimating the extent of discrimination.

Explanations of Race and Gender Relative Wage Trends

Changes in the Wage Structure

The 1980s were characterized by increasing wage inequality in the United States. This rising variance occurred both between and within education and experience groups (Katz and Murphy 1992). Specifically, the returns to education rose dramatically in the 1980s, unlike the fall in returns that occurred in the 1970s. For example, among full-time workers, real weekly wages of college-educated men with five years or less of potential experience rose 10.8 percent from 1979 to 1987. In contrast, real weekly wages *fell* by 19.8 percent for young high school graduates who did not attend college, and by 15.8 percent for young high school dropouts (Katz and Murphy 1992).

Experience-related wage differentials also increased during this period. Moreover, even within education-experience groups, wage inequality rose in the 1980s. Juhn, Murphy, and Pierce (1989) interpret this rise in within-group inequality as an increase in the returns to unobserved skills rather than as an increase in the variance of unobserved ability. This conclusion is based on the finding that older cohorts experienced similar increases in inequality to that of younger cohorts during this period. Thus, the returns to measured and unmeasured skills appear to have increased in the 1980s.

Accompanying and perhaps helping to explain these trends in inequality were changes in the industrial structure of employment. It is important to note that changes in industrial structure can have two related effects on wage inequality. First, changes in the composition of final demand can lead to changes in the overall demand for skilled labor relative to unskilled labor. For example, the growth of high-tech industries contributed to the rising premium on labor market skills (Bartel and Lichtenberg 1987); in addition, rising imports have lowered the relative demand for unskilled labor (Murphy and Welch 1991). Such changes in demand can raise the relative wages of skilled workers in all sectors, even the ones not directly involved in the initial change in product demand composition.

Second, changes in final demand can alter the industrial composition of employment. Such changes can affect a group's wages to the extent that some sectors pay higher wages ("rents") than others for similarly qualified workers. For example, the 1980s saw a virtual collapse of employment in some high-wage durable goods manufacturing industries (for example in the automobile and steel industries) and a continued rise in relative employment in service industries. Further, the fraction of the nation's employment covered by collective bargaining continued to steadily decrease (Flanagan, Kahn, Smith, and Ehrenberg 1989).

How did these changes in the structure of wages affect race and gender differentials in the 1980s? We first examine race differences.

Juhn, Murphy, and Pierce (1991) note that the rising return to education in the 1980s has widened race pay gaps, since minorities have lower education levels than whites. The authors also argue that minorities have lower unmeasured skill levels (for example, the quality of education), for which, as discussed above, the wage returns have also increased.[10] These increased wage returns are in part explained by findings that shifts in product demand have led to reductions in the demand for unskilled relative to skilled labor (Katz and Murphy 1992; Bound and Johnson 1991). For example, reductions in demand in the durable goods industries eliminated many high-paying, low-skill jobs, while increases in demand for financial services raised the demand for college-educated workers (Levy and Murnane, forthcoming).

As noted earlier, in addition to their effects on the overall demand for skill, industrial shifts can lead to changing levels of inequality due to the shrinkage or growth of high-wage sectors. Sorensen (1991) found changes in the industrial distribution of employment accounted for 5 percent of the widening of the black-white pay gap for women and 11 percent of the widening of the gap for men between 1978 and 1984.[11]

At the same time that the industrial composition of demand was changing to the detriment of the relative wages of black workers, so was union coverage. For example, among young male workers (those with less than ten years of potential labor market experience), the unionization rate in 1973 among blacks was 6 percentage points higher than for whites, controlling for education and industry; this gap in unionism was eliminated by 1988 (Bound and Freeman 1992).[12] This asymmetric pattern of deunionization lowered young blacks' relative wages. Further, Sorensen (1991) finds that among males aged 25 to 55, the relative deunionization of blacks was responsible for about 13 percent of the widening of the black-white wage gap from 1978 to 1984. For women, deunionization played very little role in racial pay gaps in the 1980s.

Finally, on the supply side, Bound and Freeman (1992) argue that one reason for the deteriorating relative wages of young, college-educated blacks in the 1980s was the increase in their relative supply.

Changing industrial structure appears to have had different effects on women's relative wages from its impact on racial differentials.

The reduction of the male-female pay gap in the 1980s occurred at the same time that the relative supply of women was rising. Further, according to Katz and Murphy (1992), in the 1963-87 period, changes in women's relative wages and the relative supply of women were positively correlated. Such a pattern suggests that relative demand and/or changes in women's relative human capital levels were part of the explanation.

First, focusing on the demand side, we note that the decline of the durable goods sector raised women's relative wages among those with less than a college education. However, in the 1980s, there were shifts favoring the relative demand for labor in "male" sectors among college graduates. Thus, the fact that women college graduates (of all cohorts) gained relative to men during that period was not due to changing output demand (Katz and Murphy 1992). As we discuss below, changes in women's human capital levels and occupational attainment play an important role here.

Shifts in industrial representation appear to have contributed to some of the decline in the gender pay gap among white workers. For example, Sorensen (1991) found that from 1978 to 1984, about 11.8 percent of the reduction in this gap was associated with industrial representation; however, O'Neill and Polachek (1991) found that over a longer period (1977 to 1989), such shifts accounted for only about 1.2 percent of the closing of the gender pay gap for white, non-Hispanic workers. Whether this difference in the estimated effects of industry is due to the different time periods covered or the different data bases and methods used (O'Neill and Polachek used the Current Population Survey, in contrast to Sorensen's use of the Michigan PSID) is an open question.[13]

Second, the decline in union representation also raised women's relative wages. For example, in 1980, white men were 9.0 percentage points more likely to be in unions than white women, while the male advantage was 8.3 percentage points among blacks; by 1990, however, the gaps had fallen to 7.1 percentage points for whites and 6.4 percentage points for blacks (Blau and Ferber 1986; U.S. Bureau of Labor Statistics 1991).

Using Sorensen's (1991) estimates in 1979 for the union log wage effect for each race-gender group, the 1980-90 changes in unionization cited above would imply reductions in male-female pay gaps of .0059 log points for whites and .0156 for blacks; these changes are about 10 to 15 percent of the total closing of the pay gaps implied in Figure 2.[14] This is similar to the finding of Even and Macpherson (forthcoming) that deunionization was responsible for about one-seventh of the decline in the gender wage gap between 1973 and 1988.

Finally, while changes in the industrial composition of employment may have favored women in certain instances, it is possible that the aforementioned rise in the returns to unmeasured skill prevented women's relative pay from rising as fast as it otherwise would have. If, even in the 1980s and 1990s, women on average have lower levels of skills (for example, those learned through general and firm-specific training) than men, then women have been swimming upstream in a labor market growing increasingly unfavorable to those with lower skill levels. Put differently, in the absence of dramatic increases in women's qualifications in the 1980s, the rising returns to skill could have lowered women's relative wages (i.e., by outweighing any positive effects of industry shifts and deunionization).

Further evidence on the impact of the overall wage structure on male-female inequality comes from an international comparison of wage determination in the 1980s using micro-data from nine industrialized countries (Blau and Kahn 1991).[15] Using a decomposition technique developed in Juhn, Murphy, and Pierce (1991), they found that in comparison to the other countries U.S. women had high levels of measured and unmeasured labor market skills (relative to males). However, the pay gap in the U.S. was wider than in most of the other countries in the sample.

A major contributing factor to this finding is the high level of wage inequality in the United States that results in a wage distribution that places a much greater penalty on those with below average skills (measured and unmeasured) than in other countries. Put differently, if the United States had the same rewards to skills (measured and unmeasured) as exist in any of the other countries in our sample, then the U.S. pay gap would be substantially smaller than it is, all else equal; further, under such a hypothetical experiment, the U.S. male-female pay gap would be among the smallest in the world.

Pay Gaps in the 1980s: Further Evidence on the Impact of Wage Structure

In our review of wage structure-based explanations for race and gender trends in relative wages in the 1980s, we considered a variety of explanations for the observed patterns. However, one problem with the existing literature is that studies tend to focus on either the race or gender difference. This makes it difficult to reach firm conclusions regarding potential differences and similarities across these two groups.[16] We thus sought to confirm the general conclusions derived from our review of the literature by undertaking an analysis of race and gender differentials over the 1970s and 1980s employing a consistent data set and framework of analysis for both groups; the 1970s are included for purposes of comparison. Specifically, we analyzed data from three years of the March Current Population Survey (CPS)—1972, 1982, and 1989, covering earnings for 1971, 1981, and 1988, respectively.[17]

Our empirical strategy was to run log annual earnings regressions with successive corrections for time inputs, human capital variables, occupation, and industry. (See Appendix A-1 for variable definitions.) The controls for time input (part-time employment, weekly work hours, and weeks worked) in effect transform the dependent variable into a (log) wage. The human capital variables include education (with, as described in Appendix A-1, splines), and potential experience (and its square). We also add controls at this stage for region, urban residence, marital status, and number of children. Occupation and industry are measured at the 1-digit level. The successive additions of new variables allow us to examine the impact of each type of factor on pay gaps.[18]

The issue which we particularly address in this analysis is the importance of industry shifts in explaining the observed trends. *The total industry effect* on male-female and black-white pay gaps is composed of two kinds of potential industry-related effects. First is a *representation effect* due to changes in the representation of each group in the various industries. If, for example, males disproportionately lost jobs in high-paying industries, then this factor would lower the male-female pay gap. Second is a *coefficient effect* due to changes in the returns to being employed in particular industries. For example, if the wage return to working in a male-dominated industry fell, then this factor would lower the male-female pay differential. The *total industry effect* is equal to the sum of the representation and coefficient effects. It may be noted that another potential impact of industry shifts on relative wages cannot be identified by this type of approach. Changes in industry demands for labor may alter the returns to skill and, to the extent that different race-gender groups are differentially endowed with these skills, the race-gender differentials.

We analyze the impact of industry in two ways. First, we compare the "+hc" and "+ind" specifications. This comparison does not control for occupation and gives perhaps a maximum effect of industry. The industry effects in this analysis account for the impact of the following kind of phenomenon: it is possible that many operatives in durable goods manufacturing were laid off and took jobs as service workers in service industries; for such workers, the full effect of the shift in industry demand includes the change in occupation as well as industry. Second, we compare the "+occ" and the "+occ/ind" specifications. This portion of the analysis examines the impact of industry changes, controlling for occupation. In this case one would examine, for example, the impact on the gender differential of male operatives losing their durable goods manufacturing jobs and changing industries but remaining in the same occupation.

Within each of these two types of specifications, the full industry effect on changing differentials is the difference in the reduction of the relevant gap (say, between 1981 and 1988) between the regression specification without and the one with industry included. This full industry effect is then decomposed into representation and coefficient effects. In decomposing industry effects, we use as units of measurement the differences in the (hours adjusted) log of earnings, as is conventional in such analyses (Bound and Freeman 1992; Blau and Beller 1992). The industry representation effect is computed as follows.

Take the case of the 1981 to 1988 changes for white men as opposed to white women. Let B_{I81} be the vector of industry regression coefficients for 1981 (these are the same for everyone); and let X_{IWM81}, X_{IWM88}, X_{IWF81}, and X_{IWF88} be, respectively, the vectors of industry dummy variables for white males in 1981 and 1988 and white females in 1981 and 1988. Then the industry representation effect on the closing of the gap (measured as the difference between the log of male and the log of female wages) from 1981 to 1988 is:

$$B_{I81}(X_{IWM88}-X_{IWM81}) - B_{I81}(X_{IWF88}-X_{IWF81}) .$$

The industry coefficient effect is then defined as the difference between the total industry effect and the representation effect.[19]

Table 1 contains estimates for the full sample of the female-male and black-white pay ratio with the varying controls. The race-gender ratios corrected for time input differ somewhat from those in Figures 1 and 2 due to differences in samples and in the definition of the earnings measure.[20] In particular, the gender ratios are slightly higher than those in Figure 2 since even among full-time workers, men typically work more hours per week than women (O'Neill 1985). In Table 1 we include both part-time and full-time workers, but control in considerable detail for gender differences in time input. However, the trends in the wage ratios (i.e., earnings ratios adjusted for time input) shown in Table 1 are similar to those in Figures 1 and 2.

For white women relative to white men there was slow progress between 1971 and 1981 and more rapid progress between 1981 and

TABLE 1

Earnings Ratios by Gender and Race, 1971-1988

	Ratios			Percent Changes		
	1971	1981	1988	1971-81	1981-88	1971-88
Women/Men						
Whites						
time input	60.0	65.0	73.8	8.4	13.5	23.1
+ hc	60.5	65.1	71.4	7.7	9.7	18.1
+ occ	61.9	67.3	73.0	8.7	8.5	17.9
+ ind	64.4	69.7	75.5	8.3	8.3	17.3
+ occ/ind	65.5	71.0	76.2	8.3	7.4	16.4
Blacks						
time input	68.4	76.8	85.9	12.2	12.0	25.6
+ hc	65.8	75.5	81.6	14.8	8.1	24.0
+ occ	74.5	79.7	83.4	7.0	4.6	11.9
+ ind	73.2	80.7	86.2	10.3	6.8	17.7
+ occ/ind	77.4	82.7	86.1	6.8	4.1	11.2
Blacks/Whites						
Males						
time input	71.0	74.6	75.7	5.1	1.6	6.7
+ hc	82.8	82.8	84.2	0.0	1.6	1.7
+ occ	86.3	86.0	88.4	−0.3	2.7	2.4
+ ind	83.8	84.0	84.8	0.3	0.9	1.2
+ occ/ind	87.3	87.0	88.9	−0.4	2.3	1.8
Females						
time input	80.9	88.0	88.2	8.7	0.2	8.9
+ hc	90.1	96.1	96.2	6.6	0.1	6.7
+ occ	103.9	102.0	100.9	−1.8	−1.1	−2.9
+ ind	95.3	97.3	96.8	2.1	−0.5	1.6
+ occ/ind	103.3	101.4	100.4	−1.8	−0.9	−2.7

1988. For black women relative to black men the percentage point decrease in the gap was somewhat larger from 1981 to 1988 than from 1971 to 1981. Further, while the percentage reduction in the gap for black women was about the same for 1981 to 1988 (12.0 percent) as for 1971 to 1981 (12.2 percent), the 1980s reduction was achieved in three fewer years, again indicating more rapid progress in the 1980s than the 1970s. For black workers relative to whites, there was progress between 1971 and 1981 with stagnation in relative wages after 1981.

We begin by discussing the contribution of industry shifts to trends in the female/male wage gap. The gender difference in log earnings controlling for time input serves as a base.[21] For whites, we obtain ambiguous results for the 1971-81 period. With occupation excluded, the gap closes faster with industry included (+ind) than with industry excluded (+hc) by .079 log points compared to .074 log points.[22] This finding would indicate that the total industry effect is to reduce the growth of white women's relative wages. However, with occupation included, adding industry lowers the growth in female relative wages (from .083 to .080), suggesting that the total industry effect is to raise women's relative wage growth somewhat. In either case, the total industry effect is relatively small in magnitude for whites in the 1970s: the total effect of industry is −6.2 ((.074−.079)/.081) to 3.7 ((.083−.080)/.081) percent of the total relative change in the female-male ratio.

Decomposing these 1970s industry effects for white women relative to white men, we find that for both specifications (i.e., occupation included or excluded), the effect of changes in representation was to lower the pay gap, while the coefficient effect raised the pay gap. In the 1970s white women's changes in their industry representation relative to men lowered the gap in log earnings by .0085 to .0129 log points; these effects represented 10.5 percent to 16.0 percent of the total hours-corrected reduction in the log earnings differential. However, in each case, industry wage premia changed to the detriment of women's relative wages and led to the total industry effects of −6.2 percent to +3.7 percent of the change in the female/male log wage gap.

For the 1980s, the main focus of the analysis, both specifications give similar answers for the industry effect on the closing of the white female-white male wage gap. The total industry effect is to reduce the female-male pay gap by 8.0 to 10.0 percent of the total reduction in the gap of .127 log points. Decomposing this industry effect, we find that 43 to 56 percent of it is due to changes in industrial representation, and 44 to 57 percent is due to coefficient changes, each of which favored women. Thus, in the 1980s, industry changes are a modest part of the explanation of the reduction in white female-white male pay gap, with the industry impact roughly equally divided between industry representation effects and inter-industry wage structure (i.e., coefficient) effects. These industry representation effects (of approximately 4 to 5 percent) are bracketed by the estimates of Sorensen (1991) and O'Neill and Polachek (1991).[23]

For black women relative to black men, controlling for occupation makes a much more important difference in the analysis of industry effects than for whites. In the 1970s black women moved significantly out of the private household occupation (in the personal services industry). Counting this development as an occupational rather than an industrial shift, which seems most appropriate to us, Table 1 shows only a small industry effect in the closing of male-female wage gaps among blacks. That is, the total industry effect accounted for about 1.8 percent of the closing of the pay gap from 1971 to 1981 and 3.9 percent from 1981 to 1988. In each period, favorable (to women) changes in industry means worked against adverse changes in coefficients. The industry representation effects accounted for 24.9 percent of the total closing of the black male-black female pay gap from 1971 to 1981 and 5.3 percent from 1981 to 1988.[24] The industry representation effect for black women is thus larger (in absolute value) than that for white women during the 1970s, and about the same magnitude as that for white women during the 1980s.

The main conclusion, then, with respect to the impact of industry shifts on gender pay gaps is that changes in the industry representation of men and women have been raising women's relative pay since at least 1971. The 1980s "deindustrialization" effect appears to be a continuation and, for whites, an acceleration of trends from the 1970s. However, countervailing forces in the 1970s such as adverse changes in industry wage coefficients and in women's relative experience levels (the latter to be discussed below) prevented women's relative pay from rising faster than it did. In the 1980s, in addition to positive industry representation effects, white women benefited from favorable changes in industry coefficients as well as from increases in their relative experience levels.

Industry effects analyzed in this way had relatively little overall impact on the changing race differences in pay when we control for occupation. In the 1970s, the total industry effect for men (.0011 log points favoring blacks) accounted for only 2.2 percent of the closing of the gap; and the total industry effect for women was only .0001 log points, or about 0.1 percent of the closing of the gap. In each case there were favorable (to blacks) shifts in industrial distribution and adverse changes in coefficients.

For men in the 1970s the industry representation effect amounted to 4.9 percent of the reduction in the black-white log wage gap; for women changes in industry means accounted for 27.0 percent of the reduction in the pay gap, a relatively large effect. The coefficient effect offset about 55 percent of the means impact for men and roughly the entire means effect for women. Not controlling for occupation, we see a large effect for black women relative to white women of moving out of the personal services industry in the 1970s.[25] But, as noted above, we believe this is more appropriately viewed as an occupational rather than an industrial shift.

Table 1 shows that in the 1980s convergence in racial pay gaps greatly slowed down, as can also be seen in Figure 1. The hours-corrected black-white earnings ratio for men rose from 74.6 percent in 1981 to 75.7 percent in 1988; for women this ratio hardly increased at all, going from 88.0 percent to 88.2 percent. Total industry effects, while large compared to these minimal rates of change in the overall black-white gap, were very small in themselves. For men the total industry impact lowered the black-white pay gap by .0044 log points (28.2 percent of the total reduction), while for women the total industry effect actually raised the gap by .0016 log points. Industry representation effects were very small but worked to reduce the black-white pay gap for both sexes: such effects were .0003 log points for men and .0006 log points for women.[26]

Our findings are similar to Sorensen's (1991) regarding the lack of importance of industry shifts for explaining changes in the black-white female pay gap. However, for men she found larger industry effects for this short time period than we have for the 1981-88 period. Specifically, industry representation and union status effects together raised the black-white pay gap for men .024 log points, or by 24 percent of the total increase in the pay gap.[27] At the beginning of the 1978-84 period, the black-white pay ratio was at its peak (Figure 1); further, the racial pay gap in this period is likely to have been heavily influenced by the recessions of 1980 and 1982-83. In contrast, our 1981-88 period does not include the first recession and includes four years of expansion after 1984. These differences in time period may explain our finding of a smaller industrial representation effect for black men vs. white men than Sorensen (1991).

Our race findings may at first appear inconsistent with the conclusion above that shifts in industry demand had a negative effect on the relative wages of blacks. However, these findings merely suggest that if such an adverse effect did occur it operated via an increase in the returns to skill, rather than specifically through coefficient and mean effects associated with the industry variables. Further, to the extent that blacks were more negatively affected than whites by these shifts, it may have been reflected in employment rather than wage effects.

Changes in Work Force Composition—The Impact of Changing Levels of Labor Market Skills

Even if the structure of the demand for labor had remained the same in the 1980s as in the 1970s, changes in labor market skills of minorities and women could still have had important effects on pay gaps. Research in the 1980s has placed considerable emphasis on such skills.

An often-noted feature of black-white pay gaps measured through 1980 is the decline in black-white wage ratios with age in any cross-section. This decline has been interpreted as reflecting improved quality and quantity of schooling of new black workers (Smith and Welch 1989). Further, in successive cross-sections through 1980, the decline in the wage ratio with age has become more pronounced, an additional finding consistent with the "new vintage" effect. In addition, Card and Krueger (1992b) find direct evidence from data on segregated schools in the South that measures of black and white school quality had substantially converged by 1966.[28]

In contrast to the pre-1980s pattern, in the 1980s, experienced black males' relative wages have risen slightly, while those of new entrants have fallen (Smith and Welch 1989, 558; Blau and Beller

1992); a similar pattern characterizes black-white differences among women (Blau and Beller 1992). These findings suggest that the vintage effect has ceased to operate in the 1980s.

Smith and Welch (1989) speculate that the relative quality of schooling for blacks entering the labor market in the 1980s may have deteriorated.[29] The evidence on this conjecture is mixed. On the one hand, O'Neill (1990a) reports that at each level of education at or above the third year of high school, racial differences in Armed Forces Qualification Test (AFQT) scores for 19- to 21-year-old males widened between 1950 and 1980; for education levels lower than the third year of high school, racial differences narrowed.[30]

On the other hand, Bound and Freeman (1992) report that between 1978 and 1986, math proficiency test scores for 17-year-old blacks rose by 12 points, compared to a 2 point rise for whites. This finding casts doubt on the hypothesis of a deterioration in relative schooling in the 1980s for blacks.[31]

It is important to point out that focusing on hourly wages can give a misleading picture of the relative labor market success of black and white workers. Although our focus is on the wage structure, some discussion of overall income is important for two reasons. First, trends in overall earnings (by far the major component of total income) give us a better picture of economic well-being than do trends in hourly wages. Second, changes in the fraction of the population that is employed influence the average productivity of those who are employed and thus our interpretation of the hourly wage differences themselves. This selectivity factor relates directly to changes in the relative labor market skills of black and white workers.

Among men, there are larger differences in average annual earnings between blacks and whites than in hourly wages. For women the racial gaps between annual and hourly earnings are similar, with the hourly gap actually slightly wider (Blau and Beller 1992). Further, black relative family incomes have deteriorated in the 1980s. For example, in 1967 median black family incomes were 59 percent of whites'; by 1975 this ratio had increased to 62 percent, reflecting the improvement in black labor market outcomes. However, by 1987 the black-white ratio in median family incomes had fallen to 56 percent (Cotton 1989). Much of this decline is associated with the growth of female-headed families among blacks, a phenomenon linked to employment problems among black males (Darity and Myers 1990).

The effect of labor force selectivity on measured wage gaps depends not only on relative employment rates. It also depends on which groups do not find or seek employment. For example, Butler and Heckman (1977) argued that the least productive would drop out of the labor force. Thus, rising relative nonemployment rates for blacks led to an overestimate of the degree of black-white convergence in wage offers. Further, Darity and Myers (1990) point out that those obtaining college educations could also drop out to continue their schooling. Again, focusing on employed workers would understate black-white wage differentials since whites are more likely to attend college than blacks.[32]

While studies have used a variety of methodologies to correct for selectivity, empirical work on this issue suggests that selectivity partially explains black gains in the 1970s; however, even after controlling for selectivity, black workers made relative gains in wage offers in the 1970s.[33]

In the 1980s selectivity appears to also explain some of the apparent deterioration in the relative wages of young black workers. That is, between 1981 and 1988, the black-white wage ratio for those with nine or fewer years' potential experience fell from 81.1 percent to 75.4 percent for men and from 91.5 percent to 87.6 percent for women. However, when we allow for changes in selectivity, the declines are smaller and in some cases are eliminated (Blau and Beller 1992). School enrollment, participation in the military, and self-employment affected sample inclusion (in addition to unemployment and nonparticipation). But these results suggest that, among younger workers in the 1980s, the white labor force was becoming more selective relative to the black labor force.[34]

The major development in the 1980s affecting the relative labor market skills of women has been the increasing work experience of the female labor force. Women's labor force participation rates rose steadily in the 1970s and 1980s. However, in the 1970s increases in female labor force participation led to reductions in the relative experience levels of the average employed woman (Polachek 1990). This development was due to the entry (or re-entry) of large numbers of women with relatively low experience levels.[35] By the 1980s, women's increasing degree of labor force commitment led to rising relative experience levels. Polachek (1990) finds that most of the acceleration in white women's relative earnings during 1980-87 relative to 1974-79 is associated with these changes in actual labor market experience.[36] Further, O'Neill and Polachek (1991) find over the 1976-87 period that changes in actual labor market experience accounted for 26.7 percent of the closing of the male-female pay gap, and changes in the returns to experience for women relative to men accounted for another 41.7 percent.[37] This latter finding reflected the growing female relative return to actual experience, which the authors interpreted as an indication of the growing labor force commitment and therefore levels of on-the-job training for women.[38]

Additional evidence consistent with the conclusions of Polachek (1990) and O'Neill and Polachek (1991) concerns lifetime labor force participation patterns for women. Prior to the 1980s, the labor force participation rate of a cohort of women would decline from ages 22 to 30, reflecting career interruptions to raise children. However, recent cohorts have actually increased their labor force participation in these age groups, reflecting an increased commitment to market work (O'Neill 1990b).[39] Further, a larger percentage of young women surveyed in the 1980s planned to be in the labor force at age 35 than was the case in 1968 (O'Neill 1990b).

These findings for women's increasing relative experience levels, lifetime participation patterns, and work plans suggest an increased commitment to market work among women. This commitment has been associated with increases in the quality of work force experience obtained by women (as suggested by their increasing relative returns to labor market experience) and in their preparation for market work. For example, in 1968, women received 8 percent of MDs, 3 percent of MBAs, and 4 percent of law degrees; by 1986, these figures had risen dramatically to 31 percent for MDs and MBAs and 39 percent for law degrees (O'Neill 1990b). And occupational segregation by sex continued to decline in the 1980s, although at a somewhat slower pace than in the 1970s, again reflecting an improvement in the quality of women's labor market experience (Blau 1988).[40]

The Effects of Public Policy

In the United States the major instances of government regulation of race and gender differences in labor market outcomes involve the Equal Pay Act of 1963, Title VII of the Civil Rights Act of 1964, and Executive Order 11246 implemented in 1965.[41] The Equal Pay Act required equal pay for equal work for men and women but was silent on the issue of employment opportunities. Title VII was comprehensive in that it banned all forms of employment discrimination (e.g., wages, hiring, layoffs, promotions) on the basis of race, gender, or national origin. The Equal Employment Opportunity Commission (EEOC) gives aid to plaintiffs in their antidiscrimination lawsuits. The Executive Order set up the Office of Federal Contract Compliance Programs (OFCCP) to monitor the hiring practices of government contractors. These companies were required to report such practices and to ensure that "affirmative action" was taken to guarantee nondiscriminatory treatment of women and minorities.

Studies evaluating the impact of government policies generally compare states with different levels of EEOC activity or contractor firms with noncontractors. Such evidence thus ignores any spillover effects to states with low EEOC activity or to noncontractors; on the other hand, OFCCP enforcement may lead to a reshuffling of employment from noncontractors to contractors with no overall change in the relative success of women or minorities. Further, the decision to bring a lawsuit or to become a government contractor may be related to existing pay differentials based on race or gender. Thus, comparisons between contractors and noncontractors or between areas with high and those with low EEOC activity may give a misleading picture of policy effectiveness. With these qualifications in mind, we note that evidence from 1970s data suggests the following conclusions regarding the effectiveness of government policies.

First, Title VII lawsuits (or their threat) in the 1960s and 1970s appear to have improved the employment and occupational status of blacks (Leonard 1984a; Heckman and Payner 1989). Second, between 1967 and 1974, enforcement of Title VII lowered male-female pay gaps and reduced occupational segregation by sex (Beller 1979 and 1982). Third, affirmative action (OFCCP) activities contributed to rising black employment and black occupational upgrading between 1974 and 1980 (Leonard 1984b; Smith and Welch 1984). However, OFCCP activities have not raised the occupational status of white women (Leonard 1989).

While there have been fewer studies of the impact of government policy in the 1980s than of its impact in the 1970s, some researchers have noted the decrease in government budgets devoted to affirmative action enforcement activity (Smith and

Welch 1984; Bound and Freeman 1992; Leonard 1990). Further, Leonard (1990) points out that the government has eliminated the threat of contract debarment as a punishment for failure to meet affirmative action requirements. In addition, back pay awards enforced on government contractors (to redress race and gender gaps) were reduced in the 1980s. Moreover, in the late 1980s, the federal government (executive branch and Supreme Court) moved to make it more difficult for plaintiffs to prove discrimination in Civil Rights Act lawsuits (Leonard 1990).[42] Finally, while the annual number of employment discrimination suits was constant during the 1980s, the number of class action suits fell (Bound and Freeman 1992).

These recent trends toward weaker enforcement of antidiscrimination laws in the 1980s appear to have had some consequences for race and gender pay gaps. First, Leonard (1990) notes that in contrast to the 1970s, between 1980 and 1984, black and female employment grew more slowly at contractors than at noncontractors. Second, Bound and Freeman (1992) note that among young males, the black-white pay gap for college-educated workers widened between 1976 and 1988. The authors attribute such losses in part to weakened affirmative pressures in the 1980s (and, as mentioned earlier, to an increased supply of such workers).

As noted, government policies in the 1970s had some effect on reducing occupational segregation by gender. However, despite continued declines, such segregation remains an important feature of the U.S. labor market (Blau 1988) and appears to continue to have major effects on male-female pay differentials.[43] Its wage effects may be due to female "crowding" into women's jobs, raising relative labor supplies there (Bergmann 1974). To the extent that such crowding represents the effects of employer (or union) exclusion rather than worker choice, government policies aimed at eliminating hiring and promotion discrimination can reduce these wage effects.[44] However, because integration of occupations can take many years, some have advocated a more immediate solution to the segregation-related portion of the gender pay gap.

This solution has been termed "comparable worth," or the principle of equal pay for jobs that are determined to be of equal value to the employer. As of 1987, 20 states had set aside money to use in making comparable worth adjustments in the salary schedules for their state government employees. In a study of the impact of comparable worth policies among two groups of public employees (Minnesota state and San Jose municipal workers), Killingsworth (1990) found that comparable worth adjustments lowered male-female pay gaps by 5.8 to 9.9 percentage points. Thus, comparable worth policies have the potential to noticeably affect the gender pay gap in a relatively short time period. However, employers responded to the new administered wages by reducing relative employment in the jobs with the highest pay adjustments. The result was a 3.5 to 6.7 percentage point fall in the female-male employment ratio, all else equal. An analysis of the implementation of comparable worth in Washington State by O'Neill, Brien, and Cunningham (1989) also finds a narrowing of the gender pay gap coupled with a decline in the share of employment in occupations receiving comparable worth pay adjustments.[45] These employment effects and the inefficiencies caused by administered wages lead many economists to oppose comparable worth policies in favor of opening up access to men's jobs (Lazear 1989).

While comparable worth policies appear to be spreading among state governments in the United States, the private sector has been largely untouched by this policy. However, in other countries, comparable worth principles have been enforced throughout the economy (OECD 1988). For example, in Australia, comparable worth was phased in during the 1972-75 period for the economy at large (Gregory and Daly 1990). This decision followed a 1969 ruling that had required equal pay for equal work.[46] Australia has had a long history of government intervention in private-sector wage determination, with minimum wages for many occupations set by tribunal. Thus, the comparable worth decision of 1972 was implemented through the existing tribunal system (Gregory and Daly 1990).

The decisions in Australia requiring equal pay for equal work (1969) and comparable worth (1972) were followed by a sharp upturn in the female-male hourly earnings ratio in manufacturing: from 1969 to 1972, this ratio rose from about 63 percent to 68 percent; by 1975, the ratio stood at about 79 percent and has been at roughly that level through 1989 (Blau and Kahn 1991). Such a dramatic cut in the pay gap provides some circumstantial evidence that Australian tribunal policies may have influenced relative pay.[47] In addition, Blau and Kahn (1991) find smaller gender pay gaps in countries with centralized wage determination systems such as Austria, Sweden, and Norway, in addition to Australia (see also Rosenfeld and Kalleberg 1990).

The evidence from Australia and from countries with centralized wage-setting systems suggests that government policies can affect gender gaps in pay. However, evidence on the negative employment effects of comparable worth in Minnesota, Washington State, and San Jose (Killingsworth 1990; O'Neill, Brien, and Cunningham 1989), as well as evidence that such policies have adversely affected female relative employment in Australia (Killingsworth 1990), remind us that such policies also impose costs.

Conclusions and Directions for Research in the 1990s

In this chapter we have reviewed research findings from the 1980s and early 1990s on race and gender pay gaps. In addition, we have presented some evidence from the Current Population Surveys (1972, 1982, and 1989) regarding the impact of shifts in the industrial composition of employment and in interindustry wage differentials on these gaps. The gender gap in pay was stable in the 1970s but fell steadily in the 1980s; the opposite patterns were observed for black-white wage differentials—a trend towards convergence in the 1970s and stability in the 1980s. Understanding these new trends comprised the unifying theme of our review. Existing studies suggest that changes in wage structure, changing relative skill levels by race and sex, and, possibly, changes in the implementation of government policies all played a role in producing the observed outcomes, although impacts were sometimes countervailing.

In our own investigation of the impact of industry shifts, we identified a total industry effect which was composed of a representation effect due to employment shifts and a coefficient effect due to changes in the returns to employment in particular industries. Our results suggest that total industry effects had little impact on the male-female pay gap during the 1970s, but accounted for a small portion of the closing of the gap for both blacks and for whites in the 1980s. In contrast, we found no evidence that total industry effects contributed to black-white wage trends in either period.

While changes in the industrial representation of women and men have been raising the relative pay of women since the 1970s, they were offset by adverse (for women) changes in industrial wage premia in the 1970s. In the 1980s, however, white women benefited from a small positive effect of changes in industry wage coefficients as well, while industry coefficient effects had only a small negative effect on the relative wages of black women which was more than offset by the convergent industry representation effect. Overall, total industry effects accounted for 11 to 16 percent of the closing of the gender gap among whites and 4 percent among blacks.

Our results for the impact of industry on race differentials suggest that to the extent that changes in the composition of demand for output have influenced these racial pay gaps, their effects have been felt across industries. So, for example, even though a reduction in the demand for unskilled labor may have originated in industries such as durable goods manufacturing, wages for unskilled workers in other industries are likely to have been adversely affected as well. It may also be noted that a related development, the movement of black women out of the private household occupation, was an important factor in raising their earnings relative to both white women and black men during the 1970s.

We conclude our review of research trends in the 1980s and early 1990s with some suggestions for future work in the area of race and gender earnings differentials. First, the use of international comparisons in statistical analyses can be greatly expanded. Since countries vary considerably in race and gender-specific policies, overall wage structures and, particularly, gender earnings ratios, such comparisons can yield considerable insights into the causes of differentials and the efficacy of various policies. Blau and Kahn's (1991, 1992) finding that wage structure (i.e., wage inequality) played a major role in explaining cross-country differences in gender ratios among a sample of industrialized countries suggests the potential fruitfulness of this approach. Also intriguing is Rosenfeld and Kalleberg's (1990) reporting of bivariate correlations (and regressions with two explanatory variables) between country characteristics and the gender pay gap, for a sample of nine countries. Larger time-series, cross-sectional data bases could be built, and the pay gap for a given country at a given time treated as a dependent variable.

Second, with the growth of immigration, racial differences take on more dimensions than the familiar black-white comparisons. The relative progress of a variety of ethnic groups is an area ripe for study in the 1990s.[48]

Third, while the use of corrections for sample selectivity or omitted productivity variable bias has become less popular in recent years, these issues still pose problems in hypotheses testing. To some degree, improved surveys can alleviate such problems by providing information on previously unobserved characteristics. Examples have included the collection of actual experience and wage offer information in data bases such as the Michigan Panel Study of Income Dynamics or the National Longitudinal Surveys. However, we can do a better job of measuring productivity than is currently done in standard data bases. Inclusion of such measures might well make omitted variable bias correction techniques less necessary.

Fourth, with the growth of computing power and the availability of large data bases, very detailed controls for industry and occupation can be constructed. We can thus produce more precise estimates of the impact of occupational segregation and industrial structure on pay gaps than has been possible in the past.

Fifth, in considering the impact of policies (for example, EEO laws), we need to take heed of Ehrenberg's (1989) warning that such policies may be endogenous. A rapid rise, for example, in women's relative earnings around the time of a change in laws may have occurred for the same underlying reasons that the laws themselves were changed. A start in the direction of modeling the behavior of wage-regulating bodies has been made by Gregory and Daly (1990) and Killingsworth (1990) and should be continued.

Finally, the analysis of race and gender wage differentials can be better integrated with recent developments in labor economics. Specifically, the "New Economics of Personnel" (as these developments were termed in the October 1987 issue of the *Journal of Labor Economics*) has examined questions of employee motivation under varying compensation schemes. Some attempts to relate such compensation methods to race and gender pay gaps have been made. For example Goldin (1986) examines the reasons women in the 1890s were more likely to be paid in piece rates than men were. And Bulow and Summers (1986) explore the implications of an efficiency wage model (in which firms find it profit-maximizing to pay above-market wage levels) for discrimination. Again, such efforts should be continued.

Acknowledgment

We are grateful for the helpful comments of Olivia Mitchell on an earlier draft of this paper.

Endnotes

1. Further, race differentials in economic welfare are understated by focusing on full-time employed workers. For example, there remain major racial differences in joblessness and in the presence of single-parent families, factors that would reduce relative black economic welfare levels even in the absence of pay gaps. See Cottom (1989) and Darity and Myers (1990).

2. See Levy and Murnane (forthcoming) for a survey of work on inequality.

3. As noted below, such methods have been controversial and have not been universally implemented. See Goldberger (1984).

4. Ashenfelter and Hannan (1986) find evidence supporting this prediction about discrimination and product market structure in the case of the banking industry.

5. O'Neill's (1990a) finding that AFQT scores have a larger effect on the log of black male than on white male wages casts some doubt on this particular version of the statistical discrimination model.

6. Arrow (1973) made a similar argument about the feedback effects of initial employer prejudices.

7. Note, however, that empirical research has generally found that, all else equal, men and women have similar quit rates. See, for example, Blau and Kahn (1981) and Viscusi (1980). Such findings do not support the premise of the Lazear and Rosen model.

8. Examples of studies using this type of selectivity correction in analyzing discriminatory wage differentials include Reimers (1983), Blau and Beller (1988), Wright and Ermisch (1991), and Sorensen (1991).

9. For example, see Kamalich and Polachek (1982) or Kahn and Sherer (1988).

10. Card and Krueger (1992b) present evidence that improvements in the relative quality of schooling for blacks through 1966 helped lower black-white wage differentials from 1960 to 1980.

11. Sorensen's (1991) wage data came from 1978 (the peak of the black-white wage ratio—see Figure 1) and 1984. Her data source was the Michigan Panel Study of Income Dynamics (PSID). She found a relatively large widening of the racial pay gaps for this limited period and sample—for women, the race gap increased by .04 log points (about 4 percentage points), while for men, the rise was .10 log points (about 11 percentage points). In estimating the effects of sectoral shifts, she measured industry using six dummy variables.

12. Among all workers, the black-white gap in percent unionized in 1980 was 7.1 percentage points for men and 9.8 percentage points for women. By 1990, the black advantage in unionization was reduced to 5.6 percentage points for men and 6.3 percentage points for women. See Blau and Ferber (1986) and U.S. Bureau of Labor Statistics (1991).

13. In addition, O'Neill and Polachek (1991) exclude Hispanics, unlike Sorensen (1991). Further, the papers used different age groups (25-55 for Sorensen and 20-59 for O'Neill and Polachek). Moreover, Sorensen (1991) uses a Heckman (1976) correction for selectivity, and, as noted earlier, coefficient estimates can be very sensitive to the implementation of such methods.

O'Neill and Polachek (1991) report very large effects of changes in industry coefficients—such changes purportedly account for 42.3 percent of the closing of the gap. However, unlike the effect of changing industrial distribution of employment, this estimate is highly dependent on which industry is the omitted category; for example, the effect of the "residual trend," which includes the impact of changes in wages in the omitted category was to *raise* the gap by 64.5 percent of the extent of its ultimate reduction. Below, we propose an alternative measure of industry coefficient effects that has been used by Bound and Freeman (1992) and that is not dependent on the choice of the omitted category.

14. The return to union membership appears to have been stable in the 1980s (see Freeman 1986). Thus, any impact of unionization on male-female pay gaps is likely due to changing relative representation rather than to changing returns.

15. The countries were, in addition to the United States, Australia, Austria, Britain, Hungary, Norway, Sweden, Switzerland, and West Germany. See also Blau and Kahn (1992).

16. In addition, most studies of race differences are limited to males; see Blau and Beller (1992) for an exception. However Blau and Beller do not examine the impact of industry shifts on the trends. As noted, Sorensen (1991) analyzes race-gender groups separately but only in detail for the 1978-84 period. Our brief examination of Current Population Survey data covers the 1971-88 years, thus providing additional coverage of the 1980s and an examination of the 1970s for comparison as well.

17. Our sample is restricted to individuals aged 18 to 64 who worked at least one week in the previous year and whose wage and salary income was at least $100. We excluded individuals with any self-employment income, members of the military, and those who were in school.

18. For convenience and brevity of reporting, we pool by race and gender and include three race-gender dummy variables (with white males the omitted category). However, as may be seen in Appendix A-1, we do allow the effects of marital status and children to differ across gender-race groups. The overall ratios reported in Table 1 are evaluated at the means of the marital status and number of children variables for each group.

19. Bound and Freeman (1992) use a similar scheme to estimate the impact of differing variables on changes in black-white wage differentials among young men.

20. The published data are for the median earnings of each group; our ratios are calculated on the basis of the geometric means. Our sample restrictions are detailed above.

21. Note that Table 1 shows for both whites and blacks in 1988 that the addition of the human capital variables reduces the female-male earnings ratio. In each case, women have higher levels of education than men, a factor contributing to this result.

22. The changes in the difference of the log of earnings are approximately equal to the percent changes in the earnings ratios shown in the final three columns of Table 1 (divided by 100).

23. Our estimated industry representation effects combine industry and union representation impacts to the extent that unionism is correlated with industry, since we are unable to control for union status. O'Neill and Polachek (1991) also did not control for unionism, while Sorensen (1991) did. It is thus perhaps surprising that Sorensen (1991) still finds the largest industry representation effects. As noted earlier, it is possible that such findings are sensitive to the choice of time period or to her use of a specific selectivity-bias correction technique.

24. Sorensen (1991) finds that industry means *raised* the male-female pay gap for blacks from 1978 to 1984 by .025 log points (even though the overall pay gap fell by .128 points); however, union status changes lowered the gap by .047 points. Thus, combining industry and union effects, as our estimates to some extent do, Sorensen's (1991) results imply that changing industry and union representation together account for 17.2 percent of the falling pay gap. This combined total is larger than our estimate of 5.3 percent for the industry representation effect over the longer 1981-88 period.

25. Blau and Beller (1992) report a similar result.

26. Not controlling for occupation, industry effects served to reduce racial gaps for both men and women in the 1980s. While such effects were larger in absolute value than they were within occupations, they remained small. For men, the total industry effect, not controlling for occupation, was .0068 log points, while for women it was .0063 log points. Industry representation effects in this specification were .0004 log points for men and .0051 log points for women, both serving to slightly reduce racial pay gaps.

27. The industry representation effect was .011, and the union status effect was .013.

28. These measures were teacher salaries, class size, and the length of the school year.

29. While a rising return to skill could explain the deterioration in black new entrants' relative wages in the 1980s, it would not by itself explain the divergent trends for experienced blacks and new black entrants. These divergent trends are consistent with a deterioration in the relative quality of schooling for blacks. However, as we note below, there may be other explanations of the deterioration in relative pay for younger blacks as well. Further, the assertion that relative quality of black schooling in the 1980s has fallen has also been challenged (see below).

30. Use of AFQT score, as opposed to school expenditures, as an indicator of school quality is controversial. On the one hand, O'Neill (1990a) found that this variable is significantly positively related to earnings for both whites and blacks, suggesting that it does measure market-related skills. On the other hand, in a review of 147 studies, Hanushek (1986) found that school expenditures did not have an influence on test scores, perhaps suggesting that expenditures do not indicate quality. However, Card and Krueger (1992b) found that school expenditures did affect the students' subsequent earnings, placing expenditures on an equal footing with test scores as labor market predictors.

31. Bound and Freeman (1992) also examine crime as a possible explanation for the deterioration in young black males' relative labor market position in the 1980s. They find that increases in crime among young blacks in the 1980s contributed to a lowering of employment rather than to lowered wages among the employed.

32. In fact, Blau and Beller (1988) find negative selectivity effects for men, results consistent with Darity and Myers' (1990) claim.

33. See, for example, Brown (1984), Smith and Welch (1989), and Blau and Beller (1992).

34. In the 1980s, older workers were much less affected by the selectivity adjustment than younger workers. Sorensen (1991) also finds a small role for selectivity in explaining rising black-white wage differentials among workers aged 25-55 in the 1978-84 period.

35. Goldin (1990) reports that a small decline in female experience levels which occurred between 1960 and 1980 "was produced by changes in the age distribution of the employed female population rather than by changes in work experience at each age" (p. 41). This "youthening" of the female labor force most likely results from the large post-1960 increases in labor force participation of younger women, including married women with preschool children, a shift which could be expected to increase women's experience and earnings in the long run. For additional evidence on experience trends for women, see O'Neill (1985), Smith and Ward (1984), and O'Neill and Polachek (1991).

36. Polachek's (1990) accounting is based on regressions that control only for education and experience. When he constrains men and women to have the same returns to these variables, actual labor market experience changes account for 75 percent of the difference in growth rates in the female-male wage ratio between 1974-79 and 1980-87. Changes in relative education levels accounted for the rest of the acceleration in the wage ratio. When he estimates separate regressions for men and women, changes in the two types of human capital together explain 92 percent of the acceleration in the wage ratio. While the increase in women's relative levels of actual work experience undoubtedly reflects an improvement in labor market skills, other explanations exist for the relationship between work experience and earnings. Specifically, Gronau (1988) finds that earnings opportunities can also affect women's propensities to accumulate labor market experience. That is, feedback effects discussed above may well be important.

37. O'Neill and Polachek (1991) pooled by race and did not allow whites and nonwhites to have different returns to the explanatory variables.

38. These coefficient changes may also reflect changes in the labor market treatment of women.

39. To some degree, such a change may reflect delayed child-bearing decisions. However, among the cohort born between 1946 and 1955 (a relatively recent one), there is no downturn in labor force participation for ages 30 to 40 (O'Neill 1990b, 28). Thus, even accounting for delayed child-bearing, there does appear to be an increased level of labor force commitment among women.

40. The potentially positive effect of decreased occupational segregation per se on relative female wages was offset during both the 1970s and 1980s by adverse (for women) changes in occupational premia. That is, increasing returns to employment in male occupations worked to lower the relative earnings of women who, despite recent gains, continued to be underrepresented in these jobs (Blau and Beller 1988 and O'Neill and Polachek 1991).

41. See Leonard (1986), Gunderson (1989), and Brown (1982) for further discussion of such governmental efforts.

42. A Civil Rights Act passed by Congress in 1991 reinstated many of the original interpretations of the civil rights laws that had been affected by these Court decisions.

43. See Johnson and Solon (1986), Sorensen (1990), Blau (1988), and Blau and Beller (1988).

44. See Reskin et al. (1986) for a survey of explanations for occupational segregation. There appears to be evidence supporting hypotheses about pre-labor market socialization and employer exclusion as causes of segregation. See also, Reskin and Roos (1990) and Strober (1984).

45. Orazem and Mattila (1990) found that the ultimate impact of comparable worth on the wage structure of employees in Iowa was greatly modified by various interest groups. Potential gains of 8.8 percentage points in female pay relative to male pay under the original plan ended up as a gain of only 1.4 percentage points after full implementation. For estimates of the potential impact of an economy-wide comparable worth policy, see Sorensen (1990) and Johnson and Solon (1986). For other empirical studies related to the comparable worth issue, see Michael, Hartmann, and O'Farrell (1989).

46. Prior to 1969, women's rates were set at 75 percent of the male pay rate (Gregory and Daly 1990).

47. There is some controversy about whether the comparable worth decision had a permanent effect on future tribunal wage awards. On the one hand, Gregory and Daly (1990) argue that there was a permanent impact. However, Killingsworth (1990) provides some econometric evidence that in the long run, wage tribunals would have eventually moved women's relative pay awards up anyway. In his view, the comparable worth decision merely sped up the process. Whichever view is correct, considerable power to move wage rates and change the male-female pay gap rests in the hands of the wage tribunals in Australia.

48. For studies of the relative wages of Hispanics, see Reimers (1983), Borjas (1982), McManus, Gould, and Welch (1983) and Carlson and Swartz (1988). For a study of the relative earnings of Asian-Americans, see Chiswick (1983).

References

Aigner, Dennis, and Glen Cain. "Statistical Theories of Discrimination in Labor Markets." *Industrial and Labor Relations Review* 30 (January 1977), pp. 175-87.

Arrow, Kenneth. "The Theory of Discrimination." In *Discrimination in Labor Markets*, eds. O. Ashenfelter and A. Rees. Princeton, NJ: Princeton University Press, 1973.

________. "Economic Dimensions of Occupational Segregation: Comment." *Signs: Journal of Women in Culture and Society* 1 (Spring 1976, pt. 2), pp. 233-37.

Ashenfelter, Orley, and Timothy Hannan. "Sex Discrimination and Product Market Competition." *Quarterly Journal of Economics* 101 (February 1986), pp. 149-73.

Bartel, Ann, and Frank Lichtenberg. "The Comparative Advantage of Educated Workers in Implementing New Technology." *The Review of Economics and Statistics* 69 (February 1987), pp. 1-11.

Becker, Gary S. *The Economics of Discrimination*. Chicago: University of Chicago Press, 1957.

________. "Human Capital, Effort, and the Sexual Division of Labor." *Journal of Labor Economics* 3 (January 1985, pt. 2), pp. S33-S58.

Beller, Andrea H. "The Impact of Equal Employment Opportunity Laws on the Male-Female Earnings Differential." In *Women in the Labor Market*, eds. C. Lloyd, E. Andrews, and C. Gilroy. New York: Columbia University Press, 1979.

________. "The Impact of Equal Opportunity Policy on Sex Differentials in Earnings and Occupations." *American Economic Review* 72 (May 1982), pp. 171-75.

Bergmann, Barbara. "Occupational Segregation, Wages and Profits When Employers Discriminate by Race or Sex." *Eastern Economic Journal* 1 (April-July 1974), pp. 103-10.

Blau, Francine D. "Discrimination Against Women: Theory and Evidence." In *Labor Economics: Modern Views*, ed. William A. Darity, Jr. Boston: Kluwer-Nijhoff, 1984.

________. "Occupation Segregation by Gender: A Look at the 1980s." Paper presented at the American Economic Association Meetings, New York City, December 1988.

Blau, Francine D., and Andrea H. Beller. "Trends in Earnings Differentials by Gender: 1971-1981." *Industrial and Labor Relations Review* 41 (July 1988), pp. 513-29.

________. "Black-White Earnings Over the 1970s and 1980s: Gender Differences in Trends." *The Review of Economics and Statistics* 74 (May 1992).

Blau, Francine D., and Marianne Ferber. *The Economics of Women, Men, and Work*, 1st ed. Englewood Cliffs, NJ: Prentice-Hall, 1986.

________. *The Economics of Women, Men, and Work*, 2nd ed. Englewood Cliffs, NJ: Prentice-Hall, 1992.

Blau, Francine D., and Lawrence M. Kahn. "Race and Sex Differences in Quits by Young Workers." *Industrial and Labor Relations Review* 34 (July 1981), pp. 563-77.

________. "The Gender Earnings Gap: Some International Evidence." Paper presented at the NBER Comparative Labor Markets Project Conference on Differences and Changes in Wage Structures, September 1991.

________. "The Gender Earnings Gap: Learning from International Comparisons." *American Economic Review* 82, no. 2 (May 1992), pp. 533-38.

Borjas, George. "The Earnings of Male Hispanic Immigrants in the United States." *Industrial and Labor Relations Review* 35 (April 1982), pp. 343-53.

Borjas, George, and Stephen Bronars. "Customer Discrimination and Self-Employment." *Journal of Political Economy* 97 (June 1989), pp. 581-605.

Bound, John, and Richard B. Freeman. "What Went Wrong? The Erosion of the Relative Earnings and Employment of Young Black Men in the 1980s." *Quarterly Journal of Economics* 107 (February 1992), pp. 201-32.

Bound, John, and George Johnson. "Wages in the United States in the 1980s and Beyond." In *Workers and Their Wages*, ed. Marvin H. Kosters. Washington, D.C.: AEI Press, 1991.

Brown, Charles. "The Federal Attack on Labor Market Discrimination: The Mouse That Roared?" In *Research in Labor Economics* 5, ed. Ronald Ehrenberg. Greenwich, CT: JAI Press, Inc., 1982.

________. "Black-White Earnings Ratios Since The Civil Rights Act of 1964: The Importance of Market Dropouts." *Quarterly Journal of Economics* 99 (February 1984), pp. 32-43.

Bulow, Jeremy, and Lawrence Summers. "A Theory of Dual Labor Markets with Application to Industrial Policy, Discrimination and Keynesian Unemployment." *Journal of Labor Economics* 4 (July 1986), pp. 376-414.

Butler, Richard, and James Heckman. "The Government's Impact on the Labor Market Status of Black Americans: A Critical Review." In *Equal Rights and Industrial Relations*, ed. Leonard J. Hausman. Madison, WI: IRRA, 1977.

Cain, Glen G. "The Economic Analysis of Labor Market Discrimination." In *Handbook of Labor Economics* 1, eds. O. Ashenfelter and R. Layard. Amsterdam: North-Holland, 1986.

Card, David, and Alan B. Krueger. "Does School Quality Matter? Returns to Education and the Characteristics of Public Schools in the United States." *Journal of Political Economy* 100 (February 1992a), pp. 1-40.

________. "School Quality and Black/White Earnings: A Direct Assessment." *Quarterly Journal of Economics* 107 (February 1992b), pp. 151-200.

Carlson, Leonard, and Caroline Swartz. "The Earnings of Women and Ethnic Minorities, 1959-79." *Industrial and Labor Relations Review* 41 (July 1988), pp. 530-46.

Chiswick, Barry R. "An Analysis of the Earnings and Employment of Asian-American Men." *Journal of Labor Economics* 1 (April 1983), pp. 197-214.

Cotton, Jeremiah. "Opening the Gap: The Decline in Black Economic Indicators in the 1980s." *Social Science Quarterly* 70 (December 1989), pp. 803-35.

Darity, Jr., William A., and Samuel L. Myers. "Black-White Earnings Gaps Have Widened: The Problem of Family Structure, Earnings Inequality and The Marginalization of Black Men." Mimeo, July 1990.

Ehrenberg, Ronald. "Commentary." In *Pay Equity: Empirical Inquiries*, eds. Robert T. Michael, Heidi I. Hartmann, and Brigid O'Farrell. Washington, D.C.: National Academy Press, 1989.

Even, William E., and David A. Macpherson. "The Decline of Private-Sector Unionism and the Gender Wage Gap." *Journal of Human Resources*, forthcoming.

Flanagan, Robert, Lawrence M. Kahn, Robert Smith, and Ronald Ehrenberg, *Economics of the Employment Relationship*. Glenview, IL: Scott, Foresman, 1989.

Freeman, Richard B. "In Search of Union Wage Concessions in Standard Data Sets." *Industrial Relations* 25 (Spring 1986), pp. 131-45.

Freeman, Richard B., and James L. Medoff. "The Impact of Collective Bargaining: Illusion or Reality?" In *Industrial Relations in the United States: A Critical Assessment*, eds. Robert McKersie, D. Quinn Mills, and Jack Stieber. Madison, WI: IRRA, 1982.

Goldberg, Matthew. "Discrimination, Nepotism and Long-run Wage Differentials." *Quarterly Journal of Economics* 97 (May 1982), pp. 307-19.

Goldberger, Arthur. "Reverse Regression and Salary Discrimination." *Journal of Human Resources* 19 (Summer 1984), pp. 293-318.

Goldin, Claudia. "Monitoring Costs and Occupation Segregation by Sex: A Historical Analysis." *Journal of Labor Economics* 4 (January 1986), pp. 1-27.

________. *Understanding the Gender Gap: An Economic History of American Women*. New York: Oxford University Press, 1990.

Gregory, R. G., and A. E. Daly. "Can Economic Theory Explain Why Australian Women Are So Well Paid Relative to Their U.S. Counterparts?" Paper presented at the 8th Conference on Women's Wages: Stability and Change in Six Industrialized Countries, Chicago, March 1990.

Gronau, Reuben. "Sex-related Wage Differentials and Women's Interrupted Labor Careers—the Chicken or the Egg." *Journal of Labor Economics* 6 (July 1988), pp. 277-301.

Gunderson, Morley. "Male-Female Wage Differentials and Policy Responses." *Journal of Economic Literature* 27 (March 1989), pp. 46-72.

Hanushek, Eric. "The Economics of Schooling: Production and Efficiency in Public Schools." *Journal of Economic Literature* 24 (September 1986), pp. 1141-77.

Heckman, James. "The Common Structure of Statistical Models of Innovation, Sample Selection Bias and Limited Dependent Variables and a Single Estimator for Such Models." *Annals of Economic and Social Measurement* 5 (1976), pp. 475-92.

———. "Sample Selection Bias as a Specification Error." *Econometrica* 47 (January 1979), pp. 153-61.

Heckman, James, and Brook S. Payner. "Determining the Impact of Federal Antidiscrimination Policy on the Economic Status of Blacks: A Study of South Carolina." *American Economic Review* 79 (March 1989), pp. 138-77.

Johnson, George, and Gary Solon. "Estimates of the Direct Effects of Comparable Worth Policy." *American Economic Review* 76 (December 1986), pp. 1117-25.

Juhn, Chinhui, Kevin M. Murphy, and Brooks Pierce. "Accounting for the Slowdown in Black-White Wage Convergence." In *Workers and Their Wages*, ed. Marvin H. Kosters. Washington, D.C.: AEI Press, 1991.

———. "Wage Inequality and the Rise in Returns to Skill." Mimeo, University of Chicago, November 1989.

Kahn, Lawrence M. "Customer Discrimination and Affirmative Action." *Economic Inquiry* 29 (July 1991a), pp. 555-71.

———. "Discrimination in Professional Sports: A Survey of the Literature." *Industrial and Labor Relations Review* 44 (April 1991b), pp. 395-418.

Kahn, Lawrence M., and Peter D. Sherer. "Racial Differences in Professional Basketball Players' Compensation." *Journal of Labor Economics* 6 (January 1988), pp. 40-61.

Kamalich, Richard F., and Solomon W. Polachek. "Discrimination: Fact or Fiction? An Examination Using an Alternative Approach." *Southern Economic Journal* 49 (October 1982), pp. 450-61.

Katz, Lawrence F., and Kevin M. Murphy. "Changes in Relative Wages, 1963-1987: Supply and Demand Factors." *Quarterly Journal of Economics* 107 (February 1992), pp. 35-78.

Killingsworth, Mark. *The Economics of Comparable Worth*. Kalamazoo, MI: W.E. Upjohn Institute for Employment Research, 1990.

Lazear, Edward P. "Symposium on Women in the Labor Market." *Journal of Economic Perspectives* 3 (Winter 1989), pp. 3-7.

Lazear, Edward P., and Sherwin Rosen. "Male-Female Wage Differentials in Job Ladders." *Journal of Labor Economics* 8 (January 1990, pt. 2), pp. S106-S123.

Leonard, Jonathan. "Antidiscrimination or Reverse Discrimination: The Impact of Changing Demographics, Title VII, and Affirmative Action on Productivity." *Journal of Human Resources* 19 (Spring 1984a), pp. 145-74.

———. "Employment and Occupational Advance Under Affirmative Action." *The Review of Economics and Statistics* 66 (August 1984b), pp. 377-85.

———. "The Effectiveness of Equal Employment Opportunity Law and Affirmative Action Regulation." In *Research in Labor Economics* 8, Part B, ed. Ronald Ehrenberg. Greenwich, CT: JAI Press, Inc., 1986.

———. "Women and Affirmative Action." *Journal of Economic Perspectives* 3 (Winter 1989), pp. 61-75.

———. "The Impact of Affirmative Regulation and Equal Employment Law on Black Employment." *Journal of Economic Perspectives* 4 (Fall 1990), pp. 47-63.

Levy, Frank, and Richard J. Murnane. "Earnings Levels and Earnings Inequality: A Review of Recent Trends and Proposed Explanations." *Journal of Economic Literature*, forthcoming.

Lewis, H. Gregg. *Union Relative Wage Effects: A Survey*. Chicago: University of Chicago Press, 1986.

Lundberg, Shelly J., and Richard Startz. "Private Discrimination and Social Intervention in Competitive Labor Markets." *American Economic Review* 73 (June 1983), pp. 340-47.

Manski, Charles F. "Anatomy of the Selection Problem." *Journal of Human Resources* 24 (Summer 1989), pp. 343-60.

McManus, Walter, William Gould, and Finis Welch. "Earnings of Hispanic Men: The Role of English Language Proficiency." *Journal of Labor Economics* 1 (April 1983), pp. 101-30.

Michael, Robert T., Heidi I. Hartmann, and Brigid O'Farrell, eds. *Pay Equity: Empirical Inquiries*. Washington, D.C.: National Academy Press, 1989.

Mincer, Jacob, and Solomon W. Polachek. "Family Investments in Human Capital: Earnings of Women." *Journal of Political Economy* 82 (March 1974), pp. S76-S108.

Murphy, Kevin M., and Finis Welch. "The Role of International Trade in Wage Differentials." In *Workers and Their Wages*, ed. Marvin H. Kosters. Washington, D.C.: AEI Press, 1991.

OECD (Organization for Economic Co-operation and Development). *Employment Outlook September 1988*. Paris: OECD, 1988.

O'Neill, June. "The Trend in the Male-Female Wage Gap in the United States." *Journal of Labor Economics* 3 (January 1985, supp.), pp. S91-S116.

________. "The Role of Human Capital in Earnings Differences Between Black and White Men." *Journal of Economic Perspectives* 4 (Fall 1990a), pp. 25-45.

________. "Women and Wages." *The American Enterprise* 1 (November/December 1990b), pp. 25-33.

O'Neill, June, Michael Brien, and James Cunningham. "Effects of Comparable Worth Policy: Evidence From Washington State." *American Economic Review* 79 (May 1989), pp. 305-09.

O'Neill, June, and Solomon Polachek. "Why the Gender Gap in Wages Narrowed in the 1980s." Unpublished manuscript, November 1991.

Orazem, Peter F., and J. Peter Mattila. "The Implementation Process of Comparable Worth: Winners and Losers." *Journal of Political Economy* 98 (February 1990), pp. 134-52.

Polachek, Solomon. "Trends in Male-Female Wages: Differences Between the 1970s and the 1980s." Paper presented at the American Economic Association Meetings, Washington, D.C., December 1990.

Reimers, Cordelia. "Labor Market Discrimination Against Hispanic and Black Men." *The Review of Economics and Statistics* 65 (November 1983), pp. 570-79.

Reskin, Barbara F., et al. *Women's Work, Men's Work: Sex Segregation on the Job*. Washington, D.C.: National Academy Press, 1986.

Reskin, Barbara F., and Patricia A. Roos. *Job Queues, Gender Queues: Explaining Women's Inroads into Male Occupations*. Philadelphia: Temple University Press, 1990.

Roberts, Harry V. "Statistical Biases in the Measurement of Employment Discrimination." In *Comparable Worth: Issues and Alternatives*, ed. Robert Livernash. Washington, D.C.: Equal Employment Advisory Council, 1980.

Rosenfeld, Rachel, and Arne Kalleberg. "Gender Inequality in the Labor Market: A Cross-National Perspective. Paper presented at the 12th World Congress of Sociology, Madrid, July 1990.

Smith, James P., and Michael P. Ward. *Women's Wages and Word in the Twentieth Century*. Santa Monica, CA: RAND Corporation, 1984.

Smith, James P., and Finis Welch. "Affirmative Action and Labor Markets." *Journal of Labor Economics* 2 (April 1984), pp. 269-98.

________. "Black Economic Progress After Myrdal." *Journal of Economic Literature* 27 (June 1989), pp. 519-64.

Sorensen, Elaine. "The Crowding Hypothesis and Comparable Worth Issue." *Journal of Human Resources* 25 (Winter 1990), pp. 55-89.

________. "Gender and Racial Pay Gaps in the 1980s: Accounting for Different Trends." Unpublished manuscript, November 1991.

Strober, Myra H. "Toward a General Theory of Occupational Sex Segregation: The Case of Public School Teaching." In *Sex Segregation in the Workplace: Trends, Explanations, Remedies*. Washington, D.C.: National Academy Press, 1984.

U.S. Bureau of Labor Statistics. *Employment and Earnings* 38 (January 1991).

Viscusi, Kip. "Sex Differences in Worker Quitting." *Review of Economics and Statistics* 62 (August 1980), pp. 388-98.

Weiss, Yorem, and Reuben Gronau. "Expected Interruptions in Labor Force Participation and Sex-Related Differences in Earnings Growth." *Review of Economic Studies* 48 (October 1981), pp. 607-19.

Wright, Robin E., and John F. Ermisch. "Gender Discrimination in the British Labour Market: A Reassessment." *Economic Journal* 101 (May 1991), pp. 508-22.

APPENDIX A-1
Variable Definitions

LNY = Natural log of annual earnings from wages and salaries.
PART = 1 if worked part time (less than 35 hours per week in the majority of weeks in the previous year); 0 otherwise.
HOURS = Usual hours last year (for 1972, hours last week).
PARTHRS = PART • HOURS.
HRSLWK = 1 if hours last week greater than zero; 0 otherwise (1972 only).
LNWW = Natural log of weeks worked in previous year.
WWHITE = 1 if white woman; 0 otherwise.
MBLACK = 1 if black man; 0 otherwise.
WBLACK = 1 if black woman; 0 otherwise.
EDUC = Number of years of school completed.
YRSLT8 = For workers with less than 8 years of schooling, the number of years less than 8; 0 otherwise.
YRSGT12 = For workers with more than 12 years of schooling, the number of years greater than 12; 0 otherwise.
EXPER = Potential experience, computed as AGE − EDUC − 6.
EXPERSQ = EXPER squared.
MSP = 1 if married spouse present; 0 otherwise.
NUMKIDS = Number of children.
MSPWW = MSP • WWHITE.
MSPBM = MSP • MBLACK.
MSPBW = MSP • WBLACK.
KIDSWW = NUMKIDS • WWHITE.
KIDSBM = NUMKIDS • MBLACK.
KIDSBW = NUMKIDS • WBLACK.
NCENT = 1 if northcentral; 0 otherwise.
SOUTH = 1 if south; 0 otherwise.
WEST = 1 if west; 0 otherwise.
URBAN = 1 if urban; 0 otherwise.

Occupation Dummies

PRO = 1 if professional; 0 otherwise.
MGT = 1 if managerial; 0 otherwise.[a]
CLER = 1 if clerical; 0 otherwise.
SALES = 1 if sales; 0 otherwise.
CRAFT = 1 if craft; 0 otherwise.
OPER = 1 if operative; 0 otherwise.
LABOR = 1 if laborer; 0 otherwise.
PHH = 1 if private household worker; 0 otherwise.
FARM = 1 if farm worker; 0 otherwise.

Industry Dummies

AGR = 1 if agriculture, forestry and fisheries; 0 otherwise.
MINING = 1 if mining; 0 otherwise.
CONSTR = 1 if construction; 0 otherwise.
DUR = 1 if durable manufacturing; 0 otherwise.
NONDUR = 1 if nondurable manufacturing; 0 otherwise.
UTIL = 1 if transportation, communications and other public utilities; 0 otherwise.
WHOLE = 1 if wholesale trade; 0 otherwise.
RETAIL = 1 if retail trade; 0 otherwise.
FIRE = 1 if finance, insurance and real estate; 0 otherwise.
PERSREC = 1 if personal (including private household), entertainment and recreational services; 0 otherwise.
PUBLIC = 1 if public administration; 0 otherwise.

[a] Includes farm managers.

CHAPTER 12

Immigration Research in the 1980s: A Turbulent Decade

GEORGE J. BORJAS
University of California—San Diego and NBER

The 1980s were turbulent years in the history of immigration to the United States. Three major events characterized the demographic and political shifts. Auspiciously enough, the decade began with the Mariel boatlift. In April 1980, Fidel Castro decided to let Cuban nationals freely migrate to the United States, and over 125,000 people quickly took advantage of this offer. The Marielitos, as they came to be known, were responsible for substantial social disruptions in the Miami area, and the uncontrolled flow rekindled the debate over the type of refugee policy that a humanitarian, democratic, welfare state should have.

The 1980s also witnessed an unsuccessful resolution to the political concern over illegal aliens that had been simmering over the past two decades. Fueled by charges that perhaps 10 to 20 million illegal aliens were overrunning the country, Congress enacted the 1986 Immigration Reform and Control Act (IRCA). This legislation had two key provisions. The first gave amnesty to about three million illegal aliens, while the second introduced a system of employer sanctions that would presumably stem the flow of additional illegal workers. It is fair to conclude that the legislation is already a failure. Although the number of illegal aliens apprehended declined immediately following IRCA, apprehensions are now back up to about one million per year, roughly the same number observed in the early 1980s.

Finally, the decade witnessed the continuation and acceleration of historic trends in both the size and composition of legal immigrant flows. During the 1950s, for instance, approximately 250,000 legal immigrants entered the United States annually, and about 53 percent of them originated in European countries. By the 1980s, the annual flow had increased to 600,000, with only 11 percent originating in Europe. These changes renewed the debate over how many visa applicants the United States should admit and how these visas should be allocated. To some extent, the debate was motivated by the growing consensus that the economic benefits from immigration would increase if the immigrant flow were more skilled. This concern led to the 1990 Immigration Act, which raised the number of persons that could be legally admitted by about 145,000 persons per year, with half of these additional visas being awarded to skilled workers.

These historic shifts in the "immigration market" were accompanied by equally important changes in our understanding of the economics of immigration, for the 1980s were also turbulent years for students of the immigrant experience. The stylized facts that dominated the discussion over the benefits and costs of immigration at the beginning of the decade were radically altered during the 1980s, and a number of new questions, issues, and perceptions replaced them.

To appreciate the magnitude of this upheaval, it is worth describing the perceived wisdom at the beginning of the decade. Two key papers (Chiswick 1978; Carliner 1980) in the economics of immigration had just been published. These papers painted a very optimistic picture of the economic contribution of immigrants to the American economy. The studies suggested that while immigrants generally arrived with an economic disadvantage (presumably because they lacked skills specific to the U.S. economy), their opportunities improved over time. This improvement, which I shall call "economic assimilation," was rapid and substantial. Within a decade or two, immigrants' earnings would approach, reach parity with, and overtake the earnings of natives of comparable socioeconomic backgrounds.

The empirical evidence had direct policy implications. First, the observation that newly arrived immigrants have very low wage rates is not a cause for concern. Within a decade or two, immigrants would reach earnings parity with American natives and thereafter actually earn more than natives. Immigrants, therefore, are unlikely to become public charges. Further, because earnings reflect productivity, the immigrant contribution to American economic performance would be substantial because immigrants are (for given socioeconomic characteristics) more productive than natives. Finally, the evidence indicated that second generation Americans performed better than their immigrant parents, so that the benefits of immigration are even larger in the long run.

There was, however, little empirical study of other equally important issues in the economics of immigration. Although the policy debate has historically focused on the hypothesis that immigrants "take jobs away" from natives, there was no evidence on this crucial question. When Greenwood and McDowell surveyed the literature as late as 1986, they concluded that "substantive empirical evidence regarding the effects of immigration is generally scarce . . . Little direct evidence is available on immigration's impact on the employment opportunities and wages of domestic workers" (Greenwood and McDowell 1986, p. 1750). Similarly, nothing was known about the fiscal consequences of immigration: Do immigrants increase the level of expenditures in social programs by more than they increase tax revenues to support such programs?

At the beginning of the 1980s, therefore, the research literature painted an optimistic (though incomplete) picture of the economic impact of immigration. By the end of the decade, many more brush strokes had been applied to the canvas, and the theme and shape of the picture had been radically altered. The study of the economics of immigration became an important topic in labor economics, and articles assessing the contribution of immigrants began to appear regularly in major scholarly journals. In addition, several books summarizing, synthesizing, and expanding the research agenda have been published recently (Simon 1989; Borjas 1990; Jasso and Rosenzweig 1990; Abowd and Freeman 1991; Borjas and Freeman 1992). This explosion of activity established a number of new stylized facts:

- The (relative) skills of successive immigrant waves declined over much of the postwar period, and this decline accelerated in the 1970s.
- It is unlikely that recent immigrants would reach parity with, let alone overtake, the earnings of natives during their working lives.
- Although there was only a weak negative correlation between the presence of immigrants in a local labor market and the earnings opportunities of natives in that

labor market, immigration may have been partly responsible for the decline in the earnings of unskilled native workers that occurred during the 1980s.

- The new immigration had an adverse fiscal impact because the recent waves use the welfare system more intensively than the earlier waves.
- There existed a strong intergenerational link between the skills of immigrants and the skills of second generation Americans, so that the huge skill differentials observed among today's immigrant national origin groups would become tomorrow's differences among American-born ethnic groups.

This chapter surveys the methodological changes that led to such a pivotal reappraisal of the economic contribution of immigrants. In a sense, it provides a history of how the analysis of new data and reanalysis of old questions changed the perceived wisdom so drastically over a short period. It is not meant to be a complete survey of the large and growing literature on the economics of immigration; it focuses, rather, on the work directly motivated by what I think are the three central economic questions in the debate over immigration policy: How do immigrants perform in the U.S. economy? What is the impact of immigrants on the economic opportunities of natives? Does the United States benefit from immigration?

Trends in Immigration

Immigration is again becoming a major component of demographic change in the United States. Table 1 shows that the flow of legal immigrants has increased steadily since the 1930s, and is rapidly approaching the historic levels reached in the early 1900s. After reaching a low of about 500,000 during the Great Depression, the flow has increased at the rate of about one million immigrants per decade. By the 1980s, the average annual flow was near 600,000 persons per year.

In addition to these legal immigrants, there has been a steady increase in the number of illegal aliens entering the United States. Just before the enactment of IRCA, the Border Patrol was apprehending over three illegal aliens per minute, for a total of about 1.8 million apprehensions in 1986. A number of demographic studies (Warren and Passel 1987; Borjas, Freeman, and Lang 1991)

TABLE 1

Flows of Immigrants Relative to Population and Labor Force, 1901-1989

Period	Flow of Immigrants (in millions)	Immigrants as Percent of Change	
		in Population	in Labor Force
		Legal Flows Only	
1901-10	8.8	55.0	51.4
1911-20	5.7	41.6	
1921-30	4.1	24.0	26.0
1931-40	.5	5.6	4.0
1941-50	1.0	5.2	7.3
1951-60	2.5	8.9	14.5
1961-70	3.3	13.6	11.1
1971-80	4.5	19.8	9.3
1981-89	5.8	26.8	16.2
		Legal and Illegal Flows	
1971-80	5.8	25.6	12.0
1981-89	8.4	38.2	23.1

Sources: John M. Abowd and Richard B. Freeman, *Immigration, Trade, and the Labor Market*, Chicago: University of Chicago Press, 1991, p. 4; U.S. Bureau of the Census, *Historical Statistics of the United States, Colonial Times to 1970*, Washington, D.C.: Government Printing Office, 1975, pp. 105, 131.

estimate the number of illegal aliens present in the United States (prior to IRCA) to be around three to four million persons, so that the flow of legal and illegal immigrants during the 1980s (reported in the last row of Table 1) was about 8.4 million persons.

As a result of the increase in the number of legal and illegal immigrants, as well as because of the decline in the fertility rate of American women and the aging of the baby boom, immigrants are an increasingly important component of new population growth and new labor market entrants. By the 1980s, both legal and illegal immigration accounted for over a third of the new population in the United States and about a quarter of all new workers.

These changes in the size of the immigrant flow are partly attributable to shifts in U.S. immigration policy. Prior to 1965, immigration was guided by the national-origins quota system. Under this system, which dates back to the 1920s, the United States allocated visa quotas to countries outside the Western Hemisphere based on the national origin composition of the U.S. population in 1920. As a result, two countries, the United Kingdom and Germany, received nearly two-thirds of all visas. In addition, immigration from Asia was essentially prohibited.

The 1965 amendments to the Immigration and Nationality Act removed the national origin requirements, made family ties to U.S. residents the key variable in the visa allocation system, and "redistributed" visas across source countries. The 1965 amendments shifted visas away from Western European countries where income levels were reaching parity with those in the United States, and hence incentives to migrate were small, to less developed countries with substantially lower income levels and correspondingly higher emigration incentives. It is not surprising, therefore, that once a few family members from non-European countries could establish "beachheads" in the United States, the size of the immigrant flow increased rapidly. As a result, the national origin mix of the immigrant population changed substantially (see Table 2).

TABLE 2
National Origin Composition of Immigrant Flow

Period	Percent of Immigrants Originating in			
	Asia	Europe	Canada	Latin America
1941-50	3.6	60.0	16.6	17.7
1951-60	6.1	52.7	15.0	24.6
1961-70	12.9	33.8	12.4	39.2
1971-80	35.3	17.8	3.8	40.3
1981-89	41.6	11.0	2.3	41.9

Source: U.S. Immigration and Naturalization Service, *Statistical Yearbook of the Immigration and Naturalization Service, 1989*, Washington, D.C.: Government Printing Office, 1990, pp. 3-4.

Immigrant Performance in the U.S. Labor Market

As noted earlier, a central question in the debate over immigration policy concerns the economic performance of immigrants in the United States. The empirical analysis designed to assess immigrant performance and assimilation was initially based on the cross-section regression model:

$$\log w_j = X_j\beta_0 + \beta_1 I_j + \beta_2 y_j + \epsilon_j, \tag{1}$$

where w_j is the wage rate of person j; X_j is a vector of socioeconomic characteristics (including education and age); I_j is a dummy variable set to unity if person j is foreign-born; and y_j gives the number of years that the immigrant has resided in the United States. If person j is a native, y_j is set to zero. Although the model typically includes higher order polynomials in some of the variables (such as age and years-since-migration), I focus on this simpler specification to highlight the central issues. Because the vector X_j controls for age or potential labor market experience (i.e., age-education-6), the coefficient β_2 measures the differential value that the U.S. labor market attaches to experience acquired in the United States versus experience acquired in the source country.

It is typically found that β_1 is negative and β_2 is positive. The original studies of Chiswick (1978) and Carliner (1980) adapted the "melting pot" hypothesis (which interestingly was a cornerstone of the original Chicago School of Sociology) to explain immigrant wage growth. When immigrants first arrive in the United States, they lack skills valued by U.S. employers, such as English proficiency, and are uninformed about the way the U.S. labor market works, where and how to apply for jobs, key characteristics of the industrial structure, etc. As a result, recently arrived immigrants are likely to have lower wages than native workers ($\beta_1<0$). Over time, immigrants pick up these skills, and their earnings begin to catch up with the earnings of demographically comparable natives ($\beta_2>0$). I will define the difference in the rates of growth in earnings between immigrants and natives to be an estimate of "economic assimilation."

The studies of the 1970 census cross-section yielded one additional finding. The estimated rate of economic assimilation was so strong that the initial wage gap between immigrants and native workers not only narrows over time, but after a decade or two immigrant earnings actually "overtake" native earnings. This overtaking was explained in terms of a selection argument: immigrants are "more able and more highly motivated" than natives (Chiswick 1978, p. 900), and immigrants "choose to work longer and harder than nonmigrants" (Carliner 1980, p. 89).

My 1985 article (Borjas 1985) puts forth an alternative interpretation of these cross-section results. Instead of focusing on economic assimilation as the engine of analysis, I argued that perhaps the cross-section data were indicating a change in cohort skills or "quality" across successive immigrant waves. In view of the postwar changes in the size and national origin composition of the immigrant flow and in the selection mechanism that allocates visas among applicants, it is unlikely that the skill composition of the immigrant flow remained constant across cohorts. If these changes generated a less skilled immigrant flow, the cross-section correlation indicating that more recent immigrants earn less than earlier immigrants may say little about assimilation, but may instead reflect innate differences in ability or skills across cohorts.

Cohort quality differentials can also arise because of nonrandom return migration by immigrants. It is estimated that perhaps a third of all immigrants leave the United States, presumably to return to their countries of origin. Suppose, for instance, that persons who "fail" in the U.S. labor market (i.e., have relatively low earnings) choose to return to their source countries. In any given cross-section, earlier immigrant waves have been filtered out and the survivors have high average earnings, while more recent waves have yet to be filtered and their average earnings are dragged down by the presence of future emigrants. Again, a positive correlation is generated between earnings and years-since-migration in the cross-section, yet this correlation says nothing about economic assimilation.

Census data unambiguously reveal that cohort skill differentials exist. Using the 1940 and the 1960-1980 decennial censuses, Table 3 reports the mean educational attainment and log wages of the most recent immigrant wave (who have been in the United States fewer than five years) in each of the censuses relative to natives. It is evident that more recent cohorts are relatively less skilled than

TABLE 3

Education and Earnings of Natives and Recent Immigrants, 1940-1980

Variable	1940	1960	1970	1980
Education of natives	8.8	10.3	11.3	12.7
Log Wage Rate of Natives	−.549	.850	1.365	2.041
Difference Between Education of Recent Immigrants and Natives	.753	.412	−.222	−.664
Difference Between Log Wage of Recent Immigrants and Natives	−.031	−.128	−.160	−.299

Note: Recent immigrants are defined as foreign-born persons residing outside the United States five years prior to the census date.

Source: George J. Borjas, "National Origin and the Skills of Immigrants in the Postwar Period," in *Immigration and the Work Force: Economic Consequences for the United States and Source Areas*, eds. George J. Borjas and Richard B. Freeman, Chicago: University of Chicago Press, 1992, Table 4.

earlier waves. Immigrants who arrived in the late 1950s, for instance, had about .4 years more schooling than natives, and earned only 12.8 percent less than natives at the time of arrival. By 1980, the newly arrived immigrants had .7 fewer years of schooling and earned 29.9 percent less than natives.

The identification of aging (i.e., assimilation) and cohort effects is a standard methodological issue in many demographic problems, and there are well-known theorems stating the conditions under which the various effects can be separately identified. It is evident that a minimum requirement is the availability of longitudinal data where a particular person is tracked over time, or the pooling of a number of cross-sections so that cohorts can be tracked across survey years. Suppose that two census cross-sections are available (e.g., the 1970 and 1980 data), and consider estimating the following regression model:

$$\log w_{nk} = X_k\delta_n + \gamma_n\pi_k + \epsilon_{nk}, \tag{2a}$$

$$\log w_{ij} = X_j\delta_i + \alpha y_j + \beta C_j + \gamma_i\pi_j + \epsilon_{ij}, \tag{2b}$$

where w_{nk} is the wage rate of native person k; w_{ij} is the wage rate of immigrant person j; X is a vector of socioeconomic characteristics; y_j gives the number of years that immigrant j has resided in the United States; C_j gives the calendar year in which the immigrant arrived; and π gives a dummy variable set to unity if the observation was drawn from the 1980 cross-section. The coefficient α gives the impact of years-since-migration and will be called the "aging" or assimilation effect; the coefficient β gives the impact of cohort membership, and will be called the cohort effect; and the coefficient γ gives the impact of aggregate economic conditions on wages and will be called the period effect. Although equations (2a) and (2b) give a highly simplified version of an aging/period/cohort effects model, the generic system easily illustrates the central issues.

The key problem is that the parameters in (2a) and (2b) cannot be identified without further restrictions. Because of the identity

$$y_j \equiv \pi_j(1980 - C_j) + (1-\pi_j)(1970 - C_j), \tag{3}$$

there is perfect collinearity between the variables y_j, C_j, and π_j in the immigrant earnings function. In order to identify two of the effects, an assumption must be made about the third. In my work, I chose the restriction that $\gamma_i = \gamma_n$, so that the immigrant/native percentage wage differential is independent of cyclical fluctuations in the wage level. Of course, other identification restrictions can be made, and a "grid" of estimated parameters can be presented for alternative restrictions. By definition, estimates of aging and cohort effects are conditional on the chosen normalization for period effects.

Figure 1 illustrates the age/earnings profiles implied by estimates of a slightly more general specification of the model using the 1970 and 1980 census data (see Borjas 1991 for details). Because recent immigrant waves have a large initial wage disadvantage, they will not reach earnings parity with natives during their working careers. Even after 30 years in the United States, the post-1965 immigrants lag far behind natives in their economic achievement.

FIGURE 1
Earnings over the Working Life for Immigrant and Native Men

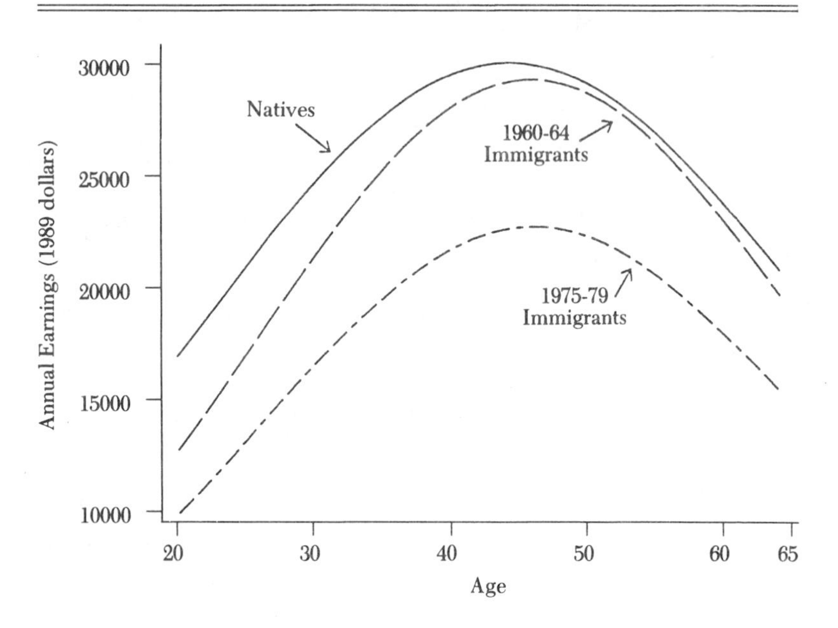

Because the policy implications of the two alternative hypotheses—assimilation versus cohort quality changes—are strikingly different, the study of identification restrictions and other estimation problems is becoming a burgeoning industry (Chiswick 1986;

LaLonde and Topel 1992). Two recent articles (Smith 1991; Friedberg 1992), for instance, generalize the model to account for the age at which an immigrant arrives in the United States. It is likely, for instance, that persons who migrate as children (and obtain much of their schooling in the United States) experience a very different assimilation process than persons who migrated as adults. The identification problem, however, does not disappear with more general specifications; in fact, it becomes more severe. Consider, for instance, the following generalization of (2a) and (2b):

$$\text{(4a)} \qquad \log w_{nk} = X_k\delta_n + \rho_n A_k + \gamma_n \pi_k + \epsilon_{nk},$$

$$\text{(4b)} \qquad \log w_{ij} = X_j\delta_i + \rho_i A_j + \alpha y_j + \beta C_j + \gamma_i \pi_j + \theta M_j + \epsilon_{ij},$$

where A indicates the person's age at the time the cross-section survey is observed, and M_j is age at migration. Equations (4a) and (4b) explicitly indicate that age is a separate controlling variable, and introduces age-at-migration linearly. The identity given by (3) still holds, so that some restriction regarding the period effect will still be required. However, the system remains unidentified because a new identity is introduced: $M_j \equiv A_j - y_j$. It is evident that an additional restriction is required to estimate the model. One possible restriction (implicitly used by both Smith and Friedberg) is that $\rho_i = \rho_n$. This restriction says that the impact of one year of pre-U.S. age (or experience) on U.S. earnings for immigrants is the same as the impact of one year of experience on earnings for natives. Although the validity of this restriction is debatable, some restriction must be imposed in order to identify the model. The lesson is clear: estimates of cohort and assimilation effects for immigrants are conditional on the imposed restrictions, and reasonable people can disagree on the validity of the underlying restrictions.

I believe the jury is still out on the question of exactly how much of the cross-section wage growth is truly assimilation and how much can be explained by cohort differentials. Most studies, however, do suggest that cohort differences are important. At the very least, the available evidence should make one quite wary of attaching any meaningful structural interpretation to cross-section regressions.

A number of studies have tried to identify the factors responsible for the skill decline across immigrant waves (Borjas 1992b; LaLonde and Topel 1992). One variable seems to be mainly responsible for the lagging economic performance of more recent waves:

the changing national origin mix of immigrants. As noted earlier, post-1965 immigrants are much more likely to originate in Latin American and Asian countries. As shown in Table 4, there are huge disparities in the relative wage of the various national origin groups. In 1980, for instance, the immigrants who had just arrived from Sweden or the United Kingdom earned about 20 percent more than natives, those from India or Iran earned about 20 percent less, while those from Mexico or Haiti earned about 50 percent less.

TABLE 4

Labor Market Performance of Immigrant Men Relative to Natives in 1980, By National Origin Group

Origin	Percentage Wage Differential Between: Immigrants and Natives	Recent Immigrants and Natives
Europe		
Germany	17.1	30.3
Greece	−17.1	−28.8
Italy	−1.2	−14.9
Poland	1.7	−30.9
Sweden	27.0	17.6
United Kingdom	23.5	21.2
Asia		
China	−19.8	−41.6
India	13.0	−18.8
Iran	−5.3	−20.0
Japan	14.6	22.4
Korea	−8.4	−26.0
Philippines	−6.8	−27.0
Americas		
Canada	13.4	19.0
Cuba	−16.7	−41.7
Dominican Republic	−37.9	−49.3
Haiti	−31.1	−48.0
Jamaica	−19.2	−30.3
Mexico	−32.8	−47.3

Note: Recent Immigrants are defined as foreign-born persons residing outside the United States five years prior to the census date.

Source: George J. Borjas, *Friends or Strangers: The Impact of Immigrants on the U.S. Economy*, New York: Basic Books, 1990, p. 232.

Two factors explain the dispersion in skills and labor market performance among national origin groups. First, skills attained in advanced, industrialized economies are more easily transferable to the American labor market. After all, the industrial structure of advanced economies and the types of skills rewarded by those labor markets greatly resemble the industrial structure of the United States and the types of skills rewarded by American employers. In contrast, the industrial structures and labor markets of less developed countries require skills that are much less useful in the American labor market. The human capital embodied in residents of those countries is, to some extent, "specific" to those countries and is not easily transferable to the U.S. labor market.

There is, however, an additional reason for the dispersion in skills among national origin groups. Suppose that immigration to the United States is mainly motivated by the search for better economic opportunities. Which individuals find it worthwhile to migrate? If the worker originates in a country that offers relatively low returns to their skills, as is common in countries with relatively egalitarian income distributions such as the United Kingdom and Sweden, the source country in effect "taxes" able workers and "insures" the least productive against poor labor market outcomes. This situation obviously generates incentives for the most able to migrate to the United States and the immigrant flow is positively selected (i.e., a "brain drain"). Conversely, if the source country offers relatively high rates of return to skills (which is typically true in countries with substantial income inequality, such as Mexico), the United States now taxes the most able and subsidizes the least productive. Economic conditions in the U.S. relative to those in the country of origin become a magnet for individuals with relatively low earnings capacities, and the immigrant flow is negatively selected.

The logic underlying these arguments is based on the well-known Roy model of occupational self-selection. Its application to the economics of immigration (see Borjas 1987, 1991) opens up a number of research questions that remain unexplored. It is, therefore, instructive to see how the main results can be derived in an extremely simple setting.

Suppose that persons in country 0 (the source country) are trying to decide if they should migrate to the United States (country 1). Suppose further that (log) earnings depend on a single factor, skills, which is completely transferable across countries. The earnings function in the two countries can be written as:

$$\log w_{i0} = \mu_0 + r_0 s_i, \tag{5a}$$

$$\log w_{i1} = \mu_1 + r_1 s_i, \tag{5b}$$

where w_{ij} gives the earnings of person i in country j; r_j is the rate of return to skills in country j; s_i gives the person's skills; and the parameters μ_0 and μ_1 are constant. It costs C_i dollars for a person to migrate to the United States. Define $K = C_i/w_{i0}$ to be a time-equivalent measure of migration costs. For simplicity, suppose that k is constant. The migration decision is then guided by the index function:

(6) $$I = \log[w_{i1}/(w_{i0}+C_i)] \approx (\mu_1-\mu_0-k) + (r_1-r_0)s_i.$$

A person migrates to the United States if $I > 0$, and remains in the source country otherwise.

This behavioral rule implies that:

(7a) Migrate if: $s_i > (\mu_0+k-\mu_1)/(r_1-r_0)$, if $r_1-r_0>0$,

(7b) $s_i < (\mu_0+k-\mu_1)/(r_1-r_0)$, if $r_1-r_0<0$.

Therefore, the relative rate of return to skills across countries determines the skill composition of the immigrant flow. If the United States offers a higher rate of return to skills than the source country, the skill composition of immigrants is truncated from below (so that they tend to be more skilled than average). Conversely, if the source country offers a higher rate of return to skills than the United States, the immigrant skill flow is truncated from above, and immigrants tend to be relatively unskilled.

A somewhat surprising implication of the model is that the *level* of the income distribution (as measured by the parameter μ) does not determine the type of selection that characterizes the immigrant flow. Differences in mean incomes (and migration costs) determine mainly the size of the flow. The reason is that differences in mean incomes affect migration incentives for everyone in the source country, but differences in prices (i.e., the rates of return to skills) target the incentives of specific subsets of the population.

This model of how immigrants are self-selected provides an interesting explanation of the decline in skills observed among successive immigrant waves. Prior to the 1965 amendments, the allocation of visas across countries was guided by the ethnic/racial composition of the U.S. population in 1920, and thus favored immigration from a number of Western European countries. The 1965 amendments removed these restrictions and led to a major increase in the number of immigrants originating in Asian and Latin American countries. The "new" immigration, therefore, is more likely to originate in countries where income inequality is relatively high and where skills are less easily transferable to the United States. Economic theory thus predicts that the earnings capacities of immigrant waves will have declined as a result of the redistribution of visas initiated by the 1965 amendments.

A major consequence of the shift towards a less skilled immigrant flow is a sizable increase in the fraction of immigrants who are welfare recipients (Borjas and Trejo 1991, 1993). Table 5 contrasts the welfare participation rates of immigrants and natives, and also documents how welfare participation varies across immigrant cohorts.

TABLE 5

Immigrant Participation in the Welfare System, 1970-80

Fraction of Households With At Least One Member Receiving Public Assistance

			Year of Immigration				
Census Year	Natives	All Immigrants	1975-80	1970-74	1965-69	1960-64	1950-59
1970	6.1	5.9	—	—	5.5	6.5	5.0
1980	7.9	8.8	8.3	8.4	10.2	9.2	7.1

Source: George J. Borjas and Stephen J. Trejo, "Immigrant Participation in the Welfare System," *Industrial and Labor Relations Review* 44 (January 1991), p. 198.

It is evident that more recent immigrant waves have higher welfare participation rates than earlier immigrant cohorts (for given length of residence in the United States). For instance, newly arrived immigrant households in the 1970 census (those who arrived between 1965 and 1969) had an overall welfare participation rate of only 5.5 percent in 1970. In the 1980 census, however, newly arrived immigrant households (who had migrated between 1975 and 1979) had a welfare participation rate of 8.3 percent. This 2.8 percentage point increase in the welfare participation rate across the two cohorts exceeds the corresponding increase of 1.8 percentage points experienced by native households over the decade. Moreover, for a given immigrant cohort, the welfare participation rate increases the longer the cohort resides in the United States. Table 5 shows that the welfare participation rate of the 1965-1969 wave nearly doubled between 1970 and 1980.

The finding that more recent cohorts use the welfare system more intensively is not surprising in view of the earlier discussion on the declining quality of successive immigrant waves. What is surprising is the seemingly perverse correlation between years-since-migration and welfare participation rates. It seems that immigrants assimilate *into* welfare. This correlation may be related to the lifting of legal restrictions, such as permanent legal residence or citizenship, that limit the participation of recent immigrants in some welfare programs. Immigrants may also believe that their chances for naturalization (and hence for sponsoring the entry of relatives through the family preference system) are jeopardized if they receive welfare. Finally, it is also possible that immigrant assimilation involves the accumulation of information not only about the labor market, but also about the income opportunities available through the welfare system.

As with the decline in relative earnings across successive immigrant waves, the changing national origin mix of the immigrant flow is largely responsible for the increasing welfare recipiency of more recent cohorts. Table 6 illustrates the huge differences in welfare recipiency across national origin groups. Only about 5 percent of the immigrants originating in Germany or the United Kingdom are on welfare in the 1980 census. Yet about 11 percent of Filipinos, 12 percent of Mexicans, 18 percent of Cubans, and 26 percent of Dominicans are welfare recipients. Among some national origin groups, therefore, welfare recipiency is disturbingly common.

Although it is evident that the new immigrants will not be relatively successful during their working lives, the cause for concern would be greatly diminished if there were substantial assimilation between the first and second generations. The early work of Chiswick (1977) and Carliner (1980) suggested such a pattern because second generation Americans earned substantially more than immigrants and also earned more than third generation Americans in the 1970 census cross-section. Table 7 reports the average (log) wages of first and second generation Americans in the 1940 and 1970 censuses (relative to the wage of third generation workers in each of the censuses).

Both cross-sections show that second generation workers have higher earnings than immigrants; in 1970 the wage advantage was

TABLE 6

Welfare Participation Rate of Immigrant Households in 1980, By National Origin Group

	Fraction of Households With At Least One Member Receiving Public Assistance	
Origin	All Immigrants	Recently Arrived Immigrants
Europe		
Germany	4.7	1.6
Greece	6.3	3.7
Italy	7.3	4.9
Poland	6.3	2.8
Sweden	5.5	1.0
United Kingdom	5.4	1.5
Asia		
China	8.7	11.2
India	2.4	1.6
Iran	2.3	1.5
Japan	5.1	1.8
Korea	6.1	6.4
Philippines	10.6	9.7
Americas		
Canada	6.3	2.2
Cuba	18.0	24.7
Dominican Republic	25.8	20.7
Haiti	10.3	6.3
Jamaica	7.9	4.4
Mexico	12.4	6.0

Note: Recent immigrants are defined as foreign-born persons residing outside the United States five years prior to the census date.

Source: George J. Borjas and Stephen J. Trejo, "Immigrant Participation in the Welfare System," ***Industrial and Labor Relations Review*** 44 (January 1991), p. 200.

about 11 percent. It would seem, therefore, that second generation Americans earn more than their parents. This conclusion, however, is premature. In a census cross-section, the family ties among the two generations are tenuous. At the time of the survey, many

TABLE 7

Log Wages of First and Second Generation Americans (Relative to Third Generation)

Group	1940	1970
First Generation	.1848	.0383
Immigrants in U.S. more than 20 years	—	.1230
Second Generation	.2344	.1507

Source: George J. Borjas, "The Intergenerational Mobility of Immigrants," *Journal of Labor Economics* 11 (January 1993), in press, Table 1.

members of the first generation have just arrived in the United States and have no native descendants yet employed in the U.S. labor market. Second generation Americans of working age can only be descendants of immigrants who have been in the country for at least two or three decades. Therefore, as long as immigrants' skills differ among cohorts, the difference between second and first generation earnings in a cross-section provides a misleading portrait of intergenerational mobility.

Comparisons of first and second generation workers, therefore, must be designed so as to increase the probability that the immigrants are the parents of the second generation Americans identified in the census (Borjas 1993). In any single census cross-section, for instance, immigrants who have been in the United States for a sufficiently long period of time (and hence can have American-born children of working age) can be compared to second generation workers. In the 1970 census, the wage advantage of second generation workers over immigrants who have been in the United States more than 20 years is only 2.8 percent.

A similar conclusion can be drawn from intercensual comparisons of first and second generation workers. Table 7 indicates that first generation workers present in the 1940 census earn about 18 percent more than third generation workers; the 1970 census, however, shows that the children of these immigrants earn only about 15 percent more than the third generation. A careful study of the census data, therefore, does not support the hypothesis that second generation workers earn substantially more than their parents.

Finally, the evidence indicates that the skill differentials observed among national origin groups in the first generation are transmitted to their ethnic offspring (Borjas 1992a, 1993). Table 8 documents this linkage by relating the earnings of second generation ethnic groups in the 1970 census to the earnings of the immigrants enumerated in the 1940 census (who are presumably their parents). The data reveal substantial dispersion among ethnic groups in the earnings of second generation Americans. In 1970, for instance, second generation workers of British ancestry earned about 20.8 percent more than third generation Americans, while second generation Canadians earned 11.4 percent more, and second generation Mexicans earned 16.1 percent less. Put differently, today's differences in skills among foreign-born national origin groups become tomorrow's skill differentials among American-born ethnic groups.

TABLE 8
National Origin and the Log Wages of First and Second Generation Americans (Relative to the Third Generation)

Origin	Relative Wage of Immigrants in 1940	Relative Wage of Second Generation in 1970
Austria	.279	.211
Canada	.252	.114
Cuba	−.004	−.025
Czechoslovakia	.277	.137
Denmark	.291	.119
France	.229	.220
Germany	.198	.128
Greece	−.103	−.189
Hungary	.247	.204
Ireland	.209	.196
Italy	.159	.137
Mexico	−.496	−.161
Netherlands	.105	.161
Norway	.270	.144
Poland	.222	.154
Portugal	.051	−.003
Romania	.295	.330
Spain	.065	.106
Sweden	.262	.178
Switzerland	.198	.117
United Kingdom	.317	.208
USSR	.276	.320
Yugoslavia	.299	.173

Source: George J. Borjas, "The Intergenerational Mobility of Immigrants," *Journal of Labor Economics* 11 (January 1993), in press, Table 3.

The 1980s began with an optimistic perception of immigrant performance in the U.S. labor market and ended with a more mixed portrayal. This reappraisal of the evidence introduced a key distinction into the literature—the distinction between cohort and assimilation effects. Because both cohort and assimilation effects are likely to exist, and because substantive policy decisions depend on their relative importance, it is almost certain that the debate over their weights will continue unabated well into the 1990s.

The Impact of Immigrants on Native Earnings

Do immigrants have an adverse effect on native earnings and employment opportunities? If so, how large is the loss in the economic welfare of natives? Finally, are all native groups equally affected by the entry of immigrants into the labor market?

These questions address some of the most important and most emotional issues in the debate over immigration policy in host countries. The fear that "immigrant hordes" displace natives from their jobs and reduce the earnings of those lucky enough to still have a job has a long (and not so honorable) history in the U.S. immigration debate. The presumption that immigrants have an adverse impact on the labor market has been and continues to be used as a key justification for policies designed to restrict the size and composition of immigrant flows into the United States.

There are two opposing views about how immigrants affect the native labor market. One asserts that immigrants have a harmful effect on the employment and earnings opportunities of natives because immigrants and natives are easily substitutable by American employers. That is, immigrants and natives tend to have similar skills, and are suited for similar types of jobs. As immigrants enter the labor market, the supply of these skills to the labor market increases, and there is more competition among the workers supplying these skills to employers. Firms, therefore, can attract workers—both immigrants and natives—at lower wage rates because these skills are now abundant in the marketplace. In addition, because of the lower wages now paid to native workers, some native workers find it worthwhile to withdraw from the labor force, and hence the number of native workers employed declines.

It is possible, however, that immigrants and natives are not interchangeable types of workers, but that they complement each other in the production process. For instance, some immigrant groups may have very low skill levels and have a comparative advantage in agricultural production. This frees up the more skilled native work force to perform tasks that require relatively more skills. The presence of immigrants increases native productivity because natives can now specialize in tasks where they too have a comparative advantage. This makes natives more valuable to firms, and increases the firm's demand for native labor. Since employers are now competing for native labor, native wage rates are bid up. In addition, some natives who previously did not find it profitable to work will now see the higher wage rate as an additional incentive to enter the labor market, and hence native employment also increases.

The impact of immigrants on native employment opportunities thus crucially depends on the underlying production technology. Suppose that the production function in a particular labor market is given by $f(L_n,L_i,K)$, where L_n indicates the quantity of native labor;

L_i that of immigrant labor; and K is the capital stock. Profit maximization implies that the wage rate of native labor is set equal to its marginal productivity, or:

$$w_n = f_n(L_n, L_i, K), \tag{8}$$

where f_n $\partial f/\partial L_n$. It is evident that the impact of immigrants on native wages will depend on the cross-derivative f_{ni}, where f_{ni} is positive or negative depending on whether the two inputs are complements or substitutes.

If the production function has constant returns to scales, marginal productivity is homogeneous of degree zero, and hence the native wage rate can be written as $w_n = g(p_i,k)$, where p_i is the fraction of the labor market that is foreign-born, and k is the capital/labor ratio. This conceptual framework suggests a simple way of establishing empirically the sign of f_{ni}. If immigrants and natives are substitutes in production, the earnings of native workers should be lower in labor markets where immigrants are in relatively abundant supply. On the other hand, if immigrants and natives are complements in production, native earnings should be relatively lower in labor markets where the supply of immigrants is scarce.

Beginning with the early work of Grossman (1982) and Borjas (1983), practically all research takes this implication of the theory as its departure point (see, for instance, the more recent work of Altonji and Card 1991, and LaLonde and Topel 1991). In particular, the studies compare native earnings in localities where immigrants are a substantial fraction of the labor force (for example, Los Angeles or New York) with native earnings in localities where immigrants are a relatively trivial fraction (for example, Pittsburgh or Nashville).

Table 9 summarizes the results of this literature. The cross-city correlations reveal that the average native wage is slightly smaller in labor markets where immigrants tend to reside. However, the decline in the native wage attributable to an increase in the supply of immigrants is numerically trivial. If one city has 10 percent more immigrants than another, the native wage in the city with the most immigrants is only .2 percent lower. A doubling of the number of immigrants in the local labor market, therefore, reduces the native wage rate by only 2 or 3 percent. The overwhelming consensus of the literature seems to be that immigrants and practically all native groups are very weak substitutes in production.

TABLE 9

The Impact of Immigrants on Native Earnings

Native Group	% Change in Native Wage as a Result of a 10 Percent Increase in the Number of Immigrants
All Native	−.2
White Men	−.2 to −.1
Black Men	−.3 to +.2
Women	.2 to +.5
Young Blacks	−.1
Young Hispanics	−.3 to .2

Source: George J. Borjas, *Friends or Strangers: The Impact of Immigrants on the U.S. Economy*, New York: Basic Books, 1990, p. 87.

These area-based studies indicate that the impact of immigration on the earnings of natives is small even in labor markets that received very large immigrant flows. On April 20, 1980, Fidel Castro declared that Cuban nationals wishing to move to the United States could leave freely from the port of Mariel, Cuba. By September 1980, about 125,000 Cubans, mostly unskilled workers, had chosen to undertake the journey. The numerical impact of the Mariel flow on Miami's population and labor force was sizable. Almost overnight, Miami's labor force had unexpectedly grown by 7 percent. Yet Card's (1990) careful analysis of the data indicates that the trend of wages and employment opportunities for Miami's population, including its black population, was barely affected by the Mariel flow. The economic conditions experienced by Miami between 1980 and 1985, in terms of wage levels and unemployment rates, were similar to those experienced by such cities as Los Angeles, Houston, and Atlanta, cities which did not experience the Mariel flow.

It is fair to conclude that the cross-city correlations have not established a single instance in which the earnings of U.S.-born workers have been strongly and adversely affected by the increase in the supply of immigrants over the last two decades. This unexpected finding raises an important question: why is the empirical evidence so at odds with the typical presumption in the public arena?

One possible (and testable) explanation of this result is that natives attenuate the negative impact of immigration by choosing to reside in other localities. Using 1980 census data, Filer (1992) finds a negative correlation between the in-migration rates of natives into particular cities and the presence of immigrants in those cities. This result suggests that natives respond to the increase in immigrant labor supply by moving elsewhere. In effect, the internal migration of natives dissipates the impact of immigration on particular labor markets and makes it difficult to determine the effects of immigration by looking at cross-city correlations.

Filer's evidence, however, is not consistent with studies of the relation between internal migration and immigration in other time periods. Using the Current Population Surveys, Butcher and Card (1991) report a positive correlation between the in-migration rates of natives to particular cities and immigration flows in the 1980s. The evidence thus suggests that the Filer results may reflect the particular historical circumstances of the late 1970s rather than a general structural pattern of response. Even if this is the case, however, it casts doubt on the validity of inferring the broad economic efforts of immigration from cross-city comparisons.

It may also be the case that the local impact of immigration is dampened by capital investments flowing into (or out of) immigrant areas. This would again have the effect of dissipating the impact of immigration on a particular labor market over the entire economy. In a sense, to the extent that workers or firms respond to the entry of immigrants by moving to areas with better opportunities, there would be little reason to expect a correlation between the labor market opportunities of natives and the presence of immigrants and hence the comparison of labor markets could be masking a "macro" impact of immigration.

Circumstantial evidence for this macro effect is present in the labor market for workers with less than a high school education. The 1980s witnessed a substantial increase in the wage gap between these unskilled workers and workers with more education. From the 1970s through the 1980s, earnings differentials between more and less educated workers skyrocketed and inequality rose among workers in given skill categories, producing a more unequal income distribution. The relative wage of high school "dropouts" declined by 10 percentage points during the 1980s.

The recent study by Borjas, Freeman, and Katz (1992) implies that the flow of less educated immigrants contributed substantially to the rise in earnings differentials across education groups. Although only about 13 percent of high school dropout workers were foreign-born in 1980, upwards of one-quarter of American workers with fewer than 12 years of schooling were immigrants in 1988. By contrast, the effect of immigration on the supply of more educated workers was relatively modest: the fraction of immigrants among college graduates increased from 8 to 11 percent over the same period.

Given reasonable responses of wages and employment opportunities to an increase in the ratio of less educated to more educated workers, this massive change in relative supplies must have had a sizable adverse impact on the economic well-being of less skilled workers. Borjas, Freeman, and Katz suggest that perhaps a third of the 10 percentage point decline in the relative weekly wage of high school dropouts between 1980 and 1988 can be attributed to the less skilled immigration flow.

This conclusion contrasts sharply with the inference drawn from the cross-city correlations. As noted above, a potential explanation for the differing implications of the Borjas, Freeman, and Katz results and the spatial analyses is that local labor markets adjust rapidly to the increased supply of immigrants (either through labor or capital flows). This hypothesis would imply that both the spatial correlations and the macro findings are "correct," but that the findings differ because they address very different questions. The cross-city correlations correctly tell us that immigrants have no measurable impact on particular labor markets, but they are not informative about the economy-wide effects of immigration.

It is evident that the recent studies raise a number of substantive and methodological questions that are only now beginning to be explored. An important component of the research agenda for the economics of immigration in the 1990s will be the resolution of the discrepancy between the cross-section and time-series results.

The Economic Impact of Immigration

Although most of the studies in the immigration literature can be interpreted as attempts to analyze various aspects of the costs and benefits of immigration, economists have been uncharacteristically shy about actually estimating the net gains of immigration to the United States. A rare exception is Simon (1989), whose calculations show that immigration is an "excellent investment" (Simon 1989, p. 128). In this section, I present a simple framework for making a back-of-the-envelope calculation of the net economic benefits of immigration.

Let me begin by providing a crude measure of the gross benefits. The immigration literature is generally silent on the question of precisely how the United States benefits from immigration. Nevertheless, it is evident that benefits would accrue if the national income of natives increased as a result of the presence of immigrants. A measure of this increase is given by standard Harberger-type calculations of producer surplus and deadweight loss. The intuition for this methodology is illustrated in Figure 2. In the absence of immigrants, the supply curve of labor is given by S and the demand curve for labor is given by D. In a competitive market, workers get paid their marginal product (w_0), and national income is given by the area under the demand curve or the trapezoid ABL_00.

What happens to national income when immigrants enter the country? The supply curve now shifts to S′ and the market wage is reduced to w_1. National income is given by the trapezoid ACL_10. Inspection of Figure 2 reveals that the total wage bill paid to immigrants is given by the rectangle L_0FCL_1, so that the increase in national income accruing to natives (which I define as the "immigration surplus") is given by the triangle BCF. Because the

FIGURE 2
Determination of the Immigration Surplus

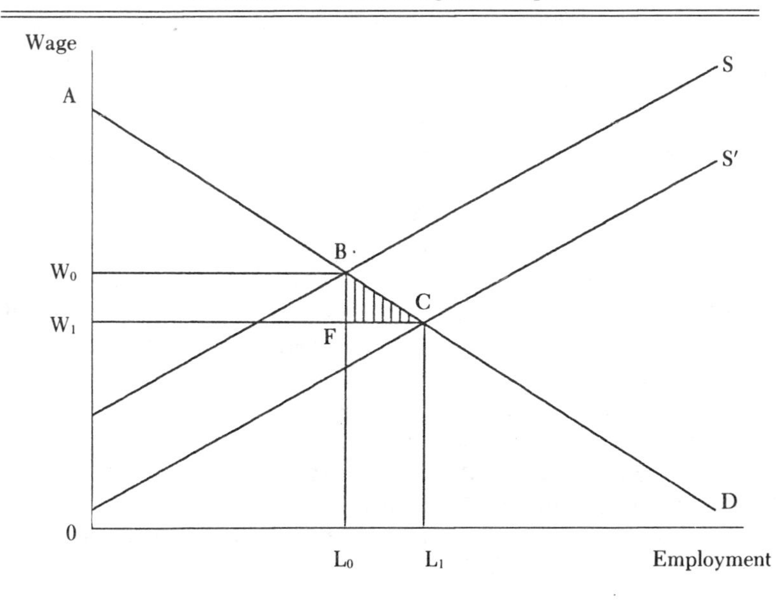

market wage equals the productivity of the last immigrant hired, immigrants increase national income by more than what it costs to employ them. Note that if the demand curve is perfectly elastic—so that immigrants have no impact on the native wage rate—immigrants would then be paid the (constant) marginal product, and natives would gain nothing from immigration. The immigration surplus exists only when native wage rates fall as a result of immigration. Although native workers get a lower wage rate, these losses are more than offset by the increase in income accruing to producers.

It is evident from Figure 2 that the immigration surplus is given by $.5\times(w_0-w_1)\times(L_1-L_0)$. A simple formula for estimating the percentage increase in national income attributable to immigration is then given by:

(9) % Change in National Income = .5 × (% Change in Labor Supply)

×(% Change in Native Wage Rate)

×(Labor's Share of National Income).

The percentage increase in the stock of workers due to immigration is about 9 percent; the percentage drop in the native wage rate as a result of immigration is at most 3 percent (based on the Borjas, Freeman, and Katz 1992 results); and labor's share in national income is about .75. This implies that immigration increases the real income of natives by only about .1 percent. The economic gains from immigration, therefore, are relatively small: about $5 billion per year.

Immigrants impose many costs on the United States, but a particularly controversial and striking example of these costs is the impact of immigration on the expenditures associated with income maintenance programs. Table 10 uses the Borjas-Trejo (1991) data on immigrant welfare recipiency to calculate the increase in welfare costs attributable to immigration under two alternative assumptions about the skill level of the immigrant stock. The first column calculates the costs by assuming that the skill level is the same as that of the average immigrant residing in the United States in 1980. The present value of cash welfare benefits (such as Aid to Families with Dependent Children) received by this typical immigrant family over their lifetime is $8,700. With 6.4 million immigrant households,

TABLE 10

Estimated Costs of Welfare Participation by Immigrants

	Assumed Skill Level of Immigrant Stock in 1980	
	That of Typical Immigrant Residing in U.S. in 1980	That of Typical Immigrant Who Migrated in 1975-1980
Welfare Receipts		
Present value of welfare costs per immigrant family over lifetime	$8700	$13,600
Total lifetime welfare costs (for 6.4 million households)	$56 billion	$87 billion
Taxes Paid		
Present value of lifetime earnings for immigrant man	$380,000	$313,000
Total earnings accruing to immigrants (for 7.6 million workers)	$2.9 trillion	$2.4 trillion
Taxes paid in all forms (40 percent of earnings)	$1.2 trillion	$960 billion
3 percent of government revenues fund cash welfare programs	$36 billion	$29 billion
Net Costs of Welfare		
Welfare receipts minus taxes paid	$20 billion	$58 billion
Net costs per year	$1.1 billion	$3.2 billion

the total cost of assistance programs for immigrants is about $56 billion.

But immigrants also pay taxes. The age/earnings profile for the typical immigrant man residing in the United States in 1980 suggests that the present value of lifetime earnings (using a discount rate of 5 percent) is $380,000. With 7.6 million working immigrants (both men and women), total earnings of immigrants are at most $2.9 trillion, of which about 40 percent, or $1.2 trillion, are paid in taxes of all forms. Because 3 percent of total revenues are allocated to fund cash welfare benefit programs, immigrants pay about $36 billion ($1.2 trillion times .03) in taxes to fund these programs. Comparing the $36 billion that immigrants contribute to welfare to the $56 billion they consume, immigrants consume $20 billion more over their lifetimes than they contribute. The welfare system causes U.S. natives to lose about $1.1 billion per year (in present value terms). The net economic gains from immigration ($5 billion–$1.1 billion), therefore, are small.

The net gain is even smaller when immigrants are relatively unskilled. As an alternative calculation, column 2 of Table 10 presents the estimated costs if the skill level of the immigrant stock is the same as that of the typical (relatively unskilled) person who migrated between 1975 and 1980. Lifetime welfare costs per household would then be $13,600, and the immigrant population would add $87 billion to welfare costs. These less skilled immigrants only earn $313,000 over their working lives, so that total earnings are about $2.4 trillion. They would then pay about $960 billion in taxes, of which $29 billion is allocated to funding cash benefit programs. The immigrants would drain the U.S. Treasury by about $58 billion over their lifetime, for a net loss of about $3.2 billion per year. Because national income increases by somewhat more, immigration is still beneficial. Note, however, that these calculations do not include the costs of other components of the welfare state, particularly health care. The introduction of these additional programs would further reduce the meager economic benefits associated with the immigration of less skilled workers.

I should stress, of course, that these calculations are extremely rough, ignore many variables, and are sensitive to a number of crucial underlying assumptions. Nevertheless, these types of calculations are, in an important sense, the end product of the economic research on immigration. As more is learned about the many channels through which immigrants influence the economy, the accuracy of the estimates will improve. The economic literature should soon be in a position to make an informed and useful contribution to the policy debate.

Acknowledgment

I am grateful to the National Science Foundation (Grant No. SES-91211538) for research support.

References

Abowd, John M., and Richard B. Freeman, eds. *Immigration, Trade, and the Labor Market*. Chicago: University of Chicago Press, 1991.

Altonji, Joseph G., and David Card. "The Effects of Immigration on the Labor Market Outcomes of Less-Skilled Natives." In *Immigration, Trade, and the Labor Market*, eds. John M. Abowd and Richard B. Freeman. Chicago: University of Chicago Press, 1991.

Borjas, George J. "The Substitutability of Black, Hispanic, and White Labor." *Economic Inquiry* 21 (January 1983), pp. 93-106.

________. "Assimilation, Changes in Cohort Quality, and the Earnings of Immigrants." *Journal of Labor Economics* 3 (October 1985), pp. 463-89.

________. "Self-Selection and the Earnings of Immigrants." *American Economic Review* 77 (September 1987), pp. 531-53.

________. *Friends or Strangers: The Impact of Immigrants on the U.S. Economy.* New York: Basic Books, 1990.

________. "Immigration and Self-Selection." In *Immigration, Trade, and the Labor Market*, eds. John M. Abowd and Richard B. Freeman. Chicago: University of Chicago Press, 1991.

________. "Ethnic Capital and Intergenerational Mobility." *Quarterly Journal of Economics* 107 (February 1992a), pp. 123-50.

________. "National Origin and the Skills of Immigrants in the Postwar Period." In *Immigration and the Work Force: Economic Consequences for the United States and Source Areas*, eds. George J. Borjas and Richard B. Freeman. Chicago: University of Chicago Press, 1992b.

________. "The Intergenerational Mobility of Immigrants." *Journal of Labor Economics* 11 (January 1993), in press.

Borjas, George J., and Richard B. Freeman, eds. *Immigration and the Work Force: Economic Consequences for the United States and Source Areas.* Chicago: University of Chicago Press, 1992.

Borjas, George J., Richard B. Freeman, and Lawrence F. Katz. "On the Labor Market Effects of Immigration and Trade." In *Immigration and the Work Force: Economic Consequences for the United States and Source Areas*, eds. George J. Borjas and Richard B. Freeman. Chicago: University of Chicago Press, 1992.

Borjas, George J., Richard B. Freeman, and Kevin Lang. "Undocumented Mexican-Born Workers in the United States: How Many, How Permanent?" In *Immigration, Trade, and the Labor Market*, eds. John M. Abowd and Richard B. Freeman. Chicago: University of Chicago Press, 1991.

Borjas, George J., and Stephen J. Trejo. "Immigrant Participation in the Welfare System." *Industrial and Labor Relations Review* 44 (January 1991), pp. 195-211.

________. "National Origin and Immigrant Welfare Recipiency." *Journal of Public Economics*, 1993, in press.

Butcher, Kristen F., and David Card. "Immigration and Wages: Evidence from the 1980s." *American Economic Review* 1 (May 1991), pp. 292-96.

Card, David. "The Impact of the Mariel Boatlift on the Miami Labor Market." *Industrial and Labor Relations Review* 43 (January 1990), pp. 245-57.

Carliner, Geoffrey. "Wages, Earnings, and Hours of First, Second and Third Generation American Males." *Economic Inquiry* 18 (January 1980), pp. 87-102.

Chiswick, Barry R."Sons of Immigrants? Are They at an Earnings Disadvantage?" *American Economic Review, Papers and Proceedings* 67 (February 1977), pp. 376-80.

________. "The Effect of Americanization on the Earnings of Foreign-Born Men." *Journal of Political Economy* 86 (October 1978), pp. 897-921.

________. "Is the New Immigration Less Skilled than the Old?" *Journal of Labor Economics* 4 (April 1986), pp. 168-92.

Filer, Randall K. "The Impact of Immigrant Arrivals on Migratory Patterns of Native Workers." In *Immigration and the Work Force: Economic Consequences for the United States and Source Areas*, eds. George J. Borjas and Richard B. Freeman. Chicago: University of Chicago Press, 1992.

Friedberg, Rachel. "The Labor Market Assimilation of Immigrants in the United States: The Role of Age at Arrival." Unpublished mimeograph, MIT, 1992.

Greenwood, Michael J., and John M. McDowell. "The Factor Market Consequences of Immigration." *Journal of Economic Literature* 24 (December 1986), pp. 1738-72.

Grossman, Jean B. "The Substitutability of Natives and Immigrants in Production." *Review of Economics and Statistics* 54 (November 1982), pp. 596-603.

Jasso, Guillermina, and Mark R. Rosenzweig. *The New Chosen People: Immigrants in the United States*. New York: Sage, 1990.

LaLonde, Robert J., and Robert H. Topel. "Labor Market Adjustments to Increased Immigration." In *Immigration, Trade, and the Labor Market*, eds. John M. Abowd and Richard B. Freeman. Chicago: University of Chicago Press, 1991.

________. "The Assimilation of Immigrants in the U.S. Labor Market." In *Immigration and the Work Force: Economic Consequences for the United States and Source Areas*, eds. George J. Borjas and Richard B. Freeman. Chicago: University of Chicago Press, 1992.

Simon, Julian L. *The Economic Consequences of Immigration*. Oxford: Basil Blackwell, 1989.

Smith, James. "Hispanics and the American Dream: An Analysis of Hispanic Male Labor Market Wages, 1940-1980." Unpublished mimeograph, RAND Corporation, 1991.

U.S. Bureau of the Census. *Historical Statistics of the United States, Colonial Times to 1970*. Washington, D.C.: Government Printing Office, 1975.

U.S. Immigration and Naturalization Service. *Statistical Yearbook of the Immigration and Naturalization Service, 1989*. Washington, D.C.: Government Printing Office, 1990.

Warren, Robert, and Jeffrey S. Passel. "A Count of the Uncountable: Estimates of Undocumented Aliens Counted in the 1980 United States Census." *Demography* 24 (August 1987), pp. 375-93.

CHAPTER 13

Work Force Preparedness

JOHN BISHOP
Cornell University

"Knowledge and Human Power are Synonymous"

—Francis Bacon

Concern about slackening productivity growth and deteriorating competitiveness has resulted in a new public focus on the skills and education of front-line workers. The introduction of "lean production" and "total quality management" is apparently raising the cognitive demands placed on blue-collar workers (Womack, Jones, and Roos 1991). Increasingly they are working in production cells in which every member of the team is expected to learn every job and to take on responsibilities formerly the sole province of supervisors, specialized technicians, and industrial engineers. Higher order thinking and problem-solving skills are believed to be in particularly short supply; so much attention has been given to mathematics and science education because it is thought that these subjects are particularly relevant to their development.

The debate has been enlivened by the availability of comparative data on mathematics and science achievement of representative samples of secondary school students for many industrialized nations. American high school students lag far behind their counterparts overseas. In the 1960s, the low ranking of American high school students in such comparisons was attributed to the fact that the test was administered to a larger proportion of American than European and Japanese youth. This excuse is no longer valid. Figures 1 through 4 plot the scores in algebra, biology, chemistry, and physics against the proportion of the 18-year-old population in the types of courses to which the international test was administered (IAEEA 1988). In the Second International Math Study, the universe from which the American sample was drawn consisted of high school seniors taking a college preparatory math course. This group, which represents only 13 percent of American 17-year-olds, is roughly comparable to the 12 percent of Japanese youth who were in the sample frame and is considerably smaller than the 19 percent of youth in the Canadian province of Ontario and the 50 percent of Hungarians who were taking college preparatory mathematics. In algebra, the mean score for this very select group of American students was about equal to the mean score of the much larger group of Hungarians and substantially below the Canadian achievement level (McKnight et al. 1987).

The findings of the Second International Science Study are even more dismal. Take the comparisons with English-speaking Canada, for example. The 18 percent of English-speaking Canadian youth taking physics knew almost as much as the 1 percent of American 17- to 18-year-olds who were taking their second year of physics (most of whom were in "advanced placement"). The 25 percent of Canadian 18-year-olds taking chemistry knew just as much chemistry as the very select 2 percent of American high school seniors taking their second chemistry course (Postlethwaite and Wiley 1992).

Clearly there is a large gap between the mathematical and scientific competence of young people from different nations. Do such gaps have major consequences for a nation's standard of living? In the view of many, they do: "Learning is the indispensable investment required for success in the 'information age' we are entering" (National Commission on Excellence 1983, 7). Morris Shamos, an emeritus professor of physics at New York University, argues, on the other hand, that "widespread scientific literacy is *not* essential to . . . prepare people for an increasingly technological society" (1988, 28). Other commentators also have questioned the relevance of algebra and geometry to the great majority of jobs that do not require technical training. It has been argued, for example, that since the great majority of employers do not currently use the new management techniques that are supposed to require a high-skill work force, preparing young people for working in high-performance work systems will make them unfitted for the boring and repetitive jobs that predominate in the labor market. This chapter examines whether evidence from labor markets supports the claims that schooling and academic achievement improve worker productivity and that the productivity benefits of quality schooling are increasing.

The paper is divided into two parts. The first examines the productivity effects of academic competencies in representative samples of current jobs—i.e., jobs which presumably reflect Taylorist-Fordist work environments rather than the new high-performance or lean-production paradigm. The second looks at trends in skill demands of jobs, in supplies of highly skilled workers, and in the payoff to skill. Recommendations for future research are presented throughout the paper.

The Impact of Academic Competencies on Worker Productivity in Current Jobs

The standard way of assessing the impact of a worker trait on productivity is to infer its effect by studying its effect on wage rates. That is what is attempted in the first section below. The surprising finding is that competence in mathematical reasoning, science, and language arts has almost no effect on wage rates during the first eight years after graduating from high school. Although these results suggest an immediate explanation for the poor performance of American students in science and higher level mathematics—the absence of significant rewards for these competencies—they appear, however, to provide only very weak support for the Excellence Commission's recommendations.

The reports that recommend educational reform, however, make claims about the *productivity*, not the *wage rate*, effects of science, mathematics, and language arts competency and these effects *are not* necessarily the same when the specific competencies of students are not signaled to the labor market by a credential (as is the case for math and science achievement in U.S. high schools).

The rest of part 1, therefore, tackles the question of productivity effects more directly by analyzing data sets in which worker competencies have been correlated with their relative job performance in specific jobs. These analyses provide support for recommendations for better preparation in math and science, but they also reinforce the findings from the analysis of wage rates regarding the important role of technical competence in blue-collar, craft, and technician jobs.

The Impact of Academic Competencies on Wages

How large are the economic returns to the academic competencies taught in high school? When do these returns appear? The

FIGURE 1
Algebra Results for 17-Year-Olds

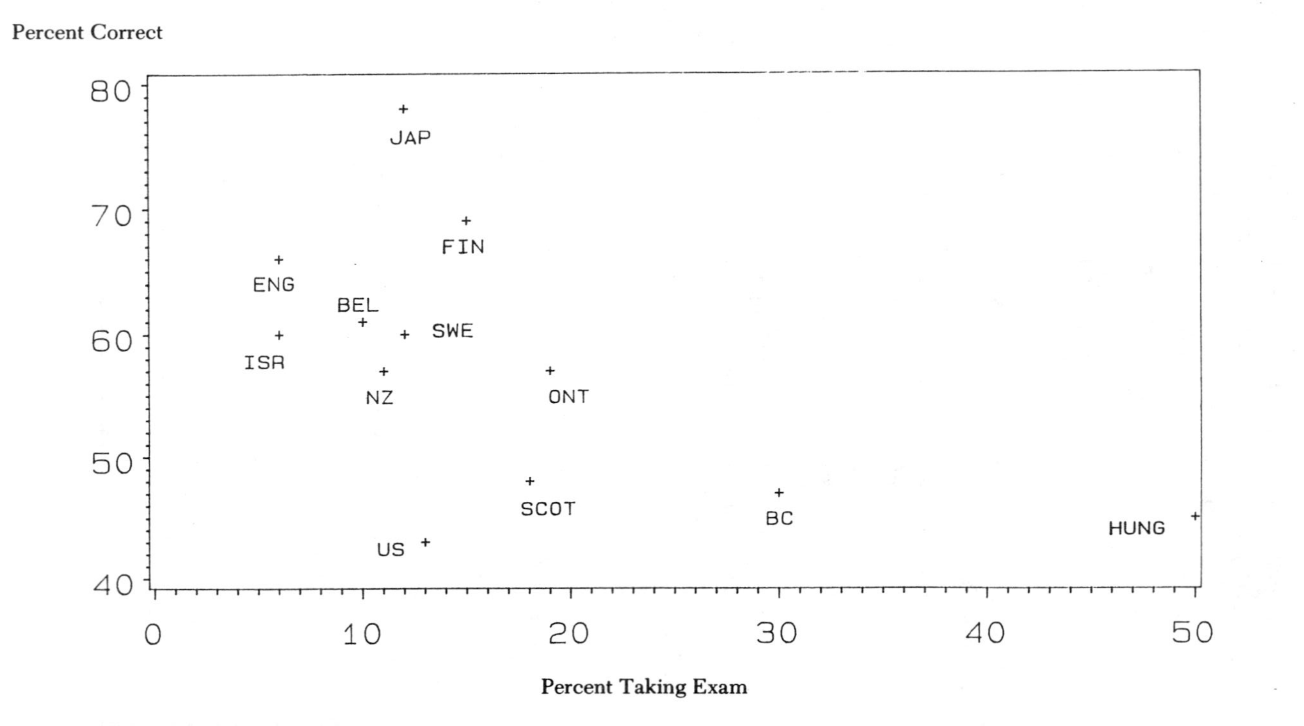

FIGURE 2
Biology Results for 18-Year-Olds

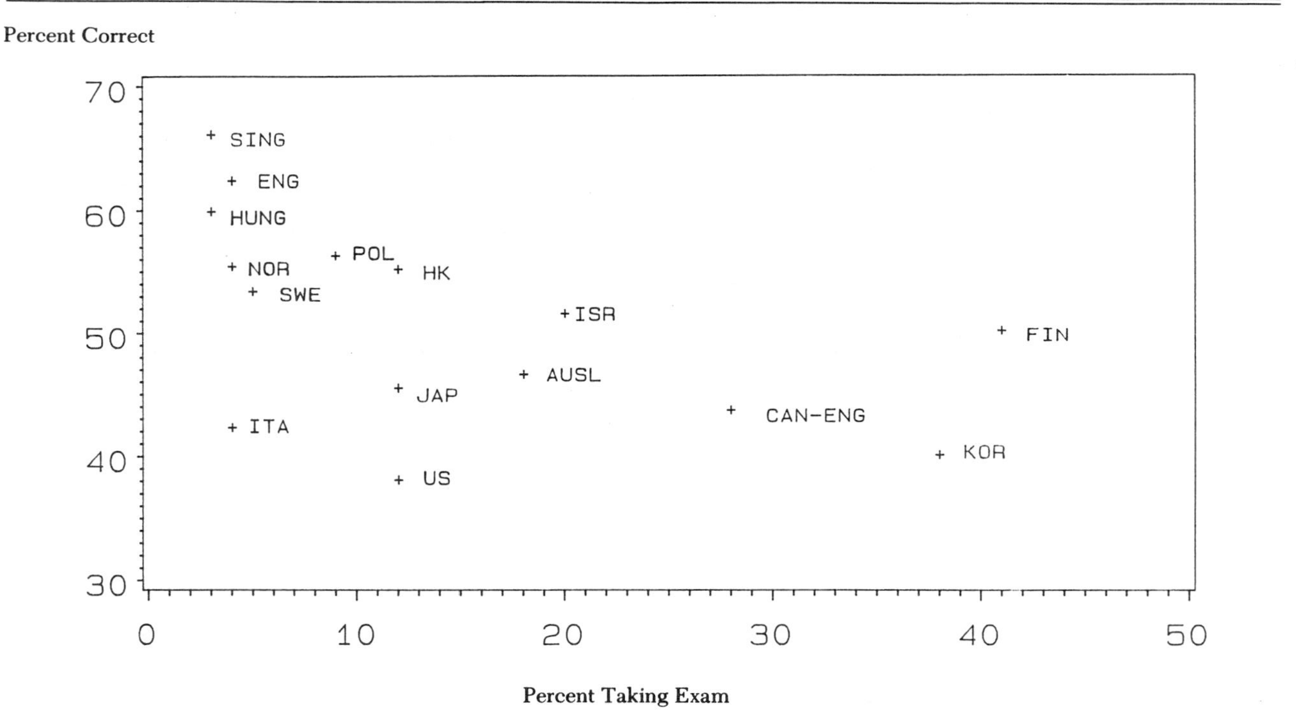

FIGURE 3

Chemistry Results for 18-Year-Olds

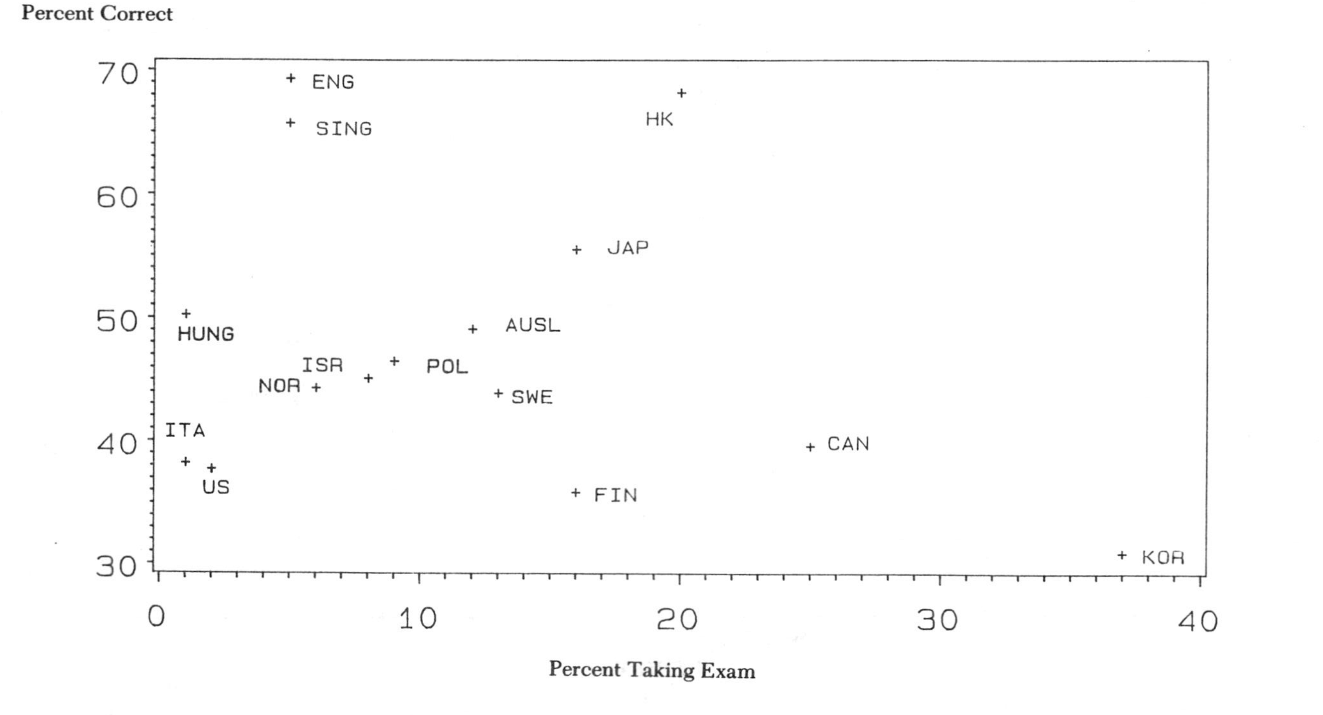

FIGURE 4
Physics Results for 18-Year-Olds

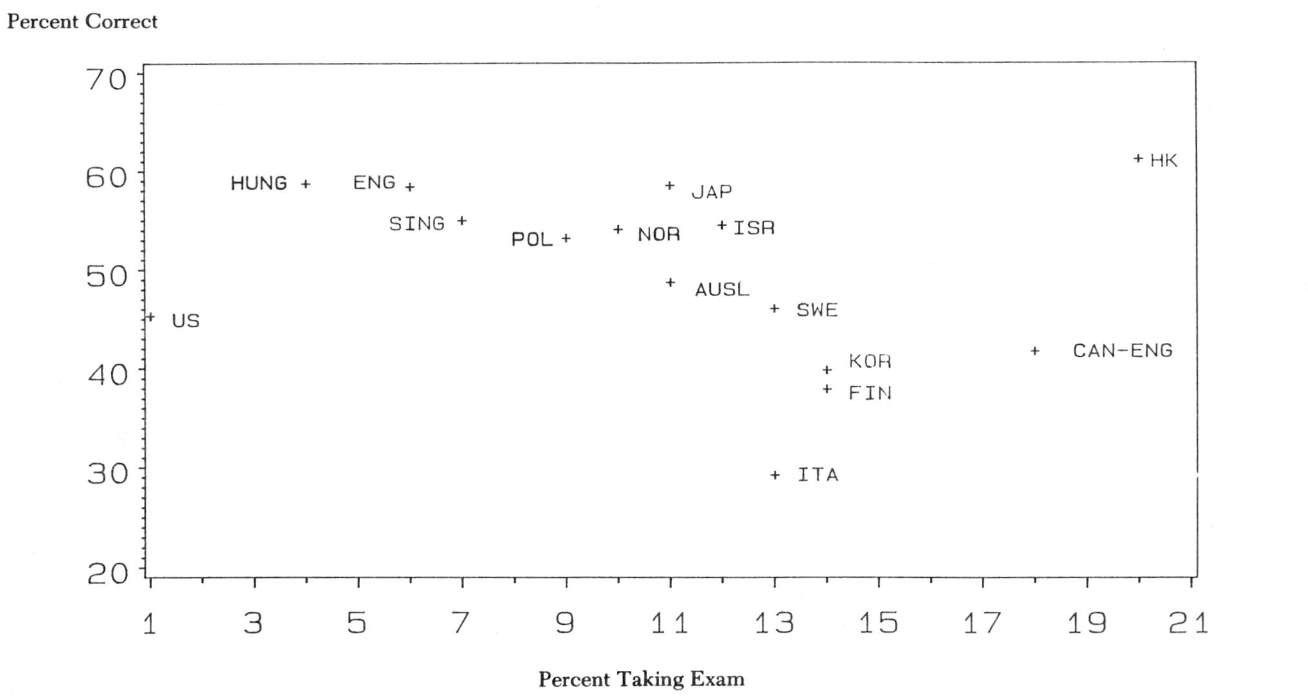

traditional way to address this issue is by estimating models predicting wage rates and earnings of young adults as a function of competence in the academic fields of mathematics, science, and language arts, and in the trade/technical arena, while controlling for years of schooling, school attendance, ethnicity, age, work experience, marital status, and characteristics of the local labor market.

The Youth Cohort data from the *National Longitudinal Survey* (NLS) are useful for analyzing this issue because they contain subtest scores from the *Armed Services Vocational Aptitude Battery* (ASVAB), a three-hour battery of tests used by the armed forces for selecting recruits and assigning them to occupational specialties. Even though the ASVAB was developed as an "aptitude" test, the current view of testing professionals is that:

> Achievement and aptitude tests are not fundamentally different. . . . Tests at one end of the aptitude-achievement continuum can be distinguished from tests at the other end primarily in terms of purpose. For example, a test for mechanical aptitude would be included in a battery of tests for selecting among applicants for pilot training since knowledge of mechanical principles has been found to be related to success in flying. A similar test would be given at the end of a course in mechanics as an achievement test intended to measure what was learned in the course. (National Academy of Sciences 1982, 27)

In a recent study (Bishop 1991), the arithmetic reasoning and mathematics knowledge subtests of the ASVAB were combined into a single mathematical reasoning construct and word knowledge and paragraph comprehension were combined into a verbal construct. The universe of skills and knowledge sampled by the mechanical comprehension, auto and shop information, and electronics subtests of the ASVAB roughly corresponds to the vocational fields of trades and industry and technical, so these subtests were aggregated into a single composite, which is interpreted as an indicator of competence in the "technical" arena. A population standard deviation on these tests is approximately equal to 4 to 5 grade-level equivalents of learning.

Two measures of labor market success were studied: the log of the 1986 hourly wage rate in the current or most recent job, and the log of yearly earnings for 1985 when they exceed $500. The sample was limited to those who were not in the military in 1979. At the time of the 1986 interview, the NLS Youth ranged from 21 to 28 years of age. An extensive set of controls was included in the estimating equations.

Holding academic competencies in 1980 constant, high school graduates were compared with high school dropouts and college graduates. Female high school dropouts with ten years of schooling earned 10 percent less than high school graduates, and college graduates earned 42 percent more. Male high school dropouts earned 21 percent less than high school graduates; college graduates earned 35 percent more. The effects of the measures of academic and technical achievement are summarized in Table 1 (see Bishop 1991 for a more complete description of the results).

The results for young men were as follows: *high-level academic competencies do not have positive effects on wage rates and earnings*. The mathematics reasoning, verbal, and science composites all had negative effects on wage rates and earnings. Speed in arithmetic computation had significant positive effects on labor market success of young men. This competency, however, is a lower order skill that is not (and should not be) a focus of high school mathematics (National Council of Teachers of Mathematics 1980). In addition, the technical composite had large and significant positive effects on wage rates and earnings.

For young women, speed in arithmetic computation and mathematical reasoning ability significantly increased wage rates and earnings. Verbal competence had very small effects and science and technical scores had no effects.

This pattern of results is not unique to this data set. Similar results were obtained in Willis and Rosen's (1979) analysis of the earnings of those who chose not to attend college, in the NBER-Thorndike data; Kang and Bishop's (1986) analysis of high school and beyond seniors; and Bishop, Blakemore, and Low's (1985) analysis of both class of 1972 and high school and beyond data. Measures of noncognitive achievement in high school such as rates of attendance, extracurricular activities, and an absence of discipline problems also fail to have positive effects on initial success in the labor market for the noncollege bound in high school and beyond data (Hotchkiss 1985; Bishop, Blakemore, and Low 1985; Rosenbaum 1989).

TABLE 1
Effect of Competencies on Log Wage Rates and Earnings

	Technical	Clerical Speed	Computation Speed	Math Reasoning	Verbal	Science	R^2	Number of Obs.	F Test on Academic Coef.
MALES									
Wages—1986	.080***	.005	.064***	−.007	−.021	−.008	.264	4272	4.35**
	(6.10)	(.51)	(5.75)	(.51)	(1.49)	(.60)			neg
Earnings—1985	.133***	.004	.119***	−.037*	.014	−.021	.358	4564	2.4
	(6.26)	(.21)	(6.55)	(1.78)	(.61)	(.93)			
FEMALES									
Wages—1986	.006	.028***	.024**	.027*	.027*	.012	.275	4080	12.6***
	(.31)	(2.60)	(2.04)	(1.94)	(1.75)	(.81)			pos
Earnings—1985	−.020	.022	.053***	.065***	.039	.009	.328	3888	11.8***
	(.64)	(1.14)	(2.60)	(2.66)	(1.40)	(.34)			pos

* $p < .05$ on a one tail test.
** $p < .025$ on a one tail test.
*** $p < .005$ on a one tail test.
T Statistics are in parentheses under the coefficient.

Source: Analysis of the 1986 National Longitudinal Survey of Youth. Sample excluded individuals who were in the military in 1979 but included both full- and part-time students if they had a job in 1985 or 1986. School attendance was controlled by four separate variables: a dummy for respondent is in school at the time of the interview; a dummy for respondent has been in school since the last interview; a dummy for part-time attendance and the share of the calendar year that the youth reported attending school derived from the NLS's monthly time log. Years of schooling was controlled by four variables: years of schooling, a dummy for high school graduation, years of college education completed, and years of schooling completed since the ASVAB tests were taken. Reports of weeks spent in civilian employment were available all the way back through 1975. For each individual, these weeks worked reports were aggregated across time and an estimate of cumulated civilian work experience was derived for January 1 of each year in the longitudinal file. This variable and its square was included in every model as was age, age squared, and current and past military experience. The individual's family situation was controlled by dummy variables for being married and for having at least one child. Minority status was controlled by a dummy variable for Hispanic and two dummy variables for race. Characteristics of the local labor market were held constant by entering the following variables: dummy variables for the four Census regions, a dummy variable for rural residence and for residence outside an SMSA, and measures of the unemployment rate in the local labor market during that year.

Rewards for academic achievement do, however, increase with age. Apparently, certain types of academic achievement improve access to jobs offering considerable training and enable workers to get more out of the training. Furthermore, academic achievement is poorly signaled to employers; so there are long delays before the labor market identifies and rewards workers who, because of their academic achievements, are exceptionally productive. When age was interacted with an overall indicator of academic achievement, positive interactions were obtained by Hauser and Daymont (1977); Taubman and Wales (1975); and Murnane, Willett, and Levy (1991). Bishop's (1991) analysis of NLS Youth data found, however, that it is the reward to computational speed which grows with age, not the reward to mathematical reasoning, verbal, and science ability as measured by the ASVAB subtests.

These results suggest an immediate explanation for the poor performance of American students in science and mathematics and possibly even for the absenteeism and discipline problems that plague American high schools. *For the 80 percent of youth who are not planning to pursue a career in medicine, science, or engineering, there are no immediate labor market rewards for developing these competencies. For the great bulk of students, therefore, the incentives to devote time and energy to the often difficult task of learning these subjects are very weak and significantly delayed.*

Do these findings also imply that if a way could be found to recruit a high-quality engineering and scientific elite (possibly by recruiting scientists and engineers from abroad or early identification of talented youth), there would be little need to worry about the poor math and science preparation of most American youth? It is to this question I now turn.

Is There Reason to Expect Wage Effects of Specific Competencies To Be the Same as Their Productivity Effects?

Are the productivity effects of achievement in science, mathematical reasoning, and English essentially zero in the types of jobs occupied by most young workers? What are the effects of technical competence on productivity?

One approach to these questions is to ask employers directly about the nature of the tasks performed in specific jobs. When the owners of small and medium-sized businesses in the United States were asked how frequently the employee most recently hired by their firm needed to "use knowledge gained of chemistry, physics or biology" in their job, 74 percent reported that such knowledge was never required and only 12 percent reported such knowledge was used at least once a week.[1] Asked how frequently the new employee had to "use algebra, trigonometry or calculus," 68 percent reported that such skills were never required by the job and only 12 percent reported they were used at least once a week.

The skills used by entry-level workers at small and medium-sized firms, however, are not decisive evidence regarding employer needs for three reasons. First, the low levels of scientific and mathematical competence in the work force available to small and medium-sized firms may have forced them to put off technological innovations such as statistical process control that require such skills, and to simplify the functions that are performed by workers who lack technical training. If better educated workers were available, entry-level workers might be given greater responsibility and become more productive. Second, the Bishop and Griffin study does not tell us what is happening at large firms or in the jobs occupied by long-tenure employees at small firms. The CEOs of many large, technologically progressive companies such as Motorola and Xerox insist that their factory jobs now require workers who are much better prepared in math and science than ever before. Third, employers may not realize how the knowledge and skills developed in high school science and mathematics classes contribute to productivity in their jobs. Without knowing which employee possesses which academic skills, they would have no way of learning from experience which scientific and mathematical skills are helpful in doing a particular job. Science and mathematics courses are thought to teach thinking, reasoning, and learning skills applicable outside the classroom and the laboratory. If these skills are indeed successfully developed by these courses, productivity might benefit even when there are no visible connections between job tasks and course content.

A second approach to estimating the effect of a trait on productivity, one favored by economists, has been to infer its effect by studying its effect on wage rates. Such an approach is not justified in this case. In the United States academic achievements in high school—particularly the fine details of achievement in a particular domain like science, mathematical reasoning, or reading ability—are not well signaled to the labor market. When competencies which are highly correlated with each other are poorly signaled to the labor market, American employers have a difficult time figuring out which competencies they need and an even more difficult time finding high school graduates with the particular constellations of academic abilities they may believe they need. As a result, the relationship between their wage offers and the imperfect signals of worker competencies available to them is unlikely to reflect the true relationship between productivity and these competencies.

The signaling failure in the United States. In Canada, Australia, Japan, and Europe, educational systems administer achievement exams which are closely tied to the secondary school curriculum. Students generally take between three and nine different examinations. These are not pass/fail minimum competency exams. On the baccalaureate, for example, there are four different levels of pass: *Très Bien, Bien, Assez Bien*, and a regular pass (Noah and Eckstein 1988). Grades on these exams are requested on job applications and typically included on one's resumé. While employers report they pay less attention to exam grades when hiring workers who have been out of school many years, it is nevertheless significant that the information remains on one's resumé long after graduation from secondary school.

In Japan, clerical, service, and blue-collar jobs at the best firms are available only to those who are recommended by their high school. The most prestigious firms have long-term arrangements with particular high schools to which they delegate the responsibility of selecting the new hire(s) for the firm. The criteria by which the high schools make their selections are, by mutual agreement, grades, and exam results. In addition, most employers administer their own battery of selection tests prior to hiring. The number of graduates that a high school is able to place in this way depends on its reputation and the company's past experience with graduates from the school (Rosenbaum and Kariya 1989).

The hiring environment for clerical, service, and blue-collar jobs is very different in the United States. American employers generally lack objective information on applicant accomplishments, skills, and productivity. Tests are available for measuring basic skills, but EEOC guidelines resulted in a drastic reduction in their use after 1971. These guidelines prohibit the use of a test on which minorities or women score below white males unless the employer can prove that the test is a valid predictor of performance for the jobs at that firm. During the 1970s each firm proposing to use a test had to do its own validity study separately on blacks and whites (Wigdor 1982). Small firms found the costs prohibitive and did not have enough employees to justify such a study. The firm also had to be able to prove that no other test or selection method was available that was equally valid but had less adverse impact. Litigation costs and the potential liability were substantial. Using an event study methodology, Joni Hersch (1991) found that corporations that were the target of a class action discrimination suit that was important enough to appear in the *Wall Street Journal* experienced a 15 percent decline in their market value during the 61-day period surrounding the announcement of the suit. Not surprisingly, companies became extremely cautious about using tests. The threat of an EEO suit caused many firms to drop tests altogether, while other firms used the test only to screen out the bottom 10 or 20 percent of job applicants, rather than to select those with the highest scores (Friedman and Williams 1982). A 1987 survey of 2,014 small and medium-sized employers who were members of the National Federation of Independent Business (NFIB) found that aptitude test scores had been obtained in only 2.9 percent of the hiring decisions studied (Bishop and Griffin, forthcoming).

Other potential sources of information on effort and achievement in American high schools are transcripts and referrals from teachers who know the applicant. Both are underused. The NFIB survey showed that for new hires with 12 or fewer years of schooling, only 5.2 percent had been referred or recommended by vocational teachers; only 2.7 percent had been referred by someone else in the high school; and transcripts had been obtained prior to the selection decision for only 14.2 percent. Transcripts are not obtained because differing grading standards in different schools and courses make them difficult to interpret, and because many high schools either do not respond to requests for transcripts or they wait too long before sending them. The only information about school experiences requested by most American employers is years of schooling, diplomas and certificates obtained, and area of specialization. Thus hiring decisions are based on easily observable characteristics, which are imperfect signals of competencies that may or may not be present. Given the limited information available to employers prior to hiring, it is not realistic to expect them to make refined decisions based on the specific combinations of academic competencies that students bring to the market.

But after a worker has been at a firm for a while, the employer presumably has learned more about the individual's capabilities and is able to observe performance on the job. Workers assigned to the same job often produce very different levels of output (Hunter, Schmidt, and Judiesch 1988). Why, one might ask, are the most productive workers not given large wage increases reflecting their higher productivity? The reason appears to be that workers and employers prefer employment contracts which offer only modest adjustments of relative wages in response to perceived differences in relative productivity. There are a number of good reasons for this preference: the unreliability of the feasible measures of individual productivity (Hashimoto and Yu 1980); the unwillingness of workers to risk a wage reduction if their supervisor decides they are not doing a good job (Stiglitz 1974); the absence of any real danger that one's best employees will be raided because the skills of these top performers can be fully used only within the firm (Bishop 1987); the desire to encourage cooperation among coworkers (Lazear 1986); and union preferences for pay structures which limit the power of supervisors. In addition, compensation for better than average job performance may be nonpecuniary—praise from one's supervisor, more relaxed supervision, or a high rank in the firm's social hierarchy (Frank 1984).

Looking at how individual wage rates varied with initial job performance among people hired for the same or very similar jobs, Bishop (1987) found that workers who were 20 percent more productive than average typically were paid only 4 percent more after a year at small nonunion firms, and that they had no wage advantage at unionized plants with 100+ employees and nonunion plants with more than 400 employees. Over time, there is some tendency for those with high test scores and good grades to be promoted more rapidly and to be employed more continuously (Wise 1975; Grubb 1990; Bishop 1990a; Bishop 1991). Since, however, worker productivity cannot be measured accurately and cannot be signaled reliably to other employers, this sorting process is slow and only partially effective. Consequently, for men and women under the age of 30, the wage rate effects of specific competencies may not correspond to their true effects on productivity and, therefore, direct evidence on productivity effects of specific competencies is required before conclusions may be drawn. We turn now to an examination of the research on the effects of academic and technical competencies on job performance, looking first at the U.S. military and then at the civilian sector.

The Impact of Academic and Generic Technical Competencies on Job Performance in the U.S. Military

Direct estimates of the relative importance of different competencies can be obtained by estimating models in which measures of job performance in the military are regressed on subtest scores of the ASVAB battery. These results can then be compared to the wage and earnings effects of ASVAB subtests presented earlier. Is technical competence an important determinant of job performance as well as wages? Do verbal skills and scientific competencies that have no effects on wage rates nevertheless have significant positive effects on job performance?

Most of the military's validity research has involved correlating scores on ASVAB tests taken prior to induction with final grades in occupationally specific training courses (generally measured at least four months after induction). When predictor and criterion are both paper and pencil tests, however, relationships may be inflated by common-methods bias. This review will, therefore, concentrate on studies which relate ASVAB test scores to a direct, hands-on measure, the Skill Qualification Test (SQT)—as good a measure of job performance in a Taylorist work setting as is available.

> SQTs are designed to assess performance of critical job tasks. They are criterion referenced in the sense that test content is based explicitly on job requirements and the meaning of the test scores is established by expert judgment prior to administration of the test rather than on the basis of score distributions obtained from administration. The content of SQTs is a carefully selected sample from the domain of critical tasks in a specialty. Tasks are selected because they are especially critical, such as a particular weapon system, or because there is a known training deficiency. The focus on training deficiencies means that relatively few on the job can perform the tasks, and the pass rate for these tasks therefore is expected to be low. Since only critical tasks in a specialty are included in

> SQTs, and then only the more difficult tasks tend to be selected for testing, a reasonable inference is that performance on the SQTs should be a useful indicator of proficiency on the entire domain of critical tasks in the specialty; that is, workers who are proficient on tasks included in an SQT are also proficient on other tasks in the specialty. The list of tasks in the SQT and the measure themselves are carefully reviewed by job experts and tried out on samples of representative job incumbents prior to operational administration. (Maier and Grafton 1981, 4-5)

Maier and Grafton data on Marine recruits. Maier and Grafton's (1981) data on the relationship between ASVAB 6/7's ability to predict SQTs were reanalyzed by Bishop (1990b). Since selection into the military and into the various specialties is a nonrandom process, mechanisms have been developed to correct for selection effects—what I/O psychologists call restriction of range (Thorndike 1949; Lord and Novick 1968; Dunbar and Linn 1986). These selection models assume that selection into a particular military occupational specialty (MOS) is based on ASVAB subtest scores (and in some cases measures of the recruit's occupational interests). For the military environment, this appears to be a reasonable specification of the selection process; for attrition is low and selection is indeed explicitly based on observable test scores. This ability to model the selection process is an advantage that validity research in the military has over research in the civilian sector.

Regressions were estimated for each of the nine major categories of military occupational specialties. Except for combat and field artillery, these MOSs have close counterparts in the civilian sector. The independent variables were the ten ASVAB 6/7 subtest scores which had counterparts in the ASVAB 8A battery used in the analysis of NLS Youth. The standardized regression coefficients from this analysis are reported in Table 2. These coefficients are an estimate of the effect of a one population standard deviation improvement in a test score on the hands-on job performance criterion measured in standard deviation units.

The effects of the four "technical" subtests—mechanical comprehension, auto information, shop information, and electronics information—are presented in the first four columns of the table. As

TABLE 2

Effect of Competencies on Job Performance (SQT)

	Mechanical Comprehension	Auto Info.	Shop Info.	Electr. Info.	Attention to Detail	Comp. Speed	Word Knowl.	Arith. Reasoning	Math Knowl.	Science	R^2
Skilled technical	0.092***	0.017	0.132***	0.174***	0.024	0.031	0.215***	0.062**	0.121***	0.057*	0.548
(1324)	(3.07)	(0.58)	(4.28)	(5.09)	(1.12)	(1.17)	(6.77)	(1.96)	(3.76)	(1.83)	
Skilled electronic	0.086	0.098	0.246***	0.045	0.084	−0.013	−0.004	−0.021	0.26***	0.072	0.426
(349)	(1.30)	(1.49)	(3.64)	(0.60)	(1.81)	(0.22)	(0.06)	(0.30)	(3.67)	(1.05)	
General (const.) maintenance	−0.004	0.082**	0.117***	0.121***	0.043*	0.068***	0.066*	−0.101***	0.441***	0.134***	0.592
(879)	(0.11)	(2.34)	(3.25)	(3.05)	(1.76)	(2.19)	(1.80)	(2.73)	(11.70)	(3.67)	
Mechanical maintenance	0.042	0.314***	0.206*	−0.089	0.055	0.235**	−0.004	−0.068	0.061	0.096	0.412
(131)	(0.38)	(2.88)	(1.84)	(0.71)	(0.72)	(2.43)	(0.03)	(0.59)	(0.52)	(0.85)	
Clerical	−0.068	0.087***	−0.030	0.065	0.015	0.085**	0.118***	0.241***	0.206***	0.064	0.425
(830)	(−1.59)	(2.05)	(−0.69)	(1.33)	(0.50)	(2.24)	(2.61)	(5.33)	(4.46)	(1.44)	
Operators and food	0.109*	0.179***	0.062	0.100***	0.050	−0.037	0.061	0.114*	0.106**	0.076*	0.414
(814)	(2.50)	(4.11)	(1.39)	(2.02)	(1.62)	(0.96)	(1.33)	(2.47)	(2.25)	(1.66)	
Unskilled electronic	0.004	0.027	0.062*	0.077**	0.036	0.053*	−0.010	0.058*	0.018	−0.025	0.052
(2545)	(0.14)	(0.87)	(1.93)	(2.15)	(1.65)	(1.92)	(0.31)	(1.75)	(0.55)	(0.76)	
Combat	0.147***	0.060***	0.080***	0.058***	0.048***	0.035**	0.069***	0.070***	0.139***	0.070***	0.358
(5403)	(8.28)	(3.38)	(4.42)	(2.86)	(3.82)	(2.23)	(3.71)	(3.74)	(7.29)	(3.82)	
Field artillery	0.059	0.047	0.030	0.134**	0.088**	−0.009	0.000	0.186***	0.230***	0.061	0.422
(534)	(1.10)	(0.89)	(0.56)	(2.21)	(2.33)	(0.19)	(0.01)	(3.28)	(3.99)	(1.10)	

Source: Reanalysis of Maier and Grafton's (1981) data on the ability of ASVAB 6/7 to predict Skill Qualification Test (SQT) scores. The correlation matrix was corrected for restriction of range by Maier and Grafton.

* $p < .05$ on a one tail test.

** $p < .025$ on a one tail test.

*** $p < .005$ on a one tail test.

T statistics are in parentheses under the coefficient.

one might anticipate, these subtests had no effect on job performance in clerical jobs. However, they had very substantial effects on job performance in all the other occupations. The impact of a one population standard deviation increase in all four of these subtests is an increase in the SQT of .415 SD in skilled technical jobs, of .475 SD in skilled electronics jobs, of .316 SD in general maintenance jobs, of .473 SD in mechanical maintenance jobs, of .450 SD for missile battery operators and food service workers, and of .170 SD in unskilled electronics jobs. If we assume the SD of true productivity averages 30 percent of the mean wage in these jobs, the impact of a simultaneous one SD increase in all four technical subtests is 11.5 percent of the wage (or about $2,875 per year) averaging across the six nonclerical, noncombat occupations.[2] The present discounted value of such a learning gain is about $50,000 (using a 5 percent real rate of discount). This is consistent with the wage rate findings presented earlier. These results imply that broad *technical literacy* is essential for workers who use and/or maintain equipment that is similar in complexity to that employed in the military.

The results for the academic subtests contrast sharply with the wage rate regressions for young males. With the sole exception of the mechanical maintenance MOS cluster, the two mathematical reasoning subtests have much larger effects on SQTs than on wage rates. *The math knowledge subtest assessing algebra and geometry is responsible for most of this effect.* Assuming that the standard deviation of true productivity is 30 percent of the wage, the impact of a simultaneous one SD increase in both mathematics reasoning subtests is 6.4 percent averaging across all seven noncombat occupations. The effects of mathematical reasoning are substantial and, unlike the wage rate findings, much larger than the effects of computational speed.

Science knowledge, which had small negative effects on wage rates, now has positive effects on hands-on measures of job performance in eight of the MOS clusters, significantly so in four clusters and in pooled data. Word knowledge has significant effects on job performance in the skilled technical, general maintenance, and clerical jobs and in combat arms. Although statistically significant, the effects of these two competencies appear to be rather modest. Assuming that the standard deviation of true productivity is 30 percent of the wage, the effect (averaged across the seven noncombat occupations) of a one SD increase in test scores is 2 percent of the wage for science and 1.9 percent for word knowledge when mathematics and technical competence are held constant.

Differences in science or verbal competency of one population SD are quite large. In these subjects, one population SD is about the magnitude of the difference between young people with 14 years of schooling and those who left school after the ninth or tenth grade. Consequently, a productivity increase of about 2 percent per population SD on the test appears to be only a modest return. This may be due to the inadequacies of the 11-minute-long ASVAB subtests used to assess these competencies. General science had only 24 items and word knowledge only 35. On the other hand, a 2 percent increase in productivity should not be dismissed as unimportant. It is about $500 per worker per year and has a present discounted value of about $8,700 (using a 5 percent real rate of interest and a 40-year working life). Studies using other samples of military recruits yield similar findings (Campbell 1986; Wise, McHenry, Rossmeissl, and Oppler 1987).

Clearly, there is a need for new research to determine whether broader and more reliable measures of verbal capacity, scientific knowledge and understanding, and the ability to solve problems have more substantial effects on job performance in nontechnical jobs than these ASVAB subtests. The military is currently conducting a massive high-quality study of the determinants of job performance in the military called *Project A*. Eighty percent of the jobs held by enlisted personnel in the military have civilian counterparts, so much of the *Project A* research has application to the civilian labor market. If the lessons are to be learned, however, research resources will have to be directed at that objective and versions of the ASVAB must be made available to employers.

The Impact of Academic and Technical Competence on Job Performance in the Civilian Sector

Ghiselli's review of validation research prior to 1973. Over the last 50 years, industrial psychologists have conducted hundreds of studies, involving many hundreds of thousands of workers, on the relationship between supervisory assessments of job performance and various predictors of performance. In 1973 Edwin Ghiselli published a compilation of the results of this research organized by type of test and occupation. Table 3 presents a summary of the raw

TABLE 3

Raw Validity Coefficients

	Mechanical Comprehension	Intelligence	Arithmetic	Spatial Relations	Perceptual Accuracy	Psychomotor Abilities
Foremen	23[c]	28[c]	20[d]	21[d]	27[d]	15[b]
Craftworkers	26[d]	25[f]	25[f]	23[f]	24[e]	19[f]
Industrial Workers	24[d]	20[f]	21[f]	21[f]	20[f]	22[f]
Vehicle Operators	22[d]	15[d]	25[c]	16[c]	17[b]	25[d]
Service Occupations	—	26[d]	28[d]	13[d]	10[d]	15[d]
Protective Occupations	23[b]	23[d]	18[c]	17[d]	21[c]	14[d]
Clerical	23[d]	30[f]	26[f]	16[c]	29[f]	16[f]

Source: Ghiselli's (1973) compilation of published and unpublished validity studies for job performance. The raw validity coefficients have not been corrected for restriction of range or measurement error in the performance rating. The perceptual accuracy category includes number comparison, name comparison, cancellation, and perceptual speed tests. They access the ability to perceive detail quickly. Psychomotor tests measure the ability to perceive spatial patterns and to manipulate objects quickly and accurately. This category of tests includes tracing, tapping, dotting, finger dexterity, hand dexterity, and arm dexterity tests.

[a] Less than 100 cases.

[b] 100 to 499 cases.

[c] 500 to 999 cases.

[d] 1,000 to 4,999 cases.

[e] 5,000 to 9,999 cases.

[f] 10,000 or more cases.

validity coefficients (correlation coefficients uncorrected for measurement error and restriction of range) for six types of tests: mechanical comprehension, "intelligence," arithmetic, spatial relations, perceptual accuracy, and psychomotor ability. As pointed out earlier, mechanical comprehension tests assess material that is covered in physics courses and applied technology courses such as auto mechanics and carpentry. The intelligence tests used in this research were paper and pencil tests assessing verbal and mathematical competency.

Intelligence tests were the best predictors of the performance of foremen. For craft occupations and semiskilled industrial jobs the mechanical comprehension tests are more valid predictors of job performance than any other test category. For protective occupations mechanical comprehension tests and intelligence tests had equal validity. For clerical jobs the best predictors of job performance were tests of intelligence, arithmetic, and perceptual accuracy. These results are consistent with the analysis of job performance in the military data reported in Table 2.

Analysis of GATB validation studies. More recent data on what predicts job performance are available from the U.S. Employment Service's program for revalidating the General Aptitude Test Battery (GATB). This data set contains data on job performance, the nine GATB "aptitudes," and background data on 36,614 individuals in 159 different occupations at 3,052 different employers. Professional, managerial, and high-level sales occupations were not studied, but the sample is quite representative of the 71,132,000 workers in the rest of the occupational distribution. It ranges from drafters and laboratory testers to hotel clerks and knitting-machine operators.

Since a major purpose of these validation studies was to examine the effects of race and ethnicity on the validity of the GATB, the firms that were selected tended to have an integrated work force in that occupation. Firms that used aptitude tests similar to the GATB for selecting new hires for the job being studied were excluded. This last requirement did not result in the exclusion of many firms.

The workers in the study were given the GATB test battery and asked to supply information on their age, education, plant experience, and total experience. Plant experience was defined as years working in that occupation for the current employer. Total experience was defined as years working in the occupation for all employers. The dependent variable was an average of two ratings on the Standard Descriptive Rating Scale (SDRS) supplied (generally two weeks apart) by the worker's immediate supervisor. The SDRS obtains supervisory ratings of five aspects of job performance (quantity, quality, accuracy, job knowledge, and job versatility) as well as an "all around" performance rating.

The mathematical achievement index was an average of normalized scores on the same arithmetic reasoning test and on a numerical computations test. Verbal ability was assessed by a vocabulary test. Perceptual ability was a normalized sum of the P and Q aptitudes of the GATB. Psychomotor ability was a normalized sum of the K, F, and M aptitudes of the GATB. The GATB does not contain subtests similar to the technical subtests of the ASVAB.

Because wage rates, average productivity levels, and the standards used to rate employees vary from plant to plant, mean differences in ratings across establishments have no real meaning. Therefore, normalized ratings deviations were predicted by deviations from the job/establishment's mean for gender, race, Hispanic, age, age squared, plant experience, plant experience squared, total occupational experience, total occupational experience squared, schooling, and test composites.[3]

The results of estimating the model are presented in Table 4. Mathematical achievement was clearly the most important determinant of job performance for all occupational categories except operatives. Uncorrected for the downward biasing effects of selection on the dependent variable, a one population standard deviation increase in mathematics achievement raised job ratings by .16 to .22 SDs in technical, craft, clerical, and service jobs. Verbal ability had no effect on job performance in craft and operative jobs. In clerical and service jobs its impact is roughly 40 percent of mathematical achievement's effect.

Spatial ability had significant positive effects on performance only for craft occupations. Perceptual speed had small effects on job performance, but the coefficients are nevertheless significant in all but technical occupations (where the sample is quite small). Psychomotor skills were significantly related to performance in all occupations, but in the better paid and more complex jobs, the magnitude of the effect was only about one-third of that of verbal and mathematical achievement together. The effect of psychomotor skills was larger in the two least skilled occupations—operatives and service except police and fire. For operatives the impact of psychomotor skills was roughly comparable to the impacts of mathematical and verbal achievement. These results are consistent with previous studies of these and other data sets (Hunter 1983).

Models were estimated containing squared terms for academic achievement and psychomotor skills but these additions did not produce significant reductions in the residual variance. When test scores are controlled, selection effects result in years of schooling having very low and sometimes negative partial correlations with job performance. On the issue of racial bias when basic skills tests are used in selection, the National Academy of Sciences concluded:

TABLE 4

Determinants of Job Performance

	Technician	High Skill Clerical	Low Skill Clerical	Craft Workers	Operatives	Service
Mathematics	.198***	.161***	.207***	.168***	.107***	.223***
	(.035)	(.033)	(.026)	(.017)	(.018)	(.039)
Verbal	.051	.073**	.070**	−.018	.012	.078*
	(.038)	(.035)	(.030)	(.020)	(.023)	(.046)
Spatial	.025	−.068***	−.002	.075***	.022	.039
Perception	(.029)	(.026)	(.021)	(.014)	(.016)	(.034)
Perceptual	.026	.106***	.103***	.048***	.082***	.063*
Ability	(.036)	(.031)	(.025)	(.018)	(.019)	(.038)
Psychomotor	.113***	.094***	.091***	.083***	.145***	.133***
Ability	(.027)	(.026)	(.021)	(.013)	(.015)	(.030)
Yrs. of	.031*	.026	−.014	−.009	−.036***	−.020
Schooling	(.016)	(.016)	(.013)	(.007)	(.008)	(.017)
Relevant	.041***	.019	.042***	.040***	.036***	.082***
Experience	(.014)	(.015)	(.012)	(.005)	(.010)	(.016)
(Relevant	−.00094**	−.00012	−.0009**	−.00025*	−.0005	−.0021***
Experience)Sq	(.00046)	(.00046)	(.0004)	(.00015)	(.0003)	(.0005)
Tenure	.085***	.113***	−.0925***	.0620***	.079***	.054***
	(.015)	(.016)	(.014)	(.0056)	(.011)	(.019)
Tenure	−.0024***	−.0031***	−.0026***	−.00156***	−.0017***	−.00131
Squared	(.0006)	(.0006)	(.0006)	(.00018)	(.0004)	(.00077)
Age	−.0024	.040***	.037***	.052***	.053***	.044***
	(.0163)	(.015)	(.010)	(.0078)	(.007)	(.013)
(Age-18)	−.00012	−.00064***	−.00062***	−.00071***	−.00072***	−.00055***
Squared	(.00021)	(.00020)	(.00013)	(.00010)	(.00009)	(.00017)
Female	.057	.063	−.024	−.396***	−.194***	.166**
	(.056)	(.072)	(.063)	(.066)	(.043)	(.073)
Black	−.138**	−.390***	−.146***	−.247***	−.216***	−.031
	(.060)	(.054)	(.042)	(.032)	(.029)	(.063)
Hispanic	.046	−.286***	.053	−.109***	−.053	−.076
	(.099)	(.086)	(.069)	(.042)	(.049)	(.108)
R. Square	.114	.167	.139	.150	.145	.153
Number of Obs.	2384	2570	4123	10016	8167	1927

* $p < .05$ on a one tail test. ** $p < .025$ on a one tail test. *** $p < .005$ on a one tail test.

Standard errors are in parentheses under the coefficient.

Source: Analysis of GATB revalidation data in the U.S. Employment Services Individual Data File. Deviations of job performance ratings from the mean for the job/establishment are modeled as a function of deviations of worker characteristics from the mean for the job/establishment. The test scores are in a population standard deviation metric. The metric for job performance is the within job/establishment standard deviation.

> Use of a single prediction equation relating GATB scores to performance criteria for the total group of applicants would not give predictions that were biased against black applicants. . . . A total-group equation is somewhat more likely to overpredict than to underpredict the performance of black applicants. (Hartigan and Wigdor 1989, 188)

The results presented in Table 4 are consistent with the National Academy of Sciences finding. In five of the six occupations, blacks are rated significantly less productive by their supervisors than white workers doing the same job (test scores and work experience held constant).

The effects of occupational experience and tenure are quite substantial for all occupations. The negative coefficients on the square terms for occupational experience and tenure imply they are subject to diminishing returns. For workers who have no previous experience in the field the expected gain in job performance (i.e., the combined effect of tenure and occupational experience) is about 12 to 13 percent of a standard deviation in the first year and about 8 to 9 percent of an SD in the fifth year. The effect of tenure on job performance stops rising and starts to decline somewhere between 16 and 24 years of tenure. Increases in occupational experience lose their positive effect on performance even later—at 37 years for operatives, at over 55 years for craft workers and high-skill clerical workers, and at 19 to 31 years for other occupations. Except for technicians, age has large curvilinear effects on job performance as well. With tenure and occupational experience held constant, age showed a significant positive effect on job performance in all except technical occupations. In these occupations, 20-year-olds with no experience at all in the field were 7.2 to 10.3 percent of an SD more productive than 18-year-olds with no experience in the field. Thirty-year-olds with no occupational experience were 4.7 to 7.4 percent more of an SD more productive than 28-year-olds with no experience in the field.

The substantial effects of age and previous occupational experience on job performance are consistent with current hiring practices which give great weight to these job qualifications. These results suggest that a job applicant who has age and relevant work experience in his favor but low test scores will often be preferable to a young applicant who has high test scores but no relevant work experience. This is particularly likely to be the case if turnover rates are high; for the productivity benefits of age and previous relevant work experience are large initially but diminish with time on the job.

Bias Problems in Validity Research. It should be recognized that the validity literature in general, and this model in particular, do not yield unbiased estimates of the true structural relationships prevailing in the full population (Brown 1982; Mueser and Maloney 1987). Validity studies based on examining which job incumbents are most productive are subject to bias for three reasons: omitted variables, the selection process that determines which new hires were retained by the firm, and the selection process by which members of the population were hired for the job.

Although the model described above is a more complete specification of the background determinants of job performance than is typically found in the validity literature, it lacks controls for important characteristics of the worker which affect worker productivity. Examples are: occupationally specific schooling; grades in relevant subjects in school; reputation of the school; the amount and quality of on-the-job training; performance in previous jobs; character traits such as reliability and need to achieve; physical strength; and a desire to work in the occupation. Exclusion of these variables from the model causes bias in the coefficients of included variables.

The second problem arises from the fact that job performance outcomes have been used to select the sample used in the analyses. Because incompetent workers were fired or induced to quit and high-performing workers were probably promoted to higher classification jobs, the job incumbents used in this study were a restricted sample of the people originally hired. The systematic nature of attrition from the job substantially reduces the variance of job performance and biases coefficients of estimated job performance models nearly half the way to zero (Bishop 1988).

The third problem concerns biases introduced by the selection that precedes the hiring decision. If hiring selections were based entirely on X variables included in the model, unstandardized coefficients would be unbiased and correction formulas would be available for calculating standardized coefficients and validities. Unfortunately, however, incidental selection based on unobservables such as interview performance and recommendations is very probable (Thorndike 1949; Olson and Becker 1983; Mueser and

Maloney 1987). In a selected sample such as accepted job applicants, one cannot argue that these omitted unobservable variables are uncorrelated with the included variables that were used to make initial hiring decisions and, therefore, that coefficients on included variables are unbiased. When someone with ten years of formal schooling is hired for a job that normally requires 12 years of schooling, there is probably a reason for that decision. The employer saw something positive in that job applicant (maybe the applicant received a particularly strong recommendation from previous employers) that led to the decision to make an exception to the rule that new hires should have 12 years of schooling. The analyst is unaware of the positive recommendations, does not include them in the job performance model and, as a result, the coefficient on schooling is biased toward zero. This phenomenon also causes the estimated effects of other worker traits used to select workers for the job, such as previous relevant work experience, to be biased toward zero. Consequently, the results just presented should not be viewed as estimates of the structural effect of schooling and previous work experience on worker productivity (Weiss and Landau 1987).

The test score results are not similarly biased, however, because *very few firms use cognitive tests to select workers and those that do were not included in the sample of firms studied specifically to avoid this source of bias.* Mueser and Maloney (1987) experimented with some plausible assumptions regarding the hiring selection process and concluded that coefficients on education were severely biased but that coefficients on test scores were not substantially changed when incidental selection effects were taken into account. There is a need for a great deal more research on the determinants of job performance, turnover, and initial hiring selections which makes use of the latest econometric methods. I suspect that in available data sets there is no real solution to the selection problem, but I hope I am wrong. This is a field that could benefit from additional simulation analyses, similar to that of Mueser and Maloney, of the effects of various selection processes.

The revision of the GATB and the Employment Service's referral system recommended by the National Academy of Sciences (Hartigan and Wigdor 1989) is going to require a massive expansion of validity research. Hopefully, this research program will add to our understanding the effects of technical competence, higher-level mathematical and scientific skills, and occupational experience, and how these patterns vary across occupations. Criterion data should be expanded to include wage rates, absenteeism, turnover intentions, employee suggestions for increasing sales or improving productivity, ratings of the employee's ability to work effectively as part of a team, and the employee's success in relating to customers and suppliers.

Prospective validity studies are needed to refine and empirically validate instruments measuring domain-specific knowledge (e.g., electronics, auto mechanics) and to expand the criterion demand to include turnover and promotions. Such models would allow us to study the effects of the selective nature of turnover on estimates of the relationship between worker competencies at time of hiring and subsequent job performance.

Policy responses to the lack of rewards for academic achievement. A number of education and business leaders have pointed out that the absence of labor market rewards for achievement in school is a major contributor to the public, parental, and student apathy about the low levels of achievement in American high schools. Recognizing this problem, the Secretary of Labor's Commission on Workforce Quality and Labor Market Efficiency recommended that "The business community should . . . show through their hiring and promotion decisions that academic achievements will be rewarded" (Commission on Workforce Quality 1989, 3).

The president's new education initiative has responded to this problem by proposing that "Employers will be urged to pay attention to [the new American achievement tests] in their hiring" (U.S. Department of Education 1991). The new American achievement tests now under development are not conventional multiple-choice tests. The assessments would be designed to evaluate the application of higher-order thinking skills to realistic problems. Essays would be written on science, literature, and history topics and portfolios of the student's best work might also be evaluated. The assessments would be aligned with course content so that studying and preparing for the assessment would result in the student developing competencies that are the objective of the course. The shift away from multiple-choice tests towards what educators call "authentic" assessment appears to be an essential part of the bargain that is being struck between the Department of Education, the 50 governors, and the education community. High-stakes assessments inevitably influence teaching and curricula. Most educators feel that many important educational goals (e.g., the ability to communicate in writing) cannot be assessed in a multiple-choice format. Consequently, new forms of more "authentic" assessment are an essential part of a high-stakes assessment system like the one proposed by the president and the National Governors Association or the one being proposed by the Secretary's Commission on Achieving Necessary Skills (SCANS 1991).

Will employers, however, be willing to base hiring decisions, in part, on the results of these new assessments? Without evidence that these assessments are valid predictors of job performance, substantial use of these assessments by employers is unlikely. There is a great deal of evidence that multiple-choice tests of verbal and mathematical competence such as the GATB and the ASVAB predict job performance in Tayloristic work environments. There is, at present, no evidence on whether constructed response tests assessing higher-order thinking skills, assessments employing essay answers, and the yet to be developed assessments of SCANS competencies have a similar ability to predict job performance. High priority should be given to research on these issues which focuses in particular on how validity patterns differ across occupations and between Tayloristic and high-performance work sites.

Assuming that employers can be persuaded to use measures of high school accomplishment in hiring, how are these accomplishments best signaled to the labor market? Probably the primary mechanisms will be direct application to employers (using competency profiles as credentials) and through the computerized job bank similar to the Worklink system being piloted in Tampa, Florida, sponsored either by an ETS-like organization or by state departments of education. Research also needs to be undertaken on how indicators of accomplishment in high school would be incorporated into the Employment Service's system of referring workers to jobs.

Trends in Payoff to Academic Competence

The evidence just reviewed implies that even in a Tayloristic-Fordist economy, mathematical and scientific competence contributes significantly to productivity. The case for higher standards in education, thus, does not depend on employers immediately switching to lean production and high-performance work systems. The pace of this transition and the magnitude of its impact on skill demands cannot be predicted at present. More research is needed.

The second argument for upgrading the quality of K-12 education is the need to increase the number of students who enter and *complete* college and in particular increase the supply of scientists and engineers who are so critical to the nation's competitiveness. It is to this issue we now turn.

The Payoff to College: Is There a Shortage of College Graduates?

In the American labor market particular types of labor shortages cause relative wages to rise; surpluses cause relative wages to decline. The wage premium for attaining a college degree fell during the 1970s—a period of surplus for college graduate labor—but then rose dramatically during the 1980s. According to May/June CPS data, real hourly wage rates of workers with 16 years of schooling and one to ten years of experience rose 14.7 (12.2) percent for males (females) between 1980 and 1988, while real wage rates of workers with 12 years of schooling and similar levels of experience fell 16 (5.4) percent for males (females) (Kosters 1989). Blackburn, Bloom, and Freeman (1989) report that between 1979 and 1987 the real full-time earnings of 25- to 34-year-old white male college graduates rose 9.2 percent, while the earnings of their high school graduate counterparts fell 9.4 percent. Katz and Murphy's (1990) study of March CPS data found that between 1980 and 1987 real weekly earnings of college graduates with one to five years of work experience rose 10.6 (12.9) percent for females (males), while the real earnings of high school graduates with similar levels of experience fell 3.2 and 15 percent, respectively. They conclude that "changes in education differentials . . . reflect changes in 'skill prices' rather than changes in group composition. We find that rapid secular growth in the relative demand for 'more skilled' workers is a key component of any consistent explanation" of these changes in wage structure.

Freeman (1991) reports that unemployment rates for college graduates were unchanged at very low levels (1.5 percent for 25- to 64-year-olds) in both 1980 and 1988, but rates rose from 4.7 to 5.4 percent for high school graduates and from 7.4 to 9.2 percent for those who had not completed high school. He concluded that "rising educational pay differentials thus understate the growing mismatch between demand and supply for labour skills in the United States" (361).

Not all analysts, however, take the view that the nation is currently experiencing a shortage of college graduates. Ronald Kutscher, Associate Commissioner of the Bureau of Labor Statistics, argues that there existed "an oversupply of college graduates during the 1980s" (Kutscher 1991). He cites as evidence for this view recent increases in the number of people with 16+ years of schooling who are coded by the Current Population Survey as having jobs which are not "traditional" for holders of a bachelor's degree. He reports that between 1983 and 1988 workers claiming to have completed 16 years of schooling increased by 41,000 in secretarial and typist jobs, by 59,000 in factory operative jobs, and by 6,000 in bartender, waiter, and waitress jobs. But what about the opposite kind of mismatch: workers who have substantially fewer years of schooling than are required by the job? This kind of mismatch also increased between 1983 and 1988. The number of workers claiming to have *fewer than 16 years* of schooling increased by 23,000 among physicians, by 18,800 among lawyers and judges, by 14,500 among college teachers, by 125,000 among other teachers, and by 99,000 among mathematical and computer scientists (U.S. Bureau of Labor Statistics 1990). These statistics would seem to imply a growing shortage of qualified college graduate workers.

But one should not give much credence to any of these estimates of mismatches between schooling and occupation. The reporting and coding of occupation are quite unreliable. Those coded as a professional, a technician, or manager by a census interviewer have a 15 to 21 percent chance of being coded in a lower-level occupation by a second interviewer a few months later (U.S. Bureau of the Census 1972). Ten percent of those who report completing 16+ years of schooling also claim not to have received a bachelor's degree. Errors in measuring education are also quite common and the incidence of such errors appears to have risen during the 1980s (Bishop and Carter 1991). Many of the discrepancies between an individual's schooling and occupation found in CPS data are caused by reporting and coding errors. How else can one explain the 9.6 percent of college teachers and the 5.4 to 6.5 percent of lawyers, physicians, and secondary school teachers who claim not to have completed 16 years of schooling (U.S. Bureau of Labor Statistics

1990)? The unreliability of individual measures of occupation and education means that counts of mismatches between schooling and occupation derived from microdata have almost no validity at all. The fact that the BLS keeps track of only one kind of mismatch makes matters worse. True mismatches between education and occupation are a lot less common than these statistics suggest.

This is not to deny that mismatches occur. College graduates are incredibly diverse and seek work in very distinct labor markets. College graduates who major in subjects which have little value in the labor market, who get Cs and Ds in undemanding courses, who are not geographically mobile, who have a substance abuse problem, or who make a poor impression in interviews will sometimes have to accept jobs which do not appear to "require" a college degree. Yet, despite the drag that these graduates represent on the mean, college graduates generally enjoy a higher wage premium now than ever before, particularly compared with those who did not attend college.

Despite the increase in college attendance rates stimulated by the high wage premium, the supply of college graduate workers is fated to grow more slowly in the 1990s than in the 1980s. The cause of the slowdown in supply is the small size of the college-age cohort during the 1990s and the growing number of retirements by workers who obtained degrees during the 1950s under the GI bill. The Bureau of Labor Statistics predicts that the rate of growth of demand for college graduate skills will slow as well (Silvestri and Lukasiewicz 1991). If their prediction is correct, the current balance between the growth of supply and demand will be maintained.

However, the BLS projection methodology is unable to anticipate the within-industry shifts in occupational employment demand that are driving the explosion of college-level occupations. The BLS grossly underpredicted the growth of professional, technical, and managerial occupations during the 1980s. Projected to account for 28 percent of employment growth, these occupations actually accounted for 52 percent of growth between 1978 and 1990. Their projections of growth for high-level occupations during the 1990s are probably biased as well. Using an econometric methodology of projecting occupational shares, Bishop and Carter (1991) predicted that the growth of professional, technical, and managerial employment would diminish during the 1990s. If this prediction is correct, the labor market for college graduates will become even tighter than it is now.

Which College Specialties Generate the Largest Economic Payoff?

College graduates who have majored in physical science, engineering, and business earn substantially more than graduates who have majored in education, humanities, or social sciences other than economics. The first four columns of Table 5 present data from the College Placement Council on how field of study affected

TABLE 5

Wage Premiums by College Major
(Relative to Bachelor's Degree in Humanities)

	Starting Salaries[a] Year				Median Earnings Males Age 21-70 BAs in 1966[b]	Average Monthly Earnings in 1984[c]
	1963	1969-70	1979-80	1991		
Bachelor's in Low-Wage Major						
Humanities	0	0	0	0	0	0
Social Sciences					14%	—
Economics	—	—	8%	15%	—	111%
Other Social Sciences	0	0	−1%	−3%	—	28%
Education	—	—	—	−13%	−9%	−6%
Biological Sciences	—	—	—	−1%	−11%	12%
Agriculture	—	—	—	4%	—	45%
Health	—	—	—	39%	—	12%
Bachelor's in High-Wage Major						
Physical Science	17%	17%	36%	24%	28%	93%
Mathematics	18%	15%	36%	24%	—	68%
Engineering					52%	114%
Chemical Eng.	23%	28%	67%	70%	—	—
Electrical Eng.	27%	24%	56%	50%	—	—
Industrial Eng.	20%	21%	53%	45%	—	—
Mechanical Eng.	24%	23%	57%	54%	—	—
Computer Science	—	—	44%	38%	—	—
Business					28%	103%
Accounting	10%	17%	21%	21%	—	—
Other Business	0	2%	11%	10%	—	—

[a] Percentage differential between the starting salary in the designated major over that received by humanities majors (College Placement Council 1985, and *CPC Salary Survey* 1991).

[b] Percentage differential for median yearly earnings of males whose highest degree is a BA or BS in the designated major relative to median earnings of humanities majors (U.S. Bureau of the Census 1967).

[c] Percentage differential for mean monthly earnings of men and women whose highest degree is a BA or BS in the designated major relative to earnings of humanities and liberal arts majors (U.S. Bureau of the Census 1987).

the starting salaries of college graduates whose placement outcomes were reported to the school's placement office for 1963, for 1969-70, for 1979-80, and for 1989 (College Placement Council 1985; 1991). The differences across fields are sometimes as large as the wage gains accruing to those obtaining higher-level degrees. Relative to majors in humanities and social sciences other than economics, engineers received 45 to 70 percent higher starting salaries in 1991, computer scientists received a 38 percent premium, physical science majors a 24 percent premium, and business majors a 10 percent premium. Studies of the earnings of adults indicate that the salaries of business majors tend to catch up with the engineers, but education and liberal arts majors remain far behind those with engineering, physical science, and business degrees (see columns 5 and 6).

Mainly because of these large wage differentials, there has been a dramatic growth in the relative supply of graduates in engineering, computer science, and business administration. For males, degrees in engineering, computer science, and business, which accounted for 33.2 percent of all BAs in 1973, rose to 50.8 percent of all bachelor's degrees in 1986. For women, degrees in engineering, computer science, and business increased from 3.5 percent to 26.6 percent of degrees awarded. In 1973, degrees in education, humanities, and social science accounted for 50.5 percent of bachelor's degrees awarded to men and 83.5 percent of the bachelor's degrees awarded to women. By 1986, these percentages had dropped to 35.1 percent and 54.7 percent, respectively. As a result, the ratio of degrees awarded in engineering and computer science to degrees awarded in humanities, social science, or education grew 5.2 percent per year in the 1970s and 10.7 percent per year in the 1980s. The ratio of business degrees to humanities, social science, and education degrees grew 5.8 percent per year in the 1970s and 5.1 percent in the 1980s.

The very rapid growth during the last 20 years of the relative supply of college graduates trained in business and engineering fields has, surprisingly, not significantly diminished the wage premiums these fields command. Trends in starting wage premiums for business and technical degrees can be followed by comparing the first four columns of Table 5. Relative to humanities majors, wage premiums for engineering degrees grew dramatically during the 1970s and then dropped slightly by 1991, but remained significantly above the levels that had prevailed in the 1960s. Wage premiums for chemistry and mathematics majors over humanities majors rose from 17 percent in the 1960s to 36 percent in 1979-80 and then fell to 24 percent in 1991. Starting wage premiums for business majors rose from essentially zero in the 1960s to 10 to 11 percent during the late 1970s and 1980s.

Trends in the effect of college major on salaries of college graduates who have been working for many years can be examined by comparing columns 5 and 6. In 1967, male college graduates 21 to 70 years old who had majored in business earned 28 percent more and engineers 52 percent more than those who had majored in humanities (U.S. Bureau of the Census 1967). In 1964, college graduates who had majored in physical science earned 93 percent more, engineers earned 114 percent more, and business majors 103 percent more than humanities majors (U.S. Bureau of the Census 1987). Clearly, the economic payoff to business and technical education is considerably greater than the payoff to majors in the humanities and social sciences other than economics, and the advantage of these fields of study has not diminished appreciably in the face of the massive increase in the number of students choosing them. There also has been a substantial shift in market demand favoring graduates with business and technical degrees over graduates with liberal arts and education degrees. In addition, the most important externalities of university education—technological advances—are generated by the education of scientists and engineers.

The earlier review in this chapter of the evidence on the wage and productivity payoff to various skills indicated very similar conclusions. Mathematical and technical skills of average workers generate much greater wage and productivity benefits than verbal and scientific skills. The policy implications of these findings are that mathematics, particularly algebra, geometry, and statistics, should receive much greater emphasis in the secondary school curriculum. Students also need to be given more exposure to computers and other technologies. There are no data on the productivity consequences of greater knowledge of history, geography, and foreign languages. The economic case for greater emphasis on English and science in high school rests largely on the pipeline argument: these competencies are necessary for success in college. For the present, however, these conclusions must remain tentative, awaiting the results of continued and much needed research on the contribution of particular skills and competencies to individual and national productivity.

Acknowledgments

The work reported herein was supported in part under the Educational Research and Development Center program, agreement number R117Q00011-91, as administered by the Office of Educational Research and Improvement, U.S. Department of Education, and a grant to Cornell from the Pew Charitable Trust. I would like to thank John Gary and George Jakubson for their assistance in creating the extract of the NLS Youth analyzed in the section on the impact of academic competencies on worker productivity. I would also like to express my appreciation to Lauress Wise, Jeffrey McHenry, Milton Maier, Jim Harris, Jack Hunter, and Frank Schmidt for their assistance in locating and interpreting the various studies of job performance in the military. The findings and opinions expressed in this report do not reflect the position or policies of the Office of Educational Research and Improvement, the U.S. Department of Education or the New York State School of Labor and Industrial Relations. It is intended to make results of Center research available to others in preliminary form to encourage discussion and suggestions.

Endnotes

[1] The survey was of a stratified random sample of the National Federation of Independent Business membership. Larger firms had a significantly higher probability of being selected for the study. The response rate to the mail survey was 20 percent and the number of usable responses was 2,014 (Bishop and Griffin, forthcoming).

[2] Studies that measure output for different workers in the same job at the same firm, using physical output as a criterion, can be manipulated to produce estimates of the standard deviation of nontransitory output variation across individuals. It averages about .14 in operative jobs, .28 in craft jobs, .34 in technician jobs, .164 in routine clerical jobs, and .278 in clerical jobs with decision-making responsibilities (Hunter, Schmidt, and Judiesch 1988). Because there are fixed costs to employing an individual (facilities, equipment, light, heat, and overhead functions such as hiring and payrolling), the coefficient of variation of marginal products of individuals is assumed to be 1.5 times the coefficient of variation of productivity. Because about two-thirds of clerical jobs can be classified as routine, the coefficient of variation of marginal productivity for clerical jobs is 30 percent $[1.5 * (.33 * .278 + .67 * .164)]$. Averaging operative jobs in with craft and technical jobs produces a similar 30 percent figure for blue-collar jobs. The details and rationale of these calculations are explained in Bishop 1988.

[3] Only deviations of rated performance ($R^m_{ij} - R^m_j$) from the mean for the establishment (R^m_j) were analyzed. The variance of the job performance distribution was also standardized across establishments by dividing ($R^m_{ij} - R^m_j$) by the standard deviation of rated performance ($SD_j(R^m_{ij})$), calculated for that firm (or 3 if the sample SD is less than 3). Separate models were estimated for each major occupation. They were specified as follows:

$$\frac{R^m_{ij} - R^m_j}{SD_j(R^m_{ij})} = \beta^o + \beta_1(T_{ij} - T_j) + \beta_2(S_{ij} - S_j) + \beta_3(X_{ij} - X_j) + \beta_4(D_{ij} - D_j) + v_2$$

where R_{ij} = ratings standardized to have a zero mean and SD of 1.
T_{ij} = a vector of the five GATB aptitude composites.
S_{ij} = the schooling of the ith individual.
X_{ij} = a vector of age and experience variables—age, age^2, total occupational experience, total occupational experience^2, plant experience, and plant experience^2.
D_{ij} = a vector of dummy variables for black, Hispanic, and female.
T_j, S_j, X_j and D_j are the means of test composites, schooling, experience variables, and race and gender dummies for the jth job/establishment combination.

References

Bishop, John H. "The Recognition and Reward of Employee Performance." *Journal of Labor Economics* 5 (October 1987, pt. 2), pp. S36-S56.

________. "Job Performance, Turnover and Wage Growth." *Journal of Labor Economics* 8 (July 1990a), pp. 363-86.

________. "The Productivity Consequences of What Is Learned in High School." *Journal of Curriculum Studies* 22 (Spring 1990b), pp. 101-26.

________. "Impact of Academic Competencies on Wages, Unemployment and Job Performance." Paper presented at the Carnegie-Rochester Conference on Public Policy, November 1991. Center for Advanced Human Resource Studies Working Paper 91-34.

________. "The Economics of Employment Testing." Center for Advanced Human Resource Research Discussion Paper 88-14, Cornell University, 1988. Forthcoming in *Testing and Public Policy*, ed. Bernard Gifford.

Bishop, John, Arthur Blakemore, and Stuart Low. *High School Graduates in the Labor Market: A Comparison of the Class of 1972 and 1980*. Columbus, OH: National Center for Research in Vocational Education, 1985.

Bishop, John, and Shani Carter. "The Worsening Shortage of College Graduate Workers." *Educational Evaluation and Policy Analysis*, Fall 1991.

Bishop, John, and Kelly Griffin. *Recruitment, Training and Skills of Small Business Employees*. Washington, D.C.: National Federation of Independent Business Foundation, forthcoming.

Blackburn, McKinley, David Bloom, and Richard Freeman. "The Declining Economic Position of Less Skilled American Men." In *A Future of Lousy Jobs?*, ed. Gary Burtless, Washington, D.C.: The Brookings Institution, 1989.

Brown, Charles. "Estimating the Determinants of Employee Performance." *Journal of Human Resources* 17 (Spring 1982), pp. 177-94.

Campbell, John P. "Validation Analysis for New Predictors." Paper presented at Data Analysis Workshop of the Committee on the Performance of Military Personnel, Baltimore, December 1986.

College Placement Council. *Inflation and the College Graduate: 1962-1985*. Bethlehem, PA: CPC, 1985.

________. *CPC Salary Survey*. Bethlehem, PA: CPC, September 1991.

Commission on Workforce Quality and Labor Market Efficiency. *Investing in People: A Strategy to Address America's Workforce Crisis*. Washington, D.C.: U.S. Department of Labor, 1989.

Commission on the Skills of the American Workforce. *America's Choice: High Skills or Low Wages!* Rochester, NY: National Center on Education and the Economy, June 1990.

Dunbar, Stephen B., and Robert L. Linn. *Range Restriction Adjustments in the Prediction of Military Job Performance.* Committee on the Performance of Military Personnel. Commission on Behavioral and Social Sciences and Education. Washington, D.C.: National Research Council/National Academy of Sciences, September 1986.

Frank, Robert. "Are Workers Paid Their Marginal Product?" *American Economic Review* 74 (September 1984), pp. 549-71.

Freeman, Richard. "Labour Market Tightness and the Mismatch between Demand and Supply of Less-Educated Young Men in the United States in the 1980s." In *Mismatch and Labor Mobility*, ed. Schioppa Fiorel. New York: Cambridge University Press, 1991.

Friedman, Toby, and E. Belvin Williams. "Current Use of Tests for Employment." In *Ability Testing: Uses, Consequences, and Controversies, Part II: Documentation Section*, ed. Alexandra K. Wigdor and Wendell R. Garner. Washington, D.C.: National Academy Press, 1982.

Ghiselli, Edwin E. "The Validity of Aptitude Tests in Personnel Selection." *Personnel Psychology* 26 (1973), pp. 461-77.

Grubb, Norton. *The Economic Returns to Postsecondary Education: New Evidence from the National Longitudinal Study of the Class of 1972.* Berkeley: University of California, School of Education, 1990.

Hartigan, John, and Alexandra Wigdor. *Fairness in Employment Testing.* Report of the Committee on the General Aptitude Test Battery. Washington, D.C.: National Academy Press, 1989.

Hashimoto, M., and B. Yu. "Specific Capital, Employment and Wage Rigidity." *Bell Journal of Economics* 11, 2 (1980), pp. 536-49.

Hauser, Robert M., and Thomas M. Daymont. "Schooling, Ability, and Earnings: Cross-Sectional Evidence 8-14 Years after High School Graduation." *Sociology of Education* 50 (July 1977), pp. 182-206.

Hersch, Joni. "Equal Employment Opportunity Law and Firm Profitability." *Journal of Human Resources* (Winter 1991), pp. 139-53.

Hotchkiss, Lawrence. *Attitudes, Behavior and Employability.* Columbus: The National Center for Research in Vocational Education, The Ohio State University, 1985.

Hunter, John. *Test Validation for 12,000 Jobs: An Application of Job Classification and Validity Generalization Analysis to the General Aptitude Test Battery.* Washington, D.C.: U.S. Employment Service, Department of Labor, 1983.

Hunter, John E., Frank L. Schmidt, and Michael K. Judiesch. "Individual Differences in Output as a Function of Job Complexity." Iowa City: University of Iowa, Department of Industrial Relations and Human Resources, June 1988.

Kang, Suk, and John Bishop. "The Effect of Curriculum on Labor Market Success Immediately After High School." *Journal of Industrial Teacher Education* (Spring 1986).

Katz, Lawrence, and Kevin Murphy. "Changes in Relative Wages, 1963-1987: Supply and Demand Factors." *Quarterly Journal of Economics* (1990).

Kosters, Marvin. "Wages and Demographics." Paper presented at Wages in the 1980s Conference, American Enterprise Institute, Washington, D.C., November 3, 1989.

Kutscher, Ronald. "Reply to Bishop and Carter on the Worsening Shortage of College Graduates." *Educational Evaluation and Policy Analysis* (Fall 1991), pp. 247-52.

Lazear, Edward P. *Pay Equality and Industrial Politics.* Palo Alto: The Hoover Institution, Stanford University, April 1986.

Longitudinal Survey of American Youth. *LSAY Codebook*, ed. Linda Pifer. Dekalb, IL: Northern Illinois University, 1988.

Lord, F., and M. Novick. *Statistical Theories of Mental Test Scores.* Reading, MA: Addison-Wesley, 1968.

Maier, Milton H., and Francis Grafton. *Aptitude Composites for the ASVAB 8, 9 and 10*. Research Report 1308, Alexandria, VA: U.S. Army Research Institute for the Behavioral and Social Sciences, May 1981.

McKnight, Curtis C., et al. *The Underachieving Curriculum: Assessing U.S. School Mathematics from an International Perspective*. A National Report on the Second International Mathematics Study. Champaign, IL: Stipes Publishing Co., January 1987.

Mueser, Peter, and Tim Maloney. *Cognitive Ability, Human Capital and Employer Screening: Reconciling Labor Market Behavior with Studies of Employee Productivity*. Columbia: University of Missouri, Department of Economics, June 1987.

Murnane, Richard, John Willett, and Frank Levy. "Skills, Skill Prices and the Mismatch Hypothesis." Paper presented at the NBER Summer Workshop on Labor Economics, July 1991.

National Academy of Sciences Committee on Ability Testing. *Ability Testing: Uses, Consequences and Controversies. Part 1: Report of the Committee*, eds. Alexandra K. Wigdor and Wendell R. Garner. Washington, D.C.: National Academy Press, 1982.

National Commission on Excellence in Education. *A Nation at Risk: The Imperative for Educational Reform: A Report to the Nation and the Secretary of Education*. Washington, D.C.: Government Printing Office, 1983.

National Council of Teachers of Mathematics. *An Agenda for Action: Recommendations for School Mathematics of the 1980s*. Washington, D.C.: National Council of Teachers of Mathematics, 1980.

Noah, Harold J., and Max A. Eckstein. "Tradeoffs in Examination Policies: An International Perspective." Paper presented at the Annual Meeting of the British Comparative and International Education Society, University of Bristol, September 15-17, 1988.

Olson, Craig A., and Brian E. Becker. "A Proposed Technique for the Treatment of Restriction of Range in Selection Validation." *Psychological Bulletin* 93, 1 (1983), pp. 137-48.

Postlethwaite, T. Neville, and David E. Wiley. *Science Achievement in Twenty-Three Countries*. London: Pergamon Press, 1992.

Rosenbaum, James. *Do School Achievements Affect the Early Jobs of High School Graduates? Results from the High School and Beyond Surveys in the U.S. and Japan*. Evanston, IL: Northwestern University, 1990.

Rosenbaum, James E., and Takehiko Kariya. "From High School to Work: Market and Institutional Mechanisms in Japan." *American Journal of Sociology* 94 (May 1989), pp. 1334-65.

Secretary's Commission on Achieving Necessary Skills. *What Work Requires of Schools*. Washington, D.C.: U.S. Department of Labor, 1991.

Shamos, Morris. "The Flawed Rationale of Calls for 'Scientific Literacy'." *Education Week* (November 23, 1988), p. 28.

Silvestri, George, and John Lukasiewicz. "Occupational Employment Projections." *Monthly Labor Review* (November 1991), pp. 64-94.

Stiglitz, Joseph E. "Risk Sharing and Incentives in Sharecropping." *Review of Economic Studies* 61 (April 1974), pp. 219-56.

Thorndike, R. L. *Personnel Selection: Test and Measurement Techniques*. New York: Wiley, 1949.

Taubman, P., and T. Wales. "Education as an Investment and a Screening Device." In *Education, Income, and Human Behavior*, ed. F. T. Juster. New York: McGraw-Hill, 1975.

U.S. Bureau of Labor Statistics. Unpublished Table F-3, 1983-1988, "Trends in the Employment of Persons Who Have 4 or More Years of College Education and the Percent They Comprise of Total Occupation Employment, by Detailed Occupation," 1990, pp. 26-38.

U.S. Bureau of the Census. "Effects of Different Reinterview Techniques on Estimates of Simple Response Variance." *Evaluation and Research Program of the U.S. Censuses of Population and Housing 1960*, Series ER 60, No. 11, Tables 30 and 46, 1972, pp. 1-100.

———. "Characteristics of Men with College Degrees: 1967." *Current Population Reports, Population Characteristics*, Series P-20, No. 201. Washington, D.C.: U.S. Government Printing Office, 1967, pp. 1-34.

———. "What's It Worth? Educational Background and Economic Status: Spring 1984." *Current Population Reports*, Series P-70, No. 11. Washington, D.C.: U.S. Government Printing Office, 1987.

U.S. Department of Education. *America 2000*. 1991.

U.S. Department of Labor, Manpower Administration. *General Aptitude Test Battery Manual*. Washington, D.C.: U.S. Government Printing Office, 1970.

Weiss, Andrew, and Henry Landau. "Validating Hiring Criteria." *National Bureau of Economic Research* Working Paper 2167. Cambridge, MA, 1987.

Wigdor, Alexandra K. "Psychological Testing and the Law of Employment Discrimination." In *Ability Testing: Uses, Consequences, and Control*, ed. Alexandra K. Wigdor, 1982. ERIC Document 213771.

Willis, Robert, and Sherwin Rosen. "Education and Self-Selection." *Journal of Political Economy* 87 (October 1979), pp. 57-536.

Wise, David A. "Academic Achievement and Job Performance." *The American Economic Review* 65 (June 1975), pp. 350-66.

Wise, L., J. McHenry, P. Rossmeissl, and S. Oppler. *ASVAB Validities Using Improved Job Performance Measures*. Washington, D.C.: American Institutes for Research, 1987.

Womack, James B., Daniel T. Jones, and Daniel Roos. *The Machine That Changed the World*. New York: Harper Perennial, 1991.

Part IV

Industrial Relations and Human Resource Regulation

Chapter 14

The Role of the State In Industrial Relations

Roy J. Adams
McMaster University

Public policy has long been a defining concern of industrial relations as a field of study.[1] Indeed, in the first half of this century the "Wisconsin School" had a large role in shaping the American welfare state (Kaufman 1988). During the 1980s the concern with public policy continued strongly. Approximately 30 percent of all of the papers presented at the annual meetings of the Industrial Relations Research Association (as well as the Canadian Industrial Relations Association) during the decade addressed the impact of government policy on problems such as unemployment, minimum wages, union organization, the effects of deregulation, immigration, etc. It was the problem, however, rather than the behavior of the government that typically was the focus of concern. Oddly, although influencing public policy is a defining characteristic of industrial relations, those in the field have paid remarkably little attention to the nature, structure, and motivation of the government as actor in the system. Government action has been treated almost exclusively as an independent variable and only rarely as the phenomenon to be explained.

Lacking a well-defined North American tradition of research into the role of the state in industrial relations, I saw my primary task in this essay to be one of providing definition to a new area of inquiry. In the first section of the paper I review the historical development of government policy toward labor. The objective is to provide a broad outline of the phenomena to be explained. In line with my own interests as well as the policy of the editors of this volume, I did not restrict my review to the United States, but instead looked at the role of the government comparatively. For the most part my general comments are meant to apply to the countries that are now regarded as economically advanced, market economy democracies.

In the second section of the paper I report the results of my research on government behavior and public policy carried out during the past decade primarily in Canada and the United States. It clearly shows that while there has been a considerable amount of work on the consequences of state action, there has been almost none on the determinants of government behavior.

The third section of the paper addresses the void in "positive" industrial relations research on the role of the state. Three "metatheories" of government behavior—pluralism, Marxism, and statism—are reviewed, as well as more specific frameworks for the analysis of aspects of government conduct concerning relations between labor and management. What I refer to as American regulation theory, an approach to understanding the behavior of government agencies, is consistent with the pluralist perspective as is strategic choice theory. Two promising approaches to the role of the state in industrial relations from a Marxist perspective are critical legal studies and French regulation theory. Statist theory, which holds that the state has interests of its own potentially contrary to those of both labor and management, is the least developed and is considered on its own.

Government Behavior Toward Labor: A Brief Historical Review

All states throughout history have had to make decisions with respect to the human relations of production (Woods 1983). As the organization that exercises generalized authority over all other organizations in society (Lindblom 1977) the state has had to decide whether unilaterally to establish terms and conditions for those involved in production of goods and services, to allow the producers to work out their own arrangements free from state involvement, or to work out a compromise between the two extremes. In medieval Britain, the state largely delegated authority to establish conditions to the guilds with respect to urban craftsmen. In the countryside, judges set wages and most other conditions were determined unilaterally by employers. During the industrial revolution, the state, reacting to the demands of expansionary capitalist entrepreneurs, withdrew from the market. Judges no longer set rural wages and guild regulations withered (Ramm 1986).

Liberal philosophy around the turn of the nineteenth century held that the state should abstain from intervention entirely so as to allow market forces to work free from constraint. Theory suggested that economic efficiency would be maximized if individual employers and employees were permitted to work out their own arrangements. However, stripped of the protection of medieval institutions, workers began to form organizations designed to protect themselves from the vagaries of the market (Slomp 1990; Rimlinger 1977). That development required another decision of the state. Should it permit worker combinations that were contrary to the assumptions of liberal economic theory or should it intervene to correct that imperfection in the market? Early in the course of industrialization, the state, in essentially all of the countries that are now classified as industrialized, market-oriented democracies, chose to intervene in order to outlaw combinations in restraint of trade (Jacobs 1986). The motivation of the state was not always entirely economic. Worker organizations also posed a political threat to the regime in power. The passage of the Combination Acts in Britain, for example, was stimulated as much by the revolution in France as by a desire to maintain markets free of combinations (Adams 1992a).

This situation is faced by contemporary governments everywhere. If government abstains from intervention in the employment relationship, then combinations designed to alter the impact of free economic forces inevitably appear. The state must then decide whether to suppress those combinations or to permit their existence. If it chooses the latter course, additional decisions must be made. Should worker and employer combinations (unions and employer associations) be allowed to contrive their own relationship or should it regulate those relations? During the second half of the 19th century, after unions and collective bargaining were legalized, most states permitted labor and management to arrive at their own arrangements (Jacobs 1986).

As a trade union membership and power grew, unions had an increasingly large influence on economic affairs, and in the period from about 1890 to 1945 most currently developed nations adopted some form of regulation with respect to labor-management relations. In the most common case, the state encouraged collective bargaining as a means of resolving labor-management disputes, but regulations were established by either legislatures or courts regarding the legality and applicability of collective agreements, the status and responsibilities of unions, and the conditions under which strikes could legally take place. Labor courts were set up in several countries in order to settle amicably individual employment disputes. Government officials often intervened in order to mediate collective disputes. In general, the object of states in this period with respect to industrial relations was to minimize social conflict while supporting a free market. At the enterprise level, first Germany and then several other countries required statutory works councils to represent the interests of employees (Hepple 1986).

After World War II public policy changed significantly. The depression of the 1930s had demonstrated serious failings of a largely unregulated market and, thus, governments began to take responsibility for active economic management. Almost universally they pledged themselves to maintain full employment and economic security (Blyth 1979) and to promote economic growth and mass consumption (Heidenheimer, Heclo, and Adams 1983; Jessop, Jacobi, and Kastendiek 1986). That meant that the state began to regulate specific terms and conditions of employment to a much greater degree than it had done prior to World War II. In that period there had been some intervention, in particular with respect to child and female labor, hours of work, and health and safety, but the quantity and scope of regulation was very limited (Ramm 1986; Hepple 1986a). Substantive intervention expanded slowly at first and then more rapidly in the decades after World War II. In the late 1960s in a milieu of rapid economic growth and very tight labor markets, substantive intervention accelerated (Gordon 1989). It continued to build until the major recession/depression of the early 1980s. By the late 70s most liberal democracies had regulations for minimum wages, maximum hours of work, holidays and vacations with pay, pensions, health insurance, disability insurance, unemployment insurance, job placement, worker access to training, human rights at work, health and safety at the workplace, and many more aspects of employment or activities related to employment such as job search and training (Dunlop 1978; Bamber and Lansbury 1987; Adams 1989).

After World War II governments of most developed countries, as part of a nexus of labor-management-state understandings, pledged to support the expansion of industrial democracy. Toward that end, statutory works councils became more widespread as a means of representing collective employee interests at the plant level, expanding their authority to co-decide employment issues. Several countries passed legislation that provided employees with representation on the directing boards of large corporations (Windmuller 1977). It became common to appoint labor and management representatives to various agencies charged with implementing policy on issues such as training, pensions, workers' compensation, and unemployment (Grant 1985).

Full employment provided labor with considerable bargaining power and workers began to make rapid advances in real wages. That, however, put pressure on prices and, constrained by the commitment to full employment, many liberal democratic states initiated a policy referred to as neo-corporatism or tripartism as a means of controlling incomes (Panitch 1977; Cooper 1982; Flanagan, Soskice, and Ulman 1983). Labor and management were invited to participate with government in the making of critical socioeconomic policy decisions in return for their moderation on wages and prices. In part the large increase in social legislation was a result of the tripartite understandings reached in many countries (Barkin 1977).

The understandings between labor, management, and the state reached after World War II applied primarily to the private sector. Civil servants were generally considered to have a special relationship with the sovereign state as employer that precluded employment relations modeled after the private sector (Schregle 1974). As a result, by the turn of the twentieth century, although the states in Europe and North America generally had recognized the legitimacy of unions, collective bargaining, and the right to strike of private sector workers, they usually did not extend that recognition to their own employees. By the 1950s, however, government employees everywhere were getting restive and demanding rights and privileges equivalent to those in the private sector (Rehmus 1975).

Those developments forced governments to make more choices. They could continue to refuse to negotiate with government employee unions as the government of Japan did, thereby precipitating continual friction, or they could recognize and bargain with representatives of their own employees as most countries did (Koshiro 1983). When the latter path was chosen, decisions again had to be made with respect to regulations. Most commonly governments placed tighter restrictions on the right of government workers to strike than they had on private sector workers (Ozaki 1987b). Also restricted was the scope of bargainable issues. For example, public service commissions rather than collective bargaining usually continued to regulate recruitment, selection, and promotion of civil servants (Ozaki 1987a).

In reaction to the Great Recession of 1981-82 and the heightened international competition—especially from Japan and the newly industrializing economies of Asia—state policy changed again. Not only did the means change, but in some countries the ends changed also. In order to compete, employers insisted that they required more flexibility and, therefore, freedom from union- and government-imposed restrictions (Boyer 1988; Wheeler 1989; Storper and Scott 1990). In response governments began to deregulate or reregulate the economy in ways congenial to business (Baglioni and Crouch 1990). They also began to privatize many government-owned businesses (Gil 1990). Some also began to move away from tripartite consultation. Because unemployment was very high in the 1980s, unions were often unable to stand up effectively against initiatives that reduced their influence and the well-being of their members.

The most extreme change in government policy occurred in Britain where the state went from a tripartite consensus policy to one of labor exclusion and from one of support of collective bargaining to one of encouraging employers to introduce economic innovations with or without the acquiescence of unions (Towers 1989; Crouch 1990). Not only did the government change its tactics for addressing socioeconomic problems, it also changed its objectives. From the postwar consensus list of goals, the neo-liberal Thatcher government discarded full employment and industrial democracy. It very aggressively pursued a policy of reregulation, by placing more constraints on unions and fewer on employers, and of privatization (MacInnes 1988). In other countries, privatization and the redoing of regulations was less extreme (Keller 1991). Unlike Britain, most countries did not formally abandon the socioeconomic consensus, although in reality goals such as full employment and universal economic democracy dropped well down on the list.

Governments during the 1980s did not unanimously act in ways contrary to the interests of labor. With the election of a labor government in 1983, Australia moved sharply toward a tripartite consensus policy (Kyloh 1989). Moreover, the initiative to innovate with a view toward the improvement of productivity was taken by Australian labor rather than by management (Niland and Spooner 1989).

In the United States several post-World War II presidents established labor-management advisory committees. Commonly, these committees were either ignored or treated as exercises in public relations (Moye 1980; Wilson 1982). Under Democratic administrations the influence of trade unions on government decision makers was greater than it was under Republican governments (Kochan and Katz 1988). However, with the exception of the war years, no system of tripartite consultation in search of consensus was successfully implemented. Although government behavior about making a socioeconomic policy did not change significantly during the 1980s, behavior with respect to collective bargaining did. In the post-World War II era, most countries' governments have insisted explicitly or implicitly that employers recognize and bargain with trade unions. In the United States, the various administrations from the mid-1930s to 1950s did the same. However, from the mid-1950s, the commitment of United States government to collective bargaining in the private sector began to slip. As employers ever more blatantly broke the law in order to escape from the strictures of collective bargaining, governments did nothing to restrain the burgeoning outlawry (Kochan, Katz, and McKersie 1985; Lawler 1990). Moreover, by busting a strike of air traffic controllers the administration of Ronald Reagan encouraged aggressive antiunion employer behavior.

In the public sector the United States followed the international movement (although less fully) toward collective bargaining. Laws were introduced in the federal as well as most state jurisdictions permitting collective bargaining for at least some employees on at least some issues. As a result, bargaining expanded significantly, but then levelled off in the 1980s (Aaron, Najita, and Stern 1988; Thornicroft 1992).

Drawing on the work of Kochan, McKersie and Cappelli (1984), one may see that any state as an actor in the industrial relations system has choices to make with respect to labor and management involvement in national socioeconomic policy, collective bargaining, and employee involvement in enterprise decisions both at the shop floor and in strategic corporate decision making. The above review suggests a sort of menu of policy choice. Either proactively or by default, every contemporary state must choose a policy pattern with respect to the other actors on each of these dimensions. One challenge for future industrial relations research is to explain existing patterns; another is to identify conditions under which they are likely to change.

Questions about the role of the state in industrial relations may be posed from both a normative perspective and a positive perspective. The positivist asks why does the state do what it does? Normative analysts ask what the state should do. To put it another way: the positive analyst seeks to determine what roles the state has chosen to fill and why; the normative analyst asks what roles should the state fill and how well is it filling them? In the sections below the state is first viewed from a normative perspective and then from a positive perspective.

The Normative Perspective

Policy Objectives and Policy Performance

Normative analysis flows from a statement of basic principles. Thus, one may ask what are the principles on which to base an analysis of the policy of liberal democratic countries? There is wide agreement (if not unanimity) that the proper role of the liberal democratic state in economic affairs is to look after the public interest. The state is considered to be the agent of the public and thus it behaves properly when it conscientiously looks after the interests of its constituency.

Industrial relations policy is not independent but derivative from more general socioeconomic policies as well as constitutional considerations. After World War II a consensus was reached among the liberal democratic nations that, in the public interest, the state should take responsibility for the achievement of a list of goals including all of the following: economic growth, full employment, economic and social security, price stability, industrial peace, and industrial democracy in the sense of participation of working people in the making of decisions that impact their conditions of work (Blyth 1979; Windmuller 1987). To a significant extent, labor and management policy flowed from this list of objectives.

Collective bargaining was generally encouraged as a means of permitting workers to participate (even if indirectly) in the making of the rules under which they worked. Many countries supplemented collective bargaining with participation via statutory works councils and employee representatives on corporate boards of directors. To achieve industrial peace various constraints were placed on the ability of unions to call strikes. Employers were generally expected to recognize and negotiate with union representatives chosen by their employees and not to interfere with the decision of their employees to join or form unions, thus taking those potentially contentious issues out of dispute. To an extent, government policy with respect to collective bargaining flowed from constitutional considerations. In Italy and France, for example, the right to strike was embedded in the constitution (Birk 1990). Many countries also made freedom of association a constitutional provision. Global standards of appropriate labor and employment policy were established by the tripartite International Labor Office in Geneva, Switzerland, and those standards had a significant effect on government behavior (Samson 1990).

To ensure universality of social and economic security, provisions with respect to issues such as unemployment insurance, pensions, and access to training were commonly legislated, although often the regulation that was instituted was one first pioneered through collective bargaining. As noted above, these policies were then commonly administered by agencies on which labor and management were represented. Tripartite consultation in search of consensus was the primary solution to achieving full employment and price stability simultaneously. Where it was successfully implemented it came to be used for a broader range of socioeconomic issues. Research concluded that countries with successful tripartite systems of policy making had lower rates of unemployment, more moderate inflation and less industrial conflict as well as higher rates of social spending than other countries (Hibbs 1978; Banting 1985). There was also some research on the conditions under which this policy might be instituted most efficaciously. It suggested that tripartite consensus policies were most easily implemented in small countries with well organized and centralized employer and union organizations (Maier 1984). Because these conditions were absent, some observers argued that incomes policies stemming from tripartite consultation were not likely to be successful in the United States (Flanagan 1980). Tripartism generally tended to be unstable primarily because of market pressures and pressures exerted on leadership by the rank and file of labor organizations.

"Corporatism" has continued to be a focus of both economic and political research in the 1980s (Calmfors and Driffill 1988; Cox and O'Sullivan 1988). The key normative question continues to be: Under what conditions is a policy of tripartism likely to be most successful? Although far from conclusive, recent work suggests an U-shape relationship between corporatism, liberalism, and economic performance, with performance being best in highly corporate and highly liberal countries, and with poorer performance by countries in-between (Paloheimo 1990).

If one accepts that the proper function of government is to pursue the public interest, then the list of consensus objectives noted above may be thought of as a yardstick against which government performance may be judged. In most respects the performance of the United States was well below international norms. Throughout most of the post-World War II period, unemployment was higher, there was more economic and social insecurity, conflict was more prevalent, and industrial democracy (as indicated by the extent of participation in collective bargaining) was more restricted than in other countries (Adams 1989; Bamber and Lansbury 1987). Economic growth rates also fell considerably behind many other countries. Only with respect to prices was the United States' performance above par. The Canadian profile was similar to that in the United States except that economic and social security was better (although worse than the European norm), unemployment and industrial conflict rates were higher but worker participation (as indicated by collective bargaining coverage) was more widespread. Sweden and Germany were very high performers on most indicators. The Swedish pattern was essentially the reverse of the United States—good on everything except prices. Germany did well on all of the indicators. Japan did well on some and not so well on others. Its economic growth was spectacular, unemployment was practically nonexistent, and prices were generally stable. On the other hand, Japan's industrial democracy was very restricted, just as it was in the United States. Economic security was excellent for the minority of people who were core employees in large corporations and government bureaucracies. Even for those outside the "lifetime employment" system, economic security was relatively high because of continuous full employment. The British pattern was about average for all developed countries on most indicators. As far as economic growth, however, Britain fared poorly.

North American Research

Most North American industrial relations research on the role of the state has been normative in character but not comparative. In the typical study the researcher focused on a particular labor problem that had been the subject of government action, gathered data on the labor-management experience following that action, and made recommendations as to how the behavior of the government could be changed in order to better meet the explicit or implicit objectives of the policy that had given rise to the action taken. In the United States studies of this type were done on a long list of issues including: equal employment opportunity, comparable worth, public-sector collective bargaining, unemployment, training, unemployment insurance, minimum wages, retirement income, immigration, collective bargaining representation elections, job creation, National Labor Relations Board caseload, the right of government employees to strike, employment-at-will, technological change, plant closings, strikes in urban transit, social security legislation, decertification of collective bargaining units, deregulation, work sharing, affirmative action, the adjustment of employment to restructuring, mediation of labor conflict, health and safety at work, the scope of collective bargaining, fringe benefits, health insurance, military educational benefits, free trade, and union growth.[2] Canadian researchers had similar preoccupations but in addition did work on more specific Canadian policy issues such as the accreditation of employer associations for bargaining purposes, public-sector wage controls, the impact of the Canadian Charter of Rights on industrial relations and first contract arbitration.

This research gave rise to many recommendations for the adoption by government of new policy approaches. Among the more notable proposals was the recommendation that there should be legislation in the United States providing dismissal only for just cause (Stieber 1983).[3] Among all of the advanced industrial countries only in the United States may employees be dismissed without reason, notice, or compensation. In Canada, under common law, employees must be given notice for dismissal without cause and three jurisdictions have introduced laws permitting dismissal only for cause (Adams, Adell, and Wheeler 1990).

During the 1980s a consensus developed among human resource management researchers that in order to function properly, new flexible production techniques would require highly involved, highly committed, and highly trained workers. Many experts also came to the conclusion that for such work processes to be widely implemented and sustained government action would be necessary. The collapse of collective bargaining in the United States also led some to suggest new means of ensuring workers a say in the establishment of the conditions under which they work.

Toward some combination of these ends, writers in both Canada and the United States suggested that policymakers should consider requiring the institution of works councils (Adams 1985; Beatty 1987; Kochan and McKersie 1989; Weiler 1990; Freeman 1990). A few recommendations were made for legislation providing workers with representation on corporate boards of directors—a radical proposal for North America but common enough elsewhere (Kochan and McKersie 1989; McKersie 1990; G. Adams 1990).

Many recommendations were made to revise the United States National Labor Relations Act or to make use of underutilized provisions in that legislation (Morris 1987; Lawler 1990). The president of the AFL-CIO even suggested that it might be a good idea if the Act were to be abolished altogether (Sloan and Witney 1988). Many observers were skeptical, however, that any change in policy designed to revitalize collective bargaining or employee participation in enterprise decision making would be made during the administration of George Bush.

In Canada labor law was a more volatile area. Right-wing governments tended to put new constraints on unions and collective bargaining, especially in the public sector (Panitch and Swartz 1985; Sack and Lee 1989) while left-wing administrations encouraged the expansion and deepening of bargaining. Several proposals for fundamental change of labor policy entered the arena of debate (Adell 1988).

Employment policy in the United States was also judged to have "failed to reach the employment goals taken for granted in the early 1960s as achievable" (Bawden and Skidmore 1989, 1. See also Mucciaroni 1990). As a result, recommendations were made for new government initiatives on hours of work, comparable worth, plant shutdowns (Ehrenberg 1989), the operation of the employment service (Bendick 1989), training (Osterman 1990), health insurance, and several other labor market issues (Levitan, Carlson, and Shapiro 1986).

Positive Analysis

Questionable Assumptions About Government Behavior

The normative analysis undertaken in the above section only makes sense if one accepts the basic premise that the proper role of the state is to pursue the public interest and if one accepts the corollary that states do in fact attempt to fulfill that role. As noted above, during the 1980s the most common type of study with respect to the state was one in which the researcher evaluated some specific government action against the explicit or assumed objects of the policy giving rise to the action and then made recommendations for improvement. This type of research is based upon certain assumptions that are almost always unstated and unconsidered. First, the researcher assumes that the state is a rational actor who has the power and motivation to make independent decisions. Second, it is assumed that the state is motivated to achieve the stated objectives of the policy and that if its current actions toward that end are not entirely effective it would welcome recommendations for improvement.

With respect to some policies, these assumptions appear to be clearly at odds with reality. For example, although full employment is explicitly a goal of the United States, the state has never aggressively attempted to reach that goal and for most of the period since the end of World War II, unemployment rates in the United States have been higher than those in other advanced democracies. The experience of Japan, Sweden, and Switzerland suggests that full employment is achievable within the context of liberal democracy. Thus, one might interpret the failure of the United States (and several other countries as well) to achieve it as a willful act contrary to the stated policy objective (Martin 1985).

Another example has to do with labor policy. It has been the formal policy of the United States to encourage the practice and procedure of collective bargaining since the passage of the Wagner Act in 1935. Until the 1950s it appeared that the object was being effectively pursued. Since then the practice of collective bargaining has been receding instead of expanding but, despite the availability of mountains of research and policy advice on how that downward trend might be reversed, policymakers have continued to allow erosion. The only conclusion can be that there is no serious commitment to achieving the stated goal and therefore normative research that assumes such a commitment based on a literal reading of the stated policy is misplaced (Kochan and McKersie 1989). Because of situations like this, in a recent essay I have suggested that industrial relations policy researchers should make a distinction between real and nominal policy (Adams 1992a).

Positive North American Research

These considerations suggest the need for positive research designed to discover why the state acts as it does with respect to industrial relations. Very little research of this kind, however, is done in North America by industrial relationists.[4] An early example of such research is the 1961 paper by Cohen that attempted to isolate the determinants of labor policy in the United States. He proposed that "the character of labor relations law is a result of the prevailing ideology of property rights and the degree of access to political power enjoyed by private power blocks" (p. 351). After reviewing the development of legislation on labor-management relations, he concluded that significant changes in policy are likely to result from major ideological and political change.

Another example in which government behavior was the dependent rather than the independent variable was Kochan's study of the correlates of public employee bargaining laws at the state level in the United States. He found that such laws were most comprehensive and were passed earliest in states with liberal political traditions where unions were strongly organized in the private sector. These were also states that spent heavily on social services and in which employees experienced above average growth in personal income during the 1960s (Kochan 1973).

On reviewing all of the volumes of the Proceedings of the meetings of the Industrial Relations Research Association that had been held during the 1980s, I could identify only one paper that clearly took a positive stance with respect to the state as an actor in the system.[5] Because it is so unusual, perhaps it is useful to review it in some depth.

The paper addressed employment training policy during the years 1978-1982. The author, A. Michael Collins (1986), identified an employment training "subgovernment" composed of "leading legislative, bureaucratic, and private actors" and of his concern was to explain the behavior of the subgovernment during the period when the Comprehensive Employment and Training Act (CETA) expired and the Job Training Partnership Act was passed. He argues that the Reagan administration attempted "to force radical change" but it was unsuccessful due to the efforts of the subgovernment and particularly to state, county, and local governments, CETA contractors, and subcontractors and "community-based organizations" representing "coalitions of minority groups, women, and labor unions" (p. 215). The Reagan administration did cut the training budget that "produced an ungainly system, its administrative structure mismatched to its financial resources" (p. 216). Nevertheless, the "core personnel" of the subgovernment were able "to keep the system alive, in anticipation of a time when the problems of persistent structural unemployment and inadequate employment training will gain a higher place on the national political agenda."

Collins' analysis was guided by a model that generated questions about "access to the legislative process, the composition and influence of the subgovernment, the subgovernment's responsiveness to outsiders, the methods used to compromise conflicting interests, and the means of controlling the agenda of policy alternatives" (p. 214). The Collins paper is a summary of a Ph.D. dissertation in public policy analysis and the theoretical citations are all to the works of political scientists, works that do not form part of the intellectual base of industrial relations. Although the objective of the Industrial Relations Research Association, when it was set up in 1947, was to provide a home for scholars from all disciplines who were interested in labor issues, in fact it was dominated from the start by economists and that domination grew over the years. As a result political scientists are all but unrepresented in the association and since they are the ones who have developed the skills of policy analysis, that form of research is all but nonexistent (Doeringer 1980; Adams 1992b).

Directions for the Future

Conceptualizing the State

Throughout most of its history, the field of industrial relations in North America has viewed the world through the prism of labor. The dominant theme during the first half of the twentieth century was the reaction of labor to the coming of industrial society (Kerr and Siegel 1955). Since then industrial relationists have continued to focus on the problems experienced by working people and the institutions that they have fashioned to address those problems. Like a blind man feeling one side of an elephant, that approach has resulted in a less than accurate perception of the whole phenomenon. During the 1980s our understanding of industrial relations was enhanced considerably as a result of research that centered on the motivation and behavior of employers as actors in the industrial relations system (Kochan, McKersie and Cappelli 1984; Kochan, Katz, and McKersie 1985). The development of the strategic choice framework and its application to employer behavior by the research group at MIT gave us a new multidimensional appreciation of American industrial relations. The need now is to move the state onto center stage. As the review above suggests, we know a good deal about public policy but not very much about the policymaker.

As a first step toward a positive research tradition on the nature of the state in industrial relations, it would seem to make sense to review the frameworks and theories used by political scientists and public policy analysts to conceptualize the state. The task is not an easy one because there is a good deal of debate and controversy over the nature of the state and several paradigms exist for the analysis of government behavior (Giles 1989; Dye 1981; King 1986). A comprehensive review is, obviously, not possible here. It is possible, however, to discuss a few approaches of particular relevance to industrial relations. Below, three conceptions of the role of the state under liberal democracy will be outlined: pluralism, Marxism, and statism. After reviewing the basic characteristics of pluralism, the potential utility of two specific frameworks consistent with the assumptions of pluralism will be discussed. Similarly, the basic parameters of Marxism will be reviewed and two specific applications of Marxist ideas will be considered. Finally, a concept of the state as an actor with interests in industrial relations separate and independent of labor and management will be discussed.

Pluralism and the Multidimensional State

As noted above, policy analysts often assume that the government is a rational, unitary actor dedicated to implementing its interpretation of the public interest. Research (and indeed some pointed reflection) indicates that the assumption is ill founded. In fact, the state is an amalgam of many parts (Miliband 1969). In the United States, for example, the state is composed of the executive branch, the two congressional houses, political parties, various agencies populated by bureaucrats, the judiciary, and the military. To be complete one must include the fifty state governments that, with variations, repeat the federal pattern, and the local authorities. More expansive versions of the state insist that government-owned institutions such as hospitals, schools, and public transport, etc., must be included. In many countries, manufacturing, extractive, and other industries are state owned and, thus, part of the state apparatus. Some analysts would go as far as to insist that for certain purposes labor and management institutions should be considered part of the state. In Canada, for example, courts will not entertain civil action on the terms of a collective agreement or on the individual contract of employment if a collective bargaining relationship has been legally established. In some jurisdictions, moreover, employees under collective bargaining may not secure their legislated labor standard rights through the courts. Instead, in British Columbia, for example, labor standards are read into collective agreements, thereby compelling the unions to take on state functions in the event of a dispute (Adams 1985). A similar doctrine is developing in the United States (Stone 1990).

Not only is the state complex, but as the leading theory of the role of the state in liberal democratic society suggests, it is not necessarily rational. Pluralist theory holds that public policy is the result of a complex interaction of interest group pressures on governmental institutions. One branch of pluralist theory holds that government agencies are neutral conduits through which interest group pressures are registered (King 1986; Giles 1989). At any point in time, government behavior is a function of the power of the dominant coalition acting upon it. This theory would explain the failure in the United States of the state to encourage vigorously collective bargaining (as it should do according to its formal policy) as the result of the strength of conservative forces acting on the government shell. Implicitly, the studies by Cohen and Kochan noted above would seem to fit into this tradition.

Another branch of pluralist thought holds that the state is not simply a neutral actor. Instead, its various parts have identifiable interests of their own as well as sources of power. From this perspective, public policy is the result of a compromise between the objects of interest groups and the objects of elements of the state itself. The analysis by Collins of training policy in the United States, noted above, would seem to fit into this school of thought. He demonstrates how the Reagan administration and the training bureaucracy had different interests. Even though the administration had substantial power, it was not able to succeed in dismantling federal programs because of the combined strength of the bureaucrats themselves and their allies in labor and community groups as well as local authorities.

American Regulation Theory

Beyond the United States there have been some interesting attempts at positive policy analysis. Of particular interest is the work of Australian Braham Dabscheck (1989, 1992) who has written on the applicability of American regulation theory to government behavior with respect to labor policy. There are several alternative versions of this theory. One version, the regulatory life cycle theory, holds that regulatory bodies go through a predictable cycle in which the regulators are very enthusiastic about ensuring compliance with the regulations early in their existence. Regulation becomes routine in middle age and mature regulatory agencies tend to be ineffective. They have a propensity to become controlled by those they regulate.

Dabscheck has applied this theory to the Australian Arbitration Commission that has power to establish wage movements in Australia. This theoretical framework would seem to have great potential as a way of analyzing the behavior of North American regulatory bodies such as the United States National Labor Relations Board. As suggested by the life cycle theory of regulation, this agency began as an enthusiastic applier of the principles of the National Labor Relations Act. In the 1960s and 1970s, as its work became more routine, it became increasingly sensitive to the concerns of the employers who were the subject of the regulations. By the 1980s the agency had become, in the judgment of some, a vehicle to protect employers from unwanted incursions of potential trade unionists. The robust manner in which some Canadian boards go about their assigned tasks stands in stark contrast and provides an interesting variation to be explained (Bruce 1989; Rose and Chaison 1989; Meltz 1985).

Strategic Choice Theory and the Role of the State in Transforming American Industrial Relations

The application by Kochan, Katz and McKersie of a revised version of industrial relations system theory to the behavior of employers during the 1970s and 1980s led to a reinterpretation of the parameters of the American industrial relations system. KKM argued that employers made decisions of critical importance to labor at three levels of the corporate hierarchy: at the top or strategic level, at the middle or level of collective bargaining, and at the shop floor level. They argued that industrial relations research, framed from the perspective of employees and unions, overly concentrated on the collective bargaining level of employer-employee interaction. They went on to argue that collective bargaining had become increasingly less critical to employee welfare during the 1970s and 1980s due to actions taken by employers at the strategic and shop floor levels. At the top many employers had decided to pursue a policy of union avoidance, in some cases opening up new nonunion plants and in others encouraging the decertification of unionized bargaining units. Nonunion employers increasingly defied the requirements of labor law. At the shop floor participatory innovations were being introduced in both unionized and nonunionized plants. In many cases the innovations marginalized trade union influence in unionized plants and were said to reduce the appeal of unions where they were not established. Even in collective bargaining the agenda tended to be set by employers rather than by trade unions as it had generally been in the past.

KKM were criticized for not paying more attention to the role of the state in the transformation from a system in which collective bargaining was considered to be the dominant institution for job regulation to one where it had become of increasingly less significance. Indeed, although the conceptual framework that they used to analyze employer behavior implied a role for the state, KKM paid no systematic attention to government behavior in their analysis.[6]

In conjunction with a theory of employer behavior that I put forth a decade ago (Adams 1981) a case may be made that the American transformation portrayed by KKM was not wrought principally by employers at all but rather that the key variable was government behavior. In my theory employers everywhere and always behave in a manner designed to maximize their control of the enterprise. This fundamental propensity to maximize control is offset to some extent by the power of labor and to a greater extent by the power of the state. One implication is that, unless checked by the government or a very powerful labor movement, employers will always attempt to escape from the fetters imposed by collective bargaining. A considerable amount of evidence from many countries supports this theory (Plowman 1991; Sisson 1987; Harris 1983).

From the 1950s onward, but especially in the 1980s, United States governments withdrew pressure from employers to recognize and bargain with unions in good faith. Several court decisions made it easier for employers to pursue a policy of control reclamation and the legislature did nothing to counter the effects of the judicial decisions (Morris 1987). The Reagan administration, in addition, decided to destroy the air traffic controllers union when it struck illegally and in so doing established a symbolic precedent that was not lost on private sector employers.

In short, if the employer propensity to maximize control is invariable, as I suggest, then the critical behavior leading to the transformation of American industrial relations was not the "strategic choices" made by employers but rather the choice made by the state to remove pressure from employers to recognize and negotiate with unions. The transformation was helped along considerably by a decade of high unemployment that undercut the already inferior power of the unions to stand against employer insurgency but the critical variable was a permissive government policy that had a predictable effect on employer behavior.

The contrary case of Canada supports this interpretation. Employers in Canada, although many of them are intimately linked with those in the United States through multinational organizations, did not go on the offensive so as to reclaim control. The state in Canada has been much more insistent that employers respect the letter and spirit of the law (Bruce 1989; Rose and Chaison 1990).[7]

Marxist and Quasi-Marxist Thought

The primary challenger to pluralism for conceptualizing the state is Marxism. Whereas pluralists hold that liberal democratic society is composed of a multitude of interest groups none of which dominate all of the others, Marxists hold that society is divided into two classes—labor and capital—and that capital interests dominate (Hyman 1975; Onimode 1985). Those who follow the tenets of Marxist political economy insist that the role of the state in liberal democratic society (or capitalist society) is to ensure conditions that allow for the accumulation by capitalists of increasing wealth and power (Offe 1975). The state is seen to be an agent of capitalist interests. Crude Marxist doctrine holds that the state "systematically pursues capitalist priorities because it is controlled . . . by powerful capitalists who shape policy to suit their own interests" (Zeitlin 1985, 19). However, most contemporary Marxist thought is more sophisticated. It asserts that governments in all countries with market economies work to maintain the capitalist system either because they are constrained by the environment to do so or because they find it to be in their interests to do so (King 1986).

The terms Marxist and Marxism have very negative connotations in North America. They are commonly associated with the harsh, discredited, Communist regimes of East and Central Europe. As a result many scholars who make use of Marxist concepts in their research neither use the designation nor think of themselves as Marxists. Many refer to their work as "critical" to distinguish it from the work of pluralists who tend to have a more affirmative attitude toward contemporary socioeconomic arrangements (Murray and Giles 1989). One such group is the critical legal studies movement in the United States.

Critical Legal Studies

A consensus had emerged by the 1940s or 1950s among the most prominent American labor policy analysts that in a democratic society employees should have the right to participate in making the rules under which they work and that collective bargaining was the most appropriate method for achieving that end (Committee for Economic Development 1961; Woods, Dion, and Crispo 1968; Aaron 1973). Public policy then should support collective bargaining. Since the National Labor Relations Act was put into effect to encourage collective bargaining it won the support of most labor analysts.

From the late 1970s onward that position was attacked by scholars associated with the critical legal studies movement. Led by Katherine Stone (1980, 1990) and Karl Klare (1978, 1981, 1990) the basic argument of the group is that analysts, legislators, and judges have formulated an ideological defense of American labor policy that, in Klare's words, has the effect of "inducing organized workers to consent to and participate in their own domination in the workplace" (1981, 455). Pluralist ideology holds that "management and labor have equal power in the workplace." As a result, under collective bargaining the workplace is "portrayed as a self-contained mini-democracy" (Stone 1980, 1515). In contrast, the critical analysts argue that the power of management far exceeds that of labor under Wagner Act-style bargaining and that the paradigm of a mini-democracy makes it difficult for that inequality to be perceived and thus for action to be taken to alter it.

In a recent essay Stone (1990) argues that collective labor policy is being slowly dismantled and is being replaced by a policy based on individual employment relations that further strengthens the power of employers.

Besides being influenced by Marxist analysis, this approach is also influenced by a subjective research tradition which holds that the proper function of social science is to reveal "deep meanings" in social relations rather than to mimic the quantitative objectivism of the natural sciences (Rosenberg 1988). As Klare notes, a major objective of the group is "to uncover the constellation of assumptions, values, and sensibilities about law, politics, and justice these texts evince, to reveal their latent patterns and structures of thought about legal and industrial issues and about the possibilities of human expression in the workplace" (1981, 451). Variations of this approach to social science research, known under titles such as hermeneutics, social action, deconstruction, and post-modernism, have spread rapidly in the past decade or so although they do not seem to have, as yet, had much influence on industrial relations. (Godard 1992a, 1992b).

French Regulation Theory

Another promising framework, inspired by Marxist thought, is French regulation theory (Aglietta 1979; Lipietz 1987; Noel 1987; Jessop 1990; Hirst and Zeitlin 1991). One of the main interests of this group is to explain what they call "regimes of accumulation." A regime of accumulation is a particular strategy carried out by business supported by regulations, policies, institutions, and habits that are referred to as "modes of regulation." These Marxian phrases may be translated into terms more familiar to industrial relationists. A regime of accumulation is essentially a strategy of production and distribution. A mode of regulation is the system of rules, habits, and norms that specify appropriate conduct by the actors in the economic system. The mode of regulation is not limited to but incorporates the industrial relations system. Note that both the French regulationists and industrial relations system theorists conceive of industrial relations as a network of rules.

Historically, two major regimes of accumulation have been identified and a third appears to be taking shape.[8] In the first regime capitalist accumulation took place primarily by expansion into new geographic areas and sectors. Competition was based on cost minimization and thus implied the payment of low wages. In pursuit of this strategy employers fought incipient unions and had the support of the government in doing so. This regime lasted until about the First World War. Government policy, in the industrializing West during the 19th and first part of the twentieth century, is explained as in support of this low-wage, expansionist strategy of business.

During the 1920s business strategy changed. Mass production (Fordism) replaced craft production and this change boosted productivity considerably. Instead of expanding into new areas and sectors, the strategy became one of selling more goods and services to those already in the capitalist sector. This strategy required high and growing purchasing power by workers. Unions and collective bargaining were consistent with this objective and thus when government policy turned to support of unions and collective bargaining and when employers recognized and entered into regular negotiations with unions the new system stabilized.

The 1980s and 1990s are regarded as a crisis period. Global competition is shaping a new business strategy. Mass production is no longer able to generate sufficient profits and growth in order for stability to be maintained. Instead it is being challenged by just-in-time, flexible production techniques (Hirst and Zeitlin 1991; Piore and Sabel 1984). The old mode of regulation appears to be inappropriate for the new regime of accumulation.

In industrial relations terminology the present period may be thought of as one in which production methods are changing as capitalists seek to find new ways to maintain high profits and growth. Old industrial relations practices do not appear to be compatible with the new methods. Thus, there is a crisis in which industrial relations are in a state of flux. Unlike some schools of Marxist thought, the French regulationists (who appear to be attempting to find a middle way between Marxism and neo-classical economic analysis) do not hold that employment relations are determined by the mode of production. Alain Lipietz (1987), one of the foremost members of the group, argues that "Regimes of accumulation and modes of regulation are *chance discoveries* made in the course of human struggles and if they are for a while successful, it is only because they are able to ensure a certain regularity and a certain permanence in social reproduction" (p. 15). To be successful "the regime of accumulation must . . . be materialized in the shape of norms, habits, laws, and regulating networks that ensure the unity of the process which guarantees that its agents conform more or less to the schema of reproduction in their day-to-day behavior and struggles" (p. 14). In short, there must be compatibility between regime of accumulation and mode of regulation but there is no guarantee that at any given place or time the two systems will be in synchronization. It is up to labor, management, and the state to "discover" production and human processes that fit together.

The French regulation analysis is global, but otherwise it is very similar to the argument made by the IR group at MIT with respect to the United States. Kochan and his colleagues have been arguing that American companies are likely to meet the international competitive challenge only if they adopt the new forms of production as well as industrial relations practices that are compatible with the new production forms. High productivity results only if production and human resources management systems are appropriately matched. They are also concerned that if left to its own volition American management will not put into effect the human resource and labor relations strategies necessary to ensure the success of the production system. In Lipietz's terms, "these seeds of the future need a favourable social and macroeconomic environment if they are to grow" (p. 137). Although the MIT group has no theory of the government action most likely to foster compatible new production/new industrial relations systems at the firm level, in recent publications they have begun to propose specific initiatives such as works councils and worker participation on boards of directors (Kochan and McKersie 1989; McKersie 1991). Additional proposals for government action consistent with the successful and sustained implementation of the new production/IR have been offered by Levine and Tyson (1990) and Adams (1992a).

Because of the close affinity between the work of the MIT group (which has been very influential in North American industrial relations) and the French regulation school, whose analysis places North America in global perspective, the latter would seem to deserve further study.

Statist Theory

In an article published in the mid-1980s, sociologist Jonathan Zeitlin (1985) suggested that a third theory of the state could be usefully applied as a means of casting light on labor relations. Zeitlin's problem was to explain the role of the state with respect to shop floor bargaining, especially in Britain. He began by noting that there was a widespread consensus in Britain "among analysts from widely different theoretical and ideological perspectives on the existence of an underlying antagonism between the state as economic manager and shop floor bargaining in defense of workers' material interests" (p. 1). Shop floor bargaining as it is conducted in Britain often results in conflict and that conflict is considered to place government economic policies in jeopardy. For that reason both Labour and Conservative governments have been antagonistic to it. The policy of the Thatcher government in the 1980s is an extreme example.

Despite this fundamental, long-term antagonism, "state actions have often contributed significantly to the growth of workplace organisation and the erosion of managerial authority on the shop floor" (p. 5). After a review of relevant British government action, Zeitlin argues that neither pluralist nor Marxist theories are able effectively to account for the complex and contradictory behavior of the state. The contradiction is, however, explainable if one makes use of a theory of the state associated primarily with several 19th century German historians referred to as "realism."

The German realists "concerned themselves not with what the state ought to be but with what particular states actually did" (p. 27). Modern practitioners of the approach, Zeitlin argues, hold that "states pursue interests distinct from, and potentially opposed to, those of *all* the contending groups which make up civil society." They have an overriding concern for "external and internal security" as well as "the maintenance of public order and political stability against potential challenges to its rule at home." As a result "state officials are continually preoccupied with the supply of financial and human resources needed to sustain their coercive and administrative apparatus" (p. 28). According to the realists, states "vary enormously in their autonomy, coherence, and ability to impose their will on their subjects" (p. 28).

The usefulness of realist theory in explaining the paradox of fluctuating state antagonism towards and support for shop floor bargaining is that "in contrast to theories which reduce the state to a passive respondent to social pressures, or deduce its behavior from a static functional analysis of social needs, a realist approach enables us to treat state leaders as independent actors with their own goals and priorities" (p. 29). Thus during times of stability the desire of the state to "maintain public order and to assure a steady flow of revenue" often leads it "as Marxists have always insisted, to support the existing structure of social and economic relations against potentially disruptive challenges from subordinate groups." On the other hand, during periods of social turbulence states may "strike bargains with subordinate groups which restore social peace at the expense of propertied elites." One may interpret government behavior in the world war periods in this light.

There are many examples, Zeitlin argues, where the "distinctive priorities" of states as independent actors led them "to pursue economic policies which can be assimilated neither to the maximization of general economic welfare nor to the promotion of the collective interest of the capitalist class" (p. 34). As an example he proposes that British foreign policy in the 1920s and again in the 1950s and 1960s led it to sacrifice "the interests of the domestic economy to financial goals connected with the stability and international role of sterling" (p. 34).

During the past decade the idea that the state should be thought of as an independent actor with its own list of priorities has begun to win an increasing number of adherents within sociology and political science (Evans, Rueschemeyer, and Skocpol 1985). Since it focuses specifically on a labor issue, Zeitlin's essay may serve as a useful model for future industrial relations research from this perspective.[9]

Theorizing the State—A Summary

Pluralists generally conceive of the state as a fragmented set of institutions through which a myriad of interest groups act.

Government behavior from this perspective is the result of the forces acting upon it. The key to understanding the role of the state is to focus on the various forces in society that seek to meet their objectives through the auspices of the state. American regulation theory, which is consistent with pluralism, provides a set of propositions designed to explain the behavior of government bureaucracies. It should help to cast insight on the action of agencies such as the American and Canadian labor relations boards. The strategic choice framework, which is essentially a modification of Dunlop's industrial relations system idea, is also consistent with pluralist ideology. To date it has been used primarily as a means of analyzing labor organizations and employers but it should prove equally useful as a guide to thinking about the role of the state with respect to the other two actors.

The main contender to pluralism as a theoretical framework for analyzing the state is Marxist theory. Its starting point is the proposition that society is divided into two antagonistic classes and that all societal institutions, including the state, are organized to maintain the dominance of the capitalist class over the working class. Critical legal theorists attempt to demonstrate that the pluralist, democratic rhetoric underlying American labor policy is inconsistent with the real purpose of the policy. As one would expect from a Marxist perspective, the true function of American policy, according to the analysis of "the Crits," is to maintain class relations beneficial to the capitalist class. French regulation theory is concerned primarily to explain why workers do not revolt under class conditions that are objectively contrary to their interests. The predominant reason offered by the regulationists is "habit." From this perspective the role of the state in industrial relations is to establish and monitor modes of regulation intended to bring the behavior of workers, consumers, and other economic actors into alignment with the needs of "capitalist accumulation." As production systems and standards change, old routines need to be broken and new ones established. Under such conditions the state can be expected to reregulate in hopes of influencing worker behavior such that new habits consistent with the needs of production will be established.

Unlike the other two conceptions which hold that the key to understanding the state is to be found outside government, statist theory directs attention inward. The behavior of the state is not simply a Skinnerian response to conditions in its environment, instead it has an agenda of its own and a will to put that agenda into place.

These three conceptions and the more specific approaches associated with them are not necessarily mutually exclusive. For example, although the concept of strategic choice in industrial relations was developed within the context of pluralist analysis, it is perfectly consistent with statist theory. Industrial relations systems from which the strategic choice framework is derivative would seem to overlap a good deal with French regulation theory.

Agenda for the Future

Historically the focus of industrial relations research in North America has been on problems experienced by people in their role as workers. In search of solutions to those problems industrial relations researchers have always been interested in actual and potential action by workers themselves, as well as action by employers and the state with respect to those problems. Traditionally, however, they have not been interested in the behavior of employers or of the state per se. In the 1980s that began to change. By looking at the world from the perspective of employees and their organizations, developments in the United States were not easy to interpret. In recognition of this limitation researchers from Massachusetts Institute of Technology developed a new conceptual framework that they applied to the labor relations behavior of employers. With the help of that framework they were able to interpret developments in the United States in a way that the old conceptions had made very difficult.

In order to make progress in the 1990s in understanding the operation of industrial relations systems it will be necessary to focus more specifically on the role of the state; not only on the impact of public policy but also on its generation and real function. We should no longer implicitly accept the proposition that the state acts in the public interest or its interpretation of the public interest. Instead we should question, analyze, and investigate its motives. We should no longer accept that "this government" is unlikely to take action appropriate to meeting stated national goals. Instead we should ask under what conditions is the government likely to pursue the appropriate policy and what needs to be done to bring about those conditions. As Mitchell concluded in her review of the labor market impact of United States federal regulation in the 1970s, "we need to know more about why regulation comes into being—how research findings and other influences find their way into labor market regulation" (1982, 180).

Government is the dominant actor in industrial relations systems. It has power resources that considerably outweigh those of either labor or business. Because of that power the state, more so than the other two actors, must be held accountable for good or bad industrial relations. In international perspective industrial relations performance in North America has not been good and the responsibility for that poor showing is predominantly that of the state. If industrial relations performance is to be improved then we must, in future, acquire a better understanding of the state as an actor in the system.

Acknowledgments

I am grateful for the useful comments made on an earlier draft of this paper by the following people: Ken Thornicroft, Hoyt Wheeler, Tom Kochan, Dave Lewin, Peter Sherer, and Bernie Adell. The final product is, of course, entirely my responsibility.

Endnotes

[1] There are many views on the definition of industrial relations as a field of study (see Adams 1992). In this essay I define the field as being composed of those academics who are members of either the Industrial Relations Research Association or the Canadian Industrial Relations Association or similar associations in other countries. Industrial relations research is research which is published in the proceedings of the meetings of industrial relations associations or in journals with industrial relations in their title. Also encompassed in "the literature" are articles and books written by members of one of the industrial relations associations on subjects similar to those addressed at the annual meetings of the associations. I realize that this is a narrow definition, but it has the advantage of being much more precise than the normal usage. Also, it seems to me that it represents, if not the entire field according to some views, the core of the field.

[2] This list of topics was gleaned from a review of the papers presented at the annual meetings of the Industrial Relations Research Association. Papers presented at the annual meetings of the IRRA and its Canadian counterpart, the Canadian Industrial Relations Association, are, it seems to me, the best indicator of the concerns of industrial relations as a field in North America. Industrial relations is also an established field in other countries such as Britain, Australia, Nigeria, and the Philippines, but it is clearly beyond the bounds of this essay to review the range of policy concerns of IR researchers in all countries in which IR is a field.

[3] In fact, scholarly proposals for government action versus employment-at-will were made in earlier decades but the issue was only widely discussed in the 1980s. In the early 1990s, an unjust dismissal statute was drafted by a group of labor law experts headed by Theodore St. Antoine.

[4] Research on the role of the state in industrial relations continues to be carried out by historians. See, for example, the work of Harris (1983), Craven (1980), Montgomery (1987), and Haydu (1988). None of these authors belong to the IRRA or CIRA. Very few historians are currently involved with industrial relations associations in North America. For the evolution of the field of industrial relations see Adams (1992).

[5] Incredibly, given the experience of the 1980s, in the recent volume of the *Industrial and Labor Relations Review* two articles appeared in which the authors attempted to explain aspects of government industrial relations behavior. In one the author attempted to identify the determinants of the passage of unjust dismissal legislation. He concluded that "when the judicial costs of firing workers are perceived to be high, unjust dismissal legislation is more likely to occur" (Krueger 1991). In the other the two authors provided an explanation for the passage of a public-sector collective bargaining act in Florida despite conditions which made that course of action seem improbable (Miller and Canak 1991).

[6] In subsequent writings they have focused more clearly on the role of the state. See, for example, Kochan and McKersie (1989), and Kochan and Katz (1988).

[7] In a letter written in response to an earlier draft of this paper, Tom Kochan accepts that a full explanation for the changes that have occurred in the U.S. industrial relations system over the past two or three decades requires reference to the behavior of the state. He argues, however, that "my restatement of the argument would be that, along with shifts in product markets and technologies came a shift in the political and regulatory environment. This confluence of pressures/opportunities provided a window for a more active management approach (strategies?) to industrial relations and thus management served as the driving party for change in practices at the firm level." I don't disagree with Kochan's restated argument. On the other hand, I do believe that it is very likely that if the U.S. state had refused to permit employer behavior contrary to the letter and spirit of the original Wagner Act employers would have behaved much differently. Even now the proposition that the U.S. labor relations system has been fundamentally transformed is not universally accepted. Had the U.S. government stood firmly against the initial moves towards outlawry by employers, discussion in the 1980s and 1990s might well have focused on incremental change in labor relations rather than fundamental transformation.

[8] Some accounts posit four instead of three regimes.

[9] In his study of the emergence of Canadian labour policy in the first decade of the twentieth century, historian Paul Craven (1980) utilizes a similar proactive concept of the state although he does not attempt to relate it to German realism.

References

Aaron, Benjamin. "Legal Framework of Industrial Relations." In *The Next Twenty-Five Years of Industrial Relations.* Madison, WI: Industrial Relations Research Association, 1973.

Aaron, Benjamin, Joyce M. Najita, and James L. Stern, eds. *Public Sector Bargaining*, second edition. Washington, D.C.: Bureau of National Affairs, Inc., 1988.

Adams, George W. "Worker Participation in Corporate Decision-Making: Canada's Future?" *Queen's Papers in Industrial Relations.* Kingston, Ontario: Queen's University Industrial Relations Centre, 1990.

Adams, Roy J. "A Theory of Employer Attitudes and Behaviour Towards Trade Unions in Western Europe and North America." In *Management Under Differing Value Systems*, eds. Gunter Dlugos, and Klaus Weiermaier. Berlin: deGruyter, 1981.

________. "Industrial Relations and the Economic Crisis: Canada Moves Towards Europe." In *Industrial Relations in a Decade of Economic Change*, eds. Hervey Juris, Mark Thompson, and Wilbur Daniels. Madison, WI: Industrial Relations Research Association, 1985a.

________. "Two Policy Approaches to Labour-Management Decision-Making at the Level of the Enterprise: A Comparison of the Wagner Model and Statutory Works Councils." In *Labour-Management Cooperation in Canada*, ed. Craig Riddell. Toronto: University of Toronto Press, 1985b.

________. "Industrial Relations Systems: Canada in Comparative Perspective." In *Union-Management Relations in Canada*, second edition, eds. John Anderson, Morley Gunderson, and Allen Ponak. Don Mills, Ontario: Addison-Wesley, 1989.

________. "State Regulation of Unions and Collective Bargaining: An International Assessment of Determinants and Consequences." Paper prepared for presentation at the World Congress of the International Industrial Relations Association. Sydney, Australia, September 1992a.

________. "The Right to Participate." *Employee Responsibilities and Rights Journal* V, 2 (forthcoming, 1992b).

________. "All Aspects of People at Work: Unity and Division in the Study of Labour and Labour Management." In *Industrial Relations Theory: Its Nature, Scope, and Pedagogy*, eds. Roy J. Adams, and Noah Meltz. Metuchen, NJ: Scarecrow Press, 1992c.

Adams, Roy, Bernard Adell, and Hoyt Wheeler. "Discipline and Discharge in Canada and the United States." *Labor Law Journal* (August 1990), pp. 596-601.

Adell, Bernard. "Law and Industrial Relations: The State of the Art in Common Law Canada." In *The State of the Art in Industrial Relations*, eds. Gerard Hebert, Hem C. Jain, and Noah M. Meltz. Toronto: University of Toronto Centre for Industrial Relations, 1988.

Aglietta, Michel. *A Theory of Capitalist Regulation: The US Experience*. London: New Left Books, 1979.

Baglioni, Guido, and Colin Crouch, eds. *European Industrial Relations, The Challenge of Flexibility*. London: Sage, 1990.

Bamber, Greg J., and Russell D. Lansbury, eds. *International and Comparative Industrial Relations*. London: Allen and Unwin, 1987.

Banting, Keith, ed. *The State and Economic Interests*. Toronto: University of Toronto Press, 1985.

Barkin, Sol. "The Total Labor Package: From Wage Bargain to Social Contract." *Journal of Economic Issues* 11 (1977), pp. 339-51.

Bawden, D. Lee, and Felicity Skidmore. *Rethinking Employment Policy*. Washington, D.C.: The Urban Institute Press, 1989.

Beatty, David. *Putting the Charter to Work*. Kingston and Montreal: McGill-Queen's Press, 1987.

Bendick, Marc, Jr. "Matching Workers and Job Opportunities: What Role for the Federal-State Employment Service? In *Rethinking Employment Policy*, eds. D. Lee Bawden and Felicity Skidmore. Washington, D.C.: The Urban Institute Press, 1989.

Birk, R. "The Law of Strikes and Lock-outs." In *Comparative Labour Law and Industrial Relations in Industrialised Market Economies*, ed. Roger Blainpain. Deventer, The Netherlands: Kluwer, 1990.

Blyth, Conrad A. "The Interaction Between Collective Bargaining and Government Policies in Selected Member Countries." In *Collective Bargaining and Government Policies*. Paris: Organization for Economic Cooperation and Development, 1979.

Boyer, Robert. *The Search for Labour Market Flexibility: The European Economies in Transition*. Oxford: Clarendon Press, 1988.

Bruce, Peter G. "Political Parties and Labor Legislation in Canada and the U.S." *Industrial Relations* 28 (Spring 1989), pp. 115-41.

Calmfors, L., and J. Driffill. "Bargaining Structure, Corporatism and Macroeconomic Performance." *Economic Policy* 6 (April 1988), p. 13-61.

Chaison, Gary N., and Joseph B. Rose. "Continental Divide: The Direction and Fate of North American Unions." *Advances in Industrial and Labor Relations*, eds. David Lewin, David Lipsky, and Donna Sockell. Greenwich, CT: JAI Press, 1990.

Cohen, Sanford. "An Analytical Framework for Labor Relations Law." *Industrial and Labor Relations Review* 14 (April 1961), pp. 350-62.

Collins, A. Michael. "Employment Training Policy and Politics, 1978-1982: From CETA to JTPA." In *Proceedings of the Thirty-Ninth Annual Meeting of the Industrial Relations Research Association*. Madison, WI: Industrial Relations Research Association, 1986.

Committee for Economic Development. *The Public Interest in National Labor Policy*. New York: Committee for Economic Development, 1961.

Cooper, Martha. *The Search for Consensus*. Paris: Organization for Economic Cooperation and Development, 1982.

Cox, Andrew, and Noel O'Sullivan. *The Corporate State*. Aldershot, U.K.: Edward Elgar, 1988.

Craven, Paul. *'An Unequal Umpire' Industrial Relations and the Canadian State 1900-1911*. Toronto: University of Toronto Press, 1980.

Crouch, Colin. "United Kingdom: The Rejection of Compromise." In *European Industrial Relations: The Challenge of Flexibility*. London: Sage, 1990.

Dabscheck, Braham. "A Survey of Theories of Industrial Relations." In *Theories and Concepts in Comparative Industrial Relations*, eds. Jack Barbash and Kate Barbash. Columbia, SC: University of South Carolina Press, 1989.

________. "Industrial Relations and Theories of Regulation." In *Industrial Relations Theory, Its Nature, Scope and Pedagogy*, eds. Roy J. Adams and Noah Meltz. Metuchen, NJ: Scarecrow, forthcoming, 1992.

Doeringer, Peter B., ed. *Industrial Relations in International Perspective, Essays on Research and Policy*. London: Macmillan, 1981.

Dunlop, John T. "Introduction." In *Labor in the Twentieth Century*, eds. John T. Dunlop and Walter Galenson. New York: Basic Books, 1978.

Dye, Thomas R. *Understanding Public Policy*, fourth edition. Englewood Cliffs, NJ: Prentice Hall, 1981.

Ehrenberg, Ronald G. "Worker's Rights: Rethinking Protective Labor Legislation." In *Rethinking Labor Policy*, ed. D. Lee Bawden and Felicity Skidmore. Washington, D.C.: The Urban Institute Press, 1989.

Evans, Peter B., Dietrich Rueschemeyer, and Theda Skocpol, eds. *Bringing the State Back In*. New York: Cambridge University Press, 1985.

Flanagan, Robert. "The National Accord as a Social Contract." *Industrial and Labor Relations Review* 34 (1980), pp. 35-50.

Flanagan, Robert J., David Soskice, and Lloyd Ulman. *Unionism, Economic Stabilization and Incomes Policy: European Experience*. Washington, D.C.: Brookings Institution, 1983.

Freeman, Richard. "Employee Councils, Worker Participation, and Other Squishy Stuff." *Proceedings of the 43rd Annual Meeting of the Industrial Relations Research Association*. Madison, WI: Industrial Relations Research Association, 1990.

Gil, Avishai. "Air Transport Deregulation and its Implications for Flight Attendants." *International Labour Review* 129 (1990), pp. 317-32.

Giles, Anthony. "Industrial Relations Theory, the State and Politics." In *Theories and Concepts in Comparative Industrial Relations*, eds. Jack Barbash and Kate Barbash. Columbia, SC: University of South Carolina Press, 1989.

Godard, John. "Beyond Empiricism: Towards a Reconstruction of IR Theory and Research." *Advances in Industrial and Labor Relations*, 1992a.

________. "Theory and Method in Industrial Relations: Modernist and Postmodernist Alternatives." In *Industrial Relations Theory. Its Nature, Scope, and Pedagogy*, eds. R. J. Adams and N. Meltz. Metuchen, NJ: Scarecrow Press, forthcoming, 1992b.

Gordon, Margaret. *Social Security in Industrialized Countries: A Comparative Analysis*. NY: Cambridge University Press, 1989.

Grant, Wyn, ed. *The Political Economy of Corporatism*. NY: St. Martin's Press, 1985.

Harris, Howell. *The Right to Manage: Industrial Relations Policies of American Business in the 1940s*. Madison, WI: University of Wisconsin Press, 1983.

Heidenheimer, Arnold J., Hugh Heclo, and Carolyn Teich Adams. *Comparative Public Policy*, NY: St. Martin's Press, 1983.

Hepple, Bob. "Welfare Legislation and Wage-Labour." In *The Making of Labour Law in Europe*, ed. Bob Hepple. London: Mansell, 1986a.

———. *The Making of Labour Law in Europe*. London: Mansell, 1986b.
Hibbs, Douglas A. "On the Political Economy of Long-Run Trends in Strike Activity." *British Journal of Political Science* 8 (1978), pp. 153-75.
Hirst, Paul, and Jonathan Zeitlin. "Flexible Specialization Versus Post-Fordism: Theory, Evidence and Policy Implications." *Economy and Society*, 20 (February 1991), pp. 2-56.
Hyman, Richard. *Industrial Relations, A Marxist Introduction*. London: Macmillan, 1975.
Jacobs, Antoine. "Collective Self-Regulation." In *The Making of Labour Law in Europe*, ed. Bob Hepple. London: Mansell, 1986.
Jessop, Bob, Otto Jacobi, and Hans Kastendiek. "Corporatist and Liberal Responses to the crisis of Postwar Capitalism." In *Economic Crisis, Trade Unions and the State*, eds. Otto Jacobi, Bob Jessop, Hans Kastendiek, and Marino Regini. London: Croom Helm, 1986.
Jessop, Bob. "Regulation Theories in Retrospect and Prospect." *Economy and Society* 19 (May 1990), pp. 153-216.
Kaufman, Bruce, ed. *How Labor Markets Work*. Lexington, MA: Lexington Books, 1988.
Keller, Berndt. "The Role of the State as Corporate Actor in Industrial Relations Systems." In *Comparative Industrial Relations, Contemporary Research and Theory*, ed. Roy J. Adams. London: Harper-Collins, 1991.
Kerr, Clark, and Abraham Siegel. "The Structuring of the Labor Force in Industrial Society: New Dimensions and New Questions." *Industrial and Labor Relations Review* 8 (1955), pp. 151-68.
King, Roger. *The State in Modern Society*. London: Macmillan, 1986.
Klare, Karl. "Judicial Deradicalization of the Wagner Act and the Origins of Modern Legal Consciousness, 1937-1941." *Minnesota Law Review* 62 (1978), pp. 265-339.
———. "Labor Law as Ideology: Toward a New Historiography of Collective Bargaining Law." *Industrial Relations Law Review* 4 (1981), pp. 405-82.
———. "Critical Theory and Labor Relations Law." In *The Politics of Law: A Progressive Critique*, ed. D. Kairys. New York: Pantheon, 1990.
Kochan, Thomas A. "Correlates of State Public Employee Bargaining Laws." *Industrial Relations* 12 (October 1973), pp. 322-37.
Kochan, Thomas A., Robert B. McKersie, and Peter Cappelli. "Strategic Choice and Industrial Relations Theory." *Industrial Relations* 23 (Winter 1984), pp. 16-39.
Kochan, Thomas A., and Harry Katz. *Collective Bargaining and Industrial Relations*, second edition. Homewood, IL: Irwin, 1988.
Kochan, Thomas A., Harry Katz, and Robert McKersie. *The Transformation of American Industrial Relations*. New York: Basic Books, 1985.
Kochan, Thomas A., and Robert B. McKersie. "Future Directions for American Labor and Human Resources Policy." *Relations Industrielles* 44 (1989), pp. 224-48.
Koshiro, Kazutoshi. "Labor Relations in Public Enterprises." In *Contemporary Industrial Relations in Japan*, ed. Taishiro Shirai. Madison, WI: University of Wisconsin Press, 1983.
Krueger, Alan B. "The Evolution of Unjust-Dismissal Legislation in the United States." *Industrial and Labor Relations Review* 44 (July 1991), pp. 644-60.
Kyloh, Robert H. "Flexibility and Structural Adjustment Through Consensus. Some Lessons from Australia." *International Labour Review* 128 (1989), pp. 103-23.
Lawler, John J. *Unionization and Deunionization*. Columbia, SC: University of South Carolina Press, 1990.
Levine, David I., and Laura D'Andrea Tyson. "Participation, Productivity, and the Firm's Environment." In *Paying for Productivity*, ed. Alan S. Blinder. Washington, D.C.: The Brookings Institution, 1990.
Levitan, Sar A., P. E. Carlson, and I. Shapiro. *Protecting American Workers: An Assessment of Government Programs*. Washington, D.C.: BNA, 1986.
Lindblom, Charles E. *Politics and Markets*. New York: Basic Books, 1977.
Lipietz, Alain. *Mirages and Miracles: The Crises of Global Fordism*. London: Verso, 1987.

MacInnes, John. *Thatcherism at Work*. Milton Keynes, U.K.: Open University Press, 1988.

Maier, Charles S. "Preconditions for Corporatism." In *Order and Conflict in Contemporary Capitalism*. Oxford: Oxford University Press, 1984.

Martin, Andrew. "The Politics of Employment and Welfare: National Policies and International Interdependence." In *The State and Economics Interests*, ed. Keith Banting. Toronto: University of Toronto Press, 1985.

McKersie, Robert B. "Governance: A Framework for Our Field." Working Paper number 3237-91-BPS. Cambridge, MA: Sloan School of Management, Masachusetts Institute of Technology, 1991.

Meltz, Noah. "Labor Movements in the United States and Canada." In *Challenges and Choices Facing American Labor*, ed. Thomas A. Kochan. Cambridge, MA: MIT Press, 1985.

Miliband, Ralph. *The State in Capitalist Society*. London: Weidenfeld and Nicholson, 1969.

Miller, Berkeley, and William Canak. "From 'Porkchoppers' to 'Lambchoppers': The Passage of Florida's Public Employee Relations Act." *Industrial and Labor Relations Review* 44 (January 1991), pp. 349-66.

Montgomery, David. *The Fall of the House of Labor: The Workplace, The State, and American Labor Activism, 1865-1925*. Cambridge: Cambridge University Press, 1987.

Morris, Charles J., ed. *American Labor Policy*. Washington, D.C.: Bureau of National Affairs, Inc., 1987.

Moye, William T. "Presidential Labor-Management Committees: Productive Failures." *Industrial and Labor Relations Review* 34 (1980), pp. 51-66.

Mucciaroni, G. *The Political Failure of Employment Policy 1945-1982*. Pittsburgh: University of Pittsburgh Press, 1990.

Murray, Gregor, and Anthony Giles. "Political Economy and Canadian Industrial Relations." *Proceedings of the 26th Conference of the Canadian Industrial Relations Association* 83-95. Laval, Quebec: Canadian Industrial Relations Association, 1989.

Niland, John, and Keri Spooner. "Structural Change and Industrial Relations: Australia." In *Proceedings of the 8th World Congress of the International Industrial Relations Association*. Geneva: International Industrial Relations Association, 1989.

Noel, Alain. "Accumulation, Regulation, and Social Change: An Essay on French Political Economy." *International Organization* 41 (Spring 1987), pp. 303-33.

Offe, Claus. "The Capitalist State and the Problem of Policy Formation." In *Stress and Contradiction in Modern Capitalism*, eds. L. Lindberg, et al. Lexington: Lexington Books, 1975.

Onimode, Bade. *An Introduction to Marxist Political Economy*. London: Zed Books, 1985.

Osterman, Paul. "Elements of a National Training Policy." In *New Developments in Worker Training: A Legacy for the 1990s*, eds. Louis A. Ferman, Michele Hoyman, Joel Cutcher-Gershenfeld, and Ernest J. Savoie. Madison, WI: Industrial Relations Research Association, 1990.

Ozaki, M. "Labor Relations in the Public Service: Methods of Determining Employment Conditions." *International Labour Review* 126 (May-June 1987a), pp. 277-99.

________. "Labour Relations in the Public Service: Labour Disputes and Their Settlements." *International Labour Review* 126 (July-August 1987b), pp. 405-22.

Paloheimo, Heikki. "Between Liberalism and Corporatism: The Effect of Trade Unions and Governments on Economic Performance in Eighteen OECD Countries." In *Labour Relations and Economic Performance*, eds. Renata Brunetta and Carlo Dell'Aringa. London: Macmillan, 1990.

Panitch, Leo. "The Development of Corporatism in Liberal Democracies." *Comparative Political Studies* 10 (1977).

Panitch, Leo, and Donald Swartz. *From Consent to Coercion: The Assault on Trade Union Freedoms*. Toronto: Garamond, 1985.

Piore, Michael, and Charles Sabel. *The Second Industrial Divide: Possibilities for Prosperity*. NY: Basic Books, 1984.
Plowman, D. H. "Management and Industrial Relations." In *Comparative Industrial Relations, Contemporary Research and Theory*, ed. Roy J. Adams. London: Harper-Collins, 1991.
Ramm, Thilo. "Laissez-faire and State Protection of Workers." In *The Making of Labour Law in Europe*, ed. Bob Hepple. London: Mansell, 1986.
Rehmus, Charles M., ed. *Public Employment Labor Relations: An Overview of Eleven Nations*. Ann Arbor, MI: University of Michigan/Wayne State University Institute of Labor and Industrial Relations, 1975.
Rimlinger, Gaston. "Labor and the Government: A Comparative Historical Perspective." *Journal of Economic History* XXXVII (1977), pp. 210-25.
Rosenberg, Alexander. *Philosophy of Social Science*. Boulder, CO: Westview, 1988.
Sack, Jeffrey, and Tanya Lee. "The Role of the State in Canadian Labour Relations." *Relations Industrielles* 44 (1989), pp. 195-223.
Samson, K. "International Labour Law." In *Comparative Labour Law and Industrial Relations in Industrialized Market Economies*, ed. Roger Blainpain. Deventer, The Netherlands: Kluwer, 1990.
Schregle, Johannes. "Labour Relations in the Public Sector." *International Labour Review* 110 (July 1974), pp. 381-404.
Sisson, Keith. *The Management of Collective Bargaining: An International Comparison*. London: Basil Blackwell, 1987.
Sloane, Arthur A., and Fred Witney. *Labor Relations*, sixth edition. Englewood Cliffs, NJ: Prentice Hall, 1988.
Slomp, Hans. *Labor Relations In Europe*. New York: Greenwood, 1990.
Stieber, Jack. "Employment-at-Will: An Issue for the 1980s." In *Proceedings of the Thirty-Sixth Annual Meeting of the Industrial Relations Research Association*. Madison, WI: Industrial Relations Research Association, 1983.
Stone, Katherine Van Wezel. "The Post-War Paradigm in American Labor Law." *Yale Law Journal* 90 (June 1981), pp. 1510-80.
________. "The Legacy of Industrial Pluralism: The Deregulation of Labour Relations in the 1980s." Paper presented to a Public Policy Workshop, University of Toronto, November 16, 1990.
Storper, Michael, and Allen J. Scott. "Work Organisation and Local Labour Markets in an Era of Flexible Production." *International Labour Review* 129 (1990), pp. 573-91.
Thornicroft, K. W. "Patterns of Teacher Bargaining in Canada and the United States." *Labor Law Journal* (forthcoming, 1992).
Towers, Brian. "Running the Gauntlet: British Trade Unions Under Thatcher." *Industrial and Labor Relations Review* 42 (1989), pp. 163-88.
Weiler, Paul C. *Governing the Workplace*. Cambridge, MA: Harvard University Press, 1990.
Wheeler, Hoyt. "Labour Market Flexibility and New Employment Patterns." In *Proceedings of the 8th World Congress of the International Industrial Relations Association*. Geneva: International Industrial Relations Association, 1989.
Wilson, Graham K. "Why is There no Corporatism in the United States?" In *Patterns of Corporatist Policy-Making*, eds. Gerhard Lehmbruch and Phillippe Schmitter. London: Sage, 1982.
Windmuller, John P., ed. "Industrial Democracy in International Perspective." *Annals of the American Academy of Political and Social Sciences* 431 (May 1977).
Windmuller, John P. *Collective Bargaining in Industrialized Market Economies: A Reappraisal*. Geneva: International Labour Office, 1987.
Woods, H. D., Gerard Dion, and John Crispo. *Canadian Industrial Relations: Report of the Task Force on Labour Relations*. Ottawa: Privy Council, 1968.
Woods, H. D. "The Problem of Labour Relations Policy." In *Proceedings of the 20th Annual Meeting of the Canadian Industrial Relations Association*. Laval, Quebec: Canadian Industrial Relations Association, 1983.
Zeitlin, Jonathan. "Shop Floor Bargaining and the State: A Contradictory Relationship." In *Shop Floor Bargaining and the State*, eds. Steven Tolliday and Jonathan Zeitlin. Cambridge: Cambridge University Press, 1985.

CHAPTER 15

Labor Law Scholarship: A Critical Survey

MATTHEW W. FINKIN
University of Illinois

The question—What has scholarship in labor and employment law been in the 1980s, and where is it going?—is posed at the confluence of two events: of considerable change in the law, and of intense debate about the nature of legal scholarship.[1] These are best developed by comparison with the literature of a generation ago.

"Traditional" Legal Scholarship

Not everything written by a scholar is an act of scholarship. Nor, as Daniel Bell, David Riesman and others have emphasized, is every intellectual exercise necessarily a scholarly one.[2] Scholarship is the practice of an academic discipline, the application of a body of learning. The questions it deals with are professional ones, and are answered, at least in part, by research; the conclusions it offers are tested by professional standards.

When one speaks of legal scholarship one is compelled to inquire into the nature of the discipline, of what is taught and learned in schools of law. And here one at once confronts vintage controversy—on whether the study of law is self-contained or should implicate a wider set of disciplines; on whether it is objective or ideologically laden. But whatever else a legal education might include, at a minimum it encompasses the transmission of the received tradition, the content of legal concepts that flow from Roman law (and its borrowings), through Anglo-Saxon and Norman times down to the reception of the common law in the early American Republic, and so to the present. Accordingly, it contemplates as well a method of analyzing legal problems: the dissection of issues into legally cognizable components, and so of distinguishing the relevant from the irrelevant,[3] either in terms of common law categories or for statutory purposes, the latter a fixture in labor law since the Wagner Act. And it has also included a manner of reasoning, of weighing competing arguments—in labor law especially, of alternative statutory readings—to assess and so to accommodate the strengths of competing interests, eventually to achieve an ostensibly optimal legal solution. It would, as James Atleson said in criticism, purport to present "a fair 'balancing' of the relevant interests."[4]

Some legal scholarship is undertaken solely to deepen or enrich our understanding. But more often traditional legal scholarship is instrumental, a bit like civil engineering, in Richard Posner's[5] analogy—or "plumbing"—in Lord Diplock's.[6] "[S]cholarly criticism," David Shapiro observed, "is not undertaken simply for the delectation of other scholars; it is designed to improve the world that is the subject of its concern."[7] Though social science research might be sought for illumination, as Derek Bok did in his work on the regulation of union elections,[8] or, more rarely, actual empirical investigation might be undertaken, as Clyde Summers did in his investigation into the law of union discipline,[9] the reasoning tends to rely primarily upon material internal to the discipline. Consequently, a recurrent suspicion has been that the problems traditional labor law scholars find interesting are mere conundrums in legal logic having scant relationship to the problems of the "real" world.[10]

The tone of the argument might be intense, even polemical (when an especially perverse decision or doctrine is criticized); or it might be detached, even Olympian. But, uncoupled from the author's rhetorical technique—sweetly to reason, to bludgeon, or to seduce—the arguments assayed are weighed ultimately by their analytical power. In sum, traditional legal scholarship does not offer new truths, like discoveries about the physical world; it proposes more persuasive ways of dealing with legal problems.

This phenomenon, of scholarship as "committed argument,"[11] is scarcely unique to the law. In the "hard" sciences as well as the social sciences and humanities, arguments are advanced for the better interpretation of the evidence at hand. The canons of responsible scholarship require the scholar to play fair: to report all the evidence; neither to distort nor to ignore. But assuming that to have been done, the conclusion offered will rise or fall on the cogency of the reasoning, on the closeness of fit of the argument to the evidence at hand. What that process entails will be illustrated momentarily.

As in other disciplines grounded in professions practiced outside the academy, the agenda for "traditional" legal scholarship is most often set by external developments—by new legislation, administrative rulings, or judicial decisions; it is rarely visionary, and has been dismissed on that very ground as "unsystematic ad hoc tinkering"[12] with the status quo. One consequence is that legal scholarship tends to be "compartmentalized":[13] it tends not to be connected in any organic way with the work that preceded it; indeed, a premium is placed upon having something genuinely new to say. Another is that traditional legal scholarship tends to have a relatively short shelf-life;[14] as the law on point becomes settled, the problem evaporates, or is eclipsed by more pressing and as yet unresolved questions. If a piece of legal writing is still cited, is still worth taking account of for other than purely historical reasons a generation after it was published, it can justifiably lay claim to be a "classic" in its field. What makes it worth taking account of is the scope and persistence of the issue, the painstaking care with which the evidence is assembled, the rigor of the analysis—whether the hard questions have been anticipated and been dealt with—and, ultimately, the power to persuade. If one were to list labor law "classics" of the 1960s, one would have to acknowledge work by Clyde Summers, Archibald Cox, Benjamin Aaron, Derek Bok, Bernard Meltzer, Julius Getman, and Howard Lesnick. If these have not always shaped the law, they have helped to shape how we think about the law.

The Literature of the 1960s

In 1960, the National Labor Relations Act enjoyed its silver anniversary, the Taft-Hartley Act was taking on a texture of administrative and judicial interpretation, the Landrum-Griffin Act was brand new, and the Civil Rights Act was not yet born. The classification system of the *Index to Legal Periodicals* reveals a body of writing dealing chiefly with the law of private-sector unionization, with separate categories provided respectively for labor law, labor management relations, collective bargaining, industrial arbitration, picketing, strikes and boycotts, unions, and wages. There was a single category for the law of "discrimination" at large, subsuming employment under that general head; and another for the individual employment relationship, classified anachronistically as "master and servant."

Legal writing of the 1960s tended to cluster about certain issues or sets of issues: the process of unionization, including unit determination, organizational activity, contract bar rules, and the like; the duty to bargain in good faith, both procedurally, as in the legality of General Electric's use of "Boulwarism," and substantively, especially concerning the reach of the duty to require bargaining over subcontracting, plant closing and relocation, and automation—the latter a pervasive concern of the period; the regulation of economic pressure, of strikes and lock-outs, and especially of the secondary boycott; the legal nature and means of enforcing collective bargaining agreements; the role of state law under the federal scheme, that is, of labor law preemption.

Sight was not altogether lost of the individual employee. Scholars evinced a fascination with the union's duty of fair representation; and Clyde Summers was writing classic pieces (by the prior definition) on the rights of individuals under collective agreements and vis-à-vis their unions. But the writing about the law of individual, non-union employment, of "master and servant," was concerned almost exclusively with liability for on-the-job injury, with the perhaps singular and, at the time, little noticed exception of Lawrence Blades' article, "Employment at Will vs. Individual Freedoms: On Limiting the Abusive Exercise of Employer Power."[15] The overwhelming concern of legal scholars of the time was the effective administration of the federal statutory system of collective bargaining which, it was assumed, would continue to be "at the center of national labor policy."[16] Thus the more speculative discussion focused upon the future role and direction of collective bargaining,[17] on whether unions had "too much" power, and so of the role of government at the bargaining table.[18]

The Literature of the 1980s

The 1990 Index of Legal Periodicals reveals a very different world. The public sector is broken out as a separate category of the literature on collective bargaining, reflecting the development of legislation and the concomitant growth of collective bargaining in that environment. Separate entries are now afforded not only for "employment discrimination," but for "age discrimination," "race discrimination," "sex discrimination," and "handicap discrimination."

Master and Servant has been replaced by "Employer and Employee," to which has been added separate classifications for "Employment At Will," "Employee Benefits," and "Employee Ownership."

The writing on the law of unionization and collective bargaining reflects the changed environment: a renewed interest in section 8(a)(2) of the labor Act, not on the eradication of "company unions" but on how that prohibition bears upon employer-sponsored plans of worker participation;[19] discussion of the reach and implications of the Court's exclusion of managerial personnel, and especially of its manner of reasoning on the managerial definition in the *Yeshiva* case;[20] on the implications of the Supreme Court's *First National Maintenance* approach to bargaining subjects and of related developments by the National Labor Relations Board for decisions over plant relocation and closing;[21] for the relation of individual to collective action under the labor Act in the wake of *City Disposal* and the Board's decision in *Meyers Industries*;[22] for the Court's shifting ground on questions of federal preemption;[23] on the increasingly anomalous status of "independent contractors";[24] and so on. In the more speculative literature, the fear of "big labor" has been replaced by rumination on whether organized labor has any future at all,[25] and of a broadened interest in labor law reform.[26] In employment discrimination, apart from a good deal of writing on technical points, the more sweeping concerns are with preferences on grounds of race and sex;[27] comparable worth;[28] and of the legal theory of discrimination, as evidenced, for example, in the use of actuarially sound sex-segregated mortality tables,[29] ability testing,[30] or the reliance more generally upon statistical proof.[31] The major explosion is the area of individual employment, especially of the erosion in the at-will rule, and of the issue of "wrongful" dismissal in the non-union workplace. One compilation of the law on point notes that in the decade of the 1980s there were over a hundred articles, notes, and comments (albeit mostly state surveys and individual case comments) dealing with that issue.[32] Other issues of individual workplace rights have drawn attention, including especially questions of employee reputation, dignity, and privacy, such as drug and other medical testing[33] and electronic workplace surveillance.[34] The scholars' particular fascination with the duty of fair representation continues unabated,[35] and portends to survive even the demise of the labor movement. The decade also witnessed a strengthening interest in labor law history[36] and, with the founding of the *Comparative Labor Law Journal* in 1978, of work in comparative labor law.

The Evaluation of "Traditional" Scholarship

The bulk of the literature continues to be of the "traditional" kind; and, better to compare it with the growing body of "non-traditional" writing, one is compelled to inquire more precisely of what it means to ask if a work has been "rigorous," has "asked itself the hard questions," has been "analytically persuasive." These questions are best explored by a comparison of two recent pieces treating very different but perennial subjects—labor law preemption and fair representation.

In 1959, the United States Supreme Court's *Garmon*[37] decision announced a sweeping doctrine of federal labor law preemption. "Administration is more than a means of regulation," the Court opined, "administration is regulation." Where the underlying conduct is even "arguably" protected *or* prohibited by the federal Act, the Court concluded that to allow the States to act would involve "too great a danger of conflict between power asserted by Congress and [the] requirements imposed by state law." It is not obvious, however, why conduct which the federal Act prohibits could not also be prohibited by the states, perhaps under an even stronger remedial scheme. But the latter was taken by the Court only to punctuate its conclusion. "[S]ince remedies form an ingredient of any integrated scheme of regulation, to allow the State a grant of remedy . . . which has been withheld" by the NLRA "accentuates the danger of conflict."

The Court's reasoning was anticipated and later approved by Archibald Cox. On the latter point, Cox observed that,

> If Congress were to make employer unfair labor practices crimes and authorize private suits for damages, the amendments would be regarded as a major change in labor policy. No less a change of policy results if a state creates the crime or right of action for damages. The NLRA provides only administrative remedies because Congress felt that they were more suited to the sensitive problems of labor relations.[38]

Professor Michael Gottesman has recently challenged Cox's conclusion.[39] *Garmon* is defensible, Gottesman argues, insofar as the conduct involved lies on a spectrum of the protected to the prohibited—such as picketing, the conduct actually involved in the *Garmon* case. One easily perceives how a state's miscalculation of where the line is to be drawn would upset the federal scheme, such that the mere danger of such interference requires a prophylactic rule. This consideration, he argues, does not apply to protected conduct that does not lie on such a spectrum, such as whether or not an employee's discharge was for union activity. The state's refusal to afford a remedy leaves the federal remedy intact; the state's affordance of an additional remedy in no way upsets the federal structure, unless Cox was right in concluding that the federal Act's remedial scheme was intended to preclude any state remedy. But Gottesman makes a compelling case that the Act's remedial scheme was driven by Congress' desire to protect the role of the NLRB, necessarily to preclude a jury trial otherwise required by the Seventh Amendment. Consequently,

> In the absence of concrete evidence that remedies were restricted for substantive reasons apart from the Seventh Amendment, there is no warrant for assuming that the Congress that enacted the Wagner Act intended to insulate employers from stronger state remedies for wrongful discharge.[40]

Without fully rehearsing his analysis, Professor Gottesman shows how the narrower view is more consistent with the Court's approach to preemption at the time the Act was passed—from which the *Garmon* decision was itself a radical departure—and is better in keeping with how the Court has dealt with preemption more recently. Consequently, Gottesman's approach is historically better grounded and doctrinally more satisfying; indeed, it would eliminate the anomaly created by *Garmon* that allows the state to afford tort relief for a discharge violative of the state's public policy, including other cases where the state's policy coincides with federal policy, save at this one point.

In contrast, note Michael Harper and Ira Lupu's equally ambitious search for a philosopher's stone to resolve the duty of fair representation.[41] The duty was created by the United States Supreme Court's 1944 decision in the *Steele* case, in part by analogy to the constitutional guaranty of equal protection of the laws. The law of equal protection was rudimentary at the time, but it has since taken on a considerable texture; and Harper and Lupu argue that that touchstone should be returned to, so to inform the limits the courts should impose upon union agreements that advantage some at the expense of others. To view fair representation "as" equal protection, they argue, is to pose this question: did the "union act in accordance with a principle that regards all as equals?"[42] Did the union accord those it represents "equal respect?"[43] The latter is developed by analogy to the constitutional law governing distinctions between citizens and aliens: our propensity "to divide the world with insiders and outsiders," Harper and Lupu argue, is a "flaw of human nature."[44] The courts should accordingly be more skeptical of union credibility "whenever the qualities of insider-outsider classification are present." For illustration, they take the case of seniority. Seniority seems at first blush to be "disrespectful" of junior workers. But, on closer inspection, such is not the case.

> [S]eniority is derived from conceptions of the good of the bargaining unit that do not disparage the intrinsic value of junior workers. Preference for senior employees over junior employees in job security and promotional opportunities can be justified by the senior employees' greater aggregate contribution to their firm, by the larger proportion of their lives that they have invested in the workplace, and by a concern for their decreasing job mobility.[45]

On the other hand, a decision by a larger group of employees to end-tail the seniority of a smaller group, acquired as a result of a business merger, would offend the duty of fair representation, for the larger group will have denied smaller equal respect: "the social empathy on which principled decision-making depends was never established."[46]

There are several infirmities in their theory. It refashions what was only one analogy, employed to create a statutory, not a constitutional, limitation into a singular prism through which all of fair representation is to be focused. Putting aside the fact that the prism is of less than crystal clarity even in the constitutional setting, the refashioning is not faithful to the historical context. Only months before the Court created the duty of fair representation, it stressed that the labor Act rested upon legislative "absorption" and "approval" of "the philosophy of bargaining as worked out in the labor movement of the United States."[47] The "practice and philosophy of collective bargaining" so absorbed and approved is concerned with the "welfare of the group," and the Court noted that a majority may act to the disadvantage of individuals or minority groups who might well do better without a union. "[T]he majority rules," said the Court, "and if it collectivizes the employment bargain, individual advantages . . . will generally in practice go in as contribution to the collective result."[48]

But Harper and Lupu refuse to look to the nature of collective bargaining, as their own treatment of seniority illustrates, for the very essence of a seniority system is the manufacture of a more or less elaborate and highly artificial structure of "insiders" and "outsiders."[49] The rules must determine the employee's eligibility for seniority, the unit or units in which seniority is acquired, and the seniority consequences of significant business decisions. The variations for these distinctions are "almost infinite"[50] and their essential function is to exclude fellow workers from competition for available jobs, as is evidenced in a rich literature that Harper and Lupu neglect.[51] It cannot be argued that the rules governing the distinction between "permanent" and "probationary," or between job progression seniority, department seniority, and plant seniority rest upon principled or neutral distinctions. Even the decision made by some unions to limit seniority and expand work sharing as an alternative to layoff has been explained by the numerical strength of short-service employees.[52] The point is that in making these classifications the union is governed by no objective principle other than the self-interest of the majority or of the union's leadership.

Gottesman's and Harper and Lupu's pieces are ambitious, they address persistent and seemingly intractable problems, and they attempt to resolve them. There the similarity ends. Gottesman has anticipated and dealt with the hard questions: he is at pains to deal with the historical setting, and with the role of the courts in reading vintage statutes under altered circumstances; and he comes to grips with the tough question of the status of the remedial scheme. Harper and Lupu slight the Court's contemporaneous conception of collective bargaining and decline to confront the serious obstacle their own example of seniority poses. Nor is this all. David Feller observed that a legal theory is important "if solutions to particular problems can be derived from it," and is sound "if the solutions it produces are more satisfactory than those which would result without it."[53] Gottesman's theory of preemption solves certain real world problems in a more satisfactory manner than the theory it would replace. Harper and Lupu's tests of "equal respect," "principled democracy," and "social empathy" are incapable of solving concrete cases.

Non-traditional Legal Writing

According to Judge Posner, the traditional legal scholarship of the 1960s came at a time of ideological quiescence, "when it was natural to think of law not in political but in technical terms."[54] In addition, he argues that there was little that other disciplines were thought to be capable of contributing to an understanding of legal problems. All that, he argues, has changed. Other disciplines—economics, game theory, statistics, philosophy, literary criticism, hermeneutics, and even musicology[55]—have been ransacked for legal insight. And the antecedent political consensus has "shattered."

> The spectrum of political opinion in law schools, which in 1960 occupied a narrow band between mild liberalism and mild conservatism, today runs from Marxism, feminism, and left-wing nihilism and anarchism on the left to economic and political libertarianism and Christian fundamentalism on the right.[56]

The literature is also colored by the desire of legal academics to be on the "cutting edge." No matter how elegant and persuasive a traditional work can be, it seems "old fashioned," "tired," "passé."[57] These new approaches, to the extent they have spoken to issues in labor and employment law, are surveyed below.

Law and Economics

At its boldest, the law and economics approach claims to be a science;[58] in more modest dress, it offers a model, an arguably more helpful way of looking at legal problems. And, for the most part, that model is a neo-classical one: it assumes that the market is the best available mechanism for aggregating private preferences, so for the maximization of wealth; and that the predominant (if not exclusive) function of law is to foster market efficiency.[59]

The bulk of the labor law writing has been devoted to such questions as the efficiency of employment discrimination law;[60] of unionization; and of non-contractual regulation of the employment relations. Despite Judge Posner's claim that the economic approach to labor law is making "rapid strides,"[61] much of the writing about unionization rarely gets beyond the traditional neo-classical critique of unions as rent-seeking cartels;[62] and the critique of legal intervention in individual employment, on grounds of efficiency,[63] is sometimes scarcely distinguishable from the arch-advocacy of laissez-faire of a century ago. One of the following excerpts is from that nineteenth-century staple—Francis Wayland's "Elements of Political Economy." The other is by Professor Richard Epstein of the University of Chicago Law School. The reader may decide which is which:

> So long as it is accepted that the employer is the full owner of his capital and the employee is the full owner of his labor, the two are free to exchange on whatever terms and conditions they see fit. . . . It is hardly plausible that contracts at will could be so persuasive in all businesses and at all levels if they did not serve the interests of employees as well as employers.[64]

> Both of these parties are equally necessary to each other. If the laborer could not procure work, or could not exchange his labor for some value which he created, he must starve. If the capitalist could not create value from the employment of his capital, he must starve also. . . . Both, therefore, come into the market on equal terms; each needs the product of the other; and, under these circumstances, they will each receive either less or more, in consequence of the conditions under which the exchange is made.[65]

Others, however, have taken a more sophisticated approach, examining the efficiency of the legal framework of collective bargaining established by the Act—of unit determination[66] and of the rules governing collective bargaining.[67] Illustrative of the latter, and useful for analytical purposes, is Cohen and Wachter's, "Replacing Striking Workers: The Law and Economics Approach."[68] They commence by asserting that the labor Act is "a statute in search of a theory." They argue that none of the traditional explanations of the Act's intent "explain or anticipate the development of labor law doctrine"; indeed, that many of the major judicial decisions are viewed as "aberrant to the traditional model." They advance their own model of the Act "as an attempt to foster efficient contracting."

In their model, employers expend what are sunk (irretrievable) investments in the firm-specific training of workers who, in effect, invest as well in their training by working for wages that are lower than their current opportunity wage in the labor market. Employees recoup that investment by receiving higher-than-opportunity wages later; if they quit, their own investment (as well as the firm's) is lost. There is, however, a potential for both parties to behave opportunistically—employers by reneging on the tacit commitment to a subsequent higher-than-opportunity wage; employees by seeking to exact a wage premium based upon the firm-specific knowledge they have acquired.

Consequently, Cohen and Wachter defend the *Mackay Radio* rule, which allows employers permanently to replace economic strikers, as a deterrent to such behavior. If the employer's wage demand is to lower the expected return on the employee's sunk investment, without regard to market conditions, the employer will be behaving opportunistically:

> In this case, striking workers would have little to fear from replacement workers, because these replacements would not accept jobs that offer a stream of future wages below competitive levels. Alternatively, any replacement workers who accepted jobs would be reluctant to make sunk investments in a firm that had developed a reputation for opportunistic behavior.[69]

But if the union is seeking to exact a wage premium, the extant wage structure would render the job more attractive to replacements.

This analysis rests upon a series of assumptions: that there is a benchmark "opportunity" wage against which both insiders and outsiders measure their interests; that putative strike replacements know that the prospective employer is (or is not) behaving opportunistically, and that their willingness to accept the job is significantly affected by their expectations with respect to such future behavior; even that the only time strikers are replaced permanently is when the strike is over wages. Suffice it to say there is virtually no evidence on when or why employers resort to permanent replacements, what they are paid vis-à-vis strikers, what jobs they tend to occupy, or how long they tend to stay; indeed, the little data that are available suggest only that employers resort to permanent replacement more frequently now than in the past, and threaten more frequently so to do.[70]

Moreover, taken on its own terms, Cohen and Wachter's model suggests an interesting scenario. Assume that a non-unionized employer assembles her employees and announces:

> When you were hired, you worked for a wage less than your opportunity wage in the labor market and I incurred certain sunk costs in training you. You agreed to work on the non-contractual though bi-lateral assumption that your wage would eventually exceed your opportunity wage and that I would not act opportunistically, because new workers would be reluctant to replace you knowing that I had so acted. Well, you were wrong. I have researched the labor market and have come to the conclusion that the supply of labor is such that I can renege on my non-contractual commitment and, if you don't like it, I can replace you all and still get an adequate supply of qualified labor at your opportunity wage. Take it or quit.

They are free to do just that. But assume instead that the workers want both to retain their jobs and keep the non-contractually promised higher-than-opportunity rate; so they unionize and strike. The function of their effort, in Cohen and Wachter's theory, is to check whether the employer had really done her homework. And in order to find out that she had, the employees will have lost their jobs permanently and the union will have ceased to exist in that workplace. It is a very odd reason for the legislature to extend statutory protection for unionization, collective bargaining, and the right to strike.

Contrary to Cohen and Wachter, a legal theory and an economic one are not one and the same. In law, a statutory "theory" refers either to a legal desideratum or to its justification; in economics, a theory is a model that "explains" and so potentially predicts certain results. If a "traditional" legal critic concludes that *Mackay Radio* converts what the Act contemplated as a periodic test of strength in an ongoing relationship into a struggle for the union's institutional survival, it would argue not that the Act's "theory" is flawed, but that *Mackay Radio* was questionable.

Critical Legal Studies

There is almost as much written about what Critical Legal Studies is about as its participants have written in the CLS vein.[71] Perhaps the best summary has been supplied by Mark Tushnet:

> [C]ritical legal studies is a political location for a group of people on the Left who share the project of supporting and extending the domain of the Left in the legal academy. On this view the project of critical legal studies does not have any essential intellectual component. . . . There should be nothing surprising about this conclusion, of course, in light of the proposition common to most CLS authors that law is politics. For, if law is politics, presumably one might also believe that legal-intellectual positions are politics too.[72]

Louis Schwartz has suggested nevertheless that CLS writing tends to share certain features: it sees the results of liberal legal balancing as indeterminate and so "incoherent"; it seeks accordingly to demolish "liberalism" which, while purporting to defend an objective balancing of competing interests, actually masks an oppressive legal system; it denies that there is any distinctive "legal" discourse, other than "stereotyped rhetorical maneuvers" that are manipulated to sustain the dominance of the powerful; and, of course, it maintains that "law is politics."[73] Note, for example, Karl Klare's attack on the public-private distinction in labor law, a distinction that declines to assimilate the actions of private entities as extensions of the state:

> The essence of the public/private distinction is the conviction that it is possible to conceive of social and economic life apart from government and law, indeed that it is impossible or dangerous to conceive of it any other way. The core ideological function served by the public/private distinction is to deny that the practices comprising the private sphere of life—the worlds of business, education and culture, the community, and the family—are inextricably linked to and at least partially constituted by politics and law.[74]

Two of the leading CLS labor law pieces play out several of the themes adverted to by Schwartz: Karl Klare has argued that the labor Act's radical potential was thwarted by the United States Supreme Court;[75] and Katherine Stone has argued that American labor law has been dominated by a philosophy of "industrial pluralism" that is doctrinally "incoherent" and serves as a "vehicle for the manipulation of employee discontent and for the legitimization of existing inequalities of power in the workplace."[76] A close reading of these pieces claimed that they were, literally, nonsense, not because of any inability intrinsic to their theories to be verified (or falsified), but because of their failure to adhere to the canons of responsible scholarship adverted to earlier.[77] The reader is free to read that critique and the resulting rejoinders[78] and make an independent assessment.

Some CLS writing is scarcely distinguishable from traditional reformism: an argument that the Landrum-Griffin Act should be read to give employees a right to vote on contract ratification;[79] an argument for statutory protection against wrongful discharge;[80] or criticism of the contemporary approach to determining what is conduct for "mutual and or protection" under the labor Act.[81] But other work illustrates some of the larger CLS themes.[82]

Take, for example, some of commentary spawned by the decision of the United States Supreme Court in *Eastex, Inc. v. NLRB*.[83] The question was whether employees had the right to distribute union literature, on the employer's premises but on their own time, that expressed positions on pending political issues. The Court sustained the employee's right so to do, but observed in passing that there may be situations where the relationship of the political message to the employees' interests as employees becomes so attenuated that it would not be statutorily protected. The NLRB's General Counsel proceeded in part upon that distinction by refusing to issue a complaint where employees were discharged allegedly for leafletting, on their own time, at a rally on behalf of a petition for political asylum for Hector Marroquin, a Mexican national assertedly "persecuted by the Mexican police in reprisal for his advocacy of democratic rights and independent trade unions."[84]

Professors James Atleson[85] and Alan Hyde[86] have separately attacked the Court's distinction. Atleson argues that it rests upon "a hallmark of liberal thought"—the public/private distinction, reiterating and emphasizing Karl Klare's assertion quoted above;[87] that it exemplifies "how neutral sounding principles operate in non-neutral ways"; and that the very fragility of the distinction can only produce "incoherent" results. Hyde shares the latter view, and argues further that the distinction is grounded in an ideology shared by the labor Board, the courts, "and the unions themselves that politics is separate from economics."

> An important element in the self-image and practice of the American Federation of Labor (AFL)—the element that

> distinguished it from its unsuccessful predecessors—was "voluntarism," the notion that trade unions should eschew political activity and rely on their own economic power. Small matter that the AFL in fact kept detailed records on legislators and participated actively in elections and politics; the ideology is more revealing than the practice.[88]

This assertion is supported by a single reference, to an unidentified union official, who made the obvious observation that American labor unions do not fill the role of labor parties. And because organized labor declined that role, Hyde suggests that labor's active political engagement is somehow inconsistent with its ideology.

Some of this criticism is sound: it is far from obvious textually that the Act draws a distinction between speech as employee and speech as citizen; the distinction is likely to prove operationally vexing, especially in mixed message cases; and, as Hyde rightly observes, if the Court's concern were grounded in impediments to production, it would be entirely possible to develop rules that would distinguish the distribution of literature from other communicative activity.

But the Court's dictum is even more questionable in terms that Atleson and Hyde do not address. It could be argued that the theory of industrial democracy underpinning the NLRA drew a close connection between the employee's liberty in the workplace, including freedom of expression on workplace issues, and the maintenance of a political democracy. The fear was that habituation to subservience in one sphere might have consequences in the other. From this perspective, and if the argument is sound, the Court's distinction becomes perverse: it would deny protection to political speech and activity, undertaken by employees away from the workplace and on their own time, when that very conduct was conceived of as the fruit of allowing protection for speech on workplace issues. And, if it is approprite to look at "the practice and philosophy" of the American labor movement as a source to inform the content of the labor Act, just as the Court said in 1944, then the law should draw from labor's rich engagement in the political process, notwithstanding its declination to form a labor party—even to its maintenance of an active foreign policy. The General Counsel's refusal to seek protection for the protest over Hector Marroquin's deportation, on the assumption that these protests had "little or no relationship to employee problems and concerns as employees," is difficult to reconcile with the AFL's vehement protest over the arrest of Mexican anarchists in 1907, to the point of its 1908 Convention resolving to seek a congressional investigation.[89]

To these writers, however, the Court is wrong for very different reasons. On the basis of a leap in logic, Hyde asks us to see the Court's declination fully to protect organized labor's political speech as a reification of organized labor's own ideology. And Atleson asks us to connect that declination to the legal permissibility of establishing a home for aged immigrants from Minsk.[90]

As Professor Edward Rubin has pointed out, even if in some sense "law is politics," it does not follow that scholarship about law is also politics.[91] But what at least part of what Critical Legal Studies gives us is not scholarship, in the sense adverted to earlier, but, just as Mark Tushnet put it, "legal intellectual positions"—a personal depiction of the world.[92]

Feminism

There are divisions, some sharp, some subtle, among feminist legal scholars.[93] Nonetheless, Cass Sunstein has usefully suggested that there are at least three distinct groupings.[94] The first, embodying traditional liberal notions of individual rights, argues that women should be legally perceived of and treated no differently from men. This "feminism of sameness" insists, in the words of one critic, "on the fundamental similarity of men and women and, hence, their essential equality."[95]

The second, often building upon the work of Carol Gilligan,[96] insists upon fundamental female differences that are not only biological and psychological but moral as well. As Sunstein put it, "In this view, women tend to value relationships and connections—an 'ethic of care'—whereas men tend to place a higher premium on abstraction, rights, autonomy, separation, formality, and neutrality—an 'ethic of justice'."[97] This "feminism of difference"—or "relational feminism"—reclaims, in the words of one sympathetic critic, the compliments of Victorian gender ideology (women as more nurturing and more moral than men) while rejecting its insults (women as more passive and less competent than men).[98]

The third, or "radical" feminism sees law as playing out a culture of male dominance that works a systematic, pervasive, and relentless oppression of women. So relentless, so pervasive, that some of these feminists view all heterosexual relations as indistinguishable from rape, and consequently debate whether lesbianism represents sexual liberation or is yet a further extension of male dominance.[99]

At some points, the feminism of individualism and the feminism of difference can converge upon the solution of a legal issue, as in the reaction to the opinion of the United States Supreme Court in *Meritor Savings Bank v. Vinson*.[100] The decision sustained the theory of sexual harassment under Title VII, including an employer's liability for "unwelcome" sexual advances; but in so doing the Court suggested that evidence of sexually provocative speech or dress would be relevant to the question of welcomeness.

If women differ from men in terms of their perception of sexual "cues," if women select clothing that is perceived by men as sexually provocative, but do so without such intent, consideration of "provocative" dress as evidence of the welcomeness of male advances would hold women accountable to a male standard; in effect, it would blame the victim for the aggressor's actions.[101] On the other hand, if most women do dress with an awareness of likely male response, at least some would not; and so to justify an employer's advances on the ground of such evidence is to attribute to the individual the characteristics of the group which, in other applications, Title VII disallows.

At other points, however, the feminism of difference would seem to conduce towards results at variance with its larger aims, as is illustrated in the literature following the decision in *EEOC v. Sears, Roebuck & Co.*[102] In order to understand how vexing the case is, a little bit of law is in order. In the absence of a policy expressly to exclude women from certain jobs, a plaintiff may attempt to prove that the employer intentionally so acted on the basis of the statistical display of women in its work force. This requires that that representation be measured against some benchmark, either of the general population or some subset. As Douglas Laycock explains,

> Most statistics in employment discrimination cases compare two populations, such as blacks and whites or men and women. One assumption that can never be relaxed is that the two populations are the same in all respects except for the possible difference under investigation and for any differences that have been controlled. If the two populations are a little bit different, the inference will be a little bit off, but usable. If the two populations are a lot different, the inference will be worthless.[103]

In the *Sears* case, women made up about 75 percent of Sears non-commission sales force; but only 27 percent of commission sales employees, who sold "big ticket" items such as furnaces, would be required to become technically proficient in knowledge of the product, and who might be required to make visits to customers' homes. The EEOC's benchmark was based upon a statistically projected female hiring rate of four women for every ten openings, based upon its analysis of applicants for all sales jobs and adjusting for six variables such as education and experience. It had not accounted, however, for any sex differential in interest between the commission and non-commission sales jobs. On average, Sears had hired three women for every ten openings. The question, then, was of the significance of that statistic, and so of the soundness of Sears' statistical benchmark.

The trial court rejected the EEOC's claim of intentional discrimination on three grounds: (1) the EEOC's benchmark failed to take account of "the interests of applicants in commission sales and products sold on commission";[104] (2) the claim of intentional discrimination was contradicted by Sears' "long and serious commitment to affirmative action" which applied to efforts to recruit women for its commission sales force;[105] and (3) the EEOC failed to produce a single witness of intentional discrimination, about which the court was simply incredulous.

It is, however, the first ground of the court's reasoning that has drawn feminist ire, at some points even to a lapse in the standard of scholarly care. Professor Williams, for example, faults the court for requiring the EEOC to prove the percentage of women interested in commission sales while "not requiring Sears to provide *equivalent proof* of the specific percentage of women who fit gender stereotypes. . . ."[106] But the burden of proof in Title VII cases always rests with the plaintiff; while free to challenge the fit claimed by the plaintiff, Sears labored under no obligation to "prove" anything. Professor Rhode, citing only secondary sources, notes that Sears "relied on tests that measured prospective employees' 'vigor' by reference to their views towards boxing, wrestling, hunting and swearing."[107] But she does not note the trial court's rejection of the relevance of that evidence on the basis of uncontroverted testimonial evidence that Sears managers paid no attention to it.[108] And, again citing a secondary source, Professor Rhode asserts that, "If, as Sears emphasized, women generally didn't seek commission positions, neither did Sears actively seek women for those positions."[109] But this ignores the evidence of Sears' extensive affirmative action plan in general, and the uncontradicted testimony from Sears' managers of their efforts to recruit women for commission sales jobs in particular.[110] And in what is the most comprehensive attack upon the "lack of interest" argument thus far, Professor Schultz commits similar lapses.[111] What vexes is the congruence of the lack of interest explanation with the tenets of the feminism of difference.

> Women tend to be more interested than men in the social and cooperative aspects of the workplace. Women tend to see themselves as less competitive. They often view noncommission sales as more attractive than commission sales, because they can enter and leave the job more easily, and because there is more social contact and friendship, and less stress in noncommission selling.[112]

As a result, some feminists launch a larger critique. Professor Schultz argues that

> Employers do not simply erect "barriers" to already formed preferences: they create the workplace structures and relations out of which those preferences arise in the first place. Thus, in resolving the lack of interest argument, courts must look beyond whether the employer has provided women the formal opportunity to enter non-traditional jobs.[113]

The role of the courts, she suggests, is to enable women "to aspire to work they have never before been able to dream of doing."[114] But she nowhere connects this desideratum to the text, history, or theory of Title VII. And others have seen the *Sears* case a basis for a more general attack upon the employment structures that, in effect, channel women into the jobs they "prefer," instead of restructuring the jobs themselves,[115] even to challenge the entire "Western wage labor system as a system of power relations that leaves women economically and socially vulnerable."[116]

Critical Race Theory

Some legal academics, identified as "the Critical Race Theory or New Race Theory group,"[117] center upon racism, which is held to be as pervasive and relentless in American legal consciousness as radical feminists hold male dominance to be.[118] Their writing, according to Richard Delgado, is characterized by the following themes:

> (1) an insistence on "naming our own reality"; (2) the belief that knowledge and ideas are powerful; (3) a readiness to question basic premises of moderate/incremental civil rights law; (4) the borrowing of insights from social science on race and racism; (5) critical examination of the myths and stories powerful groups use to justify racial subordination; (6) a more contextualized treatment of doctrine; (7) criticism of liberal legalisms; and (8) an interest in structural determinism—the ways in which legal tools and thought-structures can impede law reform.[119]

Thus far, however, their critique in labor and employment law has been largely negligible. An exception is Regina Austin's attack on a decision of the Eighth Circuit sustaining the discharge of Crystal Chambers, a pregnant, unmarried, black teacher who was considered a bad "role model" for her students—predominantly black, female teenagers in a program geared in part to discourage black teenage pregnancy.[120] Austin mounts a powerful challenge to the idea that a black teacher's unwed pregnancy would have any effect upon the sexual conduct of her students; and she places that challenge in the special sociological context of black teenagers. But she also challenges the "role model" theory on broader grounds:

> The requirement that one allow one's self to be modeled in order to keep one's job is not limited to blacks who are young fertile females. To a certain extent, the trouble Crystal Chambers encountered is a generic infliction suffered by black role models of both sexes and all ages who reject the part and become rebellious renegades or traitors to the cause of black cultural containment.[121]

Broader, but still racial grounds; which is to state the limits of the "Critical Race Theory" horizon, for one could restate the issue as whether any employer should be allowed to require employees "to be modeled," irrespective of race. If the more persuasive answer to that question is "no," then race becomes a non-issue.

Professor Austin does applaud the plaintiff as "more nearly a role model when she fought back." That approval, however, is not limited to Ms. Chambers' workplace resistance or legal struggle. "Her single motherhood," Professor Austin opines, "represented an alternative social form that one might choose deliberately, rationally, and proudly."[122] And so she speculates on whether Ms. Chambers "single pregnancy" is "potentially revolutionary and emancipatory."[123] But, if her single pregnancy, as a "representation" of rational choice, is a potentially "emancipatory" act, would that not be so because her act, a "representation," is so perceived by others? One therefore worthy of emulation in her single pregnancy? By the teenage girls under her charge?

The larger claims of New Race Theorists have lacked programmatic precision, save, interestingly, in its application to the legal-academic labor market. At least some of its proponents have claimed that "persons of color" have a unique perspective on racial-legal issues that whites cannot have.[124] This leads to the corollary that the published work of "the voice of color" must be evaluated by non-white, non-hierarchical, non-majoritarian standards;[125] in other words, that there is "black" legal scholarship and "white" legal scholarship, and that the former cannot be judged by the latter. In this way, the New Race Theorists' claim of endemic racism achieves full intellectual closure.

"Voice" and Storytelling

Professor Julius Getman has argued that legal scholars tend to speak in a certain "voice"—sometimes "professional," sometimes "scholarly," as he defines these—and argues for the greater representation of "human voice,"[126] the presentation of legal issues without "professional ornamentation," for and from the perspective of ordinary people. Some feminists and "new racial theorists" go beyond the humanization Getman calls for to make special claims for the "voice" of the oppressed and the marginalized: they "tell stories different from the ones legal scholars usually hear. . . . [t]hey reveal things about the world that we *ought* to know."[127]

How "storytelling" is employed is illustrated in a recent article by Professor Matsuda criticizing what the courts have done in cases of discrimination on the basis of foreign accent.[128] Taking as an archetypical case, *Fragrante v. City and County of Honolulu*,[129] she proceeds to tell "Manuel Fragrante's Story." Mr. Fragrante, a Philippine national, was a guerilla against the Japanese; he became an army officer and served in Vietnam; he "believed in self-reliance, hard work, and respect for authority."[130] He moved to Honolulu, became a United States citizen, applied for a clerk's job in Division of Motor Vehicles, and placed first on the civil service examination out of 700 competitors. Contrary to others, he did not think the job "beneath him."[131] He interviewed with "assured dignity." "He knew the job was his."[132] But it wasn't to be. Although he was one of five finalists for the job, it was given to another on the interviewers' conclusion that his Filipino accent would make it difficult for him to be understood. He sued for violation of Title VII, on grounds of national origin discrimination, and lost both on trial and on appeal.

The Ninth Circuit held that a refusal to hire on the basis of accent could violate the Act, citing authority to that effect; and it stressed that a "very searching look" by the trial courts was necessary to assure that an employer's explanation, that the applicant lacked an adequate level of intelligibility, is not a "cover" for unlawful discrimination. But it found no basis in the record to challenge the trial court's finding that the division had made an honest assessment of Mr. Fragrante's ability to communicate.

Professor Matsuda challenges this conclusion both on the facts and on the law. It is possible that she is correct on the first; but that would scarcely be worth almost 80 pages in the *Yale Law Journal*. On the second and more important ground, however, one may inquire of the relevance of Manuel Fragrante's "story." Professor Matsuda's "method" she tells us, is to "use personal experience . . . [to] express emotion and desire alongside logic and analysis."[133] But Mr. Fragrante's emotions and desires have no greater claim on the law's solicitude than any other job applicant's.[134] If Mr. Fragrante had been a collaborator with the Japanese, a black marketeer in Vietnam, and, not to put too fine a point on it, a despicable swine, his rights under Title VII should vary not one whit.

Personal experience she does relate; and in abundance. More of that in a moment. What of logic and analysis? Here she proposes a scheme to deal with cases where the employer's valid concern for communicative ability in certain jobs, such as university lecturer or 911 operator, may be bound up with assumptions or beliefs, even unconscious ones, about the spoken word that disfavor certain national groups. She connects her approach, and quite rightly, both to the general framework of Title VII analysis and to the law of physical or mental handicap.

The scheme she proposes is responsive to the situation where a person applies for a job, is turned down, and the job is kept open. But Mr. Fragrante was one of five finalists for the job, all of whom were at least minimally qualified. He was turned down because two others were rated higher in terms of communicative ability. Now this is a tougher problem. Assume, for example, that the minimum words per minute for a typing job is 80, but greater speed is job related. Applicant A can type 80, but not more due to a physical handicap. Applicant B, who has no handicap, can type 120. If the employer hires B, has the employer discriminated impermissibly on grounds of handicap? On the one hand, A can function in performing at the minimum speed required for the job; and so disfavoring her would seem to be handicap discrimination. But on the other hand, may not an employer select the *better* qualified, if that qualification is legitimately related to the job?

Professor Matsuda devotes several pages to urging the courts to attend very closely to the "importance of speech in a particular job . . . in order to recognize the gradation between speech as essential and speech as irrelevant."[135] But she does not extend the idea of gradation to the applicant's ability to be understood. For some jobs, university lecturer, for example, one would think some applicants better able to communicate than others. May not a university select the more intelligible applicant even though the less intelligible one does (or, with suitable accommodation, could) meet the minimum level of communicative ability required for the job? Professor Matsuda dispenses with this in one sentence, by fiat: "The court should state unequivocally that once a person's speech is found functional, the employer may not reject it because a competitor's speech is less foreign,"[136] that is, more comprehensible to a non-prejudiced audience.

Professor Matsuda denies reality, in part, on ideological grounds: the very claim of unintelligibility, she asserts, masks a dominant Anglo-linguistic hegemony. And she does so as well, as her announced method alerted us, because of her personal desires:

> Outside my office door I can hear a Caribbean voice and an African American voice involved in deep discussion as a maintenance crew works its way down the hall. Each accent is thick and deeply divergent both from the other and from the generic standard of the evening news. The

> conversation, however, is urgent and lively and the difference is no barrier. As I eavesdrop and sit in my office thinking about accents I think, "I want to live in a country that sounds like this"—a land of many voices, each bringing a gift of wisdom and culture wrapped with a gold ribbon of accent.[137]

If legal "scholarship" can be self-referential, there is no reason to separate scholarship from autobiography.[138]

The Future of Legal Scholarship

Most scholarly writing in labor and employment law is and will continue to be of the "traditional" kind—highly individual essays in the solution of legal problems that may (or may not) be of importance in the real world. To the extent other disciplines—labor economics, industrial relations, social psychology, and the like—do work that speaks to the resolution of legal issues, they will be absorbed by the future legal literature as they have been in the past.

But some of what is emerging in the legal literature is not scholarship at all, at least in the sense adverted to at the outset of this survey. It comprises, just as Mark Tushnet said, "legal-intellectual positions"—intellectualized essays about the kind of world the writers would like to see come about: a world where jobs have been restructured to facilitate or stimulate the aspirations of women; a world where organized labor seeks to become a political party; a world which gives a preference in jobs to the foreign-accented; and so on. While these essays may provoke thought and stimulate debate, they are increasingly out of touch with the more immediate realities of workplace legal problems.

One explanation for this development lies in the nature of legal journals. With a very few exceptions, law school affiliated legal periodicals are edited by law students; their decisions to publish (or not) are rarely informed by any competent professional judgment either from within the home institution's faculty or elsewhere. And if the students at "leading" law schools choose to publish the trendy work of meta-theoreticians, critical legal studies, radical feminists, New Race Theorists, or storytellers instead of mainstream legal analyses, it can be no surprise if these works pass without influencing the thought or work of real-world decisionmakers.

Endnotes

[1] Symposium on Legal Scholarship: Its Nature and Purposes, 90 Yale L.J. 955-1295 (1981); American Legal Scholarship: Directions and Dilemmas, 33 J. Legal Educ. 403-58 (1983); Law Professors, Lawyers, and Legal Scholarship, 35 J. Legal Educ. 311-420 (1985); Kissam, The Evaluation of Legal Scholarship, 63 Wash. L. Rev. 221 (1988); Rubin, The Practice and Discourse of Legal Scholarship, 86 Mich. L. Rev. 1835 (1988); Symposium: The Critique of Normativity, 139 U. Pa. L. Rev. 801-1075 (1991).

[2] D. Bell, Marxian Socialism in the United States 152 (1967); C. Jencks and D. Riesman, The Academic Revolution 242-43 (1968); E. Ladd and S. Lipset, The Divided Academy: Professors and Politics 123-24 (1975).

[3] Hyland, A Defense of Legal Writing, 134 U. Pa. L. Rev. 599, 614 (1986) ("The separation of meaningful similarities from irrelevancies is work that legal concepts, but not stories, can perform.").

[4] Atleson, The Implicit Assumptions of Labor Law Scholarship, 35 J. Legal Educ. 395, 397 (1985). To similar effect see Lesnick, Legal Education's Concern with Justice: A Conversation with a Critic, 35 J. Legal Educ. 414 (1985).

[5] Posner, The Decline of Law As Autonomous Discipline: 1962-1987, 100 Harv. L. Rev. 761, 765 (1987).

[6] Wedderburn, An Anniversary Preface, 50 Mod. L. Rev. 673, 674 (1987). ("Addresses in that era [the 1960s] to the Society of Public Teachers of Law countered Lord Diplock's insistence that law was no more than 'plumbing'. . . .").

[7] Shapiro, In Defense of Judicial Candor, 100 Harv. L. Rev. 731 (1987).

[8] Bok, The Regulation of Campaign Tactics in Representation Elections Under the National Labor Relations Act, 78 Harv. L. Rev. 38 (1964) (citing *inter alia* political science research on voter behavior in civil elections, psychological research in communications, and research in industrial relations).

[9] Summers, The Law of Union Discipline: What the Courts Do In Fact, 70 Yale L.J. 176 (1960).

[10] *See, e.g.*, Hays, Foreword, Colum. L. Rev. 1, 5 (1959):

> [I]t seems to me possible that labor lawyers sometimes conduct with great skill what may in fact be sham battles, battles in which the event is of no real importance, or even battles in which, if they were more aware of the real character of the outcome, they might be on the other side. Is our approach to labor law "too theoretical"? Would the splendid articles in this issue be even better if among the footnote citations, which show such a wealth of learning in the law, there were more references to studies made by scholars in other fields of learning? Or are they too but combatants on a darkling plain in which with present implements all of us are fairly helpless to do much more than speculate on what may happen?

[11] Fletcher, Two Modes of Legal Thought, 90 Yale L.J. 970, 986 (1981).

[12] Klare, Traditional Labor Law Scholarship and the Crisis of Collective Bargaining Law: A Reply to Professor Finkin, 44 Md. L. Rev. 731, 783 (1985) (reference omitted):

> Much of post-Realist American legal thought has been devoted to a failed attempt to sustain the proposition that legal problems give rise to determinate solutions, or at least to a fairly well-defined region of correct outcomes. The main approaches are familiar: institutional competence theory, economic efficiency analysis, rationalist moralism, and Professor Finkin's approach, the most widespread in our legal culture, namely, ad hoc, unsystematic tinkering. Though each of these approaches is more or less committed to the idea of a specialized "legal" method of analysis (as

distinct from general political or ethical discourse) through which determinate solutions can be derived to legal problems, none of these theories has come close to convincingly demonstrating the existence of such a method.

[13] Rubin, The Practice and Discourse of Legal Scholarship, 86 Mich. L. Rev. 1835, 1885 (1988).

[14] Disciplinary variation in the mortality rate of scholarship has been noted. T. Becher, Academic Tribes and Territories: Intellectual Enquiry and the Cultures of Disciplines 87-8 (1989).

[15] 67 Colum. L. Rev. 1404 (1967).

[16] H. Wellington, Labor and the Legal Process 2 (1968).

[17] *See, e.g.*, Meltzer, The New Climate for Collective Bargaining, 12 Lab. L.J. 434 (1961); Freiden, New Collective Bargaining, 50 Va. L. Rev. 1034 (1964); Fleming, New Challenges for Collective Bargaining, 1964 Wis. L. Rev. 426.

[18] Symposium: Labor Union Power and the Public Interest, 35 Notre Dame Law 591-653 (1960); Goldberg, The Role of the Labor Union in an Age of Bigness, 55 Nw. L. Rev. 54 (1960). This subject was thought worthy of conclusory comment at the close of the decade. *See* D. Bok & J. Dunlop, Labor and the American Community 466 (1970).

[19] *See, e.g.*, Kohler, Models of Worker Participation: The Uncertain Significance of Section 8(a)(2), 27 B.C.L. Rev. 499 (1986); Moberly, New Directions in Worker Participation and Collective Bargaining, 87 W. Va. L. Rev. 765 (1985); Gould, Reflections on Workers' Participation, Influence and Powersharing: The Future of Industrial Relations, 58 U. Cinc. L. Rev. 381 (1989).

[20] *See, e.g.*, Rabban, Can American Labor Law Accommodate Collective Bargaining by Professional Employees? 99 Yale L.J. 689 (1990).

[21] *See, e.g.*, Harper, Leveling the Road from *Borg-Warner* to *First National Maintenance:* The Scope of Mandatory Bargaining, 68 Va. L. Rev. 1447 (1982); George, To Bargain or Not to Bargain: A New Chapter in Work Relocation Decisions, 69 Minn. L. Rev. 667 (1985).

[22] *See, e.g.*, Bethel, Constructive Concerted Activity Under the NLRA: Conflicting Signals from the Court and the Board, 59 Ind. L.J. 582 (1984); Dolin, The *Interboro* Doctrine and the Courts, 31 Am. U. L. Rev. 551 (1982); George, Divided We Stand: Concerted Activity and the Maturing of the NLRA, 56 Geo. Wash. L. Rev. 509 (1988).

[23] *See, e.g.*, Cox, Recent Developments in Federal Labor Law Preemption, 41 Ohio St. L.J. 277 (1980).

[24] This is virtually the exclusive province of Marc Linder. *See, e.g.*, Linder, What Is an Employee? Why It Does, But Should Not, Matter, 7 Law & Inequality 155 (1989); Linder, Paternalistic State Intervention: The Contradictions of the Legal Empowerment of Vulnerable Workers, 23 U.C. Davis L. Rev. 733 (1990); Linder, Towards Universal Worker Coverage Under the National Labor Relations Act: Making Room for Uncontrolled Employees, Dependent Contractors, and Employee-Like Persons, 66 U. Det. L. Rev. 555 (1989).

[25] *See, e.g.*, Craver, The Vitality of the American Labor Movement in the Twenty-First Century, 1983 U. Ill. L. Rev. 633.

[26] *See, e.g.*, P. Weiler, Governing the Workplace: The Future of Labor and Employment Law (1990); Rabin, The Role of Unions in the Rights-Based Workplace, 25 U.S.F. L. Rev. 169 (1991).

[27] *See, e.g.*, Symposium: The Law and Economics of Racial Discrimination in Employment, 79 Geo. L.J. 1619-1782 (1991). Meltzer, The *Weber* Case: The Judicial Abrogation of the Antidiscrimination Standard in Employment, 47 U. Chi. L. Rev. 423 (1980); Rutherglen & Ortiz, Affirmative Action under the Constitution and Title VII: From Confusion to Consequence, 35 U.C.L.A. L. Rev. 467 (1988); Fallon & Weiler, *Firefighters v. Stotts:* Conflicting Modes of Racial Justice, 1984 Sup. Ct. Rev. 1.

[28] *Compare* Blumrosen, Wage Discrimination, Job Segregation, and Title VII of the Civil Rights Act of 1964, 12 U. Mich. J. L. Rev. 397 (1979) *with* Nelson *et al.*, Wage Discrimination and the "Comparable Worth" Theory in Perspective, 13 U. Mich. J. L. Rev. 231 (1980). *See also* Fischel & Lazear, Comparable Worth and Discrimination in Labor Markets, 53 U. Chi. L. Rev. 891 (1986); Holzhauer, The Economic Possibilities of Comparable Worth, *id.* at 419; Becker, Barriers Facing Women in the Wage-Labor Market and the Need for Additional Remedies: A Reply to Fischel & Lazear, *id.* at 734; Fischel & Lazear, Comparable Worth: A Rejoinder, *id.* at 950.

[29] Brilmayer, Hekeler, Laycock & Sullivan, Sex Discrimination in Employer Sponsored Insurance Plans: A Legal and Demographic Analysis, 47 U. Chi. L. Rev. 505 (1980); Benston, The Economics of Gender Discrimination in Employee Fringe Benefits: *Manhart* Revisited, 49 U. Chi. L. Rev. 489 (1982); Brilmayer, Laycock & Sullivan, The Efficient Use of Group Averages as Nondiscrimination: A Rejoinder to Professor Benston, 50 U. Chi. L. Rev. 222 (1983); and Professor Benston's reply, *id.* at 250.

[30] Kelman, Concepts of Discrimination in "General Ability" Job Testing, 104 Harv. L. Rev. 1157 (1991).

[31] *Compare* Norris, A Standard Approach to Evaluation of Multiple Regression Analysis as Used to Prove Employment Discrimination: The Plaintiff's Answer to Defense Attacks of "Missing Factors" and "Pre-Act Discrimination," 49 L. & Contemp. Probs. 65 (1986) *with* Laycock, Statistical Proof and Theories of Discrimination, *id.* at 97.

[32] 1 H. Specter & M. Finkin, INDIVIDUAL EMPLOYMENT LAW AND LITIGATION § 10.55 at 608 (1989).

[33] *See, e.g.*, Symposium on Drug Testing, 36 U. Kan. L. Rev. 641-951 (1988); Rothstein, Drug Testing in the Workplace: The Challenge to Employment Relations and Employment Law, 63 Chi.-Kent L. Rev. 683 (1987).

[34] *See, e.g.*, Barnett & Mahar, "In the Ordinary Course of Business": The Limits of Workplace Wiretapping, 10 Hastings Comm/Ent L.J. 715 (1988).

[35] *See, e.g.*, Freed *et al.*, Unions, Fairness, and the Conundrums of Collective Choice, 56 S. Cal. L. Rev. 461 (1983); Hyde, Can Judges Identify Fair Bargaining Procedures?: A Comment on Freed, Polsby and Spitzer, 57 S. Cal. L. Rev. 415 (1984), and their reply *id.* at 425.

[36] *Compare* Holt, Recovery by the Worker Who Quits: A Comparison of the Mainstream, Legal Realist, and Critical Legal Studies Approaches to a Problem of 19th Century Contract Law, 1986 Wis. L. Rev. 677 *with* Karsten, "Bottomed on Justice": A Reappraisal of Critical Legal Studies Scholarship Concerning Breaches of Labor Contracts by Quitting or Firing in Britain and the U.S., 1630-1880, 34 Am. J. Legal Hist. 213 (1990); Vander Velde, The Labor Vision of the Thirteenth Amendment, 138 U. Pa. L. Rev. 437 (1989).

[37] San Diego Building Trades Council v. Garmon, 359 U.S. 236 (1959).

[38] Cox, Labor Law Preemption Revisited, 85 Harv. L. Rev. 1337, 1343 (1972).

[39] Gottesman, Rethinking Labor Law Preemption: State Laws Facilitating Unionization, 7 Yale J. on Reg. 355 (1990).

[40] *Id.* at 409.

[41] Harper and Lupu, Fair Representation As Equal Protection, 98 Harv. L. Rev. 1211 (1985).

[42] *Id.* at 1252.

[43] *Id.* at 1221.

[44] *Id.* at 1236.

[45] *Id.* at 1237.

[46] *Id.* at 1228-29.

[47] J.I. Case v. NLRB, 321 U.S. 332, 338 (1944).

[48] *Id.* at 339.

[49] *See, e.g.*, F. Harbison, SENIORITY POLICIES AND PROCEDURES AS DEVELOPED THROUGH COLLECTIVE BARGAINING (1941).

[50] S. Slichter, UNION POLICIES AND INDUSTRIAL MANAGEMENT 116-117 (1968).

[51] *See, e.g.*, R. Schatz, THE ELECTRICAL WORKERS 118 (1983): V. Jensen, STRIFE ON THE WATERFRONT 218, 292, 336-37 (1974).

[52] S. Slichter, *supra* n.50 at 120.

[53] Feller, A General Theory of the Collective Bargaining Agreement, 61 Calif. L. Rev. 663, 664 (1973). To analogous effect see Rubin, Beyond Public Choice: Comprehensive Rationality in the Writing and Reading of Statutes, 66 N.Y.U. L. Rev. 1, 4 (1991).

[54] Posner, The Decline of Law as an Autonomous Discipline: 1962-1987, 100 Harv. L. Rev. 761, 765 (1987).

[55] Levinson and Balkin, Law, Music, and Other Performing Arts, 139 U. Pa. L. Rev. 1597 (1991).

[56] Posner, n.54 *supra* at 766.

[57] *Id.* at 773.

[58] Posner, Uses and Abuses of Economics in Law, 42 U. Chi. L. Rev. 281, 301-02 (1979).

[59] Thus the assertion that its reasoning is science-like and so presumably value-free has not gone unchallenged. *See, e.g.*, Leff, Economic Analysis of Law: Some Realism About Nominalism, 60 Va. L. Rev. 451 (1974).

[60] Some of the discussion on "comparable worth" was noted *supra* note 27. *Compare* Donohue, Is Title VII Efficient?, 134 U. Pa. L. Rev. 1411 (1986) *with* Posner, The Efficiency and Efficacy of Title VII, 136 U. Pa. L. Rev. 513 (1987) *and* Donohue, Further Thoughts on Employment Discrimination Legislation: A Reply to Judge Posner, 136 U. Pa. L. Rev. 523 (1987). Symposium: The Law and Economics of Racial Discrimination in Employment, 79 Geo. L.J. 1619-1782 (1991).

[61] Posner, The Decline of Law as an Autonomous Discipline: 1962-1987, 100 Harv. L. Rev. 761, 768 (1987).

[62] *See generally* Posner, Some Economics of Labor Law, 51 U. Chi. L. Rev. 988 (1984); Epstein, A Common Law for Labor Relations: A Critique of New Deal Labor Legislation, 92 Yale L.J. 1357 (1983). *But see* Getman and Kohler, The Common Law, Labor Law, and Reality: A Response to Professor Epstein, 92 Yale L.J. 1415 (1983); Epstein, Common Law, Labor Law, and Reality: A Rejoinder to Professors Getman and Kohler, 92 Yale L.J. 1435 (1983).

[63] *See, e.g.*, Freed and Polsby, Just Cause for Termination Rules and Economic Efficiency, 38 Emory L.J. 1097 (1984); Power, A Defense of the Employment At Will Rule, 27 St. Louis U.L.J. 881 (1983); Harrison, The "New" Terminable At-Will Employment Contract: An Interest and Cost Incidence Analysis, 69 Iowa L. Rev. 327 (1984); Heinz, The Assault on the Employment at Will Doctrine: Management Considerations, 48 Mo. L. Rev. 855 (1983).

[64] Epstein, In Defense of the Contract At Will, 52 U. Chi. L. Rev. 947, 953 (1984).

[65] F. Wayland, ELEMENTS OF POLITICAL ECONOMY 301 (1837).

[66] Leslie, Labor Bargaining Units, 70 Va. L. Rev. 353 (1984); Leslie, Multiemployer Bargaining Rules, 75 Va. L. Rev. 241 (1989); *but see* Vetter, Commentary on "Multiemployer Bargaining Rules": Searching for the Right Questions, 75 Va. L. Rev. 285 (1989).

[67] Wachter & Cohen, The Law and Economics of Collective Bargaining: An Introduction and Application to the Problems of Subcontracting, Partial Closure, and Relocation, 137 U. Pa. L. Rev. 1349 (1988); Schwab, Collective Bargaining and the Course Theorem, 72 Cornell L. Rev. 245 (1987). *Compare* Campbell, Labor Law and Economics, 38 Stan. L. Rev. 991 (1986) *with* Freeman, A Critique of Economic Consistency, 39 Stan. L. Rev. 1259 (1987).

[68] Proceedings of New York University's 43rd Annual National Conference on Labor 109 (1990).

[69] *Id.* at 118.

[70] The findings of a General Accounting Office survey are reproduced in Finkin, Labor Policy and the Enervation of the Economic Strike, 1990 U. Ill. L. Rev. 547, n.12 at 548.

[71] *See, e.g.*, Unger, The Critical Legal Studies Movement, 96 Harv. L. Rev. 561 (1983); Critical Legal Studies Symposium, 36 Stan. L. Rev. 1-674 (1984); Kennedy & Klare, A Bibliography of Critical Legal Studies, 94 Yale L.J. 461 (1984); M. Kelman, A GUIDE TO CRITICAL LEGAL STUDIES (1987).

[72] Tushnet, Critical Legal Studies: A Political History, 100 Yale L.J. 1515, 1516-17 (1991).

[73] Schwartz, With Gun and Camera Through Darkest CLS-Land, 30 Stan. L. Rev. 413 (1984).

[74] Klare, The Public/Private Distinction in Labor Law, 130 U. Pa. L. Rev. 1358, 1417 (1983).

[75] Klare, The Judicial Deradicalization of the Wagner Act and the Origins of Modern Legal Consciousness, 1937-1941, 62 Minn. L. Rev. 265 (1978).

[76] Stone, The Post-War Paradigm in American Labor Law, 90 Yale L.J. 1509, 1517 (1981).

[77] Finkin, Revisionism in Labor Law, 43 Md. L. Rev. 23 (1984).

[78] Klare, Traditional Labor Law Scholarship and the Crisis of Collective Bargaining Law: A Reply to Professor Finkin, 44 Md. L. Rev. 731 (1985); Finkin, Does Karl Klare Protest Too Much?, 44 Md. L. Rev. 1100 (1985); Klare, Lost Opportunity: Concluding Thoughts on the Finkin Critique, 44 Md. L. Rev. 1111 (1985); Stone, Re-Envisioning Labor Law: A Response to Professor Finkin, 45 Md. L. Rev. 978 (1986).

[79] Hyde, Democracy in Collective Bargaining, 93 Yale L.J. 793 (1984).

[80] Minda and Raab, Time for an Unjust Dismissal Statute in New York, 54 Brooklyn L. Rev. 1137 (1989).

[81] Fischl, Self, Others, and Section 7: Mutualism and Protected Protest Activities Under the National Labor Relations Act, 89 Colum. L. Rev. 789 (1989).

[82] J. Atleson, VALUES AND ASSUMPTIONS IN AMERICAN LABOR LAW (1983); Klare, The Quest for Industrial Democracy and the Struggle Against Racism: Perspectives for Labor Law and Civil Rights Law, 61 Or. L. Rev. 157 (1982); Klare, Workplace Democracy & Market Reconstruction: An Agenda for Legal Reform, 38 Cath. U. L. Rev. 1 (1988); Beerman and Singer, Baseline Questions in Legal Reasoning: The Example of Property in Jobs, 23 Ga. L. Rev. 911 (1989).

[83] 437 U.S. 556 (1978).

[84] Eagle Electric Mfg. Co., 114 LRRM 1284 (1983). The General Counsel also declined to proceed because the employer had argued that the employees were not dismissed for this activity, but for falsifying their employment applications. In the face of this allegation and because of the burden of proof in mixed motive cases, the General Counsel deemed it a "poor vehicle" for presenting difficult issues under *Eastex*.

[85] Atleson, Reflections on Labor, Power, and Society, 44 Md. L. Rev. 841 (1985).

[86] Hyde, Economic Labor Law v. Political Labor Relations: Dilemmas for Liberal Legalism, 60 Tex. L. Rev. 1 (1981).

[87] Text accompanying n.74, *supra*.

[88] *Hyde*, n.86 *supra* at 12 (footnote omitted).

[89] P. Taft, The A.F. of L. in the Time of Gompers 321 (1957).

[90] H. Friendly, The Dartmouth College Case and the Public-Private Penumbra 20 (1988).

[91] Rubin, The Practice and Discourse of Legal Scholarship, 86 Mich. L. Rev. 1835, 1853 (1988).

[92] *Schwartz*, n.73 *supra* at 455.

[93] See, for example, the arguments of and the extensive sources cited in: Bartlett, Feminist Legal Methods, 103 Harv. L. Rev. 829 (1990); West, Jurisprudence and Gender, 55 U. Chi. L. Rev. 1 (1988); MacKennon, Reflections on Sexual Equality Under Law, 100 Yale L.J. 1281 (1991); Rhode, Feminist Critical Theories, 42 Stan. L. Rev. 617 (1990). *But see* Harris, Race and Essentialism in Feminist Legal Theory, 42 Stan. L. Rev. 581 (1990).

[94] Sunstein, Book Review [K. MacKennon, Feminism Unmodified (1987)], 101 Harv. L. Rev. 826 (1988).

[95] Williams, Reconstructing Gender, 87 Mich. L. Rev. 797, 798 (1989).

[96] C. Gilligan, In a Different Voice (1982).

[97] Sunstein, n.94 *supra* at 827-28.

[98] Williams, *supra* n.95 at 807.

[99] Cornell, Sexual Difference, the Feminine, and Equivalency: A Critique of MacKennon's *Toward a Feminist Theory of the State* [Book Review], 100 Yale L.J. 2247 (1991).

[100] 977 U.S. 57 (1986).

[101] Littleton, Book Review [K. MacKinnon, Feminism Unmodified (1987)], 41 Stan. L. Rev. 751, 770 (1989). *See also*, Estrich, Sex at Work, 43 Stan. L. Rev. 813 (1991) (drawing analogies to the law of rape); Ehrenreich, Pluralist Myths and Powerless Men: The Ideology of Reasonableness in Sexual Harassment Law, 99 Yale L.J. 1177 (1990).

[102] 628 F. Supp. 1264 (N.D. Ill. 1986) *aff'd* 839 F.2d 302 (7th Cir. 1988).

[103] Laycock, Statistical Proof and Theories of Discrimination, 49 L. and Contemp. Prob. 97, 98 (1986).

[104] 628 F. Supp. at 1324.

[105] *Id.* at 1306-07.

[106] Williams, *supra* n.95 at 818-19 (emphasis both omitted and added).

[107] Rhode, The "No-Problem" Problem: Feminist Challenges and Cultural Change, 100 Yale L.J. 1731, 1770 (1991).

[108] 628 F. Supp. at 1317.

[109] Rhode, *supra* n.107 at 1775.

[110] 628 F. Supp. at 1306.

[111] Schultz, Telling Stories About Women at Work: Judicial Interpretations of Sex Segregation in the Workplace in Title VII Cases Raising the Lack of Interest Argument, 103 Harv. L. Rev. 1749 (1990).

[112] 628 F. Supp. at 1308.

[113] Schultz, *supra* n.111 at 1841.

[114] *Id.* at 1793.

[115] Finley, Choice and Freedom: Elusive Issues in the Search for General Justice, 96 Yale L.J. 914, 939-40 (1987).

[116] Williams, *supra* n.95 at 822.

[117] Delgado, When A Story Is Just A Story: Does Voice Really Matter?, 76 Va. L. Rev. 95 n.1 (1990); Matsuda, Voices of America: Accent, Antidiscrimination Law, and a Jurisprudence for the Last Reconstruction, 100 Yale L.J. 1329, 1331 n.7 (1991).

[118] *See, e.g.*, Crenshaw, Race, Reform, and Retrenchment: Transformation and Legitimation in Antidiscrimination Law, 101 Harv. L. Rev. 1331 (1988).

[119] Delgado, *supra* n.117.

[120] Austin, Sapphire Bound!, 1989 Wis. L. Rev. 539 *criticizing* Chambers v. Omaha Girls Club, 834 F.2d 697 (8th Cir. 1987).

[121] *Id.* at 557.

[122] *Id.* at 576.

[123] *Id.* at 578.

[124] This has provoked quite a heated debate. *Compare* Kennedy, Racial Critique of Legal Academia, 102 Harv. L. Rev. 1745 (1989) *with* Colloquy—Responses to Randall Kennedy's Racial Critique of Legal Academia, 103 Harv. L. Rev. 1844-886 (1990).

[125] *Compare* Johnson, The New Voice of Color, 100 Yale L.J. 2007 (1991) *with* Carter, Academic Tenure and "White Male" Standards: Some Lessons from the Patent Law, *id.* at 2065.

[126] Getman, Voices, 66 Tex. L. Rev. 577, 582 (1988).

[127] Delgado, When A Story Is Just A Story: Does Voice Really Matter?, 76 Va. L. Rev. 95 (1990).

[128] Matsuda, Voices of America: Accent, Antidiscrimination Law, and a Jurisprudence for the Last Reconstruction, 100 Yale L.J. 1329 (1991).

[129] 888 F.2d 591 (9th Cir. 1989). Professor Matsuda was counsel for the plaintiff.

[130] Matsuda, *supra* n.128 at 1354.

[131] *Id.* at 1336.

[132] *Id.* at 1337-38.

[133] *Id.* at 1331.

[134] *Cf.* Yudof, "Tea and the Palaz of Hoon": The Human Voice in Legal Rules, 66 Tex. L. Rev. 589, 595 (1988).

[135] Matsuda, *supra* n.128 at 1369.

[136] *Id.* at 1386.

[137] *Id.* at 1376.

[138] Culp, Autobiography and Legal Scholarship and Teaching: Finding Me in the Legal Academy, 77 Va. L. Rev. 539 (1991).

CHAPTER 16

Have OSHA and Workers' Compensation Made the Workplace Safer?

ROBERT S. SMITH
Cornell University

The Occupational Safety and Health Act (OSHA) was passed with near unanimity in 1970, and it has triggered two decades of heightened attention to safety and health issues at the workplace. Its most notable features were the authorization of the U.S. Department of Labor to promulgate and enforce workplace safety and health standards and its creation of the National Institute of Occupational Safety and Health, which was charged with the job of recommending standards based on its research of safety and health hazards. The Act also called for the creation of a temporary commission to study and recommend changes to the workers' compensation system, which is state based and has the dual goals of compensating victims and reducing workplace risk.

Changes in the attention paid to workplace risk have been dramatic over the period since 1970. More than a million safety and health inspections were conducted by federal compliance officers during these two decades, and many thousands more were performed by inspectors in states operating their own programs with federal approval. The percentage of manufacturing collective bargaining agreements with safety and health clauses rose from its level of about 70 percent in the 1957-1971 period to around 88 percent in the 1979-1987 period (Robinson 1991, p. 53). Labor-management contracts establishing joint safety and health committees in manufacturing firms went from 38 to 62 percent of the total over this same period. Changes in nonmanufacturing were even more striking. Moreover, both professional and academic interest in job safety and health showed substantial increases. In 1970, the *Wall Street Journal* published just six articles on job safety and health (one every two months), and another ten related to legislative issues involved with passage of the Occupational Safety and Health Act; in 1990, the *Journal* averaged one article a week on job safety and health issues. Likewise, academic papers on workplace safety in the social science literature rose from four in 1972 to 21 in 1990.[1]

After two decades of discussion, research, tightened regulation, and resource reallocation directed toward workplace safety and health, it is profoundly disturbing that injury rates appear to have been unaffected. The percentage of manufacturing workers experiencing lost workday injuries, for example, was 5.3 in 1988-1990, up from 4.0 in 1972; the path taken by this lost-workday case rate is shown in Figure 1, which exhibits considerable yearly variation but no hint whatsoever of a downward trend. Further, the yearly number of lost workdays per hundred manufacturing workers, shown in Figure 2, has a pronounced upward trend, rising from 73 days in 1975 to 104 days by 1990!

The failure of the overall manufacturing injury rate to fall over the past two decades, moreover, cannot easily be attributed to either changes in the interindustry mix of employment or to the failure of OSHA to give serious and early attention to risk reduction. For example, by early 1971, OSHA had targeted for intensive inspection three manufacturing industries with injury rates at least double the manufacturing average. By the end of 1972, virtually all plants in these industries with 20 or more employees had been inspected at least once, and cooperative efforts by labor, management, and the National Safety Council to remediate hazards were well under way. Injury rate trends within these targeted industries reinforce the impression that not much has changed. The lost workday case rate in the miscellaneous transportation equipment industry (which makes mobile homes) declined from 10 percent in 1972 to around 7.5 percent in the late 1980s, but rates in the lumber and wood products and meat and meat products industries were higher throughout the 1980s than in either 1972 or 1973.

The purpose of this chapter is to review and summarize what academic research has contributed to our understanding of workplace injuries.[2] In particular, it addresses the question of why injury rates have not generally declined in the last two decades despite the implementation and enforcement of the Occupational Safety and Health Act. The first section deals with patterns in the aggregate data, the second with estimates of OSHA's inspection effects, and the third with the relationship between injuries and the level of, and methods of financing, workers' compensation benefits.

A Closer Look at the Aggregate Data

The aggregate data shown in Figure 1 can be analyzed more carefully to reveal important underlying patterns that cannot easily be spotted by the eye. These patterns, or their absence, can help us to obtain a more accurate first impression about whether the attention paid to workplace risk in the past 20 years has had an observable overall effect. First, however, we must inquire about the accuracy—and possible changes in the accuracy—of the data on occupational injuries.

Questions of Data Accuracy

Data on workplace injury rates are obtained by the U.S. Bureau of Labor Statistics (BLS) from reports filed by employers. The reports are based on data recorded on an injury/illness log employers are required to keep, and they include information on the number of injuries without lost workdays, the number of injuries involving at least one day away from work, and the total days away from work.[3] Employers also report their industry, average employment levels, total labor-hours worked by their employees during the year, and the month of their first OSHA inspection (if any) during the year.

The BLS collects reports from some 285,000 establishments each year and publishes injury rates by industry, disaggregated to the four-digit level of Standard Industrial Classification (SIC). For plants of ten or fewer employees, the data are based on a sample of employers; not all employers in this group are required to report each year. For plants above that size, all of whom are surveyed, industry rates are based on a census.

The current reporting system was established by the Occupational Safety and Health Act, and it replaced a voluntary survey of 148,000, mainly large, plants conducted by BLS prior to 1971. Although the prior survey was judged to produce more accurate estimates of injury rates than, say, surveys by the National Safety Council, its voluntary nature and its categorizations of injuries

FIGURE 1
Lost Workday Case Rate

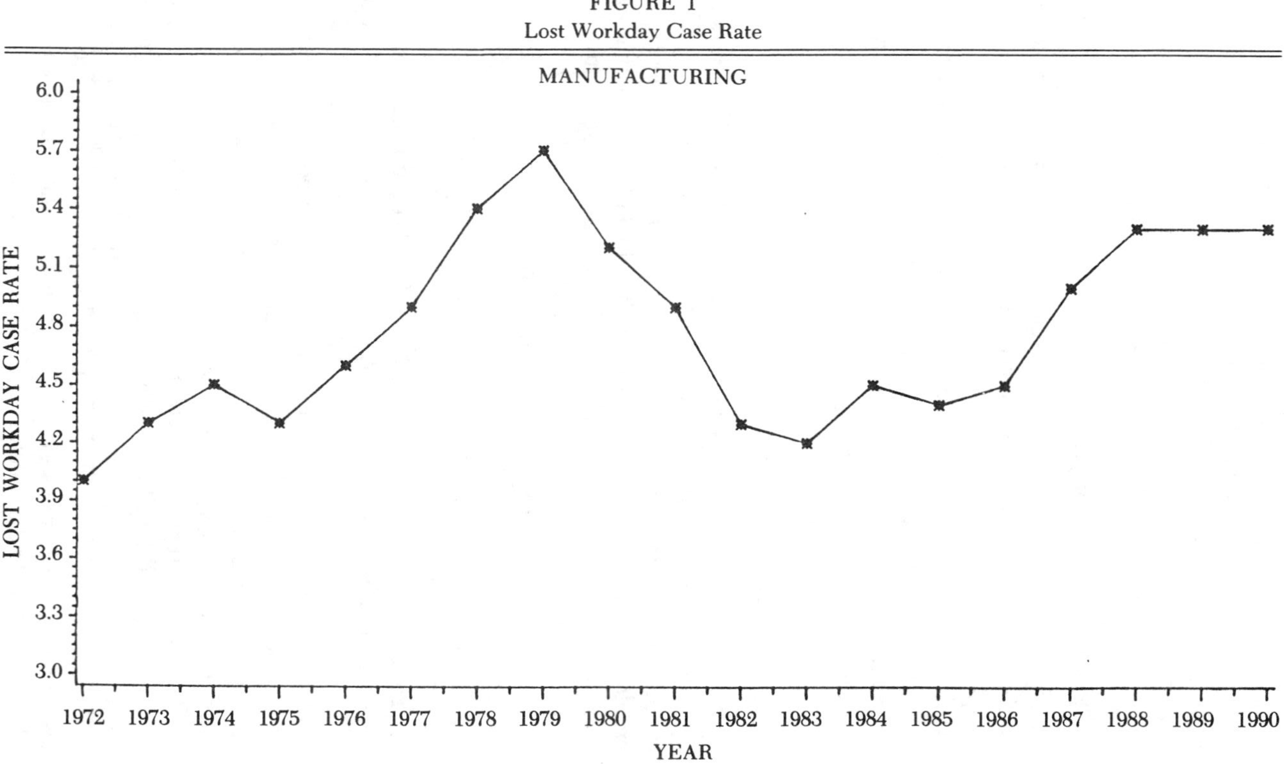

FIGURE 2
Lost Workdays Per 100 Workers

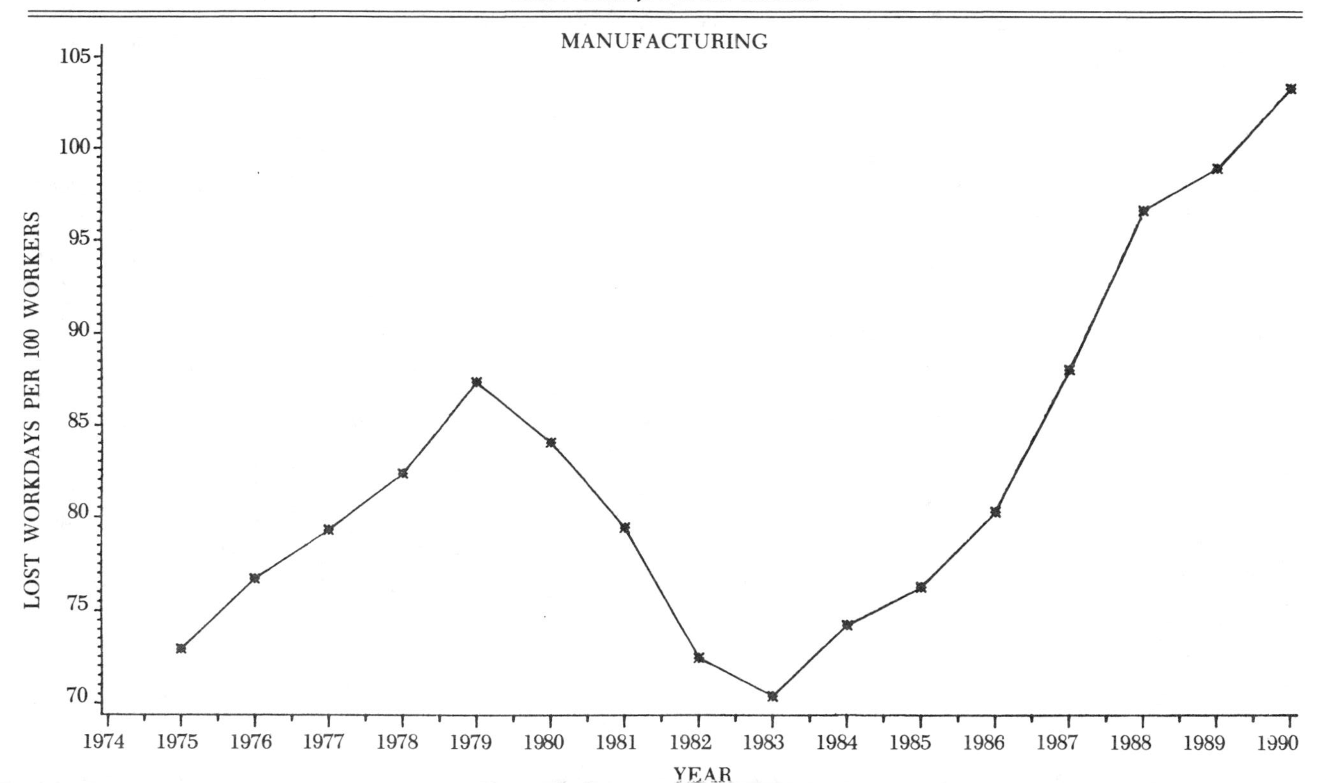

represented deficiencies that were seen as justifying the creation of a new system.[4] The new system, however, created its own problems for researchers interested in measuring the effects of the Occupational Safety and Health Act on workplace risk: the new and the old data were noncomparable. Thus, it has generally been impossible to conduct before-and-after analyses of how the Act has affected injury rates.

Despite its mandatory nature and the prospect of penalties for plants that underreport, questions about the accuracy of the BLS injury rate data have persisted. In 1985, Congress directed the Labor Department to commission a study of BLS' injury and illness data, focusing on their accuracy and reliability. The study, conducted by a panel put together by the National Research Council, found major discrepancies in the recording of traumatic (injury-related) deaths at the workplace, but it could not say whether nonfatal injury rates were biased.[5]

The discrepancy between BLS' reports of some three or four thousand traumatic deaths at work each year and the approximately 11,000 reported by the National Safety Council has long been perplexing.[6] Around half of all work-related traumatic deaths are the result of a highway motor vehicle accident, a heart attack, an assault, or a plane crash; thus, it is not difficult to imagine how the recordability of many fatalities as "work-related" could become disputable.[7] However, a pilot study by the National Research Council panel fould that 37 percent of deaths (excluding the above categories) determined to be work-related by examination of death certificates or medical examiner records were not recorded on the employer's logs. The panel concluded that traumatic occupational fatalities were probably underreported by 30 to 45 percent.[8]

Whether either fatal or nonfatal injuries are underreported, however, may be relatively unimportant for policy purposes as long as the biases are constant over time or across industries. For almost any conceivable analytical purpose, injury rates are used comparatively, and policy targets are selected based on cross-sectional or time series differences. Even a data series that underreports injuries by an unknown amount can be useful for policy or evaluative purposes, therefore, as long as there is no reason to suspect that the degree of underreporting has changed over time.

Believing that the use of plant-specific injury reports in targeting safety inspections would provide employers with strong incentives to understate injuries, BLS has gone out of its way to assure employers that their reports will not be used for enforcement purposes. It has steadfastly refused to let even OSHA have access to its raw data files. However, while BLS policies have not changed employers' reporting incentives over time, two OSHA policies adopted in the 1980s may have caused changes in the incentives to misreport. One involved the use of employer injury logs in the inspection targeting process, and the other grew out of greatly increased fines for underreporting.

From late 1981 to early 1988, OSHA utilized a two-step procedure for targeting safety inspections in manufacturing.[9] In the first stage, which used only industry-level data, OSHA selected which four-digit SIC manufacturing industries would be the focus of compliance visits. If the most recent lost-workday injury rate (LWDI) for a particular four-digit SIC industry equaled or exceeded the most recent aggregate private-sector LWDI rate, then all establishments in that industry were eligible for inspection. Industries with injury rates below the private-sector average were generally not targeted for OSHA inspections.[10]

In the second stage, when compliance officers first arrived at a plant, they examined the employer's injury log and calculated (for the past two or three years, depending on the size of the plant) the lost-workday injury rate for that particular establishment. If the establishment's own lost-workday injury rate was above the most recently available overall injury rate in manufacturing, then the officers proceeded to inspect the entire establishment. If the plant's injury rate was below the manufacturing average, the inspection was generally terminated with the records check.

Because some employers (those in low-risk industries) could be relatively confident of not being inspected, while others knew that the probabilities of a full-blown inspection depended on what was recorded on their injury log, adoption of this records-check procedure imparted differential incentives to underreport on the OSHA log.[11] A study by Ruser and Smith (1988) estimated that plants in high-hazard industries that could expect records-check inspections reduced their reported injuries by 5 to 7 percent, while plants in the low-hazard sector did not change their reporting behavior. These results were corroborated in a second paper by Ruser and Smith (1991), but only for uninspected plants. Plants that had already been inspected apparently were unlikely to change their reporting, perhaps owing to the fear of being caught by a follow-up inspection.

While the records-check procedure apparently increased the extent of underreporting after 1980, the perceived penalties for underreporting probably rose in 1986. Starting in that year, OSHA levied some large, highly publicized fines on firms that had allegedly engaged in repeated instances of willful (egregious) underreporting.[12] One beef processor, for example, was cited for over 1,000 unrecorded injuries and fined $2.6 million.[13] In 1986 and 1987 alone, at least seven large firms were each fined half a million dollars or more for recordkeeping violations. It is conceivable that the publicity surrounding these large fines for recordkeeping violations induced plants to more completely record their injuries after 1986.

A Times Series Analysis of the Aggregate Data

It is not generally possible to estimate the overall effects of the Occupational Safety and Health Act through before-and-after comparisons because, as noted above, the BLS data collected under the Act are not comparable with those collected earlier. Mendeloff (1979) and Currington (1986) used yearly manufacturing injury data from state workers' compensation systems that spanned the pre- and post-Act period, but the studies did not extend past the mid-1970s and workers' compensation data, as will become evident in the final section of this chapter, have major problems of their own.[14] Hence, the most satisfactory way to analyze aggregate time series data at this point is to see if pre-existing patterns in injury rates have been disrupted over the past 20 years.

The most notable pattern characteristic of the aggregate manufacturing injury rate is its procyclical nature. Largely because the risk of injury is greatest, other things equal, when a worker is new to the job, injury rates have historically risen during periods of declining unemployment (when businesses are both expanding employment and filling vacancies created by quits). Smith (1973) documented the strong negative relationship between the aggregate manufacturing injury rate and unemployment over the 1948-1969 period; specifically, this study found that a one-percentage-point reduction in the unemployment rate increased the injury rate by approximately 3.5 percent. No trend underlay the cyclical variability in injury rates from 1948 to 1969.

If post-1970 efforts to improve job safety have had an overall, cumulative effect, at least one of two changes in the pattern noted over the 1948-1969 period should be observed. First, a negative trend might well be expected to have replaced the trendless pattern of injury rates prior to 1970. Second, the cyclicality of rates should be damped (i.e., if the workplace is physically safer, employees' lack of experience should be of reduced importance).

Replicating the methodology used in Smith (1973), yearly changes in the aggregate manufacturing injury rate (ΔI) from 1972 to 1990 were regressed on changes in the unemployment rate (ΔU), with the intercept capturing any trend. Additionally, two dummy variables were included to take account of the cumulative effects of OSHA-related changes in the incentives to report injuries. One (D_{81}) took the value of unity in 1981 and beyond; it was included to capture the effects, discussed above, of the records-check inspection process. The other dummy variable (D_{86}) took the value of unity from 1986 and beyond, when penalties for misreporting became more severe. The results were as follows (standard errors in parentheses):

$$\underset{}{\Delta I} = \underset{(.056)}{.190} - \underset{(.033)}{.213\Delta U} - \underset{(.090)}{.346D_{81}} + \underset{(.100)}{.263D_{86}} \quad R^2 = .80$$

Durbin-Watson: 1.87

These results suggest the development of a positive trend in injury rates after 1970, even after controlling for the reporting incentive changes in the 1980s. Further, the coefficient on ΔU remains negative, statistically significant, and relatively large; the estimated coefficient of ΔU suggests that a one-percentage-point decline in the unemployment rate increases the injury rate by close to 5 percent. Finally, the coefficients of D_{81} and D_{86} suggest that reporting incentives had observable effects on the aggregate injury rate and that these effects were cumulative.[15]

While attempting to draw conclusions from a short time series of highly aggregated data may be imprudent, at least two statements seem to be warranted. First, the apparent sensitivity of the overall injury rate to reporting incentives suggests that "reporting" effects and "program" effects are probably commingled. Successful research strategies to evaluate programmatic effects must deal, therefore, with issues of reporting. Second, the result most relevant to evaluating programmatic effects is not the trend, it is the failure of the overall injury rate to become less cyclically sensitive. Trends reflect the effects of changes in the average experience or the occupational distribution of employees as well as changes in the physical hazards they face on the shop floor.[16] However, the continued higher vulnerability of new workers to injury suggests that OSHA has not reduced the relatively higher risks faced by those who are inexperienced.

Studies of OSHA's Inspection Effects

Because the Occupational Safety and Health Act fully covers the private sector, and because before-and-after comparisons are generally infeasible, a convincing study of the overall effects of the Act has not been—and may never be—done. Instead, the most credible evaluative studies have focused on the effects of OSHA inspections.

Before summarizing studies of inspection effectiveness, it is helpful to consider what the maximum potential effects might be. Federal safety policy has taken a standards-setting approach to risk reduction, and there are two major reasons to believe that compliance with existing standards would have only a limited effect on injuries. First, standards apply to permanent, physical hazards in the workplace. Some injuries (especially deaths, as noted earlier) occur off the work site, and many more are the result of either transient conditions or worker carelessness. Thus, it is not at all clear that most injuries are caused by permanent hazards to which standards could be applied. Second, the standards-setting process is cumbersome, and workplaces are both dynamic and diverse. It is inconceivable that standards can be kept up-to-date with all hazards posed by new technologies or work practices; moreover, the inefficiencies inherent in imposing uniform standards on heterogeneous workplaces are likely to provide incentives for employers and employees to jointly avoid compliance.

In recognition of the inherent limitations of standards, early studies in California, New York, and Wisconsin tried to establish a linkage between injuries and safety standard violations. Estimates by these states of the proportion of injuries occurring as a result of a safety standard violation ranged between 10 and 25 percent, although it was also estimated that between 25 and 36 percent of injuries were the result of controllable hazards to which standards were potentially applicable (Smith 1979b, pp. 166-67). Thus, it is likely that bringing plants into full compliance with OSHA standards would reduce injuries by 25 percent at the very most. The effects could increase slightly if OSHA standards were fully up-to-date.

There are two ways in which compliance can be induced through OSHA inspections. One is through the threat of penalties levied on plants in which violations are found during OSHA inspections. If the probability of inspection and the average penalty levied are high enough, deterrence can be induced in advance of inspection. Given that the average OSHA inspection finds less than one serious violation, that the average fine per serious violation is less than $300, and that most plants have a yearly inspection probability of less than 10 percent, OSHA's pre-inspection "deterrence" effect is probably very limited.[17]

The other way in which OSHA inspections can induce compliance is through identifying plants that are out of compliance and compelling them to abate their violations within a given time period (normally 30 days). Because failure to abate a violation within the period given can bring penalties of up to $7,000 per day, post-inspection abatement is normally assumed to occur.[18]

Studies Using Aggregate Industry Data

Inspection-effect studies have used two types of data. One approach has been to use inspection and injury rate data at the industry level of aggregation. These studies exploit differences in inspection probabilities and expected penalties across industries to assess the combined post-inspection "abatement" and pre-inspection "deterrence" effects on injury rates.

Using pooled time-series and cross-section data, the most straightforward method is to analyze injury rates while controlling for inspection probability and/or expected fines, industry, year, injury rates in the prior year, and non-OSHA factors that can cause injury rates to change year by year. The most recent study adopting this approach is Viscusi (1986), which used two-digit SIC data from 1973-1983 and found insignificant within-year effects of OSHA inspections. However, the study did estimate that blanketing an industry with inspections in one year would be associated with a small (3.5 percent), statistically significant decline in lost workday cases the next. There was no evidence that inspection effectiveness changed from 1973-1979 to 1980-1983, when the records-check targeting procedure was implemented. There was also no evidence that increasing expected penalties would reduce injuries.

Viscusi's conclusions about OSHA's inspection effects were necessarily guarded, but they were more optimistic than those of his first study (Viscusi 1979), which used a similar approach to study the 1972-1975 period. However, if the records-check procedure induced underreporting in the industries most likely to be inspected (see Ruser and Smith 1988), then at least some of the injury rate decline Viscusi associated with inspection intensity could be attributed to reporting changes, not reduced risk.

A more complex set of equations was estimated by Bartel and Thomas (1985), using 3-digit SIC data pooled over 1974-1978. This study simultaneously estimated equations for OSHA inspections (per worker), inspection penalties (per worker), and the lost workday case rate. It did find that greater inspection frequency significantly reduced noncompliance (as measured by OSHA's fines per worker); however, it found only weak evidence that greater compliance improved the injury rate. Specifically, the relevant point estimate suggested that full compliance would reduce the lost workday case rate by about 10 percent, but this estimate is statistically significant only at the .10 level. Bartel and Thomas concluded that the linkage between noncompliance and injuries was weak, but a "statement that OSHA standards achieve no reductions at all in injuries is probably invalid" (Bartel and Thomas 1985, p. 25). It is noteworthy that their study used data from a time period during which reporting incentives were unchanged.

Studies Using Plant-Level Data

The second approach taken in estimating OSHA's inspection effects employs longitudinal, plant-level data. The simplest, most direct approach would be to compare injury rates before and after inspection, controlling for factors other than inspection that could cause rates to change. The most natural comparison to make would be with similar plants that were not inspected. Unfortunately, OSHA seems to have targeted plants with increasing injury rates for its inspections, thus making uninspected plants a questionable comparison group.

One way to estimate inspection effects without using uninspected plants as a comparison group is to compare changes in injury rates of establishments inspected early in a given year with those of plants inspected late in the year. The fact that all plants were inspected in a given year greatly homogenizes the sample, and if within-year inspection effects occur, they should be evident for those inspected early but not for those inspected late. The early-late methodology was introduced in Smith (1979b) and has since been replicated in McCaffrey (1983) and Ruser and Smith (1991) for different time periods. All three studies controlled for industry, employment changes at the plant, and the plant's lost workday injury rate in the year prior to inspection, and all three analyzed injury rate changes both within the year of inspection and in the year following inspection. Ruser and Smith also controlled for reporting incentives induced by the adoption of the records-check inspection procedure. Altogether, the effects of inspections in 1973, 1974, 1976, 1977, and 1980-1985 have been analyzed using this approach.

Taken as a whole, these early-late studies show little or no evidence of a persistent OSHA inspection effect. Smith (1979b) found a sizable (15 percent) reduction in injury rates associated with 1973 inspections, but in none of the other years did an inspection significantly reduce injuries in either the year of inspection or the following year. The only hopeful note that emerges when the results of these studies are compared is that there is a noticeable tendency for yearly changes in the lost workday case rate to become less sensitive to changes in employment (Ruser and Smith 1991, p. 228). This result stands in contrast to the pattern that emerged when aggregate time series data pre- and post-OSHA were analyzed.

Because all three studies made use of injury rate and inspection data from the BLS survey alone, none had access to information about inspection outcomes (citations and fines). Hence, at best these studies estimated the average post-inspection "abatement" effect in which the effect is averaged over plants with no violations, those with just a few (one serious violation was the average per inspection throughout the 1970s), and those with several. Unlike the others, however, Ruser and Smith (1991) looked for pre-inspection "deterrence" effects among uninspected plants by analyzing the within-plant injury rate changes associated with the frequency of yearly OSHA inspections in the plant's industry/state/establishment-size cell. No deterrence effects were found (although, as noted earlier, the results did suggest that the records-check procedure caused those uninspected plants with the highest risk of being inspected to underreport).

Ideally, of course, one would like to estimate "abatement" effects by distinguishing those inspected plants with violations from those for which no violations were found. Performing this analysis requires matching plant-level data in the BLS survey with those in OSHA's management information system. The task is not trivial, because the two data systems have different employer identification coding schemes. However, BLS performed a match for a study by Gray and Scholz (1991), which analyzed data from large manufacturing plants over the 1979-1985 period.

The Gray and Scholz study was able to measure, over a seven-year period, the number of inspections at each plant during a given year and the number of such inspections in which penalties were imposed. It found evidence of post-inspection reductions in lost workday injuries only for inspections with penalties. These reductions persisted over the three years following inspection. After controlling for the possibility that inspections were more likely in plants with rising injury rates, they estimated that a plant inspected and penalized in one year will experience a 22 percent decline in lost workday injuries over the next three years.

Clearly, an estimated 22 percent reduction in injuries is in the credible range of OSHA's potential abatement effects, although it is at the upper end of that range. Is this result consistent with estimates from the early-late studies, which estimated average inspection effects? Because only one-third of inspections in the Gray and Scholz sample resulted in the imposition of penalties, the implied average inspection effect is a seven percent reduction in injuries. The point estimates from early-late studies, most of which cannot be confidently distinguished from zero, suggest that inspections reduce injuries by two to 15 percent; thus, the results of these studies are entirely consistent. Apparently, however, estimated effects are sufficiently imprecise to become statistically insignificant when they drop much below the 15 percent level.

The magnitudes of the above estimates stand in contrast to those in an earlier paper by Gray and Scholz (1989), which tried to estimate both deterrence and abatement effects with their data. These earlier results implied that OSHA's observed level of enforcement reduced injuries by 16 percent in the aggregate, with nine-tenths of the effect coming from deterrence. These estimates are not credible for two reasons. First, it seems clear from the foregoing studies that if OSHA inspections have had an effect at all, it cannot be easily observed by the naked eye. A 16 percent reduction in the aggregate injury rate would be readily observed. Second, it is difficult to believe that such dramatic pre-inspection deterrence could be generated by OSHA's inspection probabilities and penalty levels.

The Safety Effects of Workers' Compensation

The longest-standing set of programs designed, at least in part, to reduce workplace risk is workers' compensation. Each state has its own system for compensating the victims of occupational injury, but the systems share common features. All place liability for payment strictly on the employer, without regard to cause. All establish basic insurance premium rates by narrowly defined industries that are modified, for at least some firms, to account for firm-specific injury experience. All fully cover medical costs and indemnify injured workers for at least a portion of their lost earnings.

It is the rate-setting characteristics of workers' compensation systems that are designed to reduce workplace risk, and these characteristics have two anticipated effects.[19] The first is an "industry" effect: firms in higher-risk industries pay higher basic premiums (called "manual rates"). These premiums are charged to each firm in the industry as a fraction of its total payroll costs, so it can be argued that the higher premiums in a dangerous industry both raise the overall unit cost of its output and increase the cost of its labor relative to capital. The resulting incentives to reduce output and economize on the use of labor in high-risk industries should contribute toward an economy-wide reduction in injuries by reallocating labor from more dangerous industries to safer ones.

The second effect on safety is related to the "experience-rating" of premiums. To the extent that a firm's own injury experience is reflected in its premiums, there is an induced incentive for it to consider investing in safety. If its injuries fall, so will its workers' compensation premiums.

Experience rating, however, is imperfect. Injury rates have a random component to them, and it is difficult to distinguish a firm's "true" level of risk from this random component, except in very large firms. One result is that, in modifying a firm's manual rate, the weight given to its own experience increases with firm size. Typically, a 50 percent reduction in injury costs would result in no decline in premiums for a firm of seven employees, a five percent drop for a firm of 10, a 17 percent decline for a firm of 75, a 36 percent decline for a firm of 750, and a full 50 percent decline only for firms with 1,750 or more employees (Chelius and Smith 1987a, p. 38). Moreover, additional efforts to separate the "true" from the random component of a firm's injury rate result in its injury experience being averaged over several years—effectively delaying for over four years the full effect on premiums of a permanent decline in a firm's injury rate.

The anticipated safety effects of the workers' compensation program are based on an implicit assumption that market forces fail to assess firms for the costs of injury to their workers. Put differently, the higher insurance costs imposed on firms with more risky workplaces can optimally reduce injuries only if the labor market fails to impose on employers—through, for example, compensating wage differentials for higher risk levels—the full cost of uncompensated losses suffered by injured workers. If market forces are fully operative, reducing ex-post losses by increasing workers' compensation benefits will result in smaller (ex-ante) compensating wage differentials, and the tendency will be for employer costs, and injury rates, to remain unchanged.

Indeed, it must be noted that to the extent the market works well but experience rating is imperfect, more generous workers' compensation benefits could cause an increase in workplace risk. If the expected ex-post losses from injury are reflected in workers' wages, increased workers' compensation benefits will be accompanied by a reduction in the compensating wage differential; this reduction will be larger among higher-risk firms because their expectation of injury is greater. If insurance premiums are set at the industry level and do not vary with the experience of individual firms, both risky and relatively safe firms in each industry will face the same insurance rate increases, with the result that labor costs in risky firms fall relative to those in safer firms. Employment tends to shift toward the relatively risky employers, and the incentives for each firm to improve safety have actually been reduced.

It is unclear just how well the labor market works in providing ex-ante payment for ex-post losses. Compensating wage differentials for the risk of death have been widely found (Smith 1979a; Moore and Viscusi 1990); however, the fragility of these estimates is troubling (Kniesner and Leeth 1991), and in any case it is virtually impossible, given the nonpecuniary losses involved, to judge whether they are fully compensating. Compensating wage differentials for nonfatal risks have been more difficult to establish, although it is not uncommon to find positive wage differentials for the risk of injury and negative wage differentials associated with higher workers' compensation benefits (Moore and Viscusi 1990). One cannot, therefore, rule out the possibility that the market does assess firms for at least a portion of their injury costs.

The Empirical Effects of Increased Benefits

Dating back to the report of the U.S. National Commission on State Workmen's Compensation Laws (1972), which recommended that benefits for injured workers be increased as a way to improve employer safety incentives, analysts have striven to measure and understand the empirical relationship between workers' compensation benefits and injury rates. The results are as clear as any in the field of applied economics: there is a positive relationship between benefits and recorded injuries.

This positive relationship first appeared in the early work of Chelius (1974, 1982), which analyzed the employer data on injuries reported to BLS. In the more sophisticated of the two studies, Chelius (1982) reported that once industry and state-specific factors were controlled for, the elasticity of lost workday cases with respect to workers' compensation benefits was +0.12. The elasticity of cases not involving lost workdays was +0.07; however, it was not statistically significant. Ruser (1985) refined the measures of workers' compensation benefits, but he also found that the lost workday case rate was increased more by the generosity of benefits than was the incidence of injuries not involving lost workdays. His estimated elasticities of lost workday cases with respect to benefits were in the range of +0.12 to +0.31; elasticities for all cases (including lost workday cases) fell into the range of +0.06 to +0.28.[20] Recent papers by Ruser (1991a, 1991b) using plant-level data report results that are entirely consistent, both in quality and magnitude, with the findings of the earlier studies.

While the studies cited earlier all used employer reports of injuries to BLS, there have also been studies in which the injury data were based on employee claims made to the workers' compensation system. The early work with these data by Butler (1983) and Butler and Worrall (1983) found, across both states and time, a positive relationship between benefit levels and the number of workers' compensation claims per hundred employees. The estimated elasticity of claims with respect to benefits in Butler and Worrall, the more general of the two studies, had a lower bound of +0.40. An interesting study of a natural experiment involving an isolated cut in the benefits to some employees found similar evidence: the cut was accompanied by a decline in workers' compensation claims (Chelius and Kavanaugh 1988). More recently, Krueger (1990a) found a strong positive relationship between benefit levels and the probability that individual workers will be receiving workers' compensation payments.[21] The latter study used data that permitted controls for individual-specific factors, and Krueger's estimated elasticity of recipiency with respect to benefits was +0.70.

Explaining the tendency for increased benefits to cause increases in reported injuries has proven more difficult than measuring it because distinguishing "real" from "reporting" effects is not trivial. There are at least three aspects of the relationship between recipiency and benefits that have been analyzed.

Real Safety Effects. The actual level of workplace risk may rise with benefit levels for either of two reasons. First, an imperfectly experience-rated system may have been imposed on a perfectly functioning labor market, so that as benefits rise and workers' ex-post losses become smaller, employers' safety incentives decline. Second, as workers perceive that the costs of injury fall, they may become less careful in their behavior and more prone to injury.

A recent study has found evidence suggesting that real risk levels are not increased by higher benefits. Butler and Worrall (1991) separate workers' compensation claims into two components: payments for medical services received by injured workers and indemnity payments to them for time lost from work. As expected from prior studies, there is a positive, large, and statistically significant relationship between benefit levels and indemnity payments; specifically, a 10 percent increase in benefit levels leads to a 13 percent increase in indemnity payments. Interestingly, however, a 10 percent increase in benefit levels leads to a 3.6 percent reduction in medical cost reimbursements. This finding leads Butler and Worrall to conclude that real safety may be improved as benefits increase.

It is tempting to inquire about the relationship between workers' compensation benefits and the risks of workplace fatalities in assessing real safety effects. Fatal accidents, one would think, are objective events that are not susceptible to reporting bias. Unfortunately, whether a death is job-related is often ambiguous and contestable, so neither employer reports (as we saw earlier) nor workers' compensation filings are free of potential reporting biases. One recent study by Moore and Viscusi (1990, pp. 72, 128), however, used fatality data that were obtained from death certificates on which the cause was recorded as occupationally related. Because their data were from a source that is free of reporting bias incentives, they interpreted the negative relationship found between benefit levels and fatality rates to be evidence of a real safety effect associated with higher injury costs. Unfortunately, their fatality data were grouped at such a high level of aggregation (the one-digit level of industry) that the problem of uncontrolled heterogeneity within industries limits the confidence one can place in their result.[22]

Duration Effects. Improved benefits might elicit longer healing periods among injured workers—an outcome that could signal the kind of moral hazard problems inherent in reporting biases.[23] Gardner (1991) and Meyer, Viscusi, and Durbin (1991), for example, have analyzed the effects of "natural experiments" in three states in which benefits for some injured workers rose dramatically over a short time period while benefits for others did not. They found that, other things equal, time away from work—the "healing period"—increased when benefits rose. The estimated elasticities of duration with respect to benefits ranged from +0.3 to +0.9.

It is not clear, however, whether higher benefits should be expected to increase or decrease the average length of healing period for those who miss work due to injury. On the one hand, Worrall and Appel (1982) report that higher indemnity benefits increase the number of indemnity claims relative to medical-only claims, implying that some relatively minor cases in which no work time would otherwise have been lost are "converted" to lost-time cases. This finding is consistent with those of Chelius (1982) and Ruser (1985, 1991a), and it suggests that higher benefits might reduce the average spell for those who miss work by inducing workers to take time off for relatively minor injuries.

On the other hand, higher benefits could also lengthen the healing period of the more serious injuries already reported. As might be expected, there is ample evidence that injuries that are more difficult to diagnose or evaluate have durations that are sensitive to benefit levels. That injured workers remain off work longer when benefits are higher is well documented for cases involving low back injuries (Butler and Worrall 1985; Worrall and Butler 1985; Dionne and St. Michel 1991). In these studies the elasticities of duration with respect to benefits range from +0.18 to +0.90. For other injuries, however, the results are conflicting. Dionne and St. Michel found that higher benefits in Quebec had no effect on the healing periods of such objectively evaluated injuries as contusions, amputations, and fractures. Johnson and Ondrich (1990), on the contrary, report that a 10 percent increase in benefits elicited an 11 percent increase in the months off work associated with permanent partial injuries other than to the lower back. Moreover, Krueger (1990b) reports that a five percent increase in benefits for some workers in Minnesota increased the duration associated with their temporary total injury by eight percent (as compared to workers who did not receive the higher benefits); the increased durations were found for minor, as well as major, injuries.

Estimates of duration effects are equally confusing using BLS data on lost workdays. Chelius (1982) and Ruser (1985, 1991a), it will be recalled, found that the elasticity of lost workday cases with respect to benefit increases exceeded the elasticity for cases with no lost workdays. However, both Bartel and Thomas (1985) and Chelius (1982) found no significant relationship between benefits and the number of lost workdays per hundred workers.

In any case, increased durations cannot explain the linkage between benefits and number of claims filed (or injuries reported) per hundred workers. If real safety in the workplace either increases or remains constant, but reports of injuries rise, then one must consider the hypothesis that there exists a "reporting effect" associated with higher benefits.

Reporting Effects. For an injured worker, reporting the injury, filing a claim, and pressing for higher benefits by trying to convincingly establish a greater extent of physical impairment are time-consuming activities. If benefits are relatively low, workers may choose not to bother with the inevitable reports to be filed and medical evaluations to be undertaken. As benefits rise, injured workers may be more likely to both file claims and seek to have their injuries categorized as "permanent," thus qualifying them for larger indemnity payments. However, as benefits rise workers also have more incentives to file bogus claims, which either exaggerate the extent of their disability or seek compensation for injuries that occurred off the job.

The findings in Smith (1990) raised the possibility that some off-the-job injuries are being compensated as job-related. This study reasoned that if workers were seeking compensation for injuries occurring off the job, the injuries involved would probably be difficult to diagnose, relatively easy to conceal, and reported early in the work shift, especially on the day following a weekend. Of the three largest categories of injury, sprains and strains, which are more easily concealed and more subjectively assessed than lacerations and fractures, are reported earlier in the day. More importantly, the propensity to report strains and sprains earlier in the day is significantly increased on Mondays and on days following a three-day weekend. Smith estimated that perhaps four percent of sprains and strains are misrepresented as having occurred in the workplace.

While suggestive, Smith's evidence on misreported injuries is circumstantial, at best. Further, the study did not look for linkages between reporting patterns and benefit levels. For the most part, separating increased claims for legitimate injuries from purely bogus claims remains a challenge no study has yet surmounted. The reason is that injuries that are the most difficult to assess are also the most likely to be underreported by employees in legitimate cases when incentives to file are low. The extra time and effort required to establish both the fact of injury and its origin in the workplace, therefore, may deter the filing of both legitimate and bogus claims.

If higher benefits drive real workplace injuries down while inducing increased reporting of the frequency of injury, then at least two reporting patterns should be observed. First, claims for difficult-to-assess injuries should be more sensitive to benefit increases than claims for other injuries. The data in Table 1, which documents for four large states the rising proportion of sprain-or-strain claims that accompanied increases in benefit levels, support the existence of this pattern. Benefit levels and the "mix" of sprains and strains among all claims appear to have risen together. Krueger (1990b), however, found that the mix of injuries among Minnesota workers receiving a benefit increase was not more heavily weighted toward sprains than the mix among workers receiving no benefit increases; if anything, it was more heavily weighted toward

TABLE 1

Benefits Increases and the Proportion of Sprains/Strains Among All Claims

Year	Index of Real Benefit Levels (U.S.)	Percent of all Claims That Are for Sprains or Strains			
		New York	Florida	Michigan	Ohio
1965	100	26.6	32.6		31.9 (1966)
1970	118	28.6	35.1		30.6
1975	155	34.4	32.8	38.2 (1977)	34.1
1980	184	36.9			35.1
1982	198	38.2	38.5	44.2 (1981)	37.6

Sources: National Council on Compensation Insurance, ***Annual Statistical Bulletin, 1990***, New York: National Council on Compensation Insurance, 1990, Exhibit 1; New York, Workers' Compensation Board, *Compensated Cases Closed*, Albany: New York State, various years; Florida, Bureau of Workers' Compensation, *Analysis of Work Injuries Covered by Workers' Compensation*, Tallahassee: Florida Department of Commerce, various years; Michigan, *Compensable Injury and Illness Tabulation 1977-78, 1980-81, Compensable Injury and Illness Report*, Lansing, MI: State of Michigan, 1988; Ohio, The Industrial Commission, Division of Safety and Hygiene, *Ohio Statewide Accident Statistics*, 1980 and 1982, Columbus, Ohio: The Industrial Commission of Ohio, 1980 and 1982. Ohio data before 1980 were contained in a letter to the author from Ms. Sandy Newman, Researcher, Bureau of Workers' Compensation, dated November 1, 1991.

fractures. Clearly, more work needs to be done in understanding what types of claims are most affected by benefit increases.

Second, the reporting induced by higher benefits should affect workers' compensation claim rates—which are based on employee reports of injury, more than injury rates based on employer or medical-treatment reports. As seen indirectly by comparing the studies by Chelius (1982), Butler and Worrall (1983), Ruser (1985, 1991b), and Krueger (1990a), employee claims are more elastic with respect to benefits than are employer reports of injury to BLS. A more direct test of the hypothesis that employee reports of injuries are more elastic with respect to benefits is contained in Butler, Gardner, and Worrall (1991), which finds evidence in support of this hypothesis.

Further evidence of this second pattern is found in Butler (1983). This study reports that survivors' claims for death benefits rose quite strongly with benefits (the implied elasticity was +1.1), whereas Moore and Viscusi (1990) and Ruser (1991a), using data from a census of death certificates and employer reports to BLS, respectively, found that death rates generally declined with benefits. Given that about half of occupational fatalities either occur off the worksite or involve heart attacks and assaults, it is not difficult to imagine that the "work-relatedness" of many cases involving a fatality are perceived by the employer, insurance company, or the victim's relatives as contestable; indeed, Worrall and Butler (1986) report data showing that the probability of a given claim being contested rises with the seriousness of the injury, with death cases having the highest probability. Higher benefits, therefore, probably induce workers' survivors to seek workers' compensation awards under circumstances in which the contestability of the claim would have previously discouraged them from doing so. Combining the elasticities implied by Ruser (1991a) and Butler (1983), the pure reporting effect for fatal injuries is quite large: a 10 percent increase in benefits apparently calls forth an 18 percent increase in fatality claims strictly from cases in which a claim previously would not have been filed.

Estimating the Effects of Experience Rating

Studies analyzing the overall relationship between benefit levels and reported injuries clearly confound employee and employer inducements, which generally influence reported injuries in opposite directions. Moreover, the employer-related effects on injuries in the studies discussed earlier must operate mainly through the "industry effect";[24] unless behavior is distinguished across firm size groups, the only effects of experience rating that can be observed derive from the average degree of experience rating across industries.

To more adequately include employer effects on injuries in the analysis, one must disaggregate the injury rate by firm size category so that effects of the differential degrees of experience rating can be captured. Unfortunately, capturing the degree of experience rating poses great difficulties. Studies incorporating size into the analysis use average plant size, because data on employer characteristics are reported at the level of the plant, not the firm. Workers' compensation rates, however, are set at the level of the firm, so the degree of experience rating is affected by firm, not plant, size. For some plants, then, the degree of experience rating is implicitly understated, which biases down the estimated effects of experience rating on injury rates (some plants that are actually experience rated, and may have lower injury rates as a result, are misclassified as being less experience rated than they actually are). Of 18 two-digit manufacturing industries (other than "miscellaneous manufacturing"), only seven average 1.1 or fewer plants per company; six have 1.3 or more plants per firm.[25] Thus, the problem of misclassification is not trivial.

One set of studies has analyzed industry-wide injury rates across states or time, taking the industry average number of employees per plant into account. These studies include separate controls for benefit levels (with results described in the previous subsection), plant size, and an interaction between plant size and benefit levels. It is the latter term that is intended to capture the effects of experience rating, because higher benefits increase the marginal cost of an injury more in larger (more experience-rated) firms; the hypothesis is, of course, that the coefficient on this interaction term will be negative. This hypothesis is strongly supported by the findings of Ruser (1985) and Moore and Viscusi (1990), and weakly supported by those of Worrall and Butler (1988).

Another approach assigns plants to various size categories and analyzes injury rates across industry/state/size-category cells. Ruser (1991b) uses plant-level injury data to analyze the effects of higher benefits across different size groups; he finds that the tendency for higher benefits to increase injury rates becomes progressively smaller as plant size (experience rating) increases. Thus, while it is evident that the employee effects of higher benefits dominate employer-related incentives, employer effects apparently do increase with the degree of experience rating.

The four experience-rating studies reviewed so far estimated the average effects of the benefit-size interaction variable on injury rates across all industries. Clearly, however, there is every reason to believe that these effects will differ across industries; safety "production functions" differ, as do the prevalence of multiplant firms and the distributions of plant sizes.[26] The only study that estimates experience-rating effects on injury rates separately for each industry (Chelius and Smith 1983) was inconclusive. Only 32 of 60 estimates suggest the presence of the hypothesized experience-rating effect, and only nine of these 32 were significant at the .10 level or better. However, in the six industries in which plant size appears to most accurately reflect experience-rating incentives (industries that have 1.1 or fewer plants per company), the higher marginal cost of injuries associated with higher benefits reduced the average injury rates of larger as compared to smaller plants in 17 of 24 cases (six of the nine statistically significant reductions were in this group).

It is tempting to conclude that experience rating does offer inducements for firms to reduce injury rates, although the presence of these effects are by no means certain and the size of the effects are swamped by employee reporting effects. But are these "employer" effects of experience rating affecting just "real" safety?

There is intriguing evidence that experience rating may lead firms to undertake actions that reduce employee incentives to lengthen duration or to file claims. Krueger (1990b) finds that benefit increases in Minnesota, while lengthening the duration of temporary total injuries on average, had no effect on the healing periods for workers of self-insured firms (these firms are clearly, and fully, experience rated). Earlier, Chelius and Kavanaugh (1988), with a more limited data set, found employers that switched to self-insurance had fewer injury claims afterwards, but that the duration of claims declined even more. If experience-rated firms can adopt policies that affect the duration of the healing period, might they also adopt policies that affect the filing or approval of claims? If so, experience rating might affect more than just the real level of risk; it might also affect the reporting of injuries.

Concluding Comments

Evidence that OSHA and workers' compensation have reduced injuries in the workplace is minimal. If either program has had a benign effect on risk levels, which is itself doubtful, it is almost certain that these effects are quantitatively small. In the case of workers' compensation, real safety effects are clearly swamped by reporting effects.

It is not surprising that OSHA's effects are limited; the effects of standard setting are confined to a relatively small subset of injuries, and the inefficiencies of uniform standards imposed on heterogeneous workplaces guarantee the presence of market incentives to circumvent bureaucratic fiat. A more sensible way to reduce workplace risk is to provide more general, financial incentives for risk reduction.

Because the workers' compensation system provides generalized, financial incentives, the failure to clearly associate declines in risk with increases in injury costs is disappointing. Further attempts to isolate reporting effects from those on the real level of risk are required to clarify the size of the "real safety" response to financial incentives. Moreover, since even fully experience-rated insured firms have imperfect incentives to reduce risk, the most fruitful studies of the effects of financial incentives will probably be those that focus on the self-insured.

Most states currently allow large firms to self-insure, but access to data on the self-insured is limited. Another way to effectively expand self-insurance, which may be possible with the current impetus to deregulate workers' compensation, is for states to experiment with insurance policies that require large deductibles. Requiring employers to make large copayments would effectively remove from insurance coverage a large number of (relatively minor) injuries and more directly impose the costs of compensation on employers.[27] A carefully constructed experiment with insurance copayment requirements would probably provide the best evidence yet of the degree to which injuries can be reduced by increasing employer financial incentives.

More broadly, in our zeal to find a safety program that works, we should not lose sight of the government's responsibility to justify its involvement in workplace safety. Is the labor market really failing with respect to job safety? If so, why? Can the causes of the failure be remedied directly (by improving information or mobility, for example), or must government-generated incentives be imposed? Given the difficulty in finding real safety effects of either workers' compensation insurance or OSHA, one must face the fact that governmental good intentions are not translated into lower risk levels with any degree of certainty. Perhaps some tasks are better left to the market.

Acknowledgments

The author would like to thank Professors Richard Butler, James Chelius, Alan Krueger, and Olivia Mitchell for their thoughtful comments. They, of course, share no blame for the deficiencies that remain.

Endnotes

[1] See the *Social Science Citation Index*, relevant years.

[2] The focus of this paper is on injuries, because the data on workplace illnesses do not reflect cases of chronic disease with long gestation periods. These diseases, such as cancers and lung disorders, cannot be linked to a unique cause in a specific industry in most cases; hence, information on them is essentially unavailable.

[3] Data on various occupational illnesses are also reported but, as noted in note 2, they do not reflect most cases of chronic disease

[4] Pollack and Keimig (1987), pp. 12, 17-18.

[5] Pollack and Keimig (1987), p. 2.

[6] See, for example, *Accident Facts* (1987).

[7] *California Work Injuries* (1972), pp. 7-19. The largest single category of occupational fatalities consists of traffic accidents; in manufacturing, fatalities in this category have steadily risen from 15 percent of the total in 1950 to 35 percent in 1985 (see *Economic Report of the President*, 1987, p. 200).

[8] Pollack and Keimig (1987), pp. 56-60.

[9] The procedure described relates to inspections conducted by the federal government. Twenty-three states conduct their own inspection program under OSHA-approved guidelines. Some of these states adopted the procedure described in this paragraph and some did not.

[10] OSHA did inspect plants in these industries in response to employee complaints or to accidents involving fatalities.

[11] These incentives differed by industry, owing to different average LWDI rates. Additionally, because not all states adopted the records-check procedure, as noted in note 9, incentives to underreport also differed across states.

[12] In "egregious" cases of "flagrant disregard," OSHA decided to issue instance-by-instance citations rather than "bundling" all instances into one overall citation. Because the Occupational Safety and Health Act places limits on the fines that can be levied for each violation, "unbundling" violations permitted OSHA to vastly increase its penalties. See *Bureau of National Affairs* (1990), p. 1723.

[13] *Bureau of National Affairs* (1987), p. 851.

[14] Mendeloff found no overall effect on injuries but did find a small decrease in the risk of death. Both studies found decreases in machine-related injuries associated with the advent of the Occupational Safety and Health Act, but both also found unexplained increases in other types of injuries.

[15] When the dependent variable is in the form of yearly changes, a dummy variable captures trend effects.

[16] See Chelius (1977, Appendix A) for an interesting analysis of the rise in injury rates during the late 1960s that eventually helped to motivate Congressional passage of the Occupational Safety and Health Act. His analysis attributes most of the rise to lower unemployment and a rising proportion of younger workers in the labor force, not to a deterioration of underlying working conditions.

[17] Nonserious violations, which in recent years account for 60 percent of all citations, do not usually carry a fine (the average fine per nonserious violation was $1.60 in 1988). See Smith (1986) for data on inspections and penalties in the 1970s. For more recent data, see *Bureau of National Affairs* (1989), p. 2029.

[18] Whether plants often undo their abatement later on and slip back out of compliance has not been studied.

[19] The "reductions" contemplated can be thought of as caused either by the implementation of a workers' compensation system (going from a labor market without one) or by an increase in the workers' compensation benefits paid to injured workers.

[20] Chelius (1982), Bartel and Thomas (1985), and Ruser (1985), all found that shorter waiting periods—the length of time off work before workers' compensation benefits can be received—were associated with more reports of injuries by employers.

[21] Krueger also found that reduced waiting periods increased the probability of receipt.

[22] Ruser (1991a), using BLS data on death risk at the plant level, also found a negative and statistically significant relationship between benefit levels and death risk—but only for two of the four firm-size groups he examined. For the other two groups there was no significant relationship.

[23] Moral hazard issues, however, need not be the cause of longer healing periods. The longer periods could be the result of workers having the resources to subsidize a more complete medical recovery before having to return to work.

[24] While all these studies of injury rates across states and/or time control for the industrial mix, the industrial categories included are typically broader than the rate-setting classifications used by the workers' compensation system. Therefore, shifts in labor from risky workers' compensation classes to safer ones—the "industry effect" discussed earlier—can cause injury rates to decline within these industrial categories. However, estimating the effects of benefits on injuries after controlling for industry does not capture the effects of employment shifts among the categories used as controls.

[25] See *U.S. Bureau of the Census* (1982), Table 2, p. 5-5.

[26] Different distributions of plant sizes will affect both those studies using plant size averages as an independent variable and those using very broad plant-size categories as controls.

[27] See Chelius and Smith (1987b) for an elaboration of this proposal. This study estimates that a deductible of $3,500 per injury would remove 90 percent of all injuries from the insurance system and still provide coverage for the 10 percent of injuries that result in 85 percent of total compensation costs. Benefits to workers, of course, would remain unchanged by the presence of deductibles.

References

Accident Facts, 1987 edition. Chicago: National Safety Council, 1987.

Bartel, Ann P., and Lacy Glenn Thomas. "Direct and Indirect Effects of Regulation: A New Look at OSHA's Impact." *Journal of Law and Economics* 28 (April 1985), pp. 1-25.

Bureau of National Affairs. *Occupational Safety and Health Reporter* 17 (October 21, 1987) (No. 21).

Bureau of National Affairs. *Occupational Safety and Health Reporter* 18 (May 17, 1989) (No. 50).

Bureau of National Affairs. *Occupational Safety and Health Reporter* 19 (February 2, 1990) (No. 37).

Butler, Richard J. "Wage and Injury Rate Response to Shifting Levels of Workers' Compensation." In *Safety and the Workforce*, ed. John D. Worrall. Ithaca, NY: ILR Press, 1983.

Butler, Richard J., Harold H. Gardner, and John D. Worrall. "Moral Hazard in Workers' Compensation." Unpublished paper, Department of Economics, Brigham Young University, 1991.

Butler, Richard J., and John D. Worrall. "Workers' Compensation: Benefit and Injury Claims Rates in the Seventies." *Review of Economics and Statistics* 65 (November 1983), pp. 580-89.

________. "Work Injury Compensation and the Duration of Nonwork Spells." *Economic Journal* 95 (September 1985), pp. 714-24.

________. "Claims Reporting and Risk Bearing Moral Hazard in Workers' Compensation." *The Journal of Risk and Insurance* 53 (1991), pp. 191-204.

California Work Injuries, 1970. San Francisco: Department of Industrial Relations, 1972.

Chelius, James R. "The Control of Industrial Accidents: Economic Theory and Empirical Evidence." *Law and Contemporary Problems* 38 (Summer-Autumn 1974), pp. 700-29.

________. *Workplace Safety and Health: The Role of Workers' Compensation*. Washington, D.C.: The American Enterprise Institute for Public Policy Research, 1977.

———. "The Influence of Workers' Compensation on Safety Incentives." *Industrial and Labor Relations Review* 35 (January 1982), pp. 235-42.

Chelius, James R., and Karen Kavanaugh. "Workers' Compensation and the Level of Occupational Injuries." *Journal of Risk and Insurance* 55, no. 2 (1988), pp. 315-23.

Chelius, James R., and Robert S. Smith. "Experience-Rating and Injury Prevention." In *Safety and the Workforce*, ed. John D. Worrall. Ithaca, NY: ILR Press, 1983, pp. 128-37.

———. "Firm Size and Regulatory Compliance Costs: The Case of Workers' Compensation." *Journal of Policy Analysis and Management* 6, no. 2 (1987a), pp. 193-206.

———. *Small Business and the Financing of Workers' Compensation: Issues, Evidence and Options*. Washington, D.C.: The NFIB Foundation, 1987b.

Currington, William P. "Safety Regulation and Workplace Injuries." *Southern Economic Journal* 53, no. 1 (1986), pp. 51-72.

Dionne, Georges, and Pierre St. Michel. "Workers' Compensation and Moral Hazard." *Review of Economics and Statistics* 73, no. 2 (1991), pp. 236-44.

Economic Report of the President. Washington, D.C.: U.S. Government Printing Office, 1987.

Gardner, John A. "Benefit Increases and System Utilization: The Connecticut Experience." Unpublished paper, Workers' Compensation Research Institute, Cambridge, MA, 1991.

Gray, Wayne B., and John T. Scholz. "A Behavioral Approach to Compliance: OSHA Enforcement's Impact on Workplace Accidents." NBER Working Paper Series, no. 2813. Cambridge, MA: National Bureau of Economic Research, January 1989.

———. "Do OSHA Inspections Reduce Injuries? A Panel Analysis." NBER Working Paper Series, no. 3774. Cambridge, MA: National Bureau of Economic Research, July 1991.

Johnson, William, and Jan Ondrich. "The Duration of Post-Injury Absences from Work." *Review of Economics and Statistics* 72, no. 4 (1990), pp. 578-86.

Kniesner, Thomas J., and John D. Leeth. "Compensating Wage Differentials for Fatal Injury Risk in Australia, Japan, and the United States." *Journal of Risk and Uncertainty* 4 (January 1991), pp. 75-90.

Krueger, Alan B. "Incentive Effects of Workers' Compensation Insurance." *Journal of Public Economics* 41, no. 1 (1990a), pp. 73-99.

———. "Workers' Compensation Insurance and the Duration of Workplace Injuries." BLS Working Paper Series, no. 3253. Cambridge, MA: National Bureau of Economic Research, February 1990b.

McCaffrey, David. "An Assessment of OSHA's Recent Effects on Injury Rates." *Journal of Human Resources* 18 (Winter 1983), pp. 131-46.

Mendeloff, John. *Regulating Safety*. Cambridge, MA: MIT Press, 1979.

Meyer, Bruce D., W. Kip Viscusi, and David L. Durbin. "Workers' Compensation and Injury Duration: Evidence from a Natural Experiment." Unpublished paper, Department of Economics, Northwestern University, 1991.

Moore, Michael J., and W. Kip Viscusi. *Compensating Mechanisms for Job Risk*. Princeton: Princeton University Press, 1990.

Pollack, Earl S., and Deborah Gellerman Keimig, eds. *Counting Injuries and Illnesses in the Workplace: Proposals for a Better System*. Washington, D.C.: National Academy Press, 1987.

Report of the U.S. National Commission on State Workmen's Compensation Laws. Washington, D.C.: U.S. Government Printing Office, 1972.

Robinson, James C. *Toil and Toxics*. Berkeley, CA: University of California Press, 1991.

Ruser, John W. "Workers' Compensation Insurance, Experience-Rating, and Occupational Injuries." *Rand Journal of Economics* 16 (Winter 1985), pp. 487-503.

———. "Workers' Compensation and the Distribution of Occupational Injuries." BLS Working Paper 211. Washington, D.C.: U.S. Department of Labor, Bureau of Labor Statistics, April 1991a.

———. "Workers' Compensation and Occupational Injuries and Illnesses." *Journal of Labor Economics* 9 (October 1991b), pp. 325-50.

Ruser, John W., and Robert S. Smith. "The Effect of OSHA Records-Check Inspections on Reported Occupational Injuries in Manufacturing Establishments." *Journal of Risk and Uncertainty* 1 (December 1988), pp. 415-35.

———. "Reestimating OSHA's Effects: Have the Data Changed?" *Journal of Human Resources* 26 (Spring 1991), pp. 212-35.

Smith, Robert S. "Intertemporal Changes in Work Injury Rates." *Proceedings of the 25th Annual Meeting*, Industrial Relations Research Association. Madison, WI: IRRA, 1973, pp. 167-74.

———. "Compensating Wage Differentials and Public Policy: A Review." *Industrial and Labor Relations Review* 32 (April 1979a), pp. 339-52.

———. "The Impact of OSHA Inspections on Manufacturing Injury Rates." *Journal of Human Resources* 14 (Spring 1979b), pp. 145-70.

———. "Greasing the Squeaky Wheel: The Relative Productivity of OSHA Complaint Inspections." *Industrial and Labor Relations Review* 40 (October 1986), pp. 35-47.

———. "Mostly on Mondays: Is Workers' Compensation Covering Off-the-Job Injuries?" In *Benefits, Costs, and Cycles in Workers' Compensation*, eds. Philip S. Borba and David Appel. Boston: Kluwer Academic Publishers, 1990, pp. 115-28.

Viscusi, W. Kip. "The Impact of Occupational Safety and Health Regulation." *Bell Journal of Economics* 10 (1979), pp. 117-40.

———. "The Impact of Occupational Safety and Health Regulation." *Rand Journal of Economics* 17 (Winter 1986), pp. 567-80.

U.S. Bureau of the Census. 1982 Census of Manufacturers, vol. 1. Washington, D.C.: U.S. Government Printing Office, 1982.

Worrall, John D., and David Appel. "The Wage Replacement Rate and Benefit Utilization in Workers' Compensation Insurance." *Journal of Risk and Insurance* 49, 1982, pp. 361-71.

Worrall, John D., and Richard J. Butler. "Benefits and Claim Duration." In *Workers' Compensation Benefits: Adequacy, Equity and Efficiency*, eds. John D. Worrall and David Appel. Ithaca, NY: ILR Press, 1985, pp. 57-70.

———. "Some Lessons from the Workers' Compensation Program." In *Disability and the Labor Market*, eds. Monroe Berkowitz and M. Anne Hill. Ithaca, NY: ILR Press, 1986, pp. 95-123.

———. "Experience Rating Matters." In *Workers' Compensation Insurance Pricing*, eds. David Appel and Philip S. Borba. Boston: Kluwer Academic Publishers, 1988, pp. 81-94.

CHAPTER 17

Social Insurance and Benefits

DANIEL J.B. MITCHELL
UCLA

All developed countries provide protection against economic risk through public and/or employer-administered programs.[1] How much is provided, and the mix of public vs. private, vary substantially across national boundaries. In the United States there has been growing tension over the appropriate mix and the level of generosity. Recent debate about creating a system of national health care or about mandating employer-provided health care is but one symptom. What was the contribution in the 1980s of academic research—mainly in economics and industrial relations—to the debate over, and understanding of, social insurance and employee benefits?

It will be argued here that while much useful research was undertaken, there were deficiencies in the resulting literature. At times, narrow issues and narrow perspectives were unduly emphasized, thus widening the gap between research and application. However, the gap was two-sided. Practitioners and policymakers often failed to acquaint themselves with, or to apply, research findings or perspectives. In any case, public policy addressed the issues piecemeal, perhaps because—as will be described here—the U.S. benefits system is highly decentralized.

Finally, the question of how social insurance and benefits fit into the changing employment relationship was seldom asked. The standard model of a large firm providing benefits in the context of stable employment was eroding in the 1980s. Yet academic theorizing about benefits tended to take the standard model as given for all time and, indeed, had rationalized it as optimal. Thus, proposals to accommodate the changing employment relationship by making benefits more portable and consistent with employee mobility were unlikely to come from academics. By the end of the decade, it was primarily policymakers who were beginning to worry about such options.

Because the benefits literature is vast, this chapter concentrates on health and retirement issues. Questions of "working conditions" benefits such as vacations are not discussed, nor is the complex world of executive compensation. Finally analysis of pure tax gimmicks for the highly paid, e.g., company cars, is omitted.

Stylized Facts of Benefit Provision

What are the key characteristics of the U.S. system of benefits and social insurance? One way to respond to this question is statistically. Happily, efforts were made in the 1980s to expand the data sources available. Worthy of mention in this regard are the privately produced *EBRI Databook on Employee Benefits* (Piacentini and Cerino 1990), the U.S. Department of Labor's *Trends in Pensions* (Turner and Beller 1989), and *Health, United States* (U.S. Department of Health and Human Services 1991). Also of note are the U.S. Bureau of Labor Statistics' (BLS') regular surveys of medium-to-large firms and its expansion of the Employment Cost Index.[2]

A major data collection effort at the National Bureau of Economic Research (NBER) regarding pensions up to the late 1970s resulted in the statistical compendium *Pensions in the American Economy* (Kotlikoff and Smith 1983). By the end of the 1980s, information in this NBER volume had become somewhat dated. However, included in the tables were valuable historial data going back as far as 1950. Data-oriented articles concerning benefits and social insurance often appeared in two official journals and will undoubtedly continue to be featured in their pages: the *Monthly Labor Review* and the *Social Security Bulletin*.

Benefit Coverage

Tables 1 through 4 summarize major characteristics of the private benefit system. In Table 1, size of establishment (and firm) is shown to be positively correlated with pay levels, generally, and with benefit provision for full-time workers. Employees in big establishments not only receive more total compensation than others, they also receive a larger proportion of their pay in the form of insurance and pensions. Small establishments and firms are less likely than large ones to provide insurance or retirement benefits.

TABLE 1

Hourly Expenditures for Employee Compensation: Private Sector, March 1990

		Establishment Size (Number of Employees)			Union Status of Establishment	
	All	1-99	100-499	500 or More	Union	Nonunion
				Dollar Cost per Hour		
Total Compensation	$14.96	$13.08	$13.82	$20.02	$18.78	$14.22
Wages & salaries	10.84	9.77	10.02	13.90	12.47	10.52
Other payments*	1.43	1.05	1.25	2.38	2.17	1.28
Insurance	.92	.69	.88	1.44	1.56	.79
Pensions	.36	.29	.29	.57	.78	.28
Savings & thrift	.09	.04	.10	.19	.07	.10
Social Security	.89	.80	.84	1.15	1.08	.86
Unemployment ins.	.12	.12	.13	.12	.13	.12
Workers' comp.	.31	.32	.31	.27	.52	.27
				Percent of Total Compensation		
Total Compensation	100.0%	100.0%	100.0%	100.0%	100.0%	100.0%
Wages & salaries	72.5	74.7	72.5	69.4	66.4	74.0
Other payments*	9.6	8.0	9.0	11.9	11.6	9.0
Insurance	6.1	5.3	6.4	7.2	8.3	5.6
Pensions	2.4	2.2	2.1	2.8	4.2	2.0
Savings & thrift	.6	.3	.7	.9	.4	.7
Social Security	5.9	6.1	6.1	5.7	5.8	6.0
Unemployment ins.	.8	.9	.9	.6	.7	.8
Workers' comp.	2.1	2.4	2.2	1.3	2.8	1.9

*Leaves, vacations, wage premiums, nonproduction bonuses, other. Details need not sum to total due to rounding.

Source: U.S. Bureau of Labor Statistics, press release, USDL: 90-317, Washington, D.C., June 19, 1990; *Employer Costs for Employee Compensation in Private Industry, by Establishment Size, March 1990*, summary 91-5, April 1991.

The least likely person to receive benefits is a part-timer at a small enterprise.[3]

Unionization has an effect similar to size: union establishments feature higher compensation and are benefit-intensive (Freeman 1981). On the other hand, unionization is negatively correlated with the use of savings and thrift plans. Such programs tend to emphasize individual advance provision for retirement rather than collective entitlements. Not surprisingly, unions prefer the latter approach.

Although not shown in Table 1, public-sector employers, like unionized private employers, put more compensation into benefits than do private. Also, the kinds of benefits offered vary between the public and private sectors. For example, defined-benefit pensions are more popular (and defined contributions less popular) in public vs. private employment (Wiatrowski 1988). Historically, both union employment and public-sector employment have been associated with long job tenures and the preferences of older workers.

With regard to legally required social insurance, the size/cost relationship reverses. Larger establishments tend to spend less as a fraction of total compensation on Social Security and unemployment insurance (UI) than do smaller ones, probably because of the ceiling on taxable earnings.[4] The same is true of unionized establishments. Relative to total labor cost, workers' compensation costs fall with size of firm, suggesting economies of scale in administration. Workers' compensation is mandated private insurance in most jurisdictions. The fact that smaller firms find it proportionately more expensive undoubtedly explains their general opposition to other proposed legal mandates such as compulsory health insurance.[5] Workers' compensation costs also rise with unionization, perhaps reflecting a tendency of union workers to be located in riskier-than-average industries and occupations. In addition, unions often refer their members to attorneys who handle claims under workers' compensation and could generally be expected to inform members of their legal rights. Hence, the positive correlation is entirely reasonable.

For core employees in larger firms, both insurance and pension provision are the norm, as Table 2 illustrates. Offering medical and life insurance has become standard practice. Pensions are somewhat less common, but still cover a heavy majority of full-time workers.

TABLE 2

Percent of Full-Time Employees Participating in Selected Employee Benefit Programs, Medium and Large Firms, Private Sector, 1989

	All Employees	Prof. & Admin.*	Tech. & Clerical**	Production & Service
Medical care	92	93	91	93
Dental care	66	69	66	65
Life insurance	94	95	94	93
Pension***	81	85	81	80
Defined benefit	63	64	63	63
Defined contribution****	48	59	52	40

*Professional and administrative employees.
**Technical and clerical employees.
***Less than sum of defined benefit and defined contribution plans because some workers have both types of plans.
****Includes savings and thrift plans, deferred profit sharing, employee stock ownership, money purchase plans, and stock bonus plans.

Source: U.S. Bureau of Labor Statistics, *Employee Benefits in Medium and Large Firms, 1989*, bulletin 2363 (Washington, D.C.: GPO, 1990), p. 4.

Defined-benefit pensions—in which the benefit is typically determined by a formula relating to age, seniority, and final earnings—are the most common form. However, defined-contribution plans, which are basically employer-provided savings arrangements, are also quite common. And many workers now have both types of plans. Production and service workers are less likely than other categories to have defined-contribution plans. Union preferences for defined benefits and the lesser attractiveness of secondary tax-favored savings arrangements for blue-collar workers are significant factors in explaining the gap.

Since smaller firms are less likely than large ones to provide benefits, and since part-time workers are less likely to be eligible for benefits, Table 2 greatly overstates the coverage of private benefits for the overall wage and salary work force. Consistent and reliable economy-wide data for the United States are surprisingly hard to come by, although they tend to be much better than those reported for other countries. One study, based on Current Population Survey data, found that only 46 percent of all full-timers in the private sector were covered by some kind of pension in 1988. When coverage is defined to include only basic pension plans (and not savings plans such as 401k's), for all workers (full and part time) the figure dropped to 34 percent (Woods 1989). Even for the full-timers, the data indicated a gradual decline in coverage since the 1970s. About two-thirds of all persons with work experience in 1985 were reported covered by a work-related health insurance plan (Mitchell 1990).

The proportion of compensation received by workers in the form of direct wages and salaries has tended to fall historically, as can be seen from Table 3. Much of the decline, however, is due to increased costs of legally required social insurance. Regarding private benefits, the picture has been mixed in recent years, despite the widely held belief that the benefit share of pay inexorably rises over time. As will be discussed below, employer contributions to pensions as a percent of total compensation fell in the 1980s due to high rates of return on pension-fund assets. In contrast, health care cost containment efforts failed to stop the relative inflation of employer-provided medical plans.

TABLE 3

Trends in Components of Compensation

	Percent of Total Compensation in Each Category by Year						
	1929	1939	1949	1959	1969	1979	1989
Wages & salaries	98.7	95.5	94.9	92.4	89.6	83.9	83.6
Legally required	n.a.	n.a.	3.6	4.4	6.1	8.8	9.6
Pensions & profit sharing	n.a.	n.a.	.9	1.7	2.0	3.3	1.6
Health insurance	n.a.	n.a.	.4	1.1	1.7	3.4	4.7
Life insurance	n.a.	n.a.	.1	.3	.4	.4	.4
Other*	n.a.	n.a.	.1	.1	.1	.1	.2
Total compensation	100.0	100.0	100.0	100.0	100.0	100.0	100.0

*Consists largely of directors' fees and supplemental unemployment benefit insurance contributions.

Source: U.S. Bureau of Economic Analysis, *The National Income and Product Accounts of the United States, 1929-82: Statistical Tables* (Washington, D.C.: GPO, 1986), Tables 6.4, 6.5, 6.12, 6.13; "The U.S. National Income and Product Accounts: Revised Estimates," *Survey of Current Business* 70 (July 1990), same tables.

The final stylized statistical fact is the heavy government subsidy provided through the tax code to private employee benefits. As Table 4 shows, the federal tax revenue losses related to employer-administered retirement and insurance benefits far exceed the

TABLE 4
Tax Expenditures for Selected Employer-Provided Benefits, Fiscal Year 1990

	Revenue Loss $ billions
Pensions	$45.4
Medical	26.4
Life insurance	2.6
Accident/disability insurance	.1
ESOPs	1.9
Note: Homeowner mortgage deduction	$37.6

Source: U.S. Office of Management and Budget, *Budget of the United States Government, Fiscal Year 1992* (Washington, D.C.: GPO, 1992), Table XI-1.

more widely discussed homeowner mortgage interest deduction. Beyond the federal costs, additional tax revenue losses accrue to state governments. The major role played by the tax system in establishing and sustaining the modern American system of employer-provided benefits simply cannot be ignored.[6] Moreover, the wedge that the subsidy creates between employee value and employer cost complicates the area of benefit measurement. Even in the budget-conscious climate of the 1980s, only a few researchers were willing to suggest major cutbacks in the tax subsidy to core benefits (Munnell 1988). Perhaps this was because such suggestions seemed bound to be ignored, despite the regressive effects such subsidies often entail.

Decentralized Provision and Regulation

The most important stylized fact about the U.S. benefit system is not statistical. Rather it is the decentralized nature of the private (and some public) components of the system.[7] Legally required social insurance covers the vast majority of employees. Thus, only a small proportion of the work force (mainly in government) is not covered by Social Security. But private coverage of benefits such as pensions is at the discretion of employers. The result is a patchwork of variegated and often less-than-fully portable benefit programs. Layoffs, in particular, can put benefit coverage at risk.

A study of displaced workers who had health insurance coverage on their old jobs revealed that among those finding new jobs, about one-sixth had no coverage. Noncoverage rates were, of course, substantially higher for those remaining unemployed or out of the labor force (Podgursky and Swaim 1987; Herz 1991). The conflict between employer-linked benefits and pressures for greater employee mobility (both voluntary and involuntary) has, not surprisingly, begun to express itself in public policy initiatives.[8]

There is cross-national irony here. In the United States, where labor mobility rates have been relatively high, the private benefit system is designed for long-term job attachments. Put another way, the American benefit system has an antimobility effect, since job changing is effectively often penalized (Mitchell 1983). But in Europe, where mobility rates have long been low, the benefit system is consistent with job changing thanks to the tendency to use national benefit funds external to the firm.

U.S. benefits are also regulated on a decentralized and often uncoordinated basis. Thus, employers can escape from the rigors of state laws regulating insurance carriers by self-insuring their health benefits. Self-insurance puts them under the coverage of weaker federal regulation pursuant to the Employee Retirement Income Security Act (ERISA). It might be expected that larger firms would be best equipped to administer self-insurance. Indeed, seven out of 10 firms with 1,000 or more workers are self-insured. But the practice of self-insurance has spread as well to over one-fourth of those smaller firms that provide medical plans. Yet small firms do not have the law of large numbers in their favor when dealing with health risks (Sanchez 1991). Moreover, if a self-insured employer becomes financially unable to pay for promised benefits, adversely affected employees have relatively little recourse.

Similarly, employers can rid themselves of the rigors of ERISA-related regulation and mandatory termination insurance of defined-benefit pensions by liquidating their pensions and giving employees annuities issued by private insurance carriers. Such liquidation typically amounts to a loss of pension wealth by employees, as will be discussed later. But it also leaves them with the lesser protection of state insurance regulators. And, again, should the insurance carrier encounter financial difficulties, retirement payments are put in jeopardy since federal termination insurance no longer applies.[9]

Academic research has not focused much on regulatory incentives and misincentives of this type. The basic stylized facts of Tables 1 through 4, in contrast, are well known to researchers specializing in the compensation area. But with no one looking at the overall regulatory structure—and with regulation reacting to perceived problems on a piecemeal basis—the U.S. benefit structure ends up requiring a substantial private bureaucracy. That is, apart from governmental regulators, there need to be benefit administrators, experts, and counselors within employers. A major benefit "industry"—employers, unions, management consultants, and insurance carriers—has sprung up to lobby and interface with government regulators and lawmakers. The result has been complexity and instability of regulation.[10]

A Brief History of U.S. Benefits

Analysis of historical documents from the period before the 1930s reveals a lack of clear distinction in that early era between public vs. private provision of benefits. European systems, particularly early German social security and various collective "mutual benefit funds" in other countries, attracted considerable attention among social reformers in the United States. Even within public provision in the United States, there was no clear line drawn between what would today be considered "welfare"—e.g., programs such as AFDC which are means-tested, and those that would be viewed today as social insurance—e.g., retirement entitlements under Social Security. Proposed and actual state-run "widows' (or mothers') pension" schemes in the 1920s were an example of this ambiguity. Widows' pensions were financed out of general revenue rather than employer/employee contributions and were means-tested. Yet they eventually evolved into survivors' insurance under Social Security, which, in contrast, is funded out of employer/employee contributions and is not means-tested.

As another example, the 41 so-called "state old-age pension acts" in existence when the Social Security Act was passed in 1935 were essentially relief laws, not pensions in the modern sense (Parker 1936). These programs, the earliest of which dated from 1915, became the basis of federal-state means-tested old-age assistance, which still continues. The use of the word "pension" during and prior to the 1930s to describe private company plans, government relief programs, and social insurance illustrates the blurry lines that once separated such programs.

Benefits provided by firms were termed "welfare work" in the early part of the twentieth century. The phrase had a connotation of doing "good works." Employer welfare benefits were often seen as part of a continuum running from provision of such benefits by various fraternal, ethnic, or religious mutual aid societies to the beneficial programs of unions and to various embryonic government programs. Exactly what ideally was supposed to be in the employer's benefit "package" was also unclear. Medical insurance as it is understood today—i.e., reimbursement of doctor and hospital bills—was rare. Paid sick leave and disability were more likely to be viewed by employers as constituting the core of the health plan, perhaps combined with some kind of company clinic or "hospital." Workers' compensation, which states were increasingly mandating, was often seen as a health plan. In any case, health was not necessarily the focus of welfare work. Thus, housing, savings institutions (savings and loans, credit unions), and burial insurance might also have been part of a corporate program of welfare work.

When government stepped in and provided a previously existing private benefit, employers sometimes discontinued their programs or modified them. Thus, in a 1939 survey, about half of pension plans discontinued during the previous decade were reported to have terminated due to the passage of the 1935 Social Security Act. Of 164 pre-1935 plans still active, the proportion reported to have been "revised" due to the Act was also one-half (BLS 1940). Even today, many private pensions are formally "integrated" with Social Security, suggesting a substitution between public and private programs.

Social Security

Social Security's political popularity resulted from careful sculpting by its initiators and proponents. The distinction between the program's redistributive aspects and insurance aspects was left deliberately fuzzy, owing to popular aversion to accepting charity and relief and to distrust of government. Failure of some private pension plans during the depression, even though such plans covered only a very small fraction of the work force, helped justify government administration of Social Security. But, somewhat paradoxically, the existence of welfare programs within certain firms also served as a model for the new government program (Jacoby 1991).

Leverage from various social movements of the 1930s helped in the enactment of Social Security. Notable among these was the Townsend movement—a populist proposal aimed at ending the depression by providing the elderly with a guaranteed income conditional on both retirement and quick consumption. Social movements were again harnessed after enactment of Social Security to widen its coverage and increase benefits.

The growth of the trust fund surplus in the years immediately after the program's enactment was denounced by early Keynesians on the left as the root of the 1937 recession and by critics on the political right as a dangerous accretion of government resources. Program proponents took advantage of these charges to run down the surplus through expansion of benefits. They thereby locked in Social Security as *the* national pension system (Bernstein 1985; Achenbaum 1986). The seeds for the notion that Social Security is an inviolable "compact with the people," in Wilbur Cohen's words 50 years later, were planted at that time (Cohen 1985, p. 127).

Technical complexities of the Social Security program were also used to expand benefits. Congress was persuaded to adopt an escalator formula in the 1970s which in fact produced benefit increases exceeding the rate of inflation. This "error" was eventually corrected, but not before benefits were significantly elevated relative to wage levels. Today, even long-service workers with generous defined-benefit pensions in the private sector can expect to receive anywhere from a third to a half of retirement income from Social Security.[11] Not surprisingly, Social Security enjoys strong support from the electorate. When the system's financial crisis began to unfold in the late 1970s and early 1980s, public confidence in the program's viability began to decline. Academic discussion turned toward fundamental changes in the system which were, in some cases, outside political realities. But politicians across a broad spectrum moved quickly to fix the problem within the existing framework.

Substitution of Public for Private Benefits

For private, work-related benefits, the legal distinction concerning who pays for benefits—employer or employee—became important because of tax treatment.[12] In the late nineteenth and early twentieth centuries, however, the tax element was of little significance. And since workers moved from job to job more frequently than today, the existence of many union-run benefit plans at the time was hardly surprising. Such union plans were used as organizing tools, an idea which was revived in the 1980s by the AFL-CIO as it sought ways of offsetting membership losses.[13] But there was also an ideological element of workers controlling their own economic fates that contributed to the establishment of union-run plans. Thus, at least 25 labor-affiliated banks, through which workers could save for retirement, were in existence in the mid-1920s (BLS 1924).

Today, unemployment insurance is seen as "naturally" a state-run program. Except for the few supplemental unemployment benefit (SUB) plans in certain unionized industries, private unemployment insurance is often thought to be impossible to provide due to moral hazard and, possibly, adverse selection. However, in the 1920s and early 1930s, there were in existence company, union, and joint company-union unemployment benefit plans (BLS 1931). These were later eclipsed by the state-federal UI program created in 1935, not to mention the Great Depression.[14] But had government not stepped in, the private plans might have revived and evolved more fully.

Moral hazard and adverse selection problems exist with virtually all forms of private insurance. Some people with fire insurance burn down their property to collect from their policies; individuals with terminal health problems may attempt to acquire life insurance. Yet sufficient controls can often be put in place to make the offering of insurance feasible. The same might have been true regarding UI, particularly if offered through the employer. As in the case of other areas where public policy influenced private benefit offerings, researchers should not make the mistake of assuming that the observed outcome was inevitable.

Looking Backwards: Private Benefits Without a Government Role

It is thus useful to ask what employee benefits looked like before the age of tax incentives, government-provided social insurance, and the general expansion of regulation. In addition, it is especially useful to look at a period prior to the eruption of a major threat of unionization during World War I. Since unions were potential benefit providers, employers suddenly had wartime incentives to install benefits simply to compete with unions. But the pre-World

War I period was "uncontaminated" by such influences. Data for the pre-World War I period are, of course, limited. Nevertheless, some information is available thanks to early work by the U.S. Bureau of Labor Statistics.

Table 5 presents data collected from a 1913 BLS survey of employer "welfare work" (Otey 1913). Surveyed employers included such well-known names as Metropolitan Life, the Union Pacific Railroad, R.H. Macy & Co., H.J. Heinz, and General Electric. Consistent with the style of BLS publications of that era, the study did not present statistical tabulations. Instead, to produce Table 5, a count was made of references to 18 particular types of benefits or programs described in the 50 case studies found in the

TABLE 5

Proportion of Firms in 1913 Study with Presence of Selected Welfare Practice

Practice	All Firms	High Commitment Firms	Low Commitment Firms
Formal welfare dept. or secretary	16%	44%	0%
Employee representation plan	2	11	0
Company housing	16	0	44
Training/apprenticeship program	18	33	22
General education facilities	10	11	0
Eating facility	68	78	44
On-site medical facility or attendant	42	78	22
Other recreational/cultural facility[a]	86	89	89
Special attention to lighting/ventilation	36	56	11
Other noteworthy health and safety policies	6	22	0
Sickness/disability pay	72	100	11
Pension plan	20	22	11
Stock or profit-sharing plan	8	11	0
Death benefits	56	89	0
Accident benefits[b]	10	33	0
Mutual benefit association	54	100	0
Paid vacation plan	18	22	11
Formal link to savings institution or plan	18	44	11

[a] Presence of a locker room is not counted.

[b] Plans providing compensation for loss of limbs and similar injuries excluding sickness/disability plans.

Note: The 50 firms described in the 1913 study were ranked by the proportion of the 18 welfare programs listed above which they provided. The top nine firms on this ranking are reported as "high-commitment firms"; the bottom nine are reported as "low-commitment firms."

Source: 1913 BLS survey of employer "welfare work" (Otey 1913).

report. Selection of the 18 programs was made on the basis of judgment; these were the arrangements which the BLS report's author seemed to feel were important forms of welfare work. The 50 firms were ranked by the proportion of benefits or programs provided, and the top and bottom nine firms in the ranking were arbitrarily dubbed "high commitment" and "low commitment" firms, respectively, for their commitment (or lack thereof) to welfare work.[15]

Apart from the data on the table, four characteristics of early welfare work can be ascertained from the report. First, there was a heavy overlay of paternalism at many firms. Thus, sickness benefits at one firm (which meant paid sick leave) were denied to those whose maladies were the result of indiscretions such as bicycle racing and intoxication. A variety of cultural activities (employee choirs, libraries, social clubs, etc.) were included at some firms to uplift the untutored immigrant work forces of the period. Welfare secretaries were sometimes appointed to serve as counselors to whom employees could take their problems. But these secretaries could also serve as monitors available to weed out those who did not fit in with what would today be termed the "corporate culture."

Second, employers often saw themselves as catalysts helping employees help themselves. Thus, benefits were frequently provided through company-established and affiliated mutual aid societies to which employees paid dues. Connections with savings institutions might also be provided to encourage employees to learn the virtues of thrift. Employees would thus learn not to be overly dependent on employer beneficence for their illnesses or retirement.

Third, the benefits that today might be considered part of a core package were not so important then. Pensions existed only in about a fifth of the surveyed firms. And the rules for eligibility were such that few workers were likely ever to draw benefits. There may have been no vesting at all and no pre-funding of benefits. Payment to retirees might be discretionary with the employer. Indeed, a company might overtly proclaim that its pension system should not be regarded by workers as an entitlement.

No true medical insurance seems to have existed. It is difficult to know how much care workers might have received from the company medical facilities mentioned in the BLS report. However, these facilities appear to have been aimed mainly at on-site accidents.

Death benefits were often found in welfare programs but for sums basically limited to burial insurance. In contrast, death benefits under modern employer-provided life insurance often exceed annual salary.

Fourth, although some employers claimed to obtain productivity advantages from providing welfare work,[16] there is little evidence in the report of any systematic attempt by employers to measure these purported gains. For those companies that engaged heavily in welfare work, there was a sense that the various services offered were all "good things" to be doing. All employers could produce some rationale for what they provided; none would say they were simply giving away money. But documentation of the alleged gains was scarce.

Although contemporary benefit administration has become more professional, it is likely that similar employer responses would be found if a comparable survey were taken today. Those firms that offer benefits would say that there are gains to morale or productivity. But few would systematically endeavor to prove it. Indeed, many would dismiss the idea that their basic benefit package was designed to encourage any specific behaviors other than general appreciation of employer good will. As Lazear (1990, p. 273) has reported with regard to pensions:

> Human resource administrators often resist the idea that pensions can be used to affect incentives. Even personnel people think of pensions and other deferred compensation as a fringe with few effects other than the enhancement of the recipients' income.[17]

Government as Employer, Provider, or Mandating Authority

In the early part of the twentieth century, the question of how to provide benefits, through government or private arrangements, was less of an issue when government itself was the employer. As part of a study of possible pension arrangements for federal civil servants in 1916, the U.S. Bureau of Labor Statistics examined plans in foreign countries and at the state and local level (BLS 1916). Only four states at the time had comprehensive pension arrangements for their own workers. But 159 municipalities had pension plans. In contrast, the BLS listed only 117 private companies with pensions, 51 of which were railroads or utilities. Thus government, although servicing its own employees, was often viewed by reformers as providing a role model for private employers who, in turn, were seen as not doing enough.

The issue of government vs. private provision remains a live issue today. Politicians have generally learned that careless utterances about privatizing Social Security are to be avoided. But professional economists, presumably those without political ambitions, sometimes make such suggestions. With regard to medical insurance, there have been periodic pushes for government-run health plans. Such ideas in the American context go back to the period 1915-20 when a drive for state laws developed momentum (but ultimately failed).[18] At the time, the American Medical Association (AMA), whose later opposition to national health insurance was crucial in preventing the adoption of such a program, was still uncertain of its position. It contented itself with specifying desirable principles to be incorporated in a hypothetical program, should one be created. The AMA's ambivalence was understandable. After all, health insurance meant subsidizing the use of physicians' services. But it also might mean government regulation of what could be charged for those services.

Ultimately, AMA opposition arose from the fear of controls on fees and other matters. This opposition continued until 1990-91, when the AMA again began to look favorably at a national program of some type for the noninsured.[19] AMA opposition in the 1930s and 1940s eliminated health insurance from early proposals for the Social Security program and killed a plan pushed by President Truman after World War II. But the AMA could not kill the 1960s Medicare proposal because of the program's sympathetic targeting of the elderly and because of its sentimental link to recently assassinated President Kennedy. However, successful blockage of a federal medical program for the non-elderly left the field open to private health insurance.

The open field ultimately produced the preponderance of employer-provided health plans that exists today. Insurance carriers discovered in the World War I period—when welfare work crested—that they could sell life insurance in profitable volumes through certain large employers who provided it at no direct cost to workers. The carriers persisted in this marketing endeavor in the 1920s, even though in that era employers simply offered employees the opportunity to buy group life insurance at their own expense.

Eventually, medical insurance followed life insurance. And it ultimately became largely employer-provided thanks to the tax code. Gaps in employer-provided coverage, however, have given rise to recent calls for federal- or state-mandated programs. Under these proposals, all employers would be required to provide a basic health plan or pay into some government-created program.

Benefits for Elderly Employees and for Retirees

For elderly workers over 65, the presence of Medicare requires coordination of employer-provided health insurance with the government's program. Legislative changes in the age discrimination area effectively have made employers provide the initial coverage for such workers, with Medicare acting as supplement. But for retirees, some employers provide supplemental retiree insurance, using Medicare as the primary insurer. Employers have recently been pulling back on their retiree coverage due in part to cost and in part to new accounting standards requiring that future unfunded retiree health insurance coverage appear explicitly in corporate balance sheets. This pullback, in turn, intensified pressure for an enhanced national program.[20]

Optimality or Historical Accident?

Economists might well be troubled with the vision of the U.S. benefit system as the product of a series of historical accidents, social movements, and regulatory currents, each building on one another in a rather haphazard fashion. There is a tendency to want to see a profit/utility maximizing strategy behind the system, at least as it operates at the firm level. Of course, sociologists and historians might have trouble viewing benefits as having any firm-level optimizing rationale behind them; the social interplay of forces might seem to them to be the more natural explanation. But the historical record suggests a blend of the two approaches.

The brief summary just given reveals that a variety of complex influences has brought forth the contemporary American system. Employee "tastes" have been conditioned by past practice and are not immutable. For example, about six out of ten Americans have employment-related health insurance. This coverage comes either from their own work experience or the work of spouses or parents. Of those covered by private health insurance, but not by Medicare or Medicaid, eight out of ten have it from an employment-related source (U.S. Bureau of the Census 1990, p. 100). Given this state of affairs, it seems natural today for workers to look toward employers as *the* source of health insurance. Indeed, those firms that do not provide such benefits to regular employees, especially if they are large companies, might be seen by job seekers as signaling that they are bad places to work. It thus becomes rational for firms to offer health insurance simply because others do so. What is true for health insurance is also true for other benefits.

When benefits are not provided as expected, there is a tendency for policymakers to look for ways to induce or require recalcitrant employers to do their duty. The battle then becomes one of incentives, through the tax code or via other forms of subsidy, or mandates. Thus, the issue of mandated health insurance (and other benefits such as family leave) developed in the 1980s and continued into the 1990s. Mandates also tend to be the compromise between liberals (who prefer public to private provision, but may grudgingly accept mandates) and conservatives (who prefer private to public provision, but may reluctantly accept mandates). Finally, in an era of taxpayer resistance, mandates appear more attractive than direct government programs because they do not run through official budgets.

Research on Employer-Provided Health Insurance

The interests of researchers, practitioners, and policymakers were most closely joined in the 1980s on the topic of health care cost containment. By the end of the decade, the United States found itself spending substantially more on a per capita and percent-of-GNP basis than other advanced countries and yet achieving no obvious payoff in terms of such gross outcomes as life expectancy. There are, of course, conceptual problems with the widely used health expenditure/GNP ratio; the numerator is in gross terms while the denominator is essentially value-added. Nonetheless, the United States seemed to be doing more "caring" without achieving more "curing."[21]

Employers complained bitterly about rising costs of their health plans, although, as noted earlier, they may not have fully considered the degree to which their workers may ultimately pay for these trends. Rising medical costs added to pressure on Congress to provide coverage for those individuals who did not have employer-provided or government-provided insurance. Academics tended to explore options for cost containment within the existing system. To the extent that Congress looked for guidance on broader options which would transform the system, it was more likely to turn to the U.S. General Accounting Office and Washington types than to university academics.

Rising Health Costs

The ratio of national health expenditures to GNP rose from 4.5 percent in 1950 to 11.1 percent in 1988.[22] Although there have been occasional pauses in the upward march of this ratio, no dramatic downturns have been observed. It is easy to find ingredients in the recipe for rising health costs. With copayments ranging from zero to relatively small amounts, individuals are encouraged to consume more health services. It is difficult to provide insurance against medical risk without at the same time providing a de facto subsidy to the use of medical services. Moreover, the tax code, it is often argued, leads to excessive insurance, particularly for first-dollar amounts (as opposed to "catastrophic" care). Rising costs raise the demand for insurance, which in turn raises demand.

In addition, health consumers are at an information disadvantage in judging appropriate expenditures. They must rely on providers (physicians, hospitals, etc.) to tell them what they need. This reliance opens up a potential principal/agent problem, particularly if the agent is aware that the principal is insured and will carry little or none of the cost. Expectations of patients regarding outcomes are high and the threat of malpractice suits may produce further inducements for consumption of expensive tests. In addition, nonprofit providers may have only limited incentives to hold down costs and may stimulate use of high-quality (expensive) procedures and seek to maximize use of professional services.

The problem with these bits and pieces is that they all suggest that there should be more health services consumed as a percent of GNP, and probably at higher prices, than an uninsured and unsubsidized market would provide. But they do not necessarily suggest indefinite relative inflation and a continually rising share of GNP. Perhaps the analogy might be the union wage effect. The union differential in theory is thought to reach an equilibrium after the union fully exploits its bargaining potential. It is not expected to rise forever.

However, the empirical history of the union wage effect indicates that such theoretical steady-state equilibria are not necessarily found in practice. The U.S. union/nonunion wage differential has exhibited long waves of expansion and decline. Perhaps something like that process is at work in determining the ratio of health care expenditures to GNP. If that is the case, however, the contractionary phase has yet to be observed, despite all of the efforts since the 1960s at health care cost containment. Indeed, rising health care costs may trigger additional expenditures on other types of collateral benefits. It has been argued, for example, that "wellness" programs, employee assistance programs, and the like are a good investment for employers seeking to hold down the costs of their health care plans.[23] Research in this area has been limited, and claims of economic gains for employers are often made by advocates.

The sad fact is that it cannot be said on the basis of the empirical evidence that there is an equilibrium to the health expenditure/GNP ratio. There is even uncertainty about why individuals want health insurance, absent a tax subsidy. Is it just for the risk of catastrophic expenses? Or is there a "moral choice" element? It has been suggested, for example, that by having comprehensive insurance, individuals are spared having to trade off cost vs. benefit regarding possible treatments for loved ones. The moral choice—placing a value on someone's life—is avoided if there is insurance available that will pay for whatever treatment is available.

Are There Cost Containment Solutions?

Researchers have generally shied away from offering wholesale solutions for rising health costs. Some researchers have made suggestions for improving particular elements of the system, e.g., malpractice litigation reform. Policymakers have also focused on specific system components. An obvious example is federal encouragement of health maintenance organizations (HMOs), beginning in the early 1970s. Under the original federal HMO Act, employers were required to offer an HMO option if they offered any health plan at all, assuming there was an HMO in their area. (Amendments to the Act adopted in 1988 relax various rules and will end the dual-choice requirement in 1995.)

HMOs offer health care through their own facilities (or contracted facilities) on a flat, monthly fee basis; they thus have incentives to hold down costs. Modern HMOs are modeled after the Kaiser Plan, a program initially established for Kaiser steelworkers that gained a major foothold in California. Even today, after years of federal encouragement of HMOs, these programs remain especially concentrated in the western region (Bucci 1991). Generally, both HMOs and a related innovation—preferred provider organizations (PPOs)—have expanded at the expense of conventional fee-for-service plans. (PPOs require the insured to use a panel of selected providers or receive significantly reduced reimbursements.)

Both HMOs and PPOs have the effect of limiting consumer choice. This result seems to be part of the universal trade-off: less choice in exchange for cost containment. There is some evidence that constrained-choice plans do cut expenditures. HMOs in part ration access to care via queuing as a substitute for marginal cost pricing. Time value of the insured then acts to hold down usage of HMO services. But since consumer tastes toward queuing and other aspects of service will vary, the HMO option will work best for a homogeneous consumer population, assuming there is enough competition to provide various "qualities" of HMOs. Still, part of the apparent cost cutting effect of HMOs may simply result from their ability to "cream" the market of healthy persons.

To the extent that employers believe that HMOs and PPOs will reduce costs, research does suggest that employees can be induced to shift toward these plans, especially if the HMO or PPO option involves some reduction in patient out-of-pocket expenses. Copayments also reduce health expenditures in fee-for-service programs. Employers have incentives to reduce costs even with full recognition of the incidence effect.[24] That is because a firm that can deliver a given set of health benefits at lower cost than competitors will be at an advantage in the labor market. Such a firm could, in principle, pay lower total compensation or recruit higher quality workers.

Thus, in the 1980s, there was a proliferation of employer experimentation with second opinions, controls on hospital admissions, use of hospices, etc. But there was also a strong element of faddism in these efforts, with "managed care" (typically hiring a consultant to review and screen prospective expenditures) being the latest. American management has been prone to faddism in other labor areas: consider "total quality management" or "quality circles" as examples. Thus, it is not surprising that enthusiasm for particular health care cost containment strategies would sweep the marketplace from time to time.

In part, the faddism in health care cost containment occurs because the findings of academic researchers regarding particular approaches are modest and qualified. And what academics actually know about cost containment does not necessarily reach the practitioner market. However, consultants selling cost-constraining strategies are unlikely to be modest or qualified about the promised results. And they have strong incentives to make themselves accessible.

Third-party payers (insurance companies, government authorities in programs such as Medicare) also have incentives to hold down expenditures. Private insurers who can offer given packages at lower cost will be naturally attractive to employers for the reasons just cited. And government agencies face budgetary constraints. One common method of cost containment is to control reimbursement schedules for providers. However, there is the potential for cost containers to work against one another or to shuffle costs to some outside party. Success by Medicare and Medicaid authorities in holding down costs for their patients may lead to cost shifting toward private patients and their insurers. But there are limits to this strategy, particularly if there are profit-making providers in the market who can refuse patients and who will tend to use marginal cost pricing. The costs are then pushed to local public hospitals (which cannot turn away patients) and, thereby, to local taxpayers.

Screening potential new hires for health risks is rational from the viewpoint of employers. Thus, firms may exclude new hires with preexisting conditions from their health plans. Apart from the anti-mobility effects this exclusion creates, it also has the effect of shifting costs directly to the new hire. In fact, even copayments and deductibles have that effect. While these devices may tend to overcome the effects of overinsurance, part of the way they save money is simply by transferring costs directly to the patient. The shifting effect by itself does not reduce the national health bill, although the behavioral effect might.

Since there are incentives to screen high-risk workers out of health plans, there will undoubtedly be pressures to limit employer ability to do so through new public policies. Futuristic possibilities of risk assessment—such as genetic testing for disease susceptibility—no longer seem far off. Thus, if a mandated plan of employer-provided health care is adopted, it will almost certainly come with rules forbidding rejection of coverage on account of health status. However, unless financial transfers between insurance carriers are made (so that all employers pay a uniform premium based on average labor-force risks), there will then be temptation to discriminate in hiring against health risks. Obviously, such actions would work against other public policies such as nondiscrimination on the basis of handicap.[25]

A New Health Insurance System?

In the late 1970s, predictions were often made that national health insurance would soon be adopted. In the late 1980s, the predictions shifted toward mandated, employer-provided health insurance. Obviously, such programs are more likely to be adopted at the national level by Democratic than Republican administrations. The 1991 *Economic Report of the President* (pp. 136-43) described the misincentives inherent in health insurance and blamed overregulation at the state level for inability of private insurers to offer a "bare-bones, low-cost" policy to the uninsured. But mandates were not suggested.

However, with large employers beginning to look favorably at a national plan, and with the AMA endorsing some kind of universal program, the federal political balance is moving toward a significant change in the national health system. And at the state level, it is quite possible that the political appeal of universal coverage could attract endorsements across the political spectrum.[26] Given these shifts, there is clearly a need for academics to add overall redesign of the health insurance and delivery system to their research agenda.

Pension Research

No review of pension research in the 1980s would be complete without formal reference to the major studies of pensions and retirement behavior sponsored by the National Bureau of Economic Research (NBER). Apart from the compendium of historical data noted earlier, several symposium volumes have appeared. In addition, current studies of pensions continue to appear in the NBER's important working paper series. The NBER's sponsorship has attracted substantial attention of economists to the pension area, an interest which was reflected in the standard journals and books by other publishers.

Pensions raise issues apart from the usual concerns of labor economists and industrial relations researchers. They have an important financial side due to the large portfolios involved. The financial approach to pensions spilled into the benefit evaluation side of pensions, too. Modern finance is intimately connected with the study of risk. And pensions can be viewed as financial instruments dealing with risk, not just as saving plans. Beneficiaries are insured against the economic risk of living "too long" and thus exhausting their resources. In addition, the accumulation of pension assets has become an important form of saving. Thus, pensions must be viewed as significant components of the macro economy. And finally, of course, there is the view of pensions as a micro-level personnel practice with possible consequences for employee behavior.

The Financial View of Pensions

Although it may seem natural to Americans that defined-benefit pensions should be backed by pension trust funds, there are alternative ways of handling corporate pension liabilities. In Germany, for example, it is common practice for companies simply to carry a bookkeeping reserve of accrued pension liabilities for tax purposes but not to set up independent pension funds. The system can work so long as government and financial institutions effectively operate to avert major bankruptcies.

In the early days of pensions in the United States, unfunded plans were also not unusual. Formal pension trusts were commonplace, however, by the 1950s, but even then pensions were often not fully funded. And some pensions remained completely on a pay-as-you-go basis. Where trusts were used, but insufficient funding was applied, reserves might nevertheless mount as long as there were many more active workers than retirees. But should the firm go bankrupt, adequate funds to pay accrued pension liabilities might be lacking. "Horror stories" of elderly workers losing expected benefits were instrumental in the passage of ERISA in 1974. The new act established funding standards and created a federal agency, the Pension Benefit Guarantee Corporation (PBGC) to insure private pensions against termination.

From the finance perspective, the felt need by Congress to compel employers to fund their pensions, and to protect workers from breaches in funding, is peculiar. The returns on assets properly accumulated in pension trusts are not subject to taxation. Hence, if anything, firms should want to overfund pensions to take advantage of the tax shelter (Tepper 1981). The problem should be to keep them from overfunding. Indeed, regulators have assumed that firms will want to overfund and have adopted tax regulations to prevent it. So why don't all employers automatically fully fund their pensions up to the legal limit?

One response has been that the existence of termination insurance makes it optimal to underfund and to shift some risk to the PBGC. The difficulty with this explanation is that it neglects the historical background of underfunding that originally led to the passage of ERISA. Before creation of the PBGC, firms should have been funding to the maximum allowed by tax law. But they weren't. Were managers trying to fool shareholders by accumulating pension liabilities that they thought could not be seen through the corporate veil? Apparently not, since pension liabilities seem to be reflected in stock prices (Feldstein and Seligman 1981).

Corporate restructuring in the 1980s added to the puzzle. So-called corporate raiders sometimes took "excess" assets from pension funds and used them for other purposes. Or incumbent managers might take such assets as part of a defense against a raid.[27] Pensions could be terminated and the employees given annuities which satisfied the legal requirements of ERISA but, for reasons discussed below, inflicted losses on employees. Possibly there was a transfer of wealth from workers to shareholders in such cases. But there is some evidence that premiums paid for firms that were taken over were larger than the asset reversion, suggesting that wealth transfer was but one of several motivations behind takeovers (Pontiff, Shleifer, and Weisbach 1990).

One interpretation that might be made of the underfunding puzzle is that it represents an efficient incentive plan for employees. In effect, the retirement fate of each worker is tied up with the economic performance of the firm. But firms have other, more direct options of providing such incentives—e.g., profit sharing. The potentially drastic consequence of the (pre-PBGC) underfunded pension as an incentive—you bet your (retirement) life on the company's health—makes the pension-as-clever-profit-sharing story dubious.

In short, the underfunding of pensions is a puzzle unless corporate managers view pension promises more lightly than public policy would like them to. When unionized firms negotiated pensions in the late 1940s and 1950s, the defined-benefit form may have been chosen simply because it was compatible with immediate benefits to impending retirees. The long-term implications of pension promises may not have been fully appreciated. Firms at the time may have viewed these plans only as near-term promises to those close to retirement. They may not have seen them as absolute entitlements for workers whose retirements might lie 20 or more years in the future.

From the employer's perspective, fully funding those future retirements years in advance would have made the entitlements absolute. So, despite the tax advantages, firms may have been reluctant to make such contributions to trust funds. Even if unions did understand the long-term liabilities they were negotiating, they may have gone along with the limited-funding approach as part of a bargaining compromise. Unions obtained near-term retirement packages for their members. The future would be dealt with when it arrived.

This fuzzy commitment by employers toward pension payments is a messier view of the pension promise than many would like. But it may well be the actual answer to the underfunding mystery. Public employers, it should be noted, are not covered by ERISA and do not have to meet federal funding requirements. Underfunding of pensions by governments is a common practice, again suggesting that employers do not like ironclad commitments if they can be avoided.[28]

Social Investment

Unions played a major role in the passage of ERISA. But apart from that effort, they showed little interest in pension investment strategy until the late 1970s when the idea of "social investment" began to take hold. It was argued that pension investment policy could be used to punish antiunion employers. Related to that idea was the possibility of using pension investment for other purposes such as pressuring American multinationals to withdraw from South Africa.

Such strategies do not fit well in standard economic analysis. In principle, "bad" firms could be punished only if divestment by pension funds led to a decline in their stock prices. Unless most investors refrained from holding the stock of such firms, however, the main effect might be a portfolio shuffle; divesting social investors would sell the shares but other investors would purchase them, leaving stock prices unchanged. There certainly were portfolio reshuffles in the 1980s involving union-influenced and certain public employer pension funds. However, evidence has not been produced showing such policies reduced share prices.

Nonetheless, divestment strategies can be linked to public relations campaigns, protests at stockholder meetings, and support by pension trustees for positions and slates not favored by management. The general issue of corporate campaigns by unions was studied in the 1980s, but the particular effects of social investment could stand more research. It would be useful to disentangle the pure disinvestment threat effect from the impact of bad PR.

Closely related to social investment strategies were attempts to use pension funds to stimulate demand for union labor, particularly during periods of depressed labor markets. Pension investments were channeled in some cases to unionized construction projects. In principle, ERISA standards require that pension trustees not invest in projects with below-market returns.[29] And in theory, if the projects could produce market returns, they would not need to obtain loans from particular pension funds; other lenders would be happy to provide the funding. However, the range of returns observable in the market and the difficulty in assessing risk leave a range of discretion and the possibility of a hidden subsidy to favored projects. Again, it would be useful for researchers to examine cases of job creation via pensions. There are significant public policy issues here regarding permissible pension investment standards.

Pensions as Saving

The importance of pensions as a component of personal saving is often not well understood. Indeed, many people who look at the personal saving rate reported in the national income accounts probably do not realize that pension saving is included. In effect, pension saving is treated as merely another private decision by individuals despite the formal administrative arrangements surrounding pensions. This methodology is in keeping with a view that saving via pensions substitutes perfectly for other forms of saving over which there is more direct individual control. It also assumes that any pension saving beyond the overall level the individual would undertake can be undone through borrowing. These assumptions are open to question.

Figure 1 shows a dramatic shift in the ratio of pension benefits paid out to contributions paid in during the 1980s. The sharp rise in the ratio was due to movements in both contributions and benefits. Returns on assets rose during the 1980s. In effect, as higher returns on assets pushed up funding ratios, employers cut back on contributions.[30] Nonetheless, Figure 1 shows that net pension saving (contributions + returns on assets − payouts) fell dramatically. The acceleration of benefit payouts was an important factor in the drop. While some of the benefit increase may have been due to a maturing of pension plan liabilities, much of it was due to cash distributions to relatively young workers. ERISA vesting standards may have played a role; with lower vesting standards workers who

FIGURE 1

Ratios: Return on Assets/Contributions and Benefits/Contributions

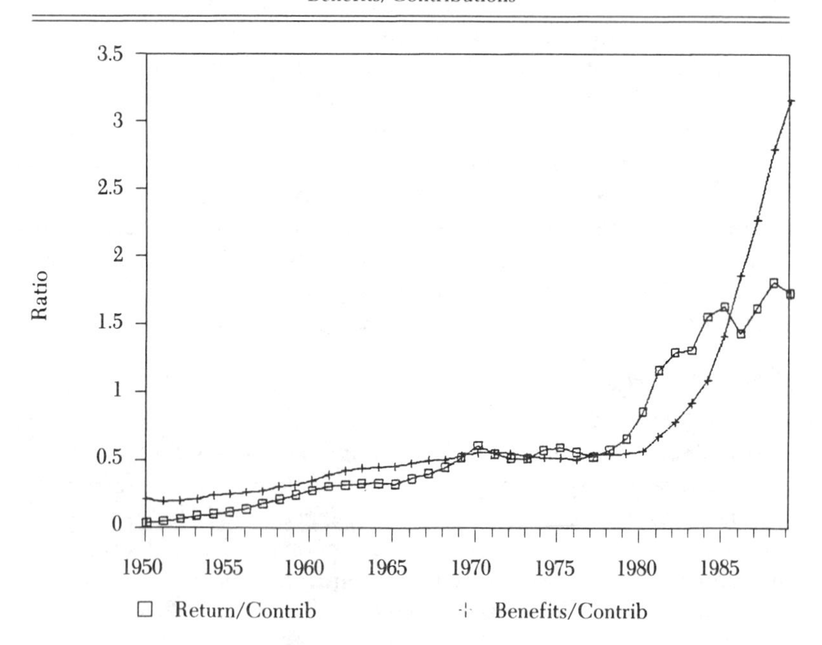

quit or were laid off were more likely to have some pension entitlement. In addition, termination and liquidation of defined-benefit pensions in the 1980s may have played a part in raising total pension distributions.

The intersection of the two lines on Figure 2 (showing saving including and excluding pensions) represents a drop from a net pension saving rate of close to 4 percent of personal disposable income down to zero by the late 1980s. However, the data of Figure 2 are only rough estimates of the actual movement.[31] Nonetheless, as Figure 2 demonstrates, the removal of the estimated pension effect from the official personal saving rate changes the magnitude and timing of reported personal saving decisions. In particular, the drop in saving after the Reagan tax cuts in 1981 appears to have been largely concentrated in pensions. The tax cuts, it may be recalled, were supposed to stimulate private saving. While there is no sign of that, the cuts do not seem to have perversely reduced the saving directly controlled by individuals.[32]

FIGURE 2

Personal Saving/Disposable Income Including and Excluding Pension Saving

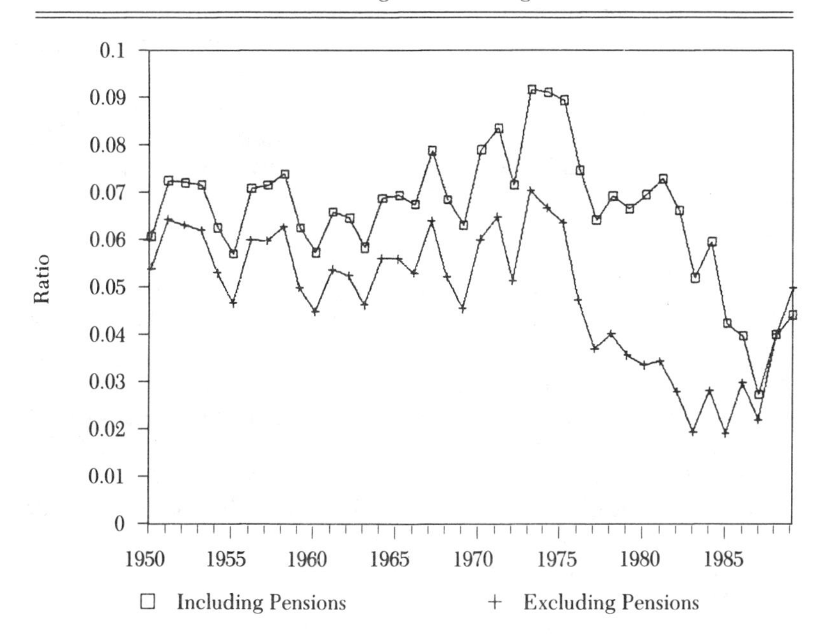

There has been some recognition of the pension-saving effect in the literature. However, the effect clearly deserves more study. Pension-saving behavior, for example, might have a bearing on the saving-interest rate elasticity or on the structure of interest rates. Finally, pensions and Social Security may have played an important role in the declining labor force participation of the elderly, especially males. Even if these programs had no effect overall on total saving, they tilt wealth toward an asset which can only be used by retiring or, in the case of a pension, at least quitting.[33] Moreover, the asset cannot generally be directly bequeathed (except to a spouse). Thus, the saving, finance, and labor force perspectives ultimately come together. Long-term macro policy relating to growth and productivity needs to take account of the pension effect.

Regulatory Issues

ERISA influences both the financial side of pensions and the benefit side. On the financial side, it establishes funding and investment standards and also creates a termination insurance mechanism through the PBGC. That the two should go together is fairly obvious (although perhaps not to those who deregulated savings and loans in the 1980s while continuing to insure their deposits!). Nonetheless, there are misincentives, particularly in the cases of firms near or in bankruptcy, to push their pension liabilities to the PBGC, the so-called PBGC "put."

Pension insurance began to show the same strains as deposit insurance in the 1980s. As liabilities are dumped at the PBGC, premiums for termination insurance are raised and regulations become more onerous. Thus, the decline in use of defined-benefit plans (which are insured) relative to defined-contribution plans (which are not) should not be surprising. Economists associated with the PBGC have looked, almost wistfully, at private solutions. Risk-adjusted premiums seem a logical solution but they do not appeal to Congress, in part because in the transition high premiums might push precariously perched plans over the edge.

Thus, the system has a dynamic towards more regulation and more discouragement of defined-benefit plans relative to defined contribution. For reasons unrelated to the PBGC's problems, such a shift would not necessarily be such a bad thing. It would deal with the labor mobility/pension portability issues discussed later.

On the benefit side, the most visible ERISA impact is on vesting. In 1986, the general vesting rule was cut by amendments to ERISA from ten to five years.[34] This shift was a binding one for most defined-benefit plans, although many defined-contribution plans already met the rule. By itself, vesting might be expected to reduce the antimobility effects of pensions, although those employees just short of the vesting period standard might delay outward mobility until they qualified. But the effect is complex because, for older workers, being vested probably also means having significant potential equity in the plan. For the median worker, who won't be very senior, the amount that is vested (or will soon be vested) is quite small.[35] Hence, the pure impact of vesting is not likely by itself to be large.

Financial rules and benefits may come together in the case of funding standards and escalator clauses. Very few private defined-benefit pensions provide formal indexation of retiree benefits. Of course, relatively few active workers have formal indexation of their wages. Nonetheless, those that do are in the union sector, the home of the big expansion of defined-benefit plans in the 1950s. Indeed, the widespread use of escalation in the union sector came at about the same time that the pension expansion occurred. Hence, the lack of private pension escalator clauses is surprising.

State and local government pension plans, which are not covered by ERISA, often do have formal indexation. This public/private discrepancy suggests that ERISA may be a significant factor in holding down explicit pension escalation. Moreover, it is not unusual in private plans to give retirees ad hoc inflation adjustments from time to time, although these typically do not fully compensate for inflation.[36] Hence, there seems to be a worker demand for inflation protection in pensions (even though the Social Security portion of retirement income is indexed).

It appears that the nonuse of formal escalation avoids strict funding standards under ERISA. Making a practice of ad hoc adjustments requires no funding, so long as it is discretionary. Given that many employers seem to prefer not fully funding their pensions, an issue discussed earlier, lack of post-retirement pension escalation is probably linked to ERISA.

Employee Behavior

Implicit contract theory suggests looking at the employment relationship as an ongoing one. In one version of the theory, workers are "underpaid" at the beginning of the contract and "overpaid" at the end (relative to productivity), as a kind of substitute for a performance bond. If workers do not perform to an adequate standard, they risk being terminated and losing the premium earnings later in their careers. At the end of their careers, since workers are overpaid, firms in this model will want to use a mandatory retirement rule to end the contract.

Within this framework, pensions fit in two ways. First, the value of the accruing pension benefit under a defined-benefit plan is typically a curve that slopes upward at an accelerating rate with tenure. Indeed, large capital losses face long-service workers who exit employment as they enter the final years of their careers. So, pensions could be the means by which the theoretical under- and overpayment is accomplished.

Second, mandatory retirement was made illegal for most workers in 1986. As a result, pensions could be used as substitutes for mandatory retirement rules by placing kinks in the benefit schedules at the desired retirement age. Indeed, workers who stay beyond normal retirement age in defined-benefit plans typically begin losing effective pension value. In short, there are various characteristics of pensions which seem to fit nicely into the implicit contracting model. A number of studies have been done suggesting that pensions are in fact part of implicit contracts.

There are two sides of the implicit contract to be looked at: the worker side and the employer side. Workers probably do look at their pensions as long-term commitments from the employer. A symptom of this view has been anger when, as part of corporate restructurings, pensions were terminated and workers given legally required substitute annuities. The legal requirement for funding and annuities is the shutdown value of the plan. In effect, the employer, to terminate a pension, is allowed to treat each employee as if he/she had suddenly quit. Those who are not vested receive nothing, even though many likely would have vested eventually. Those who were riding up the accelerating benefit curve associated with defined-benefit plans are knocked off before the curve peaks. In any implicit contract view, workers are shortchanged.

On the other hand, there is some question about how much workers know about their own pension plan provisions. Unions may increase workers' knowledge concerning pension entitlements, although evidence is unclear on this point. Still, it is a common complaint among personnel managers that workers do not understand their benefits. Without clear knowledge, the implicit contract model's anti-shirking effect is compromised.

Defined-benefit pensions do have the effect of tying workers, especially as they approach early retirement age, to the firm. Despite vesting, the accelerating benefit curve means less-than-full portability. Is this immobility effect something employers really want? One response is simply to say that if they didn't want it, they would have used defined-contribution plans instead. Possibly. But it is also possible, as noted earlier, that the defined-benefit plans were installed in the past as a way of providing quick retirement incomes to those close to retirement, something hard to provide under defined-contribution plans. There may not have been clear planning about the future.

In this view, the antimobility and imperfect portability effects of defined-benefit pensions are merely side products of decisions made long ago. Indeed, both public and private employers finding themselves in need of downsizing in the 1980s often incurred the extra costs of compensating workers for the antimobility effects of their pensions by offering them expensive early retirement bonuses. Those who do retire early are as likely to have pensions, which often last until Social Security cuts in, as those who retire later. But most plans do not normally have such features, leaving workers to depend on ordinary savings, 401k withdrawals, and distributions from defined-contribution plans. Hence, creating special incentives for early retirement, even when there are early retirement options already in the plan, can be costly to firms.

The phenomenon of employers inducing early retirements voluntarily rather than simply laying off excess workers can be taken as a sign of an implicit contract. But the need to bribe workers to give up quasi-entitlements also illustrates the difficulty employers face in figuring out what incentives they will need over periods of 20 to 30 years. Employers may have a general stake in being viewed by workers as "fair"; offering early retirement incentives in place of layoffs may be part of maintaining that image. That is a long way, however, from the carefully targeted, career-based anti-shirking pension postulated in the implicit contract model.

Similarly, firms may have used mandatory retirement rules in the past, and may now use pensions that decline in value after normal retirement age, simply to avoid the unpleasantness of sacking older workers. It's tough to look old Harry in the eye and tell him that his performance appraisal ratings are down and it's time to go. It is even tougher if Harry strikes back with an age discrimination suit. Recourse to elaborate models of career under- and overpayment may not be needed to explain pension retirement incentives.

What Is Needed in the Future?

More than anything else, research in the social insurance and benefits area in the future needs a check on reality, relevance, and need. As an example, models of the effect of Social Security on saving behavior continued in the 1980s to treat the system as if it were pay-as-you-go long after it began accumulating large reserves for the impending retirement of the baby boom. Unemployment insurance researchers continued to produce a fountain of papers on the potential impact of UI on unemployment duration. Yet the more critical issues for the UI system in the 1980s had to do with funding and coverage. Unfortunately, there seems to be no way of calling a moratorium on lines of research that have reached diminishing returns.

Research in the social insurance and benefits area during the 1980s resembled research in other aspects of economics and industrial relations. Models became more sophisticated. Researchers became more willing to consider issues which had previously been left to practitioners. All of that was to the good.

But economics also faced a crisis in the 1980s, the outlines of which are still only dimly perceived. At one time, the simple textbook model of the firm, worker, and consumer was just that—simple. It started with a few strong assumptions about rationality and proceeded in a context of frictionless markets and perfect information to strong conclusions. Sometimes the conclusions seemed silly. Economists were not naïve, however, they just did not have the mathematical skills needed to play with more complicated approaches.

Now that phase in economic research has ended. And it turns out that rationality is not very constraining. The recipe is simple: add an information cost here, a menu cost there, and a transactions cost somewhere else. Stir in some market imperfections and uncertainty. Virtually any observed outcome can then be explained as a rational response. The problem, therefore, is not insufficient modeling, but too many plausible models. And since empirical investigation often starts with known stylized facts, econometric techniques cannot be counted on to sort out which models are correct.

In the future researchers will need to talk more with practitioners. Even complex models usually have simple enough starting assumptions and/or implications to be communicated to practitioners for a reality check. The asking of practitioners what they are doing, and why, can no longer be scorned as a research tool. Examination of historical evidence and responses of other countries to similar problems is also necessary.

At the same time, practitioners in the human resource field need to begin thinking more rigorously about their own policies. Too many dollars are at risk to do otherwise. Perhaps personnel managers didn't design pensions with specific behavioral effects in mind. But such effects occur and they need to be considered. Why, for example, set up benefit systems that impede mobility when, in an era of economic instability, the ability to shed employees may be crucial?

The same is true for policymakers. They need to look at consequences of programs and rules. Academics can help in that endeavor. Is it really surprising that the PBGC is running into financial difficulties when the law creates incentives for employers to dump their pension liabilities? Were such outcomes impossible to foresee in 1974 when ERISA was passed? If small employers are added by legal mandate to the patchwork of employer-provided health plans, will that not add to the demand for medical services? If so, what is the implication for health care cost containment? And what should be done about it?

Finally, the U.S. benefit system must be viewed as a whole. Efforts to solve problems on a one-by-one basis miss the big picture. The employment relationship is changing; in the future it is likely to look more like a spot market and less like an implicit, long-term contract. In a world of corporate restructuring, exchange rate shifts, and deregulated competition, employees are put at excess risk if their health care and retirement income is tied to the fate and beneficence of a single employer.

Social insurance schemes, which are portable, fit well into this new economic order. Company-specific benefits, when they are not fully portable, do not. The latter can be made more portable through appropriate public policies. Moves are being made in some European countries to achieve this objective. The United States needs to begin moving in the same direction.

Endnotes

[1] Due to space limitations, citations throughout this chapter to literature in the field are kept to a minimum. Apologies are therefore due to the many authors who contributed to the literature in the social insurance and benefits area but whose names are not cited. An earlier version of this chapter is available from the author with full citations. Please request "Social Insurance and Benefits," working paper no. 201, UCLA Institute of Industrial Relations, 1991.

[2] The Chamber of Commerce of the United States has for many years published a survey of benefit costs. After the U.S. Bureau of Labor Statistics discontinued a similar survey in the late 1970s, the Chamber of Commerce survey was often cited regarding such costs. Unfortunately, it is difficult to obtain information concerning the Chamber's sampling practices. And the data are not readily made available to researchers. Thus, academic researchers have more typically used data from the Current Population Survey or from tax-related records of the Internal Revenue Service.

[3] Source: BLS, press release, USDL 91-260, Washington, D.C., June 10, 1991.

[4] The ceiling on UI is much lower than for Social Security. With lower turnover, there will be less tax liability since the probability that an employee will work long enough to hit the ceiling increases. Characteristics associated with low turnover (large size, unionization) will tend to reduce UI and, to a lesser extent, Social Security costs.

[5] Pension plan administration has also been found to exhibit economies of scale. See Andrews (1989), pp. 78-81. Note that smaller firms may be more likely than others to have minimum-wage workers who by law cannot absorb the incidence of health insurance costs.

[6] Some researchers have argued that if the tax subsidy were eliminated, the impact would be relatively modest. The difficulty is that once an employer-provided system has been put in place for many years, the immediate effect of a subsidy withdrawal might well be small. But this need not mean that the impact of the subsidy in creating the system was modest. Moreover, the kind of offering might well be different. In Britain, where no tax subsidy is available for private employer-provided insurance, those employers who do offer plans do so on a take-it-or-leave-it basis, typically for higher income employees.

[7] Although the UI system was created originally to be federal legislation, each state has its own set of laws and administrative procedures. Workers' compensation is almost entirely a state-run system.

[8] Examples include a Bush administration initiative to enhance pension portability in 1991 (the "POWER" proposal) and so-called "COBRA" rules adopted in the 1980s allowing continuation of health benefits (at employee expense) after layoff.

[9] The U.S. Department of Labor filed suit in 1991 attempting to force employers who terminated defined-benefit plans and replaced them with annuities to take responsibility for the failure of bankrupt insurance carriers to service these annuities.

[10] Perhaps the worst example of this instability was the enactment and then repeal of Section 89 of the Internal Revenue Code in the late 1980s. Section 89 was supposed to spread benefits to lower-paid workers and certain part-timers. Note, however, that instability has also been found at times in public policy regarding government-provided social insurance. During the 1980s, a major initiative in catastrophic health coverage for the elderly under Medicare was enacted and then repealed.

[11] Higher income workers will tend to receive relatively less from Social Security and more from their private pensions than lower income workers. This shift in mix is due to the tilt toward the lower paid in Social Security benefit schedules and to the integration of private pensions with Social Security. For data, see BLS (1990), p. 96.

[12] However, employers can now use salary reduction options largely to negate the distinction. Smaller employers are often unaware of this possibility.

[13] The modern prevalence of employer-provided plans—and the tilt in the tax code toward such plans—makes it difficult for the AFL-CIO to offer competing benefits. However, it can offer such items as discount credit cards that have no tax significance and thus are not generally offered by employers.

[14] Private unemployment insurance systems could not easily cope with systematic risk, such as depressions, through diversification. Hence, it is not surprising that private efforts failed. It is possible, however, simply to save sufficient resources so that the consequences of major layoffs can be financed. A possible analogy outside the labor market is insurance for risks such as earthquakes and other natural catastrophes.

[15] The term "high commitment" should not be taken to imply any company interest in worker participation in decision making. Indeed, only one of the 50 firms had an employee representation plan.

[16] Thus, one telephone company said it provided lunches to its operators so that they would not have indigestion from their own poorly selected meals and thus would not inflict wrong numbers on callers in the afternoon.

[17] It might be argued that the use of special early retirement options in pensions in firms trying to downsize in the 1980s disproves Lazear's argument. However, such ad hoc arrangements arose, in part, because pension planners originally failed to appreciate how much of a lock-in effect their programs had on employees. Pension planners appear to be able to correct past mistakes; it is less clear that they anticipate them.

[18] Several states created commissions to study the issue and make recommendations regarding the establishment of a state plan. The verdicts of these commissions varied from positive to negative, but no state plans were created.

[19] This reversal of position may have stemmed in part from a reading of public opinion and a sense that it would be better to influence whatever changes were coming rather than oppose them. The AMA's own polling efforts suggested considerable support for a universal system of health insurance.

[20] The idea that having to report retiree health care liabilities on the balance sheet causes businesses to withdraw such benefits does not comport with notions of perfect financial markets. Mere balance sheet reporting should not affect market valuation if market transactors already knew of the liabilities. To the extent that reporting standards are a factor, therefore, models of markets based on perfect assumption are called into question. About five million retired workers, mainly from large firms, were estimated to have retiree health plans in 1990. However, the number expected to draw such benefits (unless they are cancelled) was expected to grow rapidly (U.S. General Accounting Office, 1990).

[21] It has been noted that high-income countries may require more expenditure to produce a given amount of curing. Hence, the curing vs. caring conclusion may not be appropriately drawn from cross-national data.

[22] Source: U.S. Department of Health and Human Services (1991), p. 184.

[23] Health status is known to have significant effects on labor supply. Thus, in some cases, it might be argued that employers have an incentive to invest in providing health insurance to their employees to keep them healthy. This point is not evident, however, since presumably it would pay the employee to make the investment to avoid costly periods of absence or nonparticipation in the work force.

[24] However, firms do not have the same incentives to seek remedies that would lower costs across all employers since no competitive advantage is then derived.

[25] There is not much research available on differential health care costs by sex. Some research suggests that women's health expenditures substantially exceed men's, although some of this differential is said to be due to men's substitution of home care (by their spouses) for market-provided medical care. However, women in the work force are more similar to men in the work force than all women are to all men regarding health service usage. More work is needed in this area to determine the potential for sex-based discrimination on the basis of health care costs, especially as occupational segregation diminishes.

[26] The administration of conservative Republican Governor George Deukmejian in California began publicly exploring mandated health care in 1990. The governor pulled back from the plan when opposition began to arise. However, polls at the time suggested that the proposal would have been quite popular.

[27] The employees might have been given an ESOP in place of a pension; ESOP shares might then dilute the proportion of outstanding shares held by the raider. Changes in the law have now made it more difficult than it was in the 1980s for firms to terminate pensions and capture the excess funding.

[28] Of course, public employers receive no tax benefits from placing assets in a pension trust.

[29] There have been cases in which the U.S. Department of Labor has challenged what it considered to be sweetheart arrangements between developers and construction union pension funds.

[30] Earnings are imputed by summing the difference between contributions and benefits since 1948 and applying the yearly AAA corporate bond yield to estimate the rate of the return on the pension asset stock.

[31] The roughness of the estimate comes from the procedure used to determine pension earnings. See the previous note for details.

[32] Again, the reader is reminded that the separation of individual from pension saving violates the (questionable) notion that the two are perfect substitutes and that individuals can offset pension decisions.

[33] Social Security "taxes" earnings of retirees aged 62-69 beyond a limited level, thus restricting labor supply.

[34] Multiemployer plans have a laxer standard. In 1991, the Bush administration proposed bringing them under the same five-year rule.

[35] Median (interrupted) tenure on the job in 1987 was 4.2 years. Source: BLS, press release, USDL 87-452, Washington, D.C., October 22, 1987.

[36] Social Security benefits are indexed. So retirees will receive partial escalation of their total retirement incomes (Social Security + pension) even in the absence of ad hoc pension inflation adjustments.

References

Achenbaum, W. Andrew, *Social Security: Visions and Revisions*. New York: Cambridge University Press, 1986.

Andrews, Emily S. *Pension Policy and Small Employers: At What Price Coverage?* Washington, D.C.: Employee Benefit Research Institute, 1989.

Bernstein, Irving. *A Caring Society: The New Deal, the Worker, and the Great Depression*. Boston: Houghton Mifflin, 1985.

Bucci, Michael. "Health Maintenance Organizations: Plan Offerings and Enrollments." *Monthly Labor Review* 114 (April 1991), pp. 11-18.

Cohen, Wilbur J. "Social Security after 50 Years." In *Proceedings of the Industrial Relations Research Association*, December 1985, pp. 123-7.

Feldstein, Martin, and Stephanie Seligman. "Pension Funding, Share Prices, and National Saving." *Journal of Finance* 36 (September 1981), pp. 801-24.

Freeman, Richard B. "The Effect of Unionism on Fringe Benefits." *Industrial and Labor Relations Review*, 34 (July 1981), pp. 489-509.
Herz, Diane E. "Worker Displacement in the 1980s." *Monthly Labor Review* 114 (May 1991), pp. 3-9.
Jacoby, Sanford M. "From Welfare Capitalism to the Welfare State: The Career of Marion B. Folsom." Working paper no. 199, UCLA Institute of Industrial Relations, 1991.
Kotlikoff, Laurence J., and Daniel E. Smith. *Pensions in the American Economy*. Chicago: University of Chicago Press, 1983.
Lazear, Edward P. "Pensions and Deferred Benefits as Strategic Compensation." *Industrial Relations* 29 (Spring 1990), pp. 263-80.
Mitchell, Daniel J.B. "Employee Benefits and the New Economy: A Proposal for Reform." *California Management Review* 33 (Fall 1990), pp. 113-30.
Mitchell, Olivia S. "Fringe Benefits and the Cost of Changing Jobs." *Industrial and Labor Relations Review* 37 (October 1983), pp. 70-8.
Munnell, Alicia H. "It's Time to Tax Employee Benefits." *Proceedings of the Industrial Relations Research Association*, December 1988, pp. 374-86.
Otney, Elizabeth Lewis. *Employers' Welfare Work*. Bulletin no. 123. Washington, D.C.: GPO, 1913.
Parker, Florence E. "Experience Under State Old-Age Pension Acts in 1935." *Monthly Labor Review* 34 (October 1936), pp. 811-37.
Piacentini, Joseph S., and Timothy J. Cerino. *EBRI Databook on Employee Benefits*. Washington, D.C.: Employee Benefit Research Institute, 1990.
Podgursky, Michael, and Paul Swaim. "Health Insurance Loss: The Case of the Displaced Worker." *Monthly Labor Review* 110 (April 1987), pp. 30-3.
Pontiff, Jeffrey, Andrei Shleifer, and Michael S. Weisbach. "Reversions of Excess Pension Assets After Takeovers." *RAND Journal of Economics* 21 (Winter 1990), pp. 600-13.
Sanchez, Jesus. "Tension Over Pension Reform." *Los Angeles Times*, May 23, 1991, pp. D1, D5.
Tepper, Irwin. "Taxation and Corporate Pension Policy." *Journal of Finance* 36 (March 1981), pp. 1-13.
Turner, John A., and Daniel J. Beller, eds. *Trends in Pensions*. Washington, D.C.: U.S. Department of Labor, Pension and Welfare Benefits Administration, 1989.
U.S. Bureau of the Census. *Statistical Abstract of the United States: 1990*. Washington, D.C.: GPO, 1990.
U.S. Bureau of Labor Statistics. "Civil-Service Retirement and Old-Age Pensions." *Monthly Labor Review* 2 (June 1916), pp. 101-12.
________. "Labor Banks in the United States." *Monthly Labor Review* 18 (February 1924), p. 215.
________. *Unemployment-Benefit Plans in the United States and Unemployment Insurance in Foreign Countries*. Bulletin no. 544, Washington, D.C.: GPO, 1931.
________. "Effect of Social Security Act on Company Pensions." *Monthly Labor Review* 50 (March 1940), pp. 642-7.
________. *Press Release*. USDL 87-452, October 22, 1987.
________. *Employee Benefits in Medium and Large Firms, 1989*. Bulletin no. 2363, Washington, D.C.: GPO, 1990.
________. *Press Release*. USDL 90-317, June 19, 1990.
________. *Press Release*. USDL 91-260, June 10, 1991.
U.S. Department of Health and Human Services, National Center for Health Statistics. *Health, United States: 1990*. Washington, D.C.: GPO, 1991.
U.S. General Accounting Office. *Employee Benefits: Extent of Companies' Retiree Health Coverage*, GAO/HRD-90-92. Washington, D.C.: GAO, 1990.
U.S. President. *Economic Report of the President: 1991*. Washington, D.C.: GPO, 1991.
Wiatrowski, William J. "Comparing Employee Benefits in the Public and Private Sectors." *Monthly Labor Review* 111 (December 1988), pp. 3-8.
Woods, John R. "Pension Coverage Among Private Wage and Salary Workers: Preliminary Findings from the 1988 Survey of Employee Benefits." *Social Security Bulletin* 52 (October 1989), pp. 2-19.